Educational Psychology

Educational Psychology

A Contemporary Approach

Gary D. Borich
The University of Texas at Austin

Martin L. Tombari
University of Denver

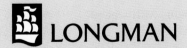

An imprint of Addison Wesley Longman, Inc.

New York • Reading, Massachusetts • Menlo Park, California • Harlow, England
Don Mills, Ontario • Sydney • Mexico City • Madrid • Amsterdam

Editor in Chief: Priscilla McGeehon
Acquisitions Editor: Virginia L. Blanford
Developmental Editor: Elaine Silverstein
Project Editor: Shuli Traub
Supplements Editor: Donna Campion
Text and Cover Designer: Rubina Yeh
Art Studio: Dillon Design Group
Photo Researcher: Michelle Ryan
Production Manager: Alexandra Odulak
Desktop Coordinator: Joanne Del Ben
Manufacturing Manager: Hilda Koparanian
Electronic Page Makeup: Americomp
Printer and Binder: Quebecor/Hawkins, Inc.
Cover Printer: Phoenix Color Corp.
Cover: Untitled, by Inge Abdulcair, age 9, Romania. Detail of "Portrait," artist unknown, age 12, Japan. Courtesy of the International Children's Art Museum.

Library of Congress Cataloging-in-Publication Data
Borich, Gary D.
    Educational psychology: a contemporary approach / Gary D. Borich, Martin L. Tombari.— 2nd ed.
        p. cm.
    Includes bibliographical references and index.
    ISBN 0-673-98287-4 (student edition) ISBN 0-673-97740-4 (instructor's edition)
    1. Educational psychology. 2. Child development. 3. Learning. 4. Classroom management.
5. Educational tests and measurements.
    I. Tombari, Martin L. II. Title.
    LB1051.B4744 1996   96–15871
    370. 15—dc20   CIP

ISBN 0-673-98287-4

345678910—ARH—999897

Contents in Brief

Contents in Detail

What Teachers Need to Know About Educational Psychology for the Twenty-First Century

In the preface to the first edition of *Educational Psychology: A Contemporary Approach*, we identified some of the many changes that were occurring or were about to occur in schools and classrooms that would affect our everyday lives. During the preparation of this second edition these changes have become even more inevitable and their impact even more dramatic.

Schools, now more than ever, must prepare learners for a high-tech world with which their teachers and parents have generally had little experience. Learners are not only becoming more diverse than at any time in our nation's history, they must live and prosper in a world in which values and ideas evolve rapidly. To adapt learners to live in this world of rapid change, our educational goals, teaching techniques, and assessment procedures must reflect the diversity of today's world.

There is little doubt among educators, employers, and parents that the primary arena in which learners will be prepared to meet rapid change in the future is the classroom of today. By virtue of its unique concern for and methods of studying human learning and development in educational settings, educational psychology will play an ever-increasing role in preparing learners for these new challenges and opportunities.

Along with schools themselves, the field of educational psychology continues to undergo rapid change. There has been a gradual updating and more focused use of individualistic and behavioral approaches to classroom learning. And most recently, cognitive and constructivist theories of learning have emerged, along with theories of how learning is affected by the social context of the classroom.

Increasingly, the traditional view of the teacher-as-technician, focusing exclusively on the individual learner, is being replaced by an emphasis on the teacher as a member of a team that includes educational specialists, other teachers, parents, and the entire community of which the learner is a part. Also underlying these new approaches to learning is a greater understanding of the roles played by culture, ethnicity, and gender. The most recent advances in cognitive and constructivist explanations of learning, the effects of culture and gender on learning, and research into the classroom as a social setting have been placed center stage in this second edition.

Along with these new directions in classroom learning, there is heightened interest in a variety of assessment strategies to measure learner achievement. Standardized tests are receiving increased scrutiny, while the rapidly advancing field of performance assessment is experiencing greatly increased research and development as a complementary approach to more traditional forms of assessment. These new assessment strategies and their relationship to cognitive and constructivist strategies of learning represent another focus of this second edition.

Educational psychologists have learned much in recent years about the science of instruction—in particular, about the role teachers, teaching practices, and learners play in constructing a classroom environment in which every learner experiences success. For a time, the teaching of educational psychology was dominated by the presentation of theory first and application second. In other words, formal principles of psychology took precedence over their application in the classroom. From research on teaching effectiveness, however, we now know that the picture is not that simple. Classrooms are enormously complex settings. The new teacher who lacks an understanding of the social forces that come into play when a group of learners comes together cannot be expected to apply theories and principles learned in the context of formal university coursework. Teacher educators have come to appreciate the role of "case knowledge"—knowledge based on the experiences of practicing teachers that conveys the wisdom of the classroom through the eyes and ears of teachers who have been there.

This text was written to reflect these and other recent changes in what teachers need to know in order to teach effectively. Our text is organized into five parts that cover the broad topics of development, learning, assessment, lesson and classroom management, and learner diversity. The title to each unit begins with the phrase *What teachers need to know about . . .* —not only to reflect the wealth of knowledge educational psychology has discovered about human learning, but to prioritize that knowledge and present it in the way that is most relevant to classroom learning. Thus, throughout this text we focus on how learning takes place in real classrooms.

Because we know that teachers tend to organize their knowledge of teaching in accord with their own experiences—or cases—rather than along theoretical lines, we have integrated theory and application throughout the chapters. In addition, this edition includes a special feature, *Applying Your Knowledge* boxes, in which we highlight practical teaching tips that are commonly known to experienced teachers but may be unknown to the beginning teacher. As in our first edition, every unit and chapter begins with a dialogue, case study, or vignette that places the information contained in the unit or chapter into a real-world context. We then weave this case knowledge throughout each chapter, building on it and enriching it with information and ideas grounded in classroom practice.

Organization of This Book

Our chapters contain much practical information not traditionally elaborated in other texts.

- The first part, **"What Teachers Need to Know About Development,"** focuses on the importance to teachers of a developmental perspective on learning and on learning problems. In contrast to some approaches to development, which draw specific classroom applications solely from theories of cognitive and affective development, we present developmental principles from the perspective of realistic case examples. Similarly, we return to this same approach in each of our other chapters.

- The second part, **"What Teachers Need to Know About Learning,"** presents the behavioral and cognitive perspectives on learning. Our discussion of behavioral learning theory and techniques emphasizes practical ways in which teachers can help learners acquire basic skills. This is followed by two new chapters in which we focus exclusively on classroom applications of cognitive and constructivist learning strategies. The first chapter in this sequence presents major advances in cognitive psychology, with particular emphasis on the important skills of problem solving, critical thinking, and reasoning, while the second addresses the practical implementation of constructivist strategies of teaching derived from the cognitive tradition. Our fourth and final chapter in this unit relates the preceding theories and constructivist concepts to the important role of human emotion and motivation in learning.

- In the third part, **"What Teachers Need to Know About Instruction and Classroom Management,"** we show how knowledge of group dynamics, positive approaches to classroom conduct, and instructional management are all essential components of effective teaching. Chapter 8 presents important principles derived from social psychology regarding classroom groups. Chapter 9 shows teachers how to use techniques of conduct management that focus on prevention and redirection rather than reaction and punishment. Chapter 10 presents important knowledge on lesson planning and instruction to guide new teachers through those difficult early weeks and months.

- Our fourth part, **"What Teachers Need to Know About Assessment,"** focuses on learner performance in a variety of contexts. We center our discussion around a model of assessment that involves both standardized and teacher-made tests. We have devoted two chapters to the latter topic—one chapter on traditional teacher-made paper-and-pencil tests, plus a unique chapter that shows teachers how to construct and grade performance assessments, including student portfolios. This chapter goes hand in hand with two earlier chapters on cognitive and constructivist approaches to provide teachers with the skills they need to carry out authentic and ongoing assessment in their classrooms.

- Our final part, **"What Teachers Need to Know About Learner Diversity,"** prepares the reader to meet the opportunities and challenges of diversity. This section presents recent research about specific learning characteristics of exceptional and at-risk learners (Chapter 14) and culturally and ethnically diverse learners (Chapter 15). We end the book with an up-to-date look at the important topic of home-school partnerships. In this chapter, we show teachers how to promote family and parent participation in the work of the classroom.

Special Content

Some highlights of the content included in this second edition text are these:
- A unique, up-to-date, two-chapter sequence on cognitive and constructivist strategies of teaching and learning. Chapter 5 covers cognitive approaches to learning, while Chapter 6 demonstrates the implementation of constructivist strategies in the classroom. These chapters comprise a current, well-integrated, practical summary of the most important research in this vital, emerging area—the two chapters alone include over 100 new references.

- A chapter on the social psychology and social dynamics of classroom groups and their effects on both classroom climate and learner achievement. This unique chapter underscores the importance of and shows teachers how to implement current trends in cooperative learning and other social-constructivist teaching methods.

- Two chapters devoted to the psychological principles that provide the foundation for positive approaches and techniques for managing the classroom.

- Three chapters on assessment—one devoted to standardized assessment and its classroom implications, another to teacher-made paper-and-pencil tests, and a third to the theory, construction, and practice of performance assessment.

- A chapter on the rapidly occurring changes in teaching the exceptional and at-risk child, including the gifted and talented, with updated research and practice on the Regular Education Initiative (REI) and the concept of normalization.

- Two chapters devoted to teaching diverse learners, with particular emphasis on culture, gender, and ethnicity (Chapter 15) and on including the family and community as partners in the work of the classroom (Chapter 16).

Pedagogical Features

Our text includes the following special features, all designed to draw the student immediately into the learning process and to make theory relevant by demonstrating practical classroom methods:

- **Applying Your Knowledge** boxes, which are new to this edition, highlight important strategies the classroom teacher can use to apply theoretical knowledge in the classroom. There are over 40 of these boxes in this second edition, and topics range from teaching reading comprehension strategies (Chapter 5), to promoting positive group norms (Chapter 8), to using "natural reinforcers" to reward learner behavior (Chapter 9), to involving parents in their children's homework assignments (Chapter 16). All are practical, research-based, and sure to provide valuable hands-on support to the beginning teacher.

- **Chapter-opening dialogues and examples** illustrate the application of principles and concepts to the real world of the classroom through the eyes and ears of practicing teachers. Case studies and vignettes interspersed throughout each chapter further extend and ground important principles and concepts to specific classroom contexts.

- **Classroom application questions** at the beginning of each chapter help students structure and organize their thinking about the contents of the chapter. Each question is repeated in the margin of the chapter, where its answer and further applications can be found.

- **"Focus on" boxes** highlight the work of contemporary educational psychologists. In our *Focus* boxes, leading researchers speak to the student directly: They describe their current work, tell how they became interested in the topics they study, and explain how their work benefits classroom teachers. These boxes show students how research is vitally important to their classroom lives. Among the scholars covered in this edition are Robert Sternberg of Yale (Chapter 5), Carl Grant of the University of Wisconsin (Chapter 15), and Concha Delgado-Gaitan of University of California–Davis (Chapter 16).

- **Chapter-opening vocabulary lists,** together with the application questions, serve as practical advance organizers for students as they begin studying each chapter.

- "**Summing Up,**" the end-of-chapter summaries, restate key concepts in an easy-to-follow outline format.

- "**For Discussion and Practice**" questions provide students with the opportunity to review what they have learned. Answers are provided in the Appendix.

- **Annotated suggested readings** at the end of each chapter highlight or expand major concepts within the chapter.

Supplements

A full range of supplemental materials has been designed to support instructors' and students' classroom needs. These include:

- **Instructor's Edition** offers a version of the text that incorporates additional resources for the convenience of the instructor. The bound-in instructor's section provides chapter overviews, outlines, key terms and concepts, exercises, and lecture discussion topics keyed to each chapter. These resources can also be found in the **Instructor's Manual.**

- **Instructor's Manual,** written by DeWayne Mason, University of California-Riverside, provides chapter overviews; intended outcomes regarding information and concepts that prospective teachers should master with each chapter; a comprehensive course outline; key terms and concepts; ideas for teaching, including exercises and lecture/discussion ideas, techniques to introduce activities; in-class applications, follow-up activities, and other pedagogical strategies; and supplemental resources, including transparency masters, case studies, and questions for quizzes.

- **Test Bank,** written by DeAnne French of the University of Texas at Austin, provides an extensive collection of questions (multiple-choice, short answer, and essay); also available in two different software programs—TestMaster (IBM and Mac) and QuizMaster appear on the same disk—that allow instructors to customize their examinations.

- **Transparencies** feature over 100 key figures, charts, and graphs from the text, as well as other sources.

- **Student Study Guide,** written by Deborah Brown of West Chester University, provides exercises keyed to learning objectives for each chapter of the text; practice tests to help students evaluate their progress; learning strategies to help students remember important concepts; case studies that present current debates in educational psychology; and field experience questions that help students to apply educational psychology theory to the practice of teaching.

- **Electronic Portfolio,** student version, created by Harry Noden of the Hudson, Ohio, school system, encourages extensive interaction with the text, experimental applications of theories in the classroom, and self-review of student progress through written responses recorded in an interactive computerized portfolio. (This is available in either Macintosh Microsoft

Word or Microsoft Works, or IBM WordPerfect. There is also a web page version.)

- **Electronic Portfolio,** faculty version, by Harry Noden provides a range of computer network options.
- **Educational Psychology Video** provides text-specific examples of classroom interactions, drawn from the following topics: "First Day of Class," "Small Group Instruction," "Classroom Behavior Management," "Working With a Discouraged Learner," and "Parent/Teacher Conference." Each is tied directly to chapter content and the learning exercises within them.

Acknowledgments

The authors wish to thank the following reviewers for providing excellent suggestions during the development of the first edition of this text: Jeanne Amlund, Penn State University; Dave Bass, Valley City State University; Douglas A. Beed, University of Montana; Brenna E. Beedle, Eastern Washington University; Karen K. Block, University of Pittsburgh; Deborah S. Brown, West Chester University; Gail C. Delicio, Clemson University; Peter R. Denner, Idaho State University; Peggy Dettmer, Kansas State University; J. Linward Doak, Eastern Kentucky University; Harold J. Fletcher, Florida State University; Marlynn M. Griffin, Georgia Southern University; Robert Hohn, University of Kansas; Philip Langer, University of Colorado; Pamela Loughon, University of North Carolina; Lee J. Messinger, Temple University; Douglas J. Stanwyck, Georgia State University; Charles E. Syester, Western Illinois University; Carol Takacs, Cleveland State University; Dennis Thompson, Georgia State University; Joan S. Timm, University of Wisconsin; Peggy Vogelson, Chestnut Hill College; Carol Walker, Catholic University of America; James M. Webb, Kent State University; Jane A. Wolfle, Bowling Green State University.

In addition, the following reviewers provided excellent feedback during this preparation of the second edition: Dianne Albright, Central Missouri State University; Kay Alderman, University of Akron; Joyce M. Alexander, Indiana University; William M. Bart, University of Minnesota; Dave Bass, Valley City State University; Gary Bonczak, Sir Sandford Fleming College, Peterborough, Ontario; Roger L. Briscoe, Indiana University of Pennsylvania; Mary Ann Capan, Western Illinois University; Diana L. Chamberlain, The University of Texas at Brownsville; Bill Fisk, Clemson University; Hal Fletcher, Florida State University; Marlynn M. Griffin, Georgia Southern University; Hope Hartman, City College-CUNY; Sharon Lee Hiett, University of Central Florida; William Lloyd McCraney, Towson State University; Anastasia S. Morrone, University of Delaware; Elizabeth Pemberton, University of Delaware; Peggy Perkins, University of Nevada at Las Vegas; Mary Ann Rafoth, Indiana University of Pennsylvania; Lawrence R. Roglen, Boise State University; Harry W. Robinson, Muskegon Community College; Christopher Skinner, Mississippi State University; Korinne Tande, Montana State University–Northern; James Webb, Kent State University; Barbara Yunker, Jacksonville State University.

Gary D. Borich

Martin L. Tombari

Educational Psychology

Introduction to Educational Psychology

This chapter will help you answer the following questions about yourself and your learners:

- What stages of development can I expect to pass through during my first year of teaching?
- How can the study of educational psychology help me develop into an expert teacher?
- How can I evaluate the knowledge acquired through the study of educational psychology and decide whether to apply it in my teaching?
- How can I use the knowledge base of educational psychology to solve specific classroom problems?

Marisa Washington is a first-year language arts teacher at Fawkes Middle School. It is February, and on this particular day she is participating in an after-school seminar on teaching writing. Dr. Cornell Gates, a former professor of Marisa, is presenting the seminar. During the break, Marisa goes up to Dr. Gates and introduces herself.

Marisa: Dr. Gates, I'm Marisa Washington. I took your class on writing about a year ago. Do you remember me?

Dr. Gates: Of course. You always sat in the last row on the left side of the room. You know what they say about students who sit in the back!

Marisa: Yeah. I think the same thing about some of my students.

Dr. Gates: This must be your first year teaching. How's it going?

Marisa: It's just like you said in class . . . the first few months are a matter of survival. Well, I think I'm past that stage now. Had you presented these ideas about writing last October, I probably would have been too overwhelmed to listen. Now I can see where I can use them.

Dr. Gates: So, you're at the point where your concerns are changing: focusing less on yourself and more on how to teach?

Marisa: That's it. I finally feel that I can plan my lessons with a focus on my presentation skills and the content. Before, every lesson plan ended with my asking, "Now, what behavior problems might this create?"

Dr. Gates: And now you ask whether the lesson will get your point across?

Marisa: Yes. Before, the things you were talking about today would have just made me worry about classroom control. Now, I'm thinking about whether they'll help me teach better.

Dr. Gates: Sounds like you're past the survival stage and beginning to focus on your teaching skills.

Marisa: I would never have said this in the fall, but I think I'm beginning to see the light at the end of the tunnel.

There is a common perception that with certification comes expertise in teaching. But it will take time for you to develop patterns of practice that will enable you to confidently and effortlessly develop and carry out effective lesson plans. As a beginning teacher you will be a developing professional, as Marisa has come to realize and as Dr. Gates has taught.

In this chapter you will also learn the meanings of these terms:

case study
concerns theory
control group
correlational study
dependent variable
descriptive research
educational psychology
ethnography
experimental group
experimental study
generalizability
hypothesis
impact stage
independent variable
operational definition
qualitative research
quantitative research
randomization
survival stage
task stage
variables

How does a beginning teacher develop into a mature, confident, and competent professional? What conditions must you experience? What knowledge must you acquire? What skills must you develop? Educators and educational psychologists have studied the developmental process of becoming a teacher and have found that it unfolds in some predictable ways. In this chapter, we will discuss the stages of development that all teachers go through on the way to becoming expert practitioners. Then we will explore the knowledge base of educational psychology, the subject of this book, and how it can help you in your classroom.

Stages of Teacher Development

At this point in your training, you probably see yourself in the role of a teacher, and you may have constructed some images or pictures of your first class. You may have promised yourself that you are going to be better than some of the teachers who taught you when you were in elementary or high school. You probably hope to be as good as some other teachers you have known. But as you begin your first regular teaching assignment you will find that there is a difference between your student teaching experience and the "real world of teaching." First, the classrooms you have been in came with a made-to-order instructional and behavior management system. All you had to do was adjust to it. Soon, no such system will exist, and you will have to create one of your own.

Second, during student teaching you have had instructional materials and lessons to draw on as aids to help you plan and teach. This may not be the case when you start your first teaching assignment. You will have to make many decisions about what, for how long, and in what manner to teach a group of learners you know little about.

Finally, your cooperating teacher has been an important advisor and confidante during your student teaching experience, someone you could approach for advice on

Student teachers can quickly move from concerns about self and self-survival to concerns about student achievement and learning.

how to teach particular learners or how to cope with the psychological and physical demands of teaching. It is possible that such a mentor may not exist in your first regular teaching assignment.

What stages of development can I expect to pass through during my first year of teaching?

The Survival Stage

This transition to the real world of teaching ushers in the first stage of teacher development, sometimes called the **survival stage** (Borich, 1993; Burden, 1986; Fuller, 1969; Ryan, 1992). The distinguishing feature of the survival stage of teaching is that your concerns will focus on your own well-being more than on the teaching task or your learners. Bullough (1989) has described this stage as "the fight for one's professional life" (p. 16). During this stage, you will typically have the following concerns:

Will my learners like me?

Will they listen to what I say?

What will parents and teachers think of me?

Will I do well when the principal observes me?

Will I ever have time to myself?

Typically, during this time you become so focused on behavior management concerns that you feel like you are struggling merely to survive the day-to-day give-and-take of classroom life. Listen to Kerrie, a first-year teacher, reflect on some assumptions she made during the fall semester of her first teaching assignment.

> . . . I thought that if you planned the curriculum really well, the management just falls into place. I really thought that when I was student teaching. If you are not well planned you are going to have problems, but planning well doesn't solve those problems; you still have management problems. At first . . . I thought that you could plan your curriculum and [good] behavior would fall into place; you could handle it as it comes. But you really can't. The other half of planning is what you will require behaviorally and you can plan for that. Now [sixth month] I plan a lot more things, like transition time and walking into the other room [to check on students]. (Bullough, 1989, pp. 25–26)

Survival stage. The first stage of teaching during which beginning teachers focus primarily on their own well-being rather than on their learners or the process of teaching.

The Task Stage

For most teachers, survival concerns and concerns about self begin to diminish rapidly during the first months of teaching, but there is no precise time when they are over. What signals their end is the transition to a new set of concerns and a gradual diminishing of concerns about your own well-being. This new set of concerns focuses on how best to deliver instruction. Various labels have been used to describe this second stage, such as the mastery stage of teaching (Ryan, 1992), consolidation and exploration (Burden, 1986), and trial and error (Sacks & Harrington, 1982). Fuller (1969) described this as the **task stage:** the stage in which the new teacher focuses on the teaching task itself.

At this stage you begin to feel confident that you can manage the day-to-day routines of the classroom and deal with a variety of behavior problems. You are at the point where you can plan your lessons without an exclusive focus on managing the classroom. Your focus turns toward improving your teaching skills and achieving greater mastery over the content you are teaching.

Task stage. The second stage of teaching in which a teacher's concerns focus on improving his or her teaching skills and mastering the content being taught.

For most teachers, concerns about survival or self diminish rapidly after several months of teaching. What follows is a new set of concerns about how to best help students learn.

Typically, your concerns during this second stage of teacher growth and development are these:

How good are my instructional materials?

Will I have enough time to cover all the content?

How can I add variety to my presentations?

Where can I get some ideas for a learning center?

What's the best way to teach writing skills?

The Impact Stage

The final stage of teacher growth and development is characterized by concerns that have to do less with management and lesson delivery and more with the impact of your teaching on learners. This point in a teacher's career is sometimes referred to as the **impact stage.** At this time, you will naturally view learners as individuals and will be concerned that each of your students fulfills his or her potential. At this stage, your principal concerns might be these:

How can I increase my learners' feelings of accomplishment?

How do I meet my learners' social and emotional needs?

What is the best way to challenge my unmotivated learners?

What skills do they need to best prepare them for the next grade?

Impact stage. The stage of teaching when instructors begin to view their learners as individuals with individual needs.

Concerns about the impact of instruction on learners' growth and development typify the final stage of the teacher's growth and development.

If you are a typical beginning teacher, your thoughts and concerns will focus at first on your own well-being and only later on the teaching task and your students. Fuller (1969), for example, found that during the early, middle, and late phases of student teaching, preservice teachers' concerns shifted from a focus on self (Will the students like me? Can I control the class?) to concerns that emphasized the teaching task (Are there sufficient instructional materials? Is there time to cover all the content?) to concerns that emphasized the needs of pupils (Are the pupils learning? Can they apply what they've learned?). Fuller speculated that concerns for *self*, *task*, and *impact* are the natural stages that most teachers pass through, representing a developmental growth pattern extending over months and even years of a teacher's career. Although some teachers pass through these stages more quickly than others and at different levels of intensity, Fuller suggested almost all teachers can be expected to move from one to another, with the most effective and experienced teachers expressing student-centered (impact) concerns at a high level of commitment.

Concerns theory grew out of the analysis of recorded transcripts of interviews with student teachers. Over an extended period of time, these records were used to identify and classify problems that student teachers experienced and the concerns they expressed about these problems. These expressed concerns, when grouped into developmental and sequential stages, showed that student teachers with the least experience were concerned about self and self-survival, while student teachers with more experience and in-service teachers were concerned about student achievement and learning.

Stated in its simplest terms, concerns theory conceptualizes the learning process for a prospective teacher as a natural flow from concerns for self (teacher) to task (teaching) to impact (pupil). The physical, mental, and emotional states of the prospective teacher play an important role in the shift of focus from self to task to impact. The lack of adequate knowledge or emotional support during the critical preteaching and student teaching peri-

Concerns theory. A view that conceptualizes the teacher's growth and development as a process of passing through concerns for self (teacher) to task (teaching) to impact (pupil).

ods can result in a slower, more labored shift of focus to task. This, in turn, can result in failure on the part of the teacher to reach a concern for his or her impact on students.

Fuller's concerns theory has several other implications. A teacher may return to an earlier stage of concern, for example, from a concern for pupils *back* to a concern for task as a result of suddenly having to teach a new grade or subject. Or, she may move from a concern for task *back* to a concern for self as a result of having to teach in a different and unfamiliar school. Thus, teacher concerns may not always be determined developmentally but can be context dependent as well. The time spent in a given stage the second time may be shorter than the first. Finally, the three stages of concern need not be exclusive of one another. A teacher may have concerns predominately in one area and still have concerns of lesser intensity in one or both of the other stages.

Educational Psychology and Teacher Growth and Development

An important question for any teacher is this: What type of knowledge and experiences are needed to pass successfully from an exclusive concern for self-survival to a concern for the impact the teacher is having on the students? Another question: What role can the study of educational psychology play in this passage from survival to impact?

Shulman (1992) identifies four types of knowledge that are crucial for teacher growth and development: (1) *practical knowledge,* which comes from student field experiences, student teaching, and regular teaching; (2) *case knowledge,* which comes from reading about what both successful and unsuccessful teachers have done; (3) *theoretical knowledge,* which comes from reading about important ideas, conceptual systems, and paradigms for thinking about teaching; and (4) *empirical knowledge,* which comes from reading what the research says about a particular subject and how to teach it.

Educational psychology is a discipline of inquiry that focuses primarily on the latter two categories of knowledge. In the remainder of this chapter, we'll look at how this knowledge is developed and used by educational psychologists to solve important classroom learning problems. But before learning how educational psychologists provide information to help teachers progress through the stages of teacher concerns, you may want to determine your own levels of concern for self, task, and impact at this point in your teaching career. In the accompanying box you will find a *Teacher Concerns Checklist.* By completing this checklist and scoring your responses according to the directions provided, you can determine which stage of concern you presently identify with most closely. You may also want to complete the checklist again at the end of your educational psychology course and compare your scores to determine how much your levels of concern have changed from self to impact.

The Tasks of Educational Psychology

Below are some common classroom problems, followed by some possible ways to deal with them. Read these problems and choose the solutions that make the most sense to you. This is not a test!

1. Desi is a first-grader who likes to write simple stories but doesn't yet know the rules for spelling. So he spells what he hears: school is *skool,*

How can the study of educational psychology help me develop into an expert teacher?

Educational psychology. A discipline that focuses on theoretical and empirical instructional knowledge.

home is *hom,* animal is *animl,* and mother is *mutha.* What should the teacher do when Desi makes these mistakes?

   a. Point out the mistakes, give the correct spelling, and have Desi practice spelling the words correctly.

   b. Don't correct the spelling mistakes. You want Desi to like writing and not worry about spelling at this point.

   c. Point out the mistakes but don't ask Desi to correct them.

2. Mr. West is a ninth-grade Spanish teacher. Several of his first-period students come late and unprepared for class, and this delays the lesson for the rest of the class. Mr. West is considering a reward system for students who are seated and ready to work on time. For each day that every student comes prepared and on time, he will set aside 10 minutes on Friday for high-interest activities. Should he use such a system?

   a. No. Most of the class comes prepared. Giving a reward for this behavior will diminish the students' internal motivation to follow class rules.

   b. Yes. The reward will help the students who are unprepared and will have no harmful effect on the rest of the class.

   c. Mr. West should use both a reward and a punishment system. Those who are unprepared should not only lose the reward but also experience logical consequences.

3. It is June and Ms. Washington is considering retaining some of her first-graders who are not ready for second-grade reading and math. What advice should we give her?

   a. Retain the students. Students who are retained generally master the skills they failed to learn in the previous grade.

   b. Retain the students. Retained students do better than students who were passed on but should have been retained.

   c. Don't retain the students. Students who were passed on but should have been retained learn more than their peers who were retained.

4. Cody frequently disrupts his seventh-grade art class. The teacher, Mr. Steinberg, is concerned because the other learners in Cody's art group are unable to concentrate and get work done. Mr. Steinberg thinks that an effective consequence for disrupting class would be to remove Cody to a "time-out" area.

   a. Time out is an effective consequence for reducing disruptive behavior like Cody's.

   b. Time out is not effective for reducing disruptive behavior.

   c. Time out is effective only when the purpose of the disruptive behavior is to get attention.

You may be surprised that there is no single correct way to deal with any of the above situations. Each has been the focus of research, and each requires more information about the situation in order to establish the best decision for learners. For example, correcting phonetic spelling mistakes has not been shown to help learners master the

Teacher Concerns Checklist

Directions. This checklist explores what teachers are concerned about at different stages of their careers. There are no right or wrong answers, because each teacher has his or her own concerns. Following are statements of concerns you might have. Read each statement and ask yourself: WHEN I THINK ABOUT TEACHING, AM I CONCERNED ABOUT THIS?

1 If you are not concerned, or the statement does not apply, write *1* in the box.

2 If you are a little concerned, write *2* in the box.

3 If you are moderately concerned, write *3* in the box.

4 If you are very concerned, write *4* in the box.

5 If you are totally preoccupied with the concern, write *5* in the box.

☐ 1. Insufficient clerical help for teachers.
☐ 2. Whether the students respect me.
☐ 3. Too many extra duties and responsibilities.
☐ 4. Doing well when I'm observed.
☐ 5. Helping students to value learning.
☐ 6. Insufficient time for rest and class preparation.
☐ 7. Not enough assistance from specialized teachers.
☐ 8. Managing my time efficiently.
☐ 9. Losing the respect of my peers.
☐ 10. Not enough time for grading and testing.
☐ 11. The inflexibility of the curriculum.
☐ 12. Too many standards and regulations set for teachers.
☐ 13. My ability to prepare adequate lesson plans.
☐ 14. Having my inadequacies become known to other teachers.
☐ 15. Increasing students' feelings of accomplishment.
☐ 16. The rigid instructional routine.
☐ 17. Diagnosing student learning problems.
☐ 18. What the principal may think if there is too much noise in my classroom.
☐ 19. Whether each student is reaching his or her potential.
☐ 20. Obtaining a favorable evaluation of my teaching.
☐ 21. Having too many students in a class.
☐ 22. Recognizing the social and emotional needs of students.
☐ 23. Challenging unmotivated students.
☐ 24. Losing the respect of my students.
☐ 25. Lack of public support for schools.
☐ 26. My ability to maintain the appropriate degree of class control.
☐ 27. Not having sufficient time to plan.
☐ 28. Getting students to behave.
☐ 29. Understanding why certain students make slow progress.
☐ 30. Having an embarrassing incident occur in my classroom for which I might be judged responsible.
☐ 31. Not being able to cope with troublemakers in my classes.
☐ 32. That my peers may think I'm not doing an adequate job.
☐ 33. My ability to work with disruptive students.
☐ 34. Understanding ways in which student health and nutrition problems can affect learning.
☐ 35. Appearing competent to parents.
☐ 36. Meeting the needs of different kinds of students.
☐ 37. Seeking alternative ways to ensure that students learn the subject matter.
☐ 38. Understanding the psychological and cultural differences that can affect my students' behavior.
☐ 39. Adapting myself to the needs of different students.
☐ 40. The large number of administrative interruptions.
☐ 41. Guiding students toward intellectual and emotional growth.
☐ 42. Working with too many students each day.
☐ 43. Whether students can apply what they learn.

words they misspelled. On the other hand, allowing children to spell phonetically makes them more accurate spellers of unfamiliar spelling words (Maribeth, 1993).

Under certain conditions, rewarding children for engaging in expected behavior has no harmful effects on intrinsic motivation (Emmer, Evertson, Clements, & Worsham, 1994). But under another set of conditions, it does. Although some children benefit from retention, most do not (Doyle, 1989). The problem is knowing what learner characteristics make them more or less likely to improve if they are retained in a grade. Finally, removing a student from a classroom for disruptive behavior makes the behavior worse in some cases and decreases it in others (Brantner & Doherty, 1983). The key is

☐ 44. Teaching effectively when another teacher is present.
☐ 45. Understanding what factors motivate students to learn.

The following items on the Teacher Concerns Checklist represent dimensions of *self, task,* and *impact:*

Self: 2, 4, 8, 9, 13, 14, 18, 20, 24, 26, 28, 30, 32, 35, 44
Task: 1, 3, 6, 7, 10, 11, 12, 16, 21, 25, 27, 31, 33, 40, 42
Impact: 5, 15, 17, 19, 22, 23, 29, 34, 36, 37, 38, 39, 41, 43, 45

To determine your score, total the number of responses in each of the three categories of concern—self, task, and impact. The higher your score in a category (out of a maximum 75 points), the more you are identified with that stage of concern. Also, by summing responses to items in each category and dividing by the number of items completed, you can compute an average rating for each of the three areas.

The sum of the scores for each of the three areas of concern can be recorded in the format below, shown here with some sample data:

Stage	Beginning	End	Change
Self	60	45	− 15
Task	45	60	+ 15
Impact	15	30	+ 15

This example shows a shift of concern from self to task and impact, which is typical of student teachers who spend about a semester in a field experience. Smaller shifts following this same pattern are not uncommon, however, after a semester of in-school observation without practice teaching. Larger shifts, particularly from task to impact, are frequently noted for beginning in-service teachers during their first two to three years of teaching.

Concerns Theory References

Borich, G. (1993). *Clearly outstanding: Making each day count in your classroom.* Boston: Allyn & Bacon (Chapter 8).

Borich, G. (1994). *Observation skills for effective teaching.* (2nd ed.). Columbus: Merrill/MacMillan (Chapter 4).

Borich, G. (1995). *Becoming a teacher: An inquiring dialogue for the beginning teacher.* Washington, DC/London: Falmer Press Ltd.

Borich, G. (1996). *Effective teaching methods.* (3rd ed.). Columbus: Merrill/MacMillan (Chapter 3).

Fuller, F.F. (1969). Concerns of teachers: A developmental conceptualization. *American Educational Research Journal, 6,* 207–226.

Fuller, F., Brown, O., & Peck R. (1966). *Creating climates for growth.* Austin: University of Texas, Research and Development Center for Teacher Education. ERIC Document Reproduction Service, ED 013 989.

Fuller, F., Pilgrim, G., & Freeland, A. (1967). *Intensive individualization of teacher preparation.* Austin: University of Texas, Research and Development Center for Teacher Education. ERIC Document Reproduction Service, ED 011 603.

Hall, G.E., & Hord, S.M. (1987). *Change in schools: Facilitating the process.* Ithaca: State University of New York Press.

Hord, S.M., Rutherford, W.L., Huling-Austin, L., & Hall, G.E. (1987). *Taking charge of change.* Alexandria: Association for Supervision and Curriculum Development.

Rogan, J., Borich, G., & Taylor, H. (1992). Validation of the stages of concern questionnaire. *Action in teacher education, 14* (2), 43–49.

Rutherford, W.L., & Hall, G.E. (1990). *Concerns of teachers: Revisiting the original theory after twenty years.* Paper presented at the annual meeting of the American Educational Research Association, Boston. (Available from W. Rutherford, College of Education, The University of Texas at Austin, Austin, TX 78712.)

Source: From Borich, 1996.

understanding the function of the disruptive behavior. We will consider these problems in greater depth when we discuss motivation (Chapter 7), group process (Chapter 8), and conduct management (Chapter 9).

Although there are no clear-cut solutions to these and similar educational problems, this does not mean that any one approach to dealing with them is as good as any other. Likewise, this lack of certainty does not relegate all your efforts to help learners to the level of trial and error. It is possible to make informed decisions about the first steps to take in dealing with classroom challenges such as these.

This is where the study of educational psychology is of most benefit to teachers.

While it may not give you a single "best" solution, educational psychology will help you devise a plan of action and a rational way to go about accomplishing your classroom goals, whether these goals involve teaching spelling, managing the behavior of a group of learners, helping learners who have learning problems, changing disruptive behaviors, or enhancing self-esteem.

By giving you a knowledge base for making intelligent choices and showing you a process for making choices, educational psychology helps you improve and become more confident about your decision making. Thus, the tasks of educational psychology and the goals of this textbook are twofold: (1) to present the knowledge necessary to effectively teach diverse groups of learners and (2) to present a process by which this knowledge can be effectively implemented in the classroom. First, let's look at how this knowledge is constructed. Then we will describe the process for making the most use of it.

The Knowledge Base of Educational Psychology

We have organized this textbook into five units, each beginning with the phrase "What Teachers Need to Know About . . . ." Each section reflects the wealth of knowledge educational psychologists have discovered about teaching and learning, prioritizes that knowledge, and presents it in a manner that is most relevant to the classroom. Since you will be using this knowledge base to make important decisions about your learners, you may well ask, "What confidence can I place on the information presented?" "How was it determined?" "How is it organized?" "Will it help me with specific and immediate problems or only with problems that have yet to occur?" The first two questions relate to the research techniques used by educational psychologists to assemble valid information. The last two questions pertain to the relevance to the classroom of theories of child development, teaching, and learning. Let's begin by examining how new knowledge about teaching and learning is acquired.

> **How can I evaluate the knowledge acquired through the study of educational psychology and decide whether to apply it in my teaching?**

Building a Knowledge Base

Asking Questions. The process of knowledge building in educational psychology begins with a question about what works best for learners. For example, is it better to correct a first-grader's spelling mistakes or to ignore them? To retain learners or to pass them on? Have learners develop their own classroom rules or have teachers do this? Use rewards to encourage learners to complete homework correctly, deduct points when they don't, or use some combination of reward and consequence? Teach self-esteem by having learners repeat positive expressions about themselves or by helping them set realistic goals and showing them how to accomplish them?

These questions are just a small sample of those addressed by educational psychologists. Sometimes the question may spring from a classroom problem that the researcher has experienced or observed. Or a particular question may come from a theory of learning or development that the researcher supports and believes may be applicable to a certain classroom problem. In any case, formulating a question is the first step in the journey for knowledge.

Defining Variables. If you examine the questions above carefully, you will notice that they have one thing in common: a curiosity about how one thing affects another.

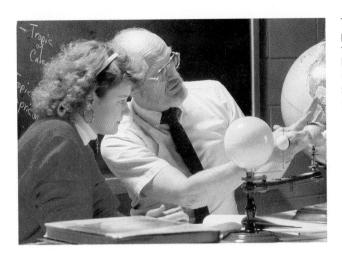

The study of educational psychology can provide teachers with research-based knowledge that can help them make important decisions and solve significant classroom problems.

For example, the question about correcting a first-grader's spelling errors really asks, "Does the manner in which you respond to a spelling mistake have an effect on learning to spell?" In other words, how does one thing (the way you respond to a spelling mistake) affect another (learning to spell). We typically call these things that affect each other **variables.**

Researchers study the way in which one variable—one teaching method, a particular classroom management technique—affects others—learning to spell, finishing seatwork. But in order to do this, they must define each variable precisely. In the question "Does the manner in which you respond to spelling mistakes have an effect on learning to spell?" there are two variables: *manner of responding* and *learning*.

Before researchers can study "manner of responding" they must identify the precise variations in the conditions being implied. For example, the variable manner of responding may be defined like this: For one group of learners the teacher will make no response following a spelling mistake; for a second group of learners the teacher will point to the spelling mistake and say "You spelled that wrong," and say no more to the learner; and for a third group of learners, the teacher will point to the mistake, say to the learner, "You spelled that word wrong," and have the learner write the correct spelling five times.

Similarly, the variable "learning" may be defined as follows: All three groups of learners will take a test consisting of two groups of 20 spelling words. One group of words will have been taught and practiced in class; the other group will be unfamiliar to the learners. The test will be given orally by the teacher, who will say each word once, use it in a sentence, and give the learners 10 seconds to write down the correct spelling.

This process of clarifying exactly what you mean when you name a variable is called *operationally defining a variable.* An **operational definition** involves describing a variable in the precise manner in which you will measure it or demonstrate it. Giving variables operational definitions is essential if the research that studies that variable is to produce usable results. Consider the following variables and reflect on how you might operationally define them: *praising learners, learning ability, following rules, self-esteem, reading achievement, knowledge of addition facts, cooperation.*

Any variable can be defined as either a dependent or an independent variable. The

Variables. Variations in conditions in a given situation.

Operational definition. The description of a variable in the precise manner in which it will be measured or demonstrated.

Independent variable. A variable that is thought to produce a desired effect or outcome.

Dependent variable. The variable that is the presumed effect of an independent variable.

independent variable (IV) is the one you believe will produce the effect or bring about the outcome you desire. It is the variable you manipulate, or change, in your experiment. The **dependent variable** (DV) is the presumed effect of the independent variable. In other words, the independent variable is what the researcher believes will cause a change in the dependent variable. If the researcher is interested in how rewards affect motivation to learn, then the type of reward is the independent variable, and learning is the dependent variable. If we want to know the effect of grade retention on reading achievement, retention is the independent variable, and reading achievement is the dependent variable. In our previous example of spelling tests, the manner of responding to mistakes is the independent variable, and learning spelling words is the dependent variable.

Hypothesis. A prediction about how the variables in a question are related to one another.

Formulating Hypotheses. Once researchers have stated the question and operationally defined the variables, they are ready to pose their research hypothesis. A **hypothesis** is a prediction of the way in which the variables are related to one another. In other words, the hypothesis describes the relationship between the independent and dependent variables. Below are some examples of hypotheses. As you read them, notice how they differ from the questions from which the hypotheses were derived:

> Learners learn unfamiliar spelling words (DV) better when spelling words are corrected (IV).

> Retaining learners (IV) in the first grade results in lower reading achievement (DV) than if they are passed on.

> Rewarding learners (IV) for behaviors they already perform makes them less likely to perform those behaviors (DV) when the rewards are taken away.

Notice that each hypothesis includes an independent and a dependent variable.

Testing the Hypothesis

Educational psychologists can choose from among a variety of methods to test hypotheses. These methods can be grouped broadly into two domains: **qualitative research,** which includes descriptive research, ethnography, and case studies; and **quantitative research,** which includes correlational and experimental studies. The distinction between these two general methods is the role played by hypotheses. Qualitative research is conducted primarily for the purpose of describing or creating hypotheses about the relationship between independent and dependent variables. Quantitative research is conducted primarily for the purpose of testing previously stated relationships between independent and dependent variables, often formulated from the results of qualitative studies.

Qualitative research. Research conducted to describe or create hypotheses about the relationship between independent and dependent variables.

Quantitative research. Research conducted to test previously stated relationships between independent and dependent variables.

Qualitative Research. The various types of qualitative studies include descriptive research, ethnographic research, and case studies.

Descriptive Research. Let's say that you are interested in studying your learners' attitudes toward providing health care services to recent immigrants, or in your fellow teachers' attitudes toward children with various types of disabilities, or in the grading methods used in your school. The purpose of your study is to describe what people do, or how learners think about a specific issue in your class or school. Such research is called **descriptive research.** Typically, you measure the variables of concern (attitudes, beliefs, grading practices) by means of questionnaires, interviews, systematic observation, or a combination of these practices. From the results you may choose to formulate specific hypotheses about the relationships between independent and dependent variables, which subsequently may be tested with the tools of quantitative research.

Ethnographic Research. In Chapter fifteen you will read about a year-long research study conducted in a classroom by a researcher who was interested in what effective teachers do to motivate culturally different learners to excel in school (Dillon, 1989). The researcher observed a class and their teacher for an entire year. She made detailed notes of what she observed and recorded her conversations with the teacher, learners, and other school personnel. She posed questions about why this particular teacher was so successful, which later formed the basis for specific hypotheses that made explicit dependent and independent variables. She then collected data that could support or refute her hypotheses, thereby combining some features of the qualitative and quantitative approaches. This research technique is called **ethnography.** Typically, ethnographic studies concentrate on life in a particular classroom or school. The researcher acts as observer, recorder, and interpreter and makes explicit his or her point of view. The results of such studies help us understand how people in that particular situation interpret and make sense of daily events or circumstances in their lives.

Case Studies. Case studies intensively study persons or situations singly or in small numbers. As such, they usually do not involve as many individuals or as extensive a data-gathering process as ethnography. For example, Tombari, Fitzpatrick, and Childress (1985) programmed a computer to give out rewards in the form of video games and used it as part of a self-management intervention to help a disruptive child. Kamps et al. (1992) studied what one particular teacher did to teach an autistic child to interact with his peers. Trovato and Bucher (1990) described how a peer tutor taught reading skills to a fourth-grade classmate. These studies generated specific hypotheses and planned interventions to determine whether the hypotheses were supported. Hence, case studies may combine elements of both qualitative and quantitative approaches.

Quantitative Research. So far we have described types of research studies that are useful for generating hypotheses about relationships between variables in specific situations: the effectiveness of one teacher's methods, the effects of rewards in a specific situation, the effects of peer tutoring in a specific classroom. While they often provide interesting hypotheses and lead researchers to ask interesting questions, such studies may lack generalizability. **Generalizability** refers to the ability to reproduce research results across contexts (e.g., laboratory conditions), settings (e.g., schools or communities), and learners (e.g., high and low achievers). To show that the results of their research are generalizable to a variety of settings, researchers must turn to quantitative research methods. We study two quantitative methods here: correlational and experimental studies.

Correlational Studies. As a prospective teacher you are probably interested in whether there is a relationship between hours spent doing homework and learner performance in school, especially since you will have to grade all that homework. Likewise,

Descriptive research. A means of measuring variables through questionnaires, interviews, or systematic observation, or a combination of these practices.

Ethnography. A research technique in which the researcher acts as an observer, recorder, and interpreter and makes his or her point of view explicit.

Case study. An intensive study of persons or situations singly or in small numbers.

Generalizability. The reproducibility of research results across contexts, settings, and learners.

you may want to know whether there is a relationship between learners' self-esteem and their performance in school. Educational psychologists have studied these relationships and others, such as the relationship between family disruption and learner behavior problems in school (Christenson & Conoley, 1993), the number of changes in children's lives and their learning and adjustment to school (Eccles, 1990), and IQ scores and math achievement (Jensen, 1980). Research studies that seek to determine whether there is a relationship between two variables are called **correlational studies.** They make use of a statistical index called the correlation coefficient, which we will learn about in Chapter 11.

Whenever you read or hear about a correlation, it is important to remember that correlations do not tell you whether one variable causes the other. For example, a correlation between homework and learner performance does not mean that giving lots of homework will cause increased performance. It simply means that some relationship between the two variables exists. Thus a statement that a correlation exists implies not causality but relationship, which can be explored further through an experimental study.

Experimental Studies. In all the types of the studies we have described so far, researchers observe and measure the variables they are interested in but do not change them in any way. In **experimental studies,** however, researchers directly change one of the variables of interest—the independent variable—to see how the change influences another variable of interest—the dependent variable. Such studies use experimental groups and control groups; learners are assigned to either group on a random basis. The **experimental group** is given a program of instruction—or some other intervention—that presumably causes changes in the dependent variable. This program or intervention is intentionally withheld from a comparably chosen **control group** in order to provide a baseline against which changes in the experimental group can be compared. The process of **randomization,** which allows large numbers of individuals to have an equal opportunity to be chosen for inclusion in the study and for participation in either the experimental or the control group, increases the generalizability of the research findings to other research contexts and learners.

For example, suppose you were designing a study to determine the effect of correcting spelling errors. You would randomly assign children to one of three groups, and each group would experience a different type of error correction: Group 1 would be corrected but given no practice; Group 2 would be corrected and made to practice the mistake, and Group 3's mistakes would be ignored. This last group is the control group, against whose results the results of the other groups would be compared.

Most of the research you will read about in this text—research on how children learn, follow classroom rules, exhibit more motivation, improve self-esteem, and get along with classmates—has been accumulated by use of experimental research techniques. These studies have used the process of randomization to achieve generalizability of results to a broad population of classrooms and learners.

Theory Building

All of the research studies we describe in this book were carried out in the context of the results of previous research. Each study was preceded by other related investigations and is followed by yet others that revisit its results and follow up on it in turn. Research

---

Correlational study. Research that tries to determine whether a relationship exists between two variables.

Experimental study. Research in which the independent variable is changed so that its effects on the dependent variable can be seen.

Experimental group. A group that is given a stimulus (such as a program of instruction) that presumably causes a change in the group members' behavior.

Control group. The baseline group against whom changes in the experimental group are compared. The experimental group's stimulus is withheld from the control group.

Randomization. A process to help insure experimental generalizability by giving large numbers of individuals an equal opportunity to be included in a study in either the experimental or the control group.

is an ongoing enterprise in which the researcher continually relates her particular study with other studies that came before it. The overall goal of the research process in any psychological discipline, such as educational psychology, is to assemble a related, coherent body of generalizations and principles that explain how people develop, learn, and are motivated. These internally consistent bodies of principles and generalizations that explain human behavior are called *psychological theories.*

In this book we will explore several important theories of development, learning, and motivation. These theories help researchers to organize information gained from their experiments and make decisions about other variables to investigate, and they also help the nonresearcher, including the classroom teacher, in two ways: (1) They help organize many seemingly unrelated facts about development, learning, motivation, and classroom management; and (2) they help us think about classroom problems in terms of previously discovered generalizations and principles that point the way to new solutions.

For example, in Chapter 7 you will learn about a particular theory of motivation called self-determination theory (Deci, Vallerand, Pelletier, & Ryan, 1991). This theory has been constructed carefully, fact by fact, over several decades. You will learn about many of these facts. But more importantly, the theory organizes these facts into generalizations, which help explain the critical attributes underlying learner motivation. When you are challenged by a learner who lacks motivation to do schoolwork, what you are likely to remember are not the isolated results of the individual research studies that contributed the facts, but the broad principles that can explain human behavior and bring meaning and purpose to these facts. It is these principles that will guide your search for new solutions to existing problems.

Now that you are acquainted with how educational psychologists assemble their knowledge base and its potential usefulness for your teaching, let's turn to the second important way in which educational psychology can help you in your classroom: the search for solutions to classroom problems.

A Process of Solving Classroom Problems

At every stage of teacher development, your students will challenge you with their various needs for achievement, social development, friendships, willfulness, and enjoyment. While most of your learners will thrive under your leadership, some will not. Learners bring to the classroom a host of individual differences, which no one program of instruction can meet. A challenge may come from a learner who is gifted in reading or math, or from a child who can't sit still, won't do work, or is considering dropping out of school. Or you may be challenged by a learner who has a strong desire to do things on her own and won't accept your authority.

How can I use the knowledge base of educational psychology to solve specific classroom problems?

Some teachers, when faced with these and other formidable challenges during the first year of teaching, become dismayed by the complexity of classroom life. They seek to return to the self-protective concerns of the survival stage of teaching. Borich (1993) describes this as turning up your "numbness amplifier" to blot out the seemingly intractable problems of your classroom rather than realizing that you can have an impact on the problem regardless of how difficult it may initially appear. Some teachers believe that the only solution is special class placement, psychological counseling, or a

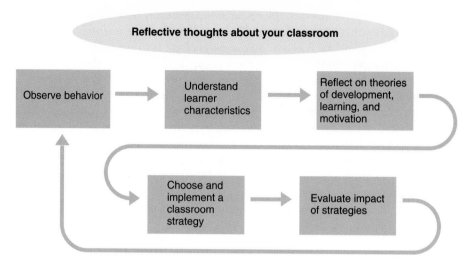

Figure 1.1
The process of reflective thinking and decision making in the classroom.

classroom transfer. Others know that while these interventions might be necessary for a given individual, the teacher also has a critical role to play in solving the problem. During this problem-solving process, educational psychology has much to offer the classroom teacher.

Figure 1.1 describes what this problem-solving process involves. The boxes in the diagram describe actions you can use to think about and solve everyday classroom problems. The oval above the boxes reflects your thoughts or considerations at different stages of problem solving. Let's look briefly at the steps you would take and the questions you would ask at each stage.

Observe Behavior

First, ask yourself what the learner is doing that is the source of the problem. Be clear about exactly what you are seeing that troubles you. Operationally define expressions such as these: She's bored; he's immature; she has no motivation; he's withdrawn. Also, be specific about your goals or objectives for the learner. Don't consider only what you want the learner *not* to do. Make yourself specify what you want the learner to do. And don't forget that your goal should be operationally defined and measurable.

Understand Learner Characteristics

Once you are clear about the problem and your goals, ask yourself how the problem and your goals relate to the developmental level of the learner (see Chapters 2 and 3). Is the behavior you see typical or atypical of the learner's age, culture, gender, or educational history? Are the goals realistic, developmentally appropriate, culturally compatible? Might there be other reasons (e.g., medical) for the behavior?

Reflect on Theories of Development, Learning, and Motivation

What are some historical and concurrent explanations of the behavior you are seeing? What learner needs may not be met? What forces outside the classroom may be playing a role in the learner's classroom behavior? What classroom conditions could be contributing to the problem? How does the learner perceive the problem? And what is he or she willing to contribute to its solution? We will consider theories of development in Part I of this book and theories of learning and motivation in Part II.

Choose and Implement a Classroom Strategy

At this stage, ask yourself what you know from research about changing this learner's behavior. What does research say is important for achieving these particular goals? What changes need to be made in classroom structure, rules, rewards, consequences, and activities to meet your own and the learner's expectations? What support can you get from the family? Part III of this book is concerned with practical application of theoretical knowledge to classroom situations.

Evaluate Impact

What does research suggest should be an adequate time to expect to see some results? What records should I keep or what records can the learner keep to document the results? How do I protect against biases that may influence me to see improvements when none occur or not to see change when change occurs? How will I know if the changes I observe are due to what goes on in my classroom and not to some influence outside the classroom? Parts IV and V of this book are concerned with evaluation of learning, the special needs of learners, and the home-school partnership. Studying these topics will provide you with a broad knowledge base against which to judge the effectiveness of your interventions.

This model of problem solving suggests that there is no classroom problem you will encounter that you cannot help resolve. A successful resolution, however, will require that you obtain the requisite knowledge and skill to *make* it happen. The course of study in which you are now enrolled and your own ongoing field experiences will start you on the path to acquiring the motivation, knowledge, and skills needed to have a lasting impact on your learners.

Summing Up

This chapter introduced you to the study of educational psychology. Its main points were these:

- New teachers pass through three interrelated stages of development, characterized by their concerns about survival, about tasks, and about the impact they are having on their learners.
- Educational psychology is a discipline that focuses on theoretical and empirical knowledge about instruction. The tasks of educational psychology are (1) to provide a knowledge base teachers need to teach diverse groups of learners and (2) to present a process teachers can use to implement this knowledge in the classroom.

- The knowledge base of educational psychology is developed through the research process, which begins with asking questions, defining variables, and formulating hypotheses.
- Educational psychologists may test hypotheses by using qualitative research methods such as descriptive studies, ethnographic studies, and case studies, or by using quantitative methods, which include correlational methods and experimental studies.
- The goal of educational psychology is to bring together the findings of many different research studies into a coherent body of theoretical knowledge about development, learning, and motivation.
- The goal of this book is to teach you to approach classroom problems by means of a problem-solving process that includes the following steps: (1) observing learner behavior, (2) understanding learner characteristics, (3) reflecting on theoretical knowledge, (4) choosing and implementing a classroom strategy, and (5) evaluating the results of the chosen strategy.

For Discussion and Practice

°1. State the three stages of teacher development and give an example of the kinds of tasks you would focus on at each stage.

°2. Define concerns theory. How did it evolve? What implications does it have for expert teachers as well as for those who are just starting out?

3. Give one example of how you have used or will use practical knowledge and case knowledge in your student teaching.

4. State a classroom problem you have encountered, either in your own education or in student teaching. Formulate a research question based on that problem.

5. Using the research question you stated in answer to question 4, define the variables involved in your problem. What is your independent variable? Your dependent variable?

6. Using the variables you defined in answer to question 5, formulate a hypothesis that states how your variables are related.

7. Is your research question most amenable to qualitative or to quantitative research? Explain your answer. What specific research method would be most useful for studying your problem?

Suggested Readings

Borich, G. (1996). *Effective teaching methods* (3rd ed.). Columbus: Merrill/Macmillan (Chapter 3). This chapter on teacher planning sets out a framework for using the concerns theory and your level of concerns for instructional planning.

Questions marked with an asterisk are answered in the appendix.

Fuller, F. F. (1969). Concerns of teachers: A developmental conceptualization. *American Educational Research Journal, 6,* 207–226. This article, which won the best research article of the year from the American Educational Research Association, describes the original research with student teachers that led to the development of the concerns theory.

Shulman, L.S. (1991). Classroom casebooks. *Educational Leadership, 49* (3), 28–31. This article illustrates how "case knowledge" is acquired and used to promote instructional theory and methods.

What Teachers Need to Know About Development

Allison Wendler is a school psychologist who provides psychological and educational assessment as well as behavior management consultation to two elementary schools, one middle school, and one senior high school. She spends one day a week at each school and reserves Fridays for catching up on report writing. Today is Friday, and she is discussing some of her cases with Darrell Walker, another psychologist.

Allison: You know, it would be a good thing if every teacher could have experience teaching at the elementary, junior, and senior high levels. Maybe that would give teachers a developmental perspective on learners.

Darrell: What do you mean?

Allison: Well, yesterday I was consulting with a kindergarten teacher. She has this boy in her class who has nighttime enuresis and wets his pants during the day. She was very concerned about it and felt it was a sign that he might be emotionally disturbed.

Darrell: And, Ms. Freud, what did you say?

Allison: I tried to explain that enuresis is not unusual, even for 5-year-olds. Kids get over it. I mean, how many twelfth-graders are wearing Pampers?

Darrell: You're not just saying let the kid grow out of it, are you? After all, most kids his age don't have that problem.

Allison: I know that, and we should do something about it, but you need to put the problem in perspective. Don't blow it up into something it isn't.

Darrell: OK, I see your point. If kindergarten teachers had more contact with older kids, maybe they would understand how quickly kids get over it.

Allison: Exactly. Now take the middle school teachers. I sometimes get referrals from sixth-grade teachers about kids who aren't adjusting. They don't finish their work, or they act out in class. These are problems, but transitions between schools can be tough on learners, and some teachers don't know how different schools can be. What seems like a behavior problem may really be an adjustment problem.

Darrell: So what you're saying is that different levels of schooling place different demands on learners, and understanding that might help teachers put a sixth-grader's adjustment problems in perspective.

Allison: Exactly. Some learning and behavior problems may not be what they seem when viewed from a developmental perspective. Some learners are less ready for the demands of a new grade or level of schooling than others and need more time and understanding to adjust.

Darrell: I see your point. Say a kid isn't ready to learn certain academic or social skills. The teacher blames the child or the lack of instruction at an earlier grade.

Allison: And another thing—if teachers could work with children of all ages they would see the whole range of problems almost every learner goes through. Then they'd be able to separate developmental or adjustment problems from more serious problems.

During the first weeks and months of teaching, many of your thoughts will focus on your learners. You will ask "Who are they?" "What can they do?" and "How much can they learn?" At this time, you will strive to understand who your learners are, what tasks they can perform, and at what level to aim your instruction (Borich, 1993, 1995; Bullough, 1989; Fuller, 1969). This is a time when you will get to know your learners as individuals and will start to recognize the kinds of tasks that can promote their individual growth and development. To do this, you will need information about your learners' cognitive and affective development. In Part I of this text we will provide you with a developmental perspective that can help you plan and implement instruction during your first weeks and months of teaching.

One area in which developmental knowledge can influence your teaching is the expectations you hold for your learners. As a teacher, you will be continually questioning whether your classroom goals and objectives are appropriate for your learners. You will want to know not only whether a particular skill is appropriate to a learner's cognitive ability, but also how much time will be required to learn it. Knowledge about a child's particular developmental level, prior developmental achievements, and the next developmental hurdles to be crossed will help you decide what to teach and how to teach it.

Developmental knowledge can also help you teach learners who are experiencing learning and adjustment problems. Developmental psychology can help you identify the many forces that affect growth, maturation, learning, and development and that affect your learners' behavior. It can also make you more understanding of the varieties of behavior you will find among learners.

In Chapter 2 we begin our study of child development with an overview of the principal developmental themes that will be addressed in the following chapter and throughout this text. We start by placing these themes in the broader context of growth, maturation, and learning to provide a developmental perspective on classroom learning and to introduce major cognitive developmental theories that will become the focus of subsequent chapters. We will also learn about the important changes in the intellectual and language development of learners that allow them to acquire information, think about the world around them, solve important problems, and control their own behavior and learning.

Your appreciation of the thinking child, gained in Chapter 2, will be expanded in Chapter 3 with an understanding of the feeling child. In Chapter 3 we will highlight the important components of personal-social development and discuss your role in enriching the emotional and social lives of your learners.

Cognitive Development

This chapter will help you answer the following questions about your learners:

- How will developmental knowledge help me set appropriate expectations for my learners?
- How will an understanding of my learners' problems affect my efforts to help them?
- Can I expect my learners to continually improve their social and intellectual skills, or will they change by developmental leaps?
- How will I know if my learners are developmentally ready for what I teach?
- What role does active involvement in classroom activities by my learners play in enhancing cognitive development?
- What adjustments must I make in the learning expectations and activities of my learners when they are in the concrete operational stage of cognitive development?
- Approximately when can I expect most of my learners to be able to reason logically and abstractly?
- How will I know that my lessons include important facts, discriminations, concepts, rules, and strategies that the learner needs to master developmental tasks?
- Have I met my learners' needs for sufficient conversation, public reasoning, shared problem solving, and cooperative projects?
- Should most of my instruction be targeted below, at, or slightly above my learners' current level of skill?
- In what ways can I enhance the language development of my learners and improve their thinking ability?
- How will learning to ask questions enhance my learners' cognitive and language development?

The following portrait of a learner named Maricela illustrates many of the principles of growth and development we will study in this and the following chapter. Let's learn a little about Maricela, starting with her very first days of life.

Portrait of Maricela

From her earliest days, Maricela showed unusual powers of concentration. She would stare for long periods at her mother's face or at light patterns on the ceiling above her as she nursed. As she grew older and learned to hold and manipulate things, she would repeat the same actions hour after waking hour.

Her parents were worried at first that her development might not be normal, since she was born two weeks prematurely and weighed only 5 pounds 6 ounces. However, Maricela's older brother, Aaron, who was 15, and her older sister, Alicia, who was 12, both weighed only about 6 pounds at birth, so the doctor assured her parents that there was nothing to worry about.

Both Maricela's parents work. Her mother, Ellene, had not worked while Maricela's brother and sister were growing up. But when Alicia started the seventh grade, Ellene decided it was time to resume her career. When Maricela was 3 months old, her mother placed her in day care. It was a difficult decision, one her mother and father considered carefully.

Maricela showed normal development during her infancy. Although she never crawled, she started walking at about the age of 13 months. Maricela said her first

In this chapter you will also learn the meanings of these terms:

accommodation
adaptation
assimilation
behavioral schemata
clinical method
concrete operational stage
developmental stage
developmental theories
equilibrium
formal operational stage
hypothetico-deductive reasoning
language acquisition device
laws of conservation
mediation
nature/nurture question
object permanence
operational schemata
organization
pragmatics
preoperational stage
schemata
sensorimotor stage
symbolic schemata
zone of proximal development

words at 10 months and began speaking in rudimentary sentences when she was about a year and a half old. She formed a strong attachment to her mother despite the fact that someone else took care of her on weekdays. At day care, she formed normal attachments with the other children in her peer group and gave every indication of being a happy, self-assured individual.

At about the age of three and a half, Maricela began to show that she could recognize shapes and colors. When blocks of varying geometric shapes and colors were placed in front of her, she would readily distinguish triangles, diamonds, and even rectangles from squares and parallelograms. She could even identify shades of different colors.

Her favorite activity was putting together a wooden puzzle of the United States. She could identify the states by name. By her fourth birthday, her parents would amaze their friends and relatives by asking Maricela questions (without the puzzle map present) such as "Which state is below Illinois?" "Which state is between California and New Mexico?" Maricela's fascination with shapes and patterns was evident even when she was a small child.

Maricela continued to be a bright, alert, happy, and enthusiastic child throughout her early childhood and preschool years. Her development went so smoothly during this time that her parents were unprepared for the problems that began at the end of kindergarten.

Maricela began complaining of frequent stomachaches and feelings of nausea for which no physician could offer a medical explanation. Most of the physicians her parents took her to provided the same conclusion about the basis of her physical complaints: anxiety.

The summer between kindergarten and first grade was calm and relaxing, and Maricela seemed to be her old self again. But the physical complaints and nausea returned at the start of first grade. A school counselor suggested that Maricela might be developing school phobia and counseled her parents to bring her to school in the morning, even if Maricela complained that she was sick. Similarly, the counselor advised Maricela's teachers to keep her in class and not send her to the nurse's office unless her problem seemed serious. This appeared to have some beneficial effect, as the physical complaints decreased.

At a parent conference in November, Maricela's teacher suggested that her parents might be pressuring her to do well in school and that this was the source of her anxiety. Maricela's older brother and sister had gone to the same school and were good students. Maricela's parents assured the teacher that they were not that type of parents. During the conference Maricela's mother mentioned that she too had experienced the same physical problems throughout most of grade school.

As Maricela grew older other problems emerged. When she changed schools in the seventh grade, her grades plummeted and her behavior became erratic. She experienced a severe loss of self-esteem and developed numerous symptoms, such as difficulty sleeping, poor appetite, frequent aches, pains, and nausea, which her doctor diagnosed as signs of depression. He prescribed a mild antidepressant, which improved Maricela's mood but also made her feel lethargic. After several months of taking the medication, she stopped, against the advice of both her physician and her mother.

She got into frequent arguments with her teachers, and rarely completed her schoolwork or homework. She seemed to lose all interest in school. Her appearance, heretofore always neat, was haggard and unkempt. Despite numerous parent-teacher conferences and frequent visits to the school counselor, nothing seemed to be able to reverse Maricela's academic, social, and personal downward slide.

When it was time for her to go to high school, Maricela told her mother that she wanted to drop out. She said she hated school, had no friends, and was picked on by teachers because she looked, dressed, and acted differently. Her parents found an alternative high school, which she agreed to attend. However, the school was too unstructured for Maricela, and after two years she had accumulated only enough credits to be a second-semester freshman. At 17, Maricela faced more than three years of high school before she would receive a diploma. She dropped out, moved into an apartment with friends, and got a job as a salesclerk in a department store.

Living away from home eventually had some beneficial results for Maricela, who realized she would not improve her job possibilities if she didn't complete high school. She enrolled in a GED program and eventually entered a community college program in early childhood education. Maricela was excited about her courses and the possibility of working with young children. She threw herself into her studies with the same fervor and dedication she had displayed for puzzle maps as a preschooler.

Maricela received an associate in arts degree from the   community college and worked for several years in a local day care center. Having decided that she would like to become the director of a day care center some day, she enrolled in a university and is now pursuing a degree in early childhood education.

Basic Questions About Maricela's Development

Developmental psychologists study changes that occur in learners like Maricela from birth to death. They examine the physical, social, language, and cognitive characteristics of learners at different ages and ask questions such as these: How do 6-year-olds and 12-year-olds differ in the ways that they learn, make friends, and get along with adults? Why do some 8-year-olds learn to reason abstractly in the third grade while others don't do so until the fourth grade? Which life stages present particular difficulty for learners?

A variety of theories attempt to explain why learners display certain characteristics or traits at some periods and not at others. These theories help us understand why a learner like Maricela might be a happy, well-adjusted child at one point in her life and an unhappy, anxious child at another. In general, **developmental theories** try to explain why children change in the ways they do and why they differ from one another.

While there are several prominent theories of child development, each seeks to answer three fundamental questions (Bee, 1995):

1. Do children display similar patterns of physical, intellectual, language, and emotional development as they mature, or do the differences outweigh the similarities? In other words, is there one typical road to development, or are there many unique paths?

2. What are the major influences on learner development? Are the major forces affecting developmental change the result of environmental circumstances? Or are the forces that exert influence over learner development primarily internal and determined at birth?

3. What is the best way to conceptualize developmental change? Is it primarily quantitative, characterized by a sequential, cumulative, hierarchi-

Developmental theories.
Theoretical approaches for explaining the process of human development. The four major theories are biological, learning, cognitive-developmental, and psychoanalytic.

cal learning of increasingly complex physical, intellectual, and social skills? Or is the nature of developmental change primarily qualitative, characterized by stages, transition points, and developmental leaps?

The answers to these questions will help you understand learners as they develop. They also provide a context for a better understanding of the learning difficulties that some of your students may encounter. Before describing the theories that have developed from these questions, let's examine more closely the issues raised by them.

Is There One Typical Road to Development or Are There Many Unique Paths?

Was Maricela's development typical? Was her memory for puzzles and recognition of shapes a predictable developmental phenomenon or a unique gift? Was her fear of school an expected individual difference that does not suggest a psychological problem? When do differences become problems?

Do you expect your learners to follow similar patterns of development? Will they show certain physical, cognitive, and social skills at about the same age? Do most learners begin to use language at 11 to 14 months, have the cognitive skills necessary to begin school at age 5 or 6, become able to reason abstractly at age 10 or 11, and reach sexual maturity by the time they are teenagers? Many of your learners will have various things in common: age, language, culture, economic circumstances, family makeup, and school experiences. Naturally there will be regularities or commonalities in their growth and development. Developmental psychologists have acquired a wealth of information about these regularities, many of which we will discuss in this and the following chapter.

But each of your learners also has a unique background, special abilities, and prior learning experiences, such as culture, language, and family child-rearing practices. Each has certain unique expectations about your classroom and about you as a teacher. The learners will react in a variety of ways to what you say and do in the classroom. In this chapter and the next we will discuss some of the ways in which learners differ in language development, rate of learning, skill in getting along with others, self-esteem, and aggression.

Developmental Patterns

The question of whether development is mainly similar or unique from one individual to another has been debated by developmental psychologists for decades (Bee, 1995; Shaffer, 1993). In general, theorists who have focused their research on physical, language, and cognitive development emphasize the common or regular features of development that all children tend to show as they grow and mature (Bee, 1995).

For example, Gesell (1928, 1954) observed children at various points in the life span to determine at which ages they walked, said their first words, jumped, and displayed other behaviors. From his work came the construction of developmental norms. *Developmental norms* represent similarities in the traits or behaviors of learners as they grow and develop. The behaviors depicted in Figure 2.1 were constructed from just such developmental norms. Charts such as this make you aware of expected patterns of growth and alert you to potential developmental problems.

Piaget (1959, 1963) and other developmental psychologists have constructed similar expectations for cognitive growth. Piaget (whose work we will study in detail later in

Learners have many things in common with one another: a shared language, culture, and socioeconomic factors. They also have experienced unique child-rearing practices, family makeup, learning experiences, and special abilities.

this chapter) has identified the sequences and stages at which learners can be expected to display certain cognitive skills.

Individual Differences

Other developmental psychologists, particularly those working in the areas of personality and social development, have been more interested in individual differences. *Individual differences* are the variations we observe among members of any group in a particular characteristic, such as temperament, energy level, friendship patterns, and parent-child attachment. Gerald Patterson (1975, 1980) studied the different patterns of aggressive behavior developed by individual children. Willard Hartup (1989) examined the development of friendship patterns in children. Susan Harter (1988, 1990) studied the reasons behind the substantial differences in self-esteem among children and adolescents. In general, these theorists emphasize that development differs more often than it is similar. They underscore that patterns of development vary significantly from culture to culture, from family to family, and even among members of the same family (Shaffer, 1993). They caution against making developmental predictions based on developmental norms such as those shown in Figure 2.1.

Why This Question Is Important for Teachers

As a teacher, you will meet an unfamiliar group of learners at the start of each school year. Your learners will have certain expectations for how they should behave toward

Months	0	2	4	6	8	10	12
Physical development	Brain cortex grows significantly		Reaches for objects	Sits alone	Stands with help	Crawls	First steps
Cognitive development	Possible limitation of some gestures		Beginning of object permanence		Object permanence well established Child can coordinate actions to solve simple problems		
Language development	Coos		Babbles	Uses gestures to communicate Understands some words			First words
Personal/ social development		Erikson's stage of trust versus mistrust					
		Spontaneous smiling	Attachment to parent		Fear of strangers/ beginning anxiety		

Years	4	5	6	7	8	9	10
Physical development	Climbs stairs one foot per step; kicks and throws ball	Hops and skips; some ball games	Jumps rope	Rides two-wheeler		Beginning puberty for some girls	Early menstruation
Cognitive development	Classifies by shape and color		Conservation of number and quantity	Inductive logic; conservation of weight		Multiple strategies for solving problems	
Language development		Continued improvement of tenses, plurals; passive voice					
Personal/ social development	Initiative versus guilt			Industry versus inferiority			
	Less attachment to parents; individual friendships develop		Role plays	Strong sex-role stereotyping	Enduring friendships appear		

Figure 2.1

Simultaneous developments from birth through adolescence.

Months	14	16	18	20	2 (years)	3
Physical development	Walk alone				Runs easily; climbs stairs one step at a time	Rides trike; uses scissors
Cognitive development	Deferred imitation Finds new solutions to problems		Beginning of symbolic thought Early pretend play			Classifies by function; 2- to 3-step play sequences Begins to take another's perspective
Language development		First two-word sentences Vocabulary growth		Two-word sentences		Three- to four-word sentences; uses grammatical markers
Personal/ social development	Autonomy versus shame and doubt					
	Stranger fear and anxiety	Peer play		Pretend play	Beginning stages of gender identity	

Years	11	12	13	14	15	16	17
Physical development	Early genital development in boys	Major pubertal changes for boys Girls: height spurt		Boys: maximum height spurt			
Cognitive development	Conservation of space/volume	Beginning formal operations	Deductive logic		Consolidation of formal operations		
Language development	Continued development in grammar and pragmatics; use of language for self-regulation						
Personal/ social development	Industry versus inferiority			Identity versus role confusion			
	Incidence of depression rises; decline in self-esteem Parent-child conflict begins at start of puberty			Maximum impact of peer group		Clear sex-role identity develops	

you and toward one another. And you will have expectations for how much your students will learn, how rapidly they will learn it, and how long they will retain the information and skills you teach them. You will also expect your learners to be sociable, confident, and committed to the instructional goals of your classroom.

You will want your expectations to be appropriate for the entire class as well as for each individual. For example, expecting a 6-year-old to reason abstractly could lead to frustration on both your part and the part of the learner. On the other hand, your awareness that sixth-graders who are just entering middle school often need a period to adjust would probably prevent you from referring students for counseling unnecessarily. Your understanding of which developmental changes are common to all children, and which differ from learner to learner, will influence the kinds of expectations you have for your learners and your behavior toward them.

In addition to its effect on your expectations, your understanding of development will help you interpret differences in the learning and social behavior of your learners. Some of your children will be outgoing; others will be shy and withdrawn. Some learners will comply with rules and requests; others will resist your authority. Most of your students will learn what you teach in the time allotted, but some will not.

At what point do these differences become cause for alarm? If you expect all learners to learn and behave similarly, you may see abnormality rather than normal individual or cultural differences. But if you have no knowledge of developmental norms, you may fail to recognize a pattern of abnormal behavior at the most opportune time to deal with it. The developmental knowledge you acquire from Part I of this text will help you develop a framework with which to interpret the differences you will observe among learners.

What Are the Major Influences on Learner Development?

Were the major influences on Maricela's development built into her at birth, or did they come from her life experiences? Was Maricela's anxiety a trait inherited from her mother or a problem caused by school and family experiences? Was her lack of commitment to school after seventh grade an inevitable unfolding of a genetically programmed problem or a reaction to some change in her life?

The Nature/Nurture Question

Developmental psychologists refer to questions such as these as the **nature/nurture question.** Those who emphasize the *nature* side of the question stress that a child's pattern of development is built in, or genetically programmed before birth. While not denying that the environment plays an important role in determining how someone behaves, psychologists who take the nature side of the debate argue that common patterns of development and certain individual differences are partially or wholly controlled by the genetic code received from the parents. To support their views, such psychologists point to studies of identical twins reared apart, which indicate that a large part of intelligence and temperament may be inherited.

Those who take the *nurture* side of the debate argue that a learner like Maricela developed primarily as a result of influences or experiences after birth. They point to such factors as family makeup and child-rearing practices, health and nutrition, family social

How will developmental knowledge help me set appropriate expectations for my learners?

Nature/nurture question. A longstanding debate about the relative importance to development of genetic influences and environmental factors.

and economic status, and school quality as important determinants of Maricela's cognitive and social development. Psychologists on the nurture side of the question often cite studies of adopted children, which show that the IQs of adopted children and their non-related siblings are surprisingly similar.

However, it would be difficult to find a psychologist today who takes a strong position on either side of the debate. Most believe that both nature and nurture—both heredity and environment—play important roles in development. Although there is no conclusive answer to the relative influence of nature and nurture on development, this issue has important implications for teaching. Let's see what they are.

Why This Question Is Important for Teachers

As a teacher, you will work with learners who display a variety of learning and behavior problems. If you teach elementary school learners, you may encounter children who, despite all efforts, find it difficult to learn to read or to use math concepts. Or you may work with learners who can't seem to sit still or follow simple rules. In any middle-school class, you may encounter learners who have developed intense anxieties about reciting before a group or taking an exam. High school learners may experience not only anxiety but also depression.

When faced with children who display learning, emotional, or behavioral problems, you must decide how to provide help or support. You will ask what caused the problems, what can be done in a classroom to ameliorate them, and how you can best prioritize your time and energy to meet the needs of both individual learners and the entire group.

> How will an understanding of my learners' problems affect my efforts to help them?

The nature/nurture question will become extremely significant for you when you attempt to answer such questions. For example, influenced by what you read in the popular press, you may believe that learning ability or temperament is largely inherited. Therefore, when faced with children who have difficulty memorizing facts, understanding concepts, or solving problems, you may attribute the problem to low native intelligence. As a result, you may not look for other reasons for poor school performance, such as low teacher expectations, poorly sequenced instruction, or lack of prerequisite learning skills. Similarly, if you view school anxiety, adolescent depression, or a short attention span as inherited conditions, you will be unlikely to examine the ways in which you can support and help a student during a difficult peroid.

Some educators place too great an importance on the genetic basis of learner problems; others deny that genetics is significant in determining individual differences in intelligence, learning ability, or personality development. In fact, behavioral geneticists have assembled a large body of evidence affirming that nature plays an important role in both cognitive and personality development (Plomin & Rende, 1991). Teachers who deny this influence may place unrealistic expectations for academic achievement or social behavior on their learners.

What Is the Best Way to Describe Developmental Change?

Examine Figure 2.1 again and notice the orderly sequence of physical, cognitive, language, and social development. The typical child sits up unassisted before she begins to stand. She learns to walk before she runs or rides a bicycle. In cognitive development, the typical infant can think about only those objects he can touch or see. As he matures, he develops the ability to think about things that are not immediately present, to imitate actions after he observes them, and to classify objects by both color and shape. Similarly, in social development children typically show a gradually increasing ability to play alongside peers, play cooperatively, develop friendships, and take another's point of view.

Developmental psychologists who have examined this seemingly orderly pattern of developmental change differ on the best way to describe it. Some believe that development consists of incremental, cumulative, quantitative change in physical capabilities and in cognitive, language, and social skills. The child's bones grow stronger, muscles acquire more mass, the brain develops more cells. The child acquires more information and has more experiences, which allow her to think in increasingly complex ways. The child's vocabulary grows, and her speaking ability becomes more sophisticated. At 2 years she has no friends, but at 8 years she has many. In other words, as the child grows and develops she gets better at thinking, reading, writing, speaking, and making friends.

Development viewed in this way has three principal attributes (Worrell & Stilwell, 1981). It is a *continuous* acquisition of new skills as the child moves from one learning context to another. Development is also *cumulative,* in that the child acquires new skills and adds them to previously learned skills to form more complex ones. Finally, development is *hierarchical,* since more complex skills cannot be learned before the prerequisite, less complex skills have been mastered. The child cannot learn long division unless he has previously learned subtraction. The child cannot learn to ride a bike until she has learned to balance.

Children experience periods of relative calm followed by periods of physical and emotional upheaval as they grow into adulthood.

Moreover, the fundamental learning processes that underlie developmental change are the same for learners of different ages. In other words, toddlers, preschoolers, and elementary and secondary school learners acquire new skills in essentially the same way. From this perspective, the development of new behavior is less dependent on the child's particular age or stage than on her mastery of the necessary prerequisite skills and exposure to learning opportunities in the environment.

Other developmental psychologists, however, believe that at different points in a child's development there are pronounced *qualitative* changes in how the child perceives the world, learns, and thinks about himself and others, or in how the child's brain or body functions. Piaget, for example, argues that older children and younger children actually approach tasks and learn in different ways.

Psychologists who view development as qualitative change are often referred to as *stage theorists.* These theorists, two of whom we will study in this chapter and the next (Piaget and Erikson), have identified discrete **developmental stages** and defined them in terms of the typical or average age at which they can be expected to begin and end. As a child moves from one stage to another, whether in terms of cognitive, language, or social development, not only will she show a change in skills (quantitative change) but, more importantly, her neurological functioning and thinking will undergo a change. At this new stage of development the child is a qualitatively different person.

> **Developmental stage.** A period of development during which a person's physical, mental, or psychological functioning is different from the periods preceding and following it.

Bee (1995), for example, views development as consisting of alternating periods or stages of rapid development followed by periods of calm and consolidation. She refers to the periods of rapid growth as *transitions.* She and other developmental psychologists (Achenbach, 1990) describe transitions as times when the child is particularly vulnerable to certain kinds of stressors from the environment (such as peer group pressure). For example, Bee believes there are two important transitions during the first 18 months of life (see Figure 2.1). One occurs at 2 months, when a major change in brain function signals a change in mother-child interaction patterns. A second transition occurs sometime between the seventh and ninth months, when the child begins to experience separation anxiety, move about independently, and communicate meaningfully with the mother.

Table 2.1 describes some major transitions that occur in the course of development. Knowledge of these transitions can often help teachers evaluate a student's behavior. For example, recall that Maricela had particular difficulties when she started kindergarten and again when she entered junior high school. As Table 2.1 shows, both of these periods are major transitions.

Why This Question Is Important for Teachers

Just as the nature/nurture debate is of interest to teachers, so too is the question whether development is best conceptualized as quantitative or qualitative change. Teachers might understandably ask the following questions of the stage theorist:

> **Can I expect my learners to continually improve their social and intellectual skills, or will they change by developmental leaps?**

- If development is characterized by qualitative changes at different ages, is the best approach with a child who shows social or behavior problems to just let him or her grow out of it?

- Are the increasing negativism and resistance to authority that characterize some children as they enter adolescence best viewed as an inevitable developmental milestone?

Table 2.1

Major Developmental Transitions

Age	Description
2 months	Change in brain function resulting from an increased number of connections between neurons results in increased social interaction with the infant's primary caretaker; manifested in smiling and cooing
7–9 months	Beginnings of separation anxiety and stranger anxiety; child can now move around independently and communicate meaningfully; may suddenly manifest fear of being put to bed alone
18–24 months	The beginning of the "terrible twos" as the child becomes increasingly willful and driven; important advances in language and cognitive development occur; the child can now maintain her attachment to parents merely by thinking about them
5–7 years	The beginnings of logical thought: the child can see the world from other people's perspectives
12 years	The major physiological and emotional changes that accompany puberty; augmented by increased cognitive and social demands
Teenage years	Negativism and resistance to change, similar to that experienced during the terrible twos; increased incidence of depression and low self-esteem; increased cognitive and social demands

- How should educators and parents deal with the depression and decrease in self-esteem that sometimes occur as a child enters adolescence?

- Do all children experience transitions or upheavals, or do only some experience turbulence followed by periods of calm?

- How much does culture (nurture) affect the ages at which transitions occur?

Teachers might also ask the following questions of those developmental psychologists who hold that development is characterized primarily by quantitative change:

- Are there any emotional or behavioral problems that children are more likely to develop at certain points in their lives than at others?

- Are learners more vulnerable to the effects of family disruption, changes in school routines, or the loss of a close friend at some ages in comparison with others?

- Does a major physiological event like puberty, or a major cognitive event such as the ability to deal with abstract symbols, signal a stressful period for the learner during which certain emotional or conduct problems might arise?

Children are growing, thinking, feeling individuals. Various theories of development have arisen that try to explain and organize information about these developmental domains.

- Are there points in a learner's development where certain changes occur that should affect the types of academic and social goals we have for learners?

- Can we attribute some of the behavior problems that learners exhibit when they enter elementary school or junior high school to a lack of learning important social skills and their prerequisites?

These questions and the issues raised by them get at the heart of why developmental knowledge and a developmental perspective on learners are important for teachers. Different theories of child development try to address these questions and resolve the issues they pose in different ways. In the remainder of this chapter and the next we will illustrate the power of those theories in describing important elements of cognitive and social development.

Cognitive Development

As we saw in Figure 2.1, the field of child development encompasses physical, language, cognitive, and personal-social development. Much of a learner's physical and language development has already occurred before he enters your classroom. Therefore, you will make your greatest impact on your learners' cognitive and social development. We turn now to specific theories of cognitive development, as well as to practical ideas you can use to facilitate your learners' cognitive development.

Let's illustrate the concept of cognitive development with an example of two learners at very different developmental stages.

It's field day at Sims Elementary School. Keith Harlow, a fifth-grade teacher, is serving drinks at the refreshment stand. Waiting is a 5-year-old kindergartner, Nirbay. Next to him is Ola, an 8-year-old second-grader.

Nirbay: I'd like a can of grape drink.
Ola: Me too.

Mr. Harlow grabs two identical cans of grape drink and reaches for the plastic cups. He picks the last of the shorter, wider cups and opens a new box of taller, narrower cups. He pours Nirbay's drink into the short cup and empties Ola's identical can into the taller cup.

Nirbay: She got more than me.
Mr. Harlow: No, she didn't. The drinks came from the same size cans. See? (He shows both empties to Nirbay.)
Nirbay: But hers is up to here. Look where mine is. She got more.
Ola (in exasperation): No, I didn't. The two cans are the same. Your cup is just wider. Can't you see?
Nirbay: She got more! I want what she got!
Mr. Harlow: OK, Nirbay, just a minute.

Mr. Harlow takes a cup like Ola's and pours Nirbay's drink into it. The levels of the drinks are now the same.

Mr. Harlow: Here, Nirbay. Is that better?
Nirbay (with a satisfied look and a glance at Ola): Uh huh! Now we're the same.

Did Nirbay and Ola have a misunderstanding, or was Nirbay just a bit slow? That question misses the point of this typical scene. Nirbay isn't stubborn or intellectually slow. He simply reasons differently than Ola. Nirbay's reasoning is tied to what he can see, but Ola's is not. She can reverse or play back in her mind how much space the fluid occupied before it was poured into the cup. She thinks qualitatively differently than does Nirbay, who, in a short time, will reason as she does.

As a teacher, you will be making choices about the types of learning you expect of your students, the activities to help bring about this learning, and the assessment techniques that show whether learning has occurred. These choices will be based on your assumptions about your learners' knowledge, understanding, and reasoning about what they see and hear. The strategies you select for teaching and testing will be most effective if they match the cognitive or thinking skills of your learners.

Cognitive development refers to changes in how children remember what they see and hear, think about problems they encounter, predict what might happen in the future, comprehend what they read, understand the similarities and differences between different objects and ideas, and create solutions for problems that puzzle them. In other words, the study of cognitive development involves understanding how children's mental skills and abilities change over time.

Many different theories attempt to explain changes in children's understanding of the world they see, the assumptions they make about it, and the logic they use to make sense of it. In this section we will describe the theory of Jean Piaget, present current research that has enhanced and extended Piaget's theory, and consider some of its limitations. We will end this chapter with a discussion of language development and its contribution to cognitive growth.

How will I know if my learners are developmentally ready for what I teach?

Theory and Method of Jean Piaget

Piaget's research involved the intensive observation of individual children (primarily his own) as they grew from birth through adolescence. We refer to this style of research, which uses observation to record the behavior of a few individuals in everyday, natural settings, as the **clinical method.** A psychologist who uses the clinical method systematically observes individual children as they interact with people and objects, generates hypotheses to interpret or explain what is observed, and asks oral questions (in the case of children who can use and understand language) to investigate each child's thinking and problem-solving behavior.

Clinical method. Research that studies a small group of subjects in everyday, natural settings.

Using this method, Piaget described how infants are born with only a few innate movements and sucking and crying reflexes to guide their behavior. Yet in a relatively short time, their physical movements become increasingly goal directed; they learn how to crawl, walk, talk, and overcome obstacles to get what they want. Soon they become planners and problem solvers; before long, they can speak and reason abstractly. Piaget was particularly interested in the cognitive development that allows for and promotes these changes. He speculated that each child was busily constructing and organizing an elaborate network of ideas and concepts, which he called cognitive structures, or *schemata.*

Schemata: Cognitive Structures for Thinking About the World

Piaget hypothesized that immediately after birth, as the child groped, cried, and sucked, he or she did so purposefully. What Piaget observed were not random movements, but rather the infant's goal-directed attempts to make sense of the world. As a child learns how to turn her head to find her mother's breast, bring her hands to her mouth, or grasp objects and suck on them, she is actually creating mental or cognitive structures that allow her to think about, organize, and make sense of experiences.

Piaget believed that the primary stimulus to cognitive development comes from the child's own attempts to make sense of new experiences.

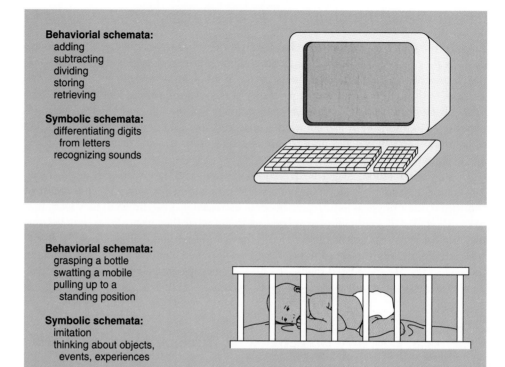

Figure 2.2
The computer and the newborn infant share some of the same characteristics of cognitive structures.

Schemata. Elaborate cognitive structures or networks made up of ideas and concepts that are used to interpret one's environment and guide behavior.

Piaget used the term **schemata** to describe these cognitive structures. Schemata (the singular is *schema*) are patterns of thought or behavior. We might also think of them as concepts or strategies that influence how the child sees the world and interacts with it.

Schemata are analogous to the software programs that allow computers to perform various tasks. A child's brain contains certain programs, or routines, that allow him to grasp objects; think about objects, events, or experiences; and perform logical operations like sequencing, matching, adding, or subtracting. Thus, computers and infants have schemata, as illustrated in Figure 2.2. The difference is that the computer's routines are programmed into it, while the child constructs schemata for herself.

Piaget identified three types of schemata through which children act upon the world, represent the world in their minds, and perform mental operations: behavioral (or sensorimotor), symbolic, and operational schemata.

Behavioral schemata. Patterns of action or sequences of behavior that the child uses to explore and respond to objects in her environment.

Behavioral (Sensorimotor) Schemata. **Behavioral schemata** are patterns of action or sequences of behavior that the child uses to explore and respond to objects in her environment. When the infant sees a mobile above her crib and purposefully swats at it to make it move, she is using a behavioral schema. Likewise, when the child grasps a bottle with both hands and brings it to her mouth, she is using a schema. In both of these instances, the infant does not think of the mobile or the bottle as an object that has an existence all its own. Rather, each is an object that is acted upon according to a behavioral schema. Behavioral schemata are most important during the first year of life.

Symbolic Schemata. At some point during the second year, children can think about objects, events, and experiences. **Symbolic schemata** allow the child to represent objects without the need to perform some type of action on them. The child can think about a pretzel he would like to eat, a truck he would like to play with, or a parent he would like to be held by.

Symbolic schemata. The mental representations of objects, events, and experiences without the need to perform some type of action on them.

Operational Schemata. By the time children enter first grade, they can perform **operational schemata,** logical operations or mental activities on objects or events, the results of which lead to some logical outcome. For example, a 6-year-old can order objects by size, perform simple mathematical calculations in her head, or imagine what a log of clay that was originally shaped like a ball would look like in its original form. She can perform these intellectual operations because of operational schemata that she has created out of experiences with concrete objects during the first five or more years of life.

Operational schemata. Mental operations performed on objects or events, the results of which lead to some logical outcome.

How Schemata Are Constructed and Changed

According to Piaget, cognitive development is the lifelong process through which learners construct and modify their own personal computer programs or schemata. They are able to do this under the guidance of two major innate intellectual functions: organization and accommodation. Two additional functions, adaptation and assimilation, allow learners to carry out the process of accommodation. Let's see how learners use all these processes.

Organization. **Organization,** as the word implies, occurs when the child combines existing schemata to form new and more complex schemata. For example, when the infant combines her looking, reaching, and grasping schemata in such a way that she gets hold of a bottle and brings it to her mouth, she has organized a new schema—visually directed reaching.

Organization of existing schemata into higher-order, more complex, and more interrelated structures occurs throughout the life span. Children who learn how to use scissors to cut out shapes, use a pencil to form letters, or coordinate various movements to ride a two-wheeler or make a basketball layup are organizing simpler behavioral schemata to form more complex ones. Likewise, the child who mimics the actions of his father shaving in the morning organizes simpler symbolic schemata for the purpose of imitating an action that he finds interesting, amusing, or useful. Finally, the child who can arrange blocks according to size or rocks according to weight is organizing already existing symbolic schemata into more complex schemata.

Organization. As a form of information processing, ordering and systematizing new information so that one can remember and use it efficiently.

Adaptation. As children grow and develop, they are constantly encountering new objects, new information, or new experiences that impel them to think about or act on their environment in new ways. **Adaptation** is the intellectual function that allows them to meet these new demands, whether they occur at home, in school, or on the playground. Children adapt to these new requirements as a result of two complementary processes called *assimilation* and *accommodation*.

Adaptation. As identified by Piaget, a central drive of humans to adapt to the world as they experience it.

Assimilation. Expanding or enriching cognitive structures with new information or perceptions.

Accommodation. Altering or adjusting cognitive structures affected by new information.

Equilibrium. The result of accommodation; the restoration of cognitive balance by altering cognitive structures to take into account new data.

Assimilation. When children try to make sense of new information or new experiences using existing behavioral, symbolic, or operational schemata, they are engaged in a process of **assimilation.** In other words, assimilation involves making sense of what is new by relating it to what is familiar.

Accommodation. **Accommodation** occurs when children succeed in modifying existing schemata in order to make sense of or account for new events, information, or experiences. For example, suppose that a child has developed a symbolic schema for "truck" as anything big with wheels that moves. She sees a van for the first time and calls it a truck. Daddy says, "Yes, that's a truck." The child *assimilates* the characteristics of a van into her truck schema.

But a few days later, the child sees a train and again says "truck." This time Daddy corrects her, saying, "No, that's a train." According to Piaget, this creates a state of disequilibrium—the child's cognitive equilibrium or balance is upset as a result of encountering new information that cannot be assimilated into an existing schema. In order to restore her cognitive balance or **equilibrium,** the child must modify her truck schema to accommodate a new category of experience—a train. She may do this by adopting the term used by her father—*train.* Figure 2.3 illustrates the complementary processes of assimilation and accommodation.

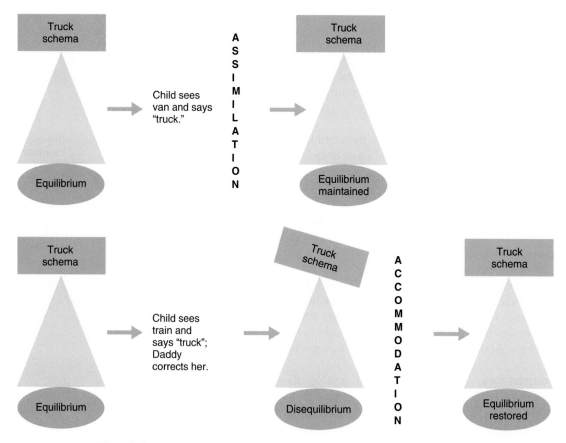

Figure 2.3
Both assimilation and accommodation maintain or restore cognitive balance.

The lifelong process of cognitive development is a continuous cycle that consists of creating schemata, enriching those schemata by assimilating new but cognitively compatible knowledge, and then altering those schemata by including new categories of experience through the process of accommodation. The creation of these new cognitive structures is guided by the two innate intellectual functions of organization and adaptation. Figure 2.4 illustrates the cyclical nature of cognitive development.

Piaget's Stage Theory of Cognitive Development

Piaget believed that the process of cognitive development unfolds through four distinct and qualitatively different stages. Figure 2.5 depicts these stages, and Table 2.2 summarizes the child's important accomplishments at each stage.

According to Piaget, these stages form an invariant developmental sequence; in other words, all children progress through them in precisely the same order and without skipping stages. Moreover, each stage is qualitatively different from the one that follows it. This means that the child must learn a unique set of schemata at each stage in order to enter the next stage.

The Sensorimotor Stage (Birth to 2 Years). At birth, the beginning of the **sensorimotor stage,** children have only a few simple reflexes (sucking, grasping, looking) to help them satisfy biological needs such as hunger. At the end of this stage, these same children can move about on their own, solve simple problems in their heads, search for and find toys and other objects that are hidden from view, and even communicate some of their thoughts to parents and peers.

Between 4 and 8 months of age, infants learn that they can make things move by banging and shaking them, which is why babies of this age love to play with rattles. Sometime between the eighth and twelfth months, they figure out how to get one thing (like a bottle) by using another (for instance, by knocking a pillow away). Between 12 and 18 months, children can represent hidden objects in their minds. They search for what they want, even when they can't see it. At the end of this period, children are beginning to use images to stand for objects. For example, a 2-year-old places her doll inside a dollhouse and imaginatively reconstructs her doll's view of the miniature rooms and furniture. This ability, called **mediation,** is an extremely important achievement, because it frees the child from the need to think about only those objects she can see around her. A child who can mediate can think about the whole world.

Current Research. Piaget lacked today's sophisticated research techniques and scientific equipment for studying early cognition. Today researchers can study the preferences of infants by tracking their eye movements, and they can use sophisticated techniques to teach infants how to manipulate their environments (for example, suck on a bottle more vigorously to see or hear more interesting sights and sounds). This research has shown that infants gain a sense of the stability of objects (called **object permanence**) much earlier than Piaget estimated—at about 4 months (Baillargeon, 1987). Meltzoff (1988) showed 9-month-old infants a video of an adult playing with toys unfamiliar to the infants. A day later, the infants imitated the adult's actions they had seen. This suggests that deferred imitation (a form of mediation) is present almost a year earlier than Piaget expected it to occur.

Although Piaget appears to have underestimated the ability of infants to take in information, store, organize, remember, and imitate it, he appears to have described correctly the sequences by which these skills develop. Furthermore, his view of the infant

Sensorimotor stage. The first of Piaget's stages of cognitive development, characterized initially by only reflex actions but later by the learning of object permanence and the beginnings of internal cognitive mediation.

Mediation. Thinking that uses symbols to represent objects or events in one's environment.

Object permanence. The knowledge that objects that are not currently visible (such as a car that has passed) still exist. This knowledge typically develops when a child has reached 6 months.

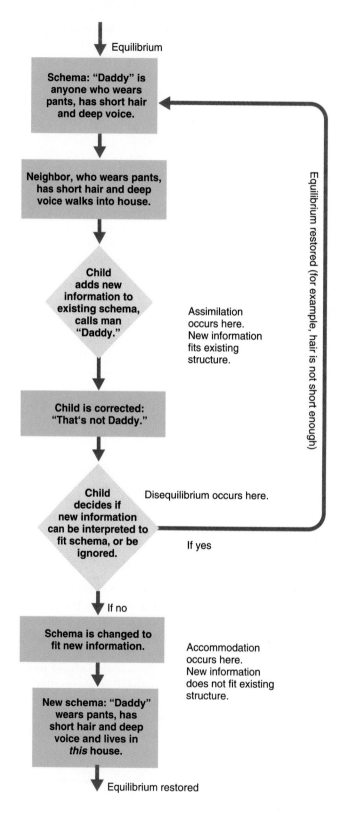

Figure 2.4
Altering schemata to assimilate new but cognitively compatible knowledge (top) or altering schemata to include incompatible knowledge (bottom) and restore equilibrium.

Equilibrium

Schema: "Daddy" is anyone who wears pants, has short hair and deep voice.

Neighbor, who wears pants, has short hair and deep voice walks into house.

Child adds new information to existing schema, calls man "Daddy."

Assimilation occurs here. New information fits existing structure.

Child is corrected: "That's not Daddy."

Child decides if new information can be interpreted to fit schema, or be ignored.

Disequilibrium occurs here.

If yes

Equilibrium restored (for example, hair is not short enough)

If no

Schema is changed to fit new information.

Accommodation occurs here. New information does not fit existing structure.

New schema: "Daddy" wears pants, has short hair and deep voice and lives in *this* house.

Equilibrium restored

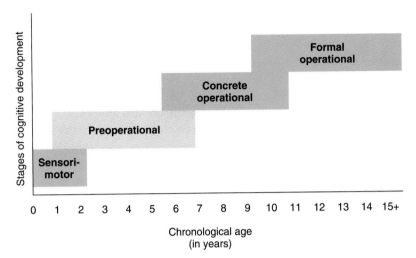

Figure 2.5
Piaget's concept of stages of cognitive development at various chronological age ranges.

as a "mini-scientist" who acts on the world and builds theories about it is very much consistent with current research findings.

The Preoperational Stage (2 to 7 Years). The **preoperational stage** builds on the accomplishments of the sensorimotor stage. Piaget postulated that a radical or qualitative change occurs at this time: the emergence of symbolic thought. We saw that toward the end of the sensorimotor period children are able to manipulate images in their heads, as shown by their ability to mediate. During the preoperational stage, they develop the ability to use symbols: they can make one thing (an image, an object, or an action) stand for something else. For example, during the preoperational period, children can make a horse out of a broom, a daddy out of a doll, or a truck or train out of a block of wood. Later (between 3 and 4 years), they play parts or roles: doctor and patient, mommy and daddy, good guys and bad guys, bus driver and passengers. Complex language, another example of the use of symbols, also emerges during this period.

Piaget emphasized that the emergence of true symbolic thought during the preoperational stage is not simply a quantitative, additive change. Rather, it is a drastic, quantum leap into a new cognitive realm, which, as Flavell (1985, p. 82) puts it, "seems nothing short of miraculous." In fact, most of Piaget's research on the preoperational period is devoted to describing this remarkable achievement in minute detail.

You may be puzzled by the term "preoperational." Operations, for Piaget, are mental actions that obey logical rules. When children arrange objects in sequence from smallest to largest, they are engaged in an operation. When they add 7 plus 8 to get 15, and realize that 15 minus 8 is 7, they have performed an operation. In the episode at the beginning of this section, Ola performed an operation when she explained that the shape of a container has no effect on the amount of the liquid that fills it. According to Piaget, children like Nirbay, who are between the ages of 2 and 7, are not ready to carry out such operations because they have not yet acquired an understanding of the laws of conservation.

Preoperational stage. The second of Piaget's stages of cognitive development; characterized by egocentrism and the increasing ability to mediate, but with a continued dependence on immediate experience.

Table 2.2

Piaget's Stages of Cognitive Development

Stage	Approximate Age	Characteristics
Sensorimotor	0–2 years	Begins to make use of imitation, memory, and thought Begins to recognize that objects do not cease to exist when they are hidden Moves from reflex actions to goal-directed activity
Preoperational	2–7 years	Gradual language development and ability to think in symbolic form Able to think operations through logically in one direction Has difficulty seeing another person's point of view
Concrete operational	7–11 years	Able to solve concrete, hands-on problems in logical fashion Understands laws of conservation and able to classify and seriate Understands reversibility
Formal operational	11–15+ years	Able to solve abstract problems in logical fashion Thinking becomes more scientific Develops concerns about social issues, identity

Source: Piaget's Theory of Cognitive Development, 3rd ed., by B. J. Wadsworth. New York: Longman Publishers USA. Copyright © 1984 by Longman Publishers USA. Reprinted with permission.

Laws of conservation. The understanding that changes in certain properties of an object (e.g., shape) do not change other properties of the object (e.g., mass).

What role does active involvement in classroom activities by my learners play in enhancing cognitive development?

Conservation is a term used to describe a child's understanding that the quantity or amount of something remains the same regardless of its original size or shape. For example, picture a child with two identical clear plastic cups of a soft drink in front of him, each cup filled to the same level, as illustrated in Figure 2.6. Pour the contents of one cup into a shallow, clear plastic bowl and pour the contents of the other cup into a tall, narrow container. Then ask the child to point to the container that has more of the drink. The child who consistently solves this type of problem correctly is said to understand the **laws of conservation.** Conservation tasks can involve solids, liquids, and continuous quantities, as shown in Figure 2.6.

Piaget has shown that children in the preoperational stage of cognitive development lack schemata to solve conservation tasks. At this stage children's reasoning is dominated by what they see. Thus, children at this stage of development typically respond to this conservation task by saying that the taller glass has more, even though nothing was added to the liquid as it was being transferred from one cup to another. As they have more and more experience playing with blocks, clay, water, and containers, children gradually alter these schemata and are able to demonstrate conservation. But this doesn't occur until they enter the concrete operational stage of development. Piaget believed that instructional attempts by adults to speed up the development of conservation schemata before the child is ready are likely to fail.

Piaget focused most of his theorizing about the preoperational stage on the child's use of symbols. Much of what he said about children during this stage focused on what they *can't* do: They can't yet consider the perspective of another (they are egocentric); they can't yet perform operations such as conservation of liquids (as Nirbay could not

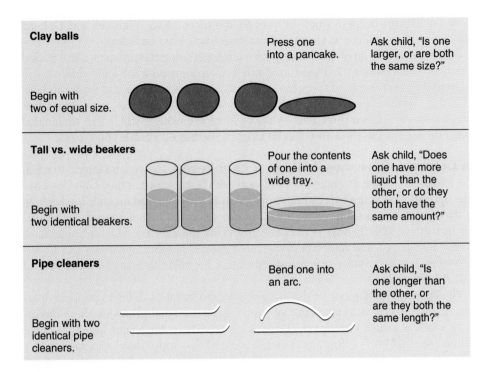

Clay balls

Begin with two of equal size.

Press one into a pancake.

Ask child, "Is one larger, or are both the same size?"

Tall vs. wide beakers

Begin with two identical beakers.

Pour the contents of one into a wide tray.

Ask child, "Does one have more liquid than the other, or do they both have the same amount?"

Pipe cleaners

Begin with two identical pipe cleaners.

Bend one into an arc.

Ask child, "Is one longer than the other, or are they both the same length?"

Figure 2.6
Different ways of determining whether a child has acquired the concept of conservation.

do); and they can't yet understand the concept of class inclusion (that the class of all dogs is different from but included within the class of animals). While the child in this stage understands that there are animals other than dogs, she doesn't understand that all dogs are animals.

Finally, the preoperational child cannot yet reason from the particular to the general, or vice versa. Instead, he reasons from particular to particular (Piaget called this *transductive reasoning*). For example, if you ask a preoperational child why it gets dark at night, he'll probably tell you "Because that's when we go to bed"; if you are driving in a car and ask the child why the trees are moving, she'll say "Because the car is moving." The child cannot yet formulate a general rule about natural phenomena or generalize beyond her immediate experience (she is *egocentric*). The cognitive structures required to perform all these operations develop during the preoperational stage.

Current Research. As with the sensorimotor stage, researchers are discovering that preoperational children are more cognitively capable than Piaget thought. Donaldson (1978), Bower and Wishart (1972), Chandler, Fritz, and Hala (1989), and Gelman and Ebeling (1989) all concluded that children around the ages of 3 and 4 are not as egocentric as Piaget suggested.

Researchers have shown that the difficulties children have with some of Piaget's classic experiments largely result from a lack of understanding of the researcher's questions. When researchers take pains to ensure that children understand these tasks, preoperational learners show that they can take the perspective of another; that is, they can begin to imagine what another viewpoint is like. Researchers such as Gelman (1972) and Bijstra, van Geert, and Jackson (1989) have shown that operations such as conservation of liquids can be performed by preoperational children. Waxman and Gelman (1986) report that children as young as 4 can understand class inclusion.

Current research on children's cognitive abilities during the preoperational period suggests two conclusions: (1) Piaget may have underestimated what some children can do during the preoperational stage; and (2) in order to exhibit more and varied abilities at this stage, researchers must first eliminate distractions, give clues, and ensure that children understand their directions. While children's thinking is still largely dominated by what they see at this time, they can be taught to be less egocentric (Bee, 1995).

The Concrete Operational Stage (7 to 11 Years). Those who intend to teach at the kindergarten or first-grade level will work with learners just as they enter the **concrete operational stage.** According to Piaget, this is the time when children become less dominated by appearances and acquire the schemata to understand arithmetic, think in symbols, classify objects into categories (like animal, vegetable, or mineral, or by color and shape), and understand the relationships between uppercase and lowercase letters. It is no wonder that formal education begins in so many societies around the world at this age.

The key accomplishments at this stage involve the learner's ability to perform operations or rules that involve mediation of words and images and to modify these mediators to reach a logical conclusion. Table 2.3 summarizes the major operations that children are capable of performing during this stage of cognitive development.

Of all the operations children can perform during the concrete operational stage, Piaget placed greatest importance on reversibility. *Reversibility* is the understanding that one's thinking processes can be reversed. For example, a first-grader understands that her model of a puppy, which was formerly a ball of clay, can be made back into a ball. A second-grader understands that 6 marbles added to his pile of 8 marbles makes a total of 14 marbles and that he can then create a pile of 8 marbles by taking 6 away from the 14. The child who grasps the basic reversibility of actions can understand other operations, such as the laws of conservation, inference, and hierarchical classification.

Implications for Teachers. Elementary school learners are far better problem solvers than are preschoolers. They can arrange objects in order; sequence numbers properly; classify objects by color, size, or shape; understand rules for both mathematics and classroom behavior; and think about both the past and the future. Nevertheless, concrete operational learners cannot perform these operations with things they cannot see or touch. In other words, their logic works only in concrete situations. Their mental operations are not yet ready for the realm of abstract ideas.

One way to illustrate this is to show an 8-year-old three dolls of ascending height whose names are Elleni, Carlos, and Aster. Show the child that Aster is taller than Carlos, and that Carlos is taller than Elleni, and the child will easily figure out that Aster is taller than Elleni. But present only a verbal description of the three dolls, and the child will have great difficulty determining the height of the first doll relative to the third doll. Thus K through 4 teachers should teach using concrete, hands-on activities that provide examples of more general rules and concepts. The accompanying box, *Teaching Concrete Operational Learners,* gives some specific examples.

Current Research. Researchers have confirmed Piaget's conclusions about the sequence and timing at which children acquire the various concrete operations and have shown that children between the ages of 7 and 11 rarely exhibit deductive logic but are adept at inductive reasoning (Tomlinson-Keasey, Eisert, Kalle, Hardy-Brown, &

Concrete operational stage. The third of Piaget's cognitive developmental stages, characterized by an understanding of the laws of conservation and a readiness to engage in other mental operations using concrete stimuli.

What adjustments must I make in the learning expectations and activities of my learners when they are in the concrete operational stage of cognitive development?

Table 2.3

Major Characteristics of the Concrete Operational Stage

Operation	Explanation	Example
Decentration	Concrete operational learners gain freedom from stimulus control: they can consider several features of a task rather than focus on only the one most obvious.	Ola recognizes that a change in one aspect of the grape drink (its depth) is compensated by a change in another aspect (its width).
Reversibility	Learners can mentally go through a series of steps to solve a problem and then reverse their thinking to return to the starting point.	Ola understands that if 7 baseball cards plus 8 new cards makes 15, then 15 minus 8 equals 7.
Conservation	Learners understand that objects remain the same in fundamental ways regardless of changes in shape or arrangement.	Ola sees a row of 10 green buttons and a row of 10 red buttons of equal length. If the spacing between the red buttons is increased so the row becomes longer, Ola realizes that there is still the same number of buttons.
Hierarchical classification	Learners can flexibly group and regroup objects into hierarchies of classes and subsets.	Ola sorts her baseball cards by team. Then she re-arranges them by position played.
Seriation	Learners use a plan to guide their arrangement of objects by height, weight, or age.	Ola weighs her rocks and arranges them in order from lightest to heaviest. Then she rearranges them from smallest to largest.
Transitive inference	Learners can seriate (arrange) objects mentally. After comparing A with B and B with C, they can infer the relationship between A and C.	Ola saw George's stack of baseball cards and noticed that he had more than she did. She now sees that Terry has fewer cards then she does. She tells Terry, "George has more cards than you."

Keasey, 1978). However, there is much debate about what causes these changes. Piaget emphasized that children, particularly at this stage, act as amateur scientists and discover the rules of operations largely on their own, using the functions of organization and adaptation. He said little about the contributions of social influences, such as peers and culture, to cognitive development. We will explore this perspective shortly, when we present the social nature of learning as formulated by Lev Vygotsky, an influential Russian developmentalist.

The Formal Operational Stage (12 Years and Older). Ola, the concrete operational thinker we introduced at the beginning of this section, has a question for her 16-year-old brother.

Ola: Why do my dinosaur toys get smaller when I put them underwater in the bathtub?
Rashid: Because light rays coming from your eyes to the water slow down and bend when they enter water. Water is more dense than air. Water makes light rays travel differently. That's why things look smaller.
Ola: But why do they look smaller?

Teaching Concrete Operational Learners

Teaching Classroom Rules. Explain your classroom rules first by having learners role-play lining up properly to leave for lunch, demonstrate changing from one learning center to another, or model how to work and play with materials. Concrete operational learners will internalize rules most quickly if they actually perform the activities involved.

Teaching Values. Stage classroom minidramas to teach values to concrete operational learners. For example, have them role-play accepting of learners with disabilities, asking for permission before using someone's property, or the appropriate reaction

when someone says something mean. Provide examples and demonstrations of appropriate actions *before* introducing the general principles from which they are derived.

Teaching Mathematical Concepts. Teach place value, or addition and subtraction facts, by having children work with manipulatives. For example, have them discover the answer to 8 plus 6 by performing the operation with beans or pasta shapes. Have the entire class collect acorns, then have them arrange all the acorns in groups of tens, the tens in groups of 100, and so on. Let the children see what 100 or 1,000 acorns looks like.

Rashid: They don't shrink. You understand that, don't you?

Ola: Yeah. I know that because when I take them out of the water they're the same size [Ola has reversible thought]. I just don't understand why they look smaller.

Formal operational stage. The fourth and final of Piaget's developmental stages, characterized by abstract thinking, logical reasoning, and other forms of higher-order conceptualization.

Rashid, who is in the **formal operational stage** of cognitive development, can take an abstract principle like "light waves travel at different speeds through substances of different density" and apply this to understanding a particular phenomenon, such as the shorter appearance of objects under water. This is an example of *deductive reasoning*, something his younger sister may not be able to do for several years.

According to Piaget, the major accomplishment of learners as they enter the formal operations stage is the development of a new and more powerful set of rules for thinking about the world: formal operations. Two features of formal operational thought that provide a new and more powerful set of rules for thinking are the ability to pose hypotheses and draw conclusions from observation (**hypothetico-deductive reasoning**) and the ability to ask "if-then" questions (*propositional thought*). These skills allow learners, beginning in middle school, to think about *possible* events, not just actual ones. They can speculate about what it might be like to go to college, and debate ethical and moral dilemmas, such as "Is it ever justifiable to take another human life?" They can think through complex if-then relationships, such as "If all animals have four legs, and if this table has four legs, then is this table an animal?" While Piaget asserted that these types of formal operations begin to develop during this period, they are not acquired all at once. Rather, they continue to emerge throughout the teenage years, with the greatest accomplishments occurring at about age 15.

Hypothetico-deductive reasoning. The ability to pose hypotheses and draw conclusions from observations.

Approximately when can I expect most of my learners to be able to reason logically and abstractly?

Current Research. Most current research in formal operations focuses on three questions: (1) Do all children reach formal operations? (2) Are young children capable of abstract reasoning? and (3) Are there any higher stages of intellectual development? (Bee, 1995; Berk, 1993; Shaffer, 1993).

Do all children reach formal operations? Try giving the following test to some of your friends:

Formal operational learners have complex thinking skills and can use learning strategies. This allows teachers to use learning techniques involving role-playing, debates, the design of experiments, and logical analysis to enhance their learners' cognitive development.

Premise 1: If there is a knife, then there is a fork.

Premise 2: There is not a knife.

Question: Is there a fork?

The correct answer to this question is "maybe." The wrong answer is "no." However, 40 to 60 percent of college students fail formal operational problems such as this one (Keating, 1979). Why? It appears that much of formal operational thought is situation specific. In other words, although college students and adults are capable of hypothetico-deductive reasoning, they tend to be better at it in the fields with which they are familiar. Thus physics majors are better able to demonstrate formal operations when dealing with physics problems than are psychology majors, who in turn are better at abstract reasoning in their discipline than are English majors, and so on (DeLisi & Staudt, 1980).

Are young children capable of abstract reasoning? Research indicates that concrete operational children can be taught abstract reasoning. For example, they can be taught how to solve propositions, such as the knife-and-fork task. Furthermore, training improves such performance (Hawkins, Pea, Glick, & Scribner, 1984). These training effects, however, are transitory. Specific training in propositional thinking lasts longer and generalizes more readily to new tasks when the trainees are in the formal operational stage (Greenbowe et al., 1981).

Are there higher stages of intellectual development? Although Piaget asserts that formal operations represents the apex of cognitive thought, Patricia Arlin (1975, 1977) disagrees. She believes that great thinkers like Einstein, Freud, and Piaget operate in a higher cognitive dimension in which they reconceptualize existing knowledge and reformulate it to come up with unique ways of thinking about the world. She calls this the *problem-finding stage* of cognitive development.

Piaget's Legacy

Piaget's insight and imaginative ideas about children have influenced how we think about cognitive development and, in particular, about child development. From Piaget's painstaking observations, we have learned that children think qualitatively differently at various stages of development and that these stages depend on the quality of the learner's experiences with the world around him. We are indebted to Piaget for the following beliefs about children and their development and learning:

1. All learning and cognitive development spring from the child's encounters with the surrounding world. Learning requires active involvement, both physical and mental, with those surrounding conditions.

2. The child is very much the agent of his or her development. Children build their own cognitive structures; they are not simply programmed at birth to think or act in certain ways.

3. Children do not passively receive knowledge in the form of facts, concepts, or procedures and amass it in their brains. Rather, they organize and transform it as they adapt new knowledge to existing cognitive structures.

4. Children think differently about the world than do adults. Although some of their perceptions may be viewed as "mistakes," they are based on a coherent way of perceiving reality, which is influenced by the schemata present at the time. Thus, the child's way of thinking changes over the course of development. Adults, therefore, should not view a child's logical errors as resulting from either an inability to think or a lack of previous learning.

Criticisms of Piaget's Theory

Developmental psychologists of different theoretical persuasions have raised two questions: (1) How do learners move into a new stage? and (2) Are there social influences on learning? In this section, we consider how two other theories, Gagné's intellectual skills hierarchy and Vygotsky's sociocultural theory, have expanded on, and in some areas contradicted, Piaget's work.

Gagné's Intellectual Skills Hierarchy. One limitation of Piaget's theory of cognitive development is that it does not explain how children move into the next stage. Are certain maturational changes necessary? Do certain skills have to be learned? To give you a greater appreciation of this criticism, let's examine a viewpoint that does appear to explain development through the stages.

Gagné's (1968, 1970, 1985) primary research interest was learning, not development. However, he applied his ideas about learning to explain how children develop cognitively. Because he approaches cognitive development as a learning theorist, his perspective has been called a developmental learning theory. Gagné (1968) views intellectual skills or cognitive capabilities as learned behaviors. This is in marked contrast to Piaget, who views intellectual skills as cognitive structures. From Gagné's perspective, the changes that take place as learners move through Piaget's developmental stages result from the accumulation of learned intellectual skills or capabilities, not altered schemata. School learners appear more capable at age 17 than at age 7 because they have learned more intellectual skills, not because they have better differentiated cognitive structures. Thus, the changes we see in learners as they acquire intellectual skills and master developmental tasks result from the cumulative effects of learning. Age and maturation are important only in that they allow the learner more opportunities to learn new things.

Gagné's position is that cognitive development proceeds continuously as the learner encounters new situations and new people. As the learner matures, people expect different things of her and interact differently with her. As a result, she can learn new behaviors such as language, walking, climbing, skating, and reading. This development is not only continuous but also cumulative. As children encounter new experiences, they add those experiences to prior experiences to form new behaviors. Earlier learned behaviors provide the foundation for later learned behaviors. Simpler learned behaviors form the basis of more complex learned behaviors.

This focus on the importance of prior learning experiences leads Gagné to another attribute of development. Development is *hierarchical:* new learning is dependent on mastery of prerequisite skills. A child must learn to keep his balance before he can ride a bike; he must learn to subtract before he can learn to divide. For Gagné, learning a new skill depends not on age or stage of development, but rather on the degree to which the learner has mastered prerequisite skills. In Chapter 4 we will return to Gagné's developmental learning theory, and in Chapter 9 we will see how it can be used to design lessons and units.

Vygotsky's Sociocultural Theory.   A second limitation to Piaget's theory is that it does not recognize the social context in which learning occurs. According to Piaget, brain maturation (combined with a learner's ability to experiment with a rich and varied environment) should lead children everywhere to reach concrete operations. Thus, Piaget has been criticized for failing to recognize that children grow up in varied social contexts that affect their experiences and the structure of their cognitive worlds. Lev Vygotsky's (1962) sociocultural theory has brought this oversight to the attention of developmental psychologists.

You've undoubtedly been told that a thorough knowledge of your students is essential for teaching them. But what is it, exactly, that you must know or understand about your learners to deal with their learning problems and promote their intellectual development? For Vygotsky the answer was straightforward: you must understand how learners think about the world and how this thinking evolves. Learners come to your classroom and encounter your lessons with certain experiences, information, concepts, and ways of thinking. Your goals and objectives may be easily assimilated into their schemata. Or, as we have studied, a process of disequilibrium, accommodation, and equilibrium may have to take place before the learner can grasp what you are teaching. While Piaget emphasized what the learner does on his or her own to alter or accommodate existing schemata to new experiences, Vygotsky focuses on what learners and adults (or peers) do together to promote learning and development.

The Role of Culture and Social Relationships.   The theme of Vygotsky's work is that a learner's cognitive development takes place in a social context. Throughout their lives learners are surrounded by parents, siblings, relatives, friends, teachers, and fellow students. They communicate with one another, stimulate one another, learn from one another. Parents and teachers, in particular, are more knowledgeable and skilled than

> How will I know that my lessons include important facts, discriminations, concepts, rules, and strategies that the learner needs to master developmental tasks?

Culture and social relationships are major stimuli to cognitive development. According to Vygotsky, cognitive development is characterized by a learner's increasing mastery of important cultural tasks presented by adults and peers.

Have I met my learners' needs for sufficient conversation, public reasoning, shared problem solving, and cooperative projects?

learners and promote their development by reading to them, explaining to them, and conversing with them. Friends and fellow learners demonstrate and explain new ideas and practices. Television, books, and movies also play an important role in the development of new intellectual skills.

Learners acquire knowledge about their culture and history from their encounters with adults, peers, and the media. This cultural knowledge includes shared beliefs, ways of viewing the world, patterns of interacting with people, and language. Therefore, cognitive development, as Vygotsky views it, is a child's increasing mastery over the culturally determined developmental tasks imposed by social agents (adults and peers). This increasing mastery may not take place in stages, as Piaget would have us believe. Nor may the principal agent of this change be the child acting as the lone investigator of the environment. Rather, the learner's cognitive development and mastery of intellectual skills may be linked primarily to his or her interactions with other people.

This linkage takes place on two levels. At the social level, the learner interacts with parents, teachers, or peers and learns the specific knowledge, beliefs, attitudes, and patterns of thinking and reasoning that are important in his culture or community. He learns language, a sense of humor, styles of conversing with people, approaches to thinking about and solving problems, and beliefs about religion, nature, and historical events.

At the next level, cultural and historical knowledge is transformed into schemata within the learner, much as Piaget would predict. At this level the child gradually learns to master developmental tasks involving reading, math, and science and learns to solve them independently because she has practiced such tasks under adult guidance. Thus, children internalize the routines or programs they use to interpret the world and master developmental tasks through their social relationships. The principal mechanism responsible for this cognitive development, according to Vygotsky, is social interaction.

The Zone of Proximal Development. In describing the process of cognitive development, Piaget used the metaphor of balance. A state of imbalance is created when a learner encounters something that cannot be assimilated into an existing schema. This state of imbalance is gradually returned to a state of balance through accommodation and assimilation.

Zone of proximal development. Vygotsky's metaphor describing the range of skills and abilities bounded by what a learner can do independently and what a learner needs adult assistance in performing.

Vygotsky's term for the area in which cognitive development takes place is the **zone of proximal development.** This zone encompasses a range of skills or abilities bounded on one side by what the learner can do independently and on the other side by the skills that the learner needs adult assistance to perform. For any learners, there are as many "zones of proximal development" as there are developmental tasks to master.

For example, let's take the area of beginning reading. Assume that a child can independently read all consonant-vowel-consonant (cvc) words, such as *pat, mat, net,* and *get.* He can also read words that have two vowels together (cvvc), such as *raid* and *bead,* but only with adult assistance. Without assistance, he will not attempt to read words that begin with consonant blends, such as *flat* or *shut.* Thus, his zone of proximal development includes all those word-recognition skills between reading one-syllable cvc words and one-syllable cvvc words. Figure 2.7 equates the zone of proximal development to that part of a baseball field in which the batter is most likely to get a hit. Some parts of the field are too far removed (too difficult) given the batter's current skill level, while others are too close (too easy). The teacher's job is to "pitch the ball"—to stimulate the learner with materials and content—in such a way that the learner scores a "hit"—delivers a correct response—at or slightly above his current level of functioning. The zone of proximal development has also been called the *zone of maximum response opportunity* (Borich, 1996) to emphasize that it provides the learner with the opportunity to climb to the next rung of the learning ladder.

> **Should most of my instruction be targeted below, at, or slightly above my learners' current level of skill?**

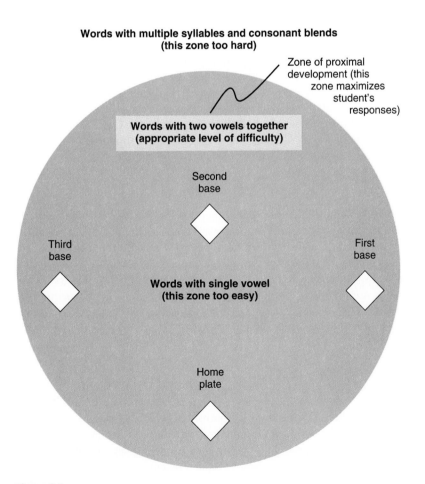

Figure 2.7
The zone of proximal development is the zone that, if stimulated by you, will bring a learner's response to the next level of refinement.

Vygotsky sees cognitive development taking place within the zone of proximal development when adults present instruction just above the learner's independent functioning level but not at a level that frustrates the learner. The zone gradually shifts upward as the learner masters new skills. In this manner, the learner and teacher gently pull and push each other in a student response–teacher reaction sequence that helps the learner climb to the next rung of the learning ladder. Thus cognitive development within the zone of proximal development involves continuously learning new skills, rather than arriving at a discrete new stage.

Neo-Piagetian Theory

Piaget's work continues to be challenged and refined. Neo-Piagetian theory, which originated in the 1960s, retains several of the ideas of the classic Piagetian system, extends some ideas, and alters others (R. Case, 1992). One contribution made by some neo-Piagetians has been to refine Piaget's concept of *vertical décalage.* Piaget used this term to describe how the sequence of substages at each level of development parallels the sequence of substages at other levels. Several theorists have developed this concept further, proposing that the same number of steps are completed at each major developmental stage, and that all steps are accomplished in the same sequence for each stage (Case, 1985; Fischer, 1980; Mounoud, 1986).

Another contribution made by neo-Piagetian theorists is that the "upper limit" of a child's cognition is influenced by the individual's maturational level and available working memory. Piaget left undeveloped the idea that specific biological factors play a large role in determining the upper limits of development. Similarly, many neo-Piagetians acknowledge that individual differences govern both the way in which children use their working memories and the way in which their thinking matures (R. Case, 1992; Lautrey, DeRibaupierre, & Rieben, 1987). Although these theorists have supported much of Piaget's work, others have questioned his ideas of cognitive development.

Summary

The greatest value of cognitive developmental theories for teachers is their ability to help us understand learning problems (Tharinger & Lambert, 1990). Piaget's, Gagné's, and Vygotsky's views enrich our developmental perspective on children's problems and provide a realistic context for them. For example, when a child is unable to master important academic or social tasks, you can use all of these theories to pinpoint the developmental tasks that are necessary before the child *can* learn. The accompanying box, *Using Developmental Theories to Analyze Learning Problems,* poses specific questions to ask from each developmental perspective.

Language Development

Earlier in this chapter we described cognitive development as the learner's increasing ability to gain freedom from stimulus control through the use of mediation. We mentioned that one of the most important tools for mediation is language. Language development plays an important role in cognitive development because it provides the symbols and rules that help us think, problem solve, and be creative.

Allowing us to be better thinkers is not the only function that language development serves. Language helps learners regulate their own behavior. It also allows learners to communicate with others and thus negotiate what they want and need from their

Using Developmental Theories to Analyze Learning Problems

Ask the following questions when analyzing specific learning problems according to each theorist's view of development.

Piaget

- Does the child have the necessary schemata to learn the task he or she is given? Are the material and techniques appropriate for the child's developmental level?
- Is the learner just entering a particular developmental stage and therefore not yet able to perform the task? Am I assuming that the learner has attained certain knowledge, concepts, and rules that he or she may not have?
- Has the child had sufficient opportunity to explore the material and actively manipulate it both cognitively and physically? Is the child in the process of accommodating new experiences to past knowledge and therefore in need of time to acquire the necessary schemata?
- Are my expectations for the learner unrealistic, given his or her age and developmental history?
- Are the material and experiences too unfamiliar or irrelevant to the child's existing schemata and prior experiences to create the disequilibrium necessary for new learning to occur?

Gagné

- What assumptions have I made about what the learner already knows or can do before I begin instruction? Is there ev-

idence from past performance that these assumptions are valid?
- Has the child received instruction in the necessary prerequisite skills?
- What cognitive demands or prerequisites are being placed on the learner by these instructional tasks?
- Do my lessons include important facts, discriminations, concepts, rules, or strategies that the learner will need in order to master subsequent tasks in the hierarchy?

Vygotsky

- Has my instruction been focused within the child's zone of proximal development? Is the child bored because he has already mastered these skills or frustrated because they are beyond what he can be expected to learn?
- Has the child's learning been too solitary? Have I met the learner's social learning needs by allowing for sufficient conversation, public reasoning, shared problem solving, and cooperative projects?
- Have I been expecting the learner to acquire knowledge that is incompatible with his or her culture? Do I use instructional methods that are culturally unfamiliar, irrelevant, or contradictory? (We will explore this issue in Chapter 15.)

environment. Learners often find themselves in new and challenging situations in which they must be understood and, in turn, understand others in order to have their needs met. As language ability develops, learners become better able to communicate with a wide variety of listeners in a variety of social contexts.

In this section, we will discuss what teachers can do to enhance these three important functions of language: thinking, self-regulation, and communication. We will also describe what makes up language, and summarize the most important explanations for how it develops. Following this discussion, we will study the effects of bilingualism and nonstandard dialects on the development of language competence.

What Are Language and Language Development?

Language is more than just a collection of sounds. Linguists (Bloom, 1973) use the term *language* to refer to the following features of a communication system:

1. Language is a system of symbols. Words stand for things. Whether it is made up of particular combinations of sounds or gestures (as in sign language), a language system

uses symbols to refer to people, places, events, and things. It is primarily these symbols, which children first begin to use between 8 and 12 months, that allow them to engage in symbolic thought when they are 18 to 24 months old.

2. Language is a system of rules. Words are used together in certain ways to produce meaningful phrases and sentences. We typically call these arrangements syntax or grammar. All speakers of any given language understand the rules, or grammar, of that language. This common grammar results in mutual understanding.

3. Language is generative or creative. Learners can create an infinite number of phrases, sentences, and expressions that enhance their ability to organize what they see, problem solve, and synthesize information to create original ways of interpreting their world.

Recall from Figure 2.1 that language development is characterized by the child's slow but steady learning of sounds, gestures, words, rules, sentences, and the generative or creative powers of language. In addition to learning sounds, symbols, and the rules of language, the child also learns the cultural rules for when and how to use them. This "know-how" knowledge is often referred to as **pragmatics,** or the practical side of language. Pragmatics includes knowledge of how to get someone's attention, how and when to change from formal to informal speech, when to ask for certain things, and in general knowing how to be a good conversationalist.

Pragmatics. The cultural rules of language usage.

How a Child Develops Language Competence

Language development occurs so gradually that we often take it for granted. Yet when we reflect seriously on the language development process, it is a wonder that it happens at all. Think for a moment about the difference between the informal language the toddler and preschooler hear on the playground and the language they eventually use in writing and speaking formally. We rarely, in normal conversation, speak to children in complete sentences, and we often use incorrect grammar. We often fail to complete our thoughts, and we add all sorts of qualifiers and parenthetical expressions to what we say. Pinker and Prince (1988) point out that the sounds, phrases, and sentences that children hear in no way allow them to infer the rules for speaking them. We do not teach children the rules of language in the same way we teach them rules for addition, subtraction, or classroom behavior. How, then, do children learn language?

There are two principal explanations for how we gradually acquire the sophisticated rules of language: learning theory, which emphasizes the role of reinforcement and imitation, and biological theory (called the nativist theory when applied to language development), which emphasizes the role of genetics. An interactionist perspective on language development that combines elements of both theories is currently gaining acceptance.

Learning Theory. Behaviorists assert that learning language is simply a process of hearing sounds, imitating them, and being reinforced for doing so. When these sounds are incorrect, a listener (usually the parent), guides or prompts the child to make correct utterances. Grammatically correct language, then, is gradually shaped by listening to and being corrected by others.

There are some problems with this perspective. First, children spontaneously produce sentences they have never heard or had modeled for them—imagine, for example, a 3-year-old telling her mother that her dinosaur would like to have some spaghetti for lunch. Second, a lot of what children hear is grammatically incorrect, yet they eventually learn correct rules of grammar without feedback or reinforcement. Finally, some of the mistakes children make, such as saying "goed" for "went" or "runned" for "ran" are incorrect generalizations of rules they probably never heard in the first place. This final problem is what originally led to the nativist view of language development.

Nativist Theory. Noam Chomsky (1965, 1975, 1986, 1988), an influential linguistic scholar, proposes that humans are innately wired for language. He postulates that humans are born with a built-in **language acquisition device** (LAD). The LAD (which Chomsky now refers to as a universal grammar) is an innate neurological process that is programmed to pick up the regular features of any language the child is exposed to (whether Swahili, Farsi, French, or Mandarin). The particular language that learners hear is filtered through this system and coded or stored as rules. These rules are then passed on to the listener as his or her language. Figure 2.8 shows how this process works.

Linguists have posed challenges to Chomsky's perspective. For example, much of a toddler's initial language utterances follow no known grammatical rules. A 2-year-old is just as likely to say "cookie Daddy" as "Daddy cookie." Postulating a LAD that abstracts rules of language and passes them on to the child appears to ignore this phenomenon (Maratsos, 1983). In addition, language competence develops far more gradually and slowly than nativist theory would have us believe.

The Interactionist Perspective. Presently, linguists and developmental psychologists concerned with language development hypothesize that children are born with certain innate abilities that predispose them to acquire varying degrees of language competence (Bohannon & Warren-Leubecker, 1989). These abilities, when combined with an environment rich in language and other experiences, can result in learners with high degrees of language competence. In contrast, environments that offer the child little language stimulation and other enriching experiences may impede the development of language competence. Thus, the learning and nativist theories conjointly explain variations in how language develops.

Language acquisition device. A built-in neurological device programmed to pick up the regular features of any language or communication.

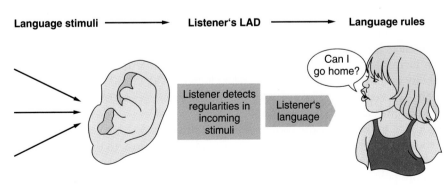

Figure 2.8
The language acquisition device (LAD).

How Teachers Can Promote Language Development

Earlier we said that language development enhances overall cognitive development by making children better thinkers and mediators, better communicators, and better regulators of their own cognitive and social behavior. Although your learners will have mastered most of the rules of language by the time they enter first grade, there are, nevertheless, significant teaching activities that can promote language development and enhance these three important outcomes. Let's explore some of these language development strategies.

How Teachers Can Enhance Mediation. As we have discussed, language provides the symbols and rules that help us think. Consequently, the more precise, elaborate, and complex a child's language expressions are, the more sophisticated will be her mediation or thinking abilities. Teachers can enhance mediation ability principally by promoting an expanded vocabulary and more complex syntactic development.

In elementary school, teachers can help their learners acquire new words and define words more precisely. This, in turn, will help learners see more clearly the relationships between words and concepts. For example, defining a bicycle as a means of transportation helps a child understand its relationship to a car, truck, or boat. These relationships would not be evident if a child's definition of *bicycle* were "something with wheels and a chain." Thus, teachers can promote both language development and cognitive development by helping learners understand the critical attributes of concepts like "bicycle," "shirt," and "cheese" rather than seeing them only in terms of their appearance or function.

In high school, mediation can be enhanced by helping learners understand both the literal and metaphorical meanings of words. For example, ask learners to explain the different ways in which a poet and an engineer might describe a bridge. What different meanings does the word then have? Such exercises help learners to think and reason in terms of metaphors and analogies and to see patterns and relationships in the world around them that may not be readily apparent.

How Teachers Can Enhance Communication. Children and adolescents must know how to use language to get what they want and need (*pragmatics*). One important example of pragmatics is knowing how to ask questions to get information. Many educators consider question-asking an important skill in cognitive development because it enables children to obtain important information as well as to regulate their own learning (Henderson & Swanson, 1977).

Researchers have found that teaching question-asking skills to school-age children results in increased participation in class discussions (Blank & Covington, 1965), in a better ability to get the teacher's attention when help is needed, and in improved problem solving (Rosser & Nicholson, 1984). The accompanying box, *Teaching Question-Asking Skills,* gives an example of how to go about it.

In addition to teaching early elementary school learners the pragmatic skill of asking questions, teachers can model for them how to phrase expressions that make it more likely a request will be granted. For example, teachers can demonstrate how to phrase a request more politely when the first one didn't obtain the result intended. For junior high and high school learners, teachers can demonstrate the pragmatics of persuasion and argument to help learners become more successful debaters.

In what ways can I enhance the language development of my learners and improve their thinking ability?

How will learning to ask questions enhance my learners' cognitive and language development?

Teaching Question-Asking Skills

Following is an example of how a teacher can promote question-asking skills in young children.

Margie: Laura and Norbert, look at this picture. Ask me some questions about it.
Laura: Why does the man look scared?
Margie: Good question! Because he's falling off his horse. Ask another question.

Norbert: How come he isn't using a saddle?
Margie: Good question! Because he likes riding bareback. Ask me another question.
Laura: What would happen if he falls into the cactus?
Margie: I like that question! The cactus spines would hurt him.

Source: Swanson & Henderson, 1977, pp. 349–350.

How Teachers Can Enhance Self-regulation. Language not only helps learners think and communicate; it also helps them control or monitor their own behavior. According to Vygotsky (1962), language helps children think about their own actions and plan what they will do. He views such *covert* or private speech as the foundation of all higher cognitive processes, including voluntary attention, planning, problem solving, and self-reflection.

You can improve learners' self-regulatory skills by pointing out the special demands of tasks, such as writing, problem solving in math, and even focusing on a task when the classroom has many distractions. You then can teach learners how to use private speech, either in the form of questions or assertive statements ("I can do this! I'll just follow the method I learned."), or to help themselves persist at their work, check their own progress, and praise themselves for a job well done.

How Does Learning Two Languages Affect Cognitive Development?

Nearly 3 million school-age children speak a language other than English at home (Berk, 1993). Many of these learners are considered to have limited English proficiency (LEP). Consequently, theoretical and practical questions are continually being asked about whether LEP students should be exposed to two languages during their preschool and early elementary school years, whether bilingualism promotes or impedes language and cognitive development, and how children can best acquire a second language.

There are basically two ways for children to become bilingual: (1) by acquiring both languages simultaneously, or (2) by learning the second language after mastering the first. Research has shown that either method results in normal language competence in both the language used at home and in the second language (Reich, 1986). Thus, parents and teachers need not fear that bilingualism adversely affects language competence. Moreover, a growing body of research suggests that bilingualism promotes overall cognitive development. Research by Hakuta, Freidman, and Diaz (1987) indicates that bilingual children, in comparison with monolingual children, show superior performance on tests of analytical reasoning, concept formation, and cognitive flexibility. Other research shows that learners who are fluent in two or more languages have a better knowledge of language structure and detail, understand that words are arbitrary symbols for actions, and can better detect grammatical errors in written and spoken communication (Bialystok, 1986; Galambos & Goldin-Meadow, 1990).

Finally, on the issue of how best to teach a second language, there seem to be some clear trends. Table 2.4 describes five different types of bilingual programs, and Figure 2.9 demonstrates the emphasis each type places on the learner's native language. Neither submersion in the second language nor immersion programs have

Table 2.4

Bilingual Programs

Type of Programs	Description
Maintenance	Help students become proficient in English while retaining and strengthening their native language. Used primarily at the elementary level, maintenance programs conduct most of the instruction in the learner's native language while maintaining close links with the child's home and non–English-speaking community. This approach usually requires large numbers of nonDEnglish learners within the school who speak the same native language and a teacher team with at least one bilingual member. Students enrolled in a maintenance program often move to a transitional program after a year or two.
Transitional	Aim to promote proficiency in English and use the student's first language as a vehicle for accomplishing this as quickly as possible. Unlike maintenance programs, transitional programs use the native language only as an aid for learning English. Transitional programs typically last two or three years, sometimes providing only a short time in which to prepare learners for the English-only classroom.
Immersion	Teach English by placing non–English-speaking learners in an English-only environment with a teacher who speaks the native language. The teacher uses the learner's native language only as an adjunct, when misunderstandings occur. Although this approach can help some learners rapidly acquire English, it can also create discontinuities between home and school, especially if the child no longer chooses to speak the native language in the home. In both immersion and submersion programs, the authority of non–English-speaking parents as significant others can be weakened.
Submersion	Place students in a classroom where only English is spoken and most students are native English speakers. Typically, the teacher makes little or no attempt to use the learner's native language as either an instructional or a communication tool. Because of the lack of engagement with the learner's native language, submersion programs can be the most disruptive to the learner's native culture and home life. They are used largely because they are among the least expensive for teaching the nonnative learner.
English as a Second Language (ESL)	Sometimes used in place of or in addition to bilingual programs at the later elementary and high school levels. Their primary focus is on remediating specific problems nonnative speakers have in learning English (for example, vocabulary, syntax, pronunciation) in the context of mostly English-only instruction. ESL classes do not teach English in the context of subject matter content, as do other types of programs, but instead are "pullout" programs, which remove learners from another class for one or more periods of the school day. The disadvantage is that students miss some instruction in the regular classroom or in another subject for part of the school day.

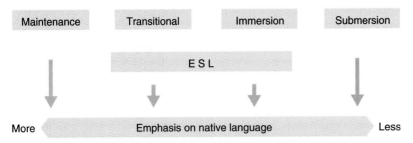

Figure 2.9
Types of bilingual programs and their relative emphasis on the native language.

been found as effective as maintenance and transition programs for teaching English to nonnative speakers (Bee, 1995; Padilla et al., 1991; Willig, 1985). In both maintenance and transition programs, learners are instructed in basic skills in their native language during the first and second years of school but are also exposed to the second language in the same classroom. Both languages are then maintained for several years before the child is expected to perform entirely in the second language in school.

Cognitive Development and Nonstandard English

All languages, including dialects and other forms of nonstandard English, are equally complex and equally capable of being used for cognitive mediation and problem solving (Dillard, 1972; Henderson, Swanson, & Zimmerman, 1974; Tharp, 1989). Linguists have demonstrated that languages cannot be ranked in terms of intellectual sophistication. Consequently, intellectual impairment or slow cognitive development cannot result from the primary language that a learner speaks, regardless of how nonstandard that language is.

In this chapter we studied how children grow and mature cognitively. With this cognitive development theory as background, we turn now to describing how children master important affective developmental tasks. In Chapter 3 we will see how learners acquire a healthy attitude about themselves, form successful relationships with peers and adults, and behave ethically and morally. We will also study how learners develop and improve self-esteem and learn prosocial behaviors through a process called social cognition.

Summing Up

This chapter introduced you to the growth and development of learners. Its main points were these:

- Developmental psychologists study changes that occur in the physical, social, language, and cognitive characteristics of learners at different ages. They describe changes in how children grow, think, speak, and relate to one another and attempt to explain these changes.
- Developmental psychologists typically are concerned with three fundamental questions about human growth: (1) Is there one road to development, or are there many unique paths? (2) Are the forces that influence learner development internal or environmentally determined? (3) Is development best characterized

by sequential, cumulative, and hierarchical changes, or by stages, transition points, and developmental leaps?

- The nature/nurture question refers to whether development results from the unfolding of an inherited genetic makeup or from the experiences and environments we encounter.

- The principal contributions of the cognitive developmental theory of Piaget were the detail with which he observed children's developmental changes and his conception of qualitative (as opposed to quantitative) differences in how children of different ages think and problem solve.

- Schemata are developed under the guidance of two innate intellectual functions: organization and adaptation.

- According to Piaget, the lifelong process of cognitive development involves creating and enriching schemata by assimilating new but compatible knowledge or by altering them to include incompatible knowledge through the process of accommodation.

- Piaget proposes that every child passes through four distinct and qualitatively different stages: sensorimotor (ages 0–2), preoperational (ages 2–7), concrete operational (ages 7–11), and formal operational (ages 11–up).

- Gagné stated that the child becomes better able to think, reason, and problem solve as he or she gets older as a result of being taught increasingly complex learning hierarchies.

- The principal theme of Vygotsky's developmental theory is that a learner's cognitive development takes place in a social context.

- The zone of proximal development encompasses the range of skills or abilities bounded on one side by the skills the learner can do independently and on the other side by the skills that a learner needs adult assistance to perform.

- Three important functions of language are to provide (1) symbols and rules that help one think, problem solve, and be creative; (2) promote cognitive strategies, the exercise of self-control, and self-monitoring; and (3) provide the means by which one can obtain what is wanted and needed from the environment.

- Language is a communication tool that includes a system of symbols, a system of rules, and a generative (expandable) or creative function.

- The language acquisition device (LAD) is a neurological process programmed to code and store the rules of any language.

For Discussion and Practice

°1. How could your understanding of the nature/nurture question help you better explain a student's behavior?

2. Using some examples of your own, explain the difference between quantitative changes in behavior and qualitative changes. Which do you believe is the better explanation for how we change and develop?

°3. Describe two developmental changes in the behavior of children that led Piaget to believe that development was qualitative and progressed in stages.

Questions marked with an asterisk are answered in the appendix.

*4. Describe what is meant by schemata, and provide an example at each of Piaget's four stages of development.

*5. Describe what is meant by organization and adaptation.

*6. Consider an area of content in your teaching field and describe how a learner would use the processes of organization and adaptation to acquire new information.

*7. Identify the primary accomplishments and limitations of Piaget's developmental stage theory.

*8. Vygotsky creates a different metaphor than Piaget to describe the context in which cognitive development takes place. What is his metaphor and how does it apply to the classroom?

*9. Identify the primary accomplishments of Vygotsky's theory of cognitive development.

*10. In your own words, how does Vygotsky's perspective on development differ from those of Piaget and Gagné?

*11. Describe the interactionist perspective, which combines the learning theory and nativist theory approaches to language acquisition. Give an example of how this broader perspective could account for some forms of language acquisition that cannot be explained by either the learning or the nativist approach alone.

*12. Using examples from your own teaching field, indicate different teaching strategies that could be used to (1) enhance your learners' mediation or thinking abilities and (2) encourage self-regulatory activities that would help your learners reflect on their own behavior.

*13. What are the differences between true bilingual instruction, total immersion, and English as a second language instruction?

Suggested Readings

Berns, Roberta M. (1993). *Child, family, community*. Fort Worth: Harcourt Brace Jovanovich. This is written for parents, teachers, and other professionals who routinely work with children. It is particularly strong in articulating the influence of family and community on children's development.

Cowan, P. A. (1978). *Piaget with feeling*. New York: Holt, Rinehart and Winston. After reading Piaget himself, there is no better guide than this to appreciating his insight and imagination.

Pinker, S. S. (1994). *The language instinct*. New York: Morrow. A fascinating and convincing account of the nativist view of language development, written by a disciple of Noam Chomsky. An extremely lively and readable introduction to developmental linguistics.

Schaffer, Davis R. (1993). *Developmental psychology* (3rd ed.). Pacific Grove, CA: Brooks Cole. This book provides a comprehensive overview of many of the most important aspects of child development. It is a particularly good source of information in the area of cognitive development.

Vygotsky, L. S. (1986). *Thought and language*. Cambridge, MA: MIT Press. Why the Soviet Union suppressed publication of this book, we will never know! After making the effort to understand his ideas, you'll appreciate his current popularity.

Personal-Social Development:
The Feeling Child

This chapter will help you answer the following questions about your learners:

- To what extent should my instructional goals include the affective development of my learners?
- Why do some children learn behaviors that repel rather than attract other children?
- What role do I play in the development of my learners' self-esteem?
- What role do friendships play in the personal-social development of my learners, and how can I enhance friendly relationships?
- Can learners be taught helping or prosocial behaviors?
- How can I enhance my learners' ability to think and reason about their own moral and ethical behavior?

As we begin our study of personal-social development, consider the following episode, described by Greenwood and Parkay (1989).

Setting: A small, relatively new high school in a rural area of a southeastern state.
Time: Lunch period on a warm autumn day.

Mr. Nash, on hall duty, is standing in the doorway because students are not permitted in the building during lunch period. Joe, a large, muscular 19-year-old-senior, whom Mr. Nash recognizes as one of his American history students, approaches the door. Mr. Nash has been warned that Joe is a troublemaker but has experienced no trouble with him to date.

Mr. Nash: You can't come in the hall now. You know students aren't allowed in here at this time.
Joe [staring belligerently]: I want some water.
Mr. Nash: You have to wait until the bell sounds. [Joe, ignoring Mr. Nash, walks to the water fountain and gets a drink.]
Mr. Nash: I told you you couldn't get water.
Joe [insolently]: I've already gotten it. [Mr. Nash says nothing more, and Joe walks outside.]

Shortly after this incident, Mr. Nash goes to the principal to obtain information about Joe. From Joe's disciplinary file, Mr. Nash discovers that he has been a problem through the years. He learns that Joe once threatened a teacher, has a reputation for fighting, and lacks respect for authority. Scholastically, Joe appears to be average. Mr. Nash also learns that Joe lives with his grandmother, that he never knew his father, and that his mother died when he was 8 years old. His grandmother is unable to discipline him, but she is concerned and cooperates with the school.

A few days later Joe comes to Mr. Nash's class late, expecting to be sent out for being tardy. Joe takes his assigned seat in the back of the classroom and pulls out a comic book. He glances at Mr. Nash as though daring him to say something, but Mr. Nash calmly ignores him and teaches the class. At the end of class, Mr. Nash calls for the papers that have been assigned. All the students except Joe hand them in. Mr. Nash says nothing as Joe walks by without his paper.

In this chapter you will also learn the meanings of these terms:

affectional bonds
empathy
horizontal relationships
modeling
perceived self-efficacy
prosocial behaviors
schema of attachment
self-concept
self-esteem
social cognition
stages of identity
vertical relationships

The next day Joe is on time for class. However, instead of taking his assigned seat, he sits in another student's seat.

Brenda: Get out of my seat, Joe! [As Joe looks at her daringly, Brenda approaches Mr. Nash in the front of the room.]
Brenda: Joe's in my seat.
Mr. Nash: Joe, you know where your seat is. Will you please sit where you belong?
Joe: I'll sit where I want to.
Mr. Nash: You'll sit where you are supposed to sit or we'll go to see the principal. [Joe grudgingly goes to his seat. An hour later, the class is dismissed.]
Mr. Nash: Joe, will you stay after class for a few minutes? [Joe hesitates, then comes to the front of the room.]
Mr. Nash: Joe, what happened to the assignment that was due yesterday?
Joe: I didn't get around to doing it. I'll turn it in later.
Mr. Nash: Why did you sit in Brenda's seat? I thought you and Brenda got along pretty well.
Joe: I was having a little fun with her, that's all. [Mr. Nash dismisses him.]

A week later Mr. Nash is in charge of admitting students to a football game. Joe walks in without paying, and Mr. Nash follows him.

Mr. Nash: You know you're supposed to pay?
Joe: So what?
Mr. Nash: I can't let you in without a ticket.

Joe ignores Mr. Nash and bolts into the stadium. The incident is reported to the principal, and Joe is escorted from the game. Joe's grandmother is called in by the principal the next day. She describes Joe as a problem at home also.

The next day in the teachers' lounge during Mr. Nash's planning period, several teachers are discussing Joe's conduct.

Mr. Nash: I'm concerned about Joe. I think he has a serious problem, and we should do something to help him.
Mr. Evans [the shop teacher]: I haven't had trouble with Joe in my class. In fact, he's one of my better students.
Mr. King [the math teacher]: He's always late for my class, and I won't let him in. You're just wasting your time on Joe.

Later, Mr. Nash meets Joe in the hall.

Mr. Nash: Come into my room; Joe, I'd like to talk to you for a minute.
Joe: What's the matter? I didn't do anything wrong.
Mr. Nash: I think you're capable of doing good work, Joe. So, what seems to be the problem?
Joe: I don't have a problem. Nobody's gonna tell me what to do.
Mr. Nash: If you're going to be a part of this school, you have to obey the rules, just like everyone else.
Joe: I'm not like everyone else.

Whether you teach in the early elementary grades, middle school, junior high, or high school, you will encounter learners like Joe. They are puzzling, complex, challenging, and frustrating to teach. They often show widely divergent patterns of behavior at different times and defy simple solutions.

Learners like Joe confront us with difficult questions. Are there enduring personality traits such as self-esteem, anxiety, and the need to challenge others that affect a person's behavior in the same way in all situations? Or is personality simply the way a person behaves in particular situations?

Like Joe, many children show a general pattern of behavior in most situations with exceptions in others. Some children, for example, are angry and uncooperative in some instances but cooperative and willing in others. How do these tendencies develop? How does a learner establish an ability to get along with others, gain self-confidence, and acquire moral and ethical behavior?

The role you play in your learners' personal and social development is as important in your teaching as your role in cognitive development. To what lengths should you go in the classroom to meet the affective needs of your learners? Should you view yourself primarily as a subject matter specialist who delivers effective lessons? Or should effective teaching include creating an atmosphere for learning in which all your students can feel comfortable and confident? These are some questions we will examine in this chapter.

> **To what extent should my instructional goals include the affective development of my learners?**

In Chapter 2 we addressed two basic questions:

1. What are the basic processes underlying development?

2. How can we better understand the cognitive developmental challenges that learners confront in school?

In this chapter we will examine two related but different questions:

1. How do children develop the ability to learn important personal-social behaviors that allow them to acquire a healthy attitude about themselves, form successful relationships with peers and adults, and behave ethically and morally?

2. How can teachers enhance self-esteem, the ability to get along with others, and ethical and moral behavior?

Three Theories of Personal-Social Development

While Joe's behavior can be examined from a variety of theories, we will study three in particular that are among the most discussed and researched. These are the biological, social learning, and psychoanalytic theories of personality and affective development. Let's review the basic ideas of these theories:

- *Biological theory* holds that differences in how we feel about ourselves, get along with others, and acquire a moral conscience are due largely to temperaments that we inherit from our parents (Bee, 1995).

- *Social learning theory* holds that personality differences are acquired through the learning process, in particular the process of modeling (Bandura, 1977b, 1986).

- *Psychoanalytic theory* holds that personality differences are the result of the complex interplay of maturational forces, cognitive development, and experience (Freud, 1905, 1965).

In this section we will explore each of these three explanations for how learners develop affectively and consider why Joe might have behaved the way he did.

The Biological Approach

The biological approach, as applied to personal-social development, holds that we inherit certain traits, or temperaments, from our parents. These temperaments describe certain predictable patterns of behavior or behavioral styles that we display in the presence of certain people, places, and events (Carey, 1981). One such temperament is *activity level*. Some individuals can be described as being energetic, up-tempo, vigorous, and having stamina and endurance, while others are low-key, laid-back, and lethargic. Your activity level can be traced to basic physiological processes, which are largely inherited (Buss & Plomin, 1986).

Adaptability to new experiences is another temperament that may be inherited (Thomas & Chess, 1977). Some of us are quick to adjust to new places and people, while others are slow to adapt and are more cautious when placed in strange and unfamiliar surroundings.

A third behavioral style or temperament is *emotionality*. Emotionality describes the degree to which individuals become quickly upset, fearful, or angry (Buss, 1989). Emotionality, along with activity level and adaptability, is assumed to be rooted in physiological processes that persist throughout childhood, adolescence, and adulthood (Bee, 1995).

Temperaments affect not only the way individuals react to their environment but also how people in the environment react to individuals with these traits. Sociable children seek out and in turn are sought by other sociable children. Conversely, temperamentally difficult children often elicit high rates of criticism and punishment from their parents and teachers.

Supporting Evidence. Temperament research is a relatively new and controversial field within developmental psychology. Psychologists often compare identical twins, who have identical biological inheritance, and fraternal twins, who share only half their genes, to obtain support for the hereditarian approach. Buss and Plomin (1986) have shown that identical twins reared apart are more similar to one another in emotionality, adaptability, and activity level than are fraternal twins reared together. Furthermore, there is some evidence that certain aspects of emotionality, adaptability, and activity level remain relatively constant as children get older (Heguik, McDevitt, & Carey, 1982).

A Biological Analysis of Joe. If we were to examine Joe's behavior from a biological perspective, we would identify certain traits that Joe possesses. For example, he appears to have a hard time getting along with others (adaptability) and becomes easily upset (emotionality). Biological theorists would then speculate that either or both of Joe's parents displayed similar temperaments and that Joe inherited these traits from them. They would examine Joe's school records for further evidence that Joe has exhibited this behavioral style over a number of years. Finally, they would analyze the persistence of Joe's problem in terms of the types of peers he is attracted to and the high rates of negative reactions he gets from peers and adults because of his temperament.

School-age learners display a variety of temperaments. Children differ in adaptability to change, activity level, and emotionality.

The Social Learning Approach

The basic assumption underlying social learning theory is that children learn and develop cognitively and affectively by observing others. We can treat social learning theory as a developmental theory because it views cognitive and affective development as dependent on the cumulative effects of three important events: (1) maturation of the child's increasing perceptual and physical abilities, (2) exposure to the increasingly complex verbal and physical behavior of models (parents, siblings, friends, teachers), and (3) an increasing ability to attend, recall, imitate, and be motivated.

In Chapter 2 we explained how children acquire new intellectual skills through social learning (Vygotsky, 1962). Children also learn affective skills through the same processes. For example, how do children learn how to take turns during a game? According to social learning theory, when children go to preschool, the skillful teacher calls their attention to the rules for playing certain games. She models taking turns and points out and praises other children who do the same. She then coaches her learners during the game to take turns and praises them for doing so. The child learns not only the behavioral skill of taking turns but also the expectation that taking turns will please others and that she can become good at it.

According to Bandura (1986), children learn social skills through a fundamental developmental process called modeling. **Modeling** involves being attentive to, remembering, imitating, and being rewarded by people, television, movies, books, and magazines. According to the social learning perspective, a child is popular not because he inherited a particular temperament but because, through modeling, he learned the behaviors involved in making and keeping friends. He also learned beliefs about the importance of friends, standards for what it means to have good friends, expectations that his efforts to make friends would be rewarded, and beliefs about his own ability to be liked by his peers.

Modeling. Demonstrating what learners are about to learn; the process of being attentive to, remembering, imitating, and being rewarded for imitating specific behaviors.

Why do some children learn behaviors that repel rather than attract other children?

Perceived self-efficacy. An appraisal or evaluation that a person makes about his or her personal competence at a particular task; an individual's personal expectations, internal standards, and self-concept.

The child who is unpopular, on the other hand, probably has not been exposed to appropriate models and has learned behaviors that repel rather than attract other children. Furthermore, she *expects* to be unsuccessful at making friends, has acquired a set of standards regarding who are and are not considered to be friends, and perceives herself to be someone who is not popular—someone who just can't make friends.

Bandura believes that the important developmental tasks that a child must master from infancy to adolescence are acquired through the social learning process. According to this theory, as children observe people and attend to the media, they are learning how to establish relationships, get along with others, acquire appropriate sex roles, and behave morally and ethically. Along with learning these behaviors, they are learning important ideas, expectations (the expected benefits to them for acting certain ways), internal standards (by seeing and hearing the standards by which others evaluate their actions), and self-concept (which Bandura refers to as **perceived self-efficacy**).

Supporting Evidence. Bandura and his followers support their theories with an extensive research base, which has accumulated over 25 years of skillfully and creatively designed studies. They have demonstrated how children become more or less aggressive depending on which models they observe (Bandura, 1973). They have also shown that the standards by which children judge the effectiveness of their own performances and those of others can be influenced by social learning processes (Zimmerman & Ringle, 1981). In addition, the extent to which learners monitor their own behavior, evaluate themselves, and praise themselves can be altered through observation of models (Glynn & Thomas, 1974; Glynn, Thomas, & Shee, 1973). Bandura also presents data showing that models can affect how competent or capable children think they are in performing tasks of varying difficulty (Bandura, 1982b). We will address the important role of modeling and its implications for instruction in Chapter 10. For now, let's see what social learning theory would say about Joe's behavior.

A Social Learning Analysis of Joe. Social learning theorists would note that Joe displays aggressive behavior toward both peers and adults. They would attribute his aggressiveness to two factors: (1) He has learned this behavior by observing aggressive models (others who physically discipline him), and (2) he has never learned the skills necessary to get along with peers and adults.

Joe also has low expectations for success in academic and social tasks. These expectations have developed through years of experiencing failure and social rejection. Each time he encounters failure, hostility from peers, or anger from teachers, his expectations are confirmed. His dislike of teachers and other authority figures prevents them from serving as role models of appropriate behavior and attitudes.

Joe's low expectations and lack of self-efficacy in academic and social settings also prevent him from learning new ways to behave around others. Joe only attracts, and is attracted to, certain types of peers. Consequently, his ability to socially learn appropriate skills, beliefs, attitudes, and expectations is limited.

The Psychoanalytic Approach

The psychoanalytic approach to personal-social development shares some characteristics with the biological and social learning approaches. Like biological theory, this approach, as we learned in Chapter 2, emphasizes that children are born with certain instinctual tendencies or drives. For Erikson (1950/1963) the genetic tendency that is most important for understanding personal-social development is the drive for identity. Although we are used to thinking of drives as sexual or life preserving, Erikson's drive for identity is a cognitive one.

Like social learning theory, Erikson's theory emphasizes the role played by the environment (particularly child-rearing processes) as it interacts with an innate drive for identity. Erikson's approach is also developmental: he holds that personality gradually develops over time as a result of the interactions between physical maturation, inborn drives, and experiences with the environment.

Unlike the biological and social learning approaches, however, Erikson's psychoanalytic approach is a theory of **stages of identity.** You were introduced to a stage theory in the previous chapter, when we studied the views of Piaget. Like any stage theory of development, Erikson's proposes that personal-social development proceeds through a series of age-related stages, some of which were identified in Chapter 2 (see Figure 2.1). Each of these stages has a central task or need that must be met before the child can enter the next stage. The stages unfold in a fixed order or sequence, which all psychologically healthy individuals follow over the life span.

Stages of identity. Discrete periods of personality development during which the individual confronts an identity crisis he or she must overcome to pass successfully to the next stage.

Erikson's Stages of Psychosocial Development. According to Erikson, the inborn drive for identity is the engine that powers personality development. By a "drive for identity," Erikson means the need each person has to know who he or she really is. This search is a lifelong quest. It starts in infancy, when you begin to form a personality as a result of your relationship with your parents. As you grew older, you expanded your relationships to encompass a wider and wider community of people, and you encountered increasingly complex social situations such as play groups, classrooms, team sports, dances, proms, and marital ceremonies. Your personality developed as a result of these encounters, as you continually attempted to solve the riddle of who you really are.

Erikson believes that as we grow older and experience new people and situations, we confront a series of identity crises. Each of Erikson's eight stages of psychosocial development challenges us with a unique identity crisis, out of which healthy personality

Erikson believed that personality develops only in the context of experience.

development occurs. If these crises are successfully met and resolved, the personality becomes strong and vigorous and better able to meet the challenge of the next stage or crisis. If, however, we fail to meet the challenge presented at one stage of development, we will be unprepared to meet the challenges of all subsequent stages. Erikson uses the metaphor of the "struggle to overcome identity crises" to explain the principal mechanism of personality development. His eight identity crises are described in the following sections and summarized in Table 3.1.

Stage 1: Infancy—Basic Trust Versus Mistrust. The infant spends her first year of life meeting the challenge of developing a sense of basic trust regarding the world around her. Depending on how her parents care for her, her response to their efforts, and her maturing physical capabilities, the infant will view the world as a predictable place that she can influence (basic trust), or a chaotic and unpredictable place over which she has little or no power (mistrust).

Stage 2: Toddlerhood—Autonomy Versus Shame and Doubt. During this stage the child develops the abilities to walk and to explore the environment. She learns to

Table 3.1

Erikson's Eight Stages of Development

Approximate Age (Years)	Ego Quality To Be Developed	Some Tasks and Activities of the Stage
0–1	Basic trust versus mistrust	Trust in mother or central caregiver and in one's own ability to make things happen; a key element in an early secure attachment.
2–3	Autonomy versus shame and doubt	Walking, grasping, and other physical skills lead to free choice; toilet training occurs; child learns control but may develop shame if issue is not handled properly.
4–5	Initiative versus guilt	Organize activities around some goal, become more assertive and aggressive. Oedipus-like conflict with parent of same sex may lead to guilt.
6–12	Industry versus inferiority	Absorb all the basic culture skills and norms, including school skills and tool use.
13–18	Identity versus role confusion	Adapt sense of self to physical changes of puberty, make occupational choice, achieve adultlike sexual identity, and search for new values.
19–25	Intimacy versus isolation	Form one or more intimate relationships that go beyond adolescent love; marry and form family groups.
26–40	Generativity versus stagnation	Bear and rear children, focus on occupational achievement or creativity, train the next generation.
40 +	Ego integrity versus despair	Integrate earlier stages and come to terms with basic identity. Accept self.

Source: The Developing Child, 7th ed. (p. 277), by H. Bee. New York: HarperCollins. Copyright © 1995, HarperCollins College Publishers. Reprinted by permission.

control biological needs for toileting and feeding. She can leave this stage with a sense of independence and autonomy or with feelings of shame about her failures and doubts regarding her ability to master her environment.

Stage 3: Early Childhood—Initiative Versus Guilt. During this stage the child's physical capabilities allow for greater freedom of movement, her cognitive abilities allow for greater language facility and the ability to control her environment through questions and requests, and her increasing abstract capabilities allow for greater use of imagination and symbolic play. These developing abilities and her parents' and teachers' reactions to them can create in her a strong sense of initiative: a desire to explore and to learn new things. On the other hand, if adults suppress, control, or ridicule the child's attempts to explore and take risks, she will react by developing feelings of guilt.

Stage 4: School Age—Industry Versus Inferiority. School places three important demands on children: to master academic tasks, to get along with others, and to follow the rules of the classroom. Children who succeed at these developmental tasks develop a sense of industry or competence (or, as Bandura would say, self-efficacy). Children who fail at these tasks acquire a basic sense of inferiority: they believe and expect that they can't do anything right.

Stage 5: Adolescence—Identity Versus Role Confusion. Adolescence is the time when a child draws upon all previous affective accomplishments and establishes a strong sense of who she is and who she hopes to be. If the child has successfully negotiated all prior identity crises, she enters adolescence with the belief that she is in control of her life and free to become whatever she chooses; with a willingness to meet new people, places, and events; and with expectations for success in whatever she tries. At this stage the child acquires not only a clear sexual identity but also an occupational identity. She adopts an appropriate sex role and realizes who and what she wants to be. If, however, the adolescent enters this stage having failed to resolve earlier identity crises, she will be

According to Erikson, children's personalities develop in stages during which they confront a variety of challenges. Healthy development at one stage depends on overcoming the challenges of the previous stages.

unable to cope with the many physical and social changes that inevitably confront her. As a result, she will leave this stage confused about who she is and what she will become.

Stages 6–8: The Adult Stages. Adulthood confronts us with three final crises: intimacy versus isolation, generativity versus stagnation, and ego integrity versus despair. While your learners will not have to confront these crises during their school years, you as a growing and developing adult will.

Before summarizing some of the evidence supporting psychoanalytic theory, we believe it is important to add that by identifying "crises" in terms of opposites (trust versus mistrust, autonomy versus shame), Erikson did not intend to imply that the ideal place to be at the end of any given stage necessarily and exclusively is with more trust, autonomy, initiative, or industry, and so forth. Both children and adults need a healthy mistrust, a healthy sense of needing other people, a healthy sense of caution in new circumstances, and a healthy realization of their limitations. In other words, it is the proper degree of each opposite that contributes to a healthy personality.

Supporting Evidence. Psychoanalytic theory is difficult to research. Its concepts and principles are general, metaphorical, and descriptive rather than analytic, and therefore they do not easily lend themselves to the methods of scientific validation. Thus, research projects designed to investigate the mechanisms underlying Erikson's approach are rare. However, research on the effects of divorce on young children (Allison & Furstenburg, 1989; Doherty & Needle, 1991; Wallerstein, 1984, 1989) shows that children of divorced parents, in comparison with children who have not experienced divorce, are at greater risk for depression, substance abuse, and emotional and behavioral disturbance. Similarly, research by Sroufe (1983, 1988) and Erickson, Sroufe, and Egeland (1985) suggests that infants and toddlers who are securely attached to their mothers when they enter preschool are better able to get along with peers, make new friends, and act sociably than less securely bonded infants and toddlers.

A Psychoanalytic Analysis of Joe. Joe's behavior suggests that he is overly aggressive, distrustful of adults, and lacking self-confidence and self-esteem. He was without his natural parents throughout much of his life and was raised by his grandmother. Some of this disruption may have occurred during the identity crisis of basic trust versus mistrust. If so, we can assume that Joe entered the toddler and early childhood stage of his life without a sense of control over his environment and with a basic distrust of people. The difficulty he experienced at this stage of development may have created feelings of shame and doubt. Having failed to resolve the crises of the first two stages of life, Joe may have entered his early childhood and school-age years uncertain of his abilities, overly dependent on adults for approval, and with low self-esteem.

A Synthesis of Theories of Personal-Social Development

Helen Bee (1995) combines the major processes of development stressed in the biological, social learning, and psychoanalytic theories into a single model of psychosocial development. Figure 3.1 represents her integrative view of the three theories of devel-

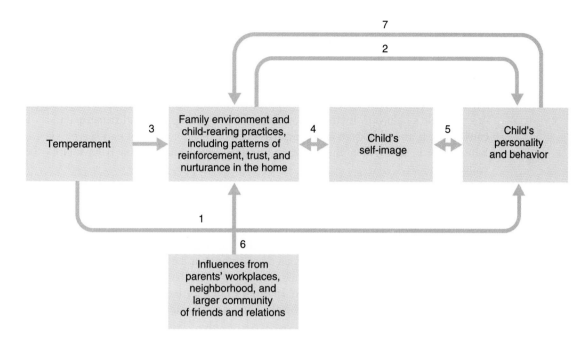

Figure 3.1
An integrative model describing the formation of individual personality. *Source:* From *The Developing Child,* 7th ed. (p. 283), by H. Bee. New York: HarperCollins. Copyright © 1995, HarperCollins College Publishers. Reprinted by permission.

opment studied in this chapter. Let's look more closely at this model of personal-social development.

Bee believes that any attempt to understand personal-social development must begin with a consideration of the child's inborn temperament. Arrow 1 represents the direct, causative effects of inborn traits on the eventual personality that we see in the child. According to Bee, the child's temperament represents an initial and permanent influence on the formation of personality. But the effect of temperament alone, as represented by Arrow 1, is insufficient to account for personality and individual behavior. Arrow 2, therefore, represents the direct effects on personality and behavior stemming from child-rearing practices and modeling processes.

What we think of as personality, however, is more than the product of these two forces. Arrow 3 represents the direct effect of the child's temperament on the family. Not only does temperament influence personality directly, but reciprocal influences involving the child's self-image occur. Arrow 4 represents the reciprocal influence of self-image and the family environment. Arrow 5 represents the reciprocal influence of self-image and personality. Thus, the child's self-image can shape as well as be shaped by personality and the family environment.

To add further to the forces that shape personality, we must remember that the child and his family are part of a larger system, consisting of the workplace, neighborhood, and larger community. Thus the family's ability to provide the stable and supportive environment essential to the development of basic trust, autonomy, initiative, industry, and identity may be affected by the economy, parental job satisfaction, and the social support networks available to the family (Arrow 6). Finally, Bee includes Arrow 7 to remind us that the child's personality and behavior not only are molded by how his parents behave but also shape the behavior of the parents. The child's attitudes, expectations, and behavior affect those who choose to be around, listen to, and play with him, and to some extent help determine who those people will be. A happy, self-confident child influences people to react in a supportive, loving manner. This, in turn, strengthens the child's behavior. By the same token, a sullen, unhappy, and distrustful child will cause parents and siblings to react negatively. Their reactions in turn may serve to maintain and even strengthen the negative attitudes, expectations, and behaviors of the child.

A Comprehensive Developmental Perspective of Joe

Bee's attempt to integrate the biological, social learning, and psychoanalytic approaches underscores the complexity of affective development and cautions us against simplistic explanations for the behavior of someone as complex as Joe. Joe's behavior can become more positive and socially acceptable. In order to help bring this about, we must understand his problems in all their complexity. Thus, any attempt to help Joe must acknowledge certain facts:

- Joe was born with certain temperaments or dispositions, which will always be an important part of his personality and behavior. However, the extent to which these impair Joe's development can be moderated by his environment.

- Joe's beliefs about people and himself have been shaped over a long period of time. While these beliefs can change, we must recognize that throughout his life Joe has been exposed to few models of socially acceptable behavior.

- Joe's current behavior causes reactions by peers and adults that only strengthen this behavior and confirm his attitudes, beliefs, and expectations of himself and those around him. It will not be sufficient for people to change how they act toward Joe. Joe must also change how he acts toward them.

- Joe has learned to approach his environment with a sense of mistrust. Any efforts to help Joe must deal with both his feelings of distrust and his attempts to frustrate those efforts.

With these perspectives of affective development as background, let's turn our attention to three important dimensions of this development: self-esteem, social relationships, and social cognition.

Self-esteem

Teacher: Can you look at me when we talk, Angela?
Angela: I don't want to look at you. I hate myself. [Angela shifts a little in teacher's direction.]
Teacher: I'm sorry you didn't get the grade you wanted. I think you may have to accept that this is a difficult course for you.

Angela: You think I should accept a D? You think a D is a good grade? I'll never be satisfied with a D!

Teacher: You make it sound as though I just made up your grade. You know I spend a lot of time on grades. I didn't give you a higher grade because you didn't earn one.

Angela: [pausing to think]: Oh, I guess you're right. It doesn't matter anyway. I'm not going to be here after this year. (Adapted from Ryan, 1992, p. 104)

Some educators and psychologists, when attempting to explain Angela's problems in school, might end up concluding that low self-esteem is at the root of them. Although it stands to reason that Angela's feelings about herself and her school achievement are related, the exact nature of this relationship is unclear. Did Angela's low self-esteem cause her to do poorly in school, or did poor achievement come first and low self-esteem follow?

Conventional wisdom holds that if children like themselves, they will make good choices for themselves. They will be good students, avoid drugs, listen to their parents and teachers, and make wise decisions about friends. This belief in the value of high self-esteem has compelled many school districts to add the development of self-esteem to their lists of school goals. At the same time, there is less agreement among educators and psychologists concerning the nature of self-esteem and how to improve it. The exact nature of self-esteem, how it develops, what accounts for differences in self-esteem among children, and its relationship to classroom achievement are the focus of this section.

Self-concept and Self-esteem

Self-concept and self-esteem are different, although many educators and psychologists use these terms interchangeably. **Self-concept** is best thought of as a *schema* or cognitive structure (a term we discussed in the previous chapter). As adults we organize our self-schemata or concepts to include a host of beliefs, feelings, and attitudes about ourselves. Some of these concepts are general (we are people, we are human beings, we have an existence outside our mind), while some are more specific. For example, we have beliefs, feelings, and attitudes about ourselves as students, workers, husbands, men, women, weekend athletes, country-western dancers, and so forth.

Like all schemata, our self-schema develops over time (Bee, 1995). The young child's self-schema is primitive and undifferentiated but includes some vague notions that he or she has an existence that is separate from others. Gradually, this schema changes. The developing child organizes her self-schema to include awareness of her sex, size, skills, likes, and dislikes. School experiences add to this schema, which gradually comes to include ideas of self ("I'm a girl"), individual ("I like sports"), and person ("I'm the athletic type"). During adolescence, according to Erikson, the self-schema takes on a future dimension as the person thinks about who she is becoming in terms of sexual, occupational, and ideological dimensions.

Self-esteem is a global evaluation or judgment of one's self-worth. When Angela declares that she hates herself, she opens up a window to her self-esteem. She indicates that she does not like who she perceives herself to be—whatever that perception may be. Harter (1988, 1990) tells us that children who make these global judgments do so on the basis of a perceived discrepancy between who they are and who they would like to be. Thus a child with low self-esteem has a standard of who she would like to be and

Self-concept. A schema individuals hold toward themselves.

Self-esteem. A global evaluation or judgment of one's worth.

perceives herself as not living up to that standard. She values some skill or quality and judges that she has little of it. She thinks that it is important to be good at some activity, such as a sport, and perceives that she is not good at it. The child with high self-esteem is satisfied with herself. She values something, has a standard to live up to, and judges that she has met that standard.

Thus, according to Harter, part of one's global judgment of self-worth, or self-esteem, is a quality or skill, or standard of performance, and a perception of how well this standard is met. A perception of discrepancy is responsible for low self-esteem. A child who values gymnastics but lacks the right body type will have lower self-esteem than a child with a similar body type who dislikes this sport. By the same token, being good at something you don't value will not boost your self-esteem.

Figure 3.2 summarizes the dimensions of self-esteem. The horizontal plane represents a continuum of value that a child places on a particular attribute. The vertical plane represents the child's perception of the extent to which he possesses that attribute. Quadrants A and D have no effect on self-esteem because the child either possesses an attribute he does not value or lacks an attribute he holds no value for. Quadrant B represents a context for high self-esteem. The child both values an attribute and perceives that he possesses it to a high degree. Quadrant C, however, represents low self-esteem, because the child perceives that he has little of an attribute that he values highly.

The Development of Self-esteem

Because self-esteem involves a judgment, a value, and a standard, it is very difficult to assess self-esteem in children before the age of 7 or 8. But as children become firmly embedded in Piaget's concrete operational stage (ages 7–11), they become better able to think abstractly about themselves. Thus, 8- and 9-year-olds routinely make judgments

Self-esteem is affected by learners' judgments of their ability to accomplish things they value. Teachers can enhance self-esteem by building an environment that promotes success.

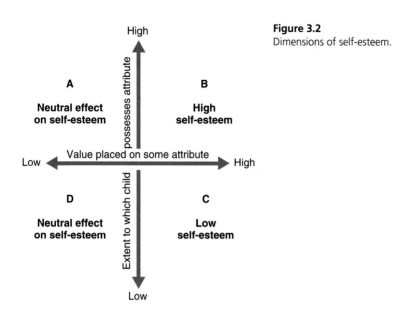

Figure 3.2
Dimensions of self-esteem.

about how well they like themselves, how happy they are, and how well they think their lives are going (Bee, 1995).

Self-esteem can take a nosedive as children enter adolescence (ages 11–13). Jacquelynne Eccles and her colleagues (Eccles, Lord, & Midgley, 1991) report a pronounced downward spiral in school achievement, motivation, and self-esteem as children enter junior high school. This is often referred to as the "seventh-grade slump."

Simmons and her colleagues (Simmons, Burgeson, Carlton-Ford, & Blyth, 1987) attribute this drop in self-esteem and achievement to the cumulative effect of all the changes that confront the child at this time. Since self-esteem involves a comparison of the self with a standard, any change in standards without a concurrent change in the skills the child needs to meet those standards can cause a drop in self-esteem.

Around the ages of 11 to 13, children can experience puberty, a change in schools, early dating, and sometimes a move to a new location or a family disruption. These changes bring about a rapid change in both the child's and society's expectations. But the new expectations or standards occur far faster than the child's ability to learn new skills to meet them. Thus, an 11- to 13-year-old child's perception of a discrepancy between what he is and what he thinks he should be can cause a decline in self-esteem.

Once the child's skill development catches up with the changing standards, self-esteem starts to rise again. Studies of self-esteem that follow teenagers throughout their school and college years show a steady improvement in perceptions of self-worth. Generally, 18- and 20-year-olds feel better about themselves than they did when they were 12- and 14-year-olds (McCarthy & Hoge, 1982; O'Malley & Bachman, 1983).

Harter's research shows not only that children differ from one another in their self-esteem but also that a child's self-esteem at one point in life may differ from that at another point (Harter, 1990). When a child's standards change, and the child becomes either more or less skillful at meeting those standards, self-esteem will shift. To what can we attribute differences in self-esteem both between and within individual children? Why do children have different standards, and when do these standards change?

Parents, teachers, and peers play a major role in the development of self-esteem. The degree to which the child's teachers, parents, or friends value athletics over academics, for example, can affect the child's own expectations in that area. Likewise, if parents and teachers place a high value on appearance, this will affect the child's standards as well. Since self-esteem involves a comparison between what children value and what they actually perceive themselves doing, children's perceptions of their own competence often account for large differences in self-esteem among children. These differences will be based on the child's direct experience of success or failure in the classroom, on dates, or during contests, and on what adults or peers say about that success or failure. Questioning a child's ability to perform, for example, may cause the child to see a greater discrepancy between what he can do and what he thinks he ought to do. The greater this discrepancy, the lower will be the child's self-esteem. Given the importance of teacher, parental, and peer statements about a child's competence or self-esteem (and assuming that the child values the skill that is being commented on), some instructional arrangements, such as certain types of ability groupings, may have potentially harmful effects on self-esteem. This occurs because such groupings can cause children to perceive a greater discrepancy than actually exists between what they are and what they think they should be (Good & Stipek, 1983). See the accompanying box, *Steps to Promoting Self-esteem in Your Classroom.*

What role do I play in the development of my learners' self-esteem?

Applying Your Knowledge:

Steps to Promoting Self-esteem in Your Classroom

1. **Be Aware That Your Own Values Can Influence How Your Learners Feel About Themselves.** Remember that when you express the desirability of one career or occupation over another, one way of dressing over another, or one social class over another you are influencing how your learners think about themselves.

2. **Be Sure That Each Learner in Your Classroom Experiences Success.** While some students may succeed where others do not, every learner should have the experience of being capable and successful in the majority of his or her work. Most of your students should feel "I can do that" when you introduce a new assignment.

3. **Questioning a Learner's Ability To Perform Can Make Him or Her Not Want To Perform.** Encourage your learners to exceed your and their expectations, and reward them for their effort, regardless of the outcome. Be sure to value those tasks that your students can perform well.

4. **If You Group Students by Ability or Achievement, Be Sure Your Grouping Is for a Specific Task and a Limited Amount of Time.** Change the members of groups often and be sure each learner has the opportunity to use his or her own unique interests and talents.

5. **Be Sensitive to Cultural Differences.** Your awareness of cultural differences will be important to how your learners feel about themselves. Make an effort to know the culture of your students, even if you do not speak their language.

6. **Carefully Evaluate the Reading Level of Your Learners and Your Reading Materials.** Be sure that there are reading assignments and printed resources available at different levels of complexity and grade levels, so that all learners feel that they can participate in the content you are teaching.

7. **Encourage Oral as Well as Written Expression.** Provide your students the opportunity to use different communication modalities, so that they feel comfortable in participating and expressing themselves with as much confidence inside the classroom as they do outside the classroom.

Physical Development and Self-esteem

As stated above, the gap between the value a learner places on some skill or quality and her perception of how much of that skill or quality she possesses is a principal determinant of self-esteem. Physical development can widen or narrow this gap and consequently plays a prominent role in a learner's self-esteem. It does this in several ways.

First, the child's growth makes new behaviors and skills possible. Before a child can write legibly, express thoughts in sketches, ride a bike, walk a balance beam, sink a foul shot, or do a backward somersault, certain physical changes are required. When these changes come late for a particular child, so too will the learning of those new behaviors that require the changes. Thus, the slow-maturing first-grader who finds himself on a soccer team with fast-maturing peers will perceive a significant discrepancy between what he values (dribbling through the defense and scoring a goal) and what he can actually do. The same holds true for slow maturers on the middle school or high school track or basketball team, and at the high school dance.

Second, the child's growth plays an important role in determining the opportunities and experiences necessary to learn new behaviors. The slow-growing child may never achieve skill in basketball because she's too small to make the team and therefore cannot benefit from the coaching and training. The uncoordinated child may be steered away from the gymnastics that he values, or the small child may find that he's discouraged from trying out for the football team.

Third, physical growth affects how others respond to the child. Children who are attractive, tall, and well coordinated receive more attention from teachers and adults than do children who are short, physically unattractive, and clumsy (Langlois & Stephan, 1981). Parents and teachers who place value on a particular physical skill, physical attractiveness, size, or artistic ability requiring physical skill will affect the learner's own expectations for himself or herself in those same areas. In the case of slow learners, this only serves to increase the gap between the quality that is valued and the amount of that quality that the learner perceives she possesses, and a drop in self-esteem is inevitable.

Are there long-term consequences to slow growth and maturation? Livson and Peskin (1980) present data showing that in adulthood, late-maturing boys showed signs of less social ease, less self-control, more uncooperativeness, and greater impulsivity than did earlier-maturing peers. Despite these data, other long-term follow-up observations of both boys and girls have shown improvements in self-esteem, self-confidence, social skill, and cognitive competence (Macfarlane, 1971).

Self-esteem and Academic Achievement

The assumption that self-esteem exerts a direct effect on school achievement has led many school districts to develop explicit goals and programs to foster its improvement (Beane, 1991). However, the research supporting this assumption is equivocal. Several studies have shown a relationship between self-esteem and school success (Hansford & Hattie, 1982; Metcalfe, 1981; Purkey, 1970; Reynolds, 1980), but they leave unresolved the question of which came first. As we have seen from our discussion, perceptions of self-worth are enhanced by successful experiences in areas in which a student places value. Nevertheless, despite the lack of conclusive research linking self-esteem and school achievement, many believe that the enhancement of self-esteem is a worthwhile goal in and of itself. Whether or not there are links between self-esteem and school achievement in the short term, the former is related to the development of a positive attitude, sociability, and adaptability, and to other traits that in turn may, over time, influence school achievement (Kash & Borich, 1978).

The most important issue, however, is not *whether* you should try to enhance your learners' self-esteem, but *how* to do so. Given the complexity of self-esteem and the subjective factors involved (what is valued, a standard of performance, and a judgment of discrepancy), we as teachers do well to be cautious about efforts to enhance self-esteem that ask children to simply repeat that they like themselves, or about a self-esteem curriculum that disregards the individual and idiosyncratic nature of each child. On the other hand, schools and teachers can play a major role in enhancing self-esteem by designing instructional arrangements that allow for cooperative learning (which we will study in Chapter 7), congruent communication (Chapter 8), heterogeneous grouping (Chapter 11), and performance assessment (Chapter 13). In other words, self-esteem should be viewed as something the child constructs for him- or herself over time by living and learning in an emotionally and intellectually supportive environment.

Social Relationships

Rebecca is a fifth-grader. She is a good student and is involved in a variety of activities, including music, soccer, and writing. Here is Rebecca's "take" on the importance of social relationships throughout her elementary school years:

Interviewer: What can you remember about friendships and social relationships when you first started school?

Rebecca: Well, in kindergarten and first grade everything is sort of loose. It's your first year with a big group of kids in a real class in a "real school." Everybody feels real proud of themselves. You don't worry about boy-girl stuff or about cliques or anything.

Interviewer: What about popularity?

Rebecca: There's popular and unpopular but you don't know it . . . you don't know the words. Popular would be like someone who doesn't have to worry about getting a turn at the paint easel. Unpopular would be someone who sort of has to cut in and be a little obnoxious to get their chance.

Interviewer: Do things change in second grade?

Rebecca: In second grade you start realizing that it's not just who is nice and who isn't. You start to notice how kids dress and who combs their hair or not. You become more conscious about what you say.

Interviewer: And what happens next?

Rebecca: When you're in third grade there really are groups . . . there were fads and if you didn't go along with them you weren't right.

Interviewer: And in fourth grade?

Rebecca: By fourth grade you have already formed solid groups and those groups are kept. You aren't going to be friends with somebody that's really obnoxious or who is in the lowest group forever.

Interviewer: What if you like a kid who is not popular?

Rebecca: You have to even out how you divide your time between the popular and unpopular kids if you want to avoid getting permanently in one group. The kids are just beginning to be really cruel to the unpopular kids. It's awfully hard to speak up for someone who is getting teased, because you don't know whether you will get someone to back you up or whether you will be alone.

Interviewer: Not a very good situation.

Rebecca: It's funny. We're all friends but underneath there's a lot of tension. (From Seifert & Hoffnung, 1987, pp. 550–551.)

Although children like Rebecca know the importance of social relationships for happiness and adjustment in school, only in the last two decades have psychologists begun to appreciate and study their significance. Developmental and educational psychologists view the establishment of successful relationships with adults and peers as one of the most reliable indicators of happiness and success in school and in later life (Cassidy & Asher, 1992).

Learning how to get along with teachers and classmates is one of the key developmental tasks that learners must master while in school. Successful relationships with parents and teachers, referred to as **vertical relationships** (Hartup, 1989), meet a learner's needs for safety, security, and protection. Successful relationships with peers, which Hartup refers to as **horizontal relationships,** are of equal developmental significance. They meet a learner's needs for belonging and allow her to acquire and practice the important social skills of cooperation, competition, and intimacy (Bee, 1995).

Vertical relationships. Students' relationships with adults, such as, parents and teachers.

Horizontal relationships. Students' relationships with peers.

Vertical Relationships

If you establish successful vertical relationships with your learners, you will notice that they:

- follow verbal requests
- imitate or model themselves after adults
- respond to praise and compliments
- seek to please
- view adults as available, reliable, and helpful
- desire to be around adults in times of trouble
- feel secure when adults are present
- want adults to teach them new things
- are willing to take chances

Hartup (1989) believes that children construct a **schema of attachment** as a result of their relationships with adults. This schema influences children's expectations and behavior regarding vertical relationships. Just as we hope that children develop a self-schema that contributes to their feelings of self-esteem, so too do we hope that children develop attachment schemata that promote positive expectations of, and positive behavior toward, parents and teachers.

Schema of attachment. Positive cognitive structure influencing vertical relationships.

Some learners, however, come to school without such a schema. They mistrust teachers. They feel insecure and threatened around them. They believe that teachers are unreliable, undependable, capricious, arbitrary, and untrustworthy (McQueen, 1992). Consequently, they are noncompliant and unresponsive to praise and encouragement; they couldn't care less about pleasing their teachers. Let's see how a child constructs such a schema or working model of attachment.

Willard W. Hartup, University of Minnesota

My interest in child development research took shape midway in my graduate career when I came to realize that children were the most interesting variables in the education equation. I had prepared earlier to be a classroom teacher but didn't realize until quite a bit later that children were more interesting to me than subject matter. At that point I changed course and took four more years to become a developmental psychologist.

Nearly a decade after deciding to study child development, I discovered the area with which I am most closely identified: peer relations. This came about because my 4-year-old son and his best friend were involved in a complex aggressive-sociable relationship with another boy that was overlaid with rich fantasizing (mostly creative ways that my son and his friend could use to destroy the other child). I became interested in the reasons that children are attracted to one another and reject one another, and conducted a series of observational and experimental studies that drew the attention of other investigators to this area. Later, I became interested in the mechanisms involved in peer socialization, and my most recent work concerns collaborative writing by friends as compared with nonfriends.

Although peer relations had been studied by investigators prior to World War II, most child psychologists in the postwar period were interested in family relations and their developmental significance. My work constituted a rediscovery of child-child relations. Along with many other investigators, I've been able to show that peer relationships have considerable developmental significance in their own right, that these relationships are linked together conjunctively with family relations in social development, and that children's friendships are both advantages and disadvantages in social development depending on who a child's friends are and the quality of these relationships.

We've come a considerable distance since I began to work in this field. Observational methods and schemes for on-line recording of observational material have been refined: Labora-

tory procedures have been worked out so that children can be used as reliable tutors or experimenters for one another; statistical models have been developed so that more than one measure can be studied at a time; and longitudinal designs can be used effectively to study causal relations developmentally. Newly available video recording equipment, sensitive recording devices, computers and computer-controlled laboratory materials, and advanced quantitative methods aided greatly in this work.

These observational methods have allowed my studies to be conducted in and around nursery and elementary schools, anywhere that children can be observed together. Supportive teachers and cooperative children are the essential ingredients of the research settings I use. Sometimes observations are made while children are at recess; at other times, children may be observed in twosomes or threesomes at a computer, at a board game, or at indoor play. Sometimes the classroom is the research laboratory.

My work contributes to practice in various ways: (1) The studies dealing with social acceptance and rejection assisted in identifying common behavioral patterns associated with socialization risk that must be familiar to teachers and special educators if they are to be effective in dealing with troubled children. (2) My studies of same-age and mixed-age relations between children showed that mixed-age socialization sometimes benefits children more than same-age socialization, especially among socially withdrawn children. These studies also showed that tutoring effects vary with age relations. (3) My studies of children's friendships show that conflicts between friends are more common than conflicts between nonfriends and that conflict management is generally better between friends than nonfriends. (4) Friends frequently make better collaborators in cognitive tasks than nonfriends; indeed, there is little evidence to suggest that friends distract one another or make poor cognitive partners, as many teachers think.

The Development of Vertical Relationships. Bowlby (1969, 1973, 1980, 1988) and Ainsworth (1972, 1982, 1989) attribute such negative schemata to a child's failure to develop affectional bonds and attachment to an adult (either parent or both parents or a caregiver) during infancy. **Affectional bonds** are long-lasting ties between a child and a parent. The child experiences the parent as a unique individual who cannot simply be replaced with someone else.

Affectional bonds. Long-lasting bonds between a child and a parent.

Out of these affectional bonds grows a state of *attachment,* an internal feeling that the parent is a safe, reliable, ever-present individual and a secure base from which the child can explore the environment. In contrast, the failure to develop affectional bonds and attachments results in feelings or internal states characterized by insecurity and mistrust of relationships. Infants and toddlers who develop internal working models or schemata of social relationships characterized by mistrust of adults sometimes enter school exhibiting antisocial behavior.

Bowlby's and Ainsworth's explanations for how relationships are formed come from the psychoanalytic tradition. As Bee's model of personality formation suggests, temperament and social learning processes also are at work. The more important question is this: What are the long-term effects of the vertical relationship schema?

Effects of Vertical Relationships on Your Learners. Table 3.2 summarizes current knowledge about the long-term effects of affectional bonds and secure attachments (Bee, 1995). It summarizes the results of numerous studies of preschool and elementary school children who were rated as securely or insecurely attached to their mothers as infants. The available evidence lends strong support to the hypothesis that early attachments exert a strong influence on learners' ability to form later successful relationships with their teachers.

Although results such as those in Table 3.2 suggest less desirable outcomes for poorly attached infants, this is not necessarily the case. As we will see in Chapters 4 through 6, on learning, the affective as well as the cognitive dimensions of learners are flexible. Just as schemata or models are constructed out of early childhood experiences, so can they be altered by later ones.

Horizontal Relationships

Most theories of affective development assign a central role to vertical relationships, particularly the social learning and psychoanalytic approaches. But that emphasis may be changing. Just as we are beginning to appreciate the role of social relationships in cognitive development, thanks to theorists such as Vygotsky (see Chapter 2), the unique effects of peer relationships in affective development are beginning to be appreciated as well.

Psychologists who study the developmental significance of peer relationships are particularly interested in what happens to children between the ages of 3, when they are still completely dependent on adults, and later adolescence, when they are almost completely independent of them. From the work of researchers such as Willard Hartup, it is now clear that children learn cooperation, healthy competition, and the ability to establish intimacy with others not only through vertical relationships but through horizontal ones as well (Hartup, 1989).

The Development of Horizontal Relationships. Horizontal relationships first appear at about the age of 3. Although infants as young as 6 months show positive inter-

Table 3.2

Characteristics Shown by Securely Attached Infants at Later Ages

Sociability. Securely attached infants get along better with their peers, are more popular, and have more friends. With strange adults they are more sociable and less fearful.

Self-esteem. They have higher self-esteem.

Relationship with siblings. They have better relationships with siblings, especially if both siblings are securely attached; if both are insecurely attached, the relationship is maximally antagonistic.

Dependency. They show less clinging and attention-seeking from a teacher and less "negative seeking" (getting attention by being bad) in preschool years.

Tantrums and aggressive behavior. They show less aggressive or disruptive behavior.

Compliance and good deportment. They are easier to manage in the classroom, requiring little overt control by the teacher, but they are not overly docile.

Empathy. They show more empathy toward other children and toward adults. They do not show pleasure on seeing others' distress, which is fairly common among avoidant children.

Behavior problems. The results are mixed, but there are a number of studies that show that securely attached infants are less likely to show behavior problems at later ages.

Problem solving. They show longer attention spans in free play and more confidence in attempting solutions to tasks with tools. They use the mother or teacher more effectively as a source of assistance.

Source: The Developing Child, 6th ed. (p. 443), by H. Bee. New York: HarperCollins. Copyright © 1992, Harper-Collins College Publishers. Reprinted by permission.

ests in other infants, and toddlers are often found playing with one another, they begin to express a true preference for peer companionship only during early childhood.

Thus, the foundation for successful peer relationships in elementary school is laid during the preschool years. During this time, children learn to play for longer periods of time with one another, pay attention to rules of equity and fairness, and look for opportunities to do things together rather than apart. Out of these experiences develops a schema that includes rudimentary expectations of loyalty and commitment to friends and a sense of mutual attachment and common interest (Hartup, 1989). Children who enter school with such a friendship schema are more likely to benefit from your efforts to build trusting peer relations than those who don't.

During the elementary school years we want this friendship schema to accommodate such notions as the importance of finding cooperative solutions during competition, a desire for low-profile modes of conflict resolution, and a forgive-and-forget approach to fights rather than the holding of grudges. Hartup (1989) emphasizes that your learners will develop these friendship-building skills primarily out of the opportunities you provide for mutual play, learning, and problem solving.

Researchers are just beginning to appreciate the importance of friendly peer relationships in learners' overall emotional development.

Eisenberg (1988, 1990) emphasizes that horizontal relationships not only help children learn how to make friends but also help them develop a set of prosocial behaviors. **Prosocial behaviors** are intentional, voluntary behaviors intended to help another person. We commonly refer to them as *altruistic* behaviors. Children who express sympathy, share a candy bar, help someone clean up a mess, or get a friend to class on time are showing prosocial behaviors. Prosocial behaviors develop primarily out of experiences with horizontal rather than vertical relationships.

As learners enter adolescence and move on to junior and senior high school, they may add the following elements to their friendship schema: (1) a willingness to share feelings and secrets with others, (2) knowledge about the feelings of others, (3) a commitment to loyalty and faithfulness, (4) an attraction toward the opposite sex, and (5) a concern for the norms and expectations of the peer group. Although conventional wisdom and the media seem to suggest that dependence on the peer group is a negative force, in most cases it is a positive one. Adolescence is the period when your learners make the necessary transition from dependence on adults to independence as young adults. Erikson and other developmental psychologists view the peer group as a necessary vehicle for safe passage during this period. So, rather than being abnormal, the intense need of teenagers for conformity may be a normal and necessary part of the process of developing personal identity and establishing intimacy with other people.

Effects of Horizontal Relationships on Your Learners. As we have emphasized, providing opportunities for learners to establish healthy relationships when they enter school helps them develop skills important in getting along with others, assisting others (altruism), and establishing intimacy. The failure to experience healthy horizontal relationships and to learn friendship-building attitudes, beliefs, intentions, and skills can have undesirable consequences, as Rebecca, in the earlier vignette, clearly

Prosocial behaviors. Intentional, voluntary behaviors intended to help others.

What role do friendships play in the personal-social development of my learners, and how can I enhance friendly relationships?

described, and as the example of Joe demonstrated. This failure is often described by the terms "unpopularity" and "social rejection."

Current evidence suggests that rejected children are more likely to be aggressive and disruptive in school (Hartup, 1989), experience intense feelings of loneliness (Cassidy & Asher, 1992), and suffer emotional disturbances in adolescence and adulthood (Dishon, Patterson, Stoolmiller, & Skinner, 1991). Nevertheless, educational psychologists have also shown that, within limits, learners can be taught some of the social skills necessary to gain acceptance by peers (Tharinger & Lambert, 1990). More importantly, by helping your learners construct their own well-functioning horizontal relationships, you eliminate the need to teach them how to acquire these relationships.

Social Cognition

What do they value? A can of hairspray. Materialistic things a lot. And yet they really care a lot about the feelings of other people in class, too—sometimes; sometimes they're really mean to each other, too. For example, . . . I had a girl come during the afternoon class who . . . said she was checking out. "I need to go home." The other girl said, "Look at that (ugly) headband she's got on." I chewed her out . . . I was so mad at her. "Do you think every girl was born with a pretty face?" She said, "Well, why are you so mad?" I said, "Because that is so mean, you don't care at all that you said that loud enough for her to hear." Some just don't have feelings that way. (Kerrie, seventh-grade teacher, quoted in Bullough, 1989, p. 119)

Kerrie is probably like most teachers. She wants her learners to value the right things. She wants them to be sensitive to one another's feelings. She becomes upset when they behave thoughtlessly and selfishly, and her reaction to her students' insensitivity is typical of what many teachers do: she scolds, criticizes, and lectures.

Some developmental and educational psychologists (Bee, 1995; Hartup, 1989; Kohlberg, 1978) suggest that goals for learners should go beyond mere academic achievement and reflect a concern that learners develop moral values, consideration for the feelings of others, and a commitment to social justice. Most educators and parents seem to agree. Increasingly, professional associations for improving teaching and curriculum, such as the Association for Supervision and Curriculum Development (ASCD), recommend that schools develop programs to teach ethics, values, community responsibility, and citizenship (Parker, 1991).

Can learners be taught helping or prosocial behaviors?

Developmental and educational psychologists have an expression for how children learn to think and become concerned about other people's actions and feelings, and how they think about what people ought to do: **social cognition.** When Kerrie expressed concern for what her learners value, and how insensitive some of them are to the feelings of others, she was disturbed about their social cognition: what they know and think about people, relationships, and right and wrong (Bee, 1995). Can teachers like Kerrie have an impact on social cognition? At what age are learners ready to think and alter aspects of their social cognition? What is the relationship between a child's ability to think about people and what they should and should not do and the ability to think and reason? Does changing how learners think about social and moral issues affect how they behave?

Social cognition. How one thinks and becomes concerned about other people's actions and feelings.

We will end our study of personal-social development with a discussion of social cognition. We will review the three major areas of social cognition: empathy, from the perspective of Martin Hoffman (1982, 1984, 1988); understanding of relationships, through the ideas of Robert Selman (1980, 1989); and moral judgment and reasoning, from the research of Lawrence Kohlberg (1978) and Carol Gilligan (1982, 1988). In addition, we will summarize what is currently known about the relationship between social cognition and social behavior.

Empathy

Whether you teach elementary, junior high, or senior high school, sooner or later you will say to one of your students, "How would you feel if someone did that to you?" In response to this question, some of your learners will greet you with blank stares, some will show puzzlement, and some will be thoroughly chastened. What you are asking of these learners is **empathy,** the ability to read someone else's feelings and match them to one's own. Empathy requires two processes: (1) determining another person's emotional state and (2) imagining how you would react to a similar emotional state. Empathy is largely a cognitive process, so when you ponder why some children show empathy and others do not, recall what was learned about cognitive development in the previous chapter.

Empathy. The ability to read someone else's feelings and match them to the observer's own feelings.

Hoffman believes that empathy develops in stages that roughly parallel the developmental stages of Piaget. Table 3.3 summarizes the changes in children's ability to empathize as they get older. These changes reflect a learner's increasing ability to think abstractly, draw inferences, and make deductions about what he or she is observing.

Hoffman's research on the development and expression of empathy has several implications for teachers concerned with this aspect of their learners' social cognition. First, a learner's ability to recognize the emotional state of another and match it to his or her own improves with age and experience. Early elementary school children, although able to recognize that a peer is experiencing distress, have difficulty relating this state to themselves. Second, failure to show empathy can be attributed to the child's level of cognitive development and to lack of social experiences that promote this development, as well as to social class and cultural differences. Undoubtedly, certain cultures and ethnic groups place different meanings on certain physical gestures and facial expressions. Moreover, different cultures place different values on the importance of interpreting the feelings of others as well as on disclosing one's own emotions (Bowers & Flinders, 1990).

Social Relationships

"That's no way to treat a friend!"

"Friends don't behave like that."

"That's no way to make a friend!"

"Come on! Let's behave like friends."

If you've heard expressions like these, you've experienced a second aspect of social cognition, friendship. Social cognition involves not only empathy—our understanding of how individuals feel—but also how we think about relationships or friendships. This aspect of social cognition concerns what children think about friends: what it means to have a friend, how to make and keep friends, and how friends should behave toward one another.

Table 3.3

Stages in the Development of Empathy

Stage 1: Global empathy. Observed during the first year. If the infant is around someone expressing a strong emotion, he may match this emotion, such as beginning to cry when he hears another infant crying.

Stage 2: Egocentric empathy. Beginning at about 12 to 18 months, when the child has a fairly clear sense of his separate self, children respond to another's distress with some distress of their own, but may attempt to "cure" the other person's problem by offering what they themselves would find most comforting. They may, for example, show sadness when they see another child hurt, and go to get their own mother (or father) for help.

Stage 3: Empathy for another's feelings. Beginning as young as 2 or 3, and continuing through elementary school, children note others' feelings, partially match those feelings, and respond to others' distress in nonegocentric ways. Over these years, children distinguish a wider and wider (and more subtle) range of emotions.

Stage 4: Empathy for another's life condition. In late childhood or adolescence, some children develop a more generalized notion of others' feelings and respond not just to the immediate situation but to the other individual's general situation or plight. So a young person at this level may become more distressed over another person's sadness if they know that sadness is chronic, or if they know that the person's general situation is particularly tragic, than if they see it as a more momentary problem.

Source: The Developing Child, 7th ed. (p. 350), by H. Bee. New York: HarperCollins. Copyright © 1995, Harper-Collins College Publishers. Reprinted by permission.

Selman's research (1989) shows that children's thinking about friendships exhibits qualitative differences as they grow from early childhood to adolescence. This analysis of the development of children's thinking about friendship describes three stages of thought, which Selman calls *levels of interpersonal understanding*. These levels are the following.

Level 0: Egocentric Level (Early Childhood). Ask a young child "What is a friend?" and you're likely to be told that a friend is "someone you like," "someone you play with," or "someone you invite to your house." If you inquire "How do you make a friend?" the child is likely to say, "Well, you just meet them and start to play." Resolving disputes at this level does not involve understanding how the other person feels or thinks; rather, it requires the understanding to "just play better" or "just stop fighting." A child's thinking at this level is concrete and reflects his or her personal perspective.

Level 1: Reciprocal Trust (Later Childhood). As children develop genuine empathy and enter Hoffman's second stage of development, a friend becomes someone who "thinks like you," "likes the same things," and is "someone you can trust." At this stage, children realize that friendship imposes mutual obligations. Friends are expected to be tolerant of one another's differences and to come to the aid of one another, even when this involves some personal risk. Friendships become characterized by qualities such as generosity and helpfulness.

Level 2: Mutual Perspective Taking (Adolescence). When adolescents talk about what makes a friend, qualities such as trust, helpfulness, and generosity are replaced by desires for mutual understanding ("We really think a lot alike"), support ("We're there for one another"), and encouragement ("She helps me be what I want to be"; "He'll forgive me no matter what I do"). A teacher can get together a group of friends who are having a conflict and encourage each to take the others' points of view. Three-way disagreements can be worked out. Such group problem solving is not possible at earlier stages of social cognition.

The implications of Selman's analysis of interpersonal understanding for teachers are similar to those of Hoffman's analysis of empathy. The accompanying box, *Encouraging Interpersonal Understanding,* provides some specific guidelines.

Moral Judgment and Reasoning

Two of the most frustrating things I've confronted this year have been derelict attitudes and morals. . . . All teachers have a personal decision to make, a line to draw between remaining silent and speaking out on particular issues. I feel that it is my obligation as a teacher, . . . to speak out on such issues as crime, theft, violence, murder, and substance abuse. When I started the year teaching in a local public high school, these issues were certainly not absent from the classrooms nor the minds of the students. It's just that when most of your students are incarcerated for these very same crimes, the subject of morality is always close at hand. (Sean, first-year teacher, from Ryan, 1992, p. 60)

Teachers like Sean are concerned about the morals and values of their students. From the earliest elementary grades to senior high school, all teachers encounter some learners who deliberately hurt others, destroy and deface property, lie, cheat, and steal. Like Sean, they ask themselves whether they need to provide moral education to their learners.

Over the past two decades numerous curricula have been developed for grades K through 12 to teach moral values (Schaefle, Rest, & Thoma, 1985). As with self-esteem, we no longer debate whether to teach values in school. Rather, the issue has become focused on what values to teach, and how to teach them. We end our examination of social

---

Applying Your Knowledge:

Encouraging Interpersonal Understanding

- Be sensitive to the cognitive demands required for different levels of thought about friendships. Do not expect a first-grader to be able to understand another child's perspective. Similarly, however, do expect and encourage empathy from adolescents.
- Provide opportunities for learners to develop friendships and work out differences, and respect social class and ethnic differences about the development of friendships and the resolution of disputes.
- Above all, as with self-esteem, allow children to construct friendships and their friendship schemata out of the direct experience of working and cooperating with others. This means, for example, encouraging cooperative learning activities, as well as encouraging different groups of children to work and play together.

cognition by reviewing research on its third dimension: how children think about what people should or ought to do.

Kohlberg's Stages of Moral Development. Over the past two decades, Laurence Kohlberg (1978) has been one of the most influential theorists and researchers in the area of social cognition dealing with judgment and moral reasoning. Kohlberg's work was heavily influenced by the writings of Piaget. Consequently, you will find many similarities between Kohlberg's analysis of moral development and Piaget's analysis of cognitive development.

To see how Kohlberg studied moral development, consider the following problem:

> In Europe, a woman was near death from a special kind of cancer. There was one drug that the doctors thought might save her. It was a form of radium that a druggist in the same town had recently discovered. The drug was expensive to make, but the druggist was charging ten times what the drug cost him to make. He paid $200 for the radium and charged $2000 for a small dose of the drug. The sick woman's husband, Heinz, went to everyone he knew to borrow the money, but he could only get together about $1000, which is half of what it cost. He told the druggist that his wife was dying and asked him to sell it cheaper or let him pay later. But, the druggist said, "No, I discovered the drug and I'm going to make money from it." So, Heinz got desperate and broke into the man's store to steal the drug for his wife. (Kohlberg & Elfenbein, 1975, p. 621)

Kohlberg told this story to children and adolescents of various ages and asked them questions designed to probe the dimensions of their moral reasoning. For example, he asked them whether Heinz should have stolen the drug, what should happen to him, what if he didn't love his wife, or what if the drug was for a dog rather than a person.

Kohlberg created a variety of these moral dilemmas and interviewed hundreds of children as well as younger and older adults in several countries. His analysis of their answers reveals a pattern of increasingly complex moral reasoning, which can be divided into three main levels with two substages at each level. Table 3.4 describes these levels.

Kohlberg's analysis of the development of moral reasoning and judgment makes two important points. First, there are clear age trends. Preschoolers and elementary school children reason primarily at stages 1 and 2. This is no surprise, given the dependence of moral reasoning on cognitive development.

Conventional reasoning emerges during adolescence and persists throughout adulthood. Postconventional reasoning is rarely found at any age level, although when it does occur it is usually found in adults. Second, although older children tend to reason relatively abstractly by drawing on general principles or values, many older adolescents and adults persist with preconventional reasoning.

Gilligan's Challenge to Kohlberg. Kohlberg's research into moral development, like Piaget's research into cognitive development, has been challenged on several fronts. For example, developmental psychologists such as Eliot Turiel report that preschoolers and first graders engage in higher levels of moral reasoning than Kohlberg's stages suggest (Nucci & Turiel, 1978; Tisak & Turiel, 1988; Turiel, 1983). Perhaps the most serious challenge to Kohlberg's theories of moral development and research methods comes from Carol Gilligan of Harvard University, who raises important issues regarding the types of people interviewed by Kohlberg and the kinds of moral dilemmas that he used to study moral judgment and reasoning (Gilligan, 1982, 1988).

Gilligan correctly points out that Kohlberg interviewed only males about their thinking on moral dilemmas. Consequently, she concludes that Kohlberg's perspective on moral development is more characteristic of males than of females. Males, according to Gilligan, view morality more from a position of rights of justice than from a position of caring, which she feels is characteristic of females. In other words, according to Gilligan, a male's analysis of moral dilemmas is dominated by considerations of the rightness or wrongness of an action (*morality of justice*) without equal consideration given to its impact on the people involved. Females, on the other hand, view moral dilemmas in terms of the responsibilities of one person to another (*morality of caring*), rather than in strict terms of abstract rights or justice. Furthermore, females tend to personalize moral dilemmas, and as a result, their reasoning attempts to resolve conflicts between responsibility to self and responsibility to others.

The nature of Kohlberg's moral dilemmas may further bias his perspective toward a morality of justice or rights rather than toward caring or responsibility. Gilligan points out that Kohlberg's dilemmas represent hypothetical situations irrelevant to the lives of the subjects he interviewed. She states that a different perspective on moral development would emerge had he presented his subjects with situations that directly affected their lives.

Gilligan concludes that these two weaknesses—the use of only male subjects and the use of abstract dilemmas—explain why Kohlberg's research tends to place more females at Stage 3 and more males at Stage 4. According to Gilligan, Kohlberg's theory of moral development is biased toward males and does not reflect the full range of considerations that diverse people employ in thinking about moral issues.

To prove her point, Gilligan (1982) studied the morality of females by interviewing women who were confronted with an actual moral dilemma: whether or not to have an abortion. Her subjects were women referred to a counseling center who were faced with the choice of continuing or terminating a pregnancy. Her analysis of their reasoning revealed the following stages of female moral development:

Level I: Orientation toward self-interest

Level II: Identification of goodness with responsibility for others

Level III: Focusing on the dynamics between self and others.

The principal feature of Level I reasoning is a pragmatic orientation: the woman focuses on doing what's best for herself. Level II reasoning is dominated by considerations that reflect a sense of responsibility for others and a capacity for self-sacrifice. Women who reason at Level III, the highest, achieve an understanding that their actions must reflect both a concern for self and a concern for others.

Researchers such as D. Kay Johnston (1988), who studied the moral reasoning of 11- to 15-year-old boys and girls, confirm that girls spontaneously adopt an orientation of caring and boys an orientation of justice. Gilligan and Attanucci (1988) found that college-age men and women employ both perspectives in their moral reasoning, but that women are far more likely to adopt a caring orientation than are men. Likewise, men are twice as likely to adopt a justice orientation as women.

The issue of whether men and women actually view the world differently and make qualitatively different moral judgments is still open to question, however. Researchers, including Muss (1988), state that studies of prosocial behavior (altruism, empathy, cooperation, and so forth) show men to be no less prosocial than women. Regardless, Gilligan's work has forced developmental psychologists to give serious consideration to the notion that some of our theories and conclusions about human development may not apply in the same ways to both males and females. Moreover, Gilligan demonstrated that any

Table 3.4

Kohlberg's Stages of Moral Reasoning

Stage	Description	Example
Level I	**Preconventional level:** Children at this level reason in terms of their own needs. Answers to moral dilemmas are based on what they can get away with. Moral values reside in good and bad acts, not people or standards. Cultural rules and labels of good and bad, right and wrong, are interpreted in terms of punishment, reward, exchange of favors, or the physical power of those who advocate the rules and labels. Children are concerned about external, concrete consequences to themselves.	
Stage 1	**Punishment and obedience orientation:** Children worry about avoiding punishment by adults or people with superior power and prestige. They are aware of rules and the consequences of breaking them. The physical consequences of an action determine its goodness or badness—"might makes right."	Heinz should not steal because he would be punished by authorities.
Stage 2	**Instrumental relativist orientation:** Children want to satisfy their own needs (and occasionally the needs of others) if they can get away with it. They are motivated by self-interest and are aware that relationships are dominated by concrete reciprocity (you scratch my back and I'll scratch yours), not loyalty, gratitude, or justice. They assume that everyone has to look out for himself and is obligated only to those who help him.	Heinz should steal because he is worried about his wife and he will feel better if she isn't sick.
Level II	**Conventional level:** Moral value resides in performing good and right roles. Children are concerned with meeting external social expectations. They value meeting the expectations of family, group, or nation by conforming to the expectations of significant people and the social order. There is active support and justification of conventional rules and roles.	
Stage 3	**Interpersonal concordance orientation:** Children earn approval by being "nice." They are concerned about living up to "good boy" and "good girl" stereotypes. Good behavior is what pleases or helps others and what is approved of by them. Children are aware of the need to consider the intentions and feelings of others; cooperation is seen in terms of the Golden Rule.	Heinz should steal because good husbands care about their wives. Other people would disapprove if he let his wife die.

comprehensive theory of moral development must encompass orientations of both care and justice, since both are important components of how humans make moral decisions.

Concluding Remarks About Social Cognition

Social cognition is the aspect of personal-social development that concerns itself with what learners think about the feelings of others (empathy), their own beliefs about friendships, and how they think they and other people should behave. As a teacher who

Stage	Description	Example
Stage 4	**Authority-maintaining orientation:** Children are motivated by a sense of duty or obligation to live up to socially defined roles, and to maintain the existing social order for the good of all. They are aware that there is a larger social system, which regulates the behavior of the people within it. They assume that the social order is the source of morality and that laws should be maintained even at personal expense.	Heinz should not steal because stealing is against the law and the laws must be maintained even at the expense of personal loss.
Level III	**Postconventional autonomous, or principled level:** Children make a clear effort to define moral values and principles that have validity and application apart from the authority of groups or individuals and apart from their own identifications. There is a concern for fidelity to self-chosen moral principles. Moral value resides in conformity to shared standards, rights, and duties.	
Stage 5	**Social-contract legalistic orientation:** Right actions tend to be defined in terms of general individual rights and standards that have been critically examined and agreed on by the whole society. There is an emphasis on procedural rules for reaching consensus because of awareness of the relativism of personal values and opinions. Aside from what society agrees on, it is possible to change the law in terms of rational considerations of social utility. Outside the legal realm, free agreement and contract are the binding elements of obligation.	
Stage 6	**Universal ethical principle orientation:** The person defines right by decisions of conscience in accord with self-chosen ethical principles that appeal to logical comprehensiveness, universality, and consistency. These principles are abstract and ethical; at heart they are universal principles of justice, of the reciprocity and equality of human rights, and of respect for the dignity of human beings as individuals. There is an orientation of letting one's conscience be a directing agent and of letting mutual respect and trust dominate interpersonal relationships.	

is concerned about the whole child and not just his or her academic achievement, you will expect your learners to respect the feelings of others, understand what it means to have friends, and behave in morally acceptable ways. However, as Bee's model of personality and behavior suggests, a learner's behavior depends on a complex combination of influences, only a part of which stems from what you do in the classroom.

We concluded our section on self-esteem by recommending that you provide the conditions for its positive growth rather than suggesting specific instructional strategies. Our recommendation for the social cognition of your learners is the same. By allowing children to learn together, encouraging them to listen to one another, providing opportunities for discussion and disagreement, and modeling empathy, respect, and morality, you will create the conditions necessary for the development of social cognition.

How can I enhance my learners' ability to think and reason about their own moral and ethical behavior?

Summing Up

This chapter introduced you to personal-social development. Its main points were these:

- Three theories that help explain how children develop affectively are biological theory, social learning theory, and psychoanalytic theory.
- Bee's attempt to integrate the biological, social learning, and psychoanalytic approaches with personal-social development considers the effects of inborn traits and the interaction between family environment, self-esteem, and factors such as the economy, parental job satisfaction, and social support networks on the development of a child's personality.
- Self-esteem is how we evaluate or feel about ourselves, or whether or not we like who we are.
- Relationships with adults that meet a learner's needs for safety, security, and protection are called vertical relationships.
- Relationships with peers that meet a learner's needs for belonging and allow him or her to acquire the social skills of cooperation, competition, and intimacy are called horizontal relationships.
- Prosocial behaviors are intentional, voluntary behaviors intended to help another. A failure to develop healthy horizontal relationships often results in the lack of prosocial behaviors.
- Social cognition is giving consideration to how other people think and expressing judgments about what they should or ought to do.
- Empathy is the ability to read someone else's feelings and match them to one's own. Empathy requires both determining another person's emotional state and imagining how one would react in a similar situation.
- Like empathy, a child's thinking about friendship is understood to deepen as the child grows from early childhood to adolescence.
- What children think people should or ought to do is called moral judgment and reasoning.
- Kohlberg's hierarchy of the developmental stages of moral reasoning includes three main levels, each with two substages, which are dependent on age and cognitive development.
- Gilligan's research suggests that any comprehensive theory of moral development should include morality relevant to both care and justice, since females tend to personalize moral dilemmas more than men and their reasoning reflects attempts to resolve conflicts between responsibility to self and responsibility to others.

For Discussion and Practice

°1. In your own words, provide a brief description of the biological, social learning, and psychoanalytic approaches to personal-social development.

°2. Cite research evidence in support of the biological approach, and identify three temperaments that, according to the biological approach, are inherited from our parents.

Questions marked with an asterisk are answered in the appendix.

°3. If you were to apply the biological approach to Joe's behavior, what might be your conclusions?

°4. Cite research evidence in support of the social learning approach. According to this approach, what three events cumulate to create affective behavior?

°5. If you were to apply the social learning approach to Joe's behavior, what might be some of your conclusions?

°6. According to Erikson, what general drive is most important for understanding personal-social development?

°7. Identify Erikson's identity crises most relevant to school-age children (stages 4 and 5) and describe how they develop.

°8. Cite research evidence in support of the psychoanalytic approach. If you were to apply Erikson's approach to Joe's behavior, what might be some of your conclusions?

°9. Using parts of the biological, social learning, and psychoanalytic approaches, provide an overview of Bee's integrated approach to personal-social development.

°10. What might be some reasons for wanting to increase children's self-esteem in the absence of research evidence indicating a strong relationship between self-esteem and school achievement?

°11. What is the difference between vertical and horizontal relationships? Give some examples of each for learners you are likely to teach.

°12. What are prosocial behaviors, and what would be some examples that Mr. Nash might expect Joe to exhibit?

°13. In your own words, what is social cognition? What is an example that might occur in your classroom?

°14. How would a child at each of Selman's three levels of interpersonal understanding describe a "friend"?

°15. Provide your own example of moral reasoning at each of Kohlberg's three levels.

16. Analyze the dilemma you considered in question 15 according to Gilligan's levels of moral reasoning.

Suggested Readings

Bee, H. (1995). *The developing child* (7th ed). New York: HarperCollins. This popular child development text contains excellent insights into the various developmental theories. It presents important scholarship in an enjoyable writing style.

Erikson, E. (1963). *Childhood and society* (2nd ed.). New York: Norton. Erikson, who was a painter by profession, writes like a highly skilled novelist. After reading this work, you may never think the same way about others—or yourself.

Seifert, K. L., & Hoffnung, R. J. (1987). *Child and adolescent development*. Boston: Houghton Mifflin. Another popular child development text; this one includes many interesting child development experiments that give the reader a flavor of this area of psychology.

What Teachers Need to Know About Learning

Professor Thomas meets with student teachers on Thursdays from 4 to 6 P.M. Today's topic is learning theory. Dr. Thomas knows he has to create some enthusiasm for an area about which few students get excited—especially after an exhausting day of student teaching.

Julie: I have a hard time seeing the value of learning theory for teachers. My cooperating teacher, Mr. Charles, saw this week's assignments for this class, and he just kind of smirked. He sees this stuff as pretty irrelevant to the classroom—and he received a teaching excellence award last year.

Leon: There were certainly good teachers before there were learning theories. They just knew their content and were excited about teaching it.

Dr. Thomas: So, your point is that you don't have to know about learning theory to be a good teacher?

Howard: I've taught some pretty good lessons so far, and I don't know anything about learning theory. Before every unit, I observe teachers at my school and talk with other teachers to get ideas. So I just don't see that learning theories are necessary.

Maria: Well, teachers may not be able to identify or talk about learning theories, but that doesn't mean they aren't influenced by them. As one of the articles pointed out, many teachers have implicit theories of learning that guide their teaching; they just don't articulate them.

Dr. Thomas: And what else did the article say? Janet?

Janet: The author felt that effective teachers use theories to guide their teaching. They work out a set of rules or principles beforehand that researchers have found valid. Less effective teachers don't have any rules or principles to guide them and probably don't know why they do certain things. So why leave it up to chance? Why not study some of the ways people learn before you begin teaching? That way you can make informed decisions rather than just doing what feels good.

Janet's view about why future teachers should know about learning theory is close to ours: Why leave it up to chance? Although explicit knowledge of learning theory may not be necessary for every lesson you teach, theory will be valuable for decision making and for understanding why some techniques promote learning more than others. As you

begin teaching, you will continually ask yourself whether you are lecturing too much, providing enough examples, using too many or too few cues, giving enough feedback, allowing sufficient time for discussion, or providing sufficient opportunities for practice. A knowledge of learning theory can help answer these questions.

Such knowledge also helps teachers explain why their classroom techniques promote learning. By providing a focus or point of observation, learning theories help teachers reflect on what they do and why they do it. Reflection is considered one of the principal ingredients of both student learning and teacher self-renewal (Borich, 1993; Sparks-Langer & Cotton, 1991; Wellington, 1991).

Our purpose in this next sequence of chapters is to help you reflect on why you make certain day-to-day decisions about how you teach. We will answer the basic question: What do teachers need to know about learning? This reflection will serve two goals: it will infuse your lessons with a coherence and consistency of techniques that will make you feel secure and confident, and it will make your learners in turn feel better and more confident about your teaching.

This unit includes those aspects of learning theory and research that are the most pertinent to classroom instruction. Chapter 4 includes what classroom teachers should know about the behavioral science approach to learning. In this chapter we concentrate on how behavioral learning principles can help you teach academic skills. We present an approach to instruction that teaches basic academic skills in a manner that places a premium on clear objectives, guided practice, errorless learning, immediate feedback, and positive consequences.

Chapters 5 and 6 cover the knowledge resulting from cognitive learning theory that is most applicable for teachers. Cognitive learning theory emphasizes what teachers can do to help their learners problem solve, remember, and understand what they read, and also assume greater responsibility for their own learning. In these chapters you will learn instructional strategies for helping your learners take in new information, make connections between this information and what has already been learned, and use this knowledge to solve important problems. In particular, Chapter 6 focuses on techniques for teaching students to solve complex, real-world problems.

Chapter 7 extends our coverage into the area of cognitive approaches to motivating learners. It focuses on how to foster internal motivation in your students. You will learn that motivating learners is a complex endeavor that places as much responsibility on the learner as it does on you.

The Behavioral Science Approach to Learning

This chapter will help you answer the following questions about your learners:

- How can I help my learners develop a positive attitude toward what I teach?
- How can I help my learners become more persistent in their efforts to learn?
- How will I know when my learners have attained the prerequisite skills required for new learning?
- How can I encourage errorless learning?
- What types of practice and feedback are required for new learning to occur?
- How will I know whether my lessons provide appropriate rewards and reinforcement?
- How do I make my learners less dependent on external rewards and more motivated to learn for learning's sake?
- What are some cautions I should be aware of when considering the use of negative consequences in my classroom?

Although educational psychologists disagree about the effectiveness of instructional methods based on behavioral science, the behavioral science approach to classroom learning has considerable significance for teaching. Its major contributions to your teaching lie in what it says about the learning of basic academic skills. We will explore the essential principles and methods of this knowledge base in this chapter.

First we will present a historical overview of the behavioral science approach to learning. From this overview, you will learn about the principles that underlie classical and operant conditioning. Then we will describe how these principles of learning can be applied to the classroom to help learners acquire important academic skills.

Overview of the Behavioral Science Approach

What should teachers know about learning in order to deliver effective instruction to their students? Behavioral scientists have clear recommendations on this matter. Before examining these ideas and their historical antecedents, let's look at how a behavioral scientist describes the ideal classroom. Here is Ogden Lindsley's vision of the twenty-first century:

> The only adult in the classroom seems to be loitering. . . . She is moving about the classroom from student to student, answering a question with a whisper here, offering a quiet suggestion there, helping with a chart decision here, and giving a pat and a smile of appreciation there. Now and then, she calls for a class one-minute practice session.
>
> The students are busy at their desks, in teams of two, timing each other's practice, jumping up to take a chart down from the wall, or to post new data. The students are noisy, shouting correct answers as fast as they can at 200 words per minute, several shouting at once at neighboring desks. . . . It is not the orderly class that student teachers were taught to manage. . . .
>
> The precision teacher performs like a coach, an advisor, and an on-line instructional designer. She arranges materials and methods for the students to teach themselves, including self-counting, timing, charting, and one-on-one direction and support. (Lindsley, 1992b, p. 51)

In this chapter you will also learn the meanings of these terms:

ABC model of learning
active responding
classical conditioning
conditioned response
conditioned stimulus
continuous reinforcement schedule
discrimination training
extinction
intermittent reinforcement schedule
interval schedule
intrinsic reinforcement
least-to-most prompting
natural reinforcers
negative reinforcement
operant conditioning
passive responding
positive reinforcement
prompts
punisher
punishment
ratio schedule
reinforcement
schedule of reinforcement
stimulus control
task analysis
unconditioned response
unconditioned stimulus

According to behavioral scientists like Lindsley, who advocates an approach called *precision teaching,* this classroom contains most of the basic conditions required for learning. These conditions are:

- An environment scientifically designed to elicit correct and rapid performance.
- A focus on observable behavior or performance.
- Opportunities for feedback and reinforcement following performance.

ABC model of learning. A model that considers antecedents in the environment that elicit desired behavior, which is then strengthened when followed by appropriate consequences.

These three essential elements make up the **ABC model of learning,** which is illustrated in Figure 4.1. The ABC model of learning refers to antecedents in the environment (A) that elicit desired behavior (B), which then becomes strengthened when followed by appropriate consequences (C). This simple model includes all the essential elements of the behavioral science approach. Think of it as an overview of the behavioral model of learning as a whole and keep its main components—antecedents, behaviors, and consequences—in mind as we examine the historical roots of behaviorism and its three major components.

Classical Conditioning

Have you ever had the experience of taking a shower when suddenly someone in the apartment above you, or in a nearby bathroom, flushes the toilet? The shower's relaxing warmth turns to scalding heat! You flinch, tense up, maybe even scream in pain. But soon the water returns to its former temperature, and you relax once again—but this time your ears are alert to the sound. When you hear the flush again, you anticipate the burning water and jump back even before the temperature changes. Your body reacts reflexively.

Your body has learned an important lesson—that there is a predictable relationship or association between two events, a sound and a change in water temperature. It has learned this association through a process called **classical conditioning.**

Classical conditioning. The process by which an unconditioned, neutral stimulus and an unconditioned response are paired repeatedly to become a conditioned stimulus that elicits a conditioned response.

Pavlov's Experiment

Ivan Pavlov, a Russian physiologist, discovered the phenomenon of classical conditioning nearly a century ago. He did this by demonstrating that dogs could "learn" to salivate at the sound of a bell that was rung before they were fed, even before they could see or smell the food. The components of the classical conditioning process are shown in Figure 4.2.

Before a dog undergoes the conditioning process, the bell is a *neutral stimulus* (NS). In other words, a bell does not automatically elicit a physiological response from a dog. Food, on the other hand, automatically causes a dog to salivate. The food, therefore, is an **unconditioned stimulus** (UCS), meaning "naturally conditioned" or "conditioned by nature." Salivation is an **unconditioned response** (UCR), a reaction that automatically follows an unconditioned stimulus.

Unconditioned stimulus. A stimulus that naturally or automatically elicits an unconditioned response.

Unconditioned response. A reaction that automatically follows an unconditioned stimulus.

During the conditioning process, the bell is rung, and food is placed in the dog's mouth just seconds later. The food causes the dog to salivate. If these events are repeated, eventually the dog will salivate at the sound of the bell alone, without tasting,

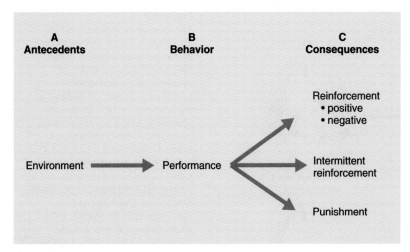

Figure 4.1
The ABC model of learning.

seeing, or smelling the food. When this occurs, the bell is no longer a neutral stimulus. Instead, it becomes a **conditioned stimulus** (CS). When a response, such as salivation, occurs following a conditioned stimulus, it is called a **conditioned response** (CR). The bell, which prior to conditioning had no effect on salivation, has become a conditioned stimulus that elicits a physiological response. While nature created the connection between food (UCS) and salivation (UCR), conditioning created the connection between salivation (CR) and the sound of a bell (CS).

Many learning theorists use the classical conditioning paradigm to explain how we learn relationships between environmental stimuli and behavioral, cognitive, and emotional responses. For example, how do we account for the following phenomena?

The smell of a certain perfume reminds you of a close friend or loved one.

You recoil at the sight of a snake when you've never encountered one before except in pictures or stories.

As a first-grader you became anxious at the sound of the school bell.

Your professor utters the word "exam" and you get a funny feeling in your stomach.

A familiar song on the radio creates mental images that change your mood.

What these events have in common is that a neutral stimulus (an odor, the sight of an animal, a sound, a spoken word, a song) has developed the power to evoke an emotional (affective), physiological (a muscle contraction), behavioral (running away), psychological (a shiver), or cognitive (an image) response. Thus, classical conditioning theorists propose that many of our behavioral, emotional, and cognitive responses to people, places, and things have been acquired through a process of classical conditioning.

For example, how might a learner develop a fear of math? Math, in and of itself, is a neutral stimulus. There is no natural connection between it and the emotional responses associated with fear (increased adrenalin flow, constriction of blood vessels, increased blood pressure, rapid breathing). However, there is a natural (unconditioned) association between being reprimanded (UCS) by a teacher or parent and the fear (UCR) that might immediately follow answering a question incorrectly or receiving a failing test

Conditioned stimulus. A stimulus that through the conditioning process has acquired the power to generate a conditioned response.

Conditioned response. In classical conditioning, a response that is elicited by some previously neutral stimulus; occurs by pairing the neutral stimulus with an unconditioned stimulus.

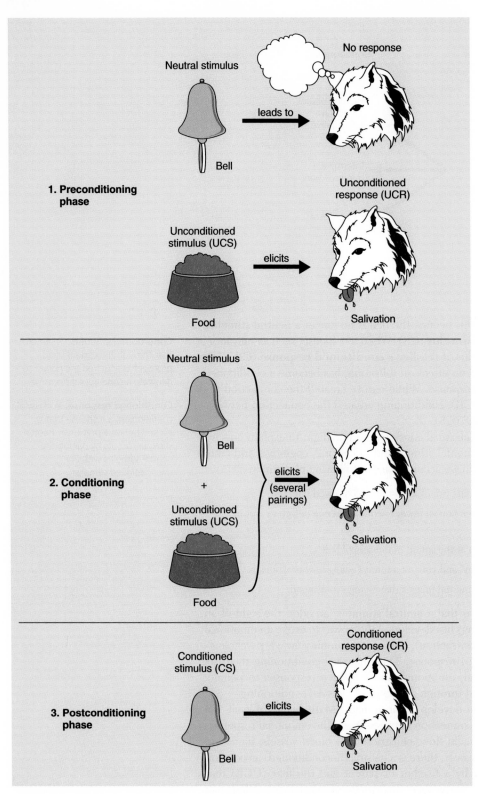

Figure 4.2
The three phases of classical conditioning. In the preconditioning phase, the unconditioned stimulus (UCS) elicits an unconditioned response (UCR). During the conditioning phase, the neutral stimulus and the UCS are paired repeatedly. In the postconditioning phase, the neutral stimulus (now called a conditioned stimulus, or CS) will elicit the original response (now called a conditioned response, or CR). *Source:* Adapted from *Developmental Psychology: Childhood and Adolescence,* by D. Shaffer, 1993, Pacific Grove, CA: Brooks/Cole. Copyright © 1993, 1989, 1982 by Brooks/Cole Publishing Company, a division of International Thomson Publishing, Inc., by permission of the publisher.

grade. Such events, repeated over time, can condition a learner to respond with intense fear at the sight of a math test—or even the announcement that one is forthcoming.

Relevance for Teachers

As a teacher, you will want your learners to acquire positive attitudes toward you and your subject. Initially, you and your learning activities will be neutral stimuli, but over time you and how you teach can become conditioned stimuli that elicit emotions (or conditioned responses) of interest and joy, evoke approach behaviors such as studying and asking questions, and even arouse physiological responses of comfort and naturalness.

Learning theorists remind us that classical conditioning processes go on in classrooms all the time. Your role is to be aware of the classical conditioning paradigm and use it to build positive associations between your teaching activities and learning. In Chapter 7 we will offer some specific recommendations to help you achieve this goal.

While the classical conditioning paradigm can explain how children learn certain emotional, behavioral, and cognitive responses to neutral stimuli, it is not as successful in explaining how children learn to be successful in Lindsley's ideal classroom: to read and solve problems, follow directions, and work productively with others. Let's look at a second learning paradigm, which can explain how learners develop these skills in their learners.

> How can I help my learners develop a positive attitude toward what I teach?

Operant Conditioning

B. F. Skinner, a Harvard psychologist, has been one of the most influential psychologists of the twentieth century. His theories and research have been applied to education, business, health care, mental health, prison reform, and military training. Skinner was thoroughly familiar with the writings of Pavlov and accepted the basic principles underlying classical conditioning. But he viewed these principles as applicable only to the learning of physiological and emotional responses—those responses (for example, salivation) that are elicited by some type of stimulus (food) and can be conditioned to another type of stimulus (bell). He called this class of behavior *respondent behavior* because it occurred in response to a stimulus.

Skinner was most interested in the learning principles governing a different class of behavior, which he called *operant behavior*. Operant behavior, in contrast to respondent behavior, is not a physiological or emotional response to something that happens in the person's environment. Rather, operant behaviors are actions that a person uses to meet the demands of the environment.

For example, riding a bicycle, going to a movie theater, pushing a vacuum cleaner, turning on the stereo, visiting a friend's house, cooking a meal, painting a picture, tuning a car engine, and writing a poem are examples of operant behaviors. These behaviors are called "operant" because they are operations that the individual carries out to help him or her deal with the environment in some way. Rather than being reactions to stimuli in the environment, they are actions or operations that the person purposely performs on the environment.

Many if not most of the operant behaviors we perform are complex, the result of years of skill acquisition. Speaking, writing, reading, problem solving, running, sewing, and making friends are complex skills, the building blocks of which can be traced to simple behaviors that the person first performed as an infant or toddler. These simple

Many complex processes can be shaped by means of operant conditioning techniques.

behaviors—grasping at a mobile, looking at a face, uttering a sound, pulling oneself up, balancing on two feet—were gradually shaped into more complex skills as a result of the interaction between the person performing the behavior and the people reacting to it.

Skinner used the expression **operant conditioning** to describe the process whereby simple operant behaviors are gradually transformed or shaped into more complex ones. Let's examine this paradigm to see first how an animal can learn a skill such as pressing a lever to get food, and then how humans can learn to speak, write, and even problem solve.

Operant conditioning. A type of learning in which the probability or likelihood of a behavior occurring is changed as a result of procedures that follow that behavior.

How Operant Conditioning Works

Figure 4.3 shows a "Skinner box"—an experimental chamber used for operant conditioning. A hungry rat is placed in the box. Inside the box is a lever, which, if pressed, releases a food pellet into a tray. There are also a red light, a green light, and an electric grid on the floor.

Suppose that your goal is to teach the rat to press the lever. When placed in the box, the rat will move about randomly. It will stand up, sniff, turn left, turn right, bump into walls, and so forth. These are all operant behaviors.

Given sufficient time, the rat will press the lever by accident and release a food pellet into the tray. Most rats will quickly learn the association between lever-pressing and

Figure 4.3
The experimental chamber referred to as the Skinner box.

food release, and they will keep pressing the lever again and again. In other words, operant conditioning will take place. If the rat is removed from the box after 30 minutes of lever-pressing and is placed back in the box the next day, it will press the lever to get food in a shorter period than it took the first time.

Now let's examine some of the basic features of operant conditioning. Figure 4.1, which illustrates the ABC model of learning, is really just another way to describe the operant conditioning process.

Reinforcement.

Reinforcement. Skinner emphasizes that what happens following a behavior determines whether it will be repeated and strengthened. He used the term **reinforcement** to refer to any event following a behavior that makes it more likely that the behavior will be repeated: the food the rat obtains reinforces the lever-pressing behavior. When the event following the behavior is desirable, so that the behavior is repeated in anticipation of a reward, **positive reinforcement** has occurred. Again, the food pellet is a positive reinforcer that makes the behavior more likely to recur.

Schedules of Reinforcement.

Schedules of Reinforcement. Skinner discovered that to get the rat to repeatedly press the lever, reinforcement had to occur on a continuous schedule—after every occasion when the rat pressed the lever. He also showed that once reinforcement stopped, the rat would soon stop pressing the lever, a process called extinction. **Extinction** is the gradual disappearance of a learned behavior when it is no longer being reinforced. This naturally led to the question of how to reinforce behavior so as to increase or speed up the initial rate of learning and make it more resistant to extinction once reinforcement was discontinued.

Skinner studied how to increase the rate of response and make learned behavior more resistant to extinction by manipulating what he called schedules of reinforcement. A **schedule of reinforcement** is a rule for when reinforcers will be given after the desired behavior is performed. Reinforcers can be given every time a behavior occurs (a **continuous reinforcement schedule**), or every now and then (an **intermittent reinforcement schedule**).

If reinforcers are given intermittently, you may choose, for example, to reinforce every other response or every third response (thus creating a **ratio schedule**), or you may decide to give the reinforcer after a set period of time, such as at the end of each 30-second or 60-second period during which the rat presses the lever (an **interval schedule**).

Ratio and interval schedules can be fixed or variable. A *fixed ratio schedule* is a rule that says, for example, "reinforce every fourth time the rat presses the lever." A *variable ratio schedule,* on the other hand, directs the experimenter to reinforce a certain proportion of responses in such a way that, on average, one out of every four responses is reinforced.

Interval schedules can also be fixed (for example, every minute) or variable (so that, on average, the rat is reinforced every 60 seconds). Figure 4.4 summarizes the various schedules of reinforcement and suggests their practical effects in the classroom.

Skinner discovered that each schedule of reinforcement had a predictable effect on rate of learning and resistance to extinction. His results are summarized in Table 4.1.

Punishment.

Punishment. What would happen to the rate of lever-pressing if, after the rat pressed the lever, a mild electric shock was delivered by means of the electric grid at the bottom of the box? Skinner found that the rat would quickly stop pressing the lever. The

Reinforcement. In operant conditioning, actions taken following a response that increase the likelihood that the response will occur again. Reinforcement can be both positive and negative.

Positive reinforcement. The condition of administering a stimulus, following a response, that increases the likelihood of that response occurring again.

Extinction. A procedure that involves identifying and eliminating the specific reinforcer for a particular inappropriate behavior.

Schedule of reinforcement. A rule for when reinforcers will be given following performance of a desired behavior.

Continuous reinforcement schedule. Reinforcement of every occurrence of a behavior.

Intermittent reinforcement schedule. A procedure by which only certain responses are followed by the delivery of a reinforcer.

Ratio schedule. Application of reinforcers after a set number of responses, such as every third response.

Interval schedule. Delivery of reinforcers after the first response made following a predetermined period of elapsed time.

How can I help my learners become more persistent in their efforts to learn?

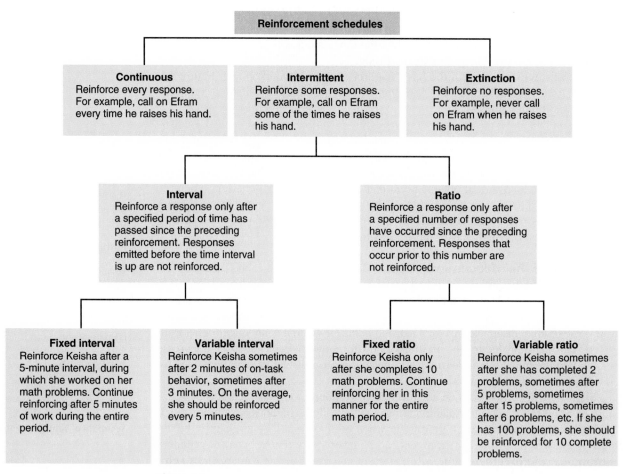

Figure 4.4
Schedules of reinforcement.

Punishment. In operant conditioning, an action taken following a response that decreases the likelihood that the response will happen again.

Negative reinforcement. A procedure that increases the likelihood of a response being repeated by removing an aversive stimulus immediately following that response.

speed with which it learned to stop pressing would depend on both the immediacy of the shock and its intensity. Skinner defined **punishment** as any action, following a response, that makes that response less likely to occur again. The key part of this definition is that punishment makes a response *less* likely to recur.

Negative Reinforcement. Punishment, which we described above, is distinguished from **negative reinforcement,** which is a way of making a response *more* likely to recur by removing an aversive (unpleasant) stimulus. For example, suppose you wanted to teach the rat to jump over a fence that divided the box in half. One means of accomplishing this would be to send an electric current through the floor on the side of the box where the rat was standing. The rat would become agitated and would eventually jump the barrier and land in the unwired portion of the box. The next time the rat was placed in the wired section and the shock was delivered, it would jump much sooner than the first time. Eventually, the rat would jump the barrier even before the shock was administered.

The rat learned to jump by means of negative reinforcement. The rat escaped or avoided a shock by performing a new behavior. In general, we tend to repeat behaviors

Table 4.1

Reinforcement Schedules and Their Effect on Rate of Learning and Resistance to Extinction

Schedule	Example	Effect on Rate of Learning	Pattern of Response Following Extinction
Continuous	Reinforce the learner every time he completes a math problem.	Learner will rapidly learn to complete math problems.	Learner will quickly stop completing math problems once reinforcement stops.
Fixed interval	Reinforce the learner every 5 minutes for working on math problems.	Learner will complete more math problems as the time for reinforcement draws near but complete fewer immediately following reinforcement.	Learner will not persist long with daily math problems. He will quickly stop doing problems once 5-minute period ends and he doesn't receive reinforcement.
Variable interval	Reinforce after various lengths of time.	These schedules generate low to moderate rates of response. After a period of adjustment to the schedule, the learner will complete a constant, stable number of problems.	Once extinction starts, the learner will continue to do math problems for longer periods of time. But there will be a slow steady decline.
Fixed ratio	Reinforce after a set number of math problems are completed.	These schedules generate rapid rates. The learner will complete math problems quickly because she gets reinforced after a fixed number of problems are completed.	Learner will not persist in doing math problems for long once she doesn't get reinforced after the total number of problems are completed.
Variable ratio	Reinforce after a varying number of math problems are completed.	These schedules produce rapid, consistent rates of performance.	Learner will persist in doing math problems the longest with this schedule.

that help us avoid, postpone, delay, or alter situations we find aversive or unpleasant. For example, when you postpone or cancel assignments or tests because students complain about them, you are negatively reinforcing their complaining behavior. If a student doesn't want you to call on her, and finds that she can get you to call on someone else by looking away, then you are negatively reinforcing her behavior.

Stimulus Control. Let's say that you want the rat to press the lever for food only when the green light comes on. In other words, you want the green light, but not the red one, to elicit or control lever-pressing behavior. This could be accomplished by reinforcing the rat with food pellets when the green light was on, but not the red one. Eventually, the rat would learn to press the lever for a reward only in the presence of a green light. This is an example of **stimulus control**—the rat's lever-pressing response has been brought under the control of the conditioned stimulus (the green light). Skinner called this type of training **discrimination training.** By reinforcing the rat only in the

Stimulus control. In operant conditioning, the control of the occurrence of a response by a dependable signal or cue, which indicates that a reinforcer will occur if the correct response is emitted.

Discrimination training. Reinforcement that occurs only in the presence of a particular stimulus in order for the subject to discriminate the occasions when a reward will occur and when it will not.

presence of a particular stimulus, the rat learns to discriminate the occasions when it will be rewarded from those when it will not.

In the classroom, this would be analogous to expecting learners to raise their hands to ask questions only when you have finished an explanation, which you signal by pausing and looking around the room. You then could bring hand raising under stimulus control by calling only on those who raise their hands and ignoring students who speak out without permission. Students quickly learn that when they raise their hands following your signal, they are more likely to be called on. Figure 4.5 provides examples of some other ways the principles of operant conditioning can apply to human behavior. Note the parallels between this figure and the components in the ABC model of learning, which were illustrated in Figure 4.1.

Relevance of Operant Conditioning for Teachers

Skinner points out that most of the behaviors that we want learners to acquire in school can be classified as operants. Complying with rules, following important routines such as lining up or changing learning groups, completing homework, writing legibly, speaking in complete sentences, dissecting a frog, reciting a poem, performing a cartwheel, getting along with others, and working independently are behaviors that teachers can gradually strengthen, shape, and refine. In addition, through discrimination training, you bring these behaviors under stimulus control—you let learners know when and under what circumstances it is appropriate to perform them.

In the remainder of this chapter, we will examine how to apply the principles of operant conditioning to help learners acquire important academic skills.

Using the Behavioral Science Approach

In the introduction to this unit we asked the question, "What does a classroom teacher need to know about learning?" According to the behavioral science approach, the teacher must be able to:

1. Focus instruction on observable learner performance.
2. Assure that learners can perform the skills that are prerequisites to that performance.
3. Elicit a rapidly paced, correct performance.
4. Use appropriate consequences following performance.

Figure 4.6 illustrates these important components of the behavioral science approach to instruction. Let's examine each of them in more detail.

Focus on Learner Performance

Behavioral scientists have traditionally defined learning as a stable change in behavior brought about by the environment. Cognitive theorists have expanded this traditional definition of learning to include such topics as cognitive changes in memory capacity, thinking, and mental processing. Behavioral scientists are opposed to this definition. Their opposition stems less from a denial that changes in cognitive (mental) activity occur than from a concern about the difficulty of measuring them.

Behaviorists believe that in order to establish a true science of instruction we must

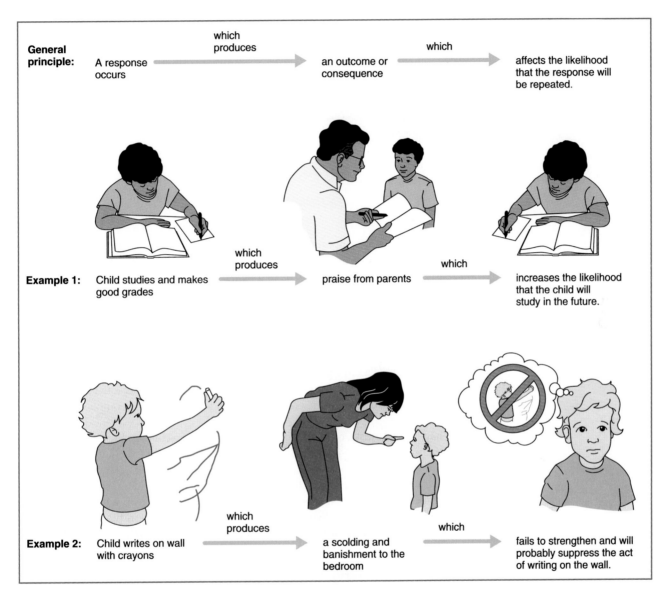

General principle: A response occurs → which produces → an outcome or consequence → which → affects the likelihood that the response will be repeated.

Example 1: Child studies and makes good grades → which produces → praise from parents → which → increases the likelihood that the child will study in the future.

Example 2: Child writes on wall with crayons → which produces → a scolding and banishment to the bedroom → which → fails to strengthen and will probably suppress the act of writing on the wall.

Figure 4.5
Basic principles of operant conditioning, showing examples of reinforcement and punishment. *Source: From Developmental Psychology: Childhood and Adolescence,* by D. Shaffer, 1993, Pacific Grove, CA: Brooks/Cole. Copyright © 1993, 1989, 1982 by Brooks/Cole Publishing Company, a division of International Thomson Publishing, Inc., by permission of the publisher.

be able to explain how what teachers do affects what learners do—not what or how they think. Cognitive activity is something we cannot measure directly. We can only infer it from observing performance—and inferences about cognitive activity can be wrong. Behaviorists believe that a focus on observable performance avoids incorrect inferences about learning and allows us to build a science of instruction on a firm foundation.

Distinctions between learning and performance and between cognitive and

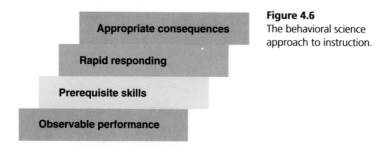

Figure 4.6
The behavioral science approach to instruction.

observable changes are important for teaching. By their strong advocacy of observable outcomes and performance objectives, behavioral scientists challenge teachers not to take learning for granted. This means that you should plan lessons with a clear vision of the important outcomes you want learners to achieve (as we will discuss in Chapter 10), and end your instruction with an assessment of those outcomes (as we will discuss in Chapters 12 and 13). Both of these recommendations are consistent with the behavioral science approach to learning. This premise of behavioral science—that the only valid measure of learning is observable performance—has been criticized by some educators and psychologists (Pasch, Sparks-Langer, Gardner, Starks, & Moody, 1991), who believe that this emphasis encourages teachers to write only those objectives that are easy to measure and thus to ignore educational outcomes involving complex intellectual skills.

Behavioral scientists, on the other hand, believe that a concern for performance will have the opposite effect—that it will persuade teachers to give more serious thought to what they want their learners to accomplish. This, in turn, will help teachers devise authentic ways to assess learning in terms of performance and thinking skills, not just the acquisition of facts. As we will see in Chapters 10 and 13, you can write clear, detailed instructional goals and objectives that can be measured reliably in the context of classroom performance and performance on real-world assessment tasks.

Ensure the Learning of Prerequisite Skills

You may be wondering how someone's intelligence, abilities, aptitudes, or learning style enters into a behavioral scientist's theory of learning. After all, if someone lacks an aptitude for math or writing, or possesses little musical or painting ability, doesn't that affect his or her learning?

What characteristics of learners should classroom teachers be concerned about when planning their lessons? Behavioral scientists have a straightforward and (given their concern for observable performance) predictable answer to these questions: Other than a learner's physical capabilities to perform the learning task, the only characteristic that is relevant to a student's learning a skill is whether the learner possesses the prerequisites for it. In other words, if you expect your students to learn how to write a paragraph, you must first ask yourself whether they can write a complete sentence, a topic sentence, and transitions between sentences. At an even more basic level, can they spell words and form letters correctly? If some of your learners cannot learn to write a paragraph skillfully and effortlessly, behavioral scientists would attribute this to a lack of prerequisite skills (or poorly designed instruction)—not to a lack of ability, aptitude, or intelligence.

Behavioral scientists believe that the source of almost all learning failures can be identified if teachers analyze both the *internal conditions* (prerequisite skills) and the *external conditions* (instructional events) of learning. For example, if one of your learners can't seem to master long division, is it because he hasn't learned how to subtract? If he is having difficulty learning subtraction skills, has he learned how to regroup? If he hasn't learned to regroup, can he identify which of two numbers is larger? At no point would the behavioral scientist conclude that the learner lacks ability or intelligence. If the teacher analyzes and probes deeply enough, eventually she can identify the source of the problem and teach or reteach the skills necessary for learning to continue.

The idea of breaking complex behaviors into smaller component behaviors originated with Skinner (1954). As we saw earlier, Skinner's experiments on shaping the behavior of rats demonstrated the usefulness of this method. Gagné (1970), however, more so than any other behavioral scientist, demonstrated the importance to classroom learning of such an analysis.

Task Analysis. The process of analyzing the internal conditions necessary for learning is called **task analysis.** The outcome of a task analysis is an arrangement of prerequisite skills into a *learning hierarchy*. You begin a task analysis by identifying what task you want your learners to perform at the end of a lesson or unit of instruction. Then ask, "In order to perform this task, what prerequisite skills must my learners already have mastered?" The answer should be the most complex, highest-level prerequisite skills.

Next, for each of these skills, identify further prerequisites. Eventually a learning hierarchy emerges, such as that shown in Figure 4.7. The questioning process you might follow for an individual learner is illustrated in this figure.

If you have trouble conducting a task analysis using the logical questioning process described above, do the task yourself and write down what you did, or observe someone doing the task and write down what you saw. Some curriculum guides are sufficiently detailed as to provide a task analysis for you.

Sequencing. Constructing a learning hierarchy is dependent on identifying the prerequisite skills in the correct sequence: you can't teach subtraction with regrouping before you teach place value. Behavioral scientists consider the sequence in which skills are taught to be especially important. They place a premium on correct responses, rapid responding, and efficiency. Therefore, incorrectly sequenced instruction results in errors, frustration, and inefficiency. Englemann (1991) cautions that the sequence of skills presented in the published curriculum you use may create problems for your learners. Thus, it will be worth your while to examine this sequence and adjust it when necessary.

Also, solving complex problems in math, writing compositions, and interpreting difficult reading passages are all tasks that require learners to perform prerequisite skills automatically and effortlessly (Mayer, 1987). Imagine the difficulty your learners would have writing an essay if they could not form letters, spell, punctuate, and construct grammatical sentences. Learners who cannot perform prerequisite skills effortlessly and with minimal errors find it difficult to transfer new learning to unfamiliar problem contexts. One of the key ingredients for transfer of new learning is the mastery of prerequisite skills.

> How will I know when my learners have attained the prerequisite skills required for new learning?

> **Task analysis.** A process for identifying the behavioral components of more complex skills and arranging them in a hierarchical sequence.

Step 1: Can Amanda distinguish lengths of a straight line?

Some problems to sample Amanda's work:

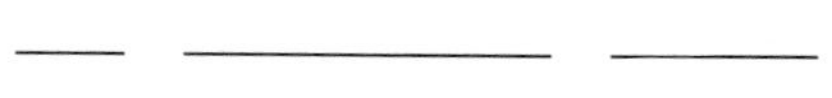

Which is the longest?   Which is the shortest?

Step 2: Can Amanda distinguish different lengths and widths of a rectangle?

Some problems to sample Amanda's work:

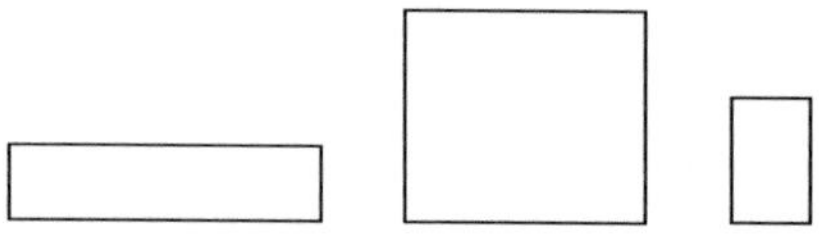

Which is the longest?   Which is the tallest?

Step 3: Can Amanda distinguish areas of rectangles by length and width?

Some problems to sample Amanda's work:

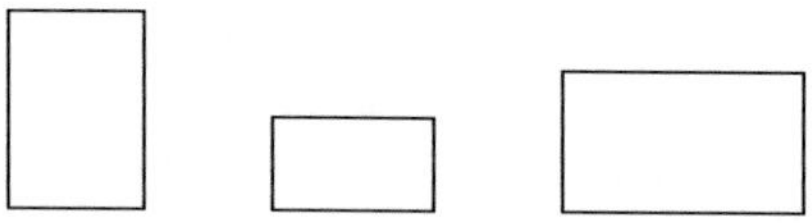

Which has the most area?   Which the least?

Step 4: Can Amanda determine whether one container has more liquid than the other, or whether both have the same amount if one is poured into the other?

Problem to sample Amanda's work:

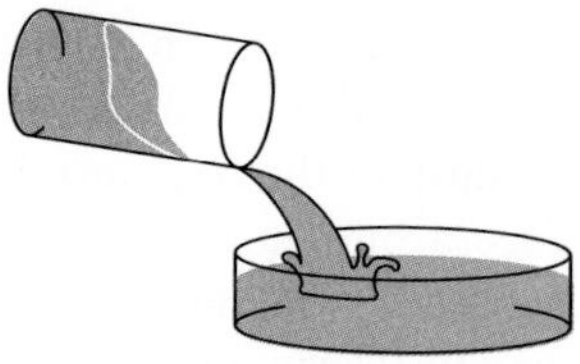

Figure 4.7

A learning hierarchy for conservation skills. *Source:* From "Contributions of Learning to Human Development," by R. M. Gagné, 1968, *Psychological Review, 75,* p. 184. Copyright © 1968 by the American Psychological Association. Adapted by permission.

Elicit Rapidly Paced, Correct Performance

As we saw in our study of operant conditioning, Skinner was able to elicit rapid correct performance by the skilled use of reinforcement and stimulus control. As you will recall, the basic elements of operant conditioning are (a) a response or behavior that you want to teach or shape, (b) an effective reinforcer, and (c) the delivery of that reinforcer immediately after performance of the desired response. The challenge—both to psychologists in the lab and to teachers in the classroom—is to elicit a correct response. Let's analyze this challenge and explore further the topic of rapidly paced, correct performance.

The skilled teacher gets learners to respond correctly by bringing correct responses under stimulus control. Exactly how is this done? How does a teacher deliver instruction in a manner that minimizes the likelihood that learners will make mistakes? Four important factors are involved.

How can I encourage errorless learning?

1. Assure the learning of prerequisite skills.
2. Present instructional material effectively.
3. Use prompts.
4. Use reinforcement.

We have already discussed the first of these factors. In this section, we explain the remaining three.

According to behavioral scientists, children learn best from instructional practices that prevent mistakes, allow rapid responding, and provide many opportunities for practice.

Effective Presentation. Behavioral scientists point out three areas for you to consider as you decide how to present instructional material: specific directions, opportunities for learner responses, and the pacing of response opportunities (Cooper, Heron, & Heward, 1987; Englemann, 1991).

Specific Directions. Let's say that you want to teach some sight words to your learners. You want them to look at a word and pronounce it correctly. Here are two examples of possible directions:

> **Example 1:** This is the word "rabbit." Say "rabbit" and point to the word.
>
> **Example 2:** This is the word "rabbit." A rabbit is a small, furry animal with big ears. It likes to eat carrots. Point to the word "rabbit" and say it.

Example 1 is a better set of directions if your objective is to bring the response "saying and pointing to the word 'rabbit' " under the stimulus control of the word "rabbit." Example 2 contains information that may distract the learner from making the correct response.

Whether you are teaching word recognition to first-graders, subtraction to second-graders, paragraph construction to sixth-graders, or problem solving in physics to eleventh-graders, instructional directions should be specific to the behavior you want your learners to acquire. So think carefully about what you want learners to do and how you will direct them to do it. Discard information and explanations that are extraneous and serve only to distract the learner.

Opportunities for Learner Response. Behavioral scientists have conducted extensive research on the idea of opportunity to respond (Delguardi, Greenwood, & Hall, 1979; Hall, Delguardi, Greenwood, & Thurston, 1982; Lindsley, 1992b). They make a useful distinction between active and passive responding. **Active responding** requires the learner to do something: write sentences, calculate answers, focus a microscope, balance a scale, weigh rocks, and record observations. **Passive responding,** on the other hand, includes such activities as listening to lectures, paying attention to peers while they are reading, watching television, and waiting for teacher assistance.

Greenwood, Delguardi, and Hall (1984) report that nearly half of a learner's day is involved in passive responding. This is unfortunate, because their research also demonstrates a strong relationship between learner achievement and active responding. Behavioral scientists, therefore, urge you to plan your lessons so that learners spend at least 75 percent of their time engaged in active responding.

Research on opportunity to respond has also found that correct responses are more likely to come under stimulus control when you design your practice material (worksheets, seatwork drills, homework assignments, and so forth) to elicit correct responses 70 to 90 percent of the time (Borich, 1996; Stephens, 1976). Many teachers purposely design materials for learner practice to be challenging—in other words, they design it so there is a strong likelihood that the learners will make mistakes. Behavioral scientists have demonstrated that learners acquire basic facts and skills faster when their opportunities for practice result in success most of the time.

Pacing of Response Opportunities. Recall Ogden Lindsley's description of the ideal classroom from the beginning of this chapter. In it, Lindsley drew our attention to the rapidity with which the learners were responding—they were "shouting correct answers as fast as they can at 200 words per minute." It is a cardinal principle of behavioral sci-

Active responding. Learner behavior that emphasizes asserting, volunteering, or actively seeking out information.

Passive responding. Learner behavior in which the learner receives or waits for information.

ence that when instruction is focused on basic academic skills, stimulus control of correct responses is more likely to occur when learners are encouraged to respond rapidly.

Although you might predict that more errors would result from fast-paced lessons, research indicates just the opposite for the acquisition of facts and action sequences. In a series of studies on the pace of reading instruction, Carnine found that rapid presentations by teachers produced greater achievement, fewer errors, and more sustained attention by learners during letter and word identification tasks than did slower presentations (Carnine, 1976; Carnine & Fink, 1978).

In summary, the behavioral science approach to learning suggests that you deliver instruction in the following ways:

- Give directions that focus only on the response you want learners to make.
- Allow learners to engage in active responding during the majority of class time.
- Design instructional material for both initial learning and practice so that learners can produce correct answers 70 to 90 percent of the time.

Use of Prompts. During instruction teachers often provide **prompts**—hints and other types of supplementary instructional stimuli to help learners make the correct responses. Because, as we have seen, the behavioral science approach is concerned with minimizing mistakes, it places a high value on the use of prompts that increase the likelihood that learners will respond correctly.

Behavioral scientists identify three categories of prompts used by teachers to shape the correct performance of their learners: verbal prompts, gestural prompts, and physical prompts. We will discuss the use of all three kinds in the following sections.

Verbal Prompts. Verbal prompts can be cues, reminders, or instructions to learners that help them perform correctly the skill you are teaching. For example, saying "Leave a space between words" to a first-grader as he is writing reminds him what you previously said about neat handwriting. Or saying "First adjust the object lens" to a learner as she is looking at a microscope slide prompts her as she is learning how to use a microscope. Verbal prompts help guide the learner to correct performance and prevent mistakes and frustration.

Gestural Prompts. Gestural prompts model or demonstrate for learners a particular skill you want them to perform. For example, if you were to point to the fine adjustment knob on the microscope and make a turning gesture with your hand, you would be prompting the student to perform this step of the process. Gestural prompts are particularly helpful when you anticipate that the learner may make a mistake. Teachers use gestural prompts routinely to remind learners how to fold a piece of paper, to grasp a pair of scissors, to raise a hand before asking a question, or to hold a pen properly when writing.

Physical Prompts. Some learners lack the fine muscle control needed to follow a demonstration and imitate the action that is being modeled. For example, the teacher might verbally describe how to form the letter "A" and demonstrate this for the learner, and the learner may still be unable to write "A" correctly. In such a case, the teacher might use her hand to guide the learner's hand as he writes. This is called a physical prompt. With a physical prompt you use hand-over-hand assistance to guide the learner

Prompts. Supplementary or additional aids that teachers use to increase the likelihood that learners will engage in successful practice.

to the correct performance. Teachers routinely use physical prompts to assist learners with handwriting, cutting out shapes, tying shoelaces, correctly holding a dissecting tool, or performing a complex dance routine.

Least-to-Most Prompting. Behavioral scientists generally recommend that you use the least intrusive prompt first when guiding a learner's performance. This is referred to as **least-to-most prompting.** Verbal prompts are considered the least intrusive, while physical prompts are considered the most intrusive (Cooper et al., 1987). Thus it would be more appropriate to first say to a learner "Don't forget the fine adjustment!" when guiding her in the use of a microscope than to take her hand and physically assist her. The reasoning behind using a least-to-most order of prompts to assist learners is that verbal prompts are easier to remove or fade than are physical prompts. Learners who are dependent on physical prompts to perform correctly will find it more difficult to demonstrate a skill independently of the teacher.

> **Least-to-most prompting.**
> Prompting learners with the least intrusive methods before progressing to relatively more intrusive forms of prompting.

At this point, let's summarize what we've learned about stimulus control and its relationship to correct responses. So far, we have learned that behavioral scientists view the eliciting of a correct response as one of the four basic elements of learning. Correct responses followed by reinforcement results in more permanent learning then correct responses intermixed with incorrect responses. Mistakes slow down the learning process and often lead to frustration and attempts by learners to avoid, or passively respond to, a learning activity.

Establishing stimulus control over learner performance is the key to errorless learning. In order to elicit rapidly paced, correct performance, you must pay particular attention to four important factors when planning your lessons:

1. Make sure your learners have mastered prerequisite skills.
2. Present your lessons in a way that will give learners frequent opportunities to make correct responses.
3. Use prompts to ensure correct responding.
4. Reinforce correct responses immediately.

Let's turn now to the fourth basic element of the behavioral science approach, which tells us how to deliver consequences to learners following their performance.

Use Appropriate Consequences Following Performance

Picture the following situation: You have just begun a unit on converting fractions to decimals with your fifth-graders. After demonstrating how to perform this skill, you pass out a worksheet with 20 problems. You give your learners 10 minutes to complete the task. As the students work, you move from desk to desk checking on their answers. You notice several students getting answers wrong. What should you do? Here are some alternatives.

1. Circle the incorrect answers, show them what they did wrong, and encourage them to do better.
2. Circle just the correct answers, point out what they did right, and encourage them to do better.
3. Circle the correct answers, and praise the students for their good work.

Teachers guide student learning through the skillful manipulation of antecedents and consequences.

4. Circle the incorrect answers, admonish the students, and have them do
    the problems again.

5. 1 and 4.

6. 2 and 3.

7. All of the above.

Educational psychologists using the behavioral science approach have researched the issue of how best to respond to the correct and incorrect responses of learners. They have
arranged the possible consequences into three general categories: (1) informational
feedback, (2) positive consequences, and (3) negative consequences. Let's examine each
and see what behavioral scientists have learned about their effectiveness in promoting
learning.

> **What types of practice and feedback are required for new learning to occur?**

Informational Feedback: Correct Responses. If a learner correctly recalls
the major historical events leading up to the Civil War, legibly forms a lowercase cursive
letter, or accurately solves an algebra equation with two unknowns showing her work,
you should do two things immediately: (1) tell the learner the answer is correct, and (2)
briefly describe what she did to obtain the correct answer. For example:

"That's right. You listed the five major events."

"Those letters are slanted correctly and you wrote them on the line."

"The answer is right and you showed all the required steps."

Behavioral scientists remind us that better learning results when you tell learners not only what they got right, but also *why* they got it right (Cooper et al., 1987).

Informational Feedback: Incorrect Answers. Learners give incorrect answers for several different reasons: carelessness, lack of knowledge, or lack of understanding. In the first case, some teachers scold or use some form of verbal punishment. Behavioral scientists and many educators strongly advise against these consequences for careless performance. Instead, they recommend that you use the following types of feedback whenever students give incorrect answers, regardless of the reason:

1. If the problem involves only knowledge of factual information, simply give the correct response.

2. If the problem involves more complex intellectual skills, point out the rules, procedures, or steps to follow.

3. Ask the learner to correct the answer.

4. Ask the learner to practice some extra problems.

Here is an example of each:

> "The correct spelling is *t-h-e-i-r.*"

> "End every sentence with a period, question mark, or exclamation point."

> "First draw the base. Then, draw the altitude. Now, retrace your steps."

> "Ask yourself: 'Who are the more talked-about people in this story?' Then answer the next set of questions."

Note that these examples do not include preaching, scolding, or focusing extensively on the student's error—even if the learner was being careless. Such responses often create feelings of anxiety and distaste for schoolwork, which encourage disengagement from the learning activity. Learning will occur more quickly if you simply tell your students what to do, have them try again, and provide practice with additional problems when an incorrect response is given (Rodgers & Iwata, 1991).

Cautions for Correcting Mistakes. Research on feedback and error correction has shown that the recommendations given above improve learning for most students. However, there are two groups of learners for whom these procedures may not be beneficial: (1) those who make a lot of mistakes and (2) those who are excessively dependent on adult guidance.

When given material that is too difficult, low-achieving learners make many errors. Such learners experience low rates of positive consequences and high rates of negative ones. Consequently, they are likely to ignore corrective feedback and simply stop working. Research on low achievers affirms that when error rates are high, little is learned from informational feedback (Kulik & Kulik, 1988; McKeachie, 1990). This finding underscores the importance of designing your instruction to produce as few errors as possible in all learners.

The second case, learners who depend greatly on adult guidance, may involve attention-seeking behavior. In other words, some learners may persist in making mistakes because of the attention they receive after doing so. Hasazi and Hasazi (1972) and Stromer (1975) speculated that when a teacher's response focuses on the mistake itself rather than on the correct answer (for example, circling reversals of letters when the learner writes *b* for *d*, or circling digits when the learner writes *32* for *23*), it may inadvertently reinforce incorrect responses.

These researchers carried out experiments in which teachers circled only correct responses and drew no attention to those that were incorrect. They found dramatic improvements in the learners' ability to write digits and letters correctly after teachers made this change alone. This surprising finding reminds us that focusing on mistakes may actually reinforce the wrong response. This may be especially true in classrooms where teachers pay more attention to children who are misbehaving (talking out of turn, not following instructions) than to those who routinely follow class rules.

Positive Consequences Following Performance. Behavioral scientists have conclusively demonstrated the crucial role played by positive consequences in promoting and strengthening learning in animals. They have shown that positive consequences play an equally critical part in the classroom learning of children (Sulzer-Azaroff & Mayer, 1986). Thus, for the classroom teacher today, the important question is not whether to use positive consequences in the classroom, but what type of consequence to use and how.

Behavioral scientists make a distinction between positive consequences and positive reinforcers. *Positive consequences,* such as smiles, praise, happy faces, "happygrams" (see Chapter 16), and prizes are enjoyable or pleasurable things that teachers (or parents) do for children to encourage their good efforts and motivate them to do better. They may or may not serve as positive reinforcers.

Something can be called a *positive reinforcer* only when it can be conclusively shown that it increases the frequency of a target behavior. When you praise a learner's correct punctuation with the intention of increasing the likelihood that she will continue her progress, you are using a positive consequence. In order to classify this consequence as a positive reinforcer, you must show that the learner continues to make progress and that your praise was the causal factor. Some teachers develop elaborate systems of positive rewards, hoping that they will energize their learners to achieve increasingly higher levels of both social and academic skills (Canter, 1989). However, the teachers believe they are using positive reinforcers when they are simply using positive consequences.

We will now extend our discussion of positive consequences following learning to address two additional issues: (1) how to use positive consequences to promote and maintain learning and (2) how to establish natural reinforcers (i.e., intrinsic motivators) for learners who require extrinsic ones.

The Expert Practice of Positive Reinforcement

Recall from our discussion of operant conditioning that positive reinforcement is the process of strengthening behavior by the presentation of a desired stimulus or reward. While this definition appears simple, reinforcement is nevertheless easily misunderstood and misused. Before we expand on the use of positive reinforcement in the classroom, let's see some examples of what it is *not.* These will help you grasp the complexity of positive reinforcement.

> Mr. Russo has snack time at 10:15 and 10:30 for his first-grade class. He gives his
> learners juice, cookies, fruit bits, and other types of reinforcers.

Mr. Baker, the principal, decided to start a positive reinforcement program. At the end of the week, each teacher would nominate his or her "best student" to receive the "Principal's Pride Award" at a ceremony each Monday morning. Parents would be invited to attend.

Mrs. Knipper allows students who finish assignments early to use the computer in the back of the room.

Mr. French has a popcorn party every Friday if the class has not broken more than five major rules the entire week.

Mrs. Reimer has a basketful of inexpensive trinkets and school supplies. She lets learners who have been particularly helpful on a given day select a prize from the basket.

Learners who read more than five books a year are treated to a special roller skating party at the end of the school year, hosted by the principal.

There is nothing wrong or inappropriate about these activities. Learners, their teachers, and parents generally like and support them. They even may have some beneficial outcomes on learning, but they are not necessarily examples of positive reinforcement. Positive reinforcement is a complex process that demands a substantial commitment of the teacher's time and effort, as we will now see.

The Process of Positive Reinforcement

When behavioral scientists speak of positive reinforcement they refer to a sequence of actions by a teacher, trainer, or behavioral specialist that has a beginning, middle, and end. When you decide to use positive reinforcement you commit yourself to this specific sequence of steps, which we describe in the accompanying box, *Administering Positive Reinforcement.* Note that very few of these steps were followed in the examples given earlier. Reread the examples now, and ask yourself how many included: baseline measurement of specific behaviors; assessment of reinforcer preferences; immediate, continuous reinforcement for the performance of specific behaviors; and a gradual fading of the use of extrinsic reinforcers to natural reinforcers.

How will I know whether my lessons provide appropriate rewards and reinforcement?

The point is that the expert practice of positive reinforcement is a demanding intellectual and physical challenge. When you decide to use it, you are committing yourself to a process that involves measurement, consistent delivery of reinforcers, and the responsibility to fade them. Because of this commitment, there may be few examples in regular school classrooms today where the science of reinforcement, as developed by behavioral scientists, is consistently and appropriately applied.

Therefore, it is important to recognize that most reward, recognition, and incentive systems used in today's schools do not constitute positive reinforcement as behavioral scientists use the term. In either case, users of positive reinforcement should be aware of the ethical issues involved in the use of extrinsic rewards, such as paying students for reading books or for staying off drugs.

Natural Reinforcers: Alternatives to Extrinsic Reinforcers

Behavioral scientists have often been criticized for creating a generation of learners who are hooked on artificial or extrinsic consequences in order to learn and behave in the

Applying Your Knowledge:

Administering Positive Reinforcement

Step 1: Determine a specific, observable behavior to strengthen and decide at what level of strength or correctness you want the behavior to occur. Behavioral scientists emphasize that we reinforce observable behaviors, not people.

Step 2: Measure the frequency or duration of this behavior before beginning to reinforce it. Without a baseline measure of the behavior, it cannot be determined whether the behavior has changed.

Step 3: Determine what reinforcers for the given behavior are likely to be the most effective.

Step 4: Give the reinforcer to the learner immediately after he or she performs the desired behavior.

Step 5: Give the reinforcer to the learner every time he or she performs the desired behavior until it reaches the desired level of strength or correctness.

Step 6: Change reinforcers or alter the teaching if the behavior does not show progress.

Step 7: Change from a continuous schedule of delivery of reinforcers to an intermittent one. This will maintain the behavior at the desired level and prevent it from weakening as the behavior is reinforced less and less.

Step 8: Gradually transfer the control of the behavior from extrinsic reinforcers to natural reinforcers.

classroom (see, for example, de Charms, 1968, 1976). However, an analysis of the writings of early behaviorists like B. F. Skinner (1953, 1974), or other behavioral scientists like Ogden Lindsley (1991, 1992a, 1992b) and Baer, Wolf, and Risley (1968), challenges this criticism. Such behavioral scientists have advocated the use of **natural reinforcers,** those that are naturally present in the setting where the behavior occurs. Thus, there are natural reinforcers for classrooms (grades), ballfields (the applause of fans), the workplace (money), and the home (story hour, parent attention). Examples of unnatural reinforcers are paying children or giving them treats for achievement in schools, or buying toys for children who behave well at home.

Skinner makes a further distinction in his definition of a natural reinforcer: he sees it as a change in stimulation resulting from the behavior itself. In other words, natural reinforcers occur when the behavior itself produces an environmental change that gives the person pleasure. For example, the natural reinforcer for hitting the correct keys on a piano is the pleasurable sound that the behavior brings. Similarly, the natural reinforcer for writing correct letters is the satisfaction the first-grader experiences when she sees the letters forming on the page. Thus to Skinner a natural reinforcer is a consequence that results from the very performance of the behavior we want the child to learn; that consequence in turn motivates the child to want to perform these behaviors again.

Children who enjoy solving puzzles are receiving natural reinforcement for doing so. Likewise, learners who write poetry, play the guitar, study history, read novels, or compete in gymnastics are receiving natural reinforcement. What these examples have in common is that children are engaging in the behaviors again and again without the need for external praise or other reinforcers delivered by another person.

Some learners are naturally reinforced by learning to write, read, color, answer questions, play sports, solve equations, answer textbook questions, and write essays, but others are not. Many learners require external reinforcers to engage in certain class-

Natural reinforcers. Reinforcers that occur naturally in the setting where a behavior occurs; also, changes in stimulation due to the behavior itself, such as hitting the correct keys on a piano when trying to play a particular song.

Positive reinforcement doesn't end with the delivery of the reinforcer. Teachers also have a responsibility to decrease learner dependence on extrinsic sources of motivation.

How do I make my learners less dependent on external rewards and more motivated to learn for learning's sake?

Intrinsic reinforcement. A strengthening of behavior that occurs in the absence of any external uses of reinforcers.

room activities that they do not find naturally reinforcing. For such children, external reinforcers have an important role to play. They can accomplish two things. They enable you to (1) shape and improve the behaviors you desire through the use of positive reinforcement and (2) transfer their control over the learner's behavior to natural reinforcers. Behavioral scientists refer to this process as *conditioning* (Horcones, 1992).

Conditioning a Natural Reinforcer. Over the past decade, the Communidad Los Horcones (Horcones, 1985, 1987, 1991, 1992) has developed a strategy for transferring the control of extrinsic reinforcers to that of natural, or intrinsic reinforcers. This process as a whole is referred to as **intrinsic reinforcement.** The group's recommendations are listed in the accompanying box, *Conditioning a Natural Reinforcer*. Note how the use of natural reinforcers relies on the learner's intrinsic motivation and thus allows you to transfer control of the behavior to the learner herself.

Positive Consequences: A Final Comment. Behavioral scientists emphasize that there is nothing wrong with extrinsic reinforcers, particularly when they are used as a means to get learning started and to condition natural reinforcers. But there are drawbacks to their use. Some learners stop studying when they are removed (Emmer, Evertson, Clements, & Worsham, 1994). They are not always available for all learners at the same time nor available for individual learners when they are needed. This is not the case with natural reinforcers.

Moreover, extrinsic reinforcers can be effective only when they are consistently delivered by another person. It is impractical to expect teachers to reinforce the most important behaviors of all learners at the right moment. Natural reinforcers allow for this possibility.

We will return to the subject of reinforcement when we study motivational theories in Chapter 7. Let's turn now to a discussion of the third type of consequence that teachers can use following learner performance: negative consequences.

Conditioning a Natural Reinforcer

Step 1: Select the target behavior. Examples are forming letters correctly, solving multiplication problems, drawing geometric figures, bisecting angles, and writing compositions.

Step 2: Identify the natural consequences of the selected behavior. For example, writing on a piece of paper produces many natural consequences: a scratching sound, the formation of letters, the filling up of a page, the gradual wearing away of a pencil point. Writing an essay has similar natural consequences, but in addition produces sentences that express thoughts, ideas, and images.

Step 3: Choose intrinsic consequences. From the list of natural consequences just given, select those that are likely to be reinforcing to the person and relevant to the purpose of the activity. For example, the formation of the letters is a more appropriate consequence to focus on than the scratching sound on the paper or the filling up of the page.

Step 4: Identify those consequences that can be more easily noticed by the learner. The more conspicuous the consequence to the learner, the easier it is to condition this as a natural reinforcer. For example, the shape of a printed word is a conspicuous consequence of correct handwriting that may serve as a natural reinforcer. Likewise, writing a complete thought, coming up with an answer that matches the one in the back of the textbook, or the satisfied feeling after finishing a task can all serve as natural reinforcers.

Step 5: Design your lessons in such a way that you make conspicuous the occurrence of natural consequences. Rather than focusing only on the right answer to a problem, point out and describe for the learner the sequence that was followed. In general, focus on how something was done, not just on the end result. Some learners may not notice or direct their attention to the natural consequences of their work. By setting up instructional conditions to do this, you allow for natural reinforcers to acquire power over behavior.

Step 6: Select appropriate backup reinforcers. In order to transfer the power of an extrinsic reinforcer over behavior to a natural consequence, you must select extrinsic or backup reinforcers. These reinforcers should have educational value, be typically available in your classroom, and, ideally, involve you in the reinforcing activity (Horcones, 1991).

Step 7: Condition the natural reinforcer. Have your learners engage in the behavior. As soon as possible, give informational feedback that points out the natural consequences you hope will become natural reinforcers. Immediately give the backup reinforcers. Gradually remove these reinforcers from the learning setting, but continue to point out and illustrate the natural consequences of what the learner did. Gradually point out the natural consequences less and less. Deliver and intermittently pair the backup reinforcers with the natural reinforcers.

The Use of Negative Consequences

We will end our discussion of the use of the behavioral science approach with the final type of consequence teachers can use: negative consequences. Here are some examples of negative consequences:

Mr. Holt's fourth-period math class was just before lunch. His students often failed to complete their seatwork during this period. He decided to delay the lunch period for any learners who did not finish their work.

Ms. Tolbert wanted to help her learners spell more accurately. She made them write each misspelled word 25 times in their notebooks.

Mr. Blandon was a stickler for correct punctuation. Any student who failed to capitalize a sentence or place a period at the end received a firm lecture on carelessness.

> Mr. Thomas decided to do something about students who weren't doing homework—students who didn't turn in homework assignments were required to do them after school.
>
> Mr. Altman sent "sad-grams" home to the parents of students who were doing poorly in his math class.

These are all examples of negative consequences, things that teachers (or other adults) do to learners after inappropriate behaviors in the hope that such behaviors will not occur again. Types of negative consequences typically used in schools are these:

Verbal reprimands: Speaking harshly to the student: "That work is sloppy and careless, and you should be ashamed of yourself for doing it."

Overcorrection: The learner not only corrects what he did wrong but engages in repetitive, boring practice on the same skill: "After you correct all the spelling mistakes, write each misspelled word correctly 50 times."

Response cost: The teacher takes away some right or privilege: "Whoever fails to complete the assignment loses the first 15 minutes of recess."

Exclusion: The learner is removed from one setting and placed in another, often called "time out": "If you don't cooperate in your groups, you will be removed and put in the back of the room for the rest of the period."

Negative Consequences Versus Punishers

Punisher. A stimulus received following a response that decreases the likelihood that the response will happen again.

Negative consequences may or may not be punishers. As we have seen, to a behavioral scientist, a **punisher** is something you do following a behavior to reduce the frequency of that behavior for as long as the punisher is used. In other words, your overcorrection of spelling mistakes is a punisher only if you keep good records that show that spelling mistakes have been substantially reduced. If not, then overcorrection is not a punisher—it is simply a negative consequence, which has no real effect on mistakes and may or may not cause the learner discomfort.

Behavioral scientists are very particular about what they call a punisher (just as they are very particular about what they call a reinforcer). Something is a punisher only if you have demonstrated that it reduces the behavior you targeted. Scolding, overcorrection, sending someone to the principal's office (exclusion), taking away recess (response cost), and even corporal punishment are all negative consequences, but they may not be punishers.

The distinction between a negative consequence and a punisher is significant for two reasons. First, some teachers persist in the use of negative consequences in the belief that they are helping their learners in some way. However, after a scolding, a learner may appear chastened and remorseful. He may even stop the inappropriate behavior for the next hour or day. But the same behavior soon reappears; the teacher, in frustration, scolds or reprimands again; and the cycle repeats itself.

Scolding in this case does not reduce the target behavior. It is not a punisher. It is simply a negative consequence, which the teacher uses to relieve frustration with the learner and which gives the illusion of effectiveness. By distinguishing between negative consequences and punishers, behavioral scientists remind us of the importance of gathering evidence that a behavior is changing before we persist in the use of any technique. They highlight an important ethical question: What is the justification for the continued use of negative consequences in the absence of proof of their effectiveness?

Second, the distinction between negative consequences and punishers is also significant because it raises the question of what is required to turn a negative consequence into an effective punisher.

What are some cautions I should be aware of when considering the use of negative consequences in my classroom?

The Use of Punishment

As often as you hear the lament "I tried positive reinforcement and it didn't work," you will hear the assertion "Punishment isn't effective." And just as we can attribute the failure of positive reinforcement to ineffective practice, so we can attribute the failure of punishment to ineffective application.

Many myths have arisen over the past two decades concerning the use of punishment in schools. These myths pertain to both the effectiveness and the ineffectiveness of punishment in reducing undesirable behavior. In the former case, we often hear statements like these: Punishment stops unwanted behavior. When all else fails, use punishment! Children must experience negative consequences for misbehavior! Spare the rod and spoil the child! In the latter case, punishment is frequently criticized because it makes children hate school or teachers, creates emotional problems, only temporarily suppresses behavior, or deals only with the symptom of the problem and not the cause.

In response to these beliefs, behavioral scientists cite hundreds of studies, carried out with both animal and human subjects over the past half century, that have led to a set of tested conclusions about punishment and its use (Cooper et al., 1987; Sulzer-Azaroff et al., 1988). Here is what these studies tell us about the use of punishment:

- Punishment can result in long-term elimination of undesirable behavior, but so can techniques that involve the exclusive use of positive reinforcement to strengthen appropriate behavior.
- Some individuals engage in severe, chronic, life-threatening behaviors that cannot be eliminated by positive reinforcement alone.

When used effectively, punishment reduces problem behavior, and, when it is used in conjunction with positive reinforcement, can promote long-term change. When used ineffectively, it raises serious ethical and legal issues.

- When punishment to eliminate inappropriate behaviors is used in conjunction with positive reinforcement to teach alternative behaviors, emotional side effects such as fear and dislike of teachers, attempts to escape or avoid school or schoolwork, or anxiety are less likely to occur.

- The failure of some nonaversive and positive reinforcement techniques to suppress undesirable behavior does not automatically justify the use of punishment. Usually this failure is due to the ineffective use of positive reinforcement.

- The failure of less intense punishment to suppress behavior does not necessarily justify the use of more intense punishment. In fact, increasing the ratio of positive reinforcement to create a contrast with punishment usually precludes the need for increased punishment.

From their studies on the effective use of punishment, behavioral scientists have identified several conditions as essential for the suppression and eventual elimination of undesirable behavior. Not surprisingly, these conditions are similar to those we identified for the successful use of positive reinforcement earlier in this chapter. They include the following:

1. Precise identification and baseline measurement of the target behavior.

2. Precise identification of an alternative, positive behavior.

3. An assessment of the most effective potential punisher for the target behavior prior to its use.

4. Consistent, immediate reinforcement and punishment on a continuous schedule until changes in both the target behavior and the alternative behavior are evident.

5. Fading of both reinforcers and punishers.

In Chapter 9, when we consider the topic of conduct management, we will return to the concept of reinforcement and examine its impact in the classroom more thoroughly.

Some Concluding Remarks

Our goal in this chapter was to present what you need to know about behavioral learning theory in order to be an effective classroom teacher. Although American educational practice is experiencing a resurgence of interest in cognitive approaches to classroom instruction, there is much of merit in the behavioral science approach that should not be lost. First, the behavioral approach emphasizes that changes in observable behavior should be the focus of your instruction and the criteria by which you judge its success. Second, behavioral scientists remind us that the most direct path to learning requires that your students have the prerequisite skills to achieve your objectives; that you design instruction that brings rapid, correct responses under stimulus control; and that you accelerate learning through the skilled use of positive reinforcement.

We have included in this chapter a description of some of the techniques involved in effective punishment. However, the behavioral scientist does not advocate the use of punishment—not because it is necessarily ineffective, but because the requirements for its expert and consistent implementation are often beyond the time constraints and resources of most classroom teachers. Also, the ineffective use of punishment raises serious ethical and legal issues.

Summing Up

This chapter introduced you to the behavioral science approach to classroom learning. Its main points were these:

- According to the behavioral science approach, the basic conditions required for learning are (1) a focus on observable performance, (2) an environment that stimulates correct and rapid performance, (3) abundant opportunities for practice and feedback, and (4) provision for positive reinforcement.
- The ABC model of learning refers to antecedents in the environment (A) that elicit desired behavior (B), which then becomes strengthened when followed by appropriate consequences (C).
- The behavioral science approach holds that the source of almost all learning failures can be identified if teachers analyze the internal conditions (prerequisite skills) and external conditions (instructional events) of learning.
- Classical conditioning is the transformation of a neutral stimulus (for example, a bell) into a conditioned stimulus (a bell that can elicit salivation), and an unconditioned response (salivation) into a conditioned response (salivation at the sound of a bell).
- Operant conditioning is reinforcement of a correct response after it has already occurred to increase the likelihood that the response will occur again.
- Stimulus control occurs when stimuli in the environment automatically bring about a response. Stimulus control is achieved by using rules, reminders, hints, prompts, demonstrations, praise, and so forth to produce as few errors and as many correct responses as possible.
- Behavioral scientists recommend that lessons be planned so that learners spend at least 75 percent of their time engaged in active responding.
- It is recommended that practice opportunities be structured so that learners can obtain the correct answer 70 to 90 percent of the time.
- Positive reinforcement occurs when increases in a desired target behavior are observed. It requires a baseline measurement of specific behavior; an assessment of reinforcer preferences; immediate, continuous reinforcement; and the gradual fading of extrinsic reinforcers.
- Natural reinforcers are those that are naturally present in the setting where the behavior occurs. They can also represent a change in stimulation due to the behavior itself; for example, hitting the correct keys on the piano.
- Negative consequences that reduce the frequency at which behavior occurs are called punishers. Verbal reprimands, overcorrection, response costs, and exclusion become punishers when they reduce the frequency of the targeted behavior.

For Discussion and Practice

°1. What three basic conditions does Ogden Lindsley believe are required for learning in an ideal classroom? Show how these are incorporated in the ABC model of learning.

°2. Define operant conditioning and give an example of how you would use it to present a lesson in your teaching area.

°3. According to the behavioral science approach to learning, other than a learner's physical capabilities to perform the task, what characteristic is relevant to student learning?

°4. What do Skinner and Gagné call the activity by which complex behaviors are broken into smaller component behaviors? How is this activity used by the classroom teacher?

°5. What is the behavioral scientist's primary goal regarding mistakes or errors in learning?

°6. Define "stimulus control" and provide an example of its use in a classroom of learners where you are likely to teach.

 7. Choose an objective in your teaching area, and provide good and bad examples of directions to learners. Why is one example better than the other?

°8. Provide three examples each of active and passive responding, and indicate the results of the research regarding their use in the classroom.

°9. During lesson presentation, on what three conditions does the behavioral scientist place most emphasis? Provide an example of each.

°10. For a topic of your own choosing, provide an example of the informational feedback you would provide after (a) a correct response and (b) an incorrect response.

°11. Distinguish between a positive consequence and a positive reinforcer, and provide an example of each.

°12. Positive reinforcement in the classroom requires what conditions of the teacher? With an example behavior in your teaching area, show how each would be implemented.

°13. In your own words, what are natural reinforcers? Provide one example relevant to the age of learners you will teach and one example relevant to your own learning.

°14. Identify and give an example of four types of negative consequences. What condition would have to be met for each to become a "punisher"?

Questions marked with an asterisk are answered in the appendix.

Suggested Readings

Journal of Applied Behavior Analysis 25 (1) (1992). This volume contains articles by present-day behavioral scientists addressing the current educational crisis. They point out how behavioral science approaches to education can improve American education.

Phillips, D. C., & Soltis, J. E. (1991). *Perspectives on learning* (2nd ed.). New York: Teachers College Press. Presents a highly readable and concisely written synopsis of all the major learning theories. It is written for classroom teachers.

Sulzer-Azaroff, B., et al. (1988). *Behavioral analysis in education,* reprint series, vol. III. Lawrence, KS: Society for the Experimental Analysis of Behavior, Inc. Describes how to use behavioral science learning techniques in schools. Many of these articles contain precise descriptions of techniques that teachers can easily read and implement.

Whaley, D. L., & Malott, R. W. (1971). *Elementary principles of behavior.* Englewood Cliffs, NJ: Prentice-Hall. One of the most readable texts available on the use of behavioral science learning theory to change behavior. It contains many examples and anecdotes.

Cognitive Learning I:
Understanding Effective Thinking

This chapter will help you answer the following questions about your learners:

- How can I teach my learners to become good thinkers?
- What cognitive learning strategies can help my learners remember what I teach?
- What cognitive learning strategies can help my learners improve their comprehension of what they read?
- Which is more important to how much my learners are able to learn: prior knowledge or intelligence?
- How can I use the information processing model of thinking to better understand how learning occurs?
- What are some ways of getting and holding my learners' attention?
- What teaching strategies can I use to enhance my learners' reception, availability, and activation of the information I present?
- Do my learners have to learn in orderly, sequential ways or can they use different sources of information simultaneously to construct their own meanings?
- Is my learners' intelligence fixed, or is it made up of many specific abilities that I can improve through instruction?

Many years ago in the village of Gidole in southern Ethiopia, there lived an old man and his three sons. The old man knew that he had only a few more years to live and he wanted to make sure that his property and possessions were left in good hands. He decided that he would leave all his worldly goods to the most intelligent of his three sons. The problem was finding out which son was the most intelligent.

One day he called his three sons to his bedroom and gave them each a dollar. He told them to go out and buy something with the dollar that would fill the entire bedroom. Then he told them that the son who could do this would inherit all his wealth.

The oldest son, Girma, went to the marketplace and bought as much hay as a dollar could buy. He carted it to the house and brought it to his father's room. But the hay filled only a corner of the room.

The second eldest son, Abebe, looked at the space taken up by the hay, thought a little, and ran out into the countryside. He bought as many large banana leaves as a dollar could buy. He carried them in a cart to his father's house and brought them to his father's room. Alas, the banana leaves filled only half of the room.

The youngest son, Tesfaye, looked at the space taken by the hay. He looked at the space taken up by the banana leaves. Then he looked at the dollar in his hand. His eyes roamed slowly over the entire room. He thought and thought. Then a smile came over his face. He ran to the market and purchased a candle and a match.

He returned to his father's room and drew the curtains. The room became dark. He placed the candle on a small wooden table next to his father's bed and lit it. The light from the candle filled the entire room! (Adapted from Bachrach, 1966)

Tesfaye is a good thinker. Cognitive psychologists might call him a good "information processor." What makes someone a good thinker or information processor? A precise answer to this question would require psychologists to examine someone like Tesfaye in the act of thinking and uncover the precise steps, mental structures, and processes involved in complex human thinking. Since these mental structures and processes cannot be observed directly, psychologists interested in the study of thinking use metaphors and models to explain what cannot be seen.

In this chapter you will also learn the meanings of these terms:

automaticity
cognitive strategies
comprehension monitoring
decay theory
declarative knowledge
displacement theory
domain-specific knowledge
dual-coding theory
elaboration
general knowledge
immediate memory
information processing model
interference theory
keyword method
long-term memory
metacognition
organization
parallel distributed processing model
procedural knowledge
propositional networks
rehearsal
schema theory
working memory

What are some of the metaphors and models that cognitive psychologists have created to explain what good thinkers do? First, they would say that good thinkers use *cognitive strategies*. An example of a cognitive strategy might be: "First try to picture or imagine the problem and picture or imagine several solutions." Undoubtedly Tesfaye did this when he scanned his father's room trying to visualize how a dollar's worth of anything could fill an entire room. Another strategy might be: "Don't jump to any conclusions. Test out what you think is the answer." Unlike his brothers, Tesfaye thought about the solution to the dilemma proposed by his father and visualized the solution before running out and purchasing the candle and match. There are many other cognitive strategies used by good thinkers to solve problems that you will learn about in this and the following chapter.

Cognitive psychologists also tell us that good thinkers are knowledgeable about and aware of their own thinking. They recognize when they are in a situation that demands the use of cognitive strategies. Good thinkers have cognitive strategies for finding out and organizing information and remembering when and where to use such strategies. In other words, good thinkers think about their own thinking.

Cognitive psychologists call this aspect of good thinking *metacognition*. If Tesfaye had thought to himself, "My father has challenged us with a real brain teaser. I'll have to use some thinking strategies to solve this problem. What's one of the first things I should do?" he would be engaged in metacognition. In this chapter you will learn how good thinkers use metacognition to regulate, control, and monitor their use of cognitive strategies (Pressley, 1995).

Thus good thinkers possess strategies for thinking as well as for regulating the use of those strategies. In addition, good thinkers have a lot of information to draw upon to enrich their thinking. Each has a storehouse of facts, concepts, rules, principles, and other associations that are built up and organized from birth to adulthood.

Cognitive psychologists use a number of different metaphors to describe this storehouse of information: *knowledge base* (Bloom, 1985); *declarative knowledge* (Gagné, Yekovich, & Yekovich, 1993), and *domain-specific knowledge* (Chi, 1978; Chi, Glaser, & Farr, 1988). Good thinkers in the fields of science, classroom teaching, auto mechanics, chess, sports, or medical diagnosis all have extensive stores of organized information to draw upon. We're unsure what specific knowledge base Tesfaye drew upon to solve his father's riddle. But at a minimum, he needed to know what a dollar could and could not buy, how much space a dollar's worth of anything uses, and the difference between the area of a room and its volume. In this chapter you will learn what cognitive psychologists have discovered about the importance of using what you know to think effectively.

Good thinkers possess the ability not only to learn information and strategies, but also to recall this information on demand and coordinate the complex ways knowledge, strategies, and metacognition interact. Cognitive psychologists have created several models to explain the processes that good thinkers use in the act of problem solving. We will study several models of complex human cognitive functioning: the basic information processing model (Gagné, Yekovich, & Yekovich, 1993), and parallel distributed processing, or new *connectionist* models (Bechtel & Abrahamsen, 1991; Rumelhart, 1992).

By now you are probably asking yourself about the connection between good thinking and intelligence. After all, Tesfaye's father developed what he thought was a type of intelligence test—he wanted to find out which son was most intelligent. Is good thinking, or good information processing, synonymous with intelligence? In the final section of this chapter we will discuss the relationship between information processing and intelligence (Gardner, 1993; Sternberg, 1989).

As a teacher, one of your goals will be to help your learners become good thinkers. In Chapter 6 we will study the question of how to teach good thinking in the classroom. There we will learn what cognitive psychologists have discovered about the best ways to teach learners to be good thinkers. We will examine two categories of cognitive instructional methods: the earlier cognitive models of instruction that incorporate notions of discovery learning (Bruner, 1961) and meaningful verbal learning (Ausubel, 1968), and the most recent models based on social learning theory (Zimmerman, 1990) and social constructivist notions (Brown & Campione, 1986; Vygotsky, 1987).

The Cognitive Approach to the Study of Learning

As you have gathered from our opening example and introduction, cognitive psychologists are concerned with studying good thinking—both the content of good thinking and its processes. You learned in Chapter 2 that good thinking requires that we find ways to represent in our minds those everyday events and actions we perceive through our senses. We called this "gaining freedom from stimulus control" and described cognitive development as the learner's gradual accumulation of cognitive skills and abilities that allow her to think about both the real and the imaginary.

We cannot see good thinking. Nor can we see its content or its processes. As a result, cognitive psychologists use metaphors to describe what they cannot see or touch. Their metaphors are ways of talking about things too abstract to describe literally or precisely. When Forrest Gump says "Life is like a box of chocolates," he is using a metaphor to describe the intangible.

Cognitive psychologists cannot see good thinking, but they can use metaphors to study and describe it.

Cognitive scientists use a variety of metaphors to describe the content and processes of good thinking. They use these expressions not with the intent of stipulating what thinking actually is like, but with the goal of offering us a suggestion. They are saying, "Since you can't see or touch good thinking, why not think of it as a computer, or a filing system, or as an information management system." If thinking with the use of a metaphor is helpful to you, then the metaphor has value.

Almost all cognitive approaches to learning are concerned with how everyday experiences are transformed or processed into mental images or sounds and stored for later use. In other words, they are concerned with how information is processed. It is logical, therefore, that cognitive psychologists have chosen the information processing model or computer as their metaphor of choice.

Regardless of the metaphor chosen to describe good thinking or good information processing, all cognitive approaches to learning share certain basic ideas. These shared ideas, or basic elements of the cognitive approach, shown in Figure 5.1, are as follows:

Relevant learner characteristics

Instructional manipulations

Cognitive processes

Cognitive outcomes

Outcome performance

The cognitive approach to learning has a unique set of beliefs and assumptions about each of these elements. Figure 5.1 illustrates that cognitive psychologists are interested not only in what learners do at the end of a lesson (outcome performance), but also in the content of their thinking (cognitive outcomes), and in how this content is altered by the processes of thinking. Moreover, their research examines how characteristics of learners (such as memory capacity or cognitive development) and instructional manipulations (such as certain teaching practices) influence good thinking. In this chapter we will study what cognitive psychologists have learned about what makes good thinking and the cognitive processes involved in good information processing. In the next chapter you will learn about those relevant learner characteristics and instructional manipulations that can help you teach good thinking. Before examining these elements of the cognitive approach, however, let's compare and contrast this approach with the behavioral approach to learning that we studied in the previous chapter.

Differences Between the Cognitive and Behavioral Approaches

Cognitive approaches to learning differ from behavioral approaches in three respects: (1) types of learning examined; (2) research methodology; and (3) extent of human learning examined. As you will recall from the previous chapter, the behavioral science approach studies observable outcome performance (for example, right and wrong answers) and how to set up a learning environment to produce more correct answers than incorrect ones. It makes no assumptions about what or how learners are thinking while they are learning. Cognitive approaches to learning, as Figure 5.1 illustrates, emphasize good thinking or good information processing and the cognitive processes and outcomes that underlie right and wrong answers.

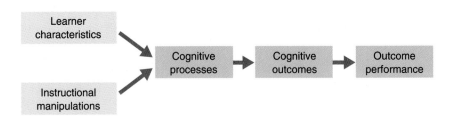

Cognitive approach

Figure 5.1
Basic elements of the cognitive approach to learning. *Source:* Adapted from *Educational Psychology: A Cognitive Approach* (p. 55), by R. E. Mayer, 1987, New York: HarperCollins. Copyright © 1987 by Little, Brown Publishers. Reprinted by permission of HarperCollins College Publishers.

Cognitive approaches to learning examine human learning exclusively. They have no interest in animal learning, which is of prime concern to behavioral scientists. Consequently, cognitive psychologists use methods that allow them to infer what people are thinking. They give people complex learning tasks and measure variables like eye movements, eye fixations, time taken to react to a stimulus, self-reports of what the learner is thinking while engaged in the act of learning, or lists of pictures or words that the learner committed to memory and recalled (Gagné, Yekovich, & Yekovich, 1993; Solso, 1988). From these sources of data, cognitive psychologists make inferences about the content and processes of human thought.

Finally, cognitive psychologists limit their interest in learning to complex human thinking, such as concept and strategy learning, decision making, problem solving, and how learners construct knowledge. Unlike behavioral scientists, they do not study simple motor responses, right or wrong answers, or simple observable behaviors. Moreover, behavioral scientists have attempted to erect a system that can account for all human learning—behavioral, emotional, and social. Cognitive psychologists, in contrast, have limited their theorizing to those aspects of human functioning related to complex thought processes.

The Content of Good Thinking

Good thinking involves three elements: strategies, metacognition, and knowledge. Expert thinkers in any field of study possess these three characteristics. As a teacher who is interested in teaching learners to be good thinkers, you will want to focus your lessons on these three areas. Let's examine what each contains.

How can I teach my learners to become good thinkers?

Cognitive Strategies

In the exercise below, fill in the blanks with terms that you have learned so far in this chapter, such as *information processing, good thinking, cognitive strategies, metacognition,* and *knowledge base.* Place your selections in the blanks in ways that make sense, but without trying to find the "best" or most correct answer.

How are ——— and ——— alike?

What is the main idea of ———?

What are the strengths and weaknesses of ——— ?

In what way is ——— related to———?

How does——— affect ——— ?

What do you think causes ——— ?

What would happen if a learner were to use ——— ?

What do I still not understand about ——— ?

King (1989) gave these generic questions to students in her undergraduate psychology class. She taught them how to use these questions in three different ways: (1) during class to learn more from her lectures, (2) after class to learn more from studying, and (3) as a basis for group discussion. She found that the use of these questions significantly improved what her students learned from her lessons.

If you use these questions on your own to learn what we are presenting in this text, you will have learned what cognitive psychologists call a cognitive learning strategy. **Cognitive strategies** are general methods of thinking that improve learning across a variety of subject areas. Cognitive strategies go beyond the processes that are naturally required for carrying out a task (Pressley, Harris, & Marks, 1992). For example, as you read this paragraph you are engaged in decoding processes (moving eyes from left to right, instantly sounding out each word, and so on). Therefore, decoding is not a cognitive strategy, because it is naturally required, or obligatory, for reading. However, if before you began to read this chapter you scanned the headings and asked yourself questions about the chapter's subject matter, and if, as you were reading, you regularly paused and asked yourself if you understood what you were reading, then you would be using cognitive strategies.

Similarly, a student is not using a cognitive strategy when he regroups and borrows to solve a subtraction problem—he is doing what is naturally required to perform the task. However, if before solving the problem and during the act of problem solving, the learner prompted himself with statements such as "What am I supposed to do? What information am I given? First, I'll draw a picture of what the problem is asking," he would be using a cognitive strategy.

There are cognitive learning strategies to improve memory, reading comprehension, math problem solving, and problem solving in general. In the following sections, we will describe a number of strategies and demonstrate how you can use them in your classroom.

Strategies to Improve Memory. As we will see in our discussion of human memory processes, learners have only a limited capacity for recalling information. Permanent recall depends on how well the learner takes in new information and stores it. Cognitive psychologists have discovered a number of strategies for improving memory that you can teach to your students. These strategies typically involve rehearsal, elaboration, and organization.

Rehearsal involves repeating to yourself what you are reading or hearing. This could involve repeating the lines in a poem, letters that spell a word, or a list of steps to be followed.

School-age learners are expected to learn the names of letters, associate sounds

---

Cognitive strategies. General methods of thinking that improve learning across a variety of subject areas.

What cognitive learning strategies can help my learners remember what I teach?

Rehearsal. Repeating to yourself what you are reading or hearing.

with particular letters and letter combinations, and memorize addition, subtraction, and multiplication steps, facts, dates, scientific terminology, and word definitions. Learners who experience difficulty memorizing such information are often helped by learning a memory strategy called **elaboration.** Learners use elaboration when they associate a particular image with something they are learning (for example, a learner recalls an image of an apple to learn the sound of the letter "a"). They might also relate something they have already learned to new material. Van Houten (1994) taught letter sounds and multiplication facts to learning disabled students using an elaboration technique that he calls *color mediation.* A child who has learned to label several colors correctly is taught to apply color labels to letters or number facts printed in a particular color (for example, red is associated with "9," or green with "p"). The number or letter in question is printed in the color associated with its verbal label. The child learns to label the letter or recall the number fact by matching it with its color.

> **Elaboration.** Associating what you are learning with a particular image or relating old learning to new.

The **keyword method** (Levin, 1985) is an elaboration strategy in which the learner transforms one or two related pieces of information into a "keyword" already familiar to her. For example, students in high school are often required to learn foreign language words and definitions. The students have two pieces of information to associate—one of which is an unfamiliar term (the foreign word). The foreign word can be transformed into something familiar, thus making its definition easier to remember. For example, to learn that *pollo* means "chicken" in Spanish, a learner would identify a word that looks or sounds like *pollo.* Either "pole" or "polo" could serve as a keyword for *pollo.* Thus the learner might imagine a chicken scratching the ground at the North Pole or a team of chickens playing polo. The potency of this memory strategy has been demonstrated in scores of studies used with learners from elementary school through college (Pressley, 1995).

> **Keyword method.** An elaboration strategy whereby the learner transforms one of two related pieces of information into a keyword familiar to him- or herself to help remember the other piece.

Organization is a term applied to memory strategies in which the learner groups or arranges the information being studied according to some system. *Chunking* is an organization strategy in which the learner places information in related groups. Another organization strategy is to arrange information into some type of outline form with

> **Organization.** Memory strategies whereby the learner groups or arranges the information being studied according to some system.

Teaching learners strategies to improve memory can have big payoffs in motivation and self-esteem, as well as in the learning of basic skills.

headings and subheadings. The accompanying box, *Teaching Memory Strategies,* contains additional examples of memory strategies. Teaching students to employ such mental organizers gives them creative alternatives by which to manipulate ideas and information, retain mental strategies for learning, and thus internally reinforce their own learning.

Comprehension monitoring.
Cognitive strategies that help learners derive meaning from what they read.

What cognitive learning strategies can help my learners improve their comprehension of what they read?

Strategies to Improve Reading Comprehension. The goal of reading instruction is to train learners not how to say words but how to get meaning out of them. **Comprehension monitoring** is a term applied to a host of strategies learners can use to derive meaning from what they read. Specific examples of comprehension strategies include *Survey, Question, Read, Recite, Review* (SQ3R) (Robinson, 1946); its somewhat more recent variation, *Preview, Question, Read, Reflect, Recite, Review* (PQ4R) (Thomas & Robinson, 1972); and *question generation* (Rosenshine & Chapman, 1992). These comprehension strategies have in common the following skills:

1. *Setting goals for reading:* Learners learn to ask themselves "What do I have to do?" and "Why am I reading this story?"

2. *Focusing attention:* Learners learn to prompt themselves with questions such as "What am I supposed to do as I read?"

3. *Self-reinforcement:* Learners learn to say to themselves "Great, I understand this. Keep up the good work," or "This strategy really works."

4. *Coping with problems:* When they encounter difficulties, learners learn to say to themselves "I don't understand this. I should go back and read it again," or "That's a simple mistake. I can correct that."

The accompanying box, *Using Reading Comprehension Strategies,* describes several other strategies that teachers of any subject area can teach to learners at the elementary or secondary school level.

Comprehension monitoring is one of a number of cognitive strategies that can help learners derive meaning from what they read.

Teaching Memory Strategies

Jingles or Trigger Sentences. *Jingles,* or trigger sentences, can cue sequential letters, patterns, or special historical dates. For example, most music students learn some variation of the phrase "Every Good Boy Does Fine" to recall the musical notes EGBDF on the lines of a treble staff. "Spring forward, fall backward" helps one remember which way to adjust clocks at the beginning and end of daylight saving time. Many school children can recite "In fourteen hundred and ninety-two, Columbus sailed the ocean blue." Such devices also can be used for recalling the steps of a mental strategy.

Narrative Chaining. *Narrative chaining* is the process of weaving a list of key words you wish to remember into a brief story. For example, if you need to memorize the key stages of a butterfly's life cycle (egg, larva, pupa, adult), you could invent a narrative such as this:

> This morning I cooked an egg for breakfast, but I heated it so long that it looked like molten lava from a volcano. A pupil from a nearby school stopped by, and when he saw my egg-turned-lava, he yelled, "I'm just a pupil! You're the adult! Couldn't you cook an egg better than that?"

In this case, lava and pupil sound enough like larva and pupa to trigger memory of the correct words in the life cycle sequence.

Number Rhyme or Peg Word. A *number rhyme* (or peg word) mnemonic system uses words that rhyme with a sequence of numbers as a basis for developing odd, imaginative mental pictures that assist in memorizing a set of other, less related words.

Using the life cycle of the butterfly as an example again, you might employ the number rhyme system this way:

> *one-sun:* Imagine a big fried egg hanging in the sky overhead in place of a shining sun.

> *two-stew:* Imagine a bubbling stew erupting from a gigantic volcano under the fried egg, drying to form molten lava.

> *three-sea:* Imagine a tiny, screaming pupil afloat on a swirling, angry sea where the hot lava sizzles as it meets the seawater.

> *four-door:* Imagine a golden door in the side of the volcano that is opened by a gentle, helpful adult who reaches out to pull the pupil from the sea near the lava that was heated by the egglike sun.

Chunking. *Chunking* refers to grouping bits of information into sets of five to seven discrete pieces. If the sets are chunked into logical categories, the information is then doubly processed in a mental framework for improved recall. A common example is memorizing a grocery list by splitting it into logical categories (dairy products, vegetables, beverages, etc.) of several items each.

Source: Reprinted with the permission of Macmillan College Publishing Company from *Effective Teaching Methods,* 3rd ed., by G. D. Borich, 1996, Copyright © 1996 by Merrill/Macmillan Publishing Company, Inc.

Strategies for General Problem Solving. Many systems for problem solving can be taught to learners (Pressley, 1995). There are problem-solving strategies to improve general problem solving (Burkell, Schneider, & Pressley, 1990; Mayer, 1987; Sternberg, 1988), scientific thinking (Kuhn, 1989), mathematical problem solving (Schoenfeld, 1989), and writing during the elementary years (Harris & Graham, 1992a) and during adolescence (Applebee, 1984; Langer & Applebee, 1987).

A problem-solving system that can be used in a variety of curriculum areas and with a variety of problems is called IDEAL (Bransford & Steen, 1984). IDEAL involves five stages of problem solving:

1. **I**dentify the problem. Learners must know what the problem is before they can solve it. During this stage of problem solving, learners ask

Applying Your Knowledge:
Using Reading Comprehension Strategies

Summarization. Teach your learners the following summarization rules:

1. Delete trivial information.
2. Delete redundant information.
3. Substitute superordinate (inclusive) terms for specific details (for example, summarize a number of descriptive details under the superordinate term "large" or "frightening").
4. Integrate a series of actions under a superordinate or all-inclusive action term (for example, summarize waking up, brushing teeth, eating breakfast, and so on as "getting up in the morning").
5. Select a topic sentence; invent a topic sentence if there is none.

Bean and Steenwyck (1984) instructed sixth-graders in the use of these rules and significantly improved their reading comprehension with a variety of reading material.

Mental Imagery. Teach your learners to create pictures or images in their minds to depict what they have read. For example, when the learner reads a potentially confusing fact, such as "an ecosystem is a specific community of living creatures and their environment," teach him to picture in his mind a natural scene that includes a variety of animals and plants. Learners can do the same for history passages, poems, current events articles, and so forth.

Sadoski (1983, 1985) taught these strategies to third- and fourth-graders and found that their recall of story details and understanding of what they read was greatly enhanced.

Story Grammar Training. Different types of texts, such as *narratives* (texts that tell stories) and *expository* texts (texts that convey information), have typical structures that students learn to recognize. For example, the structure, or *story grammar,* of a fable might go something like this: One animal encounters another animal, something happens to one of the animals or one animal does something to the other animal, the animal who was helped or harmed overcomes the obstacle or injury, the two animals meet at some future time, and one animal learns an important lesson. Mystery stories, romances, and science passages also have predictable structures. Teach your learners to ask themselves questions about this structure. For example, as they read stories, teach your learners to ask themselves:

1. Who is the main character?
2. Where and when did the story take place?
3. What did the main characters do?
4. How did the story end?
5. How did the main character feel?

Short and Ryan (1984) and Idol and Croll (1987) taught story grammars to 9- to 12-year-olds that significantly improved their reading comprehension of stories.

themselves whether they understand what the problem is and whether they have stated it clearly.

2. **D**efine terms. During this stage, learners check whether they understand what each word in the problem statement means.

3. **E**xplore strategies. At this stage, learners compile relevant information and try out strategies to solve the problem. This can involve drawing diagrams, working backward to solve a mathematical or reading comprehension problem, or breaking complex problems into manageable units.

4. **A**ct on the strategy. Once learners have explored a variety of strategies, they select one and now use it.

5. **L**ook at the effects. During the final stage of the IDEAL method, learners ask themselves whether they have come up with an acceptable solution.

The accompanying box, *Using the IDEAL Method,* provides a sample dialogue to show how a fifth-grade teacher taught her learners to use IDEAL.

Summary. There is abundant evidence that learners as young as 2 years use problem-solving strategies. Good learners at all grade levels know and use strategies to accomplish school tasks in reading, math, science, and social studies. They know how to use memory strategies to improve recall, comprehension strategies to learn more from reading, and general problem-solving strategies to improve math and science understanding. In the next section we will present research on how learners learn *when* to use cognitive strategies—an important aspect of good thinking called *metacognition.*

Metacognition

Pressley, Borkowski, and O'Sullivan (1984, 1985) reviewed a series of experiments that demonstrate that knowing how to use a cognitive strategy is no guarantee that learners will use it when they need to. In these experiments, one group of learners was taught a strategy for a particular task. A second group was taught the same strategy for the same task but was also told that using the strategy would increase learning. As predicted, learners who were informed about the usefulness of the strategy were more likely to use and remember it than those who were not informed.

O'Sullivan and Pressley (1984) found that groups of children who were given information on when and where to use a strategy for which they were trained used that strategy on a greater variety of tasks than those not given such information. From this research and that of others (Meichenbaum, 1977; Weed, Ryan, & Day, 1990), we know that the long-term use of strategies by your learners depends on how well you supplement the teaching of strategies with instruction on when and where to use them. Students who are aware of when to use strategies are said to possess **metacognition**—or knowledge about their cognition.

Development of Metacognition. While children as young as 2 years use cognitive strategies, they are not aware that they are using them and thus do not do so intentionally. The capacity to think metacognitively appears to develop as children enter the concrete operational stage of development (ages 5 to 7). Nevertheless, learners who use strategies typically fail to notice that the strategy is helping them, and often fail to use it when the opportunity arises (Pressley, 1995).

Ghatala (1986), Ghatala, Levin, Pressley, and Goodwin (1986), and Pressley and Ghatala (1990) conducted a series of studies on metacognition with school-age learners. They taught fifth- and sixth-grade learners two strategies for learning vocabulary words, one of which was clearly more effective than the others. To their surprise, the learners did not notice that one was more effective. Only when this was pointed out did the learners choose the more effective strategy for subsequent vocabulary-learning tasks.

The surprising conclusion from this research is that learners in second through sixth grades do not automatically acquire metacognitive knowledge. In other words, while engaged in using strategies, they don't automatically realize that one strategy may be better than another, spontaneously compare the effectiveness of the strategies, or use information about the effective use of the strategy to make future decisions. Learners at this age can learn to make these decisions, but they need explicit instruction.

Metacognition. Thinking about thinking; the use of cognitive strategies for finding and organizing information and remembering when and where to use them.

Using the IDEAL Method

Teacher: Today we're going to think a little more about the greenhouse problem. Remember what we talked about yesterday. The PTA is giving us money to build a greenhouse, but we have a problem about how we can get the flowers and vegetable plants to grow inside a house when they're supposed to grow outside.

Student 1: First the letter *I.* You identify the problem.

Teacher: And what do we do when we identify a problem?

Student 2: We read the problem and try to figure out what we're supposed to answer or solve.

Teacher: OK. I'll try to identify one of the problems with the greenhouse and then ask one of you to do the same. One of the problems I see is how the plants get food. Anybody else?

Student 3: I see a problem: what about when it gets cold?

Teacher: So, what's the problem?

Student 3: Well, it's how do you make sure they have the right temperature to live?

Teacher: Good! What was another thing we talked about when you think about problems?

Student 4: Letter *D!* You define any words you don't understand in the problem.

Teacher: Why is this important?

Student 4: Well, you want to make sure you really understand the problem. Sometimes we use words and think we know what they mean but we really don't. So *D* reminds us to make sure we really know what we mean when we define the problem.

Teacher: Good. I'll give you an example, then you give me one. What is a greenhouse? Are we all agreed on this?

Student 5: And the right temperature. What's that mean?

Teacher: Great. Now, what's the third thing we do when we think about solving a problem?

Teaching Metacognition. The work of Ghatala and Pressley on the development of metacognition in young children makes two main points: (1) learners as young as second grade can learn to regulate their use of cognitive strategies, but (2) they require systematic instruction to do so.

Thus, if you want your learners to use cognitive strategies to improve their learning of vocabulary, spelling, number facts, reading comprehension, or problem solving, you must not only teach these strategies systematically, but also teach learners to regulate their use. Metacognitive instruction involves teaching your learners to: (1) attend to the effectiveness of strategies, (2) attribute differences to the relative effectiveness of a particular strategy, and (3) use the more effective strategy in future decision making (Ghatala, 1986). Otherwise, learners may not use a given strategy, not notice whether it is effective, or fail to use it when they should. The accompanying box, *Teaching Metacognitive Knowledge,* provides some specific guidelines for teaching metacognition.

Summary. Learners who are taught cognitive strategies are not aware of the effect of the strategy on their learning unless they have the opportunity to compare their performances when they do and do not use the strategy. Metacognitive knowledge must go hand in hand with instruction if learners are to use strategies to improve their thinking.

As we showed in the introduction to this chapter, good thinkers not only know cognitive strategies and regulate their use, they also have knowledge of the area they are thinking about. It is to this important topic that we turn next.

Teaching Metacognitive Knowledge

1. Teach specific cognitive strategies for learning important information in each subject area. This might involve teaching specific strategies for vocabulary learning, spelling, reading comprehension, and so forth. Such strategies can involve basic rehearsal techniques, organizational strategies, or comprehension monitoring strategies. (For a comprehensive list of learning strategies see Weinstein, C. E., & Mayer, R. E. (1986). The Teaching of Learning Strategies. In M. C. Wittrock (ed.), *Handbook of Research on Teaching* (3rd ed.), pp. 315–327. New York: Macmillan.)

2. Once your learners demonstrate that they know how to use a given strategy, teach them to recognize when to use it and to monitor how it is helping them. One way to do this is to give them two equivalent tasks to learn (for example, two lists of vocabulary words; two reading passages) and have them learn one task using the strategy and the equivalent task not using the strategy.

3. Explicitly prompt the learners to attend to or monitor how the strategy is helping them and how not using the strategy affects them.

4. Have the learners record and compare how much they learned with each method.

5. Discuss with the learners how use of the strategy helped improve learning.

6. Have the learners express an intent to use the strategy the next time they are presented with a similar learning task.

7. Give the learners additional opportunities to use the strategy and monitor its effectiveness.

Knowledge

If you plan to teach history, social studies, science, literature, or the cultural arts to children in elementary, junior, or senior high school, you have probably asked yourself the following questions: Is it really important that my learners have a lot of factual information about the subject I'm teaching? What difference does a knowledge of important facts, concepts, and principles in my field make in my learners' ability to think? What can a learner with a large amount of knowledge do that a learner with limited knowledge can't? As you will see from the next section, the answer is: A lot.

The Effect of Knowledge on Learning. Suppose you gave the same memory task to two groups of learners—fourth graders and twelfth graders. If the memory task involved recalling specific information from the sports page of a daily newspaper, which group would remember more? Make your choice before reading on.

> Which is more important to how much my learners are able to learn: prior knowledge or intelligence?

Now suppose we were to tell you that the fourth graders were all sports buffs and that the twelfth graders didn't know the sports page from the society column. Now who would you predict would remember the most from the memory task? If you predicted the fourth graders, you are most likely correct.

Let's change the task. Suppose the memory task involved recalling the names of pictures of 20 common objects including a bike, a car, a ring, and a hairbrush that the learners saw for 60 seconds. Who would recall more? Here the older learners would do better. Why? The answer has to do with the role of knowledge. In the first example, the fourth graders have specific knowledge about sports. Therefore, when they read the sports page they understand and recall much more than the twelfth graders, who are unfamiliar with such terms as zone defense, nickle defense, the blue line, sacrifice, infield fly rule, and point guard.

Domain-specific knowledge.
Knowledge of facts, concepts, and principles pertaining to a specific area or topic.

General knowledge. Knowledge useful for learning across a variety of school tasks.

The fourth graders possess what cognitive psychologists call **domain-specific knowledge,** or knowledge of facts, concepts, and principles pertaining to a specific area or topic (for example, the Civil War, chess, how an engine works, cosmetology). Domain-specific knowledge is different from **general knowledge,** which is knowledge useful for learning across a variety of school tasks. Examples of general knowledge are how to write or spell, how to use a dictionary or encyclopedia, and how to use a computer. Domain-specific knowledge allows the fourth-graders to think about and process information about their domain of expertise better than learners who are unfamiliar with the domain (Chi, 1978). General knowledge, however, allows the twelfth-graders to do a better job of recognizing familiar objects.

Here's another demonstration of the importance of a knowledge base in learning. Schneider, Korkel, and Weinert (1989) and Schneider and Korkel (1989) asked 8-, 10-, and 12-year-old children to read passages about soccer, a sport popular in Germany, where they conducted their research. After reading the passages, the children were asked questions that assessed recall of specific information, the making of inferences, and detection of contradictions. Some of the children across all age levels knew a lot about soccer, some very little. In addition to measuring the soccer expertise of the children, the researchers also measured their general intelligence by means of an IQ test.

The researchers found that age had a lot to do with performance on the reading tests—12-year-olds made more correct inferences than 8-year-olds, as you would expect. But they also found that prior knowledge of soccer was associated with higher learning, regardless of age level. Knowledgeable 8-year-olds did better on the tests than did novice 12-year-olds. Even more striking was the fact that general intelligence was not a strong determinant of performance. Learners with a lot of soccer expertise and average general intelligence outperformed novice learners with high general intelligence.

These results have been confirmed in this country with both children and adult learners. Walker (1987) found that baseball experts with low general intelligence learn more from a baseball passage than do baseball novices with high general intelli-

General knowledge enables middle-school learners to perform complex tasks and solve complex problems.

gence. Ceci and Liker (1986) went to a racetrack and located both experts and novices at race handicapping who were comparable in years of education, years going to the track, and job prestige. The range of IQ in both groups was from 80 to 130. The task given to the subjects was to handicap 50 two-horse races. They were given a variety of statistics and asked to compute the odds for each of 50 races that pitted an unnamed horse against a horse that was the same in each race. The researchers found that the complexity of the reasoning of the low-IQ experts was far greater than that of the high-IQ novices.

Thus, domain-specific knowledge appears to be much more important in determining good thinking and performance on a given task than general intelligence. The message for teachers who want to teach their learners to be good thinkers is clear: Teaching cognitive strategies and metacognitive knowledge is necessary for good thinking, but it is not sufficient. You must also ensure that your learners have mastered the critical information in the area in which you want them to think well.

Types of Expert Knowledge. What types of knowledge do experts have that allow them to think so productively? Cognitive psychologists have classified knowledge in a variety of ways. We have already discussed one such type: domain-specific versus general knowledge. Another way of categorizing knowledge is declarative knowledge versus procedural knowledge. **Declarative knowledge** is another name for verbal information: the facts, concepts, principles, and theories that we learn from lectures, studying textbooks, or watching television. **Procedural knowledge** is know-how: knowledge of the action sequences involved in booting a floppy disk, writing an outline, tying your shoes, focusing a microscope, or playing a trombone. To give you a better feel for the distinction between declarative and procedural knowledge let's examine what researchers have found about the knowledge bases of expert teachers (Berliner, 1986, 1988; Carter et al., 1987, 1988; Peterson & Comeaux, 1987).

Researchers in teaching expertise typically ask experienced and beginning teachers to view videotapes of real-life classroom episodes and to then make judgments about what is happening in the classroom. The teachers record their judgments on tape or write them down. Researchers then analyze these tapes for what they reveal about the knowledge bases of expert and novice teachers. What they find is that expert teachers are able to classify the types of instruction and activities they view (discovery learning, lecture, discussion, and so forth), relate the activities of the lesson to the behavior of the learners, categorize the behavior of the learners (attention-seeking, power struggle, and so on), and suggest alternative courses of action. Novice teachers, on the other hand, have little understanding of what is going on in the classroom, see few connections between teacher behavior and learner behavior, and have few suggestions. In short, expert teachers possess a great deal of declarative knowledge about specific subject area teaching practices, curriculum materials, the characteristics and cultural backgrounds of learners, theories of instruction, and theories of learner behavior (Shulman, 1987) that allows them to make sense out of what they see in classrooms.

Other researchers who have studied the procedural knowledge of expert teachers (Calderhead & Robson, 1991; Elbaz, 1983; Emmer et al., 1994; Leinhardt & Greeno, 1986) have shown that expert teachers draw up extensive lesson plans, know how to prevent behavior problems from escalating, monitor students as they are learning, develop efficient techniques for grading papers and giving students immediate

Declarative knowledge. Verbal information: the facts, concepts, principles, and theories we learn from lectures, studying textbooks, or watching television.

Procedural knowledge. Know-how knowledge: action sequences we use to complete tasks, such as booting a floppy disk or writing an outline.

feedback on learning, and know how to ask questions that elicit reflective comments by students.

Characteristics of an Expert's Knowledge Base. So far we have learned that experts in any area have a large base of knowledge that includes both declarative and procedural knowledge. This knowledge base allows experts not only to think well, but also to think quickly. Experts are fast: they solve problems faster than novices and with fewer mistakes.

One reason they solve problems faster is because their procedural knowledge is automatic—a characteristic of the knowledge base often referred to as **automaticity** (Sternberg, 1989). Automaticity means that a procedure has been learned so thoroughly that it is carried out with little thinking and little effort. Good readers decode automatically—they don't have to think about sound/symbol associations. Good writers construct sentences automatically—they don't have to think about grammatical rules as they are writing. Expert problem solvers in math perform math operations automatically—they don't spend a lot of time thinking about how to regroup in subtraction, carry in addition, or find the least common denominator when working with fractions.

Experts also think quickly because their declarative knowledge base has *organization.* As we discussed earlier in this chapter, organization means that the declarative knowledge in a particular domain is connected and related. Early cognitive psychologists like Bruner (1966) and Ausubel (1968), as well as current researchers (Bjorklund, 1989; Rabinowitz & McCauley, 1990), speculate that as the expert's knowledge base grows, it becomes increasingly organized and related.

This organization of information is often *hierarchical:* for example, the mind organizes the information in a specific area, such as "earthquakes," from the most general principles to the most specific details. In other words, general principles of plate tectonics (geologic activity occurs where plates converge) subsume concepts (pressure, crust, tectonic plates), which, in turn, subsume specific facts (location of plates, mountain ranges, number of continents). According to these researchers, it isn't simple cognitive strategies that allow experts to reason and solve problems quickly. Rather, it is the organized nature of the information base that allows the learner to quickly access information and use it to expertly perform a task.

Educational Implications. As the saying goes, "Knowledge is power." A knowledgeable learner with an average IQ is a better thinker in a given area than is a learner with a high IQ who lacks domain-specific knowledge. Therefore, the message for teachers who want their learners to be good thinkers is clear: Teach important declarative and procedural knowledge. Make sure that you help your learners organize and categorize the verbal information so they can access it from memory quickly and efficiently. In addition, provide extensive practice with procedural knowledge so learners can perform operations like decoding text, writing sentences, or carrying out basic math procedures automatically and effortlessly.

Concluding Comments. Cognitive psychologists tell us that good thinkers or good information processors in any area of expertise have (1) an extensive knowledge base, characterized by (2) organization, and (3) automaticity. They use cognitive strategies when thinking and know when and where to use these strategies. The expert teaching of good thinking requires that teachers attend to all three components of good thinking.

Automaticity. Learning a procedure so thoroughly that it can be carried out quickly with little thinking or effort.

But how do learners come to learn, retain, and use these processes? Cognitive psychologists can't see the processes of good thinking at work. So to help understand them, they use models. In the next section, we will examine the most popular of these models—the information processing model—and study some of its more recent variations.

The Information Processing Model

In the preceding section, we learned what makes good thinking. By now you are probably asking yourself "What is the best way to teach strategies, metacognition, and knowledge to my learners?" This is also a goal of cognitive psychologists—designing instruction to make learners better thinkers. However, cognitive psychologists realize that another question must be answered before we can answer the question of how good thinking can be taught. This question is: "What does good thinking look like?"

Cognitive psychologists have some ideas about what makes up good thinking. These components were the subject of the preceding sections of this chapter. But how do knowledge, cognitive strategies, and knowledge about the use of cognitive strategies get into our heads in the first place? And once this content gets there, what happens to it? How does it get organized and sorted? Where exactly is the information stored? How is it retrieved?

All these questions have to do with how the mind works—the processes involved in good thinking. Accurate answers to these questions would greatly help us in our efforts to teach learners to think better. For example, knowing how the mind takes in new information would allow you to make better decisions about how to present new information. Knowing how the mind categorizes or organizes this information would allow you to present new information in the most efficient way.

In this section you will learn what cognitive psychologists know about how the mind takes in information, and what the mind does with that information once it has gotten in. We will examine in depth the **information processing model** to understand what it says about the flow of information into the mind. We will also discuss the **parallel distributed processing** (PDP) or *new connectionist* **model,** a model that reflects the latest hypotheses about how the mind works.

The information processing model seeks to describe what happens to information the first time it is presented to a learner. For example, the first time a ninth-grade biology student hears about the structure of the circulatory system, what happens to all the related facts, concepts, and principles? How is the biology information processed? The model shown in Figure 5.2 is a general metaphor for information flow that applies to any situation in which the mind receives new information. In this figure we see five rectangles labeled "receptors," "effectors," "immediate memory," "working memory," and "long-term memory." These boxes represent different functions, or processes, that are activated as information is being processed. They do not correspond to physical locations in the brain; they represent only functions. Arrows in the model represent the sequence in which these functions occur, while ovals stand for control processes or executive routines that govern or regulate information flow. Control processes include goal setting, strategy selection, expectations, monitoring progress, and metacognition (when we consciously regulate control processes).

Information processing model. A model of learning that examines how we learn using the "mind as computer" metaphor.

Parallel distributed processing model. A model of learning that suggests that learners may not always learn in orderly, sequential ways, but instead use sources of information simultaneously to construct their own meanings.

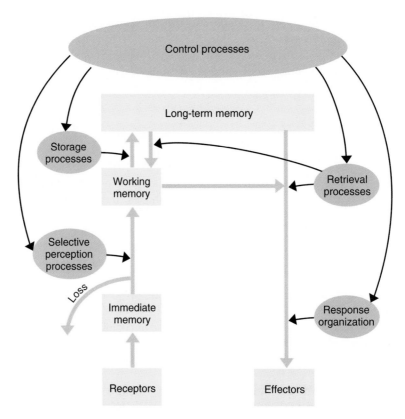

Figure 5.2
Basic elements of the human information processing system. *Source: The Cognitive Psychology of School Learning* (p. 40), by E. D. Gagné, C. W. Yekovich, and F. R. Yekovich, 1993, New York: HarperCollins. Copyright © 1993 by HarperCollins Publishers. Reprinted by permission of HarperCollins College Publishers.

Reception of Information

Information processing begins when the learner starts reading an assigned history chapter, watching a science demonstration, or listening to the explanation of the legislative process in a political science class. *Receptors* (such as rods and cones in the eyes, bones in the middle ears) take in light and sound energy, transform these different energy forms into electrical impulses, and send the impulses to the brain. These impulses are registered in **immediate memory** (IM). IM holds this wealth of sensory information for the briefest period of time—Sperling (1960) estimates a visual stimulus decays in about a fourth of a second. Nevertheless, these impulses linger just long enough for the control processes involved in selective perception to impose some organization or meaning on them. Thus, not all information coming into IM is lost.

Selective perception occurs when the learner attends to what is most important in the information coming in through the receptors and attaches some meaning to it. When the stimulus itself provides the meaning, *bottom-up processing* is said to occur (Gagné, Yekovich, & Yekovich, 1993). In other words, when the light patterns from a motorcycle are received on the rods and cones, your mind analyzes the patterns and in-

Immediate memory. Our information storage capacity that holds sensory data for less than a second before it is lost or transferred to our working memory.

How can I use the information processing model of thinking to better understand how learning occurs?

stantly recognizes it as a motorcycle—something that has meaning to you. But we also selectively perceive through *top-down processing*. For example, when a learner is reading a history assignment dealing with the Protestant Reformation, she will more quickly recognize the word "schism" because she already possesses *prior information* about schisms and has certain *expectations* for what the homework is about. Thus, selective perception, whether top-down or bottom-up, is influenced by visual, auditory, or tactile stimulus patterns, prior knowledge, and expectations.

Attention also has a great deal to do with selective perception. It is particularly important during the early stage of processing unfamiliar information. Attention maintains the learner's vigilance, which keeps the selective perception process going and enhances sensory acuity, which in turn makes one aware of new stimulus cues. Thus, gaining and holding a learner's attention, particularly at the beginning stages of a lesson, is a pivotal challenge to teachers. The accompanying box, *Grabbing and Holding Your Learners' Attention,* provides specific suggestions.

> **What are some ways of getting and holding my learners' attention?**

Working Memory

Working memory is often referred to as *short-term memory,* although there are some subtle differences between the two concepts. Pressley (1995) refers to both working memory and short-term memory as "attentional capacity." If the learner attends to and selectively perceives the data that enter immediate memory (IM), these data next enter

Working memory. The information storage capacity that receives data from immediate memory and holds it for about 10 to 20 seconds.

Applying Your Knowledge:
Grabbing and Holding Your Learners' Attention

1. Expectations are important in attention. At the start of a lesson, explanation, or demonstration, state a clear purpose and goal for the activity. For example: "Today we're going to learn how to write a capital letter *K,*" or "I'm going to show you how to find the main idea in a paragraph."

2. Our visual, auditory, and tactile senses are primed to pick up on variations in stimuli—therefore, variety will grab learners' attention, but sameness will allow their attention to wander. As you teach, vary your voice intensity, pitch, and tone, move around the room, and display colorful, visually interesting overheads, charts, or chalkboard displays.

3. Your learners' attention will be drawn to things that have emotional meaning for them. Embedding learners' names in lessons or explanations (called "name-dropping"), or including people, places, and objects that you know are important to your learners will attract and sustain their attention.

4. A common complaint of learners is "Every day we do the same old thing." Surprise them! Start the lesson differently, stand in a different place, change the room arrangement, dress differently. In other words, grab their attention by defying their expectations.

working memory (WM). Try to picture the function of WM in terms of awareness. What you are aware you are thinking about at any given moment is said to be in your WM (Gagné, Yekovich, & Yekovich, 1993). WM is of limited duration—current research suggests that it retains new information for about 10 to 20 seconds. After that, the information is either lost or transformed.

For example, we've all had the experience of getting a number from the telephone operator but having no pencil to write it down. The number gets into WM, but it is quickly lost unless you either write it down or repeat it a few times (a process called *rehearsal*). This is an example of the limited capacity of WM. Estimates are that its capacity is limited to five to nine isolated bits of information—in this example, numbers (Miller, 1956).

WM is where conscious thinking occurs—consider it a kind of mental workplace. When you try to solve a math problem in your head (for example, "If pencils cost 69 cents a dozen, how much will nine pencils cost?") you are using your WM. Because of its limited capacity and duration, WM is not a good place to perform several different mental operations at the same time. Try comprehending the main point of a sentence you are reading in a foreign language when at the same time you have to sound out and then think about the meaning of half the words. Reading comprehension occurs in working memory, which is why learners who are slow in word decoding are also weak in comprehension.

Why We Forget. Information in WM is quickly forgotten unless the learner attempts to prolong its stay. This can be done by using memory strategies of the type we referred to in the earlier box on teaching memory strategies.

Several theories try to explain why WM is of such limited duration and capacity. **Decay theory** holds that information simply leeches out of WM or dissolves. The energy impulses dissipate with the passage of time unless we rehearse the new information. While decay theory presents some vivid metaphors, it is not as convincing as displacement theory. **Displacement theory** (Miller, 1956) suggests that there are only so many "slots" in WM that can be filled. Once new information comes into WM, the existing information is pushed out and replaced by the incoming data. Displacement theory is closely related to **interference theory** (Ausubel, 1968), which posits that subsequent learning competes with prior learning and somehow interferes with what's contained in WM.

Information in WM is like information in the working memory of your computer. If you want to save it, you must transfer it to a long-term storage device. WM helps process information into a form that is acceptable for more permanent storage in long-term memory—like saving a document on the hard drive in your computer.

Implications for Teaching. The function of WM has important implications for your teaching. Two of these implications are as follows:

1. Unrelated facts are quickly forgotten unless the learner organizes them in some way or unless you help the learner to do so (remember that different learners have different storage capacities in WM).

2. The more you allow learners to think about information in WM, the more likely they are to put that information into more permanent storage. Active processing or thinking about new information, such as taking

---

Decay theory. A theory that holds that information dissolves or dissipates from our working memory unless it is rehearsed.

Displacement theory. A theory that holds that, once new information enters working memory, existing information is pushed out and replaced by incoming data.

Interference theory. A theory that holds that subsequent learning competes with prior learning and interferes with what is contained in working memory.

notes, discussion, and practice, are essential learning strategies for accomplishing this.

Long-Term Memory

Information from WM may be stored in **long-term memory** (LTM). Storage is a term or metaphor that describes a series of processes whereby new information is integrated with information that is already known or residing in LTM. The principal storage processes, as you have already learned, involve rehearsal, elaboration, and organization.

The Form of Knowledge in LTM. There is considerable discussion among cognitive psychologists about what exactly is stored in long-term memory. At one level, we know that declarative and procedural knowledge are stored there. But what form does this information take in long-term memory? This is an important question, because if we know in what form information is stored in LTM, we could present information to learners in that form to facilitate remembering. For example, if information is stored in long-term memory in the form of visual images, then teachers could help their learners to encode information visually. Cognitive psychologists propose a number of theories about how knowledge is represented in LTM: dual-coding theory, propositional networks, and schemas.

"Don't think about pink elephants." As soon as you hear this, what do you do? If you're like most people, you think about pink elephants. In thinking about *how* we think, we all depend on images to help us. We also depend on words, particularly when we can't construct an image (for example, try to imagine a heffalump). Paivio (1971, 1986) has developed a **dual-coding theory** of long-term storage. He believes that information in LTM is composed of complex networks of verbal representations and images. A good example of the verbal imaging of information is when you think about the concept "dental cavity." Your experience probably includes images of drills, excruciating pain, needles, chairs, and New Age music.

In addition to verbal images, however, you also think in terms of connected ideas (for example, "If A is bigger than B, and B is bigger than C, then A is bigger than C"). Anderson (1983) proposes that much declarative knowledge is stored in LTM in the form of extensive networks of interconnected ideas called **propositional networks.** Figure 5.3 illustrates one such network, a set of propositions about Benjamin Franklin. Cognitive psychologists propose that if we could see into a learner's brain and examine those neurons that contain information about Benjamin Franklin, it would look something like this web of ideas, concepts, and facts. If LTM actually stores information in the form of propositional networks, teaching learners how to outline and make connections during a lesson would greatly facilitate remembering.

A third hypothesis about the form of information in LTM is called **schema theory** (Anderson & Pearson, 1984). You are familiar with the concept of *schema* from Chapter 2. Recall that cognitive schemata are integrated units of knowledge. They are cognitive structures that organize large amounts of information about objects (the Taj Mahal), events (the first landing on the moon), or text readings (Willa Cather's *The Lost Lady*). Your learners have schemata for "a birthday party," "the first day of school," "the senior prom," and so forth, which organize a vast array of information about events, people, feelings, and their relationships. These schemata influence how learners perceive and make sense of what they hear and read.

Long-term memory. The information storage capacity in which new information is integrated through rehearsal, elaboration, and organization with information that is already known or residing within long-term memory.

Dual-coding theory. A theory that holds that complex networks of verbal representations and images reside within long-term memory to promote long-term retention.

Propositional networks. Extensive networks of interconnected ideas stored in long-term memory that provide representations and images that help us retain information for a long time.

Schema theory. Cognitive structures of integrated units that organize large amounts of information.

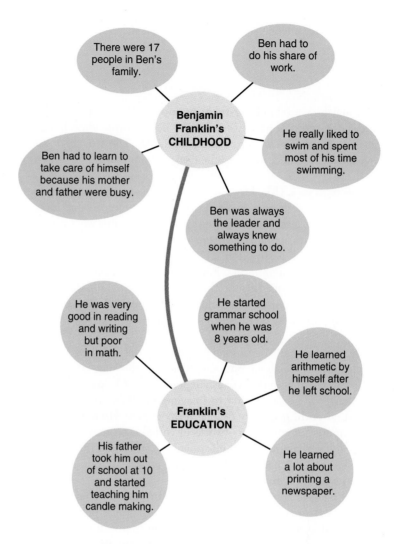

Figure 5.3
A propositional network. *Source:* D. F. Dansereau, 1988, in C. F. Weinstein, E. T. Goetz, and P. A. Alexander (eds.), *Learning and Study Strategies: Issues in Assessment, Instruction, and Evaluation,* Orlando: Academic Press. Reprinted by permission.

Capacity of LTM. Most cognitive psychologists stipulate that information in LTM lasts a lifetime (Gagné, Yekovich, & Yekovich, 1993). Then, you may be asking yourselves, how come we forget so much? Cognitive psychologists believe that your experience of forgetting things you once "knew" is due more to your failure to find a good way to retrieve the information than to any permanent loss of data.

A good example of the permanence of LTM comes from a study by Williams and Hollan (1981). They asked people who had graduated from high school between 4 and 19 years earlier to recall as many names of individuals as possible from their high school classes. At first the subjects were slow to come up with names. But as they began to use clues, such as "the kids who lived on my block," "the kids I rode to school with," or "the kids in my physics class," recall dramatically improved. The subjects in the study recalled large percentages of their graduating classes despite the fact that these classes were quite large.

Retrieval Processes. As this example shows, when we actively search our memories for information to use in a thinking task (to get it into working memory) we are engaged in *retrieval processes*. Cognitive psychologists use the term *activation* to refer to cognitive processes involved in becoming aware of what we have learned and in establishing connections between this prior learning and the task in which we are currently involved. This connection-building is facilitated by the use of retrieval cues.

Retrieval cues are hints or things we say to ourselves to help us remember what we have already learned and stored in LTM. In the experiment about remembering one's high school classmates reported above, retrieval cues were the hints, such as "the kids who lived on my block." Retrieval cues are particularly effective when the cue you are using to recall information matches information that you stored at the time of original learning. For example, the cue "who are the kids in my physics class?" would be of no help if, at the time you were taking high school physics, you never noticed who was in your class.

Tulving (1989) believes that good recall of memorized information is largely cue-dependent. You forget the meaning of a word that you once knew, such as *homunculus*, because you don't have a cue that emphasizes remembering it. You forget how to spell a particular word because you fail to use a cue that emphasizes sound. Depending on the type of recall you want (meaning, spelling, date, name, address, phone number), there are cues to match it.

Implications for Teaching

The information processing model of how the mind works is a metaphor. In this chapter, we used it to help you think about how the minds of your learners work. This model can help you think about what you can do during your lessons to help your learners better understand and retain what you are teaching.

During our discussion we highlighted various models of how information gets into the mind, how it is stored, and how it is retrieved for use in thinking. According to the information processing model, there are three conditions for meaningful learning: the cognitive processes of reception, availability, and activation. Figure 5.4 illustrates how these three conditions work together to result in meaningful learning, and the accompanying box, *Using the Information Processing Model to Promote Learning*, suggests specific strategies you can use to establish these conditions in your classroom.

> **What teaching strategies can I use to enhance my learners' reception, availability, and activation of the information I present?**

The Parallel Distributed Processing Model

Cognitive psychologists have only just begun to understand how the mind works. The information processing model has contributed greatly to the development of the cognitive science of learning. Nevertheless, alternative models of the architecture of the mind reflect both the latest advances in computer science and our understanding of cognitive processes.

McClelland and Rumelhart (1981, 1986) believe that the information processing model encourages a perspective on thinking that is inconsistent with our experience.

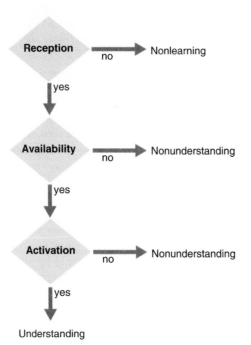

Figure 5.4
Three conditions for meaningful learning. *Source:* Adapted from *Educational Psychology: A Cognitive Approach* (p. 13), by R. E. Mayer, 1987, New York: HarperCollins. Copyright © 1987 by Little, Brown. Reprinted by permission of HarperCollins College Publishers.

According to the information processing model, the mind is a system that performs one action after another very rapidly (reception followed by flow into working memory followed by storage into long-term memory followed by retrieval and transfer to working memory, and so on).

Rumelhart's view (1992), on the other hand, is that the mind does a lot of things not one at a time, but rather all at once, much like the various processing units of a powerful computer. Inside a computer are complex arrangements of memory chips, processors, disks, switches, and drives. These components don't perform complex operations in an orderly, sequential fashion. Rather, they do a lot of things simultaneously as they solve problems.

So, too, the brain is made up of complex collections or arrangements of neurons that form *neural networks.* The brain contains many neural networks that perform a variety of specialized functions involved in complex thinking. There are neural networks for decoding text, solving arithmetic word problems, playing chess, and so forth. These networks are made up of smaller units, called *nodes,* that contain particular types of information (words, letters, sounds, images, rules) important to completing the task of the network.

No central processor or organizer (like the ovals in the information processing model in Figure 5.2) governs how these nodes work together. Instead, the nodes are simultaneously active—they activate one another; they build new connections among one another; and eventually they learn and solve the problem at hand.

As a specific example of a neural network model, Gagné, Yekovich, and Yekovich (1993) considered Marshall's work (1990) on how students distinguish among five types of arithmetic word problems. Marshall studied the five types of word problems exempli-

Using the Information Processing Model to Promote Learning

Reception. Learners must *receive* the information you want them to learn. Thus attention is of primary importance. To ensure attention:

1. Make frequent use of cues, signals, challenging questions, and other stimuli to prompt or remind your learners that they are about to learn something interesting.
2. Ask questions or call on learners frequently during your lessons, but use an unpredictable sequence. You want your learners to anticipate that they can be called on at any time during a lesson.
3. Vary your tone of voice, where you stand while teaching, and the arrangement of the room.
4. Surprise your learners.

Availability. Learners will quickly forget new information as it enters working memory unless they possess existing knowledge that they can relate it to. To ensure availability:

1. Start your lessons with reviews of information that was learned earlier.
2. Give your learners cues to help them recall what they have learned about a particular topic.
3. Ask questions to help them be more aware of what they have heard, seen, or read about the to-be-learned material.
4. Give learners summaries or overviews of lessons (called *advanced organizers* or *anticipatory sets*), which provide prior knowledge of a lesson before it actually starts.

Activation. For meaningful learning to occur, the learner must actively organize the incoming information (in other words, he must see the relationships among the facts and concepts) and relate this to information that has already been learned. This is called *building internal connections with incoming information* and *building external connections with existing information*. To ensure activation:

1. Before a lesson, show learners how the various facts, concepts, and principles are related. Use the overhead projector to show them an outline of the lessons for the coming day or week.
2. Periodically insert questions and summaries during your lessons to help them make connections to both the newly learned and previously learned material.
3. Teach cognitive strategies that help the learners become aware of the connections among what they are learning and have already learned (for example, taking lecture notes, constructing outlines).
4. Remember that conscious thinking and problem solving occur in working memory, which has a limited capacity. Teach learners strategies to prolong information in working memory and thus give them time to make comprehension automatic.

fied in Table 5.1. *Change* problems are characterized by a change in the state of one quantity. *Group* problems involve situations in which two or more groups can be logically combined into a larger group. *Compare* problems contrast the values associated with two objects. *Restate* problems require rephrasing a verbal description into a different set of quantitative terms. Finally, *vary* problems depict direct or indirect variation.

Marshall postulated that through practice and feedback in identifying these five kinds of problems, students begin to form "pattern-recognition" units that fit specific problem types. Certain features of the word problems are associated with certain types of problems. For example, phrases like "how much bigger" or "how much more" are almost always associated with "compare" problems. Thus, these phrases come to be part of the pattern-recognition unit for such problems. These units are said to exist in long-term memory.

After learning, when a student reads a new problem, he represents its features in working memory. These features then activate the same features coded in long-term memory, and the features coded in long-term memory start to activate the pattern-

Table 5.1

Five Types of
Arithmetic Word Problems

Change

Jeff loaded his printer with 300 sheets of paper. When he was done printing, there were 35 sheets of paper left. How many sheets of paper did Jeff use?

Group

Yesterday, Joe's Pizza Parlor sold 12 cheese pizzas, 15 pepperoni pizzas, and 4 vegetarian pizzas. How many pizzas were sold in all?

Compare

Carol can write 10 pages a day, and Ellen can write 5 pages a day. Who writes more—Carol or Ellen?

Restate

Rick writes twice as fast as Carol. Carol writes 10 pages a day. How fast does Rick write?

Vary

Ellen jogs 1 mile in 8 minutes. How long will it take her to run 5 miles?

Source: Marshall, 1990. Illustrated by Gagné, Yekovich, & Yekovich, 1990.

recognition unit to which they belong. Figure 5.5 shows what happens when a student reads a new word problem. The arrows at the bottom of the figure represent input from the environment (the printed problem statement). The large circle represents working memory, and the elements within this circle represent features and pattern-recognition units stored in long-term memory. Notice that elements of three different problem types (change, compare, and restate) have been activated by their connections to the representation of the current problem.

How does the learner decide which of these problem types best fits the current problem? Usually, more features of one pattern-recognition unit are activated than of any other. The unit with the most activated features is selected as appropriate. In the example in Figure 5.5, the "compare" unit has four features activated, versus only two and three for the "change" and "restate," respectively. Note that according to this model, the pattern recognition units are activated *simultaneously*. This is a characteristic assumption of neural network models.

As you can see, this model involves a great deal of metaphorical thinking, which can make the model difficult to understand and apply. However, your own experience of thinking and problem solving may help: when engaged in problem solving, you are aware of many things at once: ideas, images, facts, rules, principles, and sounds pop in

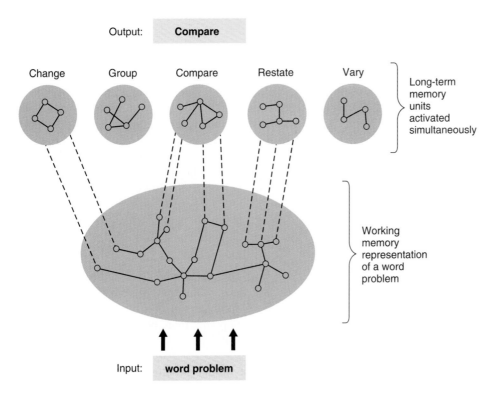

Figure 5.5
A neural-network model of word problem classification. *Source:* Adapted from Marshall, 1990.

and out of your consciousness, and eventually some closure comes about. This kind of experience suggests that the PDP model is a valid metaphor for human thought.

Teaching Implications

The neural network models of cognitive functioning suggest that the minds of your learners may not always work in orderly, sequential ways. Your learners may figure things out without being given an orderly set of rules for doing so. They may not always think rationally and logically as they are solving problems. They may construct their own meanings or make their own sense of things without considering all the facts, advantages and disadvantages, similarities and differences.

The PDP model reminds you that thinking is not simple and orderly, based on neatly stored knowledge. Rather, a lot of thinking goes on at the same time the learner is gathering new knowledge and pondering over ongoing situations. PDP theorists believe that learning depends largely on the interactions between what is in the learner's head and what is outside it. Consequently, many of the constructivist teaching approaches we will study in the next chapter have their conceptual roots in the PDP approach to cognitive processing.

Do my learners have to learn in orderly, sequential ways or can they use different sources of information simultaneously to construct their own meanings?

Cognitive Approaches to Learning and Intelligence

One of the goals of understanding how the mind works is to develop instructional methods that teachers can use to help learners become better thinkers. This goal inevitably raises the question: "If we can teach learners to think better, can we teach them to be more intelligent?" In other words, when we use the expression "good thinking" or "good information processing," do we really mean "good intelligence"? What is the difference between intelligence and the cognitive processes of good thinking? To answer this question we will examine the work of two psychologists who view intelligence from a cognitive processing perspective: Howard Gardner (1983, 1991, 1993) and Robert Sternberg (1989, 1994, 1995).

Views of Intelligence

Is my learners' intelligence fixed, or is it made up of many specific abilities that I can improve through instruction?

There are two major views of intelligence. The *classical tradition* attempts to understand the content, or *structure,* of intelligence, while the *revisionist tradition* seeks to understand its *processes.* Although we will return to the topic of intelligence in Chapter 11, let's briefly describe the former tradition and, then, because of its relevance to how the mind actually works, focus on the latter.

Intelligence as Structure. For most of the twentieth century, psychologists studying human intelligence have created tests to help them understand the underlying abilities that make up intelligence (Jensen, 1980). They asked questions such as "Is intelligence one *general* ability or many *specific* abilities (e.g., spatial ability, verbal ability, quantitative ability, etc.)?" These psychologists agree on several points:

1. Tests that contain questions to which there are clearly right and wrong answers are the best way to learn about intelligence.

2. The ability that underlies intelligence (in other words, the structure of intelligence) exists within the person and is largely inherited.

3. Intelligence is largely neurophysiological, involving such factors as the speed of transmission of nerve impulses.

4. Intelligence cannot be significantly improved through instruction or training.

Intelligence as Process. Rather than seek to understand the content or elements of intelligence, other psychologists have sought to understand what people do when they are engaged in intelligent behavior. Largely influenced by cognitive psychology, these psychologists view intelligence from an information processing framework. For them, what is important is the way in which people combine knowledge, strategies, and metacognitive processes to solve problems important to them. These theorists also share a common set of beliefs.

1. Intelligence may have a structure (abilities, and so on), but what's more important in studying and describing it is an understanding of its underlying processes.

2. Intelligence can be significantly improved by education and training.

3. Standardized tests are not the best way to explore the nature of intelligence. Instead, the best way to measure intelligence is to have people solve problems that are culturally relevant and to then examine the processes they used to do so.

4. There is a genetic component to intelligence, but it does not account for the majority of intelligent behavior.

5. Intelligence is strongly influenced by one's cultural environment. The study of intelligence must take into consideration the different environments to which people must adapt.

Two of the most prominent theorists of intelligence who work within the information processing tradition are Gardner and Sternberg. In the next sections, we will describe their recent work and discuss its relevance to classroom teaching.

Gardner's Theory of Multiple Intelligences

For Gardner (1993), intelligence involves the ability to solve problems or fashion products (compose music, write poems, choreograph a dance) that are of consequence in a particular culture or community. He rejects the notion that we can learn about intelligence by studying how people answer questions on tests. For Gardner, we can only learn about intelligence by studying the cognitive processes people use when they are solving important cultural problems or creating important cultural products.

Gardner has identified seven intelligences that are involved in solving problems and fashioning products, and he believes that all seven can be taught in school. He has also developed a curriculum to do so, called Project Spectrum (Gardner, 1993). Table 5.2 describes the seven intelligences, and Table 5.3 shows how Gardner has translated these into a school instructional program.

For Gardner, problem solving is essential to intelligence. This is consistent with many traditional notions of intelligence. However, Gardner insists that problem solving can be studied only by observing people solving problems or creating products that are important to them, not by administering standardized tests.

Gardner believes that by observing people solving the naturalistic, culturally important problems his seven intelligences represent, we will eventually map out the cognitive processes involved in good thinking. But he also predicts that no single model of cognitive functioning will be found to underlie all human problem solving. Rather, cognitive processes vary depending on the task a learner is involved in.

Sternberg's Triarchic Theory of Intelligence

Sternberg (1989, 1994) agrees with Gardner that the best way to study intelligence is to examine how people solve the problems that are important to them in their environments; that is, to study the cognitive processes by which people shape themselves and their environments to meet their needs. But he disagrees with Gardner in this important respect: Sternberg believes that regardless of the type of problem people are confronted with, they use a common set of cognitive processes to solve them. According to

Table 5.2

The Seven Intelligences

Intelligence	Possible Occupation	Core Components
Logical-mathematical	Scientist Mathematician	Sensitivity to and capacity to discern logical or numerical patterns; ability to handle long chains of reasoning
Linguistic	Poet Journalist	Sensitivity to the sounds, rhythms, and meanings of words; sensitivity to the different functions of language
Musical	Composer Violinist	Abilities to produce and appreciate rhythm, pitch, and timbre; appreciation of the forms of musical expressiveness
Spatial	Navigator Sculptor	Capacities to perceive the visual-spatial world accurately and to manipulate the mental representations that result
Bodily-kinesthetic	Dancer Athlete	Abilities to control one's body movements and to handle objects skillfully
Interpersonal	Therapist Salesperson	Capacities to discern and respond appropriately to the moods, temperaments, motivations, and desires of other people
Intrapersonal	Person with detailed accurate self-knowledge	Access to one's own feelings and the ability to discriminate among them and draw upon them to guide behavior; knowledge of one's own strengths, weaknesses, desires, and intelligences

Source: "Multiple Intelligences Go to School: Education Implication of the Theory of Multiple Intelligences," by H. Gardner and T. Hatch, 1989. *Educational Researcher, 18,* (8), pp. 4–10.

Sternberg, this is true whether the problems involve mathematical, spatial, linguistic, or interpersonal issues.

Sternberg (1989) identifies three components involved in any type of problem solving, components that represent basic information processes that act on information we take in through the senses. He calls these *metacomponents, performance components,* and *knowledge-acquisition components* (see Figure 5.6).

Metacomponents of Intelligence. When attempting to solve real-world problems, intelligent people must make decisions about which strategies to use to solve

Table 5.3

Areas of Cognitive Ability Examined in Project Spectrum

Numbers

Dinosaur Game: designed as a measure of a child's understanding of number concepts, counting skills, ability to adhere to rules, and use of strategy.

Bus Game: assesses a child's ability to create a useful notation system, perform mental calculations, and organize number information for one or more variables.

Science

Assembly Activity: designed to measure a child's mechanical ability. Successful completion of the activity depends on fine-motor skills and visual-spatial, observation, and problem-solving abilities.

Treasure Hunt Game: assesses a child's ability to make logical inferences. The child is asked to organize information to discover the rule governing the placement of various treasures.

Water Activity: used to assess a child's ability to generate hypotheses based on observations and to conduct simple experiments.

Discovery Area: includes year-round activities that elicit a child's observations, appreciation, and understanding of natural phenomena.

Music

Music Production Ability: designed to assess a child's ability to maintain accurate pitch and rhythm while singing, and to recall a song's musical properties.

Music Perception Activity: assesses a child's ability to discriminate pitch. The activity consists of song recognition, error recognition, and pitch discrimination.

Language

Storyboard Activity: measures a range of language skills including complexity of vocabulary and sentence structure, use of con-

nectors, use of descriptive language and dialogue, and ability to pursue a story line.

Reporting Activity: assesses a child's ability to describe an event with regard to the following criteria: ability to report content accurately, level of detail, sentence structure, and vocabulary.

Visual Arts

Art Portfolios: reviewed twice a year and assessed on criteria that include use of lines and shapes, color, space, detail, and representation and design. Children also participate in three structured drawing activities. The drawings are assessed on criteria similar to those used in the portfolio assessment.

Movement

Creative Movement: the ongoing movement curriculum focuses on children's abilities in five areas of dance and creative movement: sensitivity to rhythm, expressiveness, body control, generation of movement ideas, and responsiveness to music.

Athletic Movement: an obstacle course focuses on the types of skills found in many different sports, such as coordination, timing, balance, and power.

Social

Classroom Model: assesses a child's ability to observe and analyze social events and experiences in the classroom.

Peer Instruction Checklist: a behavioral checklist is used to assess the behaviors in which children engage when interacting with peers. Different patterns of behavior yield distinctive social roles, such as facilitator and leader.

Source: *Multiple Intelligence: The Theory in Practice* (pp. 91–92), by Howard Gardner, 1993, New York: Basic Books.

them; how much time to allocate to arrive at a solution; the resources necessary; the best way to monitor a solution; and how to set up a system for obtaining feedback, attending to the feedback, and making sense of it. Sternberg refers to these as *executive skills.* As you can see, they relate to the regulation and control of problem solving. Thus they are similar to the metacognitive skills we studied in the information processing model above. Conventional intelligence tests do not test these metacomponents. Nevertheless, Sternberg stipulates that these executive skills are essential features of intelligent behavior, and, more importantly, that they can be taught.

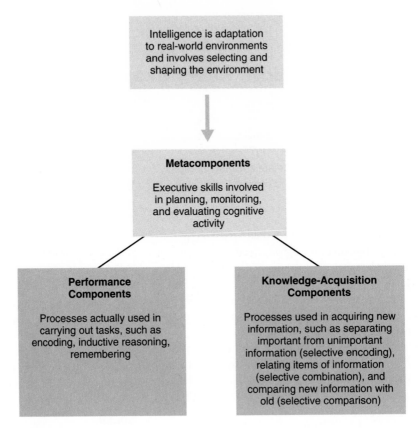

Figure 5.6
Sternberg's information processing model of intelligence, defining intelligence as adaptation to the real world. *Source:* From Sternberg, 1988.

Performance Components. Metacomponents regulate planning, monitoring, and decision making. Performance components actually carry out the processes involved in problem solving. They involve the use of cognitive strategies and include such matters as attending to stimuli, storing them in long-term memory, analyzing the features of problems, and retrieving information from working memory. These performance components work best to solve problems when they have become automated—when they are performed effortlessly and rapidly without conscious thought (for example, decoding meaning while reading). Again, conventional intelligence tests do not assess these components very well. But as we have seen in our discussion of cognitive strategies, they can be taught.

Knowledge-Acquisition Components. To solve real-world problems, learners must perform cognitive strategies with automaticity and regulate their use, and they

Robert J. Sternberg, Yale University

I became interested in my main area, the study of human intelligence, as a young child. Because of test anxiety, I did poorly on intelligence tests. I could hardly answer any questions at all. As a result, when I was in sixth grade, I was sent back to take an IQ test with fifth graders. What an embarrassment!

In seventh grade, I did a science project on mental testing. Part of it was to develop my own test. Another part was to give a test I found in the adult section of the library, the Stanford-Binet, to some of my classmates. This got me into really bad trouble. The head school psychologist found out, came to my junior high school, and yelled at me for 40 minutes, ending with his plan to burn the book if I ever brought it into school again. That event crystallized my interest in the field.

My early research on intelligence, which I started in graduate school at Stanford, emphasizes the process of intelligence rather than static psychometric factors. I developed methods of componential analysis to figure out exactly how people solved problems that required intelligence, so that one could specify the processes used, the strategies into which the processes were combined, how information was processed mentally, and how quickly and well components were executed. After using this approach for several years, I decided it was not in itself adequate, because it assumed that the kinds of problems used on conventional tests adequately measure intelligence. Eventually, my thinking shifted to the triarchic theory, according to which there are creative and practical as well as analytic aspects to intelligence. We tend to undervalue these former two aspects, especially in schools, despite their great importance for success in life.

There are a number of barriers to conducting research in intelligence. One is that it is a relatively low-prestige area in psychology. A second is that it tends to be fraught with political controversies, so that the science can get lost in debates that have nothing to do with what is being studied. A third problem is that there are enormous vested interests in maintaining the status quo. Testing companies have not always been in a great hurry to change their ways of thinking, and neither have many users of standardized tests.

Having to overcome the damage to my view of myself that resulted from my own low test scores was helpful to me, because it made me understand the effects low scores can have on people's self-esteem, sense of self-efficacy, and ability to proceed through the system. In my case, my low test scores when I was very young led to lower expectations on the part of teachers, which led to lower achievement, which I overcame only when I had a teacher in the fourth grade who had higher expectations for me.

My research has many practical applications in the classroom:

1. Teach in a way that reaches children whose profiles of intelligence suggest strengths not just in memory and analytic abilities, but also in creative and practical abilities. I have written in various places about techniques that can be used to reach children who are not traditionally school smart.

2. Testing should emphasize creative and practical as well as memory and analytic aspects of intelligence.

3. Creativity involves more than abilities. In our investment theory of creativity, we emphasize personality, motivational, and environmental factors as well as ability. Teachers need to create a classroom environment that fosters creativity. Examples of things to encourage include: (a) active definition and redefinition of problems, (b) asking yourself whether you are getting stuck in a given approach to a problem, (c) willingness to take sensible risks, (d) willingness to surmount obstacles, (e) willingness to grow, (f) finding something you really love to do, and, most important, (g) willingness to defy the crowd in one's ideas.

4. Teachers tend to prefer and more positively evaluate students whose styles match theirs. Teachers therefore need to resist their natural tendency to value students who think the way they do. Teachers also need to explicitly teach varied styles of learning and thinking. Often, teachers find that students whom they thought were not intelligent in fact are, but were not learning well because the teacher's style of teaching did not match the student's style of learning.

5. I have also emphasized the importance of questioning strategies. In particular, students should be encouraged not only to answer, but also to ask good questions. They should also explore question-answering at their own pace. Ultimately, the questions that you ask yourself are at least as important, and often more important, than your answers to the questions that others ask you.

must also acquire knowledge about the problem itself. Some of the skills involved in acquiring knowledge include distinguishing relevant from irrelevant information while reading, forming internal connections with incoming information so that concepts and principles can be formed, and building external connections with prior learning (what we have called *activation*). Sternberg believes that conventional intelligence tests can serve as good measures of the knowledge-acquisition components of intelligence. But he also believes that the skills involved in knowledge acquisition are learned and can be taught.

For Sternberg, intelligence and good information processing are one and the same. His message to teachers is clear—you can make your learners more intelligent in the following ways.

1. Give them real-world problems that are important in their culture and environment to solve.
2. Teach them general cognitive strategies that they can use to solve any problem.
3. Teach them metacognitive skills to help them regulate their use of cognitive strategies.
4. Show them how to acquire knowledge and provide practice opportunities, so that these skills become automatic.

Some Final Thoughts on Cognitive Learning Theory

We began this chapter by examining the thinking of a good information processor, Tesfaye. We saw that he knew a lot, strategized, and knew when to use these strategies. The main point of this chapter is that making your learners good thinkers involves more than helping them acquire knowledge. It requires that you both understand what is involved in good thinking and teach metacognitive strategies to enhance the cognitive processes of reception, availability, and activation. In the next chapter we will examine some of the best ways to do this in the classroom.

Summing Up

This chapter introduced you to cognitive approaches to learning. Its main points were these:

- Cognitive psychologists believe that good thinking involves the use of cognitive strategies for finding and organizing information and remembering when and where to use it.
- Cognitive scientists use a variety of metaphors to describe the content and processes of good thinking, such as the mind as a computer, filing system, or information management system.

- Cognitive psychologists focus their interest on complex human thinking, such as concept and strategy learning, decision making, problem solving, and how learners construct knowledge.
- Cognitive strategies are general methods of thinking that improve learning across a variety of subject areas.
- Rehearsal, elaboration, and organization are three strategies that can be taught to your learners to improve their memory of what you teach.
- Comprehension monitoring is a term applied to cognitive strategies that help learners get meaning from what they read and that teach them to set goals, focus their attention, self-reinforce, and cope with problems.
- Metacognition—or thinking about thinking—involves the use of cognitive strategies for monitoring our own cognitive processes, such as thinking, learning, and remembering.
- Metacognitive instruction includes teaching your learners to: (1) attend to the effectiveness of cognitive strategies, (2) attribute differences to the relative effectiveness of a particular strategy, and (3) use the more effective strategy in future decision making.
- Good thinkers have a large knowledge base that includes both declarative knowledge and procedural knowledge, as well as general knowledge.
- The key components of the information processing model are immediate, working, and long-term memory.
- The information storage capacity of your learners' working memory can be enhanced by the active processing of information, such as taking notes, discussion, practice, and comprehension monitoring.
- The parallel distributed processing model (PDP) suggests that the minds of your learners may not always work in orderly, sequential ways. This model suggests that learners may figure things out without being given an orderly set of rules, may not always think logically or rationally when solving problems, and may construct their own meanings.
- The two major traditions in the study of intelligence are the classical tradition, which attempts to understand the structure of intelligence, and the revisionist tradition, which seeks to understand its processes.
- Gardner believes that we can learn about intelligence only by studying the cognitive processes people use when they are solving important problems. He describes seven cognitive abilities that help us solve these problems: logical-mathematical, linguistic, musical, spatial, bodily-kinesthetic, interpersonal, and intrapersonal.
- Sternberg believes that, regardless of the type of problem, there is a common set of cognitive processes learners can use.

For Discussion and Practice

°1. Why have cognitive psychologists chosen various metaphors to describe how the mind works? Which is their metaphor of choice?

Questions marked with an asterisk are answered in the appendix.

°2. Regardless of the metaphor chosen, what basic elements do all cognitive approaches to learning share?

°3. In what respects do cognitive approaches to the study of learning differ from behavioral approaches?

°4. What is a cognitive learning strategy? Give an example of a cognitive learning strategy that you have used and that you would want to share with your learners.

°5. If you wanted to help your learners remember what you've taught, what three cognitive activities might you ask them to perform?

°6. If you wanted to help your learners improve their comprehension of what they've read, what skills would you teach them?

7. Write a brief classroom dialogue suitable to your subject or grade to illustrate the five stages of the IDEAL problem-solving strategy.

°8. What metacognitive instruction should you provide your learners to help them use cognitive strategies in your classroom?

°9. Provide an example of domain-specific knowledge and an example of general knowledge in your subject or grade level. On what basis did you make the distinction between these two types of knowledge?

°10. Identify two ways cognitive psychologists have classified knowledge, concepts, and principles that are built up and organized from birth to adulthood. Provide an example of each classification.

°11. What are some of the ways you could help your learners' working memory function more efficiently?

°12. Draw a weblike diagram illustrating your own version of a propositional network pertaining to the concept of "effective teaching." Of what importance are propositional networks in helping learners remember important concepts and principles?

13. Use an example suitable to your teaching field to describe how learning might occur in the form of "pattern recognition" using the neural network model illustrated by Marshall (1990).

°14. Compare and contrast the views of intelligence held by Gardner and Sternberg with the view of intelligence you grew up with. In what ways does Gardner's view of intelligence differ from Sternberg's?

Suggested Readings

Gagné, E.D., Yekovich, C.W., & Yekovich, F.R. (1993). *The cognitive psychology of school learning* (2nd ed.). New York: HarperCollins. This highly readable text tells what cognitive psychology is, how cognitive psychologists perform their work, and what they have found that is relevant to teaching. It also provides readers with a coherent explanatory framework to solve teaching and learning problems in the classroom.

Questions marked with an asterisk are answered in the appendix.

Pressley, M. (1995). *Advanced Educational Psychology For Educators, Researchers, and Policymakers.* New York: HarperCollins. Includes several excellent chapters on cognitive psychology and cognitive learning theory, with numerous examples of how to use this knowledge to improve your classroom teaching.

Solso, R. L. (1988). *Cognitive psychology* (2nd ed.). Needham, MA: Allyn & Bacon. A book for those who want to explore not only the theories underlying cognitive approaches to learning but also the research methods and findings.

Making Learners Active Thinkers

This chapter will help you answer the following questions about your learners:

- How can I help my students learn from their own beliefs and from the social environment in which they live?
- How can I emphasize primary concepts, generalizations, and underlying themes rather than isolated facts?
- How can I help my learners organize what they know in advance to get them ready to learn?
- Should I deliberately plan lessons that create conceptual conflict?
- How can I approach written work as a problem-solving activity?
- How can I make learning a joint cognitive effort between me, the learner, and the class rather than a teacher-controlled search for knowledge?
- How can I model for my learners the thinking strategies they will need to solve real-world problems?
- How can I use group discussion to allow learners to create their own representations and elaborations of the content to be learned?
- How do I plan cooperative learning lessons so that the group goal is achieved while individual group members take responsibility for their own learning?

In Chapter 5 we described what good thinkers do: they have factual and know-how knowledge, and they actively receive new knowledge and build connections to what they already know. We described several models of good thinking that stress the importance of giving learners the opportunity to construct their own knowledge and figure things out for themselves. The object of this chapter is to present you with a wealth of instructional methods for doing this. Let's begin by looking at two lessons, both designed to teach fractions. Our purpose in examining these two lessons will be to see how well each allows learners to "construct" knowledge and meaning for themselves.

Ed Robbins is teaching a unit on fractions to his fourth-grade class. During the first 12 weeks of the year, all fourth-graders learned about numbers and number theory. They covered such topics as odd, even, positive, and negative numbers. The fourth-graders are also familiar with such numerical concepts as multiples, factors, and the base 10 system for writing numbers.

On the day we observe Mr. Robbins, he is teaching a lesson about equivalent fractions as different ways of representing the same amount. During four previous lessons, his learners have studied fractions as quantities and learned how fractions that look different (for example, 1/2 and 2/4) actually represent the same amount. The present lesson is intended to reinforce this idea.

Mr. Robbins begins the lesson with a quick review of the previous lesson. On the overhead projector he shows pictures of objects such as pies and loaves of bread divided to represent different fractions of the whole. In rapid-fire fashion his learners call out the fractions. He then projects a chart with undivided whole objects and has learners come up and divide them into halves, thirds, fourths, and so on while other learners do the same on worksheets. Each learner gets immediate feedback on his or her answers.

In this chapter you will also learn the meaning of these terms:

advance organizer
authentic problems
categorization
cognitive apprenticeship
conceptual conflict
constructivism
cooperative learning
direct explanation teaching
discovery learning
intentional learners
joint cognitive venture
organization
reciprocal teaching
situated learning

Next, he signals the class to clear their desks except for a pencil and draws their attention to a large, brightly colored chart hanging from the front blackboard (shown here in Figure 6.1. He passes out a similar dittoed chart to the students. Mr. Robbins explains that for each row the students are to complete the fraction with a denominator of 100 that equals the fraction in the row. Then they are to fill in the third row with the decimal equivalent of that fraction.

Mr. Robbins first models how to do this. He demonstrates (pointing out that they have already learned this) how to make an equivalent fraction by multiplying the original fraction by a fraction that equals 1. He works several examples to be sure that his students understand the concept and can copy the examples onto their charts.

He then calls on a number of students to come to the front of the room and demonstrate several more examples for the class. Mr. Robbins asks the students to describe what they are doing as they solve the problems. He checks that the rest of the class correctly fills in the charts at their desks.

Finally, he breaks the class into small groups and directs them to fill out the remainder of the chart. He provides each group with a key to immediately check their responses when finished. As the learners engage in their seatwork, Mr. Robbins moves from group to group, checking, giving feedback, and correcting or praising as needed.

Mr. Robbins has designed this lesson to show that fractions that look different can be equal in order to point out the relationship between decimals and fractions, and to use this as a foundation for teaching the relationships between dollars, decimals, and fractions in a subsequent lesson. In the classroom next door, Kay Greer is also teaching a unit on fractional equivalents. Let's look in on her lesson.

As the lesson begins, Mrs. Greer asks Denisha to tell the class what she said yesterday about fractions. "A fraction like 1/2 isn't a number," Denisha asserts, "because it isn't on the number line." Denisha points to the number line running along the top of the front blackboard. "See! There's no 1/2. Just 1, 2, 3, 4, . . . like that!"

"Well, class, let's think about what Denisha says. Let me give you a problem and we'll study it and, then, maybe come to some conclusion about whether a fraction is a number." She turns on the overhead and projects the following for all to see.

A boy has four loaves of bread that he bought at the local supermarket. He has eight friends and he wants each friend to get an equal part of the bread. How much bread should he give each of his friends?

Mrs. Greer draws the four loaves on the overhead and watches as the children, arranged in six groups of five, copy the drawings into their notebooks. She walks around the classroom occasionally prompting groups with the question, "How much bread is each one going to get?"

The children argue among themselves: "You can't do it!" "There isn't enough bread!" "How many slices are in each loaf?" After about 10 minutes Mrs. Greer asks, "Does anyone need more time to work on this? How many are ready to discuss?"

A few raise their hands. The rest are busy drawing and redrawing loaves of bread, sketching lines across them. Several minutes go by and Mrs. Greer says, "OK, would someone like to show their solution?"

$\dfrac{1}{4}$ X $\dfrac{25}{25}$	$\dfrac{25}{100}$	0.25
$\dfrac{1}{2}$ X $\dfrac{}{50}$	$\dfrac{}{100}$	•
$\dfrac{1}{5}$ X	$\dfrac{}{100}$	•
$\dfrac{2}{5}$	$\dfrac{}{100}$	•
$\dfrac{3}{4}$	$\dfrac{}{100}$	•
$\dfrac{5}{4}$	$\dfrac{}{100}$	•
$\dfrac{3}{2}$	$\dfrac{}{100}$	•

Figure 6.1
Mr. Robbins's chart for teaching equivalent fractions.

Frank raises his hand, walks to the overhead and draws his solution. "I'm not sure it's right," he hedges. Frank draws four loaves of bread and divides each loaf into eight slices. (Frank's drawing appears in Figure 6.2.) He looks up and announces to the class, "Each friend gets four slices!"

"That's wrong!" challenges Rosa. "Each friend gets two slices, see!" She walks to the overhead, draws four loaves of bread and divides each loaf into four slices. (Rosa's drawing appears in Figure 6.3.)

"Why not just give each friend half a loaf?" asks Albert.

"Come up here and draw your solution," says Mrs. Greer. Albert walks up to the overhead and sketches his proposal to the class. "Can you write the number that each gets?" asks Mrs. Greer. Albert writes the number "1/2" for all to see.

"Well, Albert's and Rosa's slices are bigger than mine," protests Frank.

"Frank," asks Mrs. Greer, "why not write the number that shows how much of the bread your eight friends get? Albert's number is 1/2. How much is one slice as Albert sees it?" she asks the class.

"One eighth," proposes Cal. "Can you write that?" inquires Mrs. Greer. Cal comes up to the overhead and writes "1/8" next to Frank's drawing.

As children write different numbers for their solutions, Mrs. Greer asks, "Well, how can we have three different numbers for each of these solutions? We have one half, two fourths, four eighths," pointing to the different quantities and fractions on the overhead.

After several moments of silence several hands shoot up and one by one the children give explanations for the seeming discrepancy. The lesson continues in this

Loaves of bread

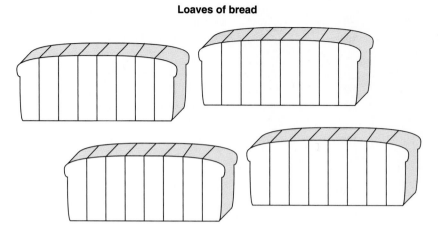

Figure 6.2
Frank's drawing. *Source: Teaching Academic Subjects to Diverse Learners* (pp. 67–69, 71, 182, 219), by M. M. Kennedy, New York: Teachers College Press. © 1990 by Teachers College, Columbia University. All rights reserved. Reprinted by permission of the publisher.

vein until five minutes before the bell. Mrs. Greer reviews what was concluded and sets the goal for the next lesson on fractions. (Adapted from Ball, 1991)

Now, let's compare the lessons of Mrs. Greer and Mr. Robbins. Both lessons had the same goal: To help learners understand the concepts of quantity and equivalence pertaining to fractions. But these two teachers have designed two very different lessons to achieve this same end.

You may have noticed that the behavioral science approach has heavily influenced Mr. Robbins's lesson (recall Chapter 4). His lesson has been designed to elicit a mini-

Loaves of bread

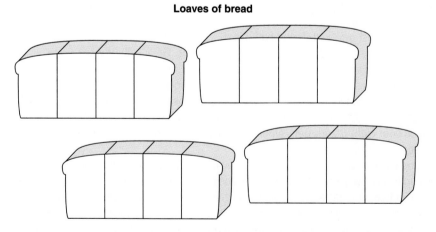

Figure 6.3
Rosa's drawing. *Source: Teaching Academic Subjects to Diverse Learners* (pp. 67–69, 71, 182, 219), by M. M. Kennedy, New York: Teachers College Press. © 1990 by Teachers College, Columbia University. All rights reserved. Reprinted by permission of the publisher.

mum of mistakes. His activities are aimed at the practice of correct responses followed by immediate feedback. For Mr. Robbins, learning involves correct responding, which is best accomplished by means of a teacher-directed or teacher-centered lesson.

Mrs. Greer, on the other hand, has a different view of learning. She is less focused on correct, rapid responses than on thought processes involving reflection, problem solving, analysis, and inquiry. Her lesson takes into consideration the fact that her learners already have information and beliefs about fractions that may or may not be correct.

Mrs. Greer wants to expose misconceptions and challenge learners to acquire new, more accurate perceptions through their own powers of reasoning. She carefully avoids providing answers. Her objective is to help learners understand fractions by influencing the cognitive processes by which they can elicit correct responses.

Recall that the information processing model of thinking you learned about in the last chapter stresses the importance of reception, availability, and activation in order for meaningful learning to occur. According to this model, any classroom lesson that hopes to produce meaningful learning and make learners good thinkers must ensure attention, acknowledge learners' prior knowledge, and ensure that learners actively engage that knowledge. In this chapter we will concentrate on activation—or how to teach learners to build internal and external bridges between what they already know and what they are about to learn.

In the previous chapter, we also reviewed the parallel distributed processing (PDP) model of thinking. Recall that this model emphasizes that learners construct their own knowledge, build their own rules and principles, and acquire unique concepts and connections among ideas and facts while thinking. Therefore, lessons aimed at teaching good thinking should allow learners to figure things out on their own. In this chapter you will learn a number of instructional approaches that allow learners the opportunity to figure things out on their own and to "construct" knowledge and meaning for themselves.

The PDP model also stresses that knowledge is acquired from social interactions. According to this model, learning and thinking are not just "in-the-head" activities. Rather, they depend on involvement with peers and adults. Therefore, the instructional methods covered in this chapter emphasize the importance of learning, thinking, and constructing knowledge in a social context.

> **How can I help my students learn from their own beliefs and from the social environment in which they live?**

Constructivism: Putting Learners in the Driver's Seat

Current cognitive models of learning and thinking (such as the information processing and PDP models) stipulate that the mind learns not by passively recording or absorbing information, but by actively trying to make sense of it. These models tell us that in the process of making sense of information, active learners build internal connections or relationships among the ideas and facts they are learning. In addition, they build external connections between the new information and what they already know. This approach to learning emphasizes the active role of the learner, in contrast to the behavioral science approach, which emphasizes the active role of the teacher. **Constructivism** is a term used by cognitive psychologists to represent this approach to learning.

Over the past decade, the term "constructivism" has come to mean more than a theory about learning. It has become associated with a theory of knowledge that says that the world is inherently complex, that there is no objective reality, and that much of

Constructivism. An approach to learning in which learners are provided the opportunity to construct their own sense of what is being learned by building internal connections or relationships among the ideas and facts being taught.

what we know is constructed from our beliefs and the social milieu in which we live. Here is how a leading constructivist, Ernst von Glasersfeld, describes this philosophy of knowing:

> From the beginning, in the 5th century B.C., the skeptics have shown that it is logically impossible to establish the "truth" of any particular piece of knowledge. The necessary comparison of the piece of knowledge with the reality it is supposed to represent cannot be made because the only rational access to that reality is through yet another act of knowing.
>
> The skeptics have forever reiterated this argument to the embarrassment of all the philosophers who tried to get around the difficulty. Nevertheless, the skeptics did not question the traditional concept of knowing.
>
> This is where constructivism, following the lead of the American pragmatists and a number of European thinkers at the turn of this century, breaks away from the tradition. It holds that there is something wrong with the old concept of knowledge, and it proposes to change it rather than continue the same hopeless struggle to find a solution to the perennial paradox. The change consists of this: Give up the requirement that knowledge represents an independent world, and admit instead that knowledge represents something that is far more important to us, namely *what we can do in our experiential world, the successful ways of dealing with the objects we call physical and the successful ways of thinking with abstract concepts.* (Glasersfeld, 1995, pp. 6–7)

In addition to being associated with a philosophical theory on the existence of knowledge, the term "constructivism" has also become associated with an educational movement that restores learners to the forefront of the instructional process. The goal of this movement is to redesign educational practice so that lessons are planned and sequenced to encourage learners to use their experiences to actively construct understanding in a way that makes sense to them. The constructivist movement in education has resulted in numerous curriculum reforms in the teaching of reading, writing, mathematics, social studies, and science (Duit, 1995; Saxe, 1995; Spivey, 1995).

In this chapter, we will use *constructivism* to refer to those instructional practices derived from research in cognitive psychology that stimulate learners to activation: practices that help build internal connections and organize information in working memory so it is more meaningful and understandable, and that build external connections between old and new information. Thus, for our purposes, constructivism is the application to classrooms of learning principles derived from cognitive models that provide learners the opportunity to construct their own ways of knowing.

Constructivist instructional practices, whether in the areas of science, social studies, mathematics, reading, or writing, have the following characteristics in common:

| How can I emphasize primary concepts, generalizations, and underlying themes rather than isolated facts? |

1. They organize learning and instruction around important ideas.
2. They acknowledge the importance of prior learning.
3. They challenge the adequacy of the learner's prior knowledge.
4. They provide for ambiguity and uncertainty.
5. They teach learners how to learn.
6. They view learning as a joint cognitive venture.
7. They assess a learner's knowledge acquisition during the lesson.

Let's examine each of these elements in more detail.

Instructional practices based on constructivist principles allow learners the opportunity to construct their own ways of knowing.

Organize Learning Around Important Ideas

Rene Jordash was unhappy with the way her world history text discussed World War I. In particular, she felt that its discussion of the causes of the war led her tenth-grade students to think that it all started because someone got shot in his carriage. She wanted her students to understand that the causes of major wars have their roots in religious, ethnic, economic, and other conflicts, which fester over long periods of time. So, to help her learners appreciate the complexity of causes underlying conflicts such as World War I, she started her third-period class with the question: "What would have happened if the Archduke Ferdinand of Austria hadn't been shot?"

Learners tend to view learning as consisting of memorizing facts, filling out worksheets, answering end-of-chapter questions, and taking tests. Extensive interviews with learners of various ages reveal that, in comparison to adults, school-age learners typically do not see learning as a goal of instruction (Bereiter & Scardamalia, 1989). In other words, they do not attend to a lesson with the explicit intention of learning, but rather with the idea of completing assignments and activities, passing tests, and doing homework.

Cognitive psychologists believe that learners' view of learning as an activity rather than a goal leads them to be passive during classroom instruction (Bereiter & Scardamalia, 1989). In other words, they sit in classrooms waiting for the spelling worksheet or biology lab sheet to be passed out, homework to be assigned, and test dates to be given. So how does a teacher help learners view learning as a goal rather than an activity? To do this, most cognitive approaches to instruction advocate that teachers focus their lessons on and make explicit to learners the primary concepts, generalizations, and underlying themes of the content they are teaching rather than focus on isolated facts or bits of information (Brooks & Brooks, 1993). Let's look at some ways teachers can do this.

Curriculum guides and textbooks don't always identify these larger ideas, generalizations, or principles for you. Often they may, instead, be compilations of facts or activities. For example, a U.S. history text typically has chapters devoted to different wars: the French and Indian War, the American Revolution, wars with Mexico, the Civil War. Students typically learn facts about these wars—names, dates, places—and fill out maps and take tests to assess that learning. A constructivist approach to teaching about important wars might instead involve students' learning about the theme of human conflict: its underlying causes and its outcomes. Wars would be presented as a *group* of events to help learners construct a larger understanding of American history.

In advocating that teachers organize instruction around primary concepts, generalizations, and underlying themes, cognitive psychologists are not denying the importance of factual knowledge; as we saw in the previous chapter, prior knowledge is considered a requirement of good thinking. Rather, they are saying that factual knowledge can be acquired in a variety of ways (for example, from reading, lectures, peers), and that the best way for learners to retain and apply this knowledge is to put it in a larger, more lifelike context that stimulates learners to reflect, organize, analyze, and problem solve.

The importance of focusing lessons around important ideas as opposed to facts has resulted in numerous curriculum reforms during the past decade. Science curricula are being developed that organize information around "conceptual themes" like cause and effect, change and conservation, diversity and variation, and energy and matter, rather than around topics such as the digestive system, the planets, nutrition, or electricity. Language arts curricula present readings in the context of themes such as fantasy/realism, reflection/impulsivity, reactive/proactive, and freedom/responsibility, rather than in genre-specific units, like poetry, prose, mythology, and nonfiction.

The rationale behind these curricular changes is that learners acquire meaning and understanding by organizing information for themselves, connecting it to other information, and storing it as networks or schemata, rather than by being told isolated bits of information. The more that lessons can be focused on larger units of knowledge—concepts, generalizations, and underlying themes—the more likely learners are to connect the new subject matter with what they already know.

Acknowledge the Importance of Prior Knowledge

Cognitive psychologists believe that learners, even at the earliest grade levels, have some information about nearly every topic they study. This information may be in the form of ideas, however vague; unconnected facts; implicit rules; or images. Frequently, this information consists of mistaken beliefs, such as "the world is flat," "the sun moves around the earth," "the cause of the Civil War was the firing on Fort Sumter," or "all microorganisms are bad." This prior knowledge affects learners' attempts to construct meaning out of what they are hearing, seeing, or reading. Unlike the behaviorists, who view the learner as passively absorbing and storing new information, cognitive psychologists assert that learners are continually engaged in trying to make sense out of what they learn.

At this point you might ask yourself, "Isn't the emphasis placed on *prior knowledge* by cognitive psychologists similar to what the behaviorists mean by *prerequisite skills?*" The answer is that although prior knowledge and prerequisite skills have some similarities, the former term, as cognitive psychologists use it, connotes far more than the latter.

Behaviorists view prior knowledge in terms of readiness for instruction. When prior knowledge is lacking, they see the teacher's role simply as one of giving it to the learners so that they can acquire new knowledge. Cognitive psychologists, on the other hand, view prior knowledge as a cognitive structure—or *schema*—which suggests deeper understandings, interconnectedness with other data, and connections to incoming knowledge. The teacher's concern with prior knowledge is not simply to fill up an empty vessel, as the behaviorists contend, but rather to help learners gain entry to that knowledge, understand its conceptions and misconceptions, and swap inappropriate cognitive structures for better ones (Floden, 1991).

Organizing Prior Knowledge. David Ausubel was one of the first American educational psychologists to advocate the importance of prior knowledge as a cognitive structure or schema for achieving meaningful learning. Ausubel (1960, 1968) held that people learn when they (1) assimilate new material into existing schemata and (2) reconstruct or accommodate new material to existing schemata by transforming it in idiosyncratic ways. He championed the concept of an "advance organizer" to provide learners with instructional supports to facilitate meaningful learning.

An **advance organizer** is a summary of the concepts, generalizations, and themes to be learned, presented at a general and inclusive level. When presented to learners at the beginning of a lesson, it can help learners both recall familiar material (material the learners had prior knowledge of) and learn unfamiliar material. (For example, the questions and classroom examples that begin each chapter of this book are advance organizers.) Ausubel believed that advance organizers help learners construct new knowledge. They do this both by providing a cue for recalling existing schemata and by providing a conceptual peg on which to hang new information.

One simple way to use advance organizers is to have learners survey chapter titles, subtitles, headings, summaries, and end-of-chapter questions *before* reading an assignment in a textbook. This stimulates prior knowledge that learners have stored in long-term memory. Then, as they read the chapter, they form connections between this knowledge and the incoming information, which promotes meaningful learning and long-term recall. The accompanying box, *Using Advance Organizers*, gives three examples of statements you could make in class to provide your learners with advance organizers for textbook readings and lessons.

Recognizing Learner Opinions, Beliefs, and Ideas. Learners who have little prior knowledge in a given area may have difficulty learning anything new. For example, suppose you were teaching a unit on World War I and you began by focusing on specific facts and details about which your learners had little prior knowledge. As a consequence, the learners would be unable to build bridges to what they already know, they would not make an effort to construct their own understanding of what is being taught, and, at best, they would passively attend to your lesson. On the other hand, if you recognize that your learners already have opinions, beliefs, or general notions about what your next lesson will cover, and if you try to organize this lesson around larger ideas that your learners can build on, they are more likely to engage in active thinking that results in meaningful learning and retention.

Anticipating Misconceptions. Cognitive psychologists caution that prior knowledge, in the form of misconceptions, may hamper the acquisition of new knowledge when these misconceptions are not anticipated by the teacher. For example, learners sometimes come to science classes with prior knowledge that is inconsistent with the content they are being asked to learn (DiSessa, 1982). Sometimes erroneous prior

How can I help my learners organize what they know in advance to get them ready to learn?

Advance organizer. A summary of the concepts, generalizations, and themes to be learned, presented at a general and inclusive level.

Applying Your Knowledge:

Using Advance Organizers

For a Chapter in a History Book. Some of the earliest visitors to America came from Europe. What drove these courageous explorers to sail across dangerous oceans in search of land they knew little about? What were they looking for, how did they get there and what did they find, what good and bad things did they bring to the new world? This chapter talks about the famous men, their ships, their journeys, their discoveries, and their successes and failures.

For a Political Science Lesson. Most nations have statements that express the basic principles on which their laws, customs, and economies are based. Today we will study three systems by which nations can guide, control, and operate their economies. The three economic systems we will study are capitalism, socialism, and communism. They often are confused with the political systems that tend to be associated with them. A political system not only influences the economic system of a country but also guides individual behavior in many other areas, such as what is taught in schools, the relationship between church and state, how people get chosen for or elected to political office, what jobs people can have, and what newspapers can print. Tomorrow we will study the political systems that go along with each of the economic systems we will study today.

For a Language Arts Lesson. Today we will learn how to avoid embarrassing errors such as this when punctuating possessives [circle an incorrectly punctuated possessive in a newspaper headline]. At the end of the period I will give each of you several additional examples of errors taken from my collection of mistakes found in newspapers and magazines. I'll ask you to make the proper corrections and report your changes to the class.

knowledge is so entrenched in the learners' minds that they continue to use mistaken ways of thinking even when alternative methods have been taught (Roth, 1990, 1991). And sometimes prior beliefs are so strong that learners ignore statements that they disagree with or they choose not to believe what they see.

To show the power of prior knowledge, Gunstone and White (1981) constructed a demonstration involving a weight and a bucket of sand, which were hanging in balance on opposite sides of a pulley and extending downward an equal distance from the wheel of the pulley. A small amount of sand was added to the bucket—so small that its addition caused no movement. Yet students who believed that the bucket would sink reported that they observed movement!

Next, the experimenters pulled the bucket down (which raised the weight) and asked students to predict what would happen if they let go of the bucket. Students predicted that the bucket would return to its original position, which it did not. Some students reacted to what they saw not by learning a new rule or generalization, but by trying to explain it away, arguing that something was wrong with the pulley.

The best way to ensure that your learners' prior knowledge works to enhance meaningful and conceptually accurate learning is to ask these questions as you prepare a unit:

1. What important ideas, principles, generalizations, or beliefs do I want my learners to construct at the end of this unit?

2. How might this topic already look to my learners? How might they already perceive it or think about it?

3. What is the best way to represent or introduce these new ideas to my learners so that they connect them with what they already know and thus challenge the adequacy of their existing knowledge?

Challenge the Adequacy of Prior Knowledge

What is the best way to get your learners to compare what they know with what you are teaching? Constructivist educators propose that teachers deliberately plan their lessons to create "conceptual conflict" (Nussbaum & Novick, 1982).

For example, imagine introducing a biology unit on the body's defense mechanisms with the following assertion: "Germs are not trying to hurt us when they settle in our bodies. They just want to live quietly, eat, and prosper." Undoubtedly, many learners view germs as targeting the body and intentionally harming it rather than as just wanting to find a way to reside peaceably in the new environment.

Conceptual conflict comes about when our existing beliefs or ways of explaining things don't produce the outcomes we predict. You were first acquainted with this idea in Chapter 2 when you read about Piaget's cognitive development theory and the process of disequilibrium. Conceptual conflict is a useful teaching tool in many different subject areas. Social studies teachers create conceptual conflict when they challenge long-established beliefs about the significance of certain events. Reading teachers create conceptual conflict when they ask learners to make predictions about what may happen next in a story. Science teachers create conceptual conflict when they ask learners to guess what will happen when a certain chemical is added.

> **Conceptual conflict.** The result when our existing beliefs or ways of explaining things don't produce the outcomes we predicted.

Some cognitive psychologists and constructivist educators suggest that the most effective way to get learners to challenge the adequacy of prior knowledge is to design lessons that deliberately create the opportunity for conceptual conflict. They believe that learners will attempt to resolve the conflict by constructing new meanings for themselves and that they will thereby retain what they have learned and apply it in new contexts (Guzzetti, Snyder, Glass, & Gamas, 1993).

Posner, Strike, Hewson, and Gertzog (1982) developed an instructional framework teachers can use to promote conceptual conflict and resolution in science instruction that is applicable to any academic discipline. The accompanying box, *Creating Conceptual Conflict,* presents their recommendations.

> **Should I deliberately plan lessons that create conceptual conflict?**

Provide for Ambiguity and Uncertainty

Constructivist educators point out that problem solving in the real world rarely results in quick, simple, and correct solutions. Rather, real-world problems are complex, messy, and unstructured, and they often have multiple solutions. Consequently, such educators argue that the problem-solving situations in which we place learners should be "authentic." **Authentic problems** are those that people encounter in the real world. They involve hands-on exercises or problems whose solutions are uncertain. Ideally, the tasks should yield multiple solutions, each with its own advantages and disadvantages. This creates the initial uncertainty and ambiguity necessary for meaningful learning to occur.

> **Authentic problems.** Problems encountered in the real world for which the expected solution is uncertain and the task then yields multiple solutions, each with advantages and disadvantages.

Many new approaches to instruction underscore the importance of ambiguity, complexity, uncertainty, and multiple solutions. Cognitive psychologists who study the development of writing skills, for example, urge that writing be viewed as problem solving (Scardamalia & Bereiter, 1986). They suggest that the task of writing involves problem exploration, planning, brainstorming, organizing ideas, testing for connections and coherence, editing, and revising. But writing typically has not been viewed as problem solving. Rather, Applebee (1984) reports that writing assignments, even in high school, tend to be limited in scope and confined to a narrow topic. The typical assignment is a first-and-final draft, one page or shorter in length, to be completed in class, and the

Applying Your Knowledge:

Creating Conceptual Conflict

- Plan lectures, demonstrations, homework assignments, and other classroom activities that deliberately create inconsistencies between the important knowledge you want students to learn and what they actually know.
- Through questions, assignments, and other assessment devices, closely monitor your learners' thinking about the to-be-learned ideas. Be alert to resistance to these alternative thinking frameworks.
- Model analytical or logical thinking for your learners to demonstrate that consistency in one's beliefs and consistency with evidence is important.
- Represent new ideas to your learners in a variety of ways: verbal, pictorial, concrete-practical, and mathematical. Point out the relationships among the various ways of representing a problem and its solution.

topic is usually chosen by the teacher to test previous learning or skills. Hence the students' task is to get the answer "right," rather than to convince, inform, or entertain a prospective audience.

Since Applebee's study, cognitive psychologists and constructivist educators have introduced numerous innovations into the teaching of writing (Atwell, 1987; Harris & Graham, 1992; Scardamalia & Bereiter, 1986). At the heart of these innovations is the notion that good writing instruction teaches learners to approach writing as a problem-solving activity. Learners are encouraged to pursue their own topics for writing rather than writing on a teacher-prescribed topic. They also learn the importance of planning: establishing goals for writing, outlining, and identifying the important information they need to gather. Finally, they learn to revise their writing in light of their goals, a process that leads writers to change their goals and be flexible in light of inconsistent or contradictory information.

How can I approach written work as a problem-solving activity?

The accompanying box, *Teaching Good Writing*, suggests that writing from a constructivist point of view is much more than learners trying to convince their teachers that they learned what they were taught. Rather, it is a process of solving an unstructured problem through planning, writing, and revising. The goal of instruction is for learners to appreciate the complexity of the writing task and to view it as a way of communicating ideas that are important to *them*.

Teach Learners How to Learn

In the previous chapter you learned that good thinkers use cognitive strategies. These strategies allow learners to acquire and construct knowledge, across a variety of situations, that can be helpful to the learner over her entire life. We reviewed strategies to

Teaching Good Writing

Scardamalia and Bereiter (1986) have developed an approach to writing that incorporates many constructivist learning principles. Their approach, which is applicable to any content area or topic, stresses teaching strategies for planning, writing, and revising. Here are some of their suggestions:

Helping Learners with the Planning Stage of Writing

1. Have learners generate an idea for writing. Give them cue cards with the following statements on them to help them improve the idea: An even better idea is ____. An important point I haven't considered yet is ____. A better argument would be ____. A different aspect would be ____. A whole new way to think of this topic is ____. No one will have thought of ____.

2. Learners should identify a goal for writing. Show your learners how to ask themselves questions about who the intended audience is, what are the needs of their audience, and what is the best way to give this audience what it wants.

3. Help learners generate content for their writing. Give your learners prompts on cards to motivate them to search their memories. For example, if they are writing about a sequence of events, the prompts might go something like this: What happened first? When did it happen? Where did it happen? To whom did it happen? and so on. Or provide cue cards with sentence openers like this: "One reason . . ." "Even though . . ." "For example, . . ." and "I think. . . ."

Helping Learners During the Writing Stage

1. Show them how to get started. If your learners are writing a nonfiction piece, give them the following list: (1) generate a topic sentence; (2) note reasons; (3) examine the reasons and ask if readers will accept each reason; (4) come up with an ending. If your learners are writing a story, give them the following questions to answer: Who is the main character? Who else is in the story? When does the story take place? Where does the story take place? What does the main character do or want to do? What do the other characters do?

2. Show your learners how to elaborate on their ideas. Teach them to cue or prompt themselves with the following statements as they are writing: *An example of this is . . . ; This is true, but it's not sufficient so . . . ; My own feelings about this are . . . ; I'll change this a little by . . . ; I could develop this idea by adding. . . .*

Helping Learners During the Revision Stage

Show them how to improve their writing. Teach your learners to revise their writing by prompting themselves with the following statements: *I'm not being clear about what I just said, so I should . . . ; I could make my main point clearer by . . . ; A criticism I should deal with in my paper is . . . ; I'm getting off the topic, so I should. . . .*

help learners remember, comprehend, write, and problem solve in a variety of academic areas.

A constructivist approach to classroom instruction includes cognitive strategies that teach students learning-to-learn skills and how to regulate those skills. Carl Bereiter, a prominent cognitive psychologist, refers to this goal of teaching as helping students become "intentional learners" (Bereiter, 1990). Students become **intentional learners** when they learn or find their own approaches or systems for achieving educational goals. Becoming an intentional learner requires the ability to find and allocate resources for learning, overcome obstacles to learning, and know how to sustain effort.

Intentional learners see themselves as being in charge of their learning—that is, they see themselves, not the teacher, as responsible for directing their learning efforts. In fact, cognitive psychologists have evidence that suggests that learners' use of cognitive strategies depends on their willingness to accept responsibility for their own learning (Bereiter & Scardamalia, 1989; Resnick, 1989). In other words, they know how to

Intentional learners. Students who find their own approaches or systems for achieving educational goals.

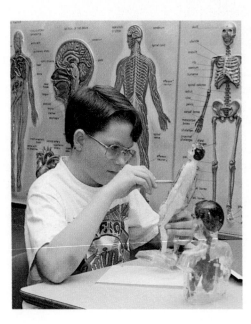

Intentional learners are students who learn or find their own approaches or systems for achieving educational goals.

monitor their understanding as they work. According to cognitive psychologists, better learners attend more closely to and assess more correctly the state of their understanding than do poorer learners (Browne, Bransford, Ferrara, & Campinone, 1983; Nelson-LeGall, Kratzer, Jones, & DeCooke, 1990; Resnick, 1989). The importance of learners' knowing cognitive strategies and how to regulate their use is summarized by Bereiter and Scardamalia (1989) as follows:

> By several different routes we arrive at the same conclusion: In order to learn what is ostensibly being taught in schools, students need to direct mental effort to goals over and above those implicit in the school activities. Without such intentional learning, education degenerates into the doing of schoolwork and other activities. (p. 385)

View Learning as a Joint Cognitive Venture

Instruction that is focused on knowledge construction is a joint cognitive effort rather than a solitary search for knowledge or an exclusively teacher-controlled activity (Bereiter & Scardamalia, 1989; Vygotsky, 1987). A **joint cognitive venture** is focused on a clear cognitive goal, and different components of the venture are carried out by different classroom participants: learner, peers, and teachers. According to cognitive instructional theory, genuine knowledge construction is not a solitary enterprise involving a learner working in isolation from peers and adults.

Research continues to document the superiority of collaborative cognitive ventures over individualistic ones (Slavin, 1990b). One benefit of collaborative learning is that less-informed learners acquire knowledge and learning strategies by observing and imitating more knowledgeable ones (Brown & Palincsar, 1989). A number of factors contribute to the importance of learning in a social context. Let's look at some of them.

Conceptual Growth. Social or group learning is a principal force for promoting conceptual growth (Brown & Campione, 1986). Group instruction forces learners to accommodate their thinking to that of others. Conceptual growth is more likely to occur when learners have to think about the alternative viewpoints of group members, elabo-

Joint cognitive venture. An activity focused on a clear cognitive goal whose various components are carried out by different classroom participants: learner, peers, and teachers.

How can I make learning a joint cognitive effort between me, the learner, and the class rather than a teacher-controlled search for knowledge?

rate and defend their own ideas in the presence of others, and debate the merits of other viewpoints.

Social Support. Groups provide social support to their members in the form of encouragement and praise. Group instruction and group problem solving allow learners to assume different responsibilities (for example, researcher, recorder, summarizer, troubleshooter, supporter). Group members encourage one another to fulfill the responsibilities of these roles so that the group can accomplish its task.

Cognitive Modeling. When students are given the opportunity to learn in a social setting, they observe the thinking processes of group members as they carry out their roles. As group members argue and discuss with one another, thinking strategies often become explicit. Research into social learning demonstrates that children can learn good thinking from one another (Zimmerman, 1990). Thus students can learn how to define problems, brainstorm solutions, identify standards, collect data, and evaluate solutions by observing what different group members do.

Shared Expertise. Group learning assignments often involve different members learning different aspects of a large body of material. For example, a group project about the life of a famous scientist might require group members to acquire knowledge about different aspects of her life: education, culture, accomplishments, important historical events during her lifetime. Each member of the group becomes a subject specialist and communicates his or her knowledge to other group members. Thus, group learning becomes an efficient vehicle for acquiring new information (Slavin, 1985).

Assess a Learner's Knowledge Acquisition During Lessons

Most educators agree that testing is an important feature of successful instruction. But testing traditionally takes place after a lesson or unit of study is completed, or at the end of a semester or marking period. Cognitive psychologists, however, believe that separating tests from lessons this way can have unfortunate results (Wiggins, 1993). First, learners do not receive feedback on the adequacy of their answers until sometimes long after their actual performance. In addition, learners may miss the connection between what happens in class and what happens on test day, reducing the motivation both to learn in class and to study for tests. When assessment is embedded within the lesson being taught, learners receive immediate feedback, more easily see the connection between what was taught and what is being tested, and see that testing is an integral part of learning. *Performance-based assessment*, which we will study in Chapter 13, is an important aspect of constructivist teaching.

The seven elements of constructivist instruction presented above represent the roots of cognitive learning theory. In the next section we will look at some additional influences on cognitive learning theory and the instructional methods that have evolved from this theory.

Classroom Instruction that Promotes Good Thinking

As we have seen, cognitive learning theory emphasizes three related aspects of learning: (1) learning is a process of knowledge construction, not a matter of simply taking in what is heard or read; (2) because learners construct new knowledge based on what they already know, learning depends on prior knowledge; and (3) learning is an inherently social activity. This section describes several teaching methods based on cognitive learning theory: discovery learning, cognitive apprenticeship, cooperative learning, and direct explanation teaching. As you read about each one, ask yourself these questions:

1. Does this method allow learners to learn for themselves, or is knowledge already digested for them?

2. Does this method acknowledge that learners have preexisting ideas, information, and beliefs, or does it assume that their minds are blank slates?

3. Does this method allow learners to acquire and construct new knowledge through extended interactions with peers and adults, or is the learner viewed as a solitary investigator?

Discovery Learning

Discovery learning. The organization of knowledge around fundamental themes and principles rather than discrete facts.

Categorization. The process by which the mind simplifies information that enters short-term memory.

Organization. How the mind arranges information in coding systems for retrieving stored knowledge.

Take a moment to reread the fraction lessons of Mr. Robbins and Mrs. Greer at the beginning of this chapter. Mrs. Greer's lesson closely followed the **discovery learning** ideas of Jerome Bruner. Bruner (1960) states that the mind organizes knowledge in a hierarchical fashion, with the more general, all-encompassing ideas at the top of the hierarchy, and the more concrete, factual ideas toward the bottom. Much of Bruner's cognitive theory is built around the idea of categorization or organization. He reasons that so much information comes in through the senses that the mind must find ways to simplify and make sense of it. **Categorization** is how the mind simplifies information that enters short-term memory. **Organization** involves arranging information in coding systems. Figure 6.4 shows an example of such a coding system for motivation. In it, different types and aspects of motivation are arranged in a hierarchy from most general at the top to most specific at the bottom.

Bruner theorizes that the mind spontaneously organizes information in a hierarchical manner with the organization of knowledge in long-term memory. He believes that all subject matter has a similar structure: facts are supported by concepts, which, in turn, are supported by generalizations. This structure of knowledge is illustrated in Figure 6.5.

These generalizations, concepts, and facts tell us how instruction should be organized. Bruner stipulates that good teaching involves helping learners *discover for themselves* the generalizations under which lie related concepts and facts, rather than simply *telling them* to the learner. This *discovery learning* is facilitated when teachers organize the knowledge they present around fundamental themes and principles rather than discrete facts. This type of organization is similar to the way in which knowledge is organized in long-term memory.

Mrs. Greer has identified the important facts, concepts, and generalizations of her unit on fractions. But rather than teach children directly the rules and techniques for mathematically manipulating fractions in order to compare them (as did Mr. Robbins), she tries to help her learners *construct* the rules and generalizations for themselves. By doing so, Mrs. Greer (and Bruner) believe that students will have greater retention, understanding, and ability to use knowledge about (in this instance) fractions to solve future problems.

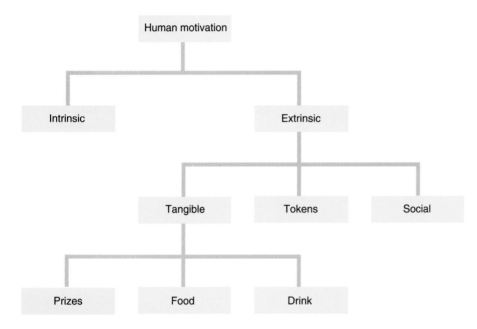

Figure 6.4
A coding system for human motivation.

   The essence of discovery learning is that the important facts, concepts, and general-izations of a subject area are not presented to learners in a final, organized form. Rather, they are taught in such a way that learners discover the relationships among facts, con-cepts, and generalizations and organize them in long-term memory on their own. Ac-cording to Bruner, teaching by the discovery method makes it more likely that learners will remember new knowledge and be able to apply it to solve real-world problems (Bruner, 1961).

Basic Features. Classroom instruction that is built around discovery learning has five important features: instructional set, motivational set, knowledge base, multiple ex-amples, and hierarchically organized curriculum. Let's see what each contains.
   Instructional set is the purpose or goal the teacher gives the learners at the start of the lesson. As we stated above, students can view learning as activities to be completed, or they can view it as an end in itself. In discovery learning, the teacher explains the pur-pose of the lesson in a way that is appropriate for the developmental level of the stu-dent. For example, you might tell kindergartners, "Today we are going to look for patterns using these blocks and buttons"; you would tell fourth-graders, "Work with these tiles to see how many different number patterns you can show. Then we'll write our results in numbers and letters"; to high school students, the message would be, "We are going to derive the equations for the graphs you drew yesterday." In this way learn-ers approach the task with the goal of acquiring understanding rather than memorizing facts, filling out a worksheet, or taking a test.
   Motivational set involves what the teacher does to stimulate, excite, or arouse learn-ers to accomplish the goal of the lesson. We will have more to say about motivation in the next chapter.

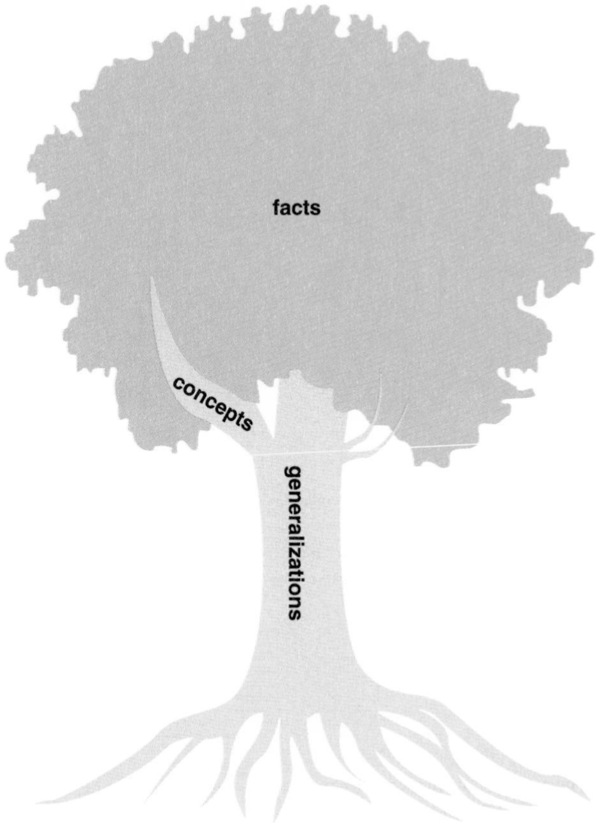

Figure 6.5
Bruner's concept of the structure of knowledge.
Source: Teaching as Decision Making: Instructional Practices for Successful Teachers (p. 33), by M. Pasch, G. Sparks-Langer, T. Gardner, A. Starko, and C. Moody (1991). New York: Longman.

Knowledge base refers to the extent of a learner's declarative and procedural knowledge relevant to the content of the lesson. As we discussed in the previous chapter, good thinkers possess a lot of knowledge. Thus, learners are more likely to see important relationships and discover important principles and generalizations if they have acquired the specific information necessary to do so.

Multiple examples means giving learners as many different instances or circumstances as possible in which the knowledge they are about to learn is included. For example, if the purpose of the lesson is to help learners discover how supply and demand affect price, you would provide a number of different examples: low interest rates cause people to refinance their mortgages, drought causes higher food prices, handmade sweaters are more expensive than mass-produced ones. Furthermore, discovery will be facilitated if you present the material through a variety of sensory modalities (audio, visual, tactile, and so forth).

A *hierarchically organized curriculum* stresses that the curriculum itself must be organized along the lines of a hierarchy of generalizations, concepts, and facts. Bruner feels that teachers must plan their lessons with an understanding of the hierarchical structure of the information they wish to convey. In that way, learners are exposed to specific facts from which they discover new concepts, from which they in turn derive generalizations.

As you read the following example of discovery learning, try to identify how it incorporates the five elements—instructional set, motivational set, knowledge base, multiple examples, and hierarchically organized curriculum.

An Example. Here is a principle of force and motion that Mr. Lyon will be teaching his junior high school science students:

> The turning effect of a force depends, in part, on how far the force acts from the center of turning (which is called the axle or pivot).

Rather than simply explaining this principle to his learners and giving them examples, Mr. Lyon devised a lesson to help them discover it on their own.

Since he would be using terms and expressions like *force, turning effect,* and *center of turning,* Mr. Lyon first ensured that his learners were familiar with the required terms. Then he brought to the classroom devices that make use of the principles of force and motion and arranged them on a table. These included nuts and bolts of various sizes, a variety of manual can openers and cans, socket wrenches of various lengths and sizes, hand-operated drills of various lengths, and paper clips.

At the start of the class he divided his students into pairs and gave each pair one paper clip. He instructed each pair to straighten the paper clip, and then have one partner hold one end and make it turn in the other partner's fingers without bending it. He asked them to note if it turned easily when the partner really squeezed the wire.

Next, he told them to make a right-angle bend in the wire about two centimeters from either end. He instructed one partner to turn the bent part as a crank, while the other squeezed the wire to keep it from turning. He asked them to note who was more successful. If both tried to turn the wire in opposite directions, who succeeded?

Finally, before allowing the pairs to experiment with the various tools and devices arranged on the table, Mr. Lyon told them that he wanted the groups to explain to him at the end of the lesson what causes a force to have a greater turning effect.

Goals for Discovery Learning Lessons. Here are some important generalizations that could serve as goals for discovery learning lessons. Think about the knowledge required of learners to discover the generalization and try to plan a lesson (with examples, visuals, and necessary apparatuses) to help them do so:

> Measurements are really comparisons with other known or accepted dimensions.

> The number of swings a pendulum makes in a given period of time depends mostly on its length.

> Major civilizations usually developed at the confluence of rivers and near natural harbors.

> Assuming no change in the quantity demanded by consumers, if producers increase the supply of a given good or service to the marketplace, then the price of that good or service can be expected to fall.

> Elderly people tend to vote in greater numbers than do voters of ages 18–21.

The accompanying box, *Teaching by the Discovery Method,* contains some suggestions for teaching generalizations like these in a discovery learning lesson.

Cognitive Apprenticeship

Classrooms traditionally have been successful places for conveying large bodies of information. They have not been as successful in teaching learners how experts gather or use that information. The notion that learners must become more skilled at gathering and using knowledge for themselves, and that the best way for them to do this is to observe experts while they are engaged in these processes, has given rise to several constructivist

Teaching by the Discovery Method

Here are some things to consider when planning and implementing a discovery lesson:

1. Choose an area you are very knowledgeable about and perhaps have already taught using more direct teaching approaches. This will ensure that you know the important facts, concepts, and generalizations that you want your learners to acquire.
2. Clearly identify the important principle, concept, generalization, or understanding that you want your learners to construct at the end of the lesson.
3. Start the lesson with a puzzling event, contradictory set of facts, or interesting object that will stimulate your learners to challenge and act on their prior beliefs.

4. Explain to your learners that the purpose of the lesson is for them to discover on their own how to resolve the puzzlement or doubt they are presently experiencing.
5. Offer a variety of materials to allow learners to act on their prior beliefs, to experiment, and to generate hypotheses.
6. Have your learners write down as best they can the generalization or rule they discovered.
7. Ask your learners to examine and discuss their thinking processes among themselves and with the entire class.
8. Lead your learners in discussions of their generalizations and the thinking processes that produced the generalizations. Present additional examples and ask them if each generalization works in these instances.

Cognitive apprenticeship. The notion that learners can best become more skilled at gathering and using knowledge for themselves by observing experts.

teaching approaches referred to as **cognitive apprenticeships** (Collins, Brown, & Newman, 1989; Pressley, 1995; Rogoff, 1990).

Cognitive apprenticeship is a model of teaching and learning that views the classroom learner as a novice who will be apprenticed to an expert. In a cognitive apprenticeship, the novice learns the cognitive strategies and metacognitive skills necessary to handle complex learning tasks. The teacher's role is not to fill the learner's mind with information, facts, and procedures, but rather to teach the "apprentices" how to explore, organize, question, and learn independently.

Cognitive apprenticeships are focused on teaching strategies and metacognition and are organized around specific learning areas such as reading, math, or writing. Thus, a novice learner learns strategies of expert thinking in a specific field: how a journalist writes, how a historian studies the past, how a mathematician solves problems. The facts and concepts that the student learns during a cognitive apprenticeship are those that are important in the expert's chosen field.

Basic Features. Cognitive apprenticeships can be organized in any field of study: science, social studies, literature, art. The most common models are in the areas of math (Schoenfeld, 1983, 1985), reading (Palincsar & Brown, 1984; Rosenshine & Meister, 1994), and writing (Scardamalia & Bereiter, 1985). All have common features: (1) they teach cognitive and metacognitive strategies, and (2) the skills learned are specific to an academic discipline (math, reading, writing, and so on). Collins, Brown, and Newman (1989) call these conditions **situated learning.** Other common elements of cognitive apprenticeships are the use of modeling, coaching, scaffolding, articulation, and reflection.

Situated learning. The teaching of cognitive and metacognitive skills specific to an academic discipline.

We have already discussed *modeling* in connection with the important work of cognitive social learning theorists. For novice learners in reading, math, or writing, modeling means they *see and hear* their teachers explain how they go about doing things. They hear their teacher thinking through a math problem. They hear and see their teacher as he reads a piece of writing and figures out how to revise it. They listen to their teacher as she explains how she determined the main ideas of a story. The challenge to the teacher is to make explicit these thinking skills, which are usually carried out automatically and covertly.

How can I model for my learners the thinking strategies they will need to solve real-world problems?

Consider how you would model for your learners the thinking strategies used to solve the following problem: "The price of bananas is four for 51 cents. What is the cost of one dozen bananas?" An expert math problem solver might think aloud to her learners like this: "Well, how do you solve a problem like this? What does the problem tell me? I know four bananas cost 51 cents. One way in which to find out how much a dozen cost is to find out the price of one banana. How can I find out how much one banana costs?"

The teacher then writes on the board while speaking to the class: "Let's see, 51 cents divided by 4 equals 12.75 cents for one banana. Now, if I multiply 12.75 cents by 12 bananas, I'll get the cost of all the bananas. So, the cost of a dozen bananas is $1.53. By finding out how much one banana costs, I can find out how much any number of bananas cost."

Coaching occurs during apprenticeships when a teacher observes his learners' attempts to imitate expert problem solving, writing, or reading while he offers feedback, hints, and guidance. As the teacher watches the learners, he may offer additional modeling, explanation, or suggestions.

Scaffolding is a technique for providing guidance to learners as they practice. The key to good scaffolding is to achieve the right balance between too much support and too little. Offering too much help to learners as they attempt to master a strategy can diminish their motivation to complete the task on their own, while providing too little assistance can quickly lead to frustration (Rosenshine & Meister, 1992).

Scaffolding occurs when a teacher recognizes that a learner is in need of assistance and offers prompts, suggestions, and hints to help the learner solve the problem. As soon as the teacher sees that the "scaffold" is working, she gradually begins to remove the prompts and cues used to construct it. Expert scaffolding requires that the teacher be familiar with the demands of the task, and that she anticipate the difficulties the learners are likely to encounter.

The accompanying box, *Using Scaffolding,* shows how a teacher uses scaffolding to teach a small group of learners how to read a contour map. Notice how the teacher guides the learners with questions, hints, and cues, and then removes this support as the learners begin to respond correctly.

Good scaffolded instruction involves getting learners to explain the reasoning they used or the steps they went through to solve a particular problem. This is your way of determining if the learner understands the process that you have modeled. This stage of cognitive apprenticeship is called *articulation.* It involves learners' explaining to the class what they are doing. For example, you might ask a learner to think out loud as he is solving a math problem. Or in reading, you might ask a learner to articulate why one sentence is a better topic sentence than another. In the example of scaffolding given in the box, the teacher might ask: "What does it mean when contour lines are very close together? How is this important in planning a trip?"

In the final stage of a cognitive apprenticeship, the teacher asks learners to compare their methods of solving a problem or their use of a particular strategy with that of an expert. This is called *reflection.* In the example of map instruction, the teacher could have given the learners a copy of the route she planned and asked them to compare it to

Using Scaffolding

Teacher: Today we're going to figure out the best route for hiking from Point A to Point B on your contour map. There were five important things to remember in doing this. Who remembers one of them?

Tammy: Notice elevation changes.

Teacher: Good. Why is that important and how do you figure that out?

Rose: The steeper the trail, the longer it takes to reach your destination. The closer the contour lines are together, the steeper is the terrain. So on this map (points to a particular area), the terrain gets real steep right here.

Teacher: What's another thing to consider when planning your route?

Toby: Water.

Teacher: What about it?

Jonathan: Where the streams are. Which way they're flowing. How fast the water is flowing.

Teacher: Do you remember how we determined the direction of flow? (No answer) It had something to do with how the contour lines look.

Tammy: I know. The stream flows in the opposite direction in which the contour lines come together.

Teacher: OK, so tell me what direction the stream is flowing.

Rose: (Starts to speak and then hesitates.)

Teacher: Find where the contour lines join. OK. What do you notice about where the lines point?

Rose: They go this way.

Teacher: So which way does the stream flow? (Rose points) Good. Now how do we gauge how fast the water is flowing in the stream? (No response) Recall that you have to consider two things. (Pause . . . no response) One is to select a mile section of the stream and the other is . . . (pauses)

Tammy: How far the land drops from beginning to end of that section.

Teacher: So, how fast is the water flowing?

---

the one they had chosen. The teacher would then ask each learner to describe the steps he or she used to plan the route, to compare them with the teacher's route.

Reciprocal teaching. Teaching that provides alternative representations or elaborations of the content to be learned through the vehicle of group discussion.

How can I use group discussion to allow learners to create their own representations and elaborations of the content to be learned?

Example: Reciprocal Teaching. Cognitive apprenticeship can be applied in your classroom with a strategy called **reciprocal teaching** (Palincsar, 1987). Reciprocal teaching provides alternative representations or elaborations of the content to be learned through the vehicle of group discussion. At the center of reciprocal teaching are group discussions in which students and teacher take turns leading discussions about the text. Gall (1984) observed that most discussion that takes place in classrooms amounts to little more than recitation of facts by students with the aid of question-and-answer sequences in which all or most of the answers are known. This leaves little opportunity for students to construct their own meaning and interpretation of content in order to reach higher levels of understanding. Most classroom discussions are further driven by content in the text, representing rapid-fire questions and answers that stay close to the facts as they are organized and presented in the textbook.

Reciprocal teaching attempts to make class discussion into a more productive and self-directed learning experience. It accomplishes this through four activities—*predicting, questioning, summarizing,* and *clarifying*—which unfold in the following sequence, as described by Palincsar and Brown (1989). In the *predicting* stage, the discussion begins by generating predictions about the content to be learned from the text based on

Reciprocal teaching provides learners with an opportunity to construct their own meanings from what they read.

(a) its title or subheading in the text, (b) the group's prior knowledge about the topic, and (c) the group's experience with similar kinds of information.

After the group members predict what they expect to learn from the text, the group reads and listens to a portion of it. Next comes the *questioning* stage, in which one learner leads a discussion of each portion of the text that was read. The discussion leader asks questions about the information in the text, and students respond and raise additional questions.

In the *summarizing* stage, the discussion leader summarizes the text, and other students are invited to comment or elaborate on the summary. In the final, *clarifying* stage, points are discussed until clarity is achieved. In this case, more predictions may be made and portions of the text may be reread for greater clarity.

The accompanying box, *Employing Reciprocal Teaching,* illustrates the four activities of predicting, questioning, summarizing, and clarifying that comprise reciprocal teaching. Notice how the teacher supports the students' participation in the dialogue. The teacher's aim is to engage as many students as possible in the learning process. This is accomplished by elaborating on student responses and allowing ample opportunity for students to participate in the dialogue from their own perspectives. As the discussion continues, more responsibility for reading and developing the dialogue is gradually given over to the students until, over time, the teacher becomes more of an advisor—or coach—whose role is to refine, not provide, the appropriate responses. By the end of the discussion, the students' responses represent their own internalizations of the text.

The goal of reciprocal teaching is to sufficiently engage students in the learning process, by whatever means, so that they become conscious of their reasoning process and refine it through their own, other students', and the teacher's modeling of that process in the context of classroom dialogues. To attain this goal, teacher and learners together must continually monitor both the meanings students are deriving from the text and the ongoing dialogue. The teacher must also continually adjust the instructional content to meet the students' current levels of understanding. As students gradually accept the shift in responsibility from teacher to student, the teacher reduces the amount of explaining, explicitness of cues, and prompting that marked the earlier part of the les-

Employing Reciprocal Teaching

Teacher: (reading from text) The pipefish change their color and movements to blend with their surroundings. For example, pipefish that live among green plants change their color to a shade of green to match the plants.

Claire: (leading the discussion) One question that I had about this paragraph is: What is special about the way the pipefish looks?

Teacher: (clarifying) Do you mean the way that it is green?

Andy: (elaborating) It's not just that it's green; it's that it's the same color as the plants around it, all around it.

Claire: (continuing) Yes, that's it. My summary of this part tells how the pipefish looks and that it looks like what is around it. My prediction is that this is about its enemies and how it protects itself and who the enemies are.

Monty: (adding to the summary) They also talked about how the pipefish moves. . . .

Keith: (rejoining) It sways back and forth.

Andy: (adding) Along with the other plants.

Teacher: (questioning) What do we call it when something looks like and acts like something else? The way that the walking stick was yesterday? We clarified this word when we talked about the walking stick.

Angel: Mimic.

Teacher: That's right. We said we would say that the pipefish mimics the . . .

Students: (together) Plants.

Teacher: OK! Let's see if Claire's predictions come true. (Class turns to the text.)

Source: Based on Palincsar & Brown, 1989, pp. 42–43.

son. Figure 6.6 lists and describes some classroom activities that represent the gradual shift of responsibility from teacher to learner during reciprocal teaching. The accompanying box, *Using Reciprocal Teaching*, presents some key summary points.

Cooperative Learning

Cooperative learning. A teaching method that uses heterogeneous groups of learners who are responsible for one another's learning with respect to a common goal.

Cooperative learning is a teaching activity that involves a heterogeneous group of students who are responsible for one another's learning of a common goal (Slavin, 1991). In most classrooms, learning is not cooperative but, rather, individualistic or competitive. *Individualistic learning* occurs when the student works independently to achieve some learning goal. The success or failure of this effort depends on the learner's efforts and is unaffected by the achievement or lack of achievement of other class members. In *competitive learning* classrooms, student performance is judged against the typical or average performance of all class members. Grades are assigned as a reference to the performance of the class as a whole.

In cooperative learning, students are organized into small groups, each with an objective to accomplish. The lessons are structured so that the group objective can only be achieved if all group members perform their assigned tasks. A learner's final grade is a combination of the group score and an individual score. Slavin (1991) has found that such groups attain higher levels of academic achievement across a variety of subject areas in comparison to more traditional classroom learning structures (Fantuzzo, King, & Heller, 1992).

Cooperative learning, like other constructivist approaches, is suitable when the teacher's goals involve the learning of problem-solving skills, cognitive strategies, meta-

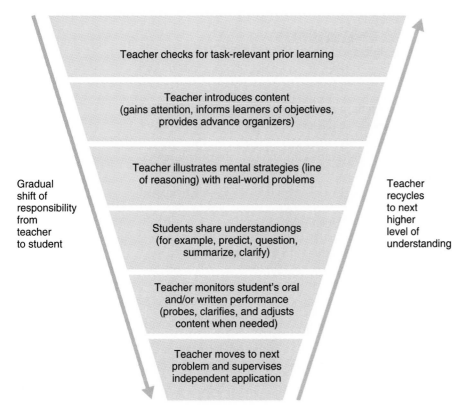

Figure 6.6
Techniques for shifting responsibility from teachers to learners. *Source:* From *Effective Teaching Methods* (3rd ed.), by G. Borich (1996). Reprinted by permission of Prentice-Hall Publishers.

cognitive knowledge, or social interaction skills. It is not an efficient method for learning factual knowledge or simple procedural routines, such as subtraction or multiplication skills (Pasch et al., 1991).

Basic Features. Cooperative learning encompasses a variety of cooperative learning models. Several specific cooperative learning activities suggested by Slavin are listed in the accompanying box, *Using Cooperative Learning Activities.* Each of these activities incorporates the most important features of a cooperative learning lesson: heterogeneous grouping, positive interdependence, individual accountability, and interpersonal skills (Cohen, 1986). Let's now look more closely at each of these.

During cooperative learning, students are arranged into *heterogeneous groups* of four to five learners. Group members should be diverse in terms of gender, ethnicity, scholastic achievement, and interpersonal skills. The teacher thereby ensures that each group contains a range of achievement levels in the subject area, gender and ethnic proportions that reflect the composition of the class as a whole, and a mixture of socially assertive and nonassertive learners. Slavin and others have found that such arrangements not only promote high levels of scholastic achievement; they also have positive effects on intergroup relations and self-esteem (Schmuck & Schmuck, 1992; Slavin, 1991).

How do I plan cooperative learning lessons so that the group goal is achieved while individual group members take responsibility for their own learning?

Applying Your Knowledge:

Using Reciprocal Teaching

- Remember that the acquisition of the strategies employed in reciprocal teaching is a joint responsibility shared by the teacher and students.
- The teacher initially assumes major responsibility for teaching these strategies (the teacher "thinks aloud" how to make a prediction, ask a question, summarize, and clarify) but gradually transfers responsibility to the students for demonstrating use of the strategies.
- All students are expected to participate in the discussion and are given the opportunity to lead. The teacher encourages participation by supporting students in a variety of ways. For example, the teacher might prompt the student, provide additional information, or alter (raise or lower) the level of demand on the student so that a response meaningful to the student can be achieved.
- Throughout the lesson, the teacher consciously monitors the success with which comprehension is occurring and adjusts the content as needed.

Cooperative learning lessons should foster *positive interdependence.* In other words, activities are planned so that group members depend on one another for the accomplishment of the group's goal. If, for example, the objective of the lesson is to conduct a critical review of *Lord of the Flies,* then each group member is assigned a different responsibility. For example, one member may examine characters; another, plot. One member may be responsible for synthesizing the ideas discussed, while another writes them down. Each member must complete his or her task, or the group will not achieve its goal. Table 6.1 lists some cooperative student roles that can be assigned to encourage positive interdependence, suggested by Johnson and Johnson (1991).

Positive interdependence can also be achieved when each learner receives a group participation grade in addition to an individual grade. For example, individuals can rate each other on a five-point scale that measures active group involvement. The average of all scores assigned by the team members would be each learner's score for individual effort. Another method is for you to rate the group's end product on a five-point scale. Sample scales for measuring group and individual effort are illustrated in Figure 6.7. Scores from these scales can be recorded either independently of one another (e.g., individual effort = 4, group product = 5) or as a ratio (e.g., 4/5 = .80). If the ratio method is chosen, each individual in the group is given the same group score, determined either by you or by averaging all group members' evaluations of each other. Ratios smaller

Using Cooperative Learning Activities

Following are examples of four cooperative learning activities you can use in your classroom.

Students Teams-Achievement Divisions

1. Teacher presents content in lecture or discussion
2. Teams work through problems/questions on worksheets
3. Teacher gives quiz over material studied
4. Teacher determines team average and individual improvement scores

Teams-Games Tournament

1. Teacher presents content in lecture or discussion
2. Teams work through problems/questions on worksheets
3. Teams play academic games against each other for points
4. Teacher tallies team points over four-week period to determine best team and best individual scores

Jigsaw

1. Students read section of text and are assigned unique topics
2. Students within teams with same topic meet in "expert groups"
3. Students return to "home" group to share knowledge of their topic with teammates
4. Students take quiz over each topic discussed
5. Individual quizzes are used to create team scores and individual improvement scores

Team-Assisted Individualization

1. Students are given diagnostic test exercise by student monitor to determine placement in materials
2. Students work through assigned unit at their own pace
3. Teammate checks text against answers and student monitor gives quiz
4. Team quizzes are averaged and number of units completed are counted by monitor to create team scores

than 1.0 indicate that the group product exceeded this individual's contribution. Ratios greater than 1.0 indicate that the individual's contribution exceeded the group product.

One reservation expressed about cooperative learning concerns whether individual learners will feel responsible for their own learning or, instead, let others do all the work. However, cooperative learning builds *individual accountability* through peer pressure and individual assessments. For the group to succeed, every member has to fulfill his or her assigned responsibilities. If one student slacks off, every group member's grade or evaluation suffers. In addition, teachers give learners individual tests or assignments to assess learning and rate the performance of each member in terms of how it contributes to overall group success. Thus, each student's final grade includes a group grade, an individual test grade, and a rating of how well he performed certain interpersonal skills important for positive group functioning.

The final feature of a cooperative learning lesson is the teaching and evaluating of *interpersonal skills.* Effective group functioning requires that learners be prepared to elicit and listen to one another's opinions, reflect on what has been said, give reasons for their statements, and allow everyone to contribute (Cohen, 1986). Thus a central feature of cooperative learning is preparing learners to cooperate. The accompanying box, *Teaching Collaborative Skills,* suggests some ways you can teach these important skills in your classroom.

1. How active was _____ in helping the group attain its final product?

_____ very active
_____ fairly active
_____ somewhat active
_____ not too active
_____ not active at all

2. How complete (or accurate, or useful, or original) is this group's final product?

_____ very complete
_____ fairly complete
_____ somewhat complete
_____ not too complete
_____ not complete at all

Figure 6.7
Simple scales for evaluating individual and group effort in a collaborative learning activity. *Source:* From *Effective Teaching Methods* (3rd ed.), by G. Borich (1996). Reprinted by permission of Prentice-Hall Publishers.

An Example. Finally, we will illustrate some of the steps you would follow to plan a cooperative learning lesson. Our example concerns a high school English teacher named Mr. Fox, who decided to include cooperative learning lessons in his unit on characterization in *Lord of the Flies.* Excerpts from the lesson described here can be seen on the videotape that accompanies this text, *What Teachers Need To Know.*

Table 6.1

Student Roles in Cooperative Learning

1. *Summarizer*—paraphrases and plays back to the group major conclusions to see if the group agrees and to prepare for (rehearse) the group's contribution before the whole class.
2. *Checker*—checks controversial or debatable statements and conclusions for authenticity against text, workbook, or references. Assures that the group will not be using unsubstantiated facts, or be challenged by more accurate representations of other groups.
3. *Researcher*—reads reference documents and acquires background information when more data are needed (for example, may conduct an interview or seek a resource from the library). The researcher differs from a checker in that the researcher provides critical information for the group to complete its task, while the checker certifies the accuracy of the work in progress and/or after it has been completed.
4. *Runner*—acquires anything needed to complete the task, such as materials, equipment, reference works. Far from a subservient role, this requires creativity, shrewdness, and even cunning to find the necessary resources, which may also be diligently sought by other groups.

5. *Recorder*—commits to writing the major product of the group. The recorder may require individuals to write their own conclusions, in which case the recorder collates, synthesizes, and renders in coherent form the abbreviated work of individual group members.
6. *Supporter*—chosen for his or her upbeat, positive outlook, the supporter praises members when their individual assignments are completed and consoles them in times of discouragement (for example, if proper references can't be found). Keeps the group moving forward by recording major milestones achieved on a chart for all the class to see, identifying progress made, and encouraging efforts of individuals, particularly those who may have difficulty participating or completing their tasks.
7. *Observer/Troubleshooter*—takes notes and records information about the group process that may be useful during whole-class discussion or debriefing. Reports to a class leader or to you when problems appear insurmountable for a group or for individual members.

Source: From Johnson & Johnson, 1991.

Establish Objectives. Mr. Fox set the following objectives for his cooperative learning lessons:

1. Students will be able to associate important human personality traits with each of the main characters.
2. Students will learn a strategy for identifying traits of characters.

Make Organizational Decisions. Mr. Fox decided to set up six groups, with five learners per group, mixed by gender, ethnicity, reading achievement, and level of assertiveness. The groups were arranged in circles, with space between the groups.

The group assignment was to reach consensus regarding what each character represents and then summarize to the class what was said within each group about the following questions:

1. How would things have been different if only girls were on the island or if there were girls *and* boys?
2. Would there be different personality traits represented among the main characters if girls were on the island?
3. If you were on the island, how would the story be different?

Prepare Materials. Each learner had a copy of the novel and a recording sheet to complete the individual assignment. Each group received a response sheet to record the results of the group assignment.

Determine Individual Roles. Mr. Fox decided to assign the following roles to group members (refer to Table 6.1): observer/troubleshooter, recorder, checker, supporter, and researcher.

Select Procedures. Mr. Fox used the following procedures to conduct the cooperative learning activity:

Reviewing: Begin class with review of main personality traits of characters.

Structuring: Explain goal of lesson. Explain group and individual responsibilities.

Modeling: Demonstrate process of character analysis. Model social skills.

Coaching: Move from group to group. Clarify, model, question, give feedback.

Fading: Gradually let groups work more and more independently.

Conduct Evaluation. Each group turned in a completed worksheet, and each student turned in his or her own worksheet analyzing each character. Using a rating sheet, Mr. Fox rated each learner's performance of the following social skills during the lesson: (1) completes role responsibility; (2) uses praise; (3) explains concisely; (4) disagrees appropriately; (5) asks for clarification.

Direct Explanation Teaching

Direct explanation teaching is a label for a variety of teaching methods that make explicit to learners at the outset of a lesson the academic competencies, strategies, generalizations, or procedures to be taught (Pressley, 1995; Roehler & Duffy, 1984). It encompasses such teaching models as *expository learning* (Ausubel & Robinson, 1969)

Direct explanation teaching. A variety of teaching methods that make explicit to learners at the outset of a lesson the academic competencies, strategies, generalizations, or procedures to be taught.

Teaching Collaborative Skills

1. **Teach learners how to communicate their own ideas and feelings.** Encourage the use of "I" and "my" to let students know it is *their* ideas and feelings that make the collaborative process work. Show how personal experiences (events observed, problems encountered, people met) constitute a valued form of information that can be used to support and justify their own ideas and feelings.

2. **Make messages complete and specific.** Each statement should include a frame of reference, perspective, or experience. For example, "I got this idea while traveling through a Pueblo Indian reservation in southern Colorado during our vacation last summer." Or, "I heard the President speak, and his main point reminded me of. . . ."

3. **Make verbal and nonverbal messages congruent with one another.** Establish a serious tone and make it clear that hidden meanings and snide remarks are not acceptable. In other words, indicate that voice and body language should always reinforce the message being conveyed and that communicating serious information comically and overdramatizing confuse both the message and the listener.

4. **Convey an atmosphere of respect and support.** Demonstrate that all students can contribute information, ideas, feelings, personal experiences, and reactions without fear of ridicule. Make clear that unsupportive behaviors are not allowed. Show that cooperation rests on sharing both emotional and physical resources, receiving help, dividing responsibility, and looking out for one another's well-being.

5. **Demonstrate how to determine if the message was properly received.** Teach your learners how to ask for feedback from listeners. For example, use phrases such as, "What do you think about what I said?" "Does what I said make sense?" "Can you see what I'm trying to say?" The more listeners are asked to paraphrase the message, the more the sender can be sure the message has been received as intended.

6. **Teach learners how to paraphrase another's point of view.** Most learners will agree or disagree with the speaker without checking to see if they have understood the message. Teach students to paraphrase messages before they decide to criticize or support them.

7. **Demonstrate how to negotiate meanings and understandings.** Often one's understanding of a message must be corrected, or fine-tuned, because the message was ambiguous, incomplete, or misinterpreted. This means that paraphrases must sometimes be recycled and brought to a higher level of understanding, for the benefit of both sender and receiver. Teach learners to use tactful phrases such as, "What I meant to say is . . ."; "What I forgot to add was. . . ."

8. **Teach participation and leadership.** Communicate the importance of the following elements of group process (Johnson & Johnson, 1991, p. 135):

   Mutual benefit—what benefits the group benefits the individual.

   Common fate—each individual wins or loses on the basis of the group's overall performance.

   Shared identity—everyone is a member of a group, emotionally as well as physically.

   Joint celebration—everyone obtains satisfaction from the progress of individual group members.

   Mutual responsibility—be concerned about group members who underperform.

and *reception learning* (Ausubel, 1977), and includes some elements of the *direct teaching model* (Rosenshine & Stevens, 1986).

Many have questioned whether direct explanation is "constructive enough" to be identified as a constructivist instructional practice. Pressley explains its constructivist roots this way:

> Direct explanation is a decidedly constructivist approach: Students do not passively learn from explanations but rather actively learn from them. They do not completely

understand what the teacher is saying or doing, but the teacher's explanation and modeling are a starting point for the student. As the student struggles with the process the teacher modeled, he or she adapts it to the particular tasks at hand and modifies it in ways that are sensible to him or her. If a classroom of children hears and watches a demonstration (e.g., of multiplication of fractions) and then practices what was taught in the lesson, there will be much struggling, adaptation, and reflection on the part of the students, with the result that at the end of the instructional day, all will have somewhat different understandings of multiplication of fractions. . . . Our view is that direct explanation is . . . the start of active exploration. (Pressley, Harris, & Marks, 1992, pp. 7–8)

Basic Features. The most critical feature of direct explanation is the teacher's description, modeling, or demonstration of cognitive strategies. The teacher models the use of cognitive strategies in an authentic context and in an authentic manner. The students hear and see the teacher struggle with the task and arrive at new strategies to accomplish it. Students thus deepen their understanding and appreciation for the significance of the "cognitive struggle" in learning when they observe teachers coping with difficult tasks (Schunk, Hanson, & Cox, 1987). The key ingredients of direct explanation teaching are up-front demonstration and explanation of the lesson goal, mental modeling of authentic problem solving, guided practice, and provision of metacognitive information. Let's learn more about each of these.

Up-front Demonstration and Explanation. Up-front demonstration and explanation of the lesson goal requires that the teacher begin the class by telling learners what they should expect to get out of the lesson. Many models of good teaching emphasize the importance of capturing learners' attention at the start of a lesson and letting them know what they are going to accomplish. Hunter (1982) refers to this as *anticipatory set*. During this phase of direct explanation teaching, the teacher presents a task to learners that requires the use of a problem-solving strategy. The teacher informs the students that they will need the strategy to complete the assignment and then explains the strategy to them.

Mental Modeling of Authentic Problem Solving. During mental modeling of authentic problem solving, the teacher thinks aloud to the learners and shows them how to apply a particular cognitive strategy. However, mental modeling involves more than just thinking aloud. It also involves saying things that indicate to learners that you are struggling or puzzling over the task. Statements like, "I'm stuck at this point. I have no idea where to go. What should I do next?" make this clear to learners. The problem should be authentic—that is, one that people encounter in their daily lives.

Guided Practice. During guided practice, the teacher uses prompts, questions, and hints to get learners to use the strategy that was modeled. Feedback, praise, and encouragement from the teacher accompany the learner's efforts. The level of assistance is determined using scaffolding techniques. As learners become more successful using the strategy, the teacher gradually fades the "scaffold" by providing fewer hints, questions, and prompts until the learner can use the strategy independently.

Metacognitive Information. In the previous chapter we discussed the importance of teaching cognitive strategies to learners so that they can become good thinkers. We also pointed out that learners do not always use strategies, despite their proven effectiveness. Therefore, during direct explanation instruction, teachers provide learners with metacognitive information about the strategy they are using. For example, one would model when and where to use them and how to notice or monitor whether they are helping. This involves (1) showing learners how to assess or monitor the effectiveness of a strategy, (2) prompting them to attribute their own improvement in performance to the strategy, and (3) prompting them to make a commitment to use the strategy in the future.

An Example. The following classroom dialogue illustrates the steps in a direct explanation lesson.

Step 1: Introduce the Lesson. "Today we're going to write something on great conquerors in history. Now, I bet you're thinking, 'I don't know anything about great conquerors.' That's a common reaction of a lot of writers, even those who write for newspapers like this one." (Holds up a copy of the local paper.) "Today you're going to learn that you know a lot more than you think. I'm going to show you how to search your memories for what you know about a topic. At the end of the lesson you will be surprised by how much you know about great conquerors and will be ready to write about them."

Step 2: Introduce the Strategy. "To show you how to do this, give me a topic to write about that you don't think I know anything about." (Student raises hand and says "rock stars of today.") "That's a good one. Now listen while I ask myself questions to search my memory for what I know about rock stars of today."

Step 3: Mental Modeling. "First, I'll try to search my memory for the name of a rock star. I can't think of the name of even one! So, I say to myself, 'Has anything happened in the news recently about a rock star?' Wait! I remember reading about Kurt Cobain! By asking myself a question about current events, I was able to remember Cobain's name. But, what do I know about Cobain and his music? So, I ask myself, 'What did the paper say?' I remember reading that he died. But what kind of music did he play? I know the article said something about his music, but I can't remember. OK. What different kinds of music are there? I know there's heavy metal, alternative rock, grunge rock. That's it. Now I remember. Cobain played grunge rock."

Step 4: Provide Guided Practice. "Now let's use this strategy for searching your memories to find out what you know about great conquerors. Look at the overhead to help you. It shows the steps I used." (Students view overhead listing cues to jog their memories.) "OK, Pete, show me how to use this strategy to find out what you know about conquerors." (Pete mentally models the use of the strategy and comes up with the names Genghis Kahn, Attila, and Caesar.) "Good job, Pete. Now, let's see if someone can use the strategy when they don't see the overhead." (Teacher turns off the projector, fading support.) "Would someone else like to use the strategy to search their memory for the names of great conquerors? Maria, what would you do first to help you recall what you know?" (Maria hesitates.) "What's something you could say to yourself to get your memory working?" (Teacher builds scaffold of support for Maria.) Maria says, "Recall stories I've read about history and wars." "That's good, Maria."

Step 5: Teach Metacognitive Knowledge. (At the end of the lesson.) "Now that you've used the strategy to search your memory, I bet you're surprised at what you remembered. Think back to the start of the lesson when you thought you didn't know anything about great conquerors." (Teacher got learners to monitor strategy effectiveness.) "Did you remember more than you thought? Well, that was the strategy working for you. (Teacher prompted learners to attribute improvement to the strategy.) "Now that you used the strategy successfully, you have to be sure to use it with other writing tasks. What other topics might you want to write about where this strategy could help you?" (Student offers suggestion.) "Current events! That's a good example. How might you use the strategy if you have to write something about the presidential election?" (Teacher provides metacognitive information about the strategy, when and where to use it, and how to monitor it.)

Summary: Designing Constructivist Learning Environments

In this chapter we have discussed a number of teaching practices that allow learners to be active during learning, construct knowledge and meaning for themselves, and control their own learning. We discussed four models of constructivist teaching: discovery learning, cognitive apprenticeship, cooperative learning, and direct explanation teaching. Whether you decide to use one of these models or "construct" your own from elements of each, a commitment to constructivist teaching will involve:

1. Focusing on lesson content that teaches metacognitive knowledge.
2. Using teaching methods that promote learner activation.
3. Presenting lessons that teach learners to seek alternative methods and explanations.
4. Allowing learners to learn with and from their peers.
5. Emphasizing intrinsic motivation for learning so that students value learning for the meaning it has in their own lives.

In the next chapter we will take up the issue of intrinsic motivation and its integral role in constructivist teaching.

Summing Up

This chapter introduced you to constructivist theory and teaching methods. Its main points were these:

- Current cognitive models of learning and thinking stipulate that the mind learns not by passively recording or absorbing, but by actively trying to make sense of information.
- *Constructivism* is a term used by cognitive psychologists for how learners acquire meaning and understanding by organizing information for themselves, connecting it to other information, and storing it as networks or schemata.
- Cognitive psychologists view prior knowledge as a cognitive structure—or schema—that learners build for themselves. The teacher's role is to help learners gain entry to that knowledge, understand its conceptions and misconceptions, and swap inappropriate cognitive structures for better ones.
- An advance organizer is a summary of the concepts, generalizations, and themes to be learned presented at a general and inclusive level.
- Authentic problems are real-world problems that involve hands-on exercises for which the solution is uncertain. Authentic learning tasks yield multiple solutions, each with advantages and disadvantages.

- Students become intentional learners when they find their own approaches or systems for achieving educational goals. This involves the ability to find and allocate resources for learning, overcoming obstacles to learning, monitoring their own work, and knowing how to sustain effort.
- Genuine knowledge construction is a joint cognitive venture focused on a clear cognitive goal. Different components of the venture are carried out by various classroom participants: learner, peers, and teachers.
- When tests are embedded within a lesson, learners receive immediate feedback, more easily see the connection between what was taught and what is tested, and understand that testing is an integral part of learning.
- Discovery learning is a teaching strategy in which learners discover the relationships among facts, concepts, and generalizations, rather than receiving them in a final, organized form.
- Cognitive apprenticeship is a model of teaching in which learners become more skilled at gathering and using knowledge for themselves by observing experts.
- Cooperative learning is a teaching strategy in which heterogeneous groups of learners work together to accomplish a common goal.
- Direct explanation teaching represents a variety of teaching methods that make explicit to learners at the outset of a lesson the academic competencies, strategies, generalizations, or procedures to be taught.

For Discussion and Practice

°1. Using your knowledge of the learning theorists studied in Chapters 4, 5, and 6, how would you categorize the respective approaches used by Mr. Robbins and Mrs. Greer to teach their lessons on fractions?

°2. In your own words and using an example from the classroom, explain what is meant by the term *constructivism.*

3. Provide an example of how you might involve your students in learning a primary concept, generalization, or underlying theme by building connections among ideas and facts.

°4. Identify several conceptual themes around which you might organize a lesson. What is the advantage of teaching concepts, generalizations, and underlying themes that span isolated bits of knowledge?

5. Identify two different advance organizers that you might use to introduce a lesson in your teaching area. How would they help your students recall prior knowledge?

°6. Explain what is meant by creating "conceptual conflict." With what Piagetian concept do you associate this term?

7. Provide some examples of lesson topics that would create conceptual conflict.

°8. Compose a writing assignment for your grade or subject that represents the ambiguity, complexity, uncertainty, and multiple solutions required for meaningful learning to occur.

Questions marked with an asterisk are answered in the appendix.

*9.   According to Bruner, what does good teaching involve? How did Mrs. Greer's lesson at the beginning of the chapter embody Bruner's concept of good teaching?

10.   Plan a lesson by indicating how you would address each of the following features to promote discovery learning: instructional set, motivational set, knowledge base, multiple examples, and hierarchically organized curriculum.

11.   Write the outline of a lesson plan for a cooperative learning activity in which you identify the lesson topic; establish its objectives; indicate your decisions pertaining to group size, arrangement, and assignment; specify materials; and determine individual student roles.

12.   Write a brief classroom dialogue using direct explanation in which you (1) conduct a demonstration and explanation and (2) mentally model an authentic problem.

Suggested Readings

Brooks, J. G., & Brooks, M. G. (1993). *The case for constructivist classrooms.* Alexandria, VA: Association for Supervision and Curriculum Development. These authors have a wealth of experience with educational programs built upon constructivist learning principles. Their text offers many concrete examples of how these principles can be put into practice.

Resnick, L.B. (Ed.). (1989). *Knowing, learning, and instruction: Essays in Honor of Robert Glaser.* Hillsdale, NJ: Lawrence Erlbaum. Essays by leading researchers in the field of cognitive approaches to classroom learning. It offers numerous real-world examples of good cognitive instruction.

Steffe, L. P., & Gale, J. (Eds.). (1995). *Constructivism in education.* Hillsdale, NJ: Lawrence Erlbaum. A series of essays by some of the leading philosophers and educators concerned about constructivism in education.

Motivation and Classroom Learning

- How can I help my learners interpret their classroom setbacks in ways that elicit renewed effort?
- What are some things teachers say to learners that can lower their motivation to succeed?
- How can learning strategies improve my students' motivation to learn?
- How can I convey to my students the motivation to say "Yes, I can do what my teacher expects"?
- How can I enhance my learners' determination to learn what I teach?
- How can I use project-based learning to motivate my learners?

B ehavioral and cognitive psychologists agree that motivation is essential for learning. Yet how to motivate learners in the classroom continues to be one of the most puzzling problems confronting the teacher. Let's look in on Professor Thomas's learning seminar as his students discuss the topic of motivation.

Betty: Well, it seems to me that motivation is becoming the scapegoat for all learning failures. That's all I hear at school . . . "These kids just aren't motivated" or "This kid just hasn't any motivation." And all the other teachers nod as if something profound has been said.

Roselia: I don't understand your problem with that. I say the same thing every day after my fourth-period class. Those kids just aren't motivated!

Betty: What gets to me is that I hear teachers talking about motivation as if they haven't any responsibility for it, or they believe it's inherited.

Kyle: I agree. We have to look at motivation as something affected by what we do and not as something out of our control.

Professor Thomas: So you agree with the behavioral science tradition on motivation?

Kyle: To the extent that it says a learner's motivation is under our control, yes. But the behaviorists view motivation as something we impose on the person through reinforcement and, if necessary, punishment. I see it as more cognitive.

Leon: So you think it's all inside the person.

Kyle: Not in the sense that we're born with it. To me motivation is how a child thinks about goals, and about his ability to reach them. As teachers, we can influence that.

Janet: But that makes motivation sound so cold and mechanistic. Motivated people have a kind of energy that seems to come from inside them. Motivation isn't just knowing where you want to go and believing you can do it. It's also having the power and vigor to get there.

Professor Thomas: Is this something a teacher can give a learner? And if so, how?

Is motivation an inherited trait like one of the three temperaments (activity, adaptability, emotionality) that we discussed in Chapter 3? Or is motivation influenced by reinforcement and consequences that strengthen some behaviors and weaken others? Is the key to motivating learners a lesson plan that captures their interest and attention? In other words, is motivation something innate that we are born with that can be strengthened by reinforcers external to the learning task, or is it something interwoven with the learning process itself? In Chapter 4 we studied how behavior can be created and strengthened by reinforcers external to the learning task. In this chapter we will focus our attention on intrinsic motivation.

In this chapter you will also learn the meanings of these terms:

antecedents
attribution theory
causal schemata
deficiency/growth needs theory
drive theory
instinct theory
intrinsic motivation
locus of causality
project-based learning
self-determination theory
self-efficacy theory
situational cues

Intrinsic motivation. Motivation to engage in an activity for its own sake.

Intrinsic motivation influences learners to choose a task, get energized about it, and persist until they accomplish it successfully, regardless of whether it brings an immediate reward. Intrinsic motivation is present when learners actively seek out and participate in activities without having to be rewarded by materials or activities outside the learning task. The first-grader who practices handwriting because she likes to see neat, legible letters like those displayed on the letter chart is intrinsically motivated. The fourth-grader who puts together puzzles of states and countries because she likes to see the finished product and wants to learn the names of the capital cities is intrinsically motivated. The ninth-grader who repeats typing drills because he likes the feel of his fingers hopping across the keys, and connects that sense with the sight of correctly spelled words on the page, has intrinsic motivation.

In this chapter we will present a framework for understanding intrinsic motivation and then link this framework to classroom strategies for building it. First, we will describe some early motivational theories that make use of the person-as-machine metaphor. Not all of these theories apply to the classroom, but learning about them will show you how different theorists have approached the problem of motivation. You are sure to find some elements of your own thinking about motivation in each of them.

Next we will examine the current cognitive approaches, which view motivation from the vantage point of the person-as-rational-thinker metaphor. Cognitive motivation theories share strong ties with cognitive learning theories. We will examine two cognitive motivation theories, *attribution theory* and *self-efficacy theory*. Both emphasize that learners need to know, understand, and appreciate what they are doing in order to become motivated. Then, along with these cognitive motivation theories, we will examine a motivational perspective called *self-determination theory,* which attempts to reconcile cognitive theory's emphasis on intrinsic motivation with more traditional notions of human needs and drives. Finally, in the last section of this chapter, you will learn to use an approach to teaching and learning called *project-based learning,* which employs the principles of intrinsic motivation to energize learners.

Before we begin, consider the two most obvious features of the behavior of motivated learners: energy and determination. Motivated learners have more than just a vision of a goal they want to achieve. They have a passion or interest for achieving that goal. Motivated learners initiate actions, expend effort, and persist in that effort. As you become acquainted with the various theories, think about how they apply to your learners and keep this question in mind: How can this theory account for the energy and direction of a motivated learner?

Person-as-Machine: Biobehavioral Motivation Theories

Teacher: Now Jared, do you see why we have to do this stuff?

Jared: It's boring. I really don't care about all this stuff!

Teacher: Jared, do you care about passing this course?

Jared: Is that a threat?

Teacher: Jared, when I was in high school, I had a teacher who said there are only two things in life that are required.

Jared: School is one of them, right?

Teacher: No, death and taxes. You gotta die and you gotta pay taxes. Everything else is optional.

Intrinsic motivation influences learners to engage actively in activities without having to be rewarded. It energizes learners to persist until they accomplish a task successfully.

Jared: So you mean I don't have to do this stuff?

Teacher: You don't have to do this stuff. You don't have to read the paper and know what's going on in the world. You don't have to graduate from high school. You don't have to get a job.

Jared: Brother . . .

Teacher: I'll be happy to help you if you want help.

Jared: I get it. I'll do it! (Adapted from Nehring, 1989, pp. 39–40)

How to win the hearts and minds of learners has been a concern of educational psychologists since the foundation of their science. In any given classroom, some learners will participate enthusiastically while others will not, but the explanation for this disparity is not always apparent. Over the years educational psychologists have used the term "motivation" to account for variations in the energy and direction of learners' behavior. But as we will see, motivation means very different things to different psychologists.

Since no one has ever seen, touched, or weighed motivation, educational psychologists typically use metaphors to help them describe this phenomenon. The use of metaphors to describe complicated mental phenomena is familiar to you from earlier chapters of this book: Piaget uses the "balance" metaphor to help explain cognitive development, and cognitive psychologists use the metaphor of the mind as an information processing system. Likewise, various other metaphors have been the principal source of motivation theory and research (Weiner, 1991).

The earliest theories of motivation assumed that the forces that give energy and direction to human behavior were beyond human control. These theories propose that either internal or external forces beyond our control cause people to display motivated or unmotivated behavior. Weiner (1991) proposes "person-as-machine" as a metaphor for describing these theories.

According to Weiner, the person-as-machine metaphor has the following attributes:

- Machines have parts (a structure).
- There is a desired end or function.
- The whole functions as a unit of mutually interacting parts to reach this end.
- The behaviors are involuntary, or without volition. Hence, the actions are like reflexes.
- The behaviors are performed without conscious awareness.
- The reactions are necessary or predetermined by a set of circumstances or activating stimuli.
- The actions are fixed and routine.
- Forces and energy are transmitted. The forces may be in balance or equilibrium (no tendency to change), or out of balance, promoting a tendency toward change. (Weiner, 1991, p. 922)

By categorizing certain theories of motivation under the person-as-machine metaphor, Weiner alerts us to various distinctive characteristics pertaining to human motivation. The theories that make use of this metaphor include *instinct theory, drive theory,* and *deficiency-growth needs theory* (Zimbardo, 1996). Let's look at what each of these theories has to say about motivation.

Instinct Theory

Instinct theory. An early school of thought about motivation that assumed that individual and collective actions and thoughts were a result of inherited and innate instincts.

Instinct theory was the earliest theory of motivation. *Instincts* are inherited, unlearned forces that help all species survive. Animals like salmon, bears, and turtles are preprogrammed at birth to engage in specific instinctive reproductive and feeding patterns. For example, salmon instinctively return to the same stream in which they were spawned to lay their eggs.

Humans are also born with instincts. The extent to which these instincts are under conscious control has been a subject of vigorous debate. Psychologists like William McDougall (1908) saw instincts as volitional and purposive:

The human mind has certain innate or inherited tendencies which are the essential springs or motive powers of all thought and action, whether individual or collective, and are the bases from which the character and will of individuals and of nations are gradually developed. . . . (p. 20)

McDougall states that instincts are inherited tendencies whose characteristics are *energy, direction,* and *action.*

Freud (1915) disagreed. According to Freud, instincts are neither conscious nor predetermined. They exist to satisfy biological needs and create a certain psychic energy or tension within the individual. This energy is bottled up, under pressure, like steam in a steam engine. It seeks release by driving us to pursue satisfactory (usually sexual) objects. Freud saw life as a struggle between the primal instincts of life (Eros) and death (Thanatos). Followers of Freud, as well as other psychologists, identified thousands of specific instincts by the 1920s (Bernard, 1924).

Instinct theory came under heavy attack in the 1920s and 1930s, especially from cultural anthropologists. These scientists pointed out that what were assumed to be human instincts were really cultural—or learned—patterns of behavior (Benedict, 1959; Mead, 1939). Instinct theory was soon replaced by drive theory as the principal explanation for the energy and direction of human action.

Drive Theory

Clark Hull is the psychologist principally identified with **drive theory** (Hull, 1943). *Drives*, according to Hull, are of two types: primary and acquired. *Primary drives* are forces within the individual that are triggered by biological needs such as hunger and thirst. These drives produce random activity (recall Skinner's animal experiments, described in Chapter 4). This activity is essentially directionless until the need is satisfied. Whatever behavior satisfies the need eventually becomes learned as a habit through the processes of drive reduction and reinforcement.

Acquired drives include desires for money, for love, to play sports, to write, or to create music. They do not spring from a biological need. Rather, they are acquired through a process of association with a primary drive. Drive theory assumes that almost all psychological motives are acquired drives.

Hull believed that all activity is directed toward reducing the tension triggered by needs and drives. Drive reduction, therefore, is the psychological mechanism underlying both activity and learning. Whatever behavior results in lessening the tension (and consequently the drive) will be repeated until it becomes habitual.

The drive theory of motivation provides the foundation for behavioral learning theory and, unlike instinct theory, still has its proponents. Extrinsic reinforcers (for example, money or good grades) are viewed as incentives that activate acquired drives. The behavior that is instrumental in getting each incentive is learned through a combination of both drive reduction and reinforcement processes.

Drive theory. A theory of motivation that is based on the assumption that all activity is directed toward reducing the tension triggered by needs and drives.

Drive theorists would explain the desire to succeed at schoolwork as an acquired drive.

Deficiency/Growth Needs Theory

Deficiency/growth needs theory.
A theory of motivation that posits that humans have an innate hierarchy of needs that drives all activity.

Abraham Maslow's perspective on motivation, **deficiency/growth needs theory,** has both similarities to, and differences from, instinct and drive theory. Like the originators of those theories, Maslow proposes that people are born with innate needs that they strive to satisfy. However, in contrast to Freud and Hull, Maslow (1943, 1970) believes that the ultimate direction of this energy is not simply satisfaction of biological needs or tension reduction but a striving for self-actualization. Consequently, his theory accentuates the positive, intellectual, uplifting (not simply hedonistic) side of human beings. For Maslow, innate forces and an innate hierarchy of needs (both deficiency needs and growth needs) give human behavior its distinctive energy and direction. Figure 7.1 illustrates Maslow's hierarchy of growth and deficiency needs, which range from primitive

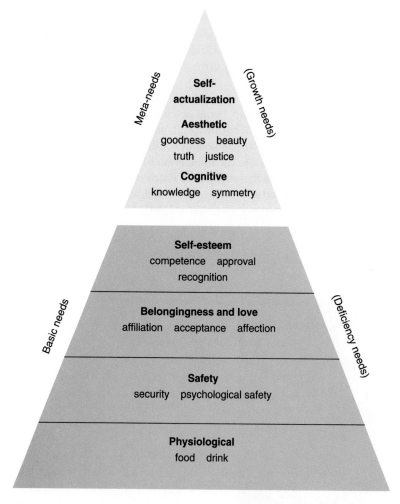

Figure 7.1
Maslow's hierarchy of needs. *Source:* Adapted from "A Theory of Human Motivation," by A. Maslow, 1943, *Psychological Review, 50,* pp. 370–396.

physiological requirements to complex aesthetic and cognitive needs, which Maslow calls *self-actualization.*

Summary

Instinct, drive, and deficiency/growth motivation theories use the machine metaphor to describe motivated behavior. These theories agree that humans, for the most part, give energy and direction to their own behaviors without thinking about it. Instinctual, inherited needs present at birth give behavior its direction. The drive to satisfy these needs explains how behavior becomes energized. Individuals are largely unaware of these two aspects of behavior.

Person-as-Rational-Thinker: Cognitive Motivational Theories

Early motivation theories, such as those just described, use biological and mechanical concepts including drives, energy, tension, and forces to explain the energy and direction of behavior. They present a picture of humans as passive and reactive, at the mercy of internal forces (needs and drives) or external forces (reinforcement and punishment) that they cannot control.

These mechanistic theories have been replaced in the last few decades by theories that use the person-as-rational-thinker metaphor (Weiner, 1980). The two principal examples of these theories are **attribution theory,** developed by Heider (1960), Kelly (1967), and Weiner (1986), and **self-efficacy theory,** whose major proponents are Bandura (1977a, 1982a) and Schunk (1991). Both of these theories posit that motivated behavior can be best explained by reference to conscious cognitive processes involving the ability to anticipate goals and rewards and to the use of judgment, evaluation, and decision making rather than unconscious biological or mechanical processes. Hence, they use the person-as-rational-thinker metaphor. They also allow us to draw parallels with the cognitive theories that we studied in the previous chapters.

Attribution theory. A perspective on motivation that assumes that people seek to understand why they succeed or fail.

Self-efficacy theory. An approach to motivation that emphasizes an individual's personal expectations, internal standards, and self-concept.

Attribution Theory

At this point in your life—if you're like everyone else—you've succeeded at some things and failed at others. Think about one of your more recent successes or triumphs. Were you successful because you really made an effort, had the ability, were lucky, or exercised some combination of the above? Another way to ask this question is this: Do you attribute your success to internal forces (effort, ability) or external forces (luck)?

Now think of one of your failures. Did you fail because you didn't work as hard as you should have, lacked the ability, simply ran into bad luck or difficulties you had no control over, or some combination of these? In other words, do you take personal responsibility for your failure or blame it on someone or something else?

Proponents of attribution theory, like Bernard Weiner (1986), begin their analysis of motivation with the assumption that people inevitably seek to understand why they succeed or fail. In doing so they attribute their accomplishments or losses to a host of antecedents: good or bad luck, difficult or easy tasks, supportive or unfriendly people,

		Locus of causality			
		Internal		**External**	
		Stability			
		Stable	Unstable	Stable	Unstable
C O N T R O L L A B I L I T Y	Uncontrollable	Ability	Mood	Task difficulty	Luck
	Controllable	Typical effort	Immediate effort	Teacher	Unusual help from others

Figure 7.2
Weiner's three-dimensional model of attributions. *Source:* "A Theory of Motivation for Some Classroom Experiences," by B. Weiner, 1979, *Journal of Educational Psychology, 71* (1). Copyright © 1979 by the American Psychological Association. Reprinted by permission.

Locus of causality. In attribution theory, a generalized belief about the causes of success and failure of our actions.

their own hard work or lack thereof, or the degree to which they possess certain abilities. These antecedents are classified in Figure 7.2 as (1) locus of causality, (2) stability, and (3) controllability.

Locus of causality refers to the origin of the cause or causes to which people attribute success or failure. The origin can be either within or outside the person. Effort and ability are internal causes—they originate from within the person. The amount of energy a person expends to accomplish a goal is under that person's control. Innate ability also comes from within and is relatively immune to outside influence. People who attribute their success or failure to either of these two causes are said to be *internally oriented.*

Luck or degree of task difficulty are the typical external causes to which we attribute success or failure. If you believe you passed your last exam because it was easy (degree of difficulty) or because the professor just happened to choose questions you had studied (luck), you are using external causes to account for your success. Similarly, if a girl attributes her failure to make the baseball team to bad weather (luck) or the weight of the baseball bat (degree of difficulty), she is using external causes for her failure. Should this be a persistent feature of her thinking, we would label her locus of causality *externally oriented.*

Stability is another dimension of causal attributes. Some causal attributes can be changed, while others cannot. You can change the amount of effort you put into a task; you can get more help; you can study a different way. These are changeable attributes. However, if you attribute failure to your lack of innate ability you implicate a cause that is relatively unchangeable and stable.

The final dimension is *controllability.* Sometimes we attribute success or failure to antecedents that are out of our control. IQ is an example of an uncontrollable cause. So is luck. Effort, on the other hand, is something we have control over.

Learners seek to understand why they succeed or fail. They may attribute success or failure to factors in or out of their control.

As you can see, attributes can be classified along all three dimensions. Luck, therefore, is an uncontrollable, unstable, external cause of success or failure, while effort is a controllable, stable, internal cause of success or failure (refer to Figure 7.2).

Attributions and Motivated Behavior. You are probably asking yourself what these causes of success or failure have to do with motivation. Weiner believes that your causal attributions affect your future efforts to succeed at any given task. According to Weiner, your attributions produce both emotional reactions regarding your future performance and expectations for success or failure. These emotional reactions and expectations explain both the energy and direction that characterize your motivated behavior. Figure 7.3 depicts Weiner's attributional model of motivation.

Attribution theory implies that the energy that drives motivated behavior comes from two sources: (1) an inherited, biologically based drive to achieve success and avoid failure (Atkinson, 1957, 1964); and (2) an emotional reaction to your cognitive appraisal of past achievements and defeats. These emotional reactions affect subsequent behavior. They either energize or restart efforts to achieve.

The direction of motivated behavior—the goals or accomplishments you pursue—derives from the following factors:

- past experiences with tasks
- the causal attribution of success or failure that you made during these tasks
- your expectations about what is likely to happen the next time you face a similar situation

For example, consider Evelyn, an eleventh-grader who is being encouraged by her teacher to take a course in calculus. Evelyn likes to try new things. She likes challenges.

Figure 7.3
Model of attributions and motivated behavior.

Her parents describe her as always having had a strong need to please and to achieve. She consistently earns high grades on both classroom and standardized math tests. Evelyn, however, is reluctant to take the course, and this puzzles both her parents and her teacher.

As it turns out, she took an advanced level algebra class in tenth grade and earned a C. She found the work difficult, and it required skills she had not learned in ninth-grade algebra. Furthermore, the teacher graded on a curve, and there were many eleventh- and twelfth-grade learners in the class. The tests were multiple choice, and Evelyn dislikes multiple-choice tests, believing they give an advantage to the good guesser over the good thinker.

Evelyn attributed her low grades to two causes: task difficulty and luck. The work was hard and so were the tests. In addition, she was unfortunately matched against older and better-prepared learners. Moreover, Evelyn felt that the tests rewarded good guessing (luck), and she considered herself a poor guesser. She felt discouraged, frustrated, and angry.

In deciding whether to take calculus, Evelyn didn't see how things would be much different. She felt unprepared for such a tough course. Some of her friends from last year had failed it. She believed the grading system and tests would be the same this year.

Weiner believes that Evelyn's feelings of anger and discouragement and her low expectations for success are the direct result of her causal attributions, not of the situation itself. Evelyn attributed her C grade to causes that were uncontrollable, unstable, and external (luck, task difficulty). Given these attributions for failure, it is no wonder that she was reluctant and unmotivated to try calculus.

Two issues arise from Evelyn's predicament. First, what leads learners like Evelyn to decide whether effort or ability, luck or task difficulty, and circumstances outside or within their control are the causes of success or failure? What are they looking at, perceiving, or sensing that influences their choice of attributions? Second, since causal inferences affect learner motivation, what can you do to influence them? As we will see, answering the first question provides clues to the second.

Antecedents of Causal Attributions. As we have pointed out, people are naturally curious about **antecedents** behind their success or failure. School learners are especially interested in this question and typically assign blame or credit to task difficulty ("That teacher is easy" or "He never passes anyone"), effort ("I was too tired to study"), luck ("I guess I studied the right things"), or mood ("I had a fight with my girlfriend and couldn't concentrate") (Bar-Tal, 1979).

> **Antecedents.** Stimuli present in an environment that make a behavior more likely to occur.

How do learners decide what causes them to pass or fail tests, get A's, C's, or F's on assignments, or receive good or poor course grades? On what basis do they assign success or failure to internal or external causes, stable or unstable characteristics, and controllable or uncontrollable factors? Weiner (1977) maintains that learners' attributions spring from three general sources of information: (1) *situational cues,* (2) *prior beliefs,* or *causal schemata,* and (3) *self-perceptions.*

Situational Cues. In any learning task, a variety of environmental factors, or **situational cues,** help learners decide why they did well or poorly. One such cue is past experience with that task. If a learner has consistently done well on spelling assignments or word problems in math, she is more likely to attribute her success to ability (which is internal, stable, and uncontrollable) than to luck. A prior record of consistent failure will produce the same attribution. By the same token, a learner with a history of getting A's, C's, and F's on compositions will probably decide that luck or effort, more than ability or task difficulty, is behind his accomplishments.

> **Situational cues.** Stimuli in the learner's behavioral environment that predispose the learner to behave in a certain manner.

Learners also note their own performance success and that of their peers when deciding why they succeeded or failed. A sixth-grader who usually gets good grades on geography tests will say that strong ability is behind her high grade on the last quiz. Conversely, if this same learner got a low grade on that quiz, as did most of her peers, she would likely attribute this to the difficulty of the test (external, stable, uncontrollable).

A third cue that learners use to explain their accomplishments is time-on-task. A ninth-grader who spent the weekend preparing for an English test and worked diligently throughout the exam period will probably conclude that his A was due to effort (internal, unstable, controllable). If this same learner got an A without studying, he might say that the test was easy (external, stable, uncontrollable).

Finally, learners note how much help they received during the task when assigning attributions for the achievement. A learner who cheated on a test and received an A would not credit ability as the causal factor, nor would the learner who received a blue ribbon for a science project that was largely the work of an older brother.

Causal Schemata. We often hear the following expressions and may in fact believe them:

Success is 10 percent inspiration and 90 percent perspiration.

Nothing comes easy.

A fool blames failure on others, a wise man on himself.

Causal schemata. Beliefs about the sequential nature of observed data in which effects are attributed to causes.

We all have certain **causal schemata,** or enduring beliefs about success and failure. We acquire them in a variety of ways—through experience, reading, listening to parents and teachers, or absorbing the wise sayings of renowned thinkers. Some learners believe that effort, not ability, is the key to success; others believe just the opposite.

Weiner (1977) asserts that attributions for success and failure depend not only on situational factors but also on the enduring beliefs learners have about what underlies achievement. Consider the student who never studies (or who we believe never studies) and gets A's on all his tests. We inevitably attribute this to natural ability, native intelligence, or IQ. It couldn't have been due to effort, we assume, because the person doesn't appear to have exerted any. By the same token, we perceive that the learner whose exceptional efforts consistently produce unexceptional results lacks ability. The learner herself may believe this.

Self-perceptions. In addition to situational factors and cognitive beliefs, learners also incorporate *self-perceptions* into their decisions about causal attributions. Learners high in self-esteem typically say that effort or ability, rather than luck or task difficulty, is the root of their success (Ames & Ames, 1984). Students high in achievement motivation usually identify effort as the key to success, while those low in this quality blame failure on luck or task difficulty.

We have identified three antecedents of the causal attributions of your learners: situation, causal schemata, and self-perception factors. Since Weiner's research demonstrates that causal attributions affect achievement behavior, and because these attributions stem from the three antecedents just given, the issue of what you can do to influence your learners' causal attributions naturally arises. Let's turn, therefore, to what attribution theory has to say about your role in motivating learners.

Teacher Influence on Attributions. Attribution theory and research tell us that the causal attributions your learners make about their accomplishments have important consequences.

- They affect future learners' expectations for accomplishing learning goals.
- They engender emotional reactions such as anger (when failure is attributed to luck), guilt or shame (when failure is attributed to effort), or discouragement (when failure is attributed to lack of ability).
- They contribute to self-esteem. Learners feel good when hard work produces success or when they believe they have a natural ability for some task.
- They affect the classroom behavior of learners.

How can I help my learners interpret their classroom setbacks in ways that elicit renewed effort?

Consequently, you will want to do everything in your power to ensure that learners attribute their classroom accomplishments and setbacks in ways that elicit effort rather than discouragement. You can accomplish this in five ways.

- Recognize that your behavior conveys attributional information to your learners and carefully monitor the attributional messages you send.
- Focus on learning strategies.
- Refrain from grouping that promotes ability as the only source of success.
- Set up instructional arrangements that promote cooperation.
- Teach realistic goal setting.

Let's examine each of these responsibilities.

Monitor Your Attributional Messages. Although ability is an internal attribute of success, it is also an uncontrollable and stable one. Immediate effort, on the other hand, is not only internal but also unstable and controllable. In other words, effort is a cause of success that a learner can do something about. Clearly, then, it is in both the teacher's and the learner's best interests to stress the role of effort over ability in achievement. Nevertheless, many teachers inadvertently communicate the opposite, particularly to low achievers.

Here are some examples:

Mr. Barker teaches seventh-grade reading. He wants his low achievers to experience success. However, their reading level is several years below that required by their reading text. He has brought fourth- and fifth-grade materials into class and given them to his slower learners. He then lavishly praises these students for correctly reading the words and answering the easy comprehension questions that follow.

Mrs. Johnson likes to challenge her learners by throwing out thought-provoking questions as she lectures and explains. She is hesitant to ask such questions of her low achievers out of concern over embarrassing them in front of the group. As a result, she has inadvertently fallen into the noticeable (to all her learners) habit of asking only yes/no questions to this group or giving them the answers when they hesitate, rather than probing, and rephrasing questions, as she does for the higher achievers.

Mr. Nkruma doesn't want his learners to doubt their ability at math, particularly those who are struggling. He wants them to believe that if they only make an effort, they can succeed. But in his concern to protect his learners from the consequences of failure, he makes excuses for them when they do poorly on tests or answer questions incorrectly in class. For example, he'll say things like "I'm sorry that you didn't do as well as you hoped," "I guess you studied the wrong material," "This was an unusually hard test," or "I probably didn't allow enough time for this test" to his learners when going over their work.

> **What are some things teachers say to learners that can lower their motivation to succeed?**

According to Good and Brophy (1991), teachers who, however well intentioned, express sympathy at their learners' failure, show surprise at their success, give excessive unsolicited help, or lavishly praise success on easy tasks are telling students that they lack ability. As McQueen (1992) points out in her discussions with low achievers, these students are painfully aware what the teacher's behavior is suggesting.

Ginott (1972) advocates that teachers practice *congruent communication* when giving feedback to learners about their achievements. An important aspect of this type of communication is the use of encouragement instead of praise. According to Ginott, encouragement has the following attributes:

- Encouraging statements are directed at a student's actions—not at his or her character or person: "Your answers show thought," not "You are a good thinker."

- Encouraging statements reflect an accurate or honest evaluation of learner performance: "Your answers to these questions are too brief and need to show more thought. The other answers are thorough, thoughtful, and show understanding of the material," not "Some of your answers are fantastic. All of them show real effort," or "I feel bad that you got such a low grade."
- Encouraging statements help learners believe in themselves and their own ability: "Your handwriting is much improved. I appreciate the effort you're putting into it," not "Here's a happy face for that neat work."
- Encouraging statements attribute learner achievement to internal rather than external factors: "You have good ideas; you should want people to understand them. That's why it's important to write clearly," not "Write grammatically correct sentences or else I'll take off a point for each mistake."

Although as a general rule you should behave as if you value effort more than ability, Spaulding (1992) advocates that teachers exercise some caution. Her reasoning is that learners who believe that their success depends almost entirely on effort may begin to doubt their ability. For example, a student may believe that learners who are competent or who have ability don't have to try very hard to succeed. But since she has to spend several hours every night practicing French in order to get good grades, she concludes that she has little ability. This reasoning may influence her to drop the study of a foreign language from her plans even though she has a genuine interest in this area.

Hermine Marshall believes that teachers who believe that lack of success should be attributed to lack of effort may cause learners to feel frustrated and hopeless (ASCD Update, 1992). She raises the issue of what to say to the child who is trying as hard as he can but not succeeding. Do you continue to imply that he's not working hard enough?

Spaulding (1992) recommends that teachers help learners understand the connection between effort and ability rather than lead them to believe that learning depends almost exclusively on either one. According to Spaulding, learners must realize that abilities are fluid. While abilities may give certain learners initial advantages, effort helps them develop. Marshall (1990) urges teachers to focus learners on the cognitive processes or strategies they use to accomplish a task, rather than putting undue emphasis on effort.

Focus on Learning Strategies.   As we saw in the last chapter, cognitive approaches to learning place as much emphasis on the processes of learning as on the outcomes. This is also true of cognitive approaches to motivation. Attribution theory, in particular, stresses that teachers point out what learners are doing during the process of learning and not just what they have accomplished.

For example, from Chapter 5 we know that attention, rehearsal, self-questioning, notetaking, practice, review, discussion, and numerous other strategies that learners engage in during instruction are important for acquiring knowledge. When you give feedback or encouragement to learners during your lessons, you should take particular pains to point out not only what they learned but what they did to accomplish it.

Similarly, when giving feedback to learners who are performing poorly, ask your learners how they came up with their answers. Marshall (ASCD Update, 1992) believes that focusing on strategies is an "attitude that teachers need to develop." She states that doing so accomplishes two things: (1) it reveals the thought processes of learners; and (2) it conveys to them that the process, as well as the product, is important. This puts the focus on learning and not just on coming up with the correct answer.

How can learning strategies improve my students' motivation to learn?

A focus on cognitive learning strategies in all facets of instruction will help learners acquire the skills and attitudes they need to succeed at academic tasks.

Refrain from Grouping that Exclusively Promotes Ability. Learners are acutely aware of, and often puzzled by, both school-wide and classroom ability grouping arrangements. Such arrangements can suggest that teachers value ability exclusive of effort. This perception on the part of learners inevitably affects their expectations of themselves, which may lead them to see no value in hard work. Attribution theory highlights a disadvantage of some types of ability grouping that may influence learners to assign greater importance for learning to ability (something they have less control over) in relation to effort or the use of learning strategies (something they have much control over) (Good & Brophy, 1991).

Promote Cooperation over Competition. In Chapter 8 we will discuss the importance of promoting cooperation among class members to build group cohesiveness. Teachers who make concerted efforts to build group cohesiveness often use a type of instructional arrangement called *cooperative learning* (Cohen, 1986; Slavin, 1987, 1990b, 1991). As we saw in Chapter 6, cooperative learning lessons assign students of varying abilities, ethnicity, and of both genders to small groups that pursue common goals together. Each member is given a role to play—one member may function as a recorder, another as a researcher, still another as a summarizer—in order to foster the group's goal.

We will return to cooperative learning arrangements and their advantages for teaching heterogeneously grouped learners in later chapters. For now, we wish to point out that in terms of causal attributions for success or failure, cooperative learning arrangements emphasize the importance of learning processes and effort at least as much as ability (Cohen, 1986; Slavin, 1990b; Spaulding, 1992). In competitive learning arrangements, on the other hand, students work alone to achieve grades and rewards, and thus tend to emphasize ability over effort and learning processes (Maehr & Midgley, 1991). Research suggests that competitive arrangements diminish intrinsic motivation (Blumenfeld et al., 1991).

Teach Realistic Goal Setting. Attribution theory tells us that learners should believe that their efforts to learn and master new tasks will not be in vain. The likelihood of this depends to a large extent on whether their goals are realistic. Failure to meet goals that are unrealistic may cause learners to doubt their abilities and to approach the learning task with a lessened commitment to learning.

Teaching learners how to set realistic goals, therefore, is an important aspect of any instructional program that aims to build intrinsic motivation. Goal setting and the beliefs of learners in their ability to achieve goals are principal elements of the next motivation theory we will discuss, the self-efficacy theory.

Summary. Attribution theory holds that the key to understanding learners' motivations for achievement can be found by analyzing their assumptions about what causes their success or failure. Additionally, this theory tells us that the most direct way to enhance learners' intrinsic motivation is to teach in ways that convince learners that success is largely due to factors under their control.

Teachers influence causal attributions that energize and give direction to learner behavior by:

- carefully monitoring their attributional messages
- focusing on learning strategies
- refraining from ability grouping
- promoting cooperation among learners
- helping learners set realistic goals.

Self-efficacy Theory

> The best-laid plans never work out. At least mine didn't. Not that first semester anyway. I thought through all the things I was taught in my education classes: clear objectives, hands-on material, guided practice, performance assessments . . . but my lessons bombed. Most of the kids in my seventh grade showed no interest in my lessons. Now I know why. They were too difficult, and the kids knew it. Everyone knew it but me. Now I plan my lessons with one thing in mind. When I tell the class what we will be doing, I want everyone to say "I'm good enough at this to do what the teacher wants." (Author, personal experience)

Self-efficacy theory holds that intrinsic motivation for academic tasks depends on learners giving a resounding "Yes!" to the question "Am I good enough to do what the teacher wants?" Bandura, one of the principal founders of self-efficacy theory, defines *self-efficacy* as "people's judgments of their capabilities to organize and execute courses of actions required to attain designated types of performance" (Bandura, 1986, p. 391). Bandura believes that learners initiate, work hard during, and persist longer at tasks they judge they are good at. This judgment is what Bandura refers to when he uses the term *self-efficacy*.

Self-efficacy is not a personality trait or disposition. There is no such thing as a self-efficacious person. It is not a biological drive or a psychological need. Instead, it is an appraisal or evaluation that a person makes about his or her personal competence to succeed at a particular task. Self-efficacy, therefore, is situation-specific. A person may have high self-efficacy for writing poetry but low self-efficacy for writing short stories. Another individual may judge herself to be competent at soccer but not at swimming. Nevertheless, the judgment, once made, goes a long way toward explaining the level of persistence and effort expended on a learning task as well as the level of achievement obtained.

You may be wondering how self-efficacy differs from attributions. Both appear to involve the cognitive process of judgment, and both affect internal motivation. Attributions, as you will recall, are perceived causes of success or failure. They influence expectations of success and subsequent behavior. Attributions are one type of information (we will soon identify others) that learners use to make their judgments about self-efficacy. An individual who succeeds at a hard task only after exerting high effort will judge himself less capable at that task than at a task of equal difficulty at which he succeeds with relatively little effort.

Antecedents of Self-efficacy Judgments. In addition to attributions, what other sources of information do learners use when appraising their self-efficacy for a given achievement? Dale Schunk (1991), a leading researcher on self-efficacy, identifies four such sources: past experience, encouragement, physiological cues, and modeling effects.

Past Experiences of Success or Failure. Suppose you are conducting a lesson on fractions. Those learners who have earned high grades on the three previous math tests will have higher self-efficacy than those who failed them. Similarly, learners who have consistently earned high marks on the last several writing assignments will have greater self-efficacy and consequently greater effort and persistence for the current writing project than will those who earned low grades.

Encouragement or Persuasion from the Teacher. Learners who believe that they are not capable of a task, such as debating, can often be persuaded that they are by a convincing and inspirational teacher. However, while persuasion can enhance self-efficacy, its effects will be fleeting if the learner's efforts produce failure.

Physiological Cues. Learners who recognize symptoms of anxiety during a spelling bee (such as rapid breathing, increased heart rate, and sweating) may interpret them as signs that they lack ability. This may lead them to lower their self-efficacy.

Modeling Effects. Learners who hear peers make positive self-efficacy statements during a learning task, and who observe successful performances, will increase their self-efficacy judgments accordingly (Schunk & Hanson, 1985; Zimmerman & Ringle, 1981). The opposite is also true. Observing failure by peers or hearing about how hard a task is causes learners to lower their estimates of self-efficacy.

Self-efficacy in the Classroom. As you can see from this list of antecedents, appraisals of self-efficacy are dynamic, ongoing, changeable judgments of competence, which learners base on a variety of personal and situational information. No one source of information determines self-efficacy. Nor are appraisals of self-efficacy, once made, necessarily firm. Rather, the learner continually weighs and combines information from a variety of sources and situations. This information includes task difficulty, number and patterns of prior successes and failures, amount of help given, current and past feelings of anxiety, credibility of the person making encouraging statements, and perceived similarity to peer models.

But a learner's favorable appraisal of ability to achieve during a lesson does not necessarily predict successful or even persistent performance. As Schunk (1989b) cautions, high self-efficacy for dissecting a frog in the absence of skill, for example, will not earn a high grade in biology class. Similarly, learners who do not value the goal that a teacher identifies for a geography lesson are unlikely to participate in it with great effort and enthusiasm regardless of their self-efficacy for map-making. Nevertheless, given sufficient skill to perform an academic task, and given that learners value the goal of that task,

Learners enjoy self-efficacy motivation when they believe in their own capabilities to succeed at a task.

their judgments of self-efficacy will be the principal determinants of the direction of their behavior and energy for it.

Now, let's apply these ideas about self-efficacy to analyzing the behavior of Evelyn, the reluctant math student. Evelyn, as we know, had a bad prior experience with an advanced math class. In addition, she attributes her failure to factors out of her control: luck and task difficulty. Consequently, her initial appraisal of self-efficacy for calculus is low. Still, she knows she has an aptitude for math based on her test scores. Moreover, she rises to challenges. In other words, she has the skill and a positive attitude. Consequently, if we could only change her self-efficacy, she might take calculus and do well.

A conversation with a counselor might help Evelyn reappraise her self-efficacy for calculus. The counselor might point out that Evelyn has good preparation and adequate skill to do well (persuasion). In addition, the counselor could encourage Evelyn to talk to her friends who took calculus last year and did well (modeling). Finally, the counselor could help Evelyn reexamine her goals for the course, which may be unclear or unrealistically high (outcome expectations).

Assuming that Evelyn takes her counselor's advice and enrolls in the course, her self-efficacy would now hinge on such factors as anxiety, continued encouragement from teachers and parents, and her actual performance, as well as the similarity she perceives between herself and her peers and her observations of their performance.

How can I convey to my students the motivation to say "Yes, I can do what my teacher expects"?

Enhancing Self-efficacy. School programs designed to influence learners' self-efficacy and change achievement-related behavior have focused primarily on three activities: goal setting, information processing, and modeling. Let's examine each and see what you can do to improve your learners' judgments of self-efficacy.

Goal Setting. Researchers of self-efficacy, such as Schunk (1991), Bandura (1988), and Elliot and Dweck (1988), have found an important link between lesson goals and self-efficacy. They have discovered that when teachers give learners a goal or help them identify their own goals for an activity, there is an initial boost in self-efficacy for that activity.

Enhancing Self-efficacy

- **Identify goals that are short-range, concrete, and challenging.** Setting specific goals for the next class or the next week is more effective than setting goals for the end of the six-week period or the semester.

- **Identify specific performance outcomes you want your learners to attain at the end of the lesson or unit.** Identifying goals in terms of specific performance indicators boosts self-efficacy ("type 30 words per minute" is better than "increase your speed"). Although easy goals may enhance self-efficacy during the initial stages of learning a new skill, learners feel better about their ability when they accomplish more challenging tasks.

- **Give learners immediate feedback on both their own performances and those of peers.** While goals give an initial boost to self-efficacy, performance feedback sustains and heightens it. Furthermore, Schunk (1983) showed that informing learners about how their peers were doing persuaded them that the goals were attainable and increased self-efficacy.

- **Let learners set their own goals whenever possible.** Schunk and Hanson (1985) found that the learners with the highest self-efficacy for subtraction were those who were allowed to set their performance goals.

This initial appraisal is soon followed by a commitment to attempt the task. As learners work toward a goal and receive feedback on their progress, their self-efficacy is validated and enhanced. As self-efficacy heightens, so do effort, persistence, and skill development. Some guidelines appear in the accompanying box, *Enhancing Self-efficacy*.

Information Processing. "I'm just not good at word problems." "I have trouble figuring out main ideas." "Reading comprehension is my real weak point." "I just can't remember a lot of what I read." You have probably heard learners make these comments. You may have even said something similar yourself at some point. They all indicate low self-efficacy for higher-level cognitive tasks.

Schunk postulated that learners who believe that they will encounter difficulty in complex learning tasks have lower self-efficacy than learners who feel confident about handling the information processing demands of these tasks. He reasons that learners who begin reading comprehension or math problem-solving activities already doubting their ability to succeed will cease efforts to master these tasks when they encounter difficulties. If, however, they sense that they understand what they are reading or are successfully solving a problem, their self-efficacy will increase, as will their motivation to persist and learn the material.

One way to help learners improve their ability to process information during reading or math activities is to teach learning strategies. As you will recall, learning strategies are systematic plans that learners use to help with the information processing demands of complex learning tasks. Such strategies, when used consciously, allow learners to sense that they are learning. The perception that they are learning enhances their self-efficacy, motivation to learn, mastery of the learning task, and willingness to use the strategies again.

Some suggestions for enhancing students' use of learning strategies are given here:

- Teach learning strategies to enhance motivation for complex learning tasks.
- Have learners observe a peer using a learning strategy, and listen to that person comment on how it helps him or her.
- Videotape your learners using a cognitive strategy and show the tape to them. This approach has been shown to enhance self-efficacy and skill learning.
- Have learners verbalize the strategy out loud as they are using it. Then gradually fade this technique so that the learner's comments become less and less audible and eventually are uttered covertly. Learners who talk about strategies as they are using them increase their attention to tasks, perceptions of learning, and self-efficacy.

Refer to Chapters 5 and 6 for more detailed information on the use of cognitive learning strategies.

Modeling. Nothing succeeds like success! A corollary to this proverb might be: Nothing reinforces success like seeing someone else succeed! And this is the major point of self-efficacy research on the impact of peer models. Such research has clearly shown that when learners see someone else succeeding, they believe more in their own capabilities (Schunk, 1989a, b; Schunk, Hanson, & Cox, 1987; Zimmerman & Ringle, 1981). In these studies the following peer modeling activities increased the self-efficacy of observers for learning tasks such as subtraction, division, word puzzles, and complex problem solving:

- hearing a peer express confidence at being able to solve a learning task
- observing a peer showing high persistence and high confidence
- hearing a peer explain how she solved a problem
- hearing a peer make helpful statements like "I need to pay more attention to what I am doing"
- seeing and hearing several peer models instead of just one
- having learners observe videotapes of themselves (called *self-modeling*) using strategies and making positive self-efficacy statements.

Teachers interested in enhancing the self-efficacy of learners should therefore make use of the abundant modeling opportunities in their classrooms.

Summary. Self-efficacy theory holds that the key to a learner's motivation for achievement lies with the learner's own beliefs in his ability to organize and execute the actions required for a successful performance. These beliefs derive from

- past experiences of success or failure
- encouragement or persuasion from others
- physiological cues, such as rapid breathing and increased heart rate, that tell the learner something about his or her capabilities to complete the task
- modeling by peers, which may make the task appear easy or difficult.

Teachers can influence the self-efficacy of learners through the teaching of realistic goal setting and learning strategies and by having peers model successful performances.

Self-determination Theory

Recall that in the introduction to this chapter we asked that as you encountered different motivational theories, you keep in mind the question "How can this theory account for the energy and direction of a motivated learner?" The cognitive motivational theories of attribution and self-efficacy have been criticized for focusing more on the direction than on the energy dimension of motivated behavior. Let's explore this important distinction.

Pintrich (1991) believes that both attribution and self-efficacy theory make motivation appear too cognitive, too abstract, too devoid of energy and passion. Similarly, Deci and his colleagues (1991) argue that most current approaches to intrinsic motivation fail to deal with the question of why learners desire certain goals or outcomes. For example, Deci believes that attribution and self-efficacy theory emphasize too strongly the role of beliefs when accounting for intrinsic motivation. He questions how these theories account for the needs of learners to feel competent and independent. He claims that such theories make the motivational process appear too rational, too cold, too isolated from the day-to-day emotions and feelings that characterize the classroom behavior of children.

Deci offers an alternative, **self-determination theory.** He contends that this theory reintroduces a component of motivation that has long been neglected by most modern cognitive motivational theories: human needs. Moreover, it does so while still assigning a critical role to the learners' thought processes. Let's examine the self-determination perspective and see how it can be applied.

Self-determination theory. An approach that holds that an attitude of determination is the foundation for motivated behavior.

Human Needs. In our presentation of attribution theory, we pointed out that a learner's intrinsic motivation for a particular task depended on her beliefs about what was responsible for past successes or failures. We outlined teaching practices that lead learners to believe that success results from factors under their control.

Self-efficacy theory tells us that learners' intrinsic motivation for a task rests with their beliefs about whether they are good at it and can achieve its goals. We learned about instructional practices that promote positive self-efficacy beliefs.

Self-determination theory is more complex. It tells us that underlying intrinsic motivation is an attitude of self-determination to accomplish a goal. This attitude is more than just a belief in one's self-efficacy, although that is a component of self-determination. Likewise, self-determination involves more than beliefs about the causes

Edward L. Deci, University of Rochester

When I was a graduate student I spent time observing children both in a nursery school and in their late elementary years. I was amazed at the difference, amazed that the younger children seemed so much more curious, so much more eager to learn. I wondered whether the experiences the older children had had in school might in some way have accounted for their lower levels of what I came to call intrinsic motivation.

When I began studying intrinsic motivation, the field of empirical psychology was still dominated by behaviorism, although the cognitive revolution had begun. I found both approaches unsatisfactory, for neither dealt with issues of motivation in ways that took account of the inherent tendency of people to grow and develop, to actualize their potentials, to self-initiate, and to engage the world in an attempt to master it.

Furthermore, the primary approach used in applying psychology to real-world problems was behavior modification. To me, that approach was inadequate: Its focus on controlling people was philosophically objectionable, and besides, it did not seem to work very well, especially for complex human problems. I found the assump-

tions and values of humanistic psychology much more congenial, and it seemed to me to be possible to use rigorous empirical methods to study human beings as living organisms—in other words, to take a humanistic view of people while studying them empirically.

At the time I started my research program I was interested in the concept of self-determination. In a sense, really, I was interested in the meaning of psychological freedom, or what the existentialists have called "authenticity." I was unwilling simply to rule this out of consideration as so many other psychologists had done; I wanted to consider it an empirical matter. So I started with the concept of intrinsic motivation because that represented to me the prototype of self-determination. I thought that if we could understand the dynamics of intrinsic motivation reasonably well, we could move on to the more complex matters of people being self-determined to do extrinsically motivated activities. That is exactly what my collaborator, Richard M. Ryan, and I have done. Now we are considering not only self-determination in extrinsically motivated behaviors but also self-determination in emotion-motivated actions.

of success or failure. Rather, self-determination theory focuses on three innate human needs: competence, relationships, and autonomy.

Competence needs involve the learner's knowledge of how to achieve certain goals and the skill for doing so. Deci believes that learners have an innate psychological need to believe that they are competent. *Relationship needs* are innate requirements for secure and satisfying connections with peers, teachers, and parents. Finally, *autonomy needs* refer to the ability to initiate and regulate one's own actions. Figure 7.4 depicts these aspects of self-determination theory.

Deci believes that classrooms promote intrinsic motivation by helping learners acquire an attitude of self-determination. In other words, they meet learners' needs for competence, relationships, and autonomy. Furthermore, self-determination theory underscores that all three needs must be satisfied if the learner is to develop an attitude of

The research on the effects of extrinsic rewards on intrinsic motivation intrigued me in part because its implications are so directly opposite to the behavior modification approach. Interestingly, there is some complementarity in the findings of the two approaches, and yet they make opposing prescriptions. The complementarity is first that both approaches have found that it is often possible to control people's behavior—that is, people will do what they have to do in order to get desired outcomes—and second that both approaches recognize that if people become dependent on rewards or other controls, and the rewards or controls are terminated, the behavior will decrease substantially.

However, the important point that has become clear from the work Rich Ryan and I have done is that when people become dependent on rewards or other controls, there are significant negative consequences for their performance and well-being. This fact has led us to recommend that rewards and other controls not be used unless they are absolutely necessary to motivate behavior, but many behaviorists, unwilling to give serious consideration to these negative consequences, continue to advocate the use of reinforcement procedures to try to control behavior.

The results of our research point clearly to the fact that the orientation teachers take toward their students—toward the learning and behavior of their students—has an important impact on the students' motivation, self-regulation, performance, and adjustment. When the teachers are controlling and evaluative, rather than understanding and supportive of autonomy, the students are likely to experience negative consequences. We do not, however, take a blaming attitude toward teachers, for teachers are themselves dealing with monumental challenges. Our research shows that teachers tend to become more controlling (i.e., they tend to be less student-centered and supportive of autonomy) when they feel pressured and directed by the administration and by other forces around them. I think the results of our research contain two important messages for teachers—two things they can put to direct use. First, teachers can understand the importance of being autonomy-supportive of their students; in other words, they can understand that the more controlling, directive, and pressuring they are with the students, the more negative the effects they will have on the students. Second, they can understand that their own controllingness is caused in part by the stresses they feel. When they lose their patience and feel irritated with their students, they can find ways to deal with their own stresses: They can find a friend to talk to and build mutually supportive relationships with others in that setting so they can help each other during the difficult times.

self-determination. Learners who believe in their own competence will not feel self-determined if the classroom does not allow them to accomplish tasks with some degree of independence. Thus, classrooms characterized by teacher-directed instructional techniques are less likely to satisfy learners' needs for autonomy than are classrooms that incorporate constructivist instructional approaches, including cooperative learning. Similarly, classrooms that rely heavily on extrinsic rewards and punishments to control behavior will not meet learners' autonomy needs.

Deci also contends that meeting a learner's needs for competence and autonomy while at the same time ignoring needs for relationships will fail to enhance self-determination and intrinsic motivation. How can this be? Doesn't a need for relationships imply a certain degree of dependence on the part of learners? And doesn't this detract from feelings and beliefs about autonomy?

Figure 7.4
Components of self-determination.

Deci resolves this seeming contradiction between needs for autonomy and needs for relationships by explaining that autonomy means that learners initiate and regulate their own learning behaviors. Self-initiation and self-regulation can develop only in a classroom where such behavior is supported and encouraged by peers and adults. Thus, self-determination theory tells us that learners will develop intrinsic motivation and the self-determination underlying such motivation only in a social milieu that supports competence and autonomy (Vygotsky, 1987, also assigns a significant role to relationships when he talks about the social nature of learning).

Enhancing Self-determination. Self-determination theory is a new and ambitious attempt to reconcile the early need and drive theories of motivation with more modern cognitive motivational perspectives that focus on a learner's attributions and beliefs. While research into the antecedents of self-determination has just begun, we can still provide some recommendations for promoting it, as shown in the accompanying box, *Promoting Self-determination.* Notice the similarities of these suggestions to those identified for effort-enhancing attributions and positive self-efficacy.

> **How can I enhance my learners' determination to learn what I teach?**

Summary. Self-determination theory tells us that learners have innate needs to feel competent, relate to other people, and be autonomous. They come to school, in other words, with built-in energy and a desire to achieve, and they possess the basic ingredients for developing the internal motivation to do so. The questions teachers should ask themselves as they scan the eager faces of their learners on the first day of school are these: "What can I do to meet their needs for competence, relationships, and autonomy? What is the best way to focus and give direction to this energy?" Self-determination theory holds that the answer to these questions lies in designing a classroom that

- places a premium on skill development
- allows learners to feel that they control this development
- encourages relationships that support the development of competence and autonomy.

With these three principles as guides, let's explore an approach to teaching and learning called project-based learning.

Promoting Self-determination

Teachers Can Help Meet Learners' Competency Needs By

- Giving positive feedback, rather than corrections and criticism, after learning.
- Congratulating learners for doing well, but only for self-initiated tasks. Deci et al. (1991) report that praising learners following performance on learning tasks they were told to do reduced feelings of autonomy and intrinsic motivation for these tasks.
- Focusing on prerequisite skills and emphasizing errorless learning (a recommendation made by behavioral learning theory, which we studied in Chapter 4).

Teachers Can Meet Learners' Needs for Relationships By

- Stressing cooperative over competitive learning.
- Involving parents in the educational process. Grolnick and Ryan (1989) report that learners whose parents are more in-volved in their education are more self-determined than those whose parents are not (see Chapter 16 on home–school partnerships).

Teachers Can Meet Learners' Needs for Autonomy By

- Minimizing the use of contingent rewards.
- Allowing learners more choices. Deadlines and other events used to pressure learners to think, feel, or behave in certain ways generally decrease self-determination and intrinsic motivation.
- Acknowledging learners' feelings about being forced to do things they don't like or in ways they don't like. Koestner, Ryan, Bernieri, and Holt (1984) report that intrinsic motivation is maintained when teachers acknowledge learners' feelings of dislike for either particular activities or ways of doing them.

Project-based Learning

Teachers who practice **project-based learning,** or build their instructional programs around projects, provide learners with an environment ideally suited to the nurturing of intrinsic motivation (Blumenfeld et al., 1991). Whether your perspective on motivation leans toward attribution theory, self-efficacy theory, self-determination theory, or all three, project-based learning offers some solutions to the age-old problem of how to give energy and direction to the classroom behavior of learners.

Before we describe project-based learning, let's briefly review attribution theory, self-efficacy theory, and self-determination theory.

- *Attribution theory* emphasizes teaching methods that assure learners that their success depends on factors they control. Teachers do this by (1) stressing the importance of the learning process, not just the product; (2) helping learners set goals; and (3) using instructional groupings to promote cooperation.

- *Self-efficacy theory* emphasizes instructional programs that help learners set their own goals, acquire learning strategies, and observe successful peer models to enhance self-efficacy beliefs and intrinsic motivation.

- *Self-determination theory* emphasizes the important role of teachers in fostering intrinsic motivation by arranging their classrooms, designing lessons,

Project-based learning. An approach to learning that argues that intrinsic motivation is marshaled, generated, and sustained in a learning environment that recognizes the importance of the interrelationships among learning tasks, learner disposition, and teachers.

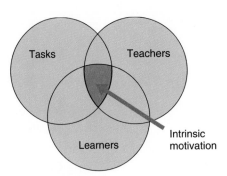

Figure 7.5
Three principal elements of project-based learning.

and speaking to learners in ways that meet their needs for competence, relationships, and autonomy. The specific recommendations for doing this are nearly identical to recommendations for promoting effort-enhancing attributions and positive self-efficacy.

Project-based learning (PBL) makes extensive use of the ideas and research of Weiner's attribution theory, Bandura's and Schunk's self-efficacy theory, and Deci's self-determination theory in designing its comprehensive approach to classroom teaching and learning. It uses these motivational approaches to help delineate the roles of its three principal components: *tasks, learners,* and *teachers,* as shown in Figure 7.5.

In PBL, intrinsic motivation is not viewed as a feature of learning tasks, a disposition of learners, or the sole responsibility of teachers. Rather, intrinsic motivation is marshaled, generated, and sustained in a learning environment where it is recognized that each of these elements has a necessary role to play, though each alone is not sufficient. When each of these components carries out its assigned role (the intersection of all three circles in Figure 7.5), intrinsic motivation results. Let's examine these components of PBL and see how each incorporates elements of the cognitive motivational theories we have studied.

The Role of Tasks

PBL assigns a critical role in the development of intrinsic motivation to the nature of the classroom learning task. It asks the question, "What kinds of tasks are most likely to induce and support learner interest, effort, and persistence?" PBL advocates the use of projects as the most appropriate vehicles for engaging learners. *Projects* have two essential components: (1) they are built around a central question or problem that serves to organize and energize classroom activities, and (2) they require learners to produce a product or outcome to successfully answer the question or resolve the problem.

Projects challenge learners with important (often real-world) problems and usually require them to draw on several diverse skill areas to solve them. A third-grade project, for example, built around the problem of nonrecyclable garbage, can involve the skills of reading, research, data gathering, data analysis, hypothesis-generating, and problem solving. Projects may be built around issues of current societal concern or questions of historical or purely intellectual interest. Good projects have the following critical characteristics.

- They are of extended duration (require several weeks to complete).
- They link several disciplines (math, reading, and writing skills, for example).

How can I use project-based learning to motivate my learners?

- They allow for a variety of solutions (the focus should be as much on process as on product).
- They involve the teacher as coach, and require small group collaboration to complete.

Blumenfeld and other proponents of PBL caution teachers that projects, by themselves, will not engage learners or motivate them to invest the effort necessary to investigate, acquire information, test solutions, and evaluate results (Anderson & Roth, 1989; Blumenfeld et al., 1991; Doyle, 1983). Rather, they must be used in a classroom milieu that supports thoughtfulness and sustained motivation.

There are, however, certain characteristics that projects must include if they are to capture the interest of learners and enhance intrinsic motivation. They must (1) present an authentic, real-world challenge, (2) allow for learner choice and control, (3) be doable—capable of being carried out within the time and resource limitations of the student and classroom, (4) require collaboration, and (5) produce a concrete result. Let's look more closely at each of these characteristics.

Present a Challenge. Both attribution and self-efficacy theory stress the importance of goals that learners want to achieve. PBL meets this important ingredient of intrinsic motivation when it offers learners an authentic, sometimes novel, and always challenging problem or question to investigate, resolve, and report on. Contrast such a project with worksheets, exercise books, end-of-chapter questions, and other routine tasks, which take up most academic time (Doyle, 1983; Goodlad, 1984; Sizer, 1984).

Allow for Learner Choice and Control. We learned about the importance of meeting learner needs for autonomy when we reviewed self-determination theory. Effective projects allow learners options regarding modes of investigation (reading, interviewing, observing, controlled experimentation), styles of reporting (written reports, audiotapes or videotapes, visual displays), solutions to problems, or types of products or artifacts to develop.

Be Doable. Learners will persevere and expend high amounts of effort if they see results (attribution theory). Similarly, they are more likely to believe that they can see a project through to a successful conclusion (self-efficacy) if it is time limited, requires readily available resources, and includes points along the way where they can receive positive feedback, make revisions, and generate further products.

Require Collaboration. Self-determination theory tells us that intrinsic motivation is nurtured in classrooms that allow learners to meet their social needs. Self-efficacy theory points out that learners acquire beliefs about their own capabilities from observing others. Projects that cannot be completed unless a small group of learners adopt different but essential roles are ideal vehicles for incorporating the principles of these motivational theories (see Chapter 6 on roles in collaborative learning activities).

Result in a Concrete Product. Projects that give learners concrete goals to work toward are more likely to sustain intrinsic motivation. Moreover, products and the process involved in producing them allow for performance-based assessment. This type of assessment allows learners to see the connection between what they do in class and what their grades are based on. This gives learners a greater sense of control over their grades, and it better meets their needs for autonomy (as identified in self-determination theory) than grades based on paper-and-pencil tests alone.

The Role of the Learner

The key to developing intrinsic motivation is not simply a matter of finding the right activity or project. Educators since the time of John Dewey (1938) have urged schools to engage learners in "hands-on" learning activities as the best way to develop intrinsic motivation. Nevertheless, many educational reforms may have failed because they only described the activities to be completed—they did not consider the role of the learners' motivational beliefs and the teacher's encouragement of those beliefs to the overall activity (Blumenfeld et al., 1991).

PBL recognizes that efforts to reform learners' tasks in school will fail unless instruction seeks to influence what learners think about the tasks and themselves. Consequently, PBL recognizes that learners will acquire important knowledge and skills from projects only if they (1) attribute their success to effort, (2) believe that they can accomplish the goals of the project, and (3) perceive themselves as competent. PBL also recognizes that learners are more likely to perceive themselves as competent if they have the prior knowledge, prerequisite skills, and learning strategies necessary for completing the projects before they begin (again, note the fit between PBL and the cognitive strategies we described in Chapters 5 and 6).

The Role of the Teacher

PBL recognizes that the teacher is the last piece in the intrinsic motivational puzzle. The teacher's unique role in PBL is that of the supporter of intrinsic motivation. Consequently, Blumenfeld and her colleagues urge teachers to support their learners' interest, efforts, and achievements by:

- avoiding statements implying that innate ability is all that is required to complete a project
- focusing learners' attention on both the process of completing the project and the end product
- making encouraging statements to learners.

Summary

In this chapter we studied two major approaches to motivation and classroom learning: person-as-machine behavioral theories and person-as-rational-thinker cognitive theories. We found the cognitive theories of attributions, self-efficacy, and self-determination to be most useful to the classroom, since each provides practical recommendations to teachers for increasing the internal motivation of their learners. Furthermore, project-based learning provided suggestions for how attribution, self-efficacy, and self-determination theories could be combined to direct the roles of tasks, learners, and teachers in providing a classroom environment that encourages intrinsic motivation.

We now turn, in Part III, to issues of classroom and instructional management. There we will see how the theories of development, learning, and motivation we have studied so far can be applied to the daily routines of classroom life.

Summing Up

This chapter introduced you to motivation and classroom learning. Its main points were these:

- Intrinsic motivation influences learners to choose a task, get energized about it, and persist until they accomplish success, regardless of whether it brings an immediate reward.
- Theories of motivation can be divided into "person-as-machine" behavioral theories and "person-as-rational-thinker" cognitive theories. The former include instinct, drive, and deficiency/growth theories; the latter include attribution, self-efficacy, and self-determination theories.
- Attribution theory presumes that people inevitably seek to understand why they succeed or fail. The antecedents to which individuals credit their successes or failures can be classified into (1) locus of causality, (2) stability, and (3) controllability.
- Locus of causality refers to the extent to which an antecedent is internal or external.
- Stability of an antecedent refers to the extent to which the antecedent can be altered by the individual or is unchangeable.
- Controllability of an antecedent refers to the extent to which the antecedent is within or outside the individual's control.
- According to attribution theory, the direction of motivated behavior derives from past experiences with tasks, causal attributions, and expectations about what is likely to happen the next time a similar situation is encountered.
- The antecedents of a learner's attributions derive from situational cues, causal schemata (or prior beliefs), and self-perceptions.
- Self-efficacy theory holds that intrinsic motivation depends on the learner's belief in his or her own capabilities to organize and execute the courses of action required to attain designated types of performance.
- The antecedents of self-efficacy judgments include past experiences of success or failure, encouragement or persuasion from the teacher, physiological cues (such as heart rate), and modeling by peers.
- Self-determination theory holds that intrinsic motivation derives from an attitude of determination to accomplish a goal. This attitude is fostered by helping the learner acquire the necessary skills, acquire secure and satisfying connections with others, and become self-initiating and self-regulating.
- Project-based learning (PBL) uses attribution, self-efficacy, and self-determination theory to build an instructional program that provides an environment for nurturing intrinsic motivation.

For Discussion and Practice

*1. How would you explain the concept of intrinsic motivation to a friend who knew nothing about theories of motivation?

Questions marked with an asterisk are answered in the appendix.

°2. In the teacher's interaction with Jared about doing "this stuff" to pass the course, what, in your opinion, explains why Jared changed his mind and decided to do what his teacher wanted?

°3. Explain why some motivational theories can be described with the "person-as-machine" metaphor.

°4. Describe the two types of drives identified by Hull, and give an example of each.

°5. Identify the five needs described by Maslow that represent the major motives that govern human behavior. From your own experience, give an example of each. Which are deficiency needs and which are growth needs?

°6. According to attribution theory, what classifications of antecedents and their variations can be used to explain success or failure?

°7. Provide an example of (a) an external, unstable, and uncontrollable cause of success or failure and an example of (b) an internal, stable, and controllable cause of success or failure.

°8. According to Weiner, from what three general sources of information do attributions spring? From your own experience, give an example of each.

°9. Identify five ways you can help your learners acquire positive attributions and, with examples from your teaching area, show how you would implement them in your classroom.

°10. According to self-efficacy theory, what four sources of information do learners use to attribute success or failure to their actions? Provide an example at your grade level of information a learner might use from each of these sources to attribute success or failure to his or her actions.

°11. Identify three ways you can help your learners enhance their self-efficacy and, with examples from your teaching area, show how you would implement them in your classroom.

°12. According to Pintrich, what criticism of attribution and self-efficacy theories does self-determination theory attempt to avoid?

°13. What three needs does self-determination theory attempt to explain that attribution and self-efficacy theories cannot?

°14. In your teaching field and grade level, provide one example each of a learner's need for competence, relationships, and autonomy.

°15. Explain one of the ways attribution theory, self-efficacy theory, and self-determination theory each contribute to project-based learning.

16. In your own teaching area, make a list of five projects that are likely to induce learner interest, effort, and persistence.

°17. What five characteristics should your list above of projects have if they are to be successful in capturing the interest, effort, and persistence of your learners? Replace any on your list that you feel do not have these qualities.

Suggested Readings

Pintrich, P. R. (Ed.). (1991). *Educational Psychologist, 26* (3 & 4). The entire issue of this journal is devoted to examining current issues and new directions in motivation theory and research.

Sizer, T. R. (1984). *Horace's compromise: The dilemma of the American high school.* Boston: Houghton Mifflin. A lively and readable examination of the problem of unmotivated high school students and what needs to be done to interest them in learning.

Spaulding, C. L. (1992). *Motivation in the classroom.* New York: McGraw-Hill. This book, written for the classroom teacher, reviews important theories and devotes several chapters to classroom activities that build intrinsic motivation.

Part

III

What Teachers Need to Know About Instruction and Classroom Management

The first two weeks were a time of adjustment. Adjusting lesson plans, classroom seating arrangements and, most challenging, adjusting discipline techniques. I knew I would have to discipline the children. I knew I wasn't supposed to be "too nice" at the beginning. . . . My main focus at the start of the year was creative and innovative lesson planning. I had left much of the discipline technique up to the fact that if the lessons were intriguing, the children would not have a need to misbehave or act out. That was true about 1 percent of the time. There was that rare occasion when all children were interested in the lesson at a single moment, but the normal situation was that there would always be someone within the classroom with a different agenda. . . . (Amy Shea, in Ryan, 1992, pp. 73–74)

Finding the right balance between not enough structure and too much is in one sense what teaching is all about. Time for one more first year story? . . . It's a few weeks later after a classroom ambience of antagonistic chaos has been firmly established. There are regular disturbances . . . and I feel unable to calm the waters. Truth be told, I am feeling battered by a stormy surf and unable to right myself in the undertow.

So, I come up with an idea how to restore control. First, I check the supply cabinet in the main office for 20 file folders. Next, I write up a list of guidelines for classroom behavior and academic work. This list goes onto a typed sheet which I staple inside each folder. With my new system students receive two grades each day: behavior and academic. The behavior grade is either 100 or 0—either the kid follows rules and is rewarded or screws up and gets a 0. At the end of the class, all academic work goes into the folder and is graded.

Day one of the new program: Students behave and do work according to plan. Everybody gets 100. I envision my forthcoming article in *Social Education:* "How to Reinforce Positive Behavior and Increase Academic Success in the Low-Track Class . . ."

By day five the program has gone to hell.

"Yo, Mr. Nehring, do I still have my hundred for today?"

"Not after that little stunt, Jack. I just wrote your name in the zero column."

"Are you sure?"

"Yes, Jack."

"Good. Now I can like totally mess up for the rest of the period and you can't do nothing about it!" (Nehring, 1989, pp. 48–49)

The overwhelming majority of beginning teachers routinely express concerns about classroom control and frequently experience discipline problems during their initial months and year in the classroom (Rogan, Borich, & Taylor, 1992). Inexperience and lack of attention to the principles of classroom management during teacher training may, in part, contribute to concerns about classroom management. But the sheer difficulty in managing a large group of diverse learners may be another reason.

At the start of each school year, every teacher faces the task of creating a group whose members are willing to do things not of their choosing with people they have not necessarily chosen as friends. The teacher assumes leadership of this group and seeks to gain their acceptance. This is a formidable task for any teacher, let alone a beginning teacher.

In Part III we will prepare you for this challenge by examining some important topics related to the social psychology of classrooms and their management. In Chapter 8 we will examine the classroom from the vantage point of the social psychologist. We will discuss the unique attributes of classroom groups, their effects on learners, and how teachers can promote the development of positive group attributes. This will lead us to how groups are formed and the leadership styles found to be effective for creating a cohesive and productive group of classroom learners.

The process of developing an effective group may take months, sometimes the better part of a semester or school year. At the same time you are steering and guiding this process, you must provide a safe and productive workplace for learners. How successful you are will depend on how well you arrange the physical environment of the classroom, set reasonable rules, teach efficient routines, and use noncoercive techniques for managing classroom behavior. These important classroom management functions will be the topic of Chapter 9.

In Chapter 10 we will examine the classroom from the perspective of instructional management. Our premise in this chapter is that the first step in good classroom management is good lesson planning. We will outline important attributes of lesson plans, including the knowledge you want learners to acquire, the cognitive or intellectual skills you expect them to demonstrate, and the attitudes and social skills your learners must develop to perform in the real world. Then we will demonstrate how effective teachers prepare lessons that help learners achieve objectives related to knowledge acquisition, thinking, and metacognition.

Together these chapters will provide you with a knowledge of social psychology and practical techniques for applying this knowledge to manage your classroom effectively and efficiently, beginning with your very first day.

Group Process in the Classroom

This chapter will help you answer the following questions about yourself and your learners:

- What goals can I work toward to make my classroom into a more cohesive group of learners?
- What are some of the ways I can put my learners at ease during the first few days of class?
- How should I respond to learners who choose to challenge my authority early in the school year?
- What types of social power can I acquire at the beginning of the year to help me form and lead a cohesive classroom?
- How can I avoid creating self-fulfilling prophecies in which my expectations about individual learners later influence my behavior toward them?
- How can I develop positive norms of conduct and learning in my classroom?
- What are some practical strategies and activities I can use in my classroom to promote trust and group cohesiveness?
- In what ways can I resolve naturally occurring conflicts arising out of the group dynamics of my classroom?

Tamara slumped into the one remaining empty chair in the teachers' lounge, exhaling loudly enough for all to hear. She said nothing and just stared blankly. After a few minutes, Christie, a fourth-grade teacher, scooted her chair over to Tamara's. Christie had been at Cedar Creek Elementary for seven years; Tamara for about seven days.

Christie: Cheer up! It's almost Friday. Wednesdays are always the hardest. Come tomorrow, there'll be only one day to go.

Tamara: So that's how it is? . . . making it 'til Friday?

Christie: What's the problem?

Tamara: I can't figure it out. Doing seatwork, copying from the book, answering repetitive questions at the end of the chapter—that's the only way I can keep my class under control. Sharing their experiences, discussing different viewpoints, or working cooperatively . . . forget that. They only behave when I keep 'em busy, like a drill sergeant. They take advantage of anything else.

Christie: That's probably all they've been accustomed to. Anything different and they'd feel insecure.

Tamara: But insecure or not, no one seems to want to be in my class. And I can tell some don't like me. Maybe I need to lighten up . . . smile all day or something and just forget about wanting to create a mature, adultlike atmosphere.

Christie: When's the last time you shared your experiences, discussed different viewpoints, or wanted to work with someone you didn't even know?

Tamara: I can't remember.

Christie: That's my point. That type of atmosphere doesn't just happen—it has to be developed. Your learners first have to feel they belong in your classroom and are accepted by you before they'll think and act without being told what to do.

Tamara: But I don't know how to make them feel accepted.

In this chapter you will also learn the meanings of these terms:

centering
coercive power
cooperative learning
distancing
expectancy (Pygmalion) effect
expert power
goal conflicts
group
group cohesiveness
group conflict
interpersonal conflicts
legitimate power
limit testing
norm crystalization
norm diffusion
norms
procedural conflicts
referent power
reward power
self-concept
self-fulfilling prophecy
social needs
social structure
stage of group formation

Tamara's dilemma is one many new teachers face. On the one hand, they want a classroom where learners trust and like one another and their teacher. They want their students to learn from one another, feel free to express themselves, respond voluntarily, and respect one another's viewpoints. On the other hand, they value academic excellence, individual achievement, and scholarship. These latter goals give rise to concerns about finishing lesson and unit plans, maintaining order, and staying on schedule. Such concerns can prevent you from investing the time to create the type of classroom climate necessary to achieve both sets of goals.

As Christie noted, a positive classroom climate doesn't just happen—it has to be developed. Such a climate arises when a teacher and learners in a classroom work together as a **group,** not as a collection of individuals. Thus, one of the most important goals for a teacher from the first day of class is group development. As we will learn in this chapter, group development and learner achievement are complementary goals: the achievement of each learner is facilitated by the development of a cohesive group.

How does a teacher go about developing a group? The first step toward this goal is becoming aware that when you enter a classroom, you are stepping into a group that may be unlike any you have experienced. The existing classroom group includes expectations, relationships, roles, interactions, and rules of behavior, all of which are largely unstated.

Our goal in this chapter is to familiarize you with group life and give you the skills you need to manage it. We will begin by examining group dynamics and group processes. Then we will study the characteristics of a group, how being in a group affects the behavior of its members, and the processes by which groups form. Finally, we will study the qualities of effective groups and what you can do to develop them in your own classroom.

Group. Two or more persons engaged in interactions around a common goal so that each member of the group influences the others.

Group Processes

In Chapters 2 and 3 you learned about various theories of developmental influences on behavior, such as heredity, temperament, and child-rearing practices. Social psychologists also examine the way our perceptions, feelings, thoughts, and actions are influenced by other people. They study how groups form and function, their unique structure and roles, and how they influence the behavior of their members. For most of the twentieth century, social psychologists have examined group processes in industry, the military, government agencies, and the field of mental health. More recently, many of these same social psychological principles have been used to study life in classrooms.

Richard and Patricia Schmuck are two researchers concerned with applying principles of group process and group dynamics to help teachers understand group life in the classroom. For the past quarter century they have researched and written about the effect of group processes on learners' emotional adjustment and academic achievement. They, along with others (Glasser, 1990; Johnson & Johnson, 1984; Schmuck & Schmuck, 1992; Slavin, 1991) believe that high levels of individual scholarship, learning, and academic achievement go hand in hand with high levels of group support and cooperation. Let's examine the classroom from this social psychological perspective.

What Is a Group?

Classes, simply by being gatherings of people, cannot necessarily be characterized as cohesive groups. For example, an adult computer literacy class whose members

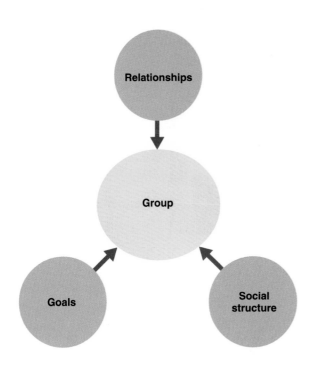

Figure 8.1
Properties of a group.

sit at individual work stations for the entire period can be expected to develop less cohesiveness than a class of third-graders who spend the entire school day together for a year. Three properties contribute to making a classroom of learners a cohesive group: (1) relationships (the interaction and interdependence of members), (2) common goals, and (3) a social structure. Figure 8.1 shows these properties. Let's look at each.

Relationships

One of the principal requirements of a group is that the members form relationships. In order to form relationships, the members of the group must interact with one another and, to a certain degree, depend on one another. The teacher who discourages interaction between members of the class, who requires that learners sit at individual desks arranged in rows for an entire grading period, and who assigns only individual seatwork will promote little interaction and interdependence and, consequently, few relationships.

This point was made by Calonico and Calonico (1972) in a study of third-grade classrooms. Their data showed that the more learners worked together, shared, and talked during academic tasks, the stronger were their feelings of friendship toward one another. Coming from the same neighborhood, being in a classroom together, and playing together during recess or lunch are no guarantees that learners will form friendships. Teachers who want learners to form a cohesive group should encourage interaction, interdependence, and cooperation during academic work.

Social psychologists tell us that groups of learners live according to certain rules of behavior, have expectations for their members, and require distinct role relationships.

Common Goals

In addition to relationships, a second attribute that contributes to a cohesive group is common goals. Individuals who come together to achieve a common purpose are more likely to form a cohesive group than individuals who do not. This attribute is less apparent in classrooms in which teachers and learners think in terms of individual rather than group achievement. Consequently, teachers who promote **group cohesiveness** should consider developing goals for the entire class to work toward. Schmuck and Schmuck (1992) propose four types of group goals: task-group, task-individual, social-emotional-group, and social-emotional-individual. Examples of these four types of goals are presented in Figure 8.2.

In this scheme, task goals are concerned with academic learning, while social-emotional goals are directed toward helping learners develop positive self-images and meet their needs for control over their environment, recognition by peers, and acceptance. The work of social psychologists suggests that teachers give consideration to both task and social-emotional goals. Research in industry shows that higher economic gains (task goals) have resulted when industrial work groups were allowed to give consideration to social-emotional processes (Kuriloff & Atkins, 1966). Schmuck (1971) also presents evidence from elementary schools that higher individual achievement results when group goals are addressed. He proposes that the highest degree of group cohesiveness will be attained in classrooms that work toward all four types of goals identified in Figure 8.2. In this manner, learners can satisfy individual needs for competence and security in the context of the support and encouragement groups provide.

Social Structure

The final attribute that contributes to group cohesiveness is called **social structure.** Social structure refers to the roles and functions assumed by members of the group. There is a social structure in every classroom: a leader and followers, a teacher and students, a

Group cohesiveness. The degree to which members of a group have relationships, common goals, and a social structure within that group.

What goals can I work toward to make my classroom into a more cohesive group of learners?

Social structure. Roles and functions that members of a group assume.

	Task	**Social-Emotional**
Group	Group projects Content discussions Setting learning goals with the class	Discussion about classroom procedures Making group agreements about classroom rules
Individual	Programmed instruction Independent assignments Reading alone	Supportiveness Acceptance Helpfulness

Figure 8.2

Goals and goal-related activities. From *Group Processes in the Classroom,* 5th ed., by R. A. Schmuck and P. A. Schmuck. Copyright © 1988 Times Mirror Higher Education Group, Inc., Dubuque, Iowa. All rights reserved. Reprinted by permission.

responsible adult and youthful members. Certain functions or responsibilities accompany each role, regardless of which individuals assume these roles.

In addition, the social structure dictates how those who assume various roles will relate to one another. These relationships can be formal: "Raise your hand and wait to be recognized before speaking"; "No one may approach my desk without permission." Or they can be informal when, for example, individual personalities and the goals of the classroom are taken into consideration. For example, although most teachers may discourage learners from calling out, a teacher may allow a less formal pattern of teacher-student talk during group discussion to encourage student spontaneity.

When considering social structure and its relationship to groups, social psychologists emphasize two points: First, a clear social structure is needed for a cohesive group to form. Classrooms in which the teacher fails to assume leadership or individual students assert control are less cohesive. Second, the individual personalities of learners and teachers should be considered when establishing how those who assume different roles relate to one another. Classrooms characterized by excessively rigid rules and relationships may find it difficult to develop high degrees of cohesiveness.

Summary

Social psychologists point out that a group has three principal attributes: relationships, common goals, and a social structure. Depending on the extent to which the teacher allows learners to interact, work toward common goals, and establish certain roles and functions, a classroom can become cohesive or fragmented.

What advantages are there for learners and teachers in a classroom with a high degree of cohesiveness? Before examining the stages of group development and what

Focus on

Richard Schmuck, University of Oregon, and Patricia Schmuck, Lewis and Clark College

During the late 1950s and early 1960s, we collaborated at the Research Center for Group Dynamics of the University of Michigan with our good friend and mentor, Ron Lippitt, who was a student of Kurt Lewin. In those days, Pat was an elementary school teacher while Dick was completing his doctoral dissertation on peer relationships and academic achievement in the classroom. Classroom group processes were just beginning to be explored by scholars, and we were intrigued, as both practitioners and researchers, with the social-emotional world of the classroom. We also were committed to making classrooms more democratic cultures. In 1969 we were asked to prepare a text, *Group Processes in the Classroom,* which was published in 1971. That first edition helped educational and school psychologists begin to recognize the importance of group dynamics to effective instruction.

In that first edition, we wanted to present theory and research on group dynamics and to give practical advice to teachers. We sought to make our theories practical and to use innovative practice to help shape our theories. We held a balance between theory and practice in the subsequent six editions. When we became parents and citizens involved in the public schools, we saw how important it was for teachers and administrators to understand the social-emotional life of the classroom and how it affected academic learning. Throughout its subsequent editions, our book chronicled our professional and personal lives in schools. Each successive edition updated the ongoing research and told new stories about our growing children, Julie (born in 1965) and Allen (born in 1968). It also told of our personal experiences such as helping to form an alternative public school, traveling to other countries, and adding new practical advice to teachers which we had gleaned from our students, research, and consulting.

The social world of the classroom is complex; it is a rich system of human interaction linking students, teachers, and the curriculum. How students communicate with one another, how the teacher organizes learning activities, how peer-group norms influence behavior, how power is shared, and how leadership is exercised all affect student learning and group climate. In our work we have tried to help teachers learn about the social complexities of classroom life; skillful teachers take account of the myriad of formal and informal relationships that affect student learning. To help them accomplish this we have worked on how and when to use cooperative learning procedures.

Today, group-process skills are the foundations of effective cooperative learning, an important teaching strategy of the 1990s. We have been active participants in the cooperative learning movement. Dick served as the first president of the International Association for the Study of Cooperation in Education from 1979 to 1982, and Pat helped convene the 1994 convention of that association in Portland, Oregon.

Since the publication of our first edition of *Group Processes in the Classroom,* we have developed related areas of scholarship to enrich teachers' understanding of classroom life. Dick has worked on organizational development in education. Pat has worked intensively on gender equity in education, focusing on women in school administration. Our latest collaborative research was a study of rural schools, *Small Districts, Big Problems,* in which we combined our loves of schools and traveling with a six-month, 10,000-mile tour of 25 small districts on the "blue highways" of America. Together, we remain committed to studying and improving classrooms, since it is within the social interaction of the classroom that learning occurs.

teachers can do to promote this development, let's look at what social psychologists have discovered about the effects groups have on their members.

Effects of Groups on Their Members

Group Effects on Learner Achievement

Would having your learners work on the same math problems in a group result in more correct answers than having them solve the same problems by themselves? In other words, does the presence of others facilitate or impede performance? This question has been asked by social psychologists (Zimbardo, 1996), and until recently they were relatively certain of the answer.

Allport (1924) and Dashiell (1935) concluded that as tasks became more cognitively complex—requiring intellectual activity, such as solving math problems—the presence of others decreased individual performance. But for tasks that required routine physical or motor skills—such as running or diving—the presence of others facilitated performance. Social psychologists explained these different findings by reference to the role played by anxiety. They reasoned that the presence of others had the effect of increasing anxiety and impairing performance when the individual was engaged in an intellectual skill that was not well learned (solving a new math problem, for example). However, when the person was doing something familiar (riding a bike, running, or diving, for example), the presence of others increased arousal or drive and improved performance.

However, research by Sharan and Sharan (1976) indicated that the presence of others during the learning of complex intellectual tasks actually produced faster learning with greater retention than the same material presented in a lecture format. In their research, learners worked cooperatively and interdependently. Schmuck and Schmuck (1992) explain these results by pointing out that the quality of the interpersonal relationships of the members of the group is the critical factor. When learners work around others they know and trust, learning is facilitated. The opposite occurs in a group of learners who neither know nor trust one another.

Subsequent research by Cohen (1984, 1986), Cohen and Intele (1981), Webb (1982), and Slavin (1984, 1990b) indicates that cooperative learning in groups produces higher levels of academic achievement involving conceptual learning and problem solving across a variety of curriculum areas than do individualistic learning formats. Webb (1982) and Cohen (1986) attribute the superiority of cooperative learning to the benefit of having to explain to others complex concepts in one's own words. The implication of this research is that when learners work interdependently and cooperatively with other learners whom they know and trust, complex cognitive learning is enhanced.

Group Effects on Motivation

Psychologists such as Maslow (1943), Dreikurs, Grunwald, and Pepper (1982), and Glasser (1986) point out that human beings have certain shared psychological needs. As we learned in Chapter 7, much of human motivation can be understood as attempts to fulfill basic human needs.

Social psychologists have added to our understanding of this human drive for fulfillment by explaining how the social context (the presence of others) contributes to motivation (Allport, 1955; Fyano, 1980; McClelland, 1975). All individuals want to

Social needs. Needs for affiliation, power, and achievement that are either not present or not as strong outside a group context.

experience recognition, have a sense of control over their environment, and feel knowledgeable to some degree. Being a member of a group, however, intensifies and alters these **social needs** so that they are expressed as a desire to be accepted as a member of a group (affiliation), a desire to have an influence over others (power), and a need to be competent (achievement). Social psychologists like Patricia and Richard Schmuck urge teachers to recognize that groups give rise to strong needs for affiliation, power, and achievement and to then use this heightened motivation to achieve academic excellence. They caution that classrooms in which these three basic needs are not satisfied may have large numbers of learners who feel rejected, listless, powerless, and incompetent. Motivational and conduct problems are thus created within the classroom.

Group Effects on the Self-concept

Self-concept. A schema that an individual holds toward him- or herself.

Social psychologists like Mead (1934) and Cooley (1956) argue that an individual's **self-concept** develops through his or her associations with other people. In other words, how one eventually comes to feel about oneself results from one's interactions with parents, siblings, peers, and teachers.

When children come to school they have the opportunity to interact with others and to learn how others perceive them; naturally they are curious about how they are perceived by teachers and peers. Social psychologists believe that children internalize views of themselves from the way others perceive them.

One study investigating this theory of self-concept was carried out by Mannheim (1957), who collected questionnaires from college students asking them what most influenced the image they held of themselves. She found that the dominant influence on her respondents' self-image came from their most immediate reference group—those with whom they lived. Her results showed that as the respondents' reference groups changed, so did the positive or negative self-image conveyed to them.

Schmuck and Schmuck (1992) emphasize the child's vulnerability to developing a low self-concept in the classroom. Their research and that of Argyus (1972) shows that low-status learners with poor grades and few friends can lose self-esteem when

Students who work in groups experience needs for belonging, power, and achievement. When these needs are satisfied, high levels of achievement and motivation result.

they have few opportunities to experience psychological success with either adults or peers. This in turn lowers their academic achievement and general psychological well-being. They also point out that some school practices related to ability grouping, labeling, and exclusion based on learning problems (to be discussed in Chapter 14) run the risk of creating low-status learners who develop negative feelings about themselves and others.

Group Effects on Emotions

Social psychologists point out that many face-to-face interactions in a group involve emotional conflicts. These emotionally charged interactions may be inevitable among group members who have needs for affiliation, power, and achievement (Coleman & Bexton, 1975).

One factor that contributes to the emotionality of a group is the experiences of the family life of its members. Individuals often generalize the feelings and patterns of interaction learned at home to groups outside the family. Willingness to cooperate, comply, and share, as well as expectations from adults or peers that learners acquire at home can influence behavior in the classroom (Dreikurs et al., 1982).

The classroom presents numerous opportunities for emotionally laden interactions of its own. It has many similarities with home life: at least one authority figure, peers with whom one must associate, and rules not of one's own making. Disagreements and conflicts can easily arise as learners seek to learn how others feel about them and try to meet their own goals. As we will see shortly, a teacher's leadership style can exacerbate or ameliorate these emotional conflicts.

Summary

Social psychologists have studied the intellectual opportunities and emotional problems created when learners come together as a group. Intellectual achievement can be enhanced or stifled depending on how comfortable a student feels around others. Drives to be accepted, influence others, and achieve in their presence can also rise to the surface. When properly channeled, these drives can produce increased levels of achievement and learner satisfaction. If frustrated, they can lead to despair, listlessness, and conflict. In the next section we examine how these drives can be channeled to form a cohesive and productive group environment.

Group Formation: A Developmental Perspective

One of the challenges confronting the classroom teacher is creating a cohesive group of learners who, at the start of the school year, may not know or choose to be with one another, are required to be in a room with a teacher who may not be of their choosing, and who may have little to say about the rules by which their behavior will be governed. Social psychologists who study group development believe that there are distinct **stages of group formation** (Mauer, 1985; Schmuck & Schmuck, 1992; Stanford, 1977; Tuckman, 1988). Teachers who want their classroom learners to work as a group—to like one another, learn from one another, and support one another's learning—must consider how a group forms and works together.

Stage of group formation. In social psychology, a period of group development in which the concerns of the group and functioning of the group are different from the periods preceding and following.

Stages of Group Development

Social psychologists such as Schutz (1958), Johnson and Johnson (1984), and Schmuck and Schmuck (1992) believe that every successful group passes through a series of stages during which it has certain tasks to accomplish or certain concerns that must be resolved. The way the group accomplishes these tasks and resolves these concerns to a large extent determines how cohesive a group it will be. Mauer (1985) describes these stages as follows:

> *Stage I: Forming.* Resolving concerns about acceptance and responsibilities.
>
> *Stage II: Storming.* Resolving concerns about shared influence.
>
> *Stage III: Norming.* Resolving concerns about how work gets done.
>
> *Stage IV: Performing.* Resolving concerns about freedom, control, and self-regulation.

Figure 8.3 illustrates these four stages. In the following sections, we describe each stage in detail and suggest specific ways that teachers can promote group development in each.

Stage I: Forming. When learners come together at the start of the school year, they usually are concerned about two issues: (1) finding their place in the social structure and (2) finding out what they are expected to do. This first issue involves concerns about "inclusion" or "group membership" (Schutz, 1958). During the first several days of class, learners (and some teachers) naturally ask, "How will I fit in?" "Who will accept or reject me?" "What do I have to do to be respected?" At this time, a phenomenon called *testing* takes place (Froyen, 1993). Learners engage in specific actions to see what kind of reaction they get from teachers and peers. This is the learner's way of finding out how the teacher and peers feel toward him. At this stage of group formation, learners are curious about one another. They want to know where other class members live, who their friends are, what they like to do after school, and where they like to go. As students learn more about one another, they begin to see how and with whom they fit in.

Putnam and Burke (1992) urge teachers to engage in activities during the first few

What are some of the ways I can put my learners at ease during the first few days of class?

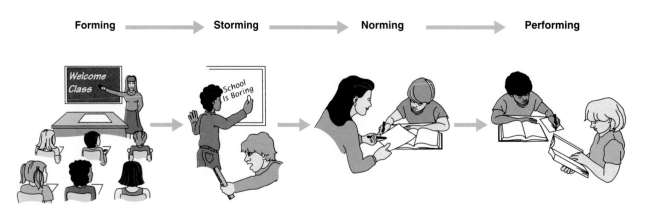

Forming   ⟶   Storming   ⟶   Norming   ⟶   Performing

Figure 8.3
Stages of group development.

When learners first come together in a group, each person may feel concerns about acceptance, influence, and competence. Skilled teachers recognize and address these concerns of their students.

weeks of school to help learners trust one another and feel like members of a group. The accompanying box, *Fostering Group Development*, describes such activities.

There is a tendency among teachers during the first stage of classroom group development to concentrate almost exclusively on concerns about work and rules to the exclusion of social concerns. However, learners who have unresolved fears about acceptance by the teacher and where they fit in the peer group will find it difficult to concentrate on academic work without first developing trust and the feeling that they are valued members of a group (Schmuck & Schmuck, 1992; Schutz, 1958).

Questions teachers can ask to promote group development during the forming stage and each subsequent stage of group development are listed in Table 8.1.

Stage II: Storming. The goal of the forming stage of group development is to help learners feel secure and perceive themselves as members of a classroom group. Healthy group life at this stage occurs if learners have accepted the teacher as their leader, made some initial commitment to follow rules and procedures, and agreed to respect other members of the class. During the storming stage of group development they begin to test the limits of these commitments (Froyen, 1993). This limit-testing may take the form of amiable challenges to academic expectations (homework, classwork, tests, and the like) and rules in order to establish the conditions under which they do and do not apply. Learners may question seating arrangements, homework responsibilities, and seatwork routines. They may want further explanations for rules that they initially agreed to follow.

Social psychologists refer to these amiable challenges to teacher authority and leadership as examples of **distancing** behavior. Distancing behavior occurs in any group where a leader initially establishes authority by virtue of his or her position rather than through competence or credibility. Thus distancing behavior represents the learners' reservations about the commitments they made during the forming stage to class expectations and group participation.

> **How should I respond to learners who choose to challenge my authority early in the school year?**

Distancing. Behaviors that challenge authority and leadership to test the limits of group commitments.

Applying Your Knowledge:
Fostering Group Development

The following actions will help you foster group cohesiveness during each stage of group development.

Forming
- Help teachers and students learn about one another and develop trust.
- Foster learners' appreciation for each others' abilities.
- Inform learners about work expectations, rules, routines, and what life in the classroom will be like.
- Promote learners' view of themselves as having a voice in the running of the classroom.
- Assess what learners know and can do.

Storming
- Don't feel threatened by or overreact to distancing or centering behavior—it will pass.
- Recognize the storming stage as a necessary part of group development.

- Monitor learners' compliance with rules, but be willing to reconsider those that aren't working.
- Avoid showing favoritism to any members of the group.

Norming
- Reinforce established classroom routines positively (see Chapter 9).
- Except for necessary reinforcement of rules, devote the greatest amount of attention to instruction.

Performing
- Reinforce learners' abilities to set their own priorities, budget their own time, and discipline themselves.
- Model reflective behavior and self-reinforcement skills.
- Structure year-end activities to prepare learners for the transition to the next school year.

Centering. The questioning by a member of a group about how that individual will personally benefit from the group; a preoccupation with fairness.

A second type of amiable limit-testing that often accompanies distancing behavior is called **centering** behavior. Centering occurs when learners start to question how they will personally benefit from being group members—in other words, they ask, "What's in it for me?" At this stage, the questions learners ask and the assertions they make reflect a preoccupation with fairness. They are quick to notice favoritism toward some members of the group.

These distancing and centering conflicts that arise between teachers and learners and between the learners themselves are a natural part of group development. Social psychologists caution teachers about feeling threatened or overreacting at this stage. The storming stage is best perceived as a desirable reflection on past commitments made by learners that must occur on the journey to developing a healthy group life. During these types of conflicts, teachers need to monitor compliance with rules and procedures, but be willing to reconsider those that may not be working. Questions that teachers can ask themselves to promote group development during the storming stage are listed in Table 8.1.

Stage III: Norming. The security learners develop at the forming stage provides them with a safe foundation to challenge the teacher's authority during the storming

Table 8.1

Important Questions About Group Development

Stage I: Forming	Stage II: Storming	Stage III: Norming	Stage IV: Performing
1. Are there activities that enable everyone to get to know about one another?	1. Are conflicts openly recognized and discussed?	1. Is there a process for resolving conflict?	1. Can this group evaluate its own effectiveness?
2. Has everyone had a chance to be heard?	2. Can the group assess its own functioning?	2. Can the group set goals?	2. Can the group and individuals solve their own problems?
3. Do learners interact with a variety of classmates?	3. Are new and different ideas listened to and evaluated?	3. Can learners express what is expected of them?	3. Do the group members have opportunities to work independently and express themselves through a medium of their own choosing?
4. Do learners and teachers listen to one another?	4. Are the skills of all members being used?	4. Is there mutual respect between teacher and learners?	4. Can individuals evaluate themselves and set goals for personal improvement?
5. Have concerns and/or fears regarding academic and behavioral expectations been addressed?	5. Do all learners have an opportunity to share leadership and responsibility?	5. What happens to learners who fail to respect norms?	5. Is the group prepared to disband?

Source: Adapted from R. A. Schmuck and P. A. Schmuck, *Group processes in the classroom,* 6th ed. Copyright © 1992 Wm. C. Brown Communications, Inc. Dubuque, Iowa. All rights reserved. Reprinted by permission.

stage. Skilled leadership during the storming stage assures learners that they will be listened to, treated fairly, and allowed to share power and influence. This assurance leads them during the norming stage to accept academic expectations, procedures, and rules for group functioning as well as the roles and functions of the various group members.

Norms are shared expectations by group members regarding how they should think, feel, and behave. Social psychologists view norms as the principal regulators of group behavior (Zimbardo, 1996). They may take the form of either written or unwritten rules that all or most members of the group voluntarily agree to follow. A classroom group has norms when learners, for the most part, agree on what is and is not socially acceptable classroom behavior.

Healthy group development at the norming stage is characterized by group behavior that is primarily focused on academic achievement. Assuming that group development has proceeded successfully up to this point, group members now are principally concerned with their own learning and that of the group. Learners feel secure and trust one another, accept their role as followers and the teacher's role as group leader, and are ready to get down to the business of the classroom. The norms that develop at this stage assure the group members that they know how to pursue and achieve their academic goals. Many teachers see the norming stage as the most satisfying and productive phase of group development.

Norms. Shared expectations among group members regarding how they should think, feel, and behave; the principal regulators of group behavior.

Stage IV: Performing. By the time the group has reached the fourth developmental stage, performing, learners feel at ease with one another, know the rules and their roles, accept group norms, and are familiar with the routines of the classroom. The principal concern for the group at this stage is establishing its independence.

Just as the storming stage of development was characterized by a testing of limits, the performing stage is characterized by learners' desire to show that they can perform independently of the teacher. Social psychologists urge teachers to encourage this desire for independence by focusing less on classroom control at this stage and more on teaching the group how to set priorities, budget time, self-evaluate, self-regulate, and self-discipline. Putnam and Burke (1992) recommend that during this stage, as compared to the others, teachers devote more time modeling to students how to reflect on what they have learned and how to evaluate their own performances.

The performing stage ends with the school year or semester. Thus, this stage represents a time of transition. Assuming all four stages of development have been successfully completed, learners will have developed relationships with one another and with their teacher. Social psychologists suggest that teachers structure year-end activities to prepare group members to make the transition to other classes and grade levels (Putnam & Burke, 1992).

Summary

Forming, storming, norming, and performing are stages by which a group develops and becomes effective in establishing relationships, common goals, and an identifiable structure. These four steps are essential in building a healthy classroom group life. In other words, at each stage certain concerns become paramount for the group, and these concerns must be resolved before the group can proceed to a more advanced level of development.

In the next section, we will discuss the criteria by which social psychologists gauge the health of a classroom group at any of the four developmental stages. We will point out the fundamental properties of a healthy developing classroom group, as indicated by social psychological research, and provide some suggestions and activities to ensure that your group possesses these ingredients. Those that are fundamental to a productive classroom climate are leadership, expectations, norms, cohesiveness, and problem solving (Schmuck & Schmuck, 1992).

Leadership

What kind of group leader do you want to be? How do you want your students to perceive you at the forming stage of group development? How will you establish your leadership so as to help learners feel comfortable with you and with each other? How will you make converts of some learners and compatriots of others? According to social psychologists (French & Raven, 1959; Raven, 1974), to accomplish this you will have to gain your students' trust and respect the "old-fashioned way . . . you will have to earn it." But exactly how is this done? French and Raven look at how you earn respect by asking the question "How do you achieve social power?" They identify five types of social power, or leadership, that a teacher or authority figure can strive for: expert, referent, legitimate, reward, and coercive power (see Figure 8.4).

What types of social power can I acquire at the beginning of the year to help me form and lead a cohesive classroom?

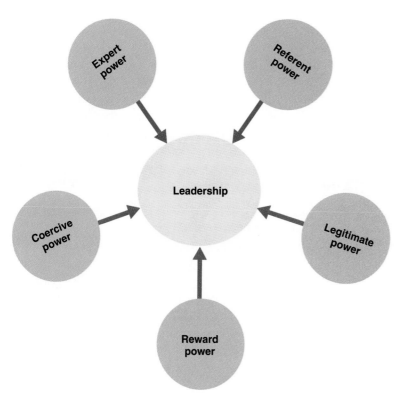

Figure 8.4
Five types of social power.

Expert Power

Certain individuals become leaders because others perceive them as experts (Borich, 1993, 1996). Successful teachers have **expert power.** Their students see them as both competent to explain and do certain things and knowledgeable about particular topics. Such influence is earned, rather than conferred by virtue of having a particular title. Teachers with expert power explain things well, show enthusiasm and excitement about what they teach, and appear confident and self-assured before their classes.

As a new teacher, you may find it difficult to establish leadership through expert power. Even though you are knowledgeable and competent, uncertainty and inexperience in front of a group may make you appear less so. Students are attuned to body language that suggests indecision and lack of confidence, and they may test the competence and challenge the authority of a teacher who appears not to be in command of the subject.

Referent Power

Students often accept as leaders teachers whom they like and respect. They view such teachers as trustworthy, fair, and concerned. The term **referent power** is used to describe leadership earned in this way. Ask any group of junior high or high school students why they like particular teachers, and they will invariably describe the teachers

Expert power. The legitimation of an individual's leadership because others perceive that individual as an expert.

Referent power. Leadership earned because of a perception of an individual's trustworthiness, fairness, and concern for members of the group.

Teachers establish leadership in a variety of ways: by appearing competent, friendly, and trustworthy and by the skillful use of rewards and logical consequences.

they like as "fair," "caring," and "someone you can talk to." Without referent power, even teachers with expert power may have their authority challenged or ignored.

Teachers sometimes say that they would rather be respected than liked, as if these two consequences were mutually exclusive. Research by Soar and Soar (1983), however, suggests that teachers can be both respected and liked. According to these researchers, teachers who were both respected and liked were associated with greater student satisfaction and higher achievement. Glasser (1986) also emphasizes that students' need for belonging in a classroom is more likely to be met by a teacher who is perceived as both warm and competent.

Legitimate Power

Legitimate power. Leadership based on a specific role rather than on the nature of an individual.

Some roles by their very nature carry with them influence and authority. Police officers, presidents, and judges exert social power and leadership by their very titles. This type of power has been referred to as **legitimate power;** unlike expert and referent power, it cannot be earned. Teachers possess a certain degree of legitimate power. Our society expects students to give teachers their attention, to respect them, and to do what they say. Most families also stress the importance of "listening to the teacher." Every new teacher begins his or her first day of class with legitimate power.

Legitimate power, therefore, gives the new teacher some breathing room during the first few weeks of school. Most students will initially obey and accept the authority of a new teacher by virtue of his or her position of authority. However, building classroom leadership solely through legitimate power—that bestowed by others—may be like building a house on a foundation of sand. The first challenge to authority may quickly erode any initial influence that legitimate power may have provided. Teachers should therefore use their legitimate power to establish referent and expert power.

Reward Power

Individuals in positions of authority can reward the people they lead. These rewards can take the form of privileges, approval, or more tangible compensation, such as money. To the extent that students desire the rewards conferred by teachers, teachers can exert a degree of leadership and authority. However, students who don't care much about good grades or teacher approval are difficult to lead solely by exerting **reward power,** since much of what is reinforcing to students can be attained outside of school without the aid of a teacher. In such cases some teachers resort to tangible reinforcers, like access to desired activities, objects, and even food. In the next chapter we will examine some of the research on the use of tangible reinforcers. In this chapter, you will learn that reward power can be an effective tool in the classroom but cannot substitute for referent or expert power.

Reward power. Leadership based on rewards or benefits that an individual can give to members of a group.

Coercive Power

By law, teachers and other school personnel are allowed to act *in loco parentis,* or with the same authority the parent has. Consequently, within limits, schools can punish students who defy the authority or leadership of the teacher by such techniques as suspension or expulsion, denial of privileges, or removal from the classroom. Teachers who rely on such techniques to maintain social power in the classroom are said to be using **coercive power.** The use of coercive power, however, may end misbehavior for a time, but at the cost of failing to develop trusting relationships or meeting students' needs for belonging. Overreliance on coercive power may lead to the formation of subgroups antagonistic to class cohesiveness, group cooperation, and achievement.

Coercive power. Leadership based on punishment or coercion.

Teachers, especially new teachers, should work to establish expert and referent power as the best way to guide group development. Expert power can be achieved by completing in-service training and graduate programs, keeping up-to-date with the literature in your field of expertise, attending seminars and workshops, and meeting state and district career ladder and mentoring requirements. It is not likely that you will have this type of influence during your first weeks of teaching. However, from the very first day of class you can exhibit referent power by giving students a sense of belonging and acceptance.

Expectations

Social psychologists emphasize that the most important content to be communicated during teacher-student interactions, whether they are formal or informal, is high expectations. Students want to receive the message that they are competent, responsible, attractive, interesting, and capable of learning what you are teaching. The expectations you hold for your learners can create the behavior you want for them. Consider the expectations a teacher is expressing to the class in each of the following statements:

How can I avoid creating self-fulfilling prophecies in which my expectations about individual learners later influence my behavior toward them?

"Tests in this class will be hard, and some probably won't make it."

"I can't understand why you're having trouble with this."

"I can see that you haven't understood a thing."

"I won't go over it again if you don't get it this time."

Social psychologists use the expression **self-fulfilling prophecy** to describe how expectancies tend to confirm themselves (Cooper, 1979). Large group settings, such as

Self-fulfilling prophecy. The correlation that has been observed between expectations and performance.

Expectancy (Pygmalion) effect.
Often referred to as a "self-fulfilling prophecy," the correlation between high teacher expectations and high learner achievement and low teacher expectations and low learner achievement.

the typical school classroom, tend to encourage the **expectancy (Pygmalion) effect.** When teachers work individually with students or in small groups, teachers receive immediate feedback that either confirms or disconfirms their expectations. However, when teachers work almost exclusively with large groups, they often lack immediate knowledge of the changes that may be occurring in their learners' behavior that can disconfirm negative expectations and biases. Consequently, their beliefs or expectancies remain unchallenged.

Good and Brophy (1991) describe how expectations lead to self-fulfillment in the following way:

- Based on what you read, hear, or see about your students, you naturally expect different achievements and social behaviors from different students.

- These expectations affect your decisions while you are teaching—you call on certain students and not others; you wait longer for some students to give answers than others; you seat students in different parts of the room; you check the work of some students more frequently; you assign easier or more difficult assignments.

- Your students eventually learn what they are and are not expected to do, and they behave accordingly.

- You therefore observe the student behavior that confirms your original expectations, and the cycle repeats itself.

Figure 8.5 describes this cycle. It can be broken only when the teacher receives consistent feedback from students that disconfirms his or her predictions. Such feedback is less likely to occur in large-group instructional formats.

A particularly alarming example of the expectancy effect was uncovered by Rist (1970) when he studied a class of ghetto students from kindergarten through second grade. Rist observed that from the time these students entered kindergarten, they were divided into three groups—"tigers," "cardinals," and "clowns"—each seated at a differ-

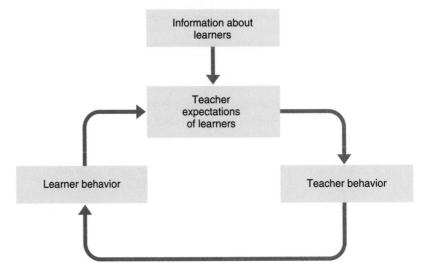

Figure 8.5
Self-fulfilling prophecy.

ent table. The kindergarten teacher initially placed the children in these groups based on their socioeconomic status and information from registration forms and from interviews with mothers and social workers. The highest-status children, the tigers, were seated closest to the teacher and quickly labeled "fast learners." The lowest status children, the clowns, were farthest removed from the teacher and were quickly led to believe that they were "slow learners."

In reality, each of the three groups had a mixture of slow and fast learners, but the slow learners who were seated farthest from the teacher seldom got the opportunity to interact with her, while those closest to the teacher frequently received her attention. Before long the abilities of each group were taken as fact rather than as creations of the teacher, so much so that it was increasingly difficult for the "clowns" to be considered anything other than slow by their teachers in subsequent grades.

At no time did the teacher seem to be aware that the arrangement was biased or that seating certain students consistently in the back of the room would reduce their contact with her. Thus, this teacher's bias became a self-fulfilling prophecy that extended even to subsequent grades and classes. Other types of self-fulfilling biases may also affect your interactions with students. For example, Gage and Berliner (1988) identified several biased ways in which teachers interact with their students. They then analyzed the extent to which experienced teachers actually exhibited these negative expectations in their classrooms. Their biases included interacting with students disproportionately in these ways:

Calling on students seated in the front half of the classroom more often than those seated in the back half of the classroom

Calling on nicer-looking students more often than average-looking students

Calling on more able students more often than less able students

Calling on nonminority group members more often than minority group members

Gage and Berliner calculated the number of student-teacher interactions that would be expected by chance for these classifications, and then from classroom observation they determined the actual number of interactions that occurred. Somewhat surprisingly, their results indicated that every teacher showed some bias in these categories. In other words, every teacher favored at least one student classification over another by naming, calling on, requiring information from, or otherwise interacting with those in some classification disproportionately to those not in that classification.

Such biases may be meaningless over a single class period but can have a significant and long-lasting emotional impact on students if continued throughout weeks, months, or the entire school year. The accumulated effect of systematic bias in a classroom can be an open message to some students that they are less desirable and less worthy of attention than others, regardless of how unintentional the bias may be. If the message is received, the result may be a change in motivation, self-concept, and even anxiety levels of some students in ways that impede any attempt to develop trusting relationships.

Studies by Schmuck and Schmuck (1992) report that sometimes biases can become so strong that even when students change their behavior significantly, the changes may not be perceived by the teacher or, when perceived, they may be misinterpreted. Thus, you may perceive your students' actual improvements in social behavior as manipulative, temporary, or motivated only to get some tangible reward. You may attribute improvements in their academic behavior to luck, cheating, or help from parents or other students rather than evidence of their growth in learning.

Inevitably, you will have different expectations for your students. Your access to academic records, report cards, and the anecdotes of previous teachers, as well as the wide range of academic and social skill levels you are likely to have in your classroom, will naturally encourage a tendency to expect less of some and more of others. You will not help but notice who grasps new concepts most quickly, and which students are the most persistent and responsible in completing classwork and homework. You cannot avoid expectations, but you can avoid their effects on learners by monitoring how you lead the class and communicate during large-group, small-group, and one-on-one interactions. Expectancy effects on the achievement and social behavior of learners can be monitored by using the checklist in the accompanying box, *Avoiding Expectancy Effects* (Cooper & Good, 1983).

Norms

Despite their immunity to the threat of a failing grade, some of my students maintained a social agenda of some kind and class participation for them represented an opportunity to cultivate relationships with the opposite sex. These students could thus be affected by shifting their seating arrangements. I did so with the intention of separating the talkative, "don't-threaten-me-with-a-failing-grade" type student from others who shared their desire to communicate and disrupt. Though I did achieve some success with the musical chairs strategy, there were definite problems with it. . . .

These noise-related problems and challenges were the most obvious and annoying of the issues that confronted me during my first few months at Meadowfield. Despite the negative effect these problems had on the class, as well as my own morale, I nevertheless managed temporarily to avoid taking a harsh stand on matters of classroom discipline. I had had several heart-to-heart discussions with my classes designed to focus

---

Applying Your Knowledge:

Avoiding Expectancy Effects

Following these guidelines will help you avoid expectancy effects in your classroom:

- Avoid calling on high-achieving students more often than low-achieving students to answer questions, read before the group, recite, or solve problems at the blackboard.
- Do not use low-achieving learners more often as message carriers, seatwork collectors, or material distributors.
- Give both high- and low-achieving students equal amounts of time to answer questions and equal numbers of prompts, hints, and leading questions.
- Give equal amounts of feedback and corrective comments to all students.
- Avoid demanding a higher level of completed and correct work from high-achieving students.

- Avoid seating high-achieving students nearer the front of the room.
- Avoid interrupting low-achieving students more frequently when they are reading, reciting, or answering questions.
- Avoid praising low-achieving students for marginal or below-average performance.
- Ask high cognitive level questions of both high and low achievers.
- Contact the parents of low-achieving learners for academic concerns, not just for behavioral concerns.
- Use similar disciplinary techniques with all learners.

attention on the problem of noise and with the hope of making it unnecessary to adopt harsh disciplinary measures.

For about a week or so after the talk, the quality of life in Room C313 improved noticeably. The situation was eventually shattered, however, by a core group of students, small but influential, for whom the desire to talk—and attract attention—was more important than the needs of everyone else. It was this group that eventually managed to restore the near chaos that at times had reigned prior to our heart-to-heart discussions. (Michael, in Ryan, 1992, pp. 152–153)

A social psychologist analyzing Michael's classroom would conclude that this class is moving toward norms that are antagonistic rather than supportive of academic achievement. In addition to leadership and expectations, social psychologists point to norms as an important barometer of healthy group development. Let's examine what they are and what you can do to influence them.

What Are Norms?

Norms describe what group members should or should not do to be socially acceptable. They tell group members what is expected of them and what they in turn should expect of others. They usually are not formally stated or written down. For example, nowhere is it written that in your college classes you should listen (and sometimes take notes) when your professor is speaking, or that you should wait to be dismissed by your teacher rather than leave before the end of class. Likewise, you know better than to read a newspaper while the professor is lecturing. You learned these behavioral expectations by observing what most other students do.

Norms play a similar role in governing behavior in elementary and secondary classrooms. But they do so differently than do rules and procedures, which are not as personally meaningful. Some positive norms are given here:

- It's OK to be seen talking to the teacher after school.
- Learners in this class should help one another with their classwork.
- We're all responsible for our own learning.
- We shouldn't gloat when one of our classmates gives a wrong answer.
- We need to respect the privacy of others.
- The most important thing for this class is learning.

Norms such as these can support academic achievement and positive relationships. Other norms can serve the opposite purpose, as we saw in Michael's class. Whether positive or negative, norms may be brought with learners on the first day of class, or they may develop as the school year proceeds. Before discussing how norms develop and what you can do to influence their development, let's see what functions norms can serve in your classroom.

Significance of Classroom Norms

Social psychologists believe that positive norms serve several functions in the classroom (Froyen, 1993; Putnam & Burke, 1992; Schmuck & Schmuck, 1992).

- Norms orient group members to which social interactions are appropriate and which are not, and then regulate those social interactions. Norms allow learners to anticipate the ways others will behave in the classroom and tell them how they are expected to behave themselves.

- Norms create group identification and group cohesiveness (Zimbardo, 1996). Group formation begins when the members agree to adhere to the norms of the group. This process begins during the forming stage of group development and ends during the norming stage.

- Norms promote academic achievement and positive relationships among class members. Academic and social goals are more likely to be achieved in classrooms with consistent norms. For example, peer group norms, when they are congruent with the teacher's norms for the class, represent one of the most important influences on school performance (Schmuck & Schmuck, 1992).

How Norms Develop

Group norms, whether in support of a teacher's goals or opposed to them, begin to develop on the first day of school, during the forming stage of group development. Zimbardo (1996) identifies two basic processes by which norms develop: diffusion and crystallization.

Norm diffusion. The formation of expectations among a group of learners as a result of past individual experiences and expectations.

Norm diffusion takes place when learners first enter a group or class. They bring with them expectations acquired from experiences in other classes, other group memberships, and other life experiences. As the learners talk and mingle with each other during breaks and recess they communicate with one another. Their various expectations for academic and social behavior are diffused and spread throughout the entire class.

Norm crystallization. The convergence of expectations into a shared perspective by the group.

Eventually, as learners engage in a variety of activities together, their expectations begin to converge and crystallize into a shared perspective regarding classroom life. This process of **norm crystallization** was shown in a classic experiment in social psychology. Sherif (1935) was interested in how the presence of other people affects perceptions. The experimental situation involved the use of a phenomenon called the *autokinetic effect*. This effect is an illusion of motion that occurs when you stare at a stationary point of light for an extended period of time. After you have stared at the light for several minutes, it appears to begin to move. Sherif asked his subjects to judge the direction and distance of the perceived movement and recorded their judgments.

Next he asked the subjects to perform the same task, this time with several other observers present. The observers, unknown to the experimental subjects, were confederates of Sherif. All the observers reported their judgments out loud. The confederates consistently reported the movement of the light in a single direction. Sherif found that his subjects then changed their judgments to conform to those of the group. Even more surprisingly, when they were alone again they continued to report that the stationary light moved in the direction identified by the other observers.

Sherif concluded that the uncertainty of the situation, combined with public sharing of opinions or judgments, encouraged the crystallization of a norm—in this case the direction of the movement of light. Once established, the norm continued to influence the perceptions of the group.

Patricia and Richard Schmuck believe that learners encounter a similar situation in the classroom. During the first few weeks of school, the classroom confronts learners with a variety of sensory experiences and many ambiguous events. Learners wonder "What will our teacher be like?" "Will she give hard work?" "Will she be fair?" "Are the other students my friends?" "Will this class be interesting?"

Learners bring to this situation certain attitudes and beliefs about teachers and classrooms. As they talk with one another, their attitudes diffuse and become shared and crystallized into classroom norms. For example, the teacher on the first day of class may unintentionally speak harshly to a learner. Learners may be confused about how to interpret this action. Those with prior negative experiences may express their feelings about the teacher. "He's someone you can't like." "Don't try to be friends." "Let's not cooperate." Eventually, these feelings and perceptions may solidify into class norms, which become resistant to change. Mike's class, which we visited earlier, was experiencing the process of norm diffusion and crystallization.

How Teachers Can Influence Classroom Norms

Social psychologists tell us that norms play an important role in determining whether learners achieve academic and social goals. As we saw earlier, positive norms can support academic achievement; negative norms can work against it. Thus, teachers should do all they can to influence the development of norms that support their classroom goals. Therefore, it is important that you know how to positively influence the development of class norms and how to identify and alter existing ones. The accompanying box, *Influencing Group Norms*, provides detailed suggestions, and Table 8.2 provides a list of

---

Table 8.2

Do As I Say, Not As I Do

The following actions can work against the development of positive classroom norms.

1. My teacher interrupts me without a word of apology, but if I interrupt my teacher, he says I am rude.
2. My teacher is a grouch and mean but expects me to be pleasant and nice.
3. My teacher expects me to like school but has dull, boring, slow-moving lessons.
4. My teacher tells me my work is poor but doesn't show me how to improve.
5. I can't read my teacher's handwriting, but he expects mine to be legible.
6. My teacher says he will allow me to do something special, but he never does.
7. My teacher says he will grade my homework, but I saw it in his wastebasket.
8. My teacher tells me to listen but never listens to me.
9. My teacher eats in the classroom, but I am not allowed to.
10. My teacher says I can't talk in the cafeteria, but he does.

Applying Your Knowledge:

Influencing Group Norms

The following techniques will help you develop positive group norms in your classroom.

- Explain to the class the concept of a group norm. Draw up a list of norms with the class. Over time, add and delete norms that either help or impede the work of the group.
- Conduct discussions of class norms and encourage learners to talk about them among themselves. Glasser (1986) suggests discussing with students ideas on how the class might be run, problems that may interfere with the group's performance, and needed rules and routines.
- Appoint or elect a class council to make recommendations for improving the group's climate and productivity. Have the group assess whether the norms are or are not working.
- Provide a model of the respect, consistency, and responsibility for learning that you want your learners to exhibit.

How can I develop positive norms of conduct and learning in my classroom?

comments from learners indicating how easily teachers can fail to model appropriate norms by communicating the message "Do as I say, not as I do."

Cohesiveness

Many teachers and administrators maintain that their job is to develop academic skills, not group cohesiveness. Social psychologists, on the other hand, believe that such a view may be shortsighted because of the relationship between academic achievement and group cohesiveness in the classroom (Schmuck & Schmuck, 1992). They assert that teachers need to be concerned that learners like not only learning but one another. They support this assertion by pointing out that learners have significant needs for affiliation by virtue of being in a classroom group.

Thus, social psychologists highlight group cohesiveness as the fourth characteristic of a healthy group that teachers should promote. They stress that group cohesiveness satisfies not only needs for affiliation but also needs for achievement. As we will see, research has established an important link between group cohesiveness, academic achievement, and group productivity.

How Cohesiveness Affects Academic Performance and Group Problem Solving

Cohesiveness refers to how individual students feel about their classroom group as a whole. Group cohesiveness is strong when each student sees himself or herself as an important part of the group. Group cohesiveness is weak when individuals in the group feel more attraction to a subgroup or to other individuals than to the entire group.

Cohesiveness exerts significant impact on your students' willingness to learn. Research on cohesiveness demonstrates that learners who perceive themselves as liked and accepted within the classroom peer structure learn more than those who do not.

A study by Lewis and St. John (1974) supports this view. These researchers studied the achievement of African-American students in classrooms where the majority of students were white. They concluded that for the African-American students to raise their grades there had to be (1) classroom norms supportive of academic achievement and (2) acceptance of African-American students by white students into the peer group. Merely being around white students who had high expectations and being part of a group with norms stressing achievement were not sufficient for the African-American students to excel. The white students had to accept them as friends as well.

Research into the effectiveness of **cooperative learning** groups suggests that such groups produce higher levels of academic achievement, particularly in terms of conceptual learning, problem solving, and metacognitive learning, than do individual, competitive learning formats (Cohen, 1985; Slavin, 1990b, 1991). The cohesiveness of these groups is a principal ingredient of their success (Cohen, 1985; Slavin, 1987, 1990b, 1991). This research indicates that teachers should prepare learners for cooperative learning through training exercises and activities that promote the development of interaction skills and trusting relationships.

Cohesiveness promotes not only individual achievement but also group productivity. Kafer (1976), working in elementary school classrooms, measured the cohesiveness

Cooperative learning. The assignment of students of varying abilities and ethnicities and of both genders to small groups with a common goal in which each member has a role.

Cohesiveness produces not only individual achievement but also group productivity in the classroom.

Table 8.3

Group Acquaintance Activities

Activity	Description
Name chain	Have students sit in a circle and, in order, say their first names and tell one thing about themselves. Each succeeding student must repeat the name of each student who preceded and one thing each person said. If Sam speaks first, followed by Maria, Maria begins her turn by saying, "That's Sam and he has a pet turtle. I'm Maria and my sister is a singer." Then, Didi, who speaks next, must identify both Sam and Maria, and so on.
What's in a name	Have students sit in small groups of five or six and tell one another something about their name: What it is, how they got it, their nickname, if people misspell or mispronounce their name, if they like their name, and what they want the class to call them.
Interviews	Start off as a whole group activity. Ask the class to list questions that would help them know a classmate better. Then students pair off, interview one another, and form new pairs.
Guess who	Have each student write a brief autobiographical sketch, which you then collect and read back to the class. Students have to guess the name of the individual whose sketch is being read. Some misleading information can be given, and students have to identify the person and then separate fact from fiction about the person.

of various small working groups. He found that the most productive groups were those that scored highest in terms of friendship patterns among group members and mutual attraction and trust. Also, Reynolds (1977) reported significant improvement in attendance in a junior high school following the establishment of a "buddy system." Learners with attendance problems identified buddies who lived near them and would remind them to go to school and be on time. After six weeks, not only did student attendance improve, but many of the buddies became close friends as well.

Promoting Group Cohesiveness

What are some practical strategies and activities I can use in my classroom to promote trust and group cohesiveness?

Group cohesiveness is most directly influenced by the friendship structure of the class. In particular, social psychologists emphasize that this structure must be diverse. In other words, learners must be friendly with as many different class members as possible. Cliques or many small independent subgroups of friends can detract from group cohesiveness.

Friendships grow out of trust. Trust develops when individuals know something about one another and have the opportunity to work and be together. Mistrust can develop in classrooms when students have little information about one another's feelings, beliefs, likes and dislikes, and other seemingly minor but interesting details such as where they live, how many are in their family, whether they have hobbies or pets, and what games and sports they like. You can actively promote the attractiveness of each student to the others by providing opportunities for them to get to know and be with one another. Some ideas for promoting diverse friendship patterns out of which cohesiveness can result are given in the accompanying box, *Promoting Group Cohesiveness*, and in Table 8.3.

Applying Your Knowledge:

Promoting Group Cohesiveness

Following are some specific techniques you can use to promote group cohesiveness in your classroom.

- Construct a bulletin board around the theme of friendships by having students bring pictures of friends. Have them take turns telling how they met the friend.
- Have your students write brief biographies. Gather all the autobiographies into a book entitled "Our Lives," and give each student a copy to read and discuss.
- Have students form a friendship circle in which they pass around something they have made (a toy, tool, model, etc.), for other students to examine and admire.
- Place the names (turned over) of your students in a box. Have each select the name of a classmate, who then becomes his or her "pal." Pals then give to or do nice things for one another. At regular intervals, each student selects one more name to add to his or her list of pals.
- Publish a student directory that includes names, hobbies, jobs, career aspirations, and so on.
- Form work groups that mix students of different backgrounds so that the same individuals are not always together.

Groups heighten the drive of all students for affiliation, achievement, and influence. These needs are best met in a class characterized by diverse friendships between students. Learning requires trust, since learning itself requires the open and free communication of ideas between and among individuals. To ignore the critical importance of cohesiveness is to ignore one of the most powerful ingredients of learning.

Problem Solving

Teachers must be prepared to deal with three types of **group conflict** in order to establish a productive group life in their classrooms. One type of conflict, which occurs during the storming stage of group development, arises out of the problems that learners bring with them to the classroom. Such problems are typically categorized by verbal and physical aggression, hostility, and defiance of authority.

A second type of conflict occurs when certain learners choose not to accept classroom rules or to abide by classroom norms, and subsequently withdraw from the group. They frequently engage in mildly disruptive attention-seeking behavior and low work productivity. These are often called conduct problems, and they typically result in con-

Group conflict. Disruptions that destabilize group relationships, structures, and goals.

flicts between the teacher and a small group of learners or one particular learner. We will discuss concepts and strategies for dealing with the first two types of conflict in the following chapter.

A third and final type of conflict arises out of the natural processes of group development. These conflicts often take the form of amiable **limit testing** during the storming stage of group development. As we saw, during this time learners often engage in distancing and centering activities. Consequently, a process for problem solving or conflict resolution is necessary during this developmental process. Therefore, problem solving, in conjunction with effective leadership, high expectations, productive norms, and group cohesiveness, is the fifth characteristic by which we gauge the health of group classroom life.

Limit testing. Challenges to teacher authority and leadership; the questioning by an individual of how he or she will personally benefit from a group. Often occurs during the storming stage of group development.

Some Examples of Group Conflict

What should you do when these incidents occur?

> During a discussion of the merits of the Vietnam War in a high school history class, one student comments that the war was immoral. Another learner says, "My father was in that war and was seriously wounded. I don't think he did anything immoral!" The two students begin to shout at one another. Other class members take sides. No one is listening to anyone else or to you anymore.

> In a first-grade class, learners are selecting books during independent reading time. Two learners want the same book. They start yelling and pushing each other. The whole class is looking at them and you.

> A seventh-grade teacher decides to reconstitute her small work groups. She gives the learners their assignments. One student comes up to her and says, "I don't want to be in the same group as Michael. He always thinks he's right and wants to do everything his way."

> A fifth-grade teacher assigns Tiffany to take the attendance slip to the office for this week. Several students complain that the teacher is playing favorites. "Why do you always give the good jobs to Tiffany?" they protest.

> An eighth-grade science teacher announces that the class is going to participate in the science fair. She gives them a list of potential projects. Several students object. "This isn't required. Why do we have to do this? My friends in Mr. Mims's class don't have to do science projects."

Social psychologists tell us that conflicts like these are inevitable aspects of group life. They occur whenever you bring together a group of individuals with diverse backgrounds, needs, and interests. These conflicts also serve an important purpose: they provide learners with an opportunity to learn how to problem solve and how to work out mutually acceptable relationships. If you suppress conflicts or fail to view them as inevitable and necessary features of group life, you may lose an opportunity to guide your class toward the performing stage of development.

Conflicts Arising Out of Group Dynamics

At the start of this chapter we defined the characteristics of a group as including common goals, relationships, and group structure. Consequently, conflicts that arise out of group dynamics usually surround goals, interpersonal relationships, and classroom procedures.

Goal Conflicts. **Goal conflicts** occur when teachers and learners, or learners among themselves, disagree about what they hope to accomplish in the classroom. A learner who comes to school primarily to be with his friends will have a goal conflict with a teacher who is concerned exclusively with academic progress. Likewise, a teacher whose primary focus is having her learners do well on a standardized basic skills test will likely have goal conflicts with learners who need to express themselves with hands-on activities and projects. Finally, learners may disagree among themselves regarding which classroom or small group goals to work toward.

Interpersonal Conflicts. As we saw earlier, being in a group heightens individual needs for affiliation, power, and achievement. As a result, face-to-face interactions in a classroom can become emotionally charged. In such an atmosphere, **interpersonal conflicts** over getting one's way, who goes first, who likes whom, or divergent opinions and ideas are inevitable.

Procedural Conflicts. As we will see in the next chapter, much of classroom life is structured by rules and routines. Sometimes these structures are dictated by the teacher; sometimes they are negotiated between learners and teacher. Regardless of how they are derived, the end result of all rules is that not everyone can do as she pleases. Thus, **procedural conflicts** over how to line up, when to use the rest room, what learners must do before leaving their seats or sharpening their pencils, the duration of recess, and so forth are common features of classroom life.

Since goal, interpersonal, and procedural conflicts can and do arise at any stage of group development, healthy groups have a process for handling such disagreements. Glasser (1986) and Putnam and Burke (1992) urge teachers to have class discussions that center on group conflict resolution. They recommend that teachers instruct their learners how to problem solve using the following guide (see Figure 8.6):

1. Agree that there is a problem. The teacher gets all members of the class to agree that there is a problem and that they will work together to solve it.

2. State the conflict. The teacher states concisely what the conflict is and assures all learners that they will have the opportunity to state their perspectives.

3. Identify and select responses. Teacher and learners brainstorm and record solutions to the problem. They assess the short-term and long-

Goal conflicts. Conflicts that arise as a result of learner-teacher or learner-learner disagreement about what should be accomplished in the classroom.

Interpersonal conflicts. Conflicts between members of a class group over individual needs for affiliation, power, and achievement.

Procedural conflicts. Disagreements between members of a group over classroom rules and routines.

In what ways can I resolve naturally occurring conflicts arising out of the group dynamics of my classroom?

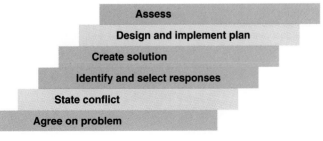

Figure 8.6
Steps in the problem-solving process.

term consequences of the solutions and discard those that have negative consequences.

4. Create a solution. The class discusses and records a solution that all basically agree will resolve the conflict.

5. Design and implement a plan. The class discusses and works out the details of when, where, and how the conflict is to be resolved.

6. Assess the success of the plan. The class identifies information that can be gathered to determine the success of the plan. Checkpoints are identified to help the class evaluate its progress. When the conflict is resolved, the value of the problem-solving process is discussed with the entire class.

Summary: The Larger Context of Classroom Management

The expert teacher must acquire three types of classroom management skills: (1) group management skills, (2) conduct management skills, and (3) instructional management skills. In this chapter we have discussed group management skills: the challenges and opportunities that you will face by virtue of being responsible for a group of individuals. Guiding group development requires an understanding of the stages of group development, the problems arising at each stage, and the effective use of group management skills to promote leadership, high expectations, norms, group cohesiveness, and problem solving. These relationships are summarized in Figure 8.7.

As a teacher you will need more than group management skills to manage your classroom. You also must be prepared to provide learners with a safe and orderly learning environment at the outset of group life. This will require that you acquire the skills of conduct management. Throughout the group development process, conduct problems with individual learners or small groups of learners will arise, and you must be prepared to deal with them quickly and effectively. These conduct management skills will be the focus of our next chapter.

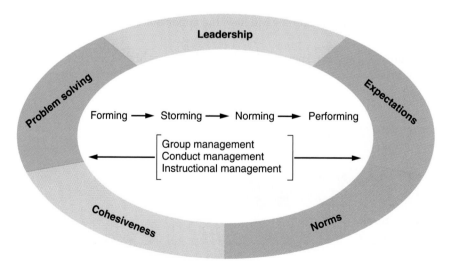

Figure 8.7
Summary of stages of group development and characteristics of a productive group climate.

Summing Up

This chapter introduced you to group process in the classroom. Its main points were these:

- Three properties make a classroom a cohesive group of learners: (1) relationships, (2) common goals, and (3) a social structure.
- Social structure refers to the roles and functions that members of the group assume, and how those who assume various roles and functions relate to one another.
- Research indicates that the presence of others during the learning of complex intellectual tasks produces faster learning with greater retention. The superiority of group learning is attributed to the benefits of having to explain to others complex concepts in one's own words.
- Although emotional conflicts within a group may be inevitable, they derive from at least two sources: (1) patterns of feelings and interaction learned at home and (2) disagreements that arise when learners discover how others feel about them and try to meet their own goals.
- There are four stages of group development: forming, when concerns about acceptance and responsibilities are resolved; storming, when concerns about shared influence are resolved; norming, when concerns about how work gets done are resolved; and performing, when concerns about freedom, control, and self-regulation are resolved.
- Two types of "limit testing" during the storming stage of group development are (1) challenges to the teacher's authority and leadership, called distancing, and (2) questioning how one will personally benefit from the group, called centering.
- Norms are expectations shared by group members regarding how they should think, feel, and behave. Norms orient group members to appropriate social interactions, create group identification and cohesiveness, and promote academic achievement and positive relationships.
- Five types of social power or leadership are expert, referent, legitimate, reward, and coercive power. All teachers should work toward expert and referent power.
- The "self-fulfilling prophecy," or "Pygmalion effect," describes how expectancies tend to confirm themselves.
- Research suggests that cohesive groups produce higher levels of academic achievement in conceptual learning, problem solving, and metacognitive learning than individual, competitive learning formats.
- Recommended steps for resolving procedural conflicts in the classroom are these: (1) agree on the problem and that the class will work together to resolve it, (2) give all individuals a chance to state the nature of the conflict, (3) identify and select responses, (4) discuss and record a solution, (5) design a plan to implement the solution, and (6) evaluate the success of the plan.

For Discussion and Practice

*1. In your own words, explain the difference between a developmental psychologist and a social psychologist with regard to how perceptions,

---

feelings, thoughts, and actions are formed. Cite a theorist from this chapter and one from Chapters 2 and 3 to help you make your distinction.

2. Describe two different groups of which you are a member, one low in cohesiveness and the other high in cohesiveness, in terms of relationships, common goals, and social structure.

3. Using Figure 8.2 as your guide, identify four activities you could assign to your class that would represent a task-group goal, a task-individual goal, a social-emotional-group goal, and a social-emotional-individual goal.

*4. Cite recent research evidence that higher achievement results when learning occurs in groups. How might you apply these findings to your classroom?

5. Using a group of which you are a member, give an example of how an individual might strive for (1) affiliation with the group, (2) power within the group, and (3) achievement as a result of the group. Identify how each of these strivings might be represented by a learner in your classroom.

*6. Give two competing explanations for how a learner develops a self-concept. Which do you believe is the stronger explanation?

*7. Identify and give an example of a principal concern at each of the four stages of group development.

*8. Give an example of a question a student might raise in your classroom exhibiting (a) distancing behavior and (b) centering behavior. What would be your response to each question?

*9. Provide examples of a norm that might exist in the following situations: at the dinner table, in a college classroom, on a date, during a test, in your classroom. What did these example norms have in common?

*10. In your own words, how does someone obtain (a) expert, (b) referent, (c) legitimate, (d) reward, and (e) coercive power? Toward which of these should a new teacher begin to work?

*11. Describe the sequence of events that would lead a teacher's expectations to become a self-fulfilling prophecy. What would be a way to break that cycle?

*12. What was the result of Gage and Berliner's research study that examined how teachers interacted with their students? Which of their categories of bias do you feel you are most prone to?

*13. Indicate the three functions norms can serve and suggest an activity you could implement in your classroom that would serve each function.

14. On the first day of class you reprimand a student for ridiculing another student who is having trouble pronouncing a word. Indicate how your behavior might become diffused and crystallized by the actions of your students to create a classroom norm.

*15. What are some of the ways you could influence the development of a norm in your classroom or alter an existing one? Which of these do you believe would be the most effective in creating a new norm, and which would be most effective in altering an existing norm?

°16. Cite the research that you believe would convince a friend that group cohesiveness affects academic achievement and productivity.

°17. Identify some ways to promote group cohesiveness in a classroom. Which do you believe would be most appropriate for your subject and grade level? (Suggest at least one other approach suitable for your classroom.)

°18. Identify the source of three different types of conflicts you are likely to encounter in your classroom. Provide one suggestion for how you might resolve each of them.

19. Provide an example of (1) a goal conflict, (2) an interpersonal conflict, and (3) a procedural conflict likely to occur in your classroom. How would you attempt to resolve each of them?

Suggested Readings

Borich, G. (1993). *Clearly outstanding: Making each day count in your classroom.* Needham, MA: Allyn & Bacon. Through the eyes and ears of three teachers, this book shows how teachers can establish positive relationships with their classes and as a result improve the effectiveness of their teaching.

Cohen, E. G. (1986). *Designing groupwork: Strategies for the heterogeneous classroom.* New York: Teachers College Press. A practical guide for teachers on how to prepare and conduct group classroom work.

Glasser, W. (1990). *The quality school: Managing students without coercion.* New York: Harper & Row. Glasser demonstrates how his theories of student needs and student motivation can be applied to restructuring American classrooms.

Schmuck, R. A., & Schmuck, P. A. (1992). *Group processes in the classroom* (6th ed.). Dubuque, IA: William C. Brown. Applies theories and research in social psychology to the understanding of classroom group processes. Contains numerous practical activities to promote group cohesiveness.

Positive Approaches to Conduct Management

This chapter will help you answer the following questions about your learners:

- How do I balance my concerns for classroom order with my concerns for classroom warmth?
- How can I communicate to a learner in a manner that does not blame, scold, or humiliate that a behavior is unacceptable?
- What are some ways I might inadvertently encourage inappropriate behavior in my classroom?
- What are some ways that the classroom environment can promote either acceptable or unacceptable behavior?
- How can I use behavior modification techniques to change the classroom conduct of learners?
- How can I arrange the visual texture and physical space of my classroom to encourage some behaviors and discourage others?
- How can I create rules in my classroom that favor a secure and orderly environment without impeding communication and trust?
- How can I establish classroom routines that are consistent with the climate I wish to promote?
- How do I stop misbehavior without disrupting the flow of a lesson?

Brown High School is a consolidated, comprehensive school with a total student body of about 550.[1] The school is brand-new; in fact, it is in the process of being completed. Workmen move in and out of classrooms daily, painting and making finishing touches on the carpentry work. Classroom equipment is sparse. In some of the classrooms, folding chairs are used in place of desks.

The total effect is one of incongruity. The outside of the school building is modern and attractive. It is shaped like a giant doughnut, with classrooms encircling an atrium. Inside, the halls are spacious and carpeted. The brightly painted rooms, which open to the halls, all appear attractive until one encounters the desks and chairs. The central office is a large, spacious room that houses the principal and his secretary. In one corner large boxes, a key plaque, and filing cabinets line the wall to the right of the counter that partially shields the principal's desk.

On this spring morning, several teachers are milling around in the office. Mrs. Towers, a confident and secure-looking woman about 45 years old, sees a fellow teacher approaching, and her face lights up in a friendly smile. She moves forward a step.

Mrs. Towers: Hi, Mrs. Gates. I've been meaning to chat with you ever since the principal introduced you at the faculty meeting. I'm Beth Towers and I teach ninth-grade science. [She extends her hand.] Welcome to Brown.
Mrs. Gates [smiling]: Oh, thank you for the welcome. I need it!
Mrs. Towers: How are things going?
Mrs. Gates [ruefully]: Well, not so well, really. I'm still a little . . . [she hesitates] a little disoriented, I guess. Somehow, everything seems so unreal.
Mrs. Towers [smiling]: Yes, I can well imagine. Changing teaching assignments to a completely different school in mid-year must be pretty frustrating.

In this chapter you will also learn the meanings of these terms:

antecedents
applied behavior analysis
behavioral setting
behaviorism
classroom management tradition
congruent communication
consequences
engaged learning time
humanistic tradition
lead management
low-profile classroom control
routine
rules
surface behaviors

---

[1]Based on an excerpt from Greenwood, Good, & Siegel, 1971.

Mrs. Gates: Oh, it is! [She looks around.] There I was last week in the school where I'd taught for years, where I knew all the children—and their parents, too—everything seemed to run so smoothly there. But, here—it's all so confused! Oh, I don't mean to imply that this is a bad place to be . . . it's just . . . different. I'm sure I'll feel right at home soon.

The first bell rings. Mrs. Gates collects her keys and starts to go. In her haste she drops a book, which Mrs. Towers retrieves for her.

Mrs. Towers: *The Lives of 10 Great Classical Composers* . . . are you going to use this with your music class?
Mrs. Gates: Oh, yes. It's so inspirational. My students loved it at Edgewater. So many of the students here seem to need to be exposed to great examples they can follow.
Mrs. Towers: Do you think that the children here will respond in the same way?
Mrs. Gates: Sure—they'll love it! You'll see. I've used this material at least six or seven times before and it's always been successful.

Mrs. Gates smiles confidently, gathers her materials, and leaves Mrs. Towers standing alone with a look of consternation on her face.

Mrs. Gates's first-period music class consists of 37 students from the seventh and eighth grades. Their ages vary from 12 to 15. When Mrs. Gates examined the cumulative records of five of the students, she found such teacher comments as "undisciplined," "unruly," "aggressive," "loud-mouthed," and "impossible."

Mrs. Gates enters the small classroom that serves as the music room. The chairs and desks are arranged in a haphazard circle around the teacher's desk. Mrs. Gates places her materials on the desk and puts a songbook on each student desk just as the last bell rings and the seventh- and eighth-grade children noisily push and shove their way into the room. Desks are moved about, chairs are pulled across the floor, and books are dropped onto the floor. Several students put their other books on top of the music books, or put the music books inside their desks.

Mrs. Gates: All right, class, go to your seats. [The talking and the jostling behavior continue.]
Mrs. Gates [focusing her attention on one child]: Rosalyn!

Rosalyn has been standing in the doorway, talking to several boys in the hall. She turns her head momentarily in Mrs. Gates's direction and calmly resumes her discussion. Mrs. Gates decides to ignore Rosalyn's behavior and turns to a child in the back of the room.

Mrs. Gates: Carlos, please sit down. [Carlos is seated on the windowsill.]
Carlos: But I am sitting down!
Mrs. Gates: Carlos, you know what I mean. In a chair, this minute! [To the rest of the class] Get to your seats!

The noise and the movement in the room continue as Mrs. Gates attempts to direct students to their assigned seats. Rosalyn finishes her conversation with the boys in the hallway and slowly takes a seat.

Mrs. Gates: Turn to page 161!
Student: We already read that; we done that part.
Mrs. Gates: I'm sorry; turn to page 168.

Student: Do we have to read again today? Why can't we do something else? [The noise level begins to build up again.]

Mrs. Gates [stridently]: All right, that's enough. This is a beautiful story about Beethoven's early life as a musical prodigy. Now, I want you to take turns reading this essay orally. Jodi, will you begin reading?

As the children read, they frequently falter and pronounce words only with great difficulty. Most appear diffident about the assignment, and they start shuffling papers on their desks. Carlos begins tapping his pencil on his desk in a distinct rhythm. Rosalyn looks up, winks at Carlos, and begins to accompany him. The beat is contagious, and Tina and Joan begin to make bobbing movements with their heads. Mrs. Gates raises her voice sharply. The students, in a hushed silence and with expressions of surprise on their faces, sit looking at Mrs. Gates. The bell rings and the children walk in clusters out of the room. A few smile sheepishly, but most have blank expressions on their faces and do not begin to talk until they enter the hallway.

Take a moment and think about your reaction to this scene. Did you feel sympathy for Mrs. Gates? Did you feel anger toward her students? Did you think Mrs. Gates deserved the respect and obedience of her students?

Or did you feel anger toward Mrs. Gates? Did you find that her teaching style is inappropriate, that she is at fault for not administering old-fashioned punishment, or that she is guilty of trying to impose her own values on children from a different social class?

Who's really to blame? The students, who lacked respect for authority? The cultural values that the students brought to their classroom? The skills and competency of the teacher, who had difficulty managing her class? Or the principal, who may have failed to understand the difference between Mrs. Gates's old and new teaching assignments? Before you answer these questions, let's ask another: Could this scene have been prevented?

The answer to this last question is a resounding "yes." What Mrs. Gates needed most was the confidence that comes from an effective classroom management plan, which can prevent such problems from occurring or quickly correct them when they do occur. Effective classroom management requires group management, as we learned in the previous chapter, and conduct management, as we will learn in this chapter. Conduct management skills involve a clear vision of where you want to take your class, the recognition that unanticipated problems may sometimes happen, and ways to deal with them when they do occur. Let's see how these ingredients come together to create the classroom management plan that Mrs. Gates should have used.

Most new teachers have certain conceptions about teaching through which they view themselves and their roles. Sometimes these conceptions take the form of metaphors—for example, teacher as coach, protector of the young, mother or father figure, adult advocate, or big brother or sister (Bullough, 1989). In this chapter, we will introduce another metaphor for teaching. We have a very special reason for introducing this metaphor, as you will see in the pages ahead. First, let's look at what it is.

Consider for a moment that you are a wilderness guide whose objective is a week of backpacking in the outdoors. The successful guide knows that the trip must be carefully planned and a sense of cohesiveness built in the group. But there is more to backpacking than planning and group cohesiveness. Blisters, water shortages, getting lost, injuries, or lack of shelter in a sudden thunderstorm, to varying degrees, can quickly turn a wilderness adventure into trouble.

Careful planning can prevent problems along the way, as can vigilance once the trip begins. But as any experienced guide knows, no amount of planning, alertness, or reflection can forestall all problems. Nature has its own way of frustrating even the best-laid plans. The wilderness guide must be adaptable to all sorts of unexpected conditions.

As a classroom guide, you will have to take charge of your environment and become skilled in reacting to unforeseen circumstances on the way to moving your hikers toward a common goal. For this you must be prepared to find new options for the quickly changing conditions in which you find yourself. Some teachers have acquired such options from the experience of surviving a poorly planned journey. But they can be acquired more easily—and less painfully—by establishing a classroom management plan that prepares you for the unexpected.

In your own experience as a classroom leader, you will have to acquire many of the skills of the wilderness guide. You will have to mold an initially unfamiliar roster of students into a cohesive group, as discussed in Chapter 8. In addition, you will have to:

- design an orderly workplace that promotes your academic goals
- develop rules that create group norms that students respect and follow
- establish a set of routines for efficiently running your workplace
- be adaptable when rules, routines, and procedures turn out to be unproductive
- maintain a workplace that fosters feelings of belonging and group solidarity
- be knowledgeable about how to seek help from other school professionals and parents.

Classroom Management Versus Classroom Control

My first teaching assignment was in an inner-city junior high school. I'll always remember what the principal said to us new teachers during orientation week: "I'll know you're a good teacher after 30 seconds of looking at your classroom through the window in your door!" What he meant was that if all the children were seated and quiet, we were good teachers. That first year I approached everything about my classroom more from the perspective of what I wanted to inhibit than what I wanted to enhance. (Author, personal experience)

It isn't surprising that most new teachers approach their first year of teaching defensively, as if their backs were always on their own 10-yard line. In teacher surveys conducted over the past 15 years, discipline problems consistently led the list of causes of teacher stress and burnout (Gallup & Clark, 1987; Gallup & Elam, 1988; Moles, 1987). Newspapers, magazines, television, and movies offer the beginning teacher a steady diet of classroom war stories. Themes of order and control dominate discussion and research into classroom organization and management (Doyle, 1986). In fact, for many educators and educational psychologists classroom management is synonymous with classroom control (Bowers & Flinders, 1990; Doyle, 1986).

However, as we will see in this chapter, management should include warmth and caring as well as control. Your decisions about classroom arrangement, rules, and routines should reflect a concern for a secure, safe, orderly environment, but not at the expense of communication and trust among your learners. As a new teacher, you will quickly come to realize that warmth and control are not mutually exclusive concerns. Effective teachers who care about their learners inevitably combine the quality of warmth with their efforts to control.

For many years, the concepts of warmth and control were considered to be at opposite ends of the same continuum. If a teacher chose to be warm, he or she could not be in control, and vice versa. However, Soar and Soar (1983) have suggested that different degrees of warmth and control may occur simultaneously, and behavior in one dimension does not necessarily preclude behavior in the other. Although many combinations of warmth and control are possible, four major profiles emerge from this conception of classroom climate, as shown in Figure 9.1.

The first is represented by quadrant A, in which the teacher may be characterized as cold and controlling. Such a teacher may humiliate and criticize students in an effort to control all aspects of their behavior. Lesser extremes represent a teacher who provides little praise or reward. This quadrant generally represents a classroom climate that is businesslike and task-oriented, with few interchanges with students that are not initiated by the teacher. It also is a classroom in which motivation to do high-level work may be inspired more by a fear of punishment, embarrassment, or, in extreme cases, humiliation than by the expectation of praise, reward, or reinforcement.

A second type of classroom climate is represented by quadrant B, in which the teacher is warm but in control. The diagram illustrates that when classroom rules are mutually determined and a consistently applied system of praise and rewards is used to motivate good behavior, warmth and control may exist simultaneously.

One danger of excessive use of rewards, however, is the creation of an almost suffocating climate in which students have little if any room to pursue a behavior or activity independently. In such a classroom, only those behaviors that the teacher has previously identified are eligible for a reward—all others are deemed less worthy. As Soar

> **How do I balance my concerns for classroom order with my concerns for classroom warmth?**

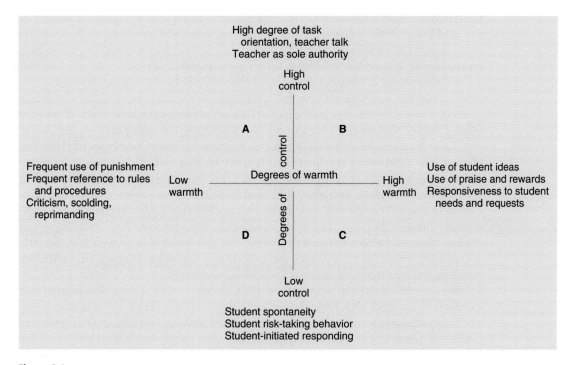

Figure 9.1
Combinations of teacher warmth and control.

and Soar (1983) have noted, this may create a classroom climate in which students have little room to pursue independent behavior because of the tightly managed praise and reward system established by the teacher. This quadrant differs primarily from quadrant A in that motivation for good behavior here comes from a well-defined and consistently applied system of praise and rewards. In quadrant A, good behavior results from a well-defined and consistently applied system of rules and/or punishment.

A third classroom climate is characterized by quadrant C, in which the teacher is warm and permissive. A teacher who falls at the lower right corner of this quadrant is one who praises and rewards students frequently while allowing them almost complete freedom in choosing the limits of their own behavior, sometimes resulting in confusion. A lesser extreme of this quadrant may represent a classroom in which praise and rewards are used freely but student spontaneity (for example, calling out) and risk-taking behavior are limited to certain times (for example, group discussion, problem-solving activities) or certain types of content (for example, social studies but not math). During these times the teacher acts as a moderator or co-discussant, guiding and directing but not controlling classroom behavior. In such a classroom, students have considerable freedom in how and when to speak, and the teacher's warm and nurturing attitude is conveyed mostly nonverbally, through a set of classroom rules that encourage individual initiative.

The fourth quadrant, D, represents a classroom that is cold yet permissive. A teacher who falls at the lower left corner of this quadrant is one who spends most of the time scolding and criticizing students but has few classroom rules to control or limit the behavior being criticized. Such an extreme climate sometimes prevails in a classroom where a substitute teacher takes over without warning. In such a classroom, students may use the teacher's unfamiliarity with the rules as an opportunity to act out, thereby initiating scolding or criticizing behavior. Since the substitute teacher is unfamiliar with the classroom rules, he cannot fall back on the established system to prevent misbehavior. And because the substitute's role is to keep order, not to create or discover the rules, much of his behavior is an attempt to "hold the line" by criticizing, reprimanding, and punishing, if need be, in order to keep the class under control.

In less extreme form, a classroom in quadrant D may be characterized by some coverage of content, interspersed with delays for classroom management of misbehavior. In general, this quadrant shows both a lack of task orientation and teacher control over the subject matter content and a high frequency of scolding, criticizing, and reprimanding.

Table 9.1 summarizes some of the characteristics of these four types of classroom climate. The table shows how particular types of teacher and student behavior characterize the dimensions of control and warmth. For the dimension of control, student spontaneity, risk-taking behavior, and student-initiated responses characterize low-control climates. Teacher talk, task orientation, and teacher authority characterize high-control climates. For the dimension of warmth, use of praise and rewards, use of student ideas, and responsiveness to student requests are associated with high warmth. Frequent reference to formal rules and procedures, use of punishment, and criticism, scolding, and reprimanding are associated with low warmth.

An effective classroom management plan blends warmth and control in ways that preclude overly rigid, dictatorial, or authoritarian forms of control, using instead a mutually agreed upon set of rules and a well-defined and consistently applied system of praise and rewards. In other words, an effective plan combines the best parts of quadrants B and C to balance warmth with control. In this chapter we will show you how to create this balance to build an effective classroom management plan.

| Table 9.1 | Four Types of Classroom Climate | | | |

A **High Control– Low Warmth**	B **High Control– High Warmth**	C **Low Control– High Warmth**	D **Low Control- Low Warmth**
High task orientation	Clearly identified and frequent use of rewards for desirable behavior	Frequent use of praise and reinforcement	Frequent scolding and criticizing
Frequent use of punishment or humiliation	Unsolicited student responses discouraged	Informal classroom rules	Few classroom rules
Lack of praise, reward, or reinforcement	High task orientation	Students have say in establishing limits of their behavior	Students frequently call out
Mostly teacher-initiated interchanges	Mostly teacher-initiated interchanges	Student spontaneity and risk-taking behavior allowed	Teacher talk focuses on minimizing misbehavior
High amount of time devoted to teacher talk	High amount of time devoted to teacher talk	Teacher acts as moderator or participant	Classroom lacks task orientation
			Frequent delays for classroom management and reprimands

Systems of Classroom Management

Anyone who reads the newspaper, listens to candidates running for public office, attends school board meetings, or overhears conversations in the teachers' lounge quickly realizes that classroom order and discipline are frequently discussed topics. A teacher's inability to control a class is one of the most commonly cited reasons for dismissal, and beginning teachers consistently rate classroom discipline among their most urgent concerns (Rogan, Borich, & Taylor, 1992).

Problems in maintaining classroom order and discipline can be exaggerated, however. Major disciplinary problems (for example, vandalism, violent fighting, and physical abuse toward teachers) are rare in most schools. Unfortunately, these incidents attract attention. Often the media report them to the exclusion of the many positive events that also occur. This chapter will address some major discipline problems, but the primary focus will be on the many less dramatic problems that without an effective classroom management plan can divert your attention from the instructional process.

Some teachers spend nearly 50 percent of their class time dealing with misbehavior that might be described as "amiable goofing off" (Jones, 1987), although these problems are minor. Thus, although you may worry about how to handle rare incidents of fighting, open defiance, property destruction, or swearing and cursing, you will actually spend most of your management time coping with students who pass notes, whisper, stare out the window, ignore your simple requests, squirm in their seats, sleep, do work unrelated to your class, or do no work at all.

Let's return for a moment to Mrs. Gates's class, where some of these misbehaviors were occurring. Imagine that on a Wednesday afternoon you get a call from the principal of Mrs. Gates's school inquiring whether you would accept a teaching job there. It

Humanistic tradition. An approach to classroom management that emphasizes the critical role of communication and problem solving between teacher and students.

Applied behavior analysis. An approach to classroom management that applies behavioristic principles to modify behavior in socially important areas.

Classroom management tradition. An approach emphasizing the organization and management of instructional activities in order to prevent misbehavior.

turns out that Mrs. Gates has resigned and they need a replacement for Monday morning. You accept the challenge and have four days to prepare for the class. What will you do?

Approaches to managing classrooms like Mrs. Gates's can be grouped into three traditions. The **humanistic tradition** emphasizes the critical role of communication and problem solving between teacher and students. This tradition is represented by the writings of Ginott (1972) and Glasser (1986, 1990). The **applied behavior analysis** tradition is best represented by the writings of O'Leary and O'Leary (1977), Alberto and Troutman (1986), Jones (1987), and Canter (1989), who apply behavioristic principles to the classroom. The third approach, which is the newest, emphasizes the teaching skills involved in organizing and managing instructional activities and in presenting content. The major proponents of this **classroom management tradition** are Kounin (1970), Brophy and Good (1986), Emmer, Evertson, Clements, and Worsham (1994), and Doyle (1986). This approach, more so than the humanistic and applied behavior analysis traditions, underscores the critical role of prevention in managing classroom behavior.

We will briefly summarize the main features of each of these traditions, point out how they can be used to manage the classroom, and evaluate each approach. First, let's identify six criteria an effective classroom management plan should contain. A comprehensive approach to classroom management should incorporate classroom strategies that accomplish the following:

- Establish positive relationships between all classroom participants. A positive, supportive classroom environment that meets student needs for belonging and acceptance is a necessary foundation for managing an orderly classroom.

- Prevent attention-seeking and work-avoidance behaviors. Time devoted to managing the classroom should be directed to engaging students in the learning process and preventing behaviors that interfere with it. Engagement and prevention include both arrangement of physical space and teaching rules and routines for working in this space.

- Redirect misbehavior quickly and unobtrusively once it occurs. Most classroom problems take the form of minor off-task and attention-seeking events. Techniques for coping with these events should not cause more disruption than the behavior itself.

- Stop persistent and chronic misbehavior with strategies that are simple enough to be used consistently. Management systems that require responses to every act of positive or negative behavior may not be practical in today's busy classrooms.

- Teach self-control. Students should be allowed the opportunity to exercise internal control before external control is imposed. When external controls are imposed, they should be implemented with plans for fading them out.

- Respect cultural differences. Verbal and nonverbal techniques for redirecting disruptive behavior do not mean the same thing to all cultural groups. Likewise, systematic strategies involving social rewards, tangible rewards, and consequences can violate important cultural norms.

Now let's learn something about each of the three approaches and analyze how well each meets these criteria.

The Humanist Tradition in Classroom Management

The principles underlying the humanist tradition come from the practice of clinical and counseling psychology. It is called *humanist* because its primary focus is the inner thoughts, feelings, psychological needs, and emotions of the individual learner. Humanist approaches emphasize allowing the student time to develop control over his or her behavior rather than insisting on immediate behavioral change or compliance. They use interventions that stress the use of communication skills, an understanding of student motives, private conferences, individual and group problem solving, and the exercise of referent and expert power.

Ginott's (1972) *cooperation through congruent communication* (also called the communication skills approach) and Glasser's (1990) *cooperation through individual and group problem solving* (also called reality therapy) are examples of the humanistic tradition. While each emphasizes a different area or set of skills that the effective classroom manager should possess, these approaches essentially represent two sides of the same coin.

Cooperation Through Congruent Communication

The cardinal principle underlying Ginott's communication skills approach is that learners can control their own behavior, if teachers allow them to do so. Teachers foster this self-control by allowing learners to choose how they wish to change their own behavior and how the class will be run. In addition, they help their students express their inner thoughts and feelings through the use of effective communication skills.

Communication skills are the primary vehicle for influencing learners' self-esteem, which in turn is the primary force underlying acceptable behavior. Therefore, this tradition tries to influence student behavior above all by enhancing student self-esteem. According to the proponents of this approach, **congruent communication** is the vehicle for promoting self-esteem. Teachers have many opportunities during the school day to engage their students in congruent communication. Such communication usually occurs during private conferences with students who misbehave. However, it can also go on during problem solving with the whole class. At such times, teachers communicate congruently when they do any of the following.

Express "Sane" Messages. Sane messages communicate to students that their behavior is unacceptable but do not blame, scold, preach, accuse, demand, threaten, or humiliate. Sane messages describe what *should* be done rather than scold what *was* done. Example: "Rosalyn, we are all supposed to be in our seats before the bell rings," *not* "Rosalyn, you're always gossiping at the doorway and coming late to class."

Accept Rather than Deny Feelings. Teachers should accept students' feelings about their individual circumstances rather than argue about them. If a student complains, "I have no friends," the teacher should accept the student's feelings of isolation, identify with the student, and say, for example, "So, you're feeling that you don't belong to any group" rather than try to convince the student that he or she has misperceived the social situation.

Congruent communication. Communication that uses statements that are directed at a learner's actions, that reflect an accurate or honest evaluation of learner performance, that help learners believe in themselves and their own abilities, and that attribute learner achievement to internal rather than external factors.

How can I communicate to a learner in a manner that does not blame, scold, or humiliate that a behavior is unacceptable?

Effective classroom management involves listening to learner concerns and responding to these concerns in ways that promote trust and make learners feel free to express what is on their minds.

Avoid Using Labels. When talking to students about what they do well or poorly, teachers should avoid terms such as "lazy," "sloppy," or "bad attitude," as well as "dedicated," "intelligent," or "perfectionist." Instead, teachers should describe what they like or don't like about students in terms of what they do. For example, "You have a lot of erasures and white-outs on your homework," *not* "Your homework is sloppy"; "You form your letters correctly," *not* "You are a good writer."

Use Praise Cautiously. Ginott believes that many teachers use praise excessively and manipulatively to control student behavior rather than to acknowledge exceptional performance. They use praise judgmentally ("Horace, you are a good student"), confuse correctness with goodness (referring to a student who completes work with a minimum of mistakes as a "good child"), praise students who display minimally acceptable behavior as a way of influencing other students ("I like the way Joan is sitting in her seat"), and praise so often that the statements lose all significance. Ginott urges teachers to use praise only to acknowledge *exceptional* performance and in terms that separate the deed from the doer. For example, "That essay showed a great deal of original thought and research."

Elicit Cooperation. Once a teacher and student have identified behavioral concerns, Ginott encourages teachers to offer alternatives to solving the problem rather than tell students what to do. "Cooperate, don't legislate" is a convenient maxim to help teachers remember this point.

Communicate Anger. Teachers are people, too. They get frustrated and angry just like anyone else. Ginott believes that teachers should express their feelings through the use of "I messages" rather than "You messages." The former focus on your feelings about the behavior or situation that angered you ("You talked when the guest speaker was lecturing, and I feel very unhappy and embarrassed by that"). The latter put the focus on the students and typically accuse and blame ("You were rude to the guest speaker"). "I messages" should be used when you own the problem—that is, when you are the one who is angry or upset.

If you were to consult Ginott about what to do Monday morning in Mrs. Gates's class, he would recommend that you have an open discussion with the students to draw their attention to the problem. Then, you would invite your students' cooperation in developing mutually agreed-upon rules and consequences. Finally, as problems arise you would have individual conferences with your students, during which you would engage them in congruent communication.

Cooperative Learning

We described Glasser's views on the importance of meeting your learners' psychological needs in Chapter 8. These needs for belonging, power, and freedom require the supportive environment that Ginott's congruent communication creates. In addition, Glasser points out that effective classroom managers create a learning environment where students want to be, develop mutually agreed upon standards of behavior that must be followed if they want to remain in this environment, and conduct problem-solving conferences with those who violate the standards.

Glasser advocates an instructional approach called *cooperative learning* as a way to make the classroom a place learners want to be. According to Glasser, classrooms that emphasize cooperative learning motivate all children to engage in learning activities. Whole-group instruction, in which students compete with one another for limited rewards, inevitably causes 50 percent of the students to be bored, frustrated, inattentive, or disruptive.

In the face of such behavior, Glasser asserts, teachers resort to "boss management." That is, they use reward and coercive power to manipulate and control their learners. Boss management (as opposed to **lead management**) jeopardizes the development of self-control, persuades students to value external rewards over the satisfaction that comes from doing good work, and, when such rewards fail to come, causes students to become disruptive, frustrated, and inattentive. Glasser (1990) summarizes the difference between bosses and leaders in the following way:

Lead management. Use of expert and referent power to develop self-control and to persuade students to enjoy the satisfaction of doing good work.

A boss drives. A leader leads.

A boss relies on authority. A leader relies on cooperation.

A boss says "I." A leader says "We."

A boss creates fear. A leader creates confidence.

A boss knows how. A leader shows how.

A boss creates resentment. A leader breeds enthusiasm.

A boss fixes blame. A leader fixes mistakes.

A boss makes work drudgery. A leader makes work interesting.

For Glasser, dealing with disruptive students is straightforward in a classroom where students experience belonging, power, and freedom—in other words, a classroom the learner would regret leaving. Faced with a student who persists in violating classroom rules the group believes are essential, the teacher should hold a brief private conference with the student during which the teacher reviews the rules, describes the disruptive behavior, asserts the need for following the rules, and makes clear the consequences for not obeying the rules (for example, removal from the room until the learner chooses to follow the rules). Glasser cautions teachers not to accept excuses from students why they can't control their own behavior. He disagrees with teachers who use socioeconomic or sociocultural conditions as excuses for learners not making the "right" choices. For Glasser there can be no excuse for disrupting an environment designed to meet learners' needs. Furthermore, when students are faced with removal from such an environment, Glasser believes they will choose, not need to be forced, to behave:

> . . . students will soon discover that you have given them every chance. If they want to stay in class, they have no choice but to follow the rules, at least until you talk things over. And if your students are satisfied most of the time, they'll want to stay. (Glasser, 1990, p. 142)

Glasser would have a clear directive for you on Monday morning as you take over Mrs. Gates's class: Begin building a more friendly workplace based on principles of cooperative learning. Some of his more specific recommendations would be the following:

- With your students, develop rules for the workplace.
- Get support from school administrators for setting aside an area to which disruptive students can be removed.
- Hold private conferences with disruptive students; stress the importance of correct choices and accept no excuses for wrong ones.
- Follow through when students must be removed, but always allow them the opportunity to return when they choose to obey class rules.

Applied Behavior Analysis in Classroom Management

Behaviorism. A school of thought in psychology whose cardinal tenet is that any conclusion made about human development must be based on scientific observations of overt behavior and the observable events that strengthen and elicit it.

Applied behavior analysis is closely linked with B. F. Skinner's (1953) theory of learning, called **behaviorism** or *operant conditioning,* which we introduced in Chapter 4. The techniques underlying the practice of *behavior modification* derive from behaviorism. The use of behavior modification techniques to change the behavior of animals has been called the *experimental analysis of behavior.* The use of these same techniques to change the socially important behaviors of learners, workers, or the public at large (for example, to encourage conservation and protection of the environment) is called *applied behavior analysis* (Lovitt, 1994). Let's review the important concepts that underlie this approach.

Changing Behavior

The applied behavior analysis approach, as it is used in schools, focuses on changing behaviors that are important for cognitive and social development. These behaviors are actions that can be seen, heard, or counted. Attitudes, values, beliefs, feelings, emotions, or self-images, all important aspects of a learner's school life, are not behaviors. Consequently, they are not the focus of applied behavior analysis.

If ever you are unsure whether something is a "behavior," put it to the "Hey, Dad! Watch me . . ." test. For example, "Hey, Dad! Watch me ride a bike" (or "do a handstand," or "solve this problem") would pass the test, since Dad can see you do it with his

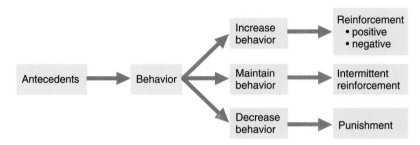

Figure 9.2
The process of behavior modification.

own eyes. But, substitute "Hey, Dad! Watch me feel good about myself" (or "have a positive attitude toward school," or "be motivated," or "have an interest in science"). These expressions fail the test, since they do not describe behaviors that Dad can observe directly.

Reinforcement

Figure 9.2 summarizes the most important components of applied behavior analysis. As this figure indicates, when your goal is to teach a new behavior, or make an existing behavior occur more frequently (for example, spell more words correctly, come to class on time more often), the behavior must be followed by some type of reinforcement during the initial stages of learning.

Recall from Chapter 4 that reinforcement can be either positive or negative. *Positive reinforcement* occurs when a teacher provides pleasant or satisfying consequences after a desired behavior and these consequences increase the likelihood that this behavior will occur again. *Negative reinforcement* occurs when a teacher ends or terminates some condition that a child perceives as threatening, fearful, or uncomfortable, after the child has engaged in some positive behavior. This increases the likelihood that the positive behavior will occur again.

Negative Reinforcement. Thorndike gave us one of the earliest demonstrations of the power of negative reinforcement when he used it to teach a cat how to escape a puzzle box. He placed the cat in an enclosed box, a situation that most cats find uncomfortable. To get out of the box, the cat had to pull a cord hanging from the top of the box. As soon as the cat pulled the cord, a door opened and the cat escaped. The next time Thorndike placed the cat in the same box, the animal pulled the cord more quickly. It had learned a useful behavior that helped it escape an unpleasant situation— an example of negative reinforcement.

While teachers plan ways to use positive reinforcement to teach children useful behaviors, they rarely arrange situations to use negative reinforcement for this purpose. This is because the use of negative reinforcement first requires that the child be put in an unpleasant situation and then taught how to get out of it. Such an approach is contrary to recommendations made by both applied behavior analysts and school personnel that teachers give preference to positive (nonaversive) techniques for improving the conduct of their learners (Donnellan & LaVigna, 1990).

However, teachers must be aware of the principle of negative reinforcement in their classrooms because many of them are inadvertently using it to reinforce *inappropriate* behaviors. For example, consider the common situation in which a learner experiences something in the classroom that he wants to escape or avoid: difficult work, dull workbook exercises, or a teacher he perceives as punitive and unfair. Such a learner may complain, refuse to do work, change his seat without permission, fall asleep, or disrupt the class to delay or escape the unpleasant event. If the teacher changes the learner's assignment when he complains, or puts him in the hallway when he is disruptive, that is negatively reinforcing the learner's behavior and thus increasing the likelihood that it will recur.

As this example illustrates, teachers can easily fall into the "negative reinforcement trap" that some learners unconsciously set. In fact, applied behavior analysts like Brian Iwata (1987) speculate that more inappropriate behavior is learned through negative than through positive reinforcement. In other words, students are more likely to avoid or escape something undesirable than to be rewarded with attention for doing something appropriate.

Intermittent Reinforcement. When you are satisfied with a particular behavior and its frequency, *intermittent reinforcement* can be applied to maintain the behavior at its present level. For example, suppose that at the start of the school year, a student consistently came late and unprepared. You started a program to reinforce this student for coming to class prepared and on time. The student now has met the goal. You can maintain this behavior by reinforcing the student's behavior on an intermittent schedule (for example, every fourth day), as we discussed in Chapter 4.

Antecedents

Antecedents are events (or stimuli) that, when present, increase the likelihood that a particular behavior will occur. For example, seeing the teacher seated at her desk talking to a student may be an antecedent for a student in the back of the room to fool

> **What are some ways I might inadvertently encourage inappropriate behavior in my classroom?**

Antecedents. Stimuli present in an environment that make a behavior more likely to occur.

In deciding how to respond to inappropriate behavior, teachers must determine what is the best reinforcer for a particular individual's behavior and what is the most appropriate consequence for disruptive behavior.

around with the person sitting next to her. Similarly, an antecedent to misbehavior in a class might be the teacher turning his back to write on the chalkboard. To give a positive example, turning on the overhead projector may be an antecedent for some students to take out their notebooks and start copying without the teacher needing to ask them. Posting rules for all to see and reminding learners of these rules before a lesson can be an antecedent for some students to engage in learning-related behaviors.

Antecedents are an important aspect of classroom conduct management because their presence or absence often makes the difference in whether students engage in appropriate learning and social behaviors. Antecedents acquire this ability to control behavior by their repeated association with the rewards or **consequences** that typically follow behavior. For example, seeing the teacher with her back to the class is an antecedent for certain types of disruptive behavior because, in the past, whenever the teacher turned her back and students misbehaved they were rewarded with attention from peers (positive reinforcement) or by avoiding work (negative reinforcement).

Similarly, teachers often want students to raise their hands and wait to be called on (behavior) following a question (antecedent). To develop this association between question asking and hand raising, teachers explain and model the behaviors they expect, praise students who respond appropriately, and call on students who raise their hands. They ignore students who call out answers without first raising their hands. If teachers use this important procedure consistently, children learn that following a question, they must raise a hand if they are to get recognized by the teacher.

Here are some antecedents to appropriate and inappropriate behavior often observed in classrooms:

> **Seating arrangement:** Whenever Mike sits near Jamal he is likely to talk and not complete work; sitting near the window or door is an antecedent to not paying attention, but sitting near the teacher is an antecedent to getting work done.

> **Teacher proximity:** The farther a teacher is from students, the more likely they are to engage in off-task behaviors; students are more likely to listen and participate in the lesson when the teacher faces them; during independent seatwork activities, students work best when the teacher walks around the room and monitors their work.

> **Style of asking questions:** Students are more likely to pay attention when the teacher asks a question, pauses, looks at the entire class, and then calls on someone.

> **Activity transitions:** Students are more likely to engage in disruptive behavior during transitions from one activity to another.

> **Nature of the activity:** Students pay attention during whole group activities and discussions but disrupt during individual seatwork (or vice versa).

> **Person leading the lesson:** Students pay attention when the teacher leads the lesson but misbehave for substitute teachers and student teachers.

> **Teacher's manner to students:** Students typically talk back to the teacher after she has harshly criticized a response, made fun of a student, or unjustly accused a student of misbehavior.

These and other antecedents to good and bad behavior are important to you as a teacher because they suggest low-profile, nonintrusive ways of preventing the behavior. For example, rather than interrupt your lesson to stop the misbehavior of two students who are sitting near each other, you can change their seats beforehand. Similarly, walking

Consequences. Stimuli or events that follow behavior; consequences can be negative or positive.

What are some ways that the classroom environment can promote either acceptable or unacceptable behavior?

around the room to prevent misbehavior is preferable to constantly calling out the names of students who misbehave while you are seated at your desk doing paperwork.

Using Applied Behavior Analysis to Improve Classroom Behavior

Applied behavior analysts recommend the following strategies for improving the classroom behavior of your learners:

1. Identify precisely both the inappropriate behavior you wish to change and the appropriate behavior you want to take its place. As we emphasized above, applied behavior analysis requires observable definitions of classroom problems and goals. Be sure to state positively the alternative behavior in which you want the student or students to engage. For example, if students are looking out the window or talking with one another during seatwork, the appropriate statement would be "Complete your assignments," *not* "No talking or whispering or staring out the window." This last statement violates the so-called Dead Person's Rule: If the behavior can be performed better by a dead person, it is not an appropriately stated goal. Negatively stated goals ("No talking," "No getting out of your seat," "No calling out") should be restated positively: "Take notes while the teacher is speaking," "Complete seatwork," "Raise your hand and wait to be called on," "Look at me when I am talking to you."

2. Identify the antecedents to both inappropriate and appropriate behavior and make the necessary changes. The following are examples of changes in classroom antecedents that can accomplish the goals above: changing seating arrangements to bring you closer to the students, to eliminate certain distractions (what's going on outside the classroom), or to separate students who misbehave; using an overhead projector so that your back is never turned to the class; walking around the room and monitoring students whenever you assign seatwork; reviewing rules at the start of class to remind students of expected behavior; preparing students for activity transitions so that they go smoothly; giving students warm-up activities to eliminate dead time at the start of a class; commenting on student responses in an encouraging manner.

3. Identify the goal of the inappropriate behavior and discontinue actions on your part (or those of peers) that reinforce it. Students typically misbehave with two goals in mind: (1) to gain positive reinforcement from you or their peers or (2) to escape or delay classroom situations that they find unpleasant, undesirable, or boring. One strategy for dealing with misbehavior is to ensure that the student is not positively reinforced for misbehavior. This typically involves such teacher actions as ignoring misbehavior whose purpose is to gain attention (a response sometimes called *extinction*), seeing to it that peers don't attend to misbehavior, and not giving students preferred activities when they misbehave to get them.

When the goal of misbehavior is to escape or avoid classroom activities and responsibilities, the general strategy is for you to be careful not to let this happen. Be sure students are held accountable for work they don't complete; follow through on assignments rather than forgetting about them in the face of noncompliance; do not shorten assignments in response to student complaints.

4. Set up procedures to reinforce the behavior you want to replace the inappropriate behavior. In addition to changing antecedents and avoiding reinforcing inappropriate behavior, applied behavior analysts recommend that you set up procedures to systematically reinforce the appropriate behavior you want students to demonstrate. We described procedures for using and fading reinforcers in Chapter 4.

How can I use behavior modification techniques to change the classroom conduct of learners?

When choosing reinforcement procedures to teach appropriate classroom behavior, use reinforcers that are natural to the school setting, such as extra time to do homework, lunch with the principal or favorite teacher, extra recess, playing an educational game, time to use the library for pleasure reading, or access to computers. Such reinforcers, called *natural reinforcers,* are readily available in schools at almost no cost. Consequently, you will use them more consistently than reinforcers that must be purchased and brought into the school setting. The accompanying box, *Using Natural Reinforcers,* provides additional suggestions.

5. Use punishment as a last resort. Most behavior problems can be dealt with without punishment (Donnellan & LaVigna, 1990). For some learners, however, more restrictive strategies may be required. Thus, if you have tried the strategies above and still not been able to change learner behavior for the better, you might, under appropriate guidance and supervision from a school psychologist or counselor, consider the following strategies for reducing inappropriate behavior, together with the positive strategies described above:

- **Removal from the classroom setting:** Remove the student to a setting where he or she cannot gain access to positive reinforcement (a "time out"). Time outs should be used only when the goal of the misbehavior is positive reinforcement (e.g., attention), not when the goal of the behavior is to escape the lesson or class. It should be used for a brief period of time (10 to 30 minutes). Following the end of the time-out period the student should be returned to the classroom and expected to engage in the classroom activities that are going on at that time. If a particular student's misbehavior is motivated to escape the classroom and becomes so disruptive that he must be removed, make sure he completes work missed during the time-out period.

Applying Your Knowledge:
Using Natural Reinforcers

Here are some practical strategies for natural reinforcement:
"Catch-em-being-good." Praise students who complete work, or who raise their hands, while ignoring those who are off-task or calling out.
Contracts. Set up individual agreements or contracts with students whereby they can gain access to preferred activities or other rewards that have educational value. For example, a student might be rewarded with extra computer time if he completes all his work on time.
Lotteries. Hold a lottery at the end of the week. During the week, students earn "lottery tickets" for engaging in appropriate behavior. At the end of the week, the student with the winning ticket in the draw earns a desirable reinforcer, such as extra recess time or a small gift.

Applied behavior analysis suggests that punishment should be used only as a last resort.

- **Loss of privileges:** Denying a student a desired activity because he has misbehaved can be effective in reducing misbehavior; for example, missing part of recess, coming in early from lunch, staying a few extra minutes after school, and so forth.
- **Restitution:** This strategy involves the student performing such activities as repairing things that were broken, cleaning objects that were soiled or disfigured, paying for things that were stolen, or apologizing to others for behaving inappropriately toward them.
- **Positive practice:** Have students write essays in which they explain their misbehavior, why it was not a good choice of actions, what they should do instead, and why this would be useful to them; or have students practice the appropriate behavior they should have performed.

If you were to invite an applied behavior analyst to help you with Mrs. Gates's classroom, she would first take a "wait-and-see approach," assuming that much of the misbehavior was elicited by actions on Mrs. Gates's part that serve as antecedents. Since the students will meet a new teacher on Monday, some of their behavior may change. The behavior analyst would wait to see which disruptive behaviors emerge, analyze the antecedents for these behaviors, decide what is reinforcing them, and then develop an intervention that uses punishment only as a last resort.

Table 9.2 lists a sequence of questions an applied behavior analyst would answer before selecting an intervention to modify a behavioral problem. The table addresses both the antecedents and consequences of problems and is intended to help you analyze problems and pose appropriate interventions.

Table 9.2

Table 9.2

Questions to Answer Before Selecting an Intervention Using the Applied Behavior Analysis Approach

	Antecedents	**Consequences**
Analysis Questions	1. What in the person's environment may be eliciting the problem behavior?	2. What happens following the problem behavior that may be causing it to persist?
	3. What appears to elicit positive behavior that is an alternative to the problem behavior?	4. What typically follows this positive behavior when (and if) it occurs?
Intervention Questions	5. What can you do to stop the problem behavior or prevent this behavior from occurring?	6. What will you do after the problem behavior occurs to make it less likely to happen again?
	7. How can you arrange the environment to make a positive behavior more likely to occur?	8. What will you do after the positive behavior occurs to make it more likely to happen again?

The Classroom Management Tradition

Throughout much of the latter half of this century, classroom discipline was focused on the question of how best to respond to student misbehavior. The humanistic and the applied behavior analysis approaches to classroom management shared the spotlight during this period. As we have seen from the previous sections, both of these traditions are primarily reactive rather than preventative systems of classroom management. That is, they tend to emphasize solutions to misbehavior *after* it occurs, rather than before. The 1970s and 1980s, however, provided another approach to classroom management that framed the question of classroom control and warmth not in terms of reaction but in terms of prevention. This approach was based on classroom research that examined what effective teachers do to prevent misconduct and what less effective teachers do to create it.

The research basis for this tradition began with projects carried out by Kounin (1970), by the Research and Development Center for Teacher Education at the University of Texas at Austin (Emmer et al., 1994), and by the Institute for Research on Teaching at Michigan State University (Brophy, 1986, 1988). Some of this research involved the observation and analysis of both experienced and inexperienced teachers while they taught. The major conclusion was that the distinction between more and less effective classroom managers can be made more by what they do to prevent misbehavior than by how they respond to it. In this section we will explain how the researchers came to this conclusion and the characteristics of effective classroom managers they found. First, let's look at one study of classroom management and how it was conducted.

In a study by Emmer, Evertson, and Anderson (1980), 27 third-grade teachers in eight elementary schools were recruited for a year-long observation. Based on their average rates of student engagement and student off-task behavior (measured after the first three weeks of school), the teachers were classified into two groups: more effective managers and less effective managers. The teachers who were categorized as effective classroom managers had significantly higher student engagement rates (more students actively engaged in the goals of the lesson) and significantly lower student off-task behaviors (fewer reprimands and warnings) throughout the school year. Finally, observation data pertaining to the classroom management procedures of these teachers during the first three weeks of school were used to compare the two groups. These included data on room arrangement, classroom rules, consequences of misbehavior, responses to inappropriate behavior, consistency of teacher responses, monitoring, and reward systems. In addition, observers counted the number of students who were on-task or off-task at 15-minute intervals to determine the extent to which students were attending to the teacher.

The more effective managers established themselves as instructional leaders early in the school year. They worked on rules and procedures until students had fully learned them. Instructional content was important for these teachers, but they also emphasized group cohesiveness and socialization into a common set of classroom norms. By the end of the first three weeks, their classes were ready for the rest of the year.

In contrast to the more effective managers, the less effective managers did not have well-worked-out procedures in advance. This was most evident among the first-year teachers who were being observed. For example, the researchers described one new teacher who had no procedures for using the bathroom, pencil sharpener, or water fountain. As a result, the children came and went at will, complicating the teacher's instructional tasks.

Rules and routines are the nuts and bolts of a classroom management program that focuses on prevention. Effective classroom managers teach rules and routines with the same expertness that they use to teach knowledge and concepts.

Like the better managers, most of the poorer managers had rules, but they presented the rules and followed up on them differently. In some cases, the rules were vague: "Be in the right place at the right time." In other cases, they were introduced casually and without discussion, leaving it unclear to most children when and where a rule applied.

The less effective managers were also ineffective monitors of their classes. This was caused in part by the lack of efficient routines for activities. In other cases this was the result of teachers removing themselves from the active surveillance of the whole class to work at length with a single child. A major result of the combination of vague and untaught rules and poor procedures for monitoring and establishing routines was that students were frequently left without sufficient guidance to direct their own activities.

One further characteristic of the less effective managers was that the consequences of good behavior and inappropriate behavior were either not in evidence in those classrooms or not delivered in a timely manner. For example, teachers sometimes issued general criticisms that failed to identify a specific offender or a particular event. Some of these teachers frequently threatened or warned children but did not follow through, even after several warnings. This allowed children to push the teacher to the limits, causing more problems. Other teachers issued vague disciplinary messages ("You're being too noisy") that were not sufficiently focused to capture the attention of the children for whom they were intended.

It was easy to see how deficiencies in the areas of rules, establishment of routines, monitoring, and a praise-and-reward structure negatively affected the overall management and organization of the classroom. Most of the time these deficiencies became "windows of opportunity" that prompted a wider range of pupil misconduct, off-task behavior, and disengagement from the goals of the classroom. After only a few weeks had elapsed, undesirable patterns of behavior and low teacher credibility had become established in the less effective managers' classrooms.

From this and related studies of classroom management (Evertson, Emmer, Clements, & Worsham, 1994; Evertson & Emmer, 1982), we learn that effective classroom managers possess three broad classes of effective teaching behaviors:

- They devote extensive time before and during the first few weeks of school to planning and organizing their classrooms to minimize disruption and enhance work engagement.

- They approach the teaching of rules and routines as methodically as they approach teaching their subject areas. They provide students with clear instructions about acceptable behavior, and they monitor student compliance with these instructions carefully during the first few weeks of school.

- They inform students about the consequences of breaking rules and enforce these consequences consistently.

How would this tradition analyze Mrs. Gates's class? Recall that this tradition has a lot to say about ways to prevent behavior problems but offers few immediate, short-term solutions after a problem has occurred. In other words, it offers no quick fixes, since it emphasizes planning in anticipation of such problems, not their resolution afterwards. A comprehensive plan incorporating elements of all three traditions is needed to make Mrs. Gates's classroom a positive environment for learning. We will present such a perspective in the next section.

Edmund T. Emmer, The University of Texas at Austin

I became interested in the areas of classroom management and discipline for several reasons. Much of the early research on teacher effectiveness had identified components of management as a central dimension of the teacher's role in creating a good environment for learning. I was also fortunate to be working at the Research and Development Center for Teacher Education with several colleagues who shared my interest in this area. The Center received funding for studies of teaching effectiveness, enabling us to develop a program of research that had classroom management as a central focus. My interest in the area is also personal. As a teacher, I realized the importance of being able to establish and maintain an orderly setting in which diverse students work and learn. I also believed that doing so was much more complicated than some of the platitudes that I had been fed while I was learning to teach: Be consistent, be fair, be firm, etc. Not that such advice was incorrect, but it didn't communicate useful information.

One of the unique aspects of the classroom management research was our focus on the beginning of the year as a critical time. Most prior research on management and discipline had adopted a cross-sectional approach. Researchers entered classrooms well after the school year had begun in order to study correlates of managerial outcomes. Although some of that research, most notably that of Kounin and his colleagues, had identified some valuable teacher management components, it was not clear how such behaviors developed over time or to what extent other factors such as pupil differences might be involved. One of our goals in this research was to conduct extensive observations at the beginning of the year as well as later. Although difficult to arrange because of the large numbers of observers and the sensitivity of some teachers and schools to "outsiders" during the first week or so, these observations proved to be very valuable in allowing us to document and describe the socialization process that occurs in many effective teachers' classrooms. We were also able to use the beginning-of-year data to contrast sub-samples of teachers who had very different classroom climates later in the year, and to find that much of the roots of later disorder were established early by what the less effective manager did (and did not do).

An interesting aspect of the research was observing teachers within the same school who had very different student behavior in their classrooms. In several cases I observed two elementary teachers at the same grade level. In one classroom, students would work very productively, staying engaged during academic activities, and generally looking like a classroom in which I would be happy to have my own children reside. In the other classroom, the teacher would struggle to keep children on-task, and disruptions were frequent. Similar cases also occurred at the secondary level. After noting numerous instances of such "natural" experiments, we undertook some analyses in which we matched pairs of teachers' classes based on several factors in order to control the possibility that entering students' characteristics would account for the behavioral differences.

A very interesting aspect of these analyses was the finding that the student behaviors in the classes were very similar during

An Integrated Approach to Classroom Management

As we have seen, all three approaches have both advantages and limitations. Table 9.3 summarizes the three approaches along the six criteria we set out at the beginning of the chapter. It's clear from the table that while each approach has made significant contributions, effective classroom managers blend together the best parts of different approaches (Doyle, 1986; Emmer et al., 1980; Evertson & Emmer, 1982). We now turn to an integration of all three traditions of classroom management.

the first week of school, in spite of clear managerial differences between the teachers. However, during the second and third weeks of school, more off-task behavior began to be evident in the less effectively managed classes. The seeds of discipline problems are planted early but do not germinate immediately. To use a different metaphor, the honeymoon period lasts a week or so. Good student behavior during the first week of school may not persist, and teachers should not be fooled by it! One of the problems for new teachers is that their management mistakes are not always accompanied by immediate feedback, and that their consequences make their appearance gradually.

Teachers can apply this research to create a classroom setting that will enhance their curricular goals. As teachers, we all want classrooms in which students are cooperative and academically engaged, and do not disrupt others. Creating such a classroom is not achieved by following platitudes or simply creating a list of rules for student behavior (although clear expectations will help). Rather, good classroom management is accomplished by thoroughly planning a set of features, implementing them during the first week or weeks (in more complex classes), and maintaining the system. In particular, areas that should be planned before school begins include the *teacher's expectations for behavior, consequences,* the *physical setting,* and *first week activities.* Each of these areas should be analyzed as it applies to your own teaching situation. For example, if you plan to use discussion activities, you should think carefully about what you want students to *do* during that activity. Should they raise hands and wait to be called upon before contributing? What should students do who are not called on? Will movement out of seat be permitted? Will participation be graded? You will need to be prepared to discuss your discussion guidelines with students when you first use the activity in your class. If you want student input on your guidelines, you will at least need to think through those features that should be considered.

A cardinal rule to observe is that if you want students to behave in a certain way, you should be prepared to *teach* such behavior to the students the first time it is needed. Teaching a behavior may require only a simple explanation. It may also require a visual aid (e.g., written on a poster), a demonstration, a discussion, or student input. To teach a behavior, you will also need to provide students with feedback to help them understand what is expected. You should be prepared to deal with problems when they first occur. Students learn to behave inappropriately, too. We found that more effective managers during the first several weeks visually monitored their students and promptly addressed inappropriate behavior. Less effective managers were not as observant of their classrooms and did not deal with problems soon enough. Thus, students in their classes might have learned that they could get away with misbehavior. When problems are addressed promptly, they can be handled with simple measures such as eye contact, proximity, a brief desist, or redirection. Waiting too long may produce an escalated problem that requires more extensive interventions, which can disrupt activities, give undesirable attention, and undermine your management system.

Setting Up the Classroom Workplace

During the first week of school, do you want your students to do more listening or more talking? Do you want them to be calm and quiet or excited and talkative? Do you want them to focus on your questions or listen to your answers? Do you want to promote talking or listening, independent or cooperative work, self-study or group problem solving? The way you arrange your classroom—align furniture, place partitions, decorate walls and bulletin boards, and "soften" the environment—will have as much to do with achieving these goals as the rules and routines you create to establish a classroom management plan.

How can I arrange the visual texture and physical space of my classroom to encourage some behaviors and discourage others?

Table 9.3

Comparison of Three Traditions

Criterion	Humanist Tradition	Behavior Analysis Tradition	Classroom Management Tradition
Building trusting relations	Explicit on building trusting relations between teacher and students; not helpful on relationships among peers	Does not address this criterion	Does not address this criterion
Preventing misbehavior	Emphasizes how to react to students who misbehave; does not address prevention	Does not address prevention	Tradition focuses strongly on planning and anticipation of classroom behavior
Redirecting minor misbehavior	Emphasizes individual problem solving; some suggested techniques may be impractical for classroom teachers	Emphasizes complicated interventions that are appropriate for more serious infractions	Tradition focuses strongly on simple, unobtrusive techniques to redirect minor misbehavior
Stopping major disruptive behavior	Ginott suggests the teacher invite the student's cooperation in addressing the problem; Glasser's removal-from-the friendly-workplace technique may be more effective	Suggests behavior modification plans that may include punishment or elaborate reinforcement schemes; may be impractical for the classroom teacher to carry out	Focuses on preventing major disruptions, not on rectifying them once they occur
Teaching self-control	Face-to-face communication skills encourage the teaching of self-control	Suggested interventions require individualized programs carried out by trained professionals	Does not address this criterion
Responding to cultural differences	Does not address this criterion	Does not specifically address this criterion	Does not address this criterion

Behavioral setting. The immediate environment in which a behavior occurs.

Psychologists use the term **behavioral setting** to refer to the way in which particular environments elicit specific behaviors. You will have numerous choices to make about how to arrange your classroom—your behavioral setting. Each choice will encourage certain student behaviors and discourage others. The first step in designing your behavioral setting is to identify what you want your students to do when they are in it.

Your behavioral and instructional goals for students will vary from day to day and from month to month as you identify learner needs and provide the necessary learning experiences to meet them. As your goals vary, so must the behavioral setting you arrange to bring about these goals.

As a rule, you will want to match your behavioral goals with your behavioral setting. Thus, the room arrangement you choose is important in communicating to your students the kind of behaviors you are trying to elicit. For example, the room arrangement shown in Figure 9.3 would be more appropriate for acquiring knowledge, concepts, and rules than for developing relationships and learning to cooperate. These latter goals may

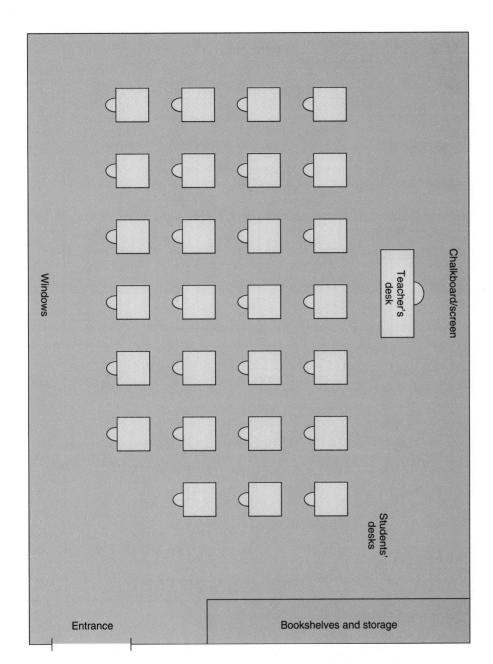

Figure 9.3
A classroom arrangement emphasizing the acquisition of knowledge, rules, and concepts.

be more appropriately met in a classroom arranged along the lines of that in Figure 9.4. With this arrangement, you can expect more expression of student opinion, increased student talk, and greater spontaneity in student responses. As the internal features of your classroom turn from a traditionally formal arrangement to this less formal one, so too will the social climate of the classroom. Because this arrangement suggests that interpersonal communication and sharing are permitted, then they undoubtedly will occur.

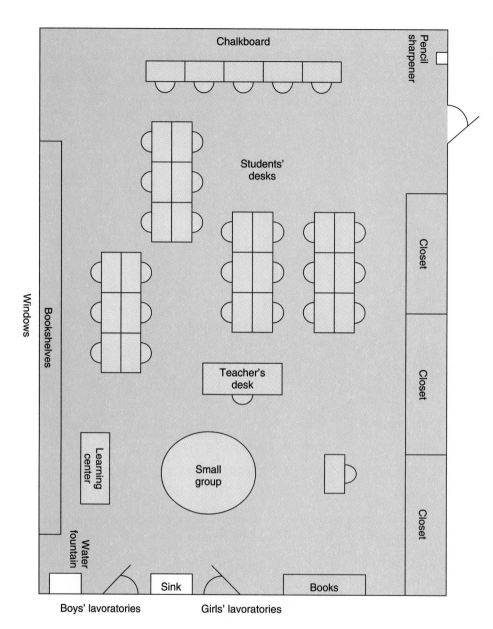

Figure 9.4
A classroom arrangement emphasizing positive relations and cooperative learning.

Sometimes more than one classroom arrangement can exist simultaneously, as when both the acquisition of knowledge and cooperation and sharing may be your goals. In this case the arrangement shown in Figure 9.5 would be appropriate.

The arrangement of space tends to dictate patterns of student involvement. For example, the arrangement in Figure 9.3 could be expected to encourage speaking in sequential order, one-to-one involvement with the teacher, and individual seatwork in which the textbook is treated as the primary source of learning (Phillips, 1983). But be-

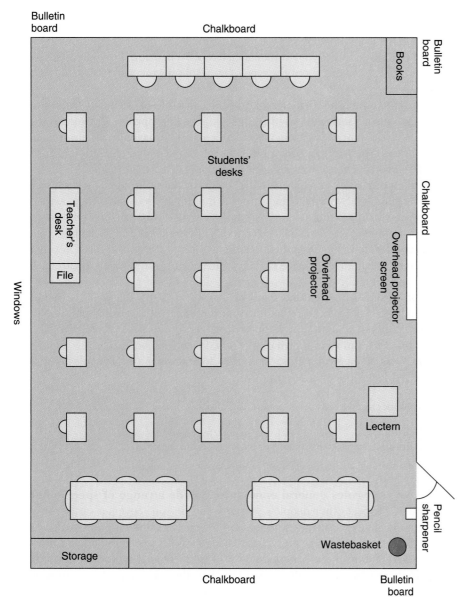

Figure 9.5
A compromise classroom arrangement allowing both knowledge acquisition and cooperative learning.

cause of differences in culture or ethnicity, some students may be less responsive to some classroom arrangements than to others. For example, an arrangement like that in Figure 9.3, which limits the teacher to calling on individual students, who then must respond in front of the entire group (Erickson & Mohatt, 1982), will elicit different responses from students of different cultures or ethnicities. Thus, classroom arrangement should be responsive to both instructional goals and cultural expectations, a topic we will study in Chapter 15.

Rules. General statements defining acceptable and unacceptable behaviors.

How can I create rules in my classroom that favor a secure and orderly environment without impeding communication and trust?

Rules for Running the Workplace

Just as no one behavioral setting is best for all students and every teacher, there is no one best set of rules to direct your students' behavior. When you develop **rules** you are making a personal statement about the type of atmosphere you want to promote in your behavioral setting.

If you want to establish an orderly, businesslike, task-oriented climate, rules such as "Speak and leave your seat only when recognized" are appropriate. But such rules are inappropriate if you want a classroom where students are expected to discuss, obtain resources in different parts of the room, problem solve, and cooperate with one another.

Here are several general suggestions for developing classroom rules.

● **Make your rules consistent with the classroom climate you seek to promote.** The beginning of your teaching career is the time to recognize your own values and preferences for managing your classroom. Articulate your personal philosophy of classroom management and have your classroom rules reflect it. For example, refer to Figure 9.1 and decide in which parts of quadrant B or C you want to be. Do you want your classroom climate to emphasize slightly more control than warmth (quadrant B) or the reverse (quadrant C)?

● **Don't establish rules that can't be enforced.** A rule that says "No talking or getting out of your seat" may be difficult to enforce when your personal philosophy encourages independent thinking, problem solving, and group work. Unfairness and inconsistency may result in your applying rules you do not fully believe in.

● **Set only necessary rules.** There are four reasons to have rules, and each should reflect at least one of these purposes:

Enhance work engagement and minimize disruption

Promote safety and security

Prevent disturbance to other students or other classroom activities

Promote acceptable standards of courtesy and interpersonal relations.

● **Make your rules general enough to include a range of specific behaviors.** The rule "Respect other people's property and person" covers a variety of problems, such as stealing, borrowing without permission, and throwing things. Similarly, the rule "Follow the teacher's requests immediately" allows you to put an end to a variety of off-task, disruptive behaviors that no list of rules could anticipate or cover. Similarly, be careful not to state a rule so generally that the specific problems to which it pertains remain unclear to your learners. For example, a rule that states simply "Show respect" or "Obey the teacher" may be sufficiently vague as to be ignored by most of your learners and to thus be unenforceable by you.

Engaging Students in the Learning Process

Classrooms are busy places. Materials have to be checked in and out, activities begun and ended, learners moved through their lessons, and assignments given, completed, and evaluated. Groups are formed, arranged, and rearranged. In the midst of these activities, students need things, forget things, borrow things. They get thirsty, hungry, tired, and sick. They have to use the bathroom.

Routine. A procedure organized around a particular time, concept, or place that helps guide learners through the day.

This complexity requires systematic routines. A **routine** is a set of rules organized around a particular time (for example, beginning of the day), context (for example, group work), or place (for example, library, learning center, or playground) that helps guide your learners through the day. The key to keeping your learners engaged and you in control of this complexity is effective teaching of the routines that keep your classroom productive and efficient.

The amount of time learners spend thinking about, acting on, or working with a learning task is referred to as **engaged learning time** (Savage, 1991). Engaged learning time is different from the amount of time you may have planned for teaching a particular lesson or activity. For example, you may have allocated 35 minutes for a particular activity, but your students may spend only 15 minutes of that time actively engaged in the learning task.

What happened to the other 20 minutes? Most likely they were used up passing out materials, making announcements, giving directions, dealing with student requests to leave the room or to borrow materials, cleaning up, and handling discipline problems. In the studies of effective classroom managers we cited earlier, the teachers who were most successful at maximizing engaged learning time were those who taught routines to their students during the first few weeks of school (Emmer et al., 1994). There is also a significant relationship between engaged learning time and achievement, providing perhaps the most persuasive argument for using well-established routines. Let's look at some examples of routines and discuss how you can establish your own.

Table 9.4 provides some examples of classroom routines (many other possible routines, such as those for grading, leaving the room, use of school facilities, and academic feedback, are omitted here). With each routine comes a set of procedures or informal rules pertaining to specific areas of concern. For example, your "beginning class routine" may include what your students should be doing while you are taking attendance (sit still without talking, check over homework or last assignment, read silently from text, for instance). It can also include how a student should enter the room after the bell has rung (for example, come to you, go directly to his or her seat, or go see the counselor) and how handouts, tests, and assignments are to be dispensed (for example, first in each row passes them to those behind, student helpers come to your desk, each helps himself or herself from stacks conveniently placed in the front and back of the room). The procedures you establish under each routine will depend on your own circumstances and instructional style.

Teaching a routine takes time and energy, but routines established in advance of your first day of teaching will also save you time later and give your students a sense of organization and order. Routines allow you more time to teach and more time for your learners to become engaged in the learning process, since the routines will enhance the speed and efficiency with which things get done. Routines are especially effective with time-consuming noninstructional activities, which can sometimes take up to 50 percent of the time you initially allocate to a particular topic or lesson (Jones & Jones, 1990). Think for a moment about the time that might have been saved in Mrs. Gates's class, had she had a routine for the beginning of class. Routines should be taught with as much planning and thoroughness as your learning objectives, and then followed up by monitoring their effectiveness (Jones & Jones, 1990; Pasch, Sparks-Langer, Gardner, Starko, & Moody, 1991).

Maintaining Work Engagement

A concern for trusting relationships and a behavioral setting suited to the goals of your instruction, together with a carefully crafted set of rules and routines, will get you off on the right foot during the first weeks of school. Some students, however, may choose not

Engaged learning time. The amount of time learners spend thinking about, acting on, or working with a learning task.

How can I establish classroom routines that are consistent with the climate I wish to promote?

Table 9.4

Examples of Classroom Routines

Routine	Steps
Beginning of class	1. Attendance
	2. Tardies
	3. Distributing materials
Work requirement	1. Heading of paper
	2. Use of pen vs. pencil
	3. Neatness, legibility
	4. Incomplete work
Seatwork	1. Attention to task
	2. Obtaining help
	3. What to do when work is completed
	4. Movement and talking
	5. Obtaining materials
Group activity	1. Expected behavior of group members
	2. Expected behavior of other students
	3. Sharing of resources
	4. Individual responsibilities
	5. Choosing a leader
Ending of class	1. Putting away supplies and equipment
	2. Cleaning up
	3. Writing assignments
	4. Dismissal
Interruptions	1. Talk among students
	2. Turning in work
	3. Handing back assignments
	4. Getting back work
	5. Out-of-seat rules
Checking assignments in class	1. Students exchanging papers
	2. Marking and grading papers
	3. Turning in assignments

to follow your rules and routines. They may be disinterested in school, lack the skills to profit from the lesson, or simply want to escape from the classroom. Some of these disruptions will be minor, last for only a short time, and resolve themselves. But others will persist. If they do, it is important that you respond in ways that promote a positive learning climate.

Low-Profile Classroom Management

Rinne (1984) has used the expression **low-profile classroom control** to refer to coping strategies used by effective teachers to stop misbehavior without disrupting the flow of a lesson. These techniques are effective for **surface behaviors** (Levin & Nolan, 1991), minor disruptions that represent the majority of disruptive classroom actions. Examples of surface behaviors are laughing, talking out of turn, passing notes, daydreaming, not following directions, combing hair, doodling, humming, and tapping. These are the normal developmental behaviors that children do when confined to a small space with large numbers of other children. They are not indicative of underlying emotional disorders or personality problems. However, they can disrupt the flow of a lesson and the work engagement of others if left unchecked.

Figure 9.6 depicts the components of low-profile classroom control, a set of techniques that requires *anticipation* by the teacher to prevent problems before they occur; *deflection* to redirect disruptive behavior that is about to occur; and *reaction* to stop disruptions immediately after they occur. Let's look at each. We also list some of the most time-honored of these techniques in the accompanying box, *Employing Low-Profile Classroom Control.*

Anticipation.   Alert teachers have their antennae up to sense changes in student motivation, attentiveness, arousal levels, or excitability as these changes happen or even as they are about to happen. They are aware that at certain times of the year (before and after holidays), week (just before a major social event), or day (right after an assembly or physical education class), the class will be less ready for work than usual. Skilled classroom managers are alert not only to changes in the group's motivational or attention level but also to changes in specific individuals that may be noticed as soon as they enter class.

Low-profile classroom control. A set of coping strategies and techniques used to stop misbehavior, especially surface behaviors, without disrupting the flow of a lesson.

Surface behaviors. Normal developmental behaviors children find themselves doing when confined to a small space with large numbers of other children.

> **How do I stop misbehavior without disrupting the flow of a lesson?**

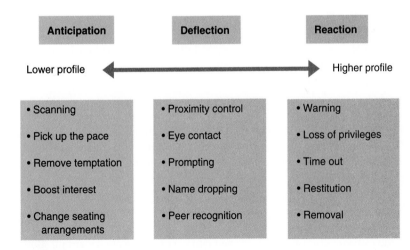

Figure 9.6
Characteristics of low-profile control.

Employing Low-Profile Classroom Control

Here are some suggestions for each stage of the control process.

Anticipation

- Maintain a reserve of activities that are likely to boost students' interest during times when it is difficult to stay focused on normal day-to-day activities.
- Force yourself to be more positive or eager in the face of waning student enthusiasm. For example, raising and lowering the pitch of your voice or moving to different parts of the room more frequently can be effective.
- When necessary, quickly change seating arrangements to minimize antagonisms when arguments between students occur.

Deflection

- Prompt the student by reminding the class of the rule that's about to be broken. For example: "We're all supposed to be doing math now."

- Use *name dropping:* insert the target student's name into your explanation or lecture. For example, "Now if Angela were living in Boston at the time of the Boston Tea Party, she might have. . . ."
- Recognize a peer who is engaged in appropriate behavior. For example: "Notice how Greg has already finished all three problems."

Reaction

- React quickly, quietly, and consistently to misbehavior.
- Reaction should begin with a reminder and proceed quickly to a warning and then, if necessary, to immediate consequences.

At these times anticipation involves visually scanning back and forth to quickly size up the seriousness of a potential problem and head it off before it emerges or becomes a bigger problem. For example, you may decide to pick up the pace of the class to counter a perceived lethargy after a three-day weekend, or remove magazines or other objects that may distract attention before a long holiday. Anticipation involves not only knowing what to look for but where and when to look for it. It also involves having a technique ready, no matter how small, for changing the environment quickly and without notice to your students to prevent the problem from occurring or escalating.

Deflection. As noted, good classroom managers sense when disruption is about to occur. They are attuned to verbal and nonverbal cues that in the past have preceded disruptive behavior. For instance, a student may glance at a friend, close his textbook abruptly, sit idly, squirm, ask to be excused, sigh with frustration, or grimace. Although not disruptive by themselves, these behaviors may signal that other, more disruptive behavior is about to follow.

Some teachers can deflect these behaviors by simply moving nearer to the student who may be about to misbehave, thus preventing a more disruptive episode from occurring. Other teachers make eye contact with the learner and use certain facial expressions such as raised eyebrows or a slight tilt of the head to communicate a warning. Both these techniques effectively use nonverbal signals to deflect a potential problem. Verbal signals, such as prompting or name dropping, can also be effective (see the box). As the

Teachers need to develop skills in anticipating, deflecting, and reacting to inappropriate behavior. Many different verbal and nonverbal abilities are required of an effective classroom manager.

potential for the problem to escalate increases, the effective manager shifts from nonverbal to verbal techniques to keep pace with the seriousness of the misbehavior about to occur.

Reaction. Anticipation and deflection can efficiently and unobtrusively prevent actions that disrupt the flow of a lesson. They allow students the opportunity to correct themselves, thus fostering the development of self-control. However, the classroom is a busy place, and the many demands on your attention may make a behavior difficult to anticipate or deflect.

When disruptive behavior that cannot be anticipated or unobtrusively redirected occurs, your primary goal is to end the disruptive episode as quickly as possible. Effective classroom managers, therefore, must at times react to a behavior by providing a warning and a consequence. Glasser (1990) points out that an effective consequence for breaking a rule is temporary removal from the classroom—provided that your classroom is a place where that student wants to be. Other possible consequences are loss of privileges, school detention, loss of recess, or loss of another activity that the learner would miss.

When disruptive behavior occurs, your reaction sequence might proceed as follows:

1. As soon as a student is disruptive, acknowledge a nearby classmate who is performing the expected behavior: "Carlos, I appreciate how hard you are working on the spelling words." Then wait 15 seconds for the disruptive student to change his or her behavior.

2. If the disruption continues, say, "Michael, this is a warning. Complete the spelling assignment and leave Carrie alone." Wait 15 seconds.

3. If the student doesn't follow the request after this warning, say, "Michael, you were given a warning. You must now leave the room [or you must stay inside during lunch or cannot go to the resource center today]. I'll talk to you about this during my free period."

Dealing with Chronic Disruptive Behavior

The low-profile techniques of anticipation, deflection, and reaction should promote lesson flow when used skillfully. When these techniques do not work for a particular student or group of students, it may be a signal that the needs of the student (for example, for belonging, as discussed in Chapter 8) are not being met. When disruptive behavior persists and you are sure you have taken all reasonable steps to deal with it (for example, followed the anticipation-deflection-reaction approach), you should consult a school counselor or school psychologist. Many school districts have professionals either on staff or under consultant contracts who can handle such matters.

Culturally Responsive Classroom Management

One of the most interesting and encouraging advances in the understanding of classroom management is the emerging field of cultural compatibility and behavior management. The writings and research of Tharp (1989), Dillon (1989), and Bowers and Flinders (1990) present convincing arguments that members of different cultures react differently to the nonverbal and verbal behavior management techniques discussed in this chapter, including proximity control, eye contact, warnings, and classroom arrangement. Furthermore, they cite numerous examples of varying ways in which teachers from one culture interpret disruptive behaviors of children from another culture.

In Chapter 15 we will deal with the issues of culturally responsive teaching in more detail. For now, it is important for you to know simply that many behavioral management techniques are culturally sensitive and that the effective classroom manager matches the technique not only with the situation but also with the cultural history of the learner.

Summing Up

This chapter introduced you to positive approaches to classroom management. Its main points were these:

● A classroom management plan prevents behavior problems from occurring and prepares you to respond efficiently and effectively to unanticipated classroom events.

- Different degrees of control and warmth can occur simultaneously. Behavior in one dimension does not preclude behavior in the other. This makes possible a management plan that promotes both control and warmth.
- Research shows that as much as 50 percent of class time can be spent dealing with misbehavior that might be described as "amiable goofing off," or "surface behavior."
- The humanist classroom management tradition allows the student time to develop control over his or her behavior by focusing on inner thoughts, feelings, and emotions. The humanist approach is strongest in promoting individual problem solving and self-control. It is weakest in preventing misbehavior from occurring and in addressing major disruptive behavior.
- The applied behavior analysis tradition focuses on changing behavior through the use of reinforcement and consequences. Applied behavior analysis is strongest in stopping major disruptive behavior and, to a lesser extent, in teaching self-control. It is weakest in building trusting relations and in preventing problems before they occur.
- The classroom management tradition focuses on anticipating and preventing misbehavior by establishing a classroom environment in which misbehavior is less likely to occur. The classroom management tradition is strongest in preventing misbehavior before it occurs and in preventing minor misbehaviors from escalating. It is weakest in stopping major disruptive behavior that is already occurring.
- More effective and less effective classroom managers can be distinguished more by how they prevent misbehavior than by how they respond to misbehavior that occurs.
- Effective classroom managers organize their classrooms to minimize disruptive behavior and enhance work engagement, teach rules and routines as methodically as they teach content, inform students about the consequences of breaking rules, and enforce rules consistently.
- A *routine* is a set of rules organized around a particular time, concept, or place that helps guide learners through the day. Routines can apply to particular times of the day (beginning of day), contexts (group work), or places (in and out of the classroom).
- Low-profile classroom control entails anticipation, deflection, and reaction.

For Discussion and Practice

*1. Identify the behaviors in Mrs. Gates's class that might be described as surface behaviors or as amiable goofing off.

*2. If you were given the responsibility of helping Mrs. Gates, what are four behavioral expectations that you would implement immediately?

*3. Describe what you would do in your own classroom to combine the quality of warmth with the quality of control.

Questions marked with an asterisk are answered in the appendix.

4. Characterize a hypothetical teacher's behavior in each of the four quadrants in Figure 9.1, using specific behaviors and events. With which quadrant do you most readily identify?

°5. Describe in your own words the humanistic, applied behavior analysis, and classroom management traditions, citing at least one author and reference for each.

°6. What characteristics does Ginott's congruent communication contain? Which do you feel would be the most difficult to implement in your classroom? Which would be the easiest?

°7. Identify some specific recommendations Glasser (1990) would provide Mrs. Gates in helping her better manage her classroom.

°8. Give an example of each of the following from your own classroom experience: (a) positive reinforcement, (b) negative reinforcement, (c) intermittent reinforcement, (d) antecedent.

9. Give an example of each of the five strategies an applied behavior analyst would recommend for improving the behavior of your learners.

°10. Describe some of the characteristics Emmer, Evertson, and Anderson (1980) found to be associated with effective managers and some they found to be associated with ineffective managers.

11. Construct a plan for dealing with Mrs. Gates's class using the classroom management tradition. What would you do first, second, third, and so on, beginning on Monday morning?

°12. Using the appropriate descriptors provided in Table 9.1, identify some of the behaviors that would characterize the classroom arrangements shown in Figures 9.3 and 9.4.

°13. What is the difference between engaged learning time and allocated time?

°14. Identify four areas in which establishing a routine would be essential to an orderly first week of school.

°15. In your own words, define low-profile classroom control. Provide one example each of anticipation, deflection, and reaction for low-profile classroom control, using a classroom dialogue.

16. Provide one example of a culturally sensitive behavior management technique. State with whom it might and might not be effective.

Suggested Readings

Bowers, C. A., & Flinders, D. J. (1990). *Responsive teaching: An ecological approach to patterns of language, culture, and thought.* New York: Teachers College Press. An original and thoughtful analysis of how cultural patterns of thought and language effect a teacher's classroom management decisions.

Charles, C. M. (1992). *Building classroom discipline: From models to practice* (3rd ed.). New York: Longman. A comprehensive survey of the major theoretical approaches to classroom discipline. Presents helpful suggestions for developing your own personalized system of classroom management.

Emmer, E. T., Evertson, C. M., Clements, B. S., & Worsham, M. E. (1994). *Classroom management for sec-

ondary teachers (3rd ed.). Englewood Cliffs, NJ: Prentice-Hall. Presents detailed, step-by-step activities and principles for planning and organizing junior and senior high school classrooms. The recommendations are derived from observations of the best practices of effective teachers.

Jones, V. F., & Jones, L. S. (1990). *Comprehensive classroom management* (3rd ed.). Nedham, MA: Allyn & Bacon. Presents a comprehensive discussion of the classroom management tradition and offers many practical suggestions to both elementary and secondary school teachers on ways to promote positive behavior.

Instructional Management

This chapter will help you answer the following questions about your learners:

- How can I use goals to motivate and energize my learners?
- How can I write objectives at higher levels of behavioral complexity, such as analysis, synthesis, and decision making?
- What are some of the ways to capture student interest at the start of a lesson?
- How do I teach by modeling?
- How can I conduct an effective demonstration?
- How can I help students take responsibility for their own learning?
- What can I do to make my learners look forward to practicing their skills?
- How can prompts be used to help guide learners to a first response?
- What are some ways to use questions to encourage learners to respond correctly?
- How can technology make independent practice and transfer a practical classroom goal?
- How can I help my learners transfer what I teach to new situations and settings?

Lori Freeman heads the science department at Sierra Blanca Junior High School.[1] She has been teaching courses in physical science, life science, and ecology for 16 years to a diverse group of seventh- and eighth-grade learners, mostly from working-class and lower middle-class families. Both she and her colleagues will tell you that Ms. Freeman is as excited about her subject and her students as she was on her first day of teaching.

It is the second week in February, and Ms. Freeman is teaching a unit on photosynthesis. Years ago an experienced teacher advised Ms. Freeman to plan her most exciting units between Christmas and Easter, the time of year when both students and faculty experience the winter doldrums. Following this advice, Ms. Freeman has given a lot of thought to her goals, objectives, and instructional activities for this unit. Rather than start the first lesson with a presentation on the importance of food for plants, Ms. Freeman decides that a discussion on food for people would be more interesting. She begins to engage her class of 28 learners in a dialogue about which of a variety of substances can be considered food. Her students are seated in groups of five or six with their attention drawn to an overhead transparency of a prepared list of substances. Ms. Freeman begins with a brisk pace of questions, clarifications, and explanations while moving about the room to keep her students' attention.

The class has little trouble agreeing that substances like carrots, milk, and potatoes are food. But the class is puzzled over whether water is food. Ms. Freeman lets the debate continue for a few minutes and then changes the overhead to a definition of food, which reads, *Food: substances that contain energy in the form of calories for living things.* After a brief explanation, she asks the students to record the definition in their notebooks. Then Ms. Freeman returns to the issue of whether water is food, given the definition they have just seen. Most students agree that water is not food. Carla, however, remains unconvinced, calling out, "It's a kind of food." Some heated discussion follows, but the issue remains unresolved as Ms. Freeman ends the lesson with instructions to copy the next day's assignment from the board.

In this chapter you will also learn the meanings of these terms:

anticipatory set
coaching
commanding stimuli appeal
direct instruction
discrepancy appeal
emotional appeal
fading
goals
guided practice
independent practice
indirect instruction
instructional events
instructional management
modeling
objectives
prompts
psychophysical appeal
self-directed instruction
structuring
transfer of learning

[1]Adapted from Anderson, 1991.

The following day Ms. Freeman decides to review the previous day's discussion by asking if there are any questions. Carla states that her older brother, who is a college student, told her that food has to have calories and pointed out that water doesn't have any. "So I guess water isn't food," she explains to the class.

Carla's comments about water provide a transition to a brief explanation and discussion about the role of water in our lives. Ms. Freeman turns on the overhead again and asks the students several questions about how plants get food. The students are puzzled at first. Then someone blurts out, "We fertilize them." Another says that his parents insert little food sticks in the potted plants at home. Each student response is recorded on the transparency.

"Well, do the plants reach out and grab these food sticks and munch on them like some kind of snack?" challenges Ms. Freeman. The class laughs, but most are still puzzled. Ms. Freeman then asks them to write in their notebooks their thoughts about how plants get food. She gives them about 10 minutes, during which time she moves about the room checking work, answering and asking questions, encouraging more complete answers, and reminding them of the facts they have learned. Two minutes before the activity is to end, she reminds them to finish their work.

"OK, now let's have some of your ideas," Ms. Freeman asks. She writes on the transparency *How Plants Get Food.* "Tell me what you wrote. How do you think plants get food? Donald?" Ms. Freeman lists Donald's ideas: carbon dioxide from the air, light from the sun, oxygen from the air, minerals from the soil or from food sticks, water from rain.

In the ensuing discussion, Ms. Freeman guides her students to the understanding that plants make their food through the minerals they absorb from water. As the lesson ends, Ms. Freeman makes the association between what they have just learned and the process of photosynthesis. Subsequent explanations and laboratory tasks provide examples and real-life demonstrations of the process of photosynthesis.

Introduction

Educational psychologists have always focused much attention on identifying what successful teachers like Ms. Freeman do to promote student learning. By analyzing the classroom behavior of effective teachers, researchers have identified certain regularly occurring patterns of teacher behavior. These patterns of expert practice are evident regardless of whether the subject is reading, science, social studies, math, art, or any other subject.

Ms. Freeman's lesson did not just happen. It was undoubtedly the result of much hard work and self-reflection. Nor is it likely that any other teacher could have substituted for her on this day and achieved the same kind of interaction between teacher and learners. This lesson went smoothly because it was part of a much larger pattern of practice that extended across the entire school year. What was this pattern of practice?

Ms. Freeman's pattern of practice involved many different aspects of teaching. Included among them were the principles of group management we discussed in Chapter 8. Her learners felt secure enough to express their own ideas and to disagree with the viewpoints of others because Ms. Freeman had taken the time to develop high expectations for all her students, classroom norms that value learning and group cohesiveness.

Included also in Ms. Freeman's pattern of practice were rules and routines of conduct management, discussed in Chapter 9. Her learners moved smoothly from one activity to another, listened to Ms. Freeman and to each other, and spoke at appropriate times because of the conduct management procedures Ms. Freeman already had in place.

But in addition to her expertise in group and conduct management, Ms. Freeman also showed a pattern of expert practice that we will refer to as **instructional management.** This includes two broad components of teaching skill: (1) expertise in planning for instruction and (2) expertise in delivering instruction. Before teaching her lesson, Ms. Freeman had made important planning decisions about its **goals** and **objectives.** These goals and objectives gave Ms. Freeman and her learners a purpose or reason for the activities they were pursuing. They also made it easier to gauge the learners' progress.

Finally, Ms. Freeman and her learners were able to achieve their goals and objectives because of her expert pattern of practice in delivering instruction. As you will learn in this chapter, the effective delivery of instruction includes four general categories of teaching skills: (1) structuring, (2) modeling, (3) coaching, and (4) fading.

One of your goals as a beginning teacher will be to build successful patterns of practice in your classroom. These will involve the learning climate you create, the classroom management procedures you establish, the goals and objectives you choose, and the teaching activities of structuring, modeling, coaching, and fading you employ to achieve a positive impact on your learners. By carefully studying this chapter and observing patterns of expert practice during your field placements and student teaching, you will be able to build successful patterns of practice. When these activities become enriched with an understanding of learner assessment (to be discussed in Part IV), you will have acquired the patterns of expert practice of an effective teacher.

Goals: Giving Instruction a Purpose

Since I began teaching, my English 9B classes have been one struggle after the next. Not only do all of my students have distinct personalities, but they have a variety of skill levels as well. When I announced we would be reading *Romeo and Juliet,* some students—mostly girls—rejoiced at the prospect. Others groaned, "Why?" It was more a plea than a question. "Because," was my response, *"Romeo and Juliet* is required reading for all ninth graders as stated in the curriculum guide."

Meaningless. They didn't buy it. That was my first mistake. I had not really thought about why I was teaching the play. I only knew that I was going to teach it because the guide said so, and I had not anticipated that the majority of my students would want to know why. (Vickie White, in Shulman, 1991, p. 28)

Since your students will silently ask themselves "Why do I have to learn this stuff?" it is only reasonable to ask "Why am I teaching it?" There are several ways to answer this question. One is that you are teaching a lesson so that your students can attain a certain outcome—recognize the sounds of consonant blends, add two-digit numbers, or focus a microscope. This answer involves the identification of the behavioral outcomes your learners will acquire at the end of your lesson. But such an explanation says little about the importance of the behavior or skill you want your students to attain. Imagine answering Vickie's students' question about why they have to learn "this stuff" with the answer "So you'll know about Romeo and Juliet!" We know what will follow: "But why do we have to know that?" Vickie's students will continue to search for a purpose or meaning for the activity she has chosen. Finding none, they will disengage themselves from her lesson.

Instructional management. Two broad components of teaching skill: (1) expertise in planning for instruction and (2) expertise in delivering instruction.

Goals. Educational priorities that focus on the subject matter, societal concerns, and/or learner interests and are used to guide the formation of objectives.

Objectives. Statements that specify the skills learners acquire in order to achieve important goals.

The Relevance of Educational Goals

Educational goals provide a sense of mission and purpose. The more aware you are of your mission and purpose in teaching an area of content, the more you will be able to inspire your students to learn it, unlike Vickie, who was unable to relate what she was teaching to a larger purpose that could be understood by her students. Your ability to articulate goals conveys to learners your sense of purpose, from which they can make a commitment to learn. This is why goals are important—they energize and motivate students to become actively engaged in and committed to the learning process. The accompanying box, *Writing Instructional Goals*, gives examples of goals that might energize students to make a commitment to learn. As you read them, reflect on how well they answer the question "Why am I teaching this?"

Notice that these goal statements, although written for the teacher, are expressed from the learner's point of view. In other words, goals identify what your students will learn from your instruction. For example, the statement "The teacher will show students examples of logical arguments" would fail as an educational goal because it describes what you will do, not what your students will learn. "Learners will acquire the

How can I use goals to motivate and energize my learners?

Applying Your Knowledge:

Writing Instructional Goals

The following are examples of clear instructional goals for a variety of content areas and levels.

Social Studies

1st-grade unit on "People Who Made America"
Goal: Learners will appreciate that people are different and why that's good.

3rd-grade unit on "Our Community"
Goal: Learners will understand what makes up a community, what holds a community together, and why communities are important to their lives.

7th-grade unit on "Local History"
Goal: Learners will understand the advantages and disadvantages of placing regional interests over national ones.

11th-grade unit on "U.S. History Since 1965"
Goal: Learners will be prepared to live with the uncertainty that not all problems have solutions.

Science

1st-grade unit on "The World Around Us"
Goal: Learners will realize there are logical answers to questions such as "Mommy, why is the sky blue?"

4th-grade unit on "Living Things"
Goal: Learners will understand the relationships between how an organism looks, the structure of the organism, and the ways in which it functions, so they can see how life is sustained.

11th-grade unit on "Coping with Innovation and Change"
Goal: Learners will be able to recognize and learn ways of dealing with the rapid pace of technology in our everyday lives.

Mathematics

1st-grade unit on "Addition Facts"
Goal: Learners will understand that mathematics derives from the things we see around us.

4th-grade unit on "Percentages"
Goal: Learners will be able to apply mathematics to solving problems regarding daily nutritional needs.

7th-grade unit on "Measurement"
Goal: Learners will appreciate how measurement allows the planning and construction of spaces that are comfortable to live in.

10th-grade unit on "Geometric Propositions"
Goal: Learners will acquire the ability to construct a convincing argument.

ability to construct a convincing argument" qualifies as a goal statement because it identifies what is expected of your students.

How do you choose goals for learners? What is the best way to find proper goals, given the diversity and complexity that exist across subjects and grades? Several approaches to formulating educational goals have been developed to help you. One approach comes from the work of Tyler (1974).

Tyler's Goal Development Approach

Tyler's approach to generating educational goals has had a major influence on curriculum development over the past three decades. Tyler believes that as society becomes more complex there are more things for people to learn. But the time available to learn this ever-expanding amount of knowledge and skills continually decreases. Consequently, educators must make informed choices about which goals are worth teaching.

Tyler identified five factors to consider when a teacher establishes priorities for what students should learn. First, goals must include:

- the subject matter we know enough about to teach (subject matter mastery)
- societal concerns, which represent what is valued in both the society at large and the local community
- personal interests of the students, and the abilities and knowledge they bring to school.

Second, these goals must be refined to match

- your school and community's educational philosophy
- what instructional theory and research tell us can be taught.

Tyler's approach to establishing educational goals is illustrated in Figure 10.1.

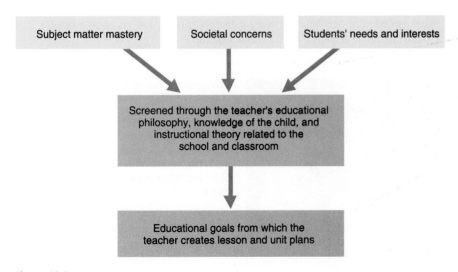

Figure 10.1
Tyler's considerations in goal selection.

From Educational Goals to Classroom Accomplishments

Broad educational goals can provide direction for unit and lesson planning, communicate the importance of your instruction to administrators and parents, and energize your learners to higher levels of commitment and performance. They can also provide a practical framework around which to organize and sequence your instruction.

While goals answer the question "Why am I teaching this?" they do not specify what or how you will teach on any given day. Goals give you little direction as to what strategies you might use to achieve them and do not indicate when—or even if—they are met. A satisfactory answer to these questions requires the preparation of lesson objectives.

Objectives: Giving Goals a Direction

As we have seen, identifying educational goals is the first step in unit and lesson planning. In the course of your teaching, you will be responsible for preparing and managing extended sequences of instruction, called *units,* and day-by-day activities, called *lessons.* Units comprise interrelated sequences of lessons, which may cover one, two, or more weeks of instruction. Lessons represent the content for a single class day. Table 10.1 shows a portion of the content outline from a middle school science text, *Earth Science* (Addison-Wesley, 1987). Let's look at what it offers as a guide to unit and lesson planning—and what it doesn't offer!

Content outlines like that in Table 10.1 are useful for identifying topics to be covered in a unit or lesson. However, they typically do not provide information about the more fundamental issue of what your students must do with what they have learned. In other words, will you expect your students to recall important facts, such as definitions of weathering and erosion? Or will you expect your students to master such concepts as fault, plate tectonics, and continental drift? Or is the purpose of your unit to teach students to acquire important generalizations concerning the relationship between plate tectonics, faults, and earthquakes and use these generalizations to problem solve?

Deciding what you want your students to accomplish during a lesson or unit of instruction requires answering the following questions:

- What knowledge or content (facts, concepts, principles, rules) is essential for learner understanding of the subject matter?

Goals help teachers realize a purpose for their teaching and help learners see a reason for exerting a genuine effort to achieve. Without a clear understanding of why a skill is being taught, instruction can become directionless and purposeless.

Table 10.1

Content Outline from a Middle-School Science Text

Unit 5: Landscapes

I. Chapter 9: The Earth's Changing Surface
   A. Weathering
      1. Comparing rocks and solids
      2. Comparing liquids and solids
   B. Physical weathering
      1. Comparing weathering rates
      2. Static versus dynamic rates

II. Chapter 10: The Restless Crust
   A. Volcanic activity
      1. Lava viscosity
      2. Volcanic cones and topographic maps
   B. Stress, structure, and earthquakes
      1. Folded structures
         a. Relationship between synclines and anticlines
         b. Other types of folded structures
      2. Faults
         a. Recognizing geologic faults
         b. Measuring their movement

III. Chapter 11: Plate Tectonics
   A. Interior of the earth
      1. Relationship between present continents and Pangaea
      2. Changes over time
   B. Theory of continental drift
   C. Sea floor spreading theory
   D. Plate tectonics theory

- What intellectual skills are necessary for the learner to use this knowledge or content?
- What habits of mind or attitudes are important for learners to perform successfully with this knowledge or content?

To help you answer these questions, we will consider the work of two psychologists, Robert Gagné and Benjamin Bloom, whose ideas have significantly shaped our understanding of how the mind works. Most importantly, their ideas have contributed to a design for unit and lesson planning that moves teachers from an exclusive focus on self—what you will do—to a concern for your impact on learners—what your students will be able to accomplish. Let's look at what each of them has to say.

Gagné's Classification of Learning Outcomes

According to Gagné, the precise identification of a learning outcome is the first step in the learning process. This allows the teacher to determine the prerequisite skills for that outcome and to arrange these skills in the form of a learning hierarchy (a process called *task analysis*). As you will recall from Chapter 4, a *learning hierarchy* is an arrangement of behavioral outcomes or motor skills (action sequences), from the most complex at the top of the hierarchy to the least complex at the bottom.

To develop a learning hierarchy, you must first identify a learning outcome. Gagné has classified learning outcomes into five types: verbal information, intellectual skills, cognitive strategies, attitudes, and motor skills (see Table 10.2). As you study a curriculum guide or content outline for the subject you will teach, you can categorize your expectations for learners into one or more of these five learning outcomes.

Table 10.2

Gagné's Classification of Learning Outcomes

Category	Description
Verbal information	When you require your learners to memorize the alphabet, months of the year, important dates, etc., you are specifying *verbal information* as an outcome of your instruction. Verbal information also includes expressing this knowledge in the form of labels, words, ideas, or statements. Facts are examples of verbal information. Verbal information provides many of the building blocks for the development of concepts, rules, and generalizations.
Intellectual skills	Intellectual skills incorporate the learning of discriminations, concepts, simple rules, and generalizations (which are complex rules). *Discriminations* involve teaching learners to distinguish the sight and sound of "b" from "d," the color red from green, igneous from sedimentary rock, palmate from pinnate venation, etc. A discrimination, in most cases, is a building block for the formation of concepts. For example, before you can form the concept of types of rocks, or textures, or sounds, you must first be able to see, touch, and hear the differences.
Cognitive strategies	We discussed cognitive strategies in Chapter 5. As you will recall, this type of learning involves the learning of a sequence of steps to solve a problem, comprehend a reading passage, or write an essay. It also requires the prior learning of concepts and rules as the basis of problem solving.
Attitudes	If you want your learners to develop preferences for certain things, appreciations for particular ideas, work habits, ways of getting along with others, etc., you are interested in *attitudes* as an outcome of learning.
Motor skills	*Motor skills* are precise, accurate movements of small or large muscles. They are often grouped into *action sequences:* learning to tie shoes, ride a bike, copy letters, cut out a circle, bisect an angle, dissect a frog, focus a microscope, finger a guitar, or stitch shut a wound. While each of these actions may involve the prior learning of information, intellectual skills, and attitudes, they typically require the prerequisite learning of more simple actions.

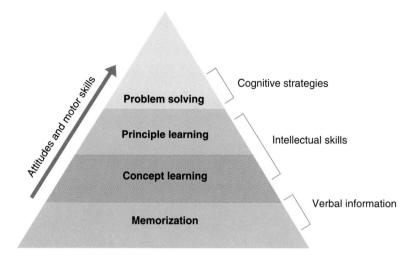

Figure 10.2
Gagné's hierarchy of learning.

Classifying a particular learning outcome into its proper category helps you develop learning hierarchies. Figure 10.2 presents the general structure of a learning hierarchy, which usually takes the form of a pyramid, with higher-order outcomes (for example, a cognitive or problem-solving strategy) at the apex and more basic learning outcomes (for example, verbal information) at the base. Attitude and motor skills may be taught at any level of the hierarchy and then reinforced as more complex learning evolves. Each lower level of the hierarchy is a prerequisite to achieving a higher level of learning.

Thus, according to Gagné, a successful problem solver must first learn the important facts, concepts, and principles of which the problem is composed. Likewise, a learner finds it impossible to acquire a principle, for example, unless he or she has first learned the concepts to which the principle applies. Concept learning, in turn, requires the learner to "memorize" bits of information in order to be able to put them together in a meaningful way to form the concept.

In Table 10.3 we return to our earth science curriculum outline to illustrate how a hierarchy of learning can help answer the question "What do I want my students to do with what I've taught?" What you are to teach has been given you by the textbook and curriculum guide; what you want your students to be able to do has yet to be defined. Study the examples of behavioral outcomes at each level of the hierarchy in Table 10.3 to see whether they define what the learner should be able to do.

The learning hierarchy illustrated in Figure 10.2 shows which types of learning are required before other, more complex learning can take place. Imagine how frustrated your students would be if you were to teach plate tectonic theory without first teaching them the concepts they need to understand it. Gagné's hierarchy demonstrates that much of the subject matter taught in schools can be placed in the form of a hierarchy of learning, such as the one illustrated in Table 10.3 and Figure 10.2. Consequently, as a teacher you must ensure that whichever type of learning you want your learners to acquire, they have been given the prerequisite knowledge or skills to achieve it.

Table 10.3

Behavioral Outcomes for Each Level of Gagné's Hierarchy

Level	Behavioral Outcome
Problem solving	Predict which areas of the earth would experience significant rearrangements if there were rapid heating of the earth's core.
Principles	Below are listed the generalizations needed to solve this problem: 1. Most geologic activity occurs where tectonic plates converge. 2. The convergence of tectonic plates creates weakness in the earth's crust. 3. Heating at the earth's core creates upward pressure on the earth's crust.
Concepts	In order to understand and apply these generalizations to solving the problem, some of the concepts that must be learned are: earth's crust earth's core tectonic plates convergence pressure geologic activity
Memorization	In order to acquire these concepts, students must have information (definitions, names, places, etc.) or experiences that allow them to find similarities and differences between the facts, presented in a way that enhances information storage and retrieval.

Depending on what type of learning (memorization, concepts, principles, or problem solving) you expect your students to master, there are more or less effective techniques and activities to teach it. For example, you will use different instructional methods to help learners acquire concepts than you will to help them form generalizations or to problem solve. The accompanying box, *Matching Instructional Approaches to Learning Outcomes,* indicates some of the instructional approaches that classroom researchers (Brophy, 1986; Brophy & Good, 1986; Clark & Peterson, 1986) have found effective in helping learners acquire different learning outcomes.

Bloom's Analysis of Learning Outcomes

Gagné's analysis of learning illustrates the diversity of expectations we can have for learners. Nevertheless, his categories of learning are broad and do not indicate specific behaviors that indicate whether learners are acquiring verbal information, forming concepts, applying generalizations, problem solving, or developing positive attitudes.

Bloom and colleagues, and others (Bloom, Englehart, Hill, Furst, & Krathwohl, 1956; Harrow, 1969; Krathwohl, Bloom, & Masia, 1964), have developed systems for classifying learning outcomes and identifying behaviors that can be expected of learners. These systems lend greater specificity to the work of Gagné. These authors refer to their respective classification schemes as *taxonomies of behavioral objectives,* since they are intended as targets or goals of instruction. Accordingly, they have categorized objectives into three domains: the *cognitive domain,* which represents intellectual abilities and skills, including those identified by Gagné; the *affective domain,* which represents atti-

Matching Instructional Approaches to Learning Outcomes

Teaching Facts, Rules, or Action Sequences:

1. Teach the whole group using a lecture format.
2. Ask frequent questions and give feedback.
3. Encourage independent learner practice, review, and rehearsal.
4. Organize information into meaningful chunks, and point out relationships between the facts.

Teaching Concepts and Generalizations:

1. Organize the information in advance to provide a meaningful framework for learners.
2. Use cycles of inductive and deductive methods.
3. Provide both examples of the concept and nonexamples.
4. Ask discovery (inquiry) types of questions.
5. Encourage student ideas and contributions.

6. Provide opportunities for students to apply newly learned concepts.
7. Ask students to evaluate how well they have acquired the concepts and generalizations.

Teaching Problem Solving:

1. Provide opportunities for students to explain, predict, compare, analyze, generalize, test hypotheses, and evaluate.
2. Ask difficult questions that encourage reflection.
3. Use small groups to teach the most difficult skills.
4. Encourage student-to-student discussion.
5. Model how you solve a problem by thinking out loud to your learners.
6. Provide plenty of opportunities to practice solving problems.
7. Make learners aware of their own thinking.

---

tudes, beliefs, and values; and the *psychomotor domain,* which represents bodily movement and physical performance.

The taxonomy of cognitive objectives is specifically associated with the work of Bloom et al. (1956). Like Gagné, these authors assume that the levels of their taxonomy are hierarchical. That is, higher-level mental operations are assumed to include, and to be dependent on, lower-level operations. Each level of the taxonomy of cognitive objectives has different characteristics and includes action verbs to represent the mental processes that represent them. Table 10.4 identifies and describes the levels included in the affective and psychomotor domains.

Bloom's cognitive domain includes six levels: knowledge, comprehension, application, analysis, synthesis, and evaluation. In the following sections we describe each level of the cognitive domain.

Knowledge. Objectives at the knowledge level require learners to remember or recall information such as facts, terminology, problem-solving strategies, and rules. Some action verbs and examples that describe learning outcomes at the knowledge level are:

define	list	identify
recognize	select	state
label	match	name

For example, the following learning outcomes are included in the knowledge domain:

- The student will *state* the four major food groups, without error, by Friday.

> **How can I write objectives at higher levels of behavioral complexity, such as analysis, synthesis, and decision making?**

Table 10.4

Levels of the Affective and Psychomotor Domains

Affective Domain

Level	Description
Receive	The learner is *aware of* or passively attends to certain phenomena and stimuli (i.e., listening, being attentive to).
Respond	The learner *complies with* given expectations by attending or reacting to certain stimuli or phenomena (i.e., obeys or participates as expected).
Value	The learner *displays behavior consistent with a single belief or attitude* in situations where he is not forced to comply or obey (i.e., demonstrates a definite preference, displays a high degree of certainty and conviction).
Organization	The learner *is committed to a set of values* and displays or communicates his or her beliefs or values (i.e., develops a rationale for a set of values, makes judgments about sets of values).
Characterization	The total *behavior of the learner is consistent* with the values he or she has internalized (i.e., develops a consistent philosophy of life, exhibits respect for the property of others, demonstrates an aversion to drugs, shows a commitment to school).

Psychomotor Domain

Level	Description
Imitation	When the learner is exposed to an observable action he begins to make covert imitation of that action. This is then followed by overt performance of an act and the capacity to repeat it. The performance, however, *lacks neuromuscular coordination* or control and hence is generally in a crude and imperfect form (i.e., impulse, overt repetition).
Manipulation	Emphasizes the development of *skill in following directions,* performing of selected actions, and fixation of performance through necessary practice. At this level the learner is capable of performing an act according to instruction rather than just on the basis of observation, as is the case at the level of imitation (i.e., following directions).
Precision	The proficiency of performance reaches a higher level of refinement in reproducing a given act. The learner performs the skill *independently of a model or a set of directions.* Accuracy, proportion, and exactness in performance become significant (i.e., reproduction, control, errors reduced to a minimum).
Articulation	Emphasizes the *coordination* of a series of acts by establishing appropriate sequence and accomplishing harmony or internal consistency among different acts (i.e., performance involves *accuracy and control* plus elements of speed and time).
Naturalization	A high level of proficiency in the skill or performance of a single act is required. The behavior is performed with the least expenditure of psychic energy. The act is routinized to such an extent that it results in an *automatic and spontaneous* response (i.e., performance becomes *natural and smooth*).

Sources: From *A Taxonomy of the Psychomotor Domain: A Guide for Developing Behavioral Objectives,* by A. Harrow, 1969, New York: David McKay; *Taxonomy of Educational Objectives: The Classification of Educational Goals. Handbook II: Affective Domain,* by D. Krathwohl, B. Bloom, and B. Masia, 1964, New York: David McKay.

- From memory, the student will *match* United States generals with their most famous battles with 80 percent accuracy.

Comprehension. Objectives at the comprehension level require some degree of understanding. Learners are expected to be able to change the form of a communication, translate, restate what has been read, see connections or relationships between parts of a communication (interpretation), or draw conclusions from information or see the consequences of it (inference). Some action verbs that describe learning outcomes at the comprehension level are:

defend	summarize	infer
explain	estimate	predict
extend	distinguish	paraphrase

Here are some examples of learning outcomes at the comprehension level:

- By the end of the semester, the student will *summarize* the main events of a story in grammatically correct English.
- The student will *distinguish* between the realists and the naturalists, citing examples from the readings.

Application. Objectives written at the application level require the learner to use previously acquired information in a setting other than the one in which it was learned. Application differs from comprehension in that application requires the presentation of a problem in a different and often applied context. Thus, the student can rely on neither the content nor the context in which the original learning occurred to solve the problem. Some action verbs that describe learning outcomes at the application level are:

change	compute	modify
prepare	use	solve
relate	demonstrate	organize

Some examples of application-level objectives are:

- On Monday, the student will *demonstrate* for the class an application to real life of the law of conservation of energy.
- Given equations not covered in class, the student will *solve* them on paper with 85 percent accuracy.

Analysis. Objectives written at the analysis level require the learner to identify logical errors (for example, point out a contradiction or an erroneous inference) or to differentiate between facts, opinions, assumptions, hypotheses, and conclusions. At this level, students are expected to draw relationships between ideas and to compare and contrast. Some action verbs that describe learning outcomes at the analysis level are:

deduce	break down	relate
outline	infer	diagram
illustrate	point out	subdivide

Some examples of objectives written at the analysis level are:

- Given a presidential speech, the student will be able to *point out* the positions that attack an individual rather than that individual's program.
- Given absurd statements (for example, "A man had the flu twice. The first time it killed him. The second time he got well quickly."), the student will be able to *illustrate* the contradiction.

Synthesis. Objectives written at the synthesis level require the learner to produce something unique or original. At the synthesis level, students are expected to solve an unfamiliar problem in a unique way or to combine parts to form a unique or novel solution. Some action verbs that describe learning outcomes at the synthesis level are:

compile	create	develop
devise	predict	produce
compose	design	formulate

Following are some objectives written at the synthesis level:

- Given a short story, the student will *formulate* a different but plausible ending.
- Given a problem to be solved, the student will *design* on paper a scientific experiment to address the problem.

Evaluation. Objectives written at the evaluation level require the learner to form judgments and make decisions about the value of methods, ideas, people, or products that have a specific purpose. Students are expected to state the bases for their judgments (for example, the criteria or principles they used to reach their conclusions). Some action verbs that describe learning outcomes at the evaluation level are:

appraise	criticize	justify
support	validate	contrast
defend	judge	argue

Following are some objectives written at the synthesis level:

- Given a previously unread paragraph, the student will *judge* its value according to the five criteria discussed in class.
- Given a description of a country's economic system, the student will *defend* it, basing arguments on principles of democracy.

Delivering Instruction

In the previous section you learned about the importance of specifying goals and objectives for your learners. We pointed out that goals energize you and your students to achieve high degrees of effort and learning. We discussed how objectives specify what students are expected to do to demonstrate learning.

There is another important use for goals and objectives: they can determine your choice of instructional methods. Simply stated, *instructional methods* are patterns of practice that recur in classrooms time and again. They include, for example, the meth-

Table 10.5

Three Instructional Methods and Some Related Teaching Skills

Instructional Methods

Teaching Skills	Direct Instruction	Indirect Instruction	Self-Directed Instruction
Structuring	At the start of the lesson, the teacher focuses the learner's attention on the learning of certain facts, rules, and action sequences.	At the start of the lesson, the teacher focuses the learner's attention on problems to be solved, decisions to be made, or relationships to be discovered.	At the start of the lesson, the teacher focuses on how one learns how to learn the material to be presented.
Modeling	The teacher models actions, demonstrates the component skills of a more complex action, and shows the organization of the information to be learned.	The teacher models the process of inquiry, problem solving, or decision making.	The teacher models how one thinks about what is about to be learned.
Coaching	Using primarily lecture and whole group learning formats, the teacher leads the learners through a lesson, maintaining attention, interest, and momentum with a brisk and lively pace.	In either whole group or small group formats, the teacher uses questioning skills to probe for deeper understanding, raise contradictions, point out differences, and elicit personal experiences and examples from the learners' lives.	The teacher uses reciprocal teaching techniques to help students acquire the ability to make predictions, ask themselves questions, and summarize their own learning.
Fading	The teacher ensures tranfer by allowing learners to practice and apply their newly learned facts, rules, and action sequences to a variety of examples and situations.	The teacher ensures transfer by giving learners opportunities to apply their newly learned concepts, patterns, and abstractions to a variety of examples and situations and to engage in self-evaluation.	The teacher ensures transfer of their newly learned cognitive strategies by giving learners opportunities to generate their own examples and situations in which metacognition is used, and to self-evaluate its usefulness.

ods of direct (or didactic) instruction, indirect (or inquiry) instruction, and self-directed (or self-regulated) instruction. Each of these general methods includes certain specific teaching skills, among which are *structuring, modeling, coaching,* and *fading.* These skills are described in Table 10.5 together with the instructional methods with which they are most commonly used.

For instance, if your objective is to have students acquire facts (for example, names and dates of battles of the Civil War), rules (for forming possessives), or action sequences (for focusing a microscope), you will most likely use **direct instruction,** which involves some questioning, clarifying, and explaining. But if your objective is to teach concepts (for example, photosynthesis), patterns (global warming), or abstractions (environmental responsibility), you will most likely use **indirect instruction,** which involves constructivist teaching methods discussed in Chapter 5. If, however, your

Direct instruction. Instructional methods that present information explicitly through lecturing, questioning, and demonstration. Direct instruction is particularly suited to the acquisition of facts, rules, and action sequences.

Indirect instruction. Instructional methods best suited for the learning of concepts, patterns, and abstractions. Indirect instruction involves the expression of learner ideas, teacher-mediated discussion, and group problem solving.

Structuring	Modeling	Coaching	Fading
• Focusing attention • Holding attention	• Gaining attention • Facilitating retention • Eliciting production • Providing motivation	• Establishing accountability • Providing practice • Guiding practice • Motivating	• Prompt fading • Reinforcer fading • Providing independent practice

Figure 10.3
Specific teacher behaviors for structuring, modeling, coaching, and fading.

objective is to teach strategies for learning (for example, a model for learning to solve equations that can be used time and again), you will most likely adopt the method of **self-directed instruction,** which incorporates the skills of metacognition (thinking about thinking), subvocal rehearsal, guided practice, and self-evaluation that you learned about in Chapter 5. In this chapter we will study each of these general instructional methods and the specific teaching skills they require.

As noted in Table 10.5, our three instructional methods require the four specific teaching skills of structuring, modeling, coaching, and fading. Specific teacher behaviors used in executing each of these skills are identified in Figure 10.3. Regardless of the instructional method you are using, you will want to be familiar with structuring, modeling, coaching, and fading. As you look across the rows of Table 10.5, you will find that while each method requires the same teaching skills, these skills are used for different purposes. For example, the direct instruction method calls on the teacher to use modeling to help learners acquire facts, rules, and action sequences, such as those required by certain motor skills. By comparison, the self-directed method requires that the teacher draw on his or her expertise in modeling to show learners how to think about their own thinking in order to acquire a strategy for learning. In the next section, we will study the teaching skills of structuring, modeling, coaching, and fading. We will demonstrate how successful teachers use these skills to capture student attention, convey purpose, communicate information, keep lessons moving at a brisk and lively pace, and provide opportunities for transferring what has been learned to new and different contexts.

Self-directed instruction. An instructional method that places much of the responsibility for learning on the learner by using metacognition, subvocal rehearsal, guided practice, and self-evaluation.

The Events of Instruction

Instructional events are key elements of the teaching process that allow learners to acquire and transfer new information and skills. Gagné, Briggs, and Wagner (1992) suggest nine key instructional events:

Instructional events. Elements of the teaching process that allow learners to acquire and transfer new information and skills.

1. Gaining attention
2. Informing the learner of the objective
3. Stimulating the recall of prerequisite learning
4. Presenting the stimulus material
5. Guiding learning

6. Eliciting the desired behavior
7. Providing feedback
8. Enhancing retention
9. Promoting transfer

Hunter (1982) proposes a similar sequence of events, called the *mastery teaching program*. According to Hunter, the key instructional events are these:

1. Review
2. Anticipatory set
3. Objectives and purpose
4. Input and modeling
5. Checking for understanding
6. Guided practice
7. Closure
8. Independent practice and reteaching

Recently, there has been debate over whether the events of instruction, as outlined by Gagné, Briggs, and Wagner and by Hunter, are appropriate only for the learning of the facts, rules, and action sequences often taught with the direct instructional method. Slavin (1991), for example, states that instructional sequences such as Hunter's may be inappropriate when the objectives of instruction deal with inquiry or problem solving, which often are the focus of indirect instruction. However, regardless of the goals or objectives of instruction, certain key teaching activities should occur across methods if learning is to be acquired and transferred.

Table 10.6 shows how the key teaching skills of structuring, modeling, coaching,

Table 10.6

Three Perspectives on Events of Instruction

Gagné, Briggs, & Wagner	Borich & Tombari	Hunter
Gaining attention ——————→	Structuring ←——————	Review
Informing learner of objective		Anticipatory set
Stimulating recall		Objectives and purpose
Presenting material ——————→	Modeling ←——————	Input and modeling
Guiding learning		Checking for understanding
Eliciting behavior ——————→	Coaching ←——————	Guided practice
Providing feedback		Closure
Enhancing retention ——————→	Fading ←——————	Independent practice
Promoting transfer		

Focus on

Madeline Hunter, University of California, Los Angeles

I graduated as a clinical psychologist, and my first job was at the Los Angeles Childrens' Hospital. There, in a case study conference, I gave a "super diagnosis" of a child's problem. The attending school staff looked at me coldly and said, "So, what do we do tomorrow morning?" That question changed my life—for what good is a diagnosis without a prescription? So I became a school psychologist and found that all teachers had taken an Ed Psych course and learned about salivating dogs and pecking pigeons, none of it taught as a basis for "tomorrow morning" decisions in teaching. Consequently, I began translating psychological research into the language of teaching. Most recently, I have been translating brain research from the language of neurology into the language of teaching (pedagogy), so that teachers can enable students to learn more efficiently and effectively.

Many people do not realize that on the basis of valid theory, the teacher must make professional decisions. Every decision a teacher makes (or delegates to students) falls into one of three categories. The first is *content:* What is the intended learning? Here, new curriculum work in literacy for understanding and communicating with others, and learning to integrate and generalize math, science, and social studies to current problems, is giving us choices as to what is worth learning. Authentic assessment tells us where to begin and when to proceed.

The second category of professional decisions, *learning behaviors,* is focused on what a student is doing so that his or her brain generates meaning for the new learning. Although a student may have a preference for a certain learning style, it is the teacher's responsibility to help the student develop proficiency in many ways of learning rather than being limited to a few. Also, this decision must include student demonstrations that learning has occurred (authentic assessment). From the first two decisions, content and learning behavior, is derived the learning target (objective, outcome), which validates that students have acquired the knowledge, process, skill, or attitude intended and which contribute to a productive, satisfying life.

The third decision, *teaching behavior,* is based on research-validated cause-and-effect relationships between teaching and learning. These generalizations are grouped under (1) increasing students' motivation (effort) to learn, (2) accelerating the rate and degree of that learning, (3) enhancing retention, and (4) transfer of that learning, which makes problem solving, creativity, and productive, satisfying decisions possible. Of all the school factors, the teachers' ability to make and implement valid professional decisions is the most important in students' achievement.

Teachers constantly ask, "Why didn't we learn this in our previous teacher education classes?" The answer is that psychology is a relatively new science. Only in the last two decades has research on the human brain and how it functions been advanced enough to reveal the relationship between the professional decisions of a teacher and the learning success of all students.

and fading compare with the instructional events of Gagné, Briggs, and Wagner and of Hunter. Notice that these teaching skills apply not only to the instructional events of these authors but also to each of our three general instructional methods.

The Expert Practice of Structuring

Structuring. Getting learners ready to learn by selecting, organizing, and previewing the content to be presented.

Structuring is the process of getting learners ready to learn by selecting, organizing, and previewing the content to be presented. Structuring is that part of a lesson during which the teacher exerts the most control over the learning process. During structuring, it is essential that the teacher be skilled at capturing the attention of learners and focusing it on the outcome of the lesson. If not fully alert, learners will find it difficult to remember the information given, understand the goal of the lesson, or participate in the instructional process—all of which are essential for learning and transfer to occur.

How do you gain a learner's attention? Your voice, your actions, and your visual displays have to compete with hundreds of other stimuli that also are vying for your learners' attention. How can you get students to attend? What does it mean to "pay attention"?

Learners who pay attention usually demonstrate several skills.

- They orient themselves to you and what you direct them to (for example, the overhead projector, the blackboard, the text).
- They focus their attention on the relevant aspects of what they are attending to (for example, the problem you are describing, the responses of another student, the picture in the text).
- They ignore distracting stimuli (for example, another student or the sounds of a nearby classroom).
- They remain alert during the lesson (for example, they maintain their engagement with the lesson despite a desire to return to a more passive state).

Structuring focuses learners on the first two of the skills above. These involve (1) focusing attention by directing the eyes, ears, and body posture of learners to a relevant stimulus and (2) holding their attention long enough to establish a learning set. We will explore the third and fourth attention-gaining skills under the expert practice of coaching. For now, let's turn to the first two skills: focusing and holding your learners' attention.

Focusing Attention. Before you can communicate the purpose or objective of a lesson, you must focus the eyes and ears of your learners. This is difficult at the start of class if your learners are taking out materials, finishing their homework, asking questions of one another, or catching up on the latest gossip with their friends.

Research on attention has focused on four properties of instructional stimuli that cause learners to make an attending response, such as shifting one's body posture, changing the direction of a gaze, scanning the visual field, or holding a fixed stare (Solso, 1988). From this research, we can identify four appeals that can be used to make instructional content more attractive to learners. They are (1) psychophysical appeal, (2) emotional appeal, (3) discrepancy appeal, and (4) commanding stimuli appeal.

Psychophysical Appeal. A **psychophysical appeal** is any variation in the color, size, intensity, or pitch of stimuli in your learners' visual field that causes them to make an attending response. The most accessible and efficient stimuli for you to vary are those coming from your own body: your voice, gestures, posture, movement, facial expressions. You can most efficiently focus your learners' attention by changing your voice inflection, moving as you talk, and varying your posture or gestures.

Emotional Appeal. Just as we have emotional responses associated with our names, learners have emotional responses to certain sights, sounds, words, and smells. The skillful teacher uses the **emotional appeal** of these stimuli to focus learners' attention by calling on them by name, commenting from time to time on a unique article of their

> **What are some of the ways to capture student interest at the start of a lesson?**

Psychophysical appeal. Any variation in the color, size, intensity, or pitch of stimuli in the visual field of learners that results in the learners' making an attending response.

Emotional appeal. A characteristic of an instructional stimulus that draws on the emotional response of learners to focus learner attention.

clothing, using words in the student's second or native language, and introducing certain sights, sounds, and smells that may relate to the topic of a lesson.

Discrepancy Appeal. Our attention is often drawn to stimuli that make a **discrepancy appeal** by means of the element of surprise—something novel or unique grabs our attention. The history teacher who dresses up in an authentic costume to illustrate a period in history, the science teacher who creates an unusual noise or smell at the start of an experiment, the math teacher who begins by presenting an unsolvable problem, the language teacher who deliberately misspells a word to be used in the day's lesson, or the speech teacher who stages a shouting match with a student before a lesson on listening skills to demonstrate inattention—all are using the property of discrepancy to focus the attention of learners.

Commanding Stimuli Appeal. Teachers often use a **commanding stimuli appeal** to get learners to comply with a request. Statements such as "Now listen closely" or "All books and pens away," when delivered assertively, are likely to be followed. Some teachers have their students vote on a code word during the first week of school, which when spoken assertively by the teacher gets everyone to stop what they are doing and look at the teacher.

Holding Attention. The expert practice of structuring involves not only focusing the attention of learners but also giving them something to focus on. This is accomplished by building a *learning set.* Hunter (1982) refers to this phase of the lesson as the **anticipatory set.** Its purpose is to make the goal or objective of the lesson relevant to the learners, to put the lesson into a context the learners can relate to, and to get their minds off other distracting stimuli. During this time learners recall past learning by drawing a picture, by summarizing something they saw or heard, by reading a short passage, or by writing down an idea—all with the intent of relating past with present learning.

Anticipatory sets often take the form of *advance organizers* (Ausubel, 1968). Recall from Chapter 5 that an advance organizer gives learners an overview of what is to come

Discrepancy appeal. The use of novel, unique, or surprising stimuli to focus the attention of learners.

Commanding stimuli appeal. The use of assertive commands or statements by an instructor to focus learner attention.

Anticipatory set. An organized framework usually presented to learners at the beginning of a lesson that helps them relate past with present learning and that places the lesson into a context that the learners can relate to and focus on.

Gaining learners' attention and holding it is one of the principal ingredients of expert instructional practice. Teachers use a variety of structuring techniques to accomplish this.

that helps them store, label, and package the content for retention and later use. For example, "Listen to this story and think of the three things the duckling did."

The Expert Practice of Modeling

Once your learners' attention is on you, you have the opportunity to model what your students are about to learn. **Modeling** is a teaching activity that involves demonstrating to learners what you want them to do (in the form of action sequences), say (in the form of facts and concepts), or think (in the form of problem solving or learning-to-learn strategies).

When used correctly, modeling can help learners acquire a variety of intellectual and social skills more easily and efficiently than can verbal explanations alone. Modeling is particularly effective for younger learners, who may not be able to follow complex verbal explanations, and who may need to see how something is done before they can actually do it.

Bandura and his colleagues have studied how and why we learn from models (Bandura, 1969, 1977b; Rosenthal & Zimmerman, 1978; Zimmerman, 1989). Recall from Chapter 3 that their research on modeling is referred to as *social learning theory,* which attempts to explain how people learn from observing others. From their work we know that children can learn not only attitudes, values, and standards of behavior from observing adults and peers but also intellectual skills.

Some of this learning takes place by directly imitating what a model (for example, a teacher) is doing, while other learning takes place by inferring why the model is acting a certain way or what type of person the model is. For example, learners acquire certain values about the importance of learning, caring for others, doing work neatly, or respecting other cultures by observing how their parents, friends, and teachers actually behave in the real world and then inferring from their observations how they too should behave. Although teachers model all the time, we know that some forms of modeling are better than others. Zimmerman and Kleefeld (1977) found that teachers who were taught the practice of modeling were far more effective at helping young children to learn than those who were not.

How One Learns From Models. Four psychological processes need to occur for students to learn from modeling:

1. Attention
2. Retention
3. Production
4. Motivation.

Figure 10.4 shows how these processes work in sequence when students learn from models. Let's take a closer look at them to discover how students learn from what they see.

Attention. Demonstrations are of value only if learners are looking at and/or listening to them. In other words, without *attention* there can be no imitation or observational learning. In the previous section we highlighted the importance of gaining a learner's attention. Modeling requires not only that you gain your learners' attention, but that you

Modeling. Demonstrating what learners are about to learn; the process of being attentive to, remembering, imitating, and being rewarded for imitating specific behaviors.

How do I teach by modeling?

Attention → Retention → Production → Motivation

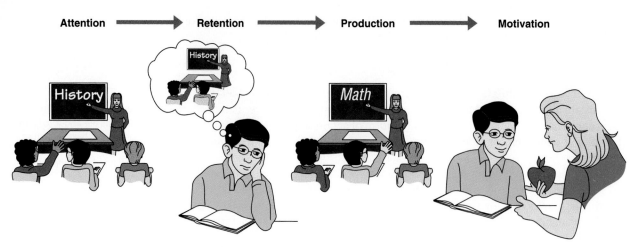

Figure 10.4
How one learns from models.

retain it throughout the lesson. Bandura (1977b) found that teachers hold their learners' attention better under these conditions:

- The model is someone who has expert and referent power (as discussed in Chapter 8).
- The model is demonstrating something that has functional value to the learner; learners pay little attention to those things for which they see no immediate relevance.
- The demonstration is simplified by subdivision into component parts, and it is presented in a clearly discernible step-by-step fashion.

Retention. Teachers model because they want their learners to be able to repeat the same actions when they are no longer present. For example, teachers typically model when they demonstrate how to add a column of numbers, sound out a word, or evaluate a short essay. But the transfer of these actions to the learner will occur only if the learner remembers what she saw or heard. Demonstrations from which imitation is to occur must be planned with the goal of retention in mind.

Learners are more likely to remember demonstrations that:

- are linked to previous skills or ideas they have already learned. The more meaningful the demonstration, the more likely it is to be retained. ("Remember how yesterday we added one-digit numbers in a column? Well, today we will use the same procedure on numbers that have two or more digits.")
- include concise labels, vivid images, code words, or visual mnemonics that help learners hold new learning in memory. ("Look at how I shape my lips when I pronounce this next word.")
- are immediately rehearsed. Rehearsals can be overt, as when the teacher asks learners to say or do something immediately following the demonstration, or covert, as when the learner visualizes or mentally creates an image of what was demonstrated. ("Now, everyone read the next passage to themselves, repeating silently the sequence of steps I just demonstrated.")

Production. The third component of the modeling process occurs when learners actually do what the teacher demonstrated. In this stage, the mental images or verbal codes that the learner retained in memory direct the learner's performance. These images or codes are recalled by the practice situation the teacher creates and by the verbal cues given. Having been evoked, these images guide the actual performance of what was learned during the demonstration.

Learners are more likely to produce what they saw if:

- production follows closely the retention phase. ("OK, now that you've practiced remembering the correct sequence of steps I demonstrated, let's use them to interpret the meaning of the following passage.")

- the practice situation contains cues or stimuli that evoke the retained mental images or verbal codes. ("This next word requires you to position your lips exactly as you saw me do in the last example.")

- the performance immediately follows mental rehearsal. ("Let's switch to several new examples that you haven't seen before.")

The production phase allows the teacher to observe the learner and give feedback on how well he or she has mastered the behavior. Giving learners information about the correctness of their actions—without expressing negativity or dissatisfaction—has been shown to increase the likelihood of a correct performance (Vasta, 1976).

Motivation. The final stage of learning through modeling occurs when learners experience desirable outcomes following their performance. Desirable outcomes usually take the form of teacher praise, which motivates learners to later repeat what they have just seen. Learners are less likely to repeat the actions of a model if they have experienced punishing or unsatisfying consequences following their initial attempts to imitate the model.

Learners are more likely to repeat the actions of a model immediately and also to transfer it to new situations over time if the teacher:

- gives praise and encouragement rather than criticism immediately after the performance. ("Your answer is partly correct; think some more about what we've just discussed" as opposed to "Your answer is wrong. You're not listening again.")

- directs the praise at specific aspects of the performance. ("I like how you left enough space between your words" as opposed to "That's neat writing.")

- gives directions rather than corrections after an incorrect performance. ("Remember, the first step is to generate a hypothesis" as opposed to "You don't state the research design before you generate a hypothesis!")

The last two stages of the modeling process (production and motivation) are typically incorporated into the expert practice of coaching. They are included here as a reminder that your learners will acquire and use new intellectual skills learned through modeling only if such skills are practiced and reinforced.

Guidelines for Effective Demonstrations. Now that we have pointed out the important psychological processes responsible for learning through imitation and observation, we will highlight the teaching skills necessary to use social learning theory to present effective demonstrations. At some point you probably encountered a teacher who was particularly effective at demonstrating what he or she wanted you to learn. You have

A significant portion of a teacher's time is spent modeling skills and giving effective demonstrations. When using modeling or demonstrations, teachers must consider such psychological processes as attention, retention, production, and motivation.

How can I conduct an effective demonstration?

also had teachers whose demonstrations left you confused. What did the former do to instill the confidence and skills needed to perform the behavior that the latter did not? The answer lies with what makes a good demonstration.

Research on what makes a good demonstration indicates that an expert modeler is a skilled explainer (Good & Brophy, 1991). The accompanying box, *Conducting Effective Demonstrations,* give specific guidelines for demonstrations, and Figure 10.5 summarizes these guidelines.

Coaching. An aspect of instruction by which the teacher helps learners master particular skills through the skillful use of practice and prompts.

The Expert Practice of Coaching

Coaching is that stage of the instructional process during which the learner converts memories into actions as a result of the modeling process. This is the aspect of instruc-

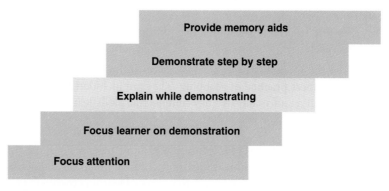

Provide memory aids

Demonstrate step by step

Explain while demonstrating

Focus learner on demonstration

Focus attention

Figure 10.5
Guidelines for an effective demonstration.

Conducting Effective Demonstrations

Follow these guidelines for presenting vivid and effective demonstrations.

- **Focus learners' attention.** Begin your demonstration only when your learners' attention is focused on you. Then direct the learners' attention to what you want them to see.
- **Stress the value of the demonstration.** Briefly and concisely point out why the learners should observe what you are about to show them. Then relate new learning to prior learning to show its relationship to content already successfully mastered.
- **Talk in conversational language while demonstrating.** Back up to cover unfamiliar concepts, repeat actions when needed, use analogies to bridge content gaps, and use examples to reinforce what has been learned. Then probe for understanding.
- **Make the steps simple and obvious.** Break complex actions into simple steps that can be followed one at a time. Point out what will be done next, and then describe the action as you perform it, thinking out loud to describe how the action actually is performed.
- **Help learners remember the demonstration.** Go slowly ("Stop me if I'm going too fast"), exaggerate certain actions ("See how puffy my lips are when I pronounce this word"), highlight distinctive features ("Look at the strange coloring of the specimen"), and give simple memory aids to help learners retain what they see ("Notice the height of the lens from the specimen slide").

tion we usually think of as teaching. Coaching is the most physically and mentally demanding of the four teaching activities and typically takes up the most time in a lesson.

Effective coaching requires:

- establishing accountability
- providing opportunities for practice
- guiding practice by prompting and questioning
- motivating.

Figure 10.6 summarizes these steps; here we will describe them in detail.

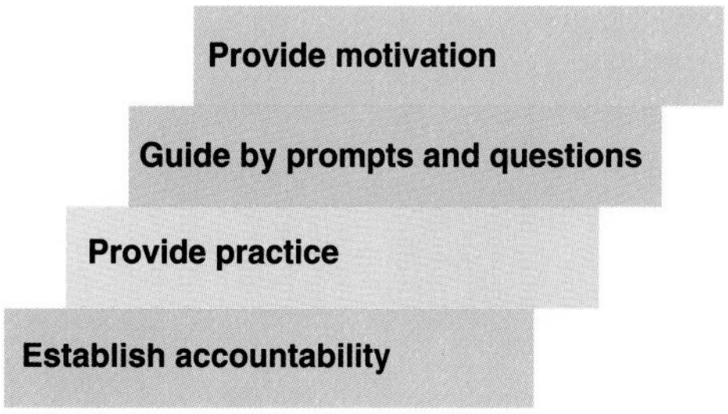

Provide motivation

Guide by prompts and questions

Provide practice

Establish accountability

Figure 10.6
Expert coaching.

Establishing Accountability. The following extract from a student teacher's diary describes a common teaching problem:

> School seems to mean so little for many of my kids. They can do the work but they just sit there and wait to be reminded or threatened. Take Bart. He comes into class, looks at me when I'm giving the class assignment, but then sits and does nothing until I remind him to get to work. He works for a while and then stops until the next reminder. What work he does is about 25 percent correct. During discussions he never listens to what anyone else is saying. I have about five or six Barts in every one of my eighth-grade classes. (Beth, student teacher)

This excerpt describes what many beginning teachers encounter when it is time for practice or classwork. It is tempting to assume, like Beth, that the problem is motivation: the students just don't care. Research by Kounin (1970) and Emmer, Evertson, Clements, and Worsham (1994), however, point us in another direction. They suggest that incomplete, sloppy, or missed assignments and an "I don't care" attitude may reflect the teacher's failure to make learners feel accountable during the coaching stage of the lesson.

Accountability is the degree to which teachers communicate to learners the classwork they are expected to complete during a specific period of time. The more learners are told what they are responsible for, the greater the accountability for learning. From research by Emmer et al. (1994), we learn that there are three aspects to accountability: (1) communication, (2) monitoring, and (3) feedback. The accompanying box, *Establishing Accountability*, details the steps you can take.

How can I help students take responsibility for their own learning?

Applying Your Knowledge:
Establishing Accountability

The following actions will allow you to increase your learners' accountability.

Communication. Inform learners what they are to do and ensure that each learner understands the skills she is expected to perform. Do this by calling on several students of different ability levels to check on the extent to which they understand the class assignment before giving the signal to begin.

Monitoring. Circulate around the room to see that work has been started and is being done correctly. Monitoring should occur whether the classroom assignment involves independent seatwork, small group problem solving, or copying from the blackboard.

Feedback. Learners feel more accountable for learning when they receive immediate feedback on their performances. Efficient routines for providing feedback may include peer feedback, self-evaluation, or teacher feedback.

Toward the end of Beth's student teaching she became much more skilled at establishing accountability. Here is an excerpt from her cooperating teacher's evaluation of her performance during her last week of student teaching:

> Beth, like many new teachers, tended to hide immediately after giving an assignment. She would sit at her desk and avoid even looking at students. She hoped that the students would begin work immediately and everyone would know exactly what to do. She hadn't developed the skill of anticipating problems and giving clear step-by-step directions. No sooner would she sit down than students would swarm to her desk with questions about what they were expected to do.
>
> As time passed, she learned to move about the room during the work activity, question learners who were having problems, and encourage those who were doing well. Now, even when the class is working quietly, she continues to move about the room encouraging, praising, and prompting.

Providing Opportunities for Practice. The purpose of practice is to engage learners actively in the learning process. During structuring and modeling, students listen, observe, covertly rehearse, or make brief responses to your questions as you check for understanding. But they have not yet had the opportunity to practice and master the skills you modeled, the information you conveyed, or the problem-solving techniques you demonstrated. During the coaching phase of instruction, learners begin to practice the objectives of your lesson.

Practice has historically been associated with drill (Ornstein, 1992) and direct instructional methods (Borich, 1996). It has been strongly emphasized in behavioristic approaches to learning that stress the importance of building stimulus-response connections (Hilgard & Bower, 1981). Mastery learning and errorless learning methods also incorporate extensive practice and drill (Bloom, 1981).

However, practice is essential for accomplishing the goals of any instructional method—direct, indirect, or self-directed. Depending on the instructional method used and the desired objective, practice can take many forms. During direct instruction, practice may take the form of repeating multiplication tables or letters of the alphabet. It may also involve independent seatwork and the use of workbooks. Practice during indirect instruction may occur when the teacher places learners in small groups to solve science or math problems cooperatively. It may also occur when students complete problem-solving handouts and worksheets. During self-directed learning, practice may take the form of reciprocal teaching within the naturally occurring dialogue of the classroom, as we saw in Chapter 6. It may also involve completing extended projects and investigations at a learning center, at home, or in the library.

Regardless of the type of practice activity used, there are several guidelines for promoting effective practice:

> **What can I do to make my learners look forward to practicing their skills?**

● **Students should understand the reasons for practice.** Practice often turns into busywork, which can create boredom, frustration, and noncompliance. Learners should approach classroom practice with the enthusiasm experienced by an athlete in training. This is more likely to occur if (1) the purpose of the practice has been made known to learners ("We will need to be proficient at solving these problems in order to go on to our next activity") and (2) practice occurs during as well as after new learning ("Let's stop right here, so you can try some of these problems yourselves").

● **Effective practice is delivered in a manner that is brief, nonevaluative, and supportive.** Eliciting practice involves more than simply saying "OK. Take out your books, turn to page 78, and answer questions 1, 3, 7, and 9. You have 20 minutes." Rather, your introduction to a practice activity should accomplish three objectives: (1) inform the learners that they are going to practice something they are capable of succeeding at ("You've done part of this before, so this shouldn't be much different"), (2) dispel anxiety about doing the task through the use of nonevaluative and nonthreatening language ("You've got part of it right, Anita; now, think some more and you'll have it"), and (3) let the learners know that you will be around to monitor their work and support their efforts ("I will be around to help, so let me know if you have a problem").

● **Practice should be designed to ensure success.** Practice makes perfect only when it is done correctly. If your learners are making many math, punctuation, or problem-solving mistakes, practice is making *im*perfect. Design your practice to produce as few errors as possible. For example, worksheets should be developed to ensure that at least 80 to 90 percent of the problems are completed correctly.

● **Practice should be arranged to allow students to receive feedback.** As we learned earlier in our discussion of modeling, feedback exerts a powerful effect on learning. Develop procedures and routines for rapid checking of work so that learners know as soon as possible how well they are performing. Having peers correct one another's practice is an efficient way to give feedback. Also, having answer sheets handy so that learners can check their own work can be a simple and effective means of providing feedback.

● **Practice should have the qualities of progress, challenge, and variety.** Kounin (1970) found that the key to preventing learners from becoming bored was to design practice opportunities that allow them to see that they are making progress ("Don't forget to check your answers with the key on the board"). In addition, practice should be introduced in a challenging and enthusiastic manner ("This will really test your understanding with some new and interesting kinds of problems"). Finally, practice exercises should include a variety of examples and situations.

Learners need practice. During the coaching phase of instruction, teachers motivate learners to want to practice, give them many opportunities to do so, and guide practice by prompts and questions.

Guiding Practice by Prompting and Questioning. We typically think of practice as a solitary activity during which learners master skills that have been explained or demonstrated by the teacher. This type of practice is often referred to as **independent practice.** However, other forms of practice involve the active participation of both teacher and learners, whether one-to-one or in groups. This type of practice is called **guided practice.**

During guided practice, the teacher provides activities that encourage learners to organize a first, crude response to information that has been modeled or demonstrated. Teachers typically stimulate this type of practice with the use of prompts and questions.

Prompts. Learners will not always follow your directions to initiate a particular response or demonstrate a particular skill. This is particularly so with younger learners who are practicing unfamiliar action sequences such as tying a shoelace, booting a disk into a computer, writing the letters of the alphabet, using scissors to cut out a picture, or solving a long division problem. At various times during practice, learners need additional support from the teacher to produce the kinds of physical or intellectual skills for which practice was designed. **Prompts** are supplementary aids that teachers use to increase the likelihood that learners will engage in successful practice.

Prompts typically take the form of verbal directions ("Remember what you're supposed to do first?"), gestures (the teacher points to the lever that engages the disk drive), or physical guidance (the teacher holds the child's hand and guides it gently as the child forms the letter *H*). Teachers who are skilled at prompting are careful to provide only the minimum amount of assistance necessary to make the action happen. This is called *least-to-most* prompting (Cooper, 1979). Prompts must gradually be diminished so that the learner can perform the task independently.

Questions. We opened this chapter with Ms. Freeman's middle-school science class. Let's return there now to observe the coaching phase of her lesson.

> **Ms. Freeman:** How do plants get their energy from the soil? Are there little Snickers Bars in the dirt and do the plants reach out and chew them?
> **Terry:** It's like minerals and nutrients.
> **Ms. Freeman:** But are they food? Do they contain energy?
> **Heather:** Well, we throw scraps of food away in the soil like banana peels and apple cores, and they contain minerals the plants eat.
> **Ms. Freeman:** How do the banana peels and apple cores that contain the minerals get into the plant?
> **Terry:** The plant sucks them in through its roots.
> **Ms. Freeman:** But how? Does water that comes through the roots carry the minerals? What do you say, Carla?
> **Carla:** Yes, that's it. Plants need water to grow, so water must help them get the food they need. But then, wouldn't water be a kind of food?
> **Ms. Freeman:** Think about this: Do plants make their own food, or are they given food by the water they receive?

Notice how Ms. Freeman guides her learners as they practice thinking through a problem and how she uses questions to heighten interest and stimulate thinking. To Ms. Freeman, questions are not simply a tool for cross-examining students or catching

---

Independent practice. The solitary attempt of a learner to master skills.

Guided practice. Teacher-provided activities used to encourage learners to organize a response to what has been modeled or demonstrated, often with prompts and questions.

Prompts. Supplementary or additional aids that teachers use to increase the likelihood that learners will engage in successful practice.

How can prompts be used to help guide learners to a first response?

Asking Questions during Guided Practice

Plan Your Questions in Advance. Although talk-show hosts make it appear as if their questions are spontaneous and unrehearsed, this seldom is the case. In reality, ad-libbing and spontaneity can lead to dead time. The type of questions you select, their level of difficulty, and the sequence in which you ask them should be based on your lesson objectives.

Make Questions Concise, Clear, and to the Point. Effective oral questions are like effective writing: every word should be necessary. Pose questions in the same natural conversational language you would use with any close friend.

Allow Time for Students to Think (wait time 1). Many teachers do not allow learners enough time to answer a question before calling on someone else or moving to the next question. Gage and Berliner (1988) and Rowe (1974) report that, on average, teachers only wait about 1 second for learners to respond. Borich (1996) and Ornstein (1992) recommend that you increase the wait time to 3 or 4 seconds for lower-level questions and to as much as 15 seconds for higher-level questions.

Keep the Students in Suspense. First deliver the question, then mention the student's name. Similarly, randomly select the students you want to answer your questions. You want your learners to feel that they could be called on at any time.

Give Students Sufficient Time to Complete Their Responses Before Redirecting the Question or Probing (wait time 2). Wait time 2 is the time you wait following a student answer before probing for deeper understanding or redirecting the question when the answer is incomplete or wrong. To maintain lesson momentum, teachers often interrupt a learner before she or he has finished responding.

Provide Immediate Feedback to the Learner. Acknowledge correct answers by providing encouragement, elaborating on the response, further probing, or moving on to another question. Most important, communicate to the learner that you heard and evaluated the answer. Follow up on incorrect or incomplete answers with probes or by redirection of the question to another student.

What are some ways to use questions to encourage learners to respond correctly?

those who are inattentive. Rather, they are the principal mechanism by which she steers her learners to take maximum advantage of their opportunities to practice. The accompanying box, *Asking Questions during Guided Practice*, provides detailed guidelines for using questions during this phase.

Interactive and Technology-driven Methods of Practice. Practice, whether independent or guided, can also be provided by programmed instruction, peer and cross-age tutoring, computer-assisted instruction, interactive videodisc, and telecommunications networks. These interactive methods and techniques usually have in common the following features:

- They allow rapid movement within and across content, depending on the learners' success.
- They allow students to proceed at their own pace and level of difficulty.
- They provide immediate feedback about the accuracy of responses.
- They gradually shift the responsibility for learning from teacher to student.

Students tend to learn better when they solve real-life problems. As a result, many schools are reorganizing curricula to support independent judgment, critical thinking, and real-world problem solving (Boyer, 1993). Instead of practicing on hypothetical problems, students increasingly are using tutorial methods and communication technologies to address many of the same issues and problems as do professionals. Thanks to advances in computer chip design and fiberoptic technologies, the power of information technology is rapidly being integrated into the school curriculum.

For example, advances in digitalization have made it possible to combine text, sound, and video to create multimedia environments for the personal computer that establish authentic practice environments. Information superhighways allow high-speed transfer of text, voice, and video across schools, geographical regions, and countries to provide real problem-solving contexts. These information highways allow students the opportunity to:

How can technology make independent practice and transfer a practical classroom goal?

- **search far beyond their local libraries.** For example, students can browse through holdings on "early flight" in the Library of Congress, visually take a tour of a space station circling in space, or ask questions of a curator at the Air and Space Museum via electronic mail.

- **become more specialized and focused on current issues.** For example, students can query a database being compiled by the *New York Times* on a fast-breaking story, scan a recent index of *Scientific American* for the latest advances on gene splicing, or communicate via electronic mail with a researcher stationed in Antarctica.

- **cooperate with other learners at a distance.** Learners may team up with students in another school, state, or nation to share information of mutual interest, such as acid rain, deforestation, or the global economy.

- **work with mentors outside their own school.** Learners can explore connections between academic work and job opportunities or see how principles and concepts are used at more advanced levels, such as in subsequent courses, in the workplace, or in different community contexts.

These methods and technologies provide possibilities for creating authentic practice experiences that only a decade ago were unimaginable. Increasingly, they are being used to encourage independent judgment, critical thinking, and real-world problem solving by allowing the learner to question and prompt human and textual resources that before were accessible only to professionals working in the field. They also reduce a school's dependence on quickly dated texts and workbooks, which may not provide the learner with sufficient practice opportunities for gradually shifting the responsibility for learning from teacher to student. The accompanying box, *Providing Practice Opportunities with Technology,* describes some ways that learners can practice during the structuring, modeling, and coaching phases of instruction.

Motivating Learners. Successful groups of learners, no less than successful teams of athletes, demand that their coaches be skilled motivators. The expert practice of coaching, therefore, requires that teachers be skilled at motivating learners. The learning that is elicited and strengthened during guided practice must be maintained, generalized, and transferred outside of practice. Your knowledge of motivation acquired in Chapter 7 and your ability to instill it in your learners will help this take place.

Providing Practice Opportunities with Technology

Programmed Instruction. *Programmed instruction* refers to written instructional materials that students work on by themselves at their own level and at their own pace. Programmed instruction materials typically break skills down into small subskills like those that might be identified in a learning hierarchy (Figure 10.2.) Questions and prompts along the way actively engage learners in formulating responses. The learner is given immediate knowledge of the correctness of his or her answer, usually directly beneath or near the question or prompt.

Programmed instruction has not been found to be more effective than conventional methods when it is used as the sole source of instruction (Bangert, Kulik, & Kulik, 1983; Slavin, 1984). However, when self-instructional materials cover familiar content and learners work in mixed-ability learning teams (called Team Assisted Individualization; Slavin et al., 1984), programmed materials have been found effective (Good, Grouws, & Egmeier, 1983; Slavin, 1985; Slavin & Karwait, 1984).

Computer Assisted Instruction (CAI). Computer assisted instruction provides many of the same practice opportunities of programmed instruction. CAI programs are available at many different grade levels and content areas to give students practice, assess understanding, and provide remediation if needed. The advantage of CAI over written programmed materials is that the accuracy of student responses can be quickly assessed, and the sequence and difficulty of the activities can be changed to correspond with the learners' current level of functioning. Thus practice can be individualized—more time can be spent on a particular topic or skill, or the program can return to an earlier sequence of instruction to review prerequisite learning.

CAI can provide color pictures, charts, and diagrams that can motivate learners and enhance the authenticity of the practice experience. Most computer assisted instruction is now presented to learners on personal computers in the classroom with software developed by textbook publishers. As with other individualized learning methods, CAI has been found most effective when it provides practice opportunities for content already presented during the structuring, modeling, and coaching phases of instruction (Atkinson, 1984; Kulik & Kulik, 1984).

Interactive Videodiscs and CD-ROM. Interactive videodiscs (laser discs) and CD-ROM share the same advantages over both written and computer assisted programmed material. These new laser technologies can present to the learner any combination of text, diagrams, slides, maps, films, and animations on demand, thereby greatly increasing the flexibility of the recorded content over traditional programmed instruction. They can also hold different soundtracks—for example, one in English and another in Spanish. The learner can freeze frames indefinitely and locate any frame or sequence of frames on the disc almost instantaneously.

Because of these characteristics, interactive videodiscs and CD-ROM technology are particularly suited to simulating and modeling higher-order thinking skills and real-life experiences, such as laboratory experiments, physical motion, and even noises and sounds that can make learning come alive. For this reason, these technologies are quickly becoming the preferred medium for providing interactive individualized practice activities. Since these are new technologies, researchers have just begun to study their effects in the classroom. However, their effectiveness has been documented most frequently in the field of science.

Fiberoptics/Telecommunications. This technology offers the greatest opportunity to stimulate the senses through multimedia, making the learning environment more fluid and personalized. Often referred to as the "living curriculum," the combination of laser technology and telecommunications has many of the features of interactive videodisc technology, with the added advantage that no longer must the subject matter being studied exist on a videodisc inside a personal computer. Access to information along communication superhighways connects the learner rapidly with human and textual resources across schools and geographical locations.

From teacher input during the structuring, modeling, and coaching phases of instruction, the learner creates his or her own curriculum by selecting information pathways that increasingly bring authentic detail and professional expertise to the problem at hand. In this manner, responsibility for the retention and application of content passes gradually from the teacher to the learner, encouraging cooperative ventures with other students, professionals, and resources.

The Expert Practice of Fading

Although all four teaching activities include elements of transfer of learning, **fading** is the event that most directly achieves it. The expert practice of fading, whether used during direct, indirect, or self-directed instruction, involves two steps:

1. The removal of any external supports required to activate learning (for example, prompts and reinforcers).
2. The provision of independent practice that promotes transfer.

Fading. The removal of external learning supports and the simultaneous provision of independent practice to promote transfer.

Prompt Fading. The teaching of many action sequences, such as testing a hypothesis, forming correct letters in handwriting, tying knots, focusing a microscope, or dissecting a frog, frequently requires prompts to guide correct responses. Likewise, prompts are frequently required to help learners develop oral language proficiency, essay writing, and problem-solving skills. These prompts may be verbal, gestural, or physical.

You can fade verbal prompts by gradually using fewer words or shorter explanations, allowing more time for learner response, or lowering the sound of your voice as the student begins to work more skillfully and independently. We often fade gestural prompts by gradually shortening the length of the gesture from a full arm sweep, for example, to a short pointing response. Physical prompts can be faded by slowly moving your assistance from hand-over-hand, to guiding the wrist, to lightly touching the forearm, to lightly tapping the elbow. Delaying the fading of prompts can lead to *prompt dependency*. Conversely, removing prompts too soon can create frustration and anxiety in the learner.

Reinforcer Fading. The purpose of reinforcer fading is to gradually transfer the motivation for performing a skill from extrinsic reinforcers (such as food, tokens, stickers, and praise) to intrinsic reinforcers. It is more desirable and natural for learners to read because they enjoy it than because their parents give them a dollar for every book they read. Likewise, we want learners to keep the classroom neat and to play sports or musical instruments for the enjoyment of the activity rather than to obtain a grade. As you will recall, we outlined specific procedures for reinforcer fading in Chapter 4.

Providing Independent Practice That Promotes Transfer. The following first-person account describes one of the most vexing problems in teaching: how to help students demonstrate their learning in new situations and settings.

> Yesterday afternoon I had the most frustrating experience. I was walking to the subway after school and I ran into Gabriel, one of my ESL (English as a Second Language) students. We had just spent the last two days drilling the future tense of "going to," as in "What are you going to do tomorrow?" So I said, "Gabriel, what are you going to do tonight?" And do you know what he said after two days of drill and practice? "I went to finish my homework tonight." Not "want" . . . but "went." He completely mixed up the past and future tenses. I don't know how these kids are ever going to learn this stuff. (Author, personal experience)

Transfer of learning is the phrase used to describe this problem. Teachers want their students to transfer their learning, or generalize it from the classroom to the world

Transfer of learning. The process whereby skills learned in one situation or under one set of conditions are demonstrated in a different situation or under a different set of conditions.

How can I help my learners transfer what I teach to new situations and settings?

outside the classroom. Of what value is learning how to speak or write grammatically correct English, solve math problems, type with accuracy, read poetry, plan a menu, or use logic if these skills are practiced only in a classroom under the guidance of a teacher?

Transfer of learning is a central concern whether you are engaged in direct, indirect, or self-directed instruction—that is, whether you want learners to acquire facts, rules, and action sequences; concepts, patterns, and abstractions; or learn how to learn. Regardless of which instructional method you choose or what the goal or objective of instruction is, effective instruction should culminate in the learner's demonstrating her learning in a new or different context.

The purpose of guided practice during coaching is to help learners acquire new intellectual, social, and motor skills. The purpose of independent practice during fading is to help learners transfer those skills to real-world contexts. Achieving this goal requires teachers to design independent practice with transfer in mind. Independent practice that promotes transfer should:

- emphasize mastery by beginning after learners have mastered the original task that has been modeled for them
- have real-world similarity by being completed under the same time constraints and with the same distractions that exist in the real world
- provide variety by giving learners as many different examples and situations as possible on which to practice, using a variety of sources, such as fiction, editorials, poetry, and magazines
- offer flexibility by changing the conditions, locations, and peers under which practice occurs
- promote self-direction by asking learners to identify examples where they can use their skills, such as measurement, punctuation, money management, scientific inquiry, and classifying objects, and to monitor their own progress.

In the chapters ahead we will present several means by which you can determine the degree to which you have acquired the expert practices of structuring, modeling, coaching, and fading.

Summing Up

This chapter introduced you to methods of instructional management. Its main points were these:

- The five factors to consider when establishing priorities for what students should learn are: (1) subject matter we can teach; (2) societal concerns; (3) needs, interests, and abilities of students; (4) the educational philosophy of the school and community; and (5) instructional theory and research.
- According to Gagné, learning outcomes can be divided into verbal information, intellectual skills, cognitive strategies, attitudes, and motor skills.
- Gagné's hierarchy of learning presumes that lower-level outcomes (for example, memorization) are prerequisite to achieving any higher level of learning.

- According to Bloom et al., Krathwohl et al., and Harrow, respectively, learning outcomes can be divided into the cognitive domain, which represents intellectual abilities and skills; the affective domain, which represents attitudes, beliefs, and values; and the psychomotor domain, which represents bodily movement and physical performance.
- The taxonomy of objectives in the cognitive domain includes six levels of objectives: knowledge, comprehension, application, analysis, synthesis, and evaluation.
- Teaching methods are regularly occurring patterns of practice that promote learning and transfer. They include the direct, indirect, and self-directed forms of instruction. Each teaching method may include the specific teaching activities of structuring, modeling, coaching, and fading.
- Structuring is a teaching activity in which the teacher captures the attention of the learners and focuses them on the outcome of the lesson.
- Modeling is a teaching activity that involves demonstrating to learners what you want them to do (in the form of action sequences), say (in the form of facts and concepts), or think (in the form of problem-solving or learning-to-learn strategies).
- The four psychological processes that need to occur if students are to learn from modeling are (1) attention, (2) retention, (3) production, and (4) motivation.
- Coaching is a teaching activity during which the learner converts images or memories into actions. Coaching involves establishing accountability, providing opportunities for practice, guiding practice by prompting and questioning, and motivating.
- A solitary activity in which the learner masters the skills that have been explained or demonstrated is referred to as independent practice. An activity that involves the active participation of both teacher and learner, together or in groups, is referred to as guided practice.
- Fading is a teaching activity that gradually diminishes prompts and external reinforcers to activate learning and promote transfer.

For Discussion and Practice

°1. In your own words, describe the purpose of goals and objectives.

2. Prepare three goals for the subject or grade you will teach that exhibit a relationship between subject matter mastery, societal concerns, and students' needs and interests. Justify the responsiveness of each goal to all three considerations.

°3. What are Gagné's five types of learner outcomes? Give an example of each for the subjects you will be teaching.

4. What would be your answer to the student question "Why do I have to learn this stuff?"

Questions marked with an asterisk are answered in the appendix.

°5. What is the order or sequence of intellectual skills implied by Gagné's hierarchy of learning? Explain why this sequence is important.

6. For a subject you will teach, provide an example of a problem-solving exercise that would require learners to combine facts, concepts, and principles in a real-world context.

°7. Identify six levels of the taxonomy of cognitive objectives and at least one mental operation each could require.

8. Prepare an objective in your subject area and grade level for each level of the affective domain.

°9. Identify three general instructional methods. In your own words, describe a pattern of teaching skills that you might use with each instructional method.

°10. What were some of the ingredients of Ms. Freeman's lesson that made it a success? What instructional method or methods was she using?

°11. What are the key events of the teaching process according to Gagné, Briggs, and Wagner?

°12. Which events of instruction proposed by Hunter correspond with the skills of structuring, modeling, coaching, and fading?

°13. Identify and give examples in your content area or grade level of four ways a teacher could vary instruction to increase student attention.

°14. Identify and give examples in your content area or grade level of the four psychological processes that must occur in order for students to learn from modeling.

°15. What are five guidelines for creating an effective demonstration? Describe how each would be implemented for a lesson in your field, using specific examples.

°16. Explain in your own words and with the aid of examples the concepts of (a) prompt fading and (b) reinforcer fading.

°17. Describe an example of independent practice that includes all the characteristics required to promote transfer.

°18. What does the phrase "transfer of learning" mean? Provide an example in your teaching field.

°19. What are five ways independent practice can promote transfer? Provide examples in your teaching field of how you would accomplish each in the classroom.

Suggested Readings

Borich, G. (1996). *Effective teaching methods* (3rd ed.). Columbus, OH: Merrill/Macmillan. This book reviews the research basis for the effective teaching practices discussed in this chapter and provides methods for implementing them in the classroom.

Kennedy, M. C. (Ed.). (1991). *Teaching academic subjects to diverse learners.* New York: Teachers College Press. This book contains chapters by subject area specialists in the areas of science and mathematics.

The various authors discuss effective teaching methods specific to these disciplines. They also address the challenges that classes of diverse learners present to teachers.

Pasch, M., Sparks-Langer, G., Gardner, T. G., Starko, A. J., & Moody, C. D. (1991). *Teaching as decision-making: Instructional practices for the classroom teacher.* New York: Longman. This text contains numerous practical exercises to help teachers with instructional planning. It emphasizes the day-to-day decisions that teachers must make when choosing goals, objectives, and strategies for learners.

Part

IV

What Teachers Need to Know About Assessment

Stan Rossman teaches science at Fawkes Middle School. He has three sections of seventh-grade earth science and two sections of eighth-grade physical science. This is his second year at Fawkes. It is Friday, just before the end of the second six-week grading period. Stan is going over the results of a unit test in physical science with his fourth-period class. Let's listen in as he explains to his class how he graded the test.

Stan: This test was worth 100 points. There were 25 multiple-choice questions each worth 2 points, and 2 essay questions worth 25 points each. As you can see from the overhead, five of you got As, seven Bs, ten Cs, three Ds, and three Fs. Any questions?

Stu: I didn't have enough time. It was too long a test for only 50 minutes. [Several other students nod.]

Stan: I hear you, but 12 of you got As and Bs. They seemed to have enough time.

April: It just seems like there was a lot of stuff on the test we didn't spend much time on in class. I studied a lot from my class notes, but it didn't help that much.

Stan: Well, I told you that you were responsible for everything in Chapters 8, 9, and 10, even if we didn't cover all of it in class.

April: But I figured most of the test would be over what we did cover in class.

Stan: Well, next time don't make that assumption. Just study everything in the book.

Fasil: In class and in lab I got everything right. I understood the experiments and I completed every lab assignment. But on the test, I just didn't know it. It was like you had us do one thing in class and another on the test.

Stan: I understand what you're saying, but if you knew the material you would know it regardless.

Fasil: I just think I know more than my grade shows!

As a teacher, the time when you do the most soul-searching will occur after you give back the results of your tests. If your learners didn't do as well as you or they expected, you may begin to question whether your learning objectives were too ambitious, whether you taught the material well enough, or whether you sufficiently motivated all your learners to do their best. Your learners will also raise questions—about their own abilities and study habits, and your ability to make a fair test. When your learners' test scores are not what you or they expect, you will want to be sure that your test accurately measured what you taught.

Teachers make classroom tests for two purposes: (1) to assess learner achievement and (2) to make judgments about the effectiveness of their teaching. If you know that you have a good test (which, as you will learn in this unit, means that it reliably and validly measures what you have taught), you can begin to make decisions about which of your learning objectives have been achieved, which you need to review, and whether you should continue or change your instructional approach. But if you have doubts about the test itself, you will be unable to make important decisions about your learners or your teaching.

In this unit you will learn the skills you need to confidently make classroom tests and assign grades based on those tests. After studying this unit you will be able to make a test that both you and your learners will judge fair and accurate.

Since the results of classroom tests naturally raise questions about ability to learn, we begin this unit with a discussion of human learning ability. In Chapter 11 we review definitions of learning ability, how best to measure it, and the advantages and disadvantages of standardized testing. We will also discuss the effects of heterogeneously and homogeneously grouping learners for instruction, and the research that has considered this important issue.

Chapter 12 introduces the concept of content validity. There you will learn how to create paper-and-pencil tests that measure what you have taught and what your learners know. After studying this chapter, you will know how to build a classroom test that has appropriate time limits, that asks questions that reflect the objectives you have taught, and whose emphasis matches the emphasis given those objectives. You will also learn important principles and rules of grading, including the averaging of grades from different types of assignments and tests.

In Chapter 13 you will learn how to construct authentic performance tests. Performance tests ask your learners to exhibit adultlike skills and responsibilities that reflect the processes and thinking skills used by professionals working in the real world. In this chapter we will also show you how to reliably and accurately grade performance tests and student portfolios and chart your learners' achievements. Let's begin our discussion of what teachers need to know about assessment with a discussion of learning ability and how it relates to your classroom.

Assessing for Learning: Ability and Standardized Assessment

This chapter will help you answer the following questions about your learners:

- How do I explain the results of standardized tests to learners and parents?
- How do I use a norms table to determine how well my learners are performing?
- How will I know if a standardized test is a reliable and valid measure of a learner's ability?
- How do I answer the question: "Is there a relationship between IQ and what my students learn in school?"
- Are ability tests fair to learners from various cultures and ethnic backgrounds?
- Can knowing my learners' IQs help me make day-to-day instructional decisions in my classroom?
- How can I use the cognitive approach to learning to understand and improve my students' performance?
- What can my school do to ensure that both high- and low-ability learners experience the same effective instruction?

After about three weeks of teaching, just about the time you begin to prepare your first progress reports, you will experience firsthand what many of your professors and education courses have been saying: some learners pick things up a lot faster than others.

Like any concerned teacher, you will ponder ways to meet your students' individual learning needs. You will ask yourself: How can I accelerate the learning of slower learners and still meet the needs of the faster students? Why do some learn more quickly than others even when all appear equally motivated? How can I identify fast and slow learners to provide each group with instruction matched to their abilities?

Here's what Ron Brandt, executive editor of *Educational Leadership*, says about his early efforts to promote individualized instruction matched to student ability.

> I realize now I was mistaken when I pushed a version of individualized instruction in the 1960s and 1970s. I wasn't alone: eminent psychologists, noted consultants, federal officials, and lots of other practitioners thought as I did. We accepted the findings of social science, bolstered by our own experience, that individuals differed greatly in learning ability. To cope with these differences, it made sense to organize instruction sequentially, provide self-explanatory materials, and devise ways for teachers to manage the operation. That way, students could "progress at their own pace."
>
> Those of us who organized such programs may not have been entirely wrong, but in just two decades I have come to think very differently. For example, it now appears that learning ability is modifiable, and that it is not a single general factor. Cognitive psychologists now emphasize the social nature of learning, which makes highly questionable a system in which students work alone most of the time. Indeed, the aim of many educators these days is to make the classroom a community of inquiry, just the opposite of an assortment of unrelated individuals. Perhaps most important, our expectations are changing. With new economic conditions we are beginning to see that preparation for college and preparation for work are not necessarily exclusive aims. We even see the possibility, as many advocates insist, that the same high standards should apply to all. (Brandt, 1992, p. 5)

Brandt goes on to question not only individualized instruction based on the notion of learning ability, but also tracking: grouping learners into different classes according to scores on standardized tests of learning ability. Despite some agreement among educational psychologists and school administrators, those most affected by changes in this practice—parents, teachers, and students—do not always share this view. Jim Nehring, a high school teacher, is one of them.

In this chapter you will also learn the meanings of these terms:

age-equivalent scores
correlation coefficient
general ability tests
group ability tests
heterogeneous grouping
homogeneous grouping
index of item difficulty
index of item discrimination
individual ability tests
instructional validity
multiple ability tests
norm group
normal distribution
norms
percentile rank
predictive validity
principle of indirect measurement
psychometric approach
qualitative item analysis
quantitative item analysis
redundancy principle
reliability
standard deviation
standardization
standard scores
test-retest reliability
tracking
validity

Our current school superintendent doesn't believe in tracking. "All kids should be taught in the same class," he says. "Tracking stigmatizes students, according to the research. It arbitrarily lowers teacher expectations. Heterogeneous grouping," he says, "is where it's at. . . ." Classes at Amesley High School used to be "homogeneous"; that means kids were placed in different classes depending on how able or motivated we figured they were. . . . Anyway, at Amesley High, homogeneous grouping is no more. At least until the superintendent, current or future, becomes persuaded by the other body of research that sees merit in tracking. Meanwhile, the teachers are up in arms since they've been teaching to tracked groups for the last million years and all of a sudden are expected to teach both Andrew and Esther in the same class at the same time. There's been a good deal of scrambling at Amesley as teachers try out any and all varieties of lesson plans that will simultaneously challenge Andrew to, say, understand Marx's theory of class struggle while enlightening Esther with the correct spelling for wuz. (Brandt, 1992, p. 17)

We will return to the ability grouping, or tracking, controversy later in this chapter. For now, in order to fully appreciate the debate, let's explore the question of how intellectual or learning ability is assessed.

First, we will examine the practice of assessing learning ability through the use of the standardized IQ, or ability test. In the following pages, you will learn how these tests are constructed, administered, and interpreted. We will then use our understanding of these assessment tools to answer three important questions:

- How much does classroom learning depend on the skills measured by standardized IQ tests?
- Are IQ tests fair to learners from diverse cultures and backgrounds?
- Do such tests provide information useful for instructional purposes?

Let's begin by examining the relationship between intelligence and learning ability.

Assessing Ability to Learn

A careful reading of the works of Binet and Simon (1916), Wechsler (1975), Thorndike (1913), Guilford (1985), and Gardner (1983) suggests that intelligence is a global aspect of personality. What we call "intelligence" includes not only the abilities to learn academic subjects, deal with abstractions, and solve problems, but also the abilities to withstand stress and distraction, be motivated, remain emotionally stable, be interested in learning, be socially competent, and display physical grace.

Thorndike, Cunningham, Thorndike, and Hagen (1991) believe that much of the present-day controversy surrounding the use of ability tests can be attributed to the unfortunate use of the term "intelligence" in association with them. These researchers assert that so-called IQ (intelligence) tests are indicators of academic learning ability, not measures of a global personality trait called intelligence.

Today the issue of assessing someone's IQ or ability to learn is controversial. Although the goal that stimulated the development of the first standardized IQ test was to provide better services to learners who could not benefit from traditional classroom instruction, doubts concerning the effective use of the IQ test to accomplish this goal have never been greater (Haney, 1981; Reschly, 1981; Reynolds & Kaiser, 1990; Thorndike et al., 1991). Psychologists, educators, parents, students, and political leaders are increasingly voicing concerns that IQ tests may restrict more than expand an individual's access to learning opportunities (Garcia, 1981). In this chapter, you will learn about their advantages and limitations in assessing learning ability and about alternatives to their use.

What Is an Ability?

Why do some children grasp intellectual skills faster than others? Why do some children learn to read, solve math problems, or compose essays with less effort than some of their peers? The usual answer given is that some learners have more "ability" than others.

Attributing differences in children's learning to an "ability" to learn, however, begs the question of what, exactly, *is* an "ability." For most of the twentieth century, educational psychologists have defined an "ability" as a psychological trait or characteristic that is internal, stable, and unchangeable. Thus "ability" has been assumed to underlie achievement in music, art, athletics, reading, mathematics, science, and writing, as well as many other fields. Furthermore, "ability" has been assumed to be largely present at birth and not acquired through experience or training.

Some researchers, however, differ with this definition of ability. For example, Bergan and Dunn (1976) view an ability as a repertoire of intellectual skills that expands and grows and improves as learners study, practice, and work hard. Bergan and others (Carroll & Horn, 1981) are critical of today's ability tests, which are based on vague definitions that fail to specify the behaviors involved in performing the specific actions tested. These authors disagree with developers of early ability tests about what underlies differences in school learning.

Assumptions of the Psychometric Approach

These pioneers of ability testing began a tradition of measurement called the **psychometric approach.** The psychometric approach comprises a set of beliefs or assumptions about psychological phenomena, as well as a technology for measuring them. Almost all current ability and academic achievement tests are derived from this set of beliefs, which include the following assumptions:

● **We can measure a psychological attribute or trait by systematically observing and recording its effects.**

For example, no one has ever *seen* "temperature." Yet we all know that it exists. Why? Because we can see its effects. When a column of mercury is exposed to heat, it rises in a predictable fashion. Likewise with an ability. Although we have never *seen* "ability," we can observe its effects. We do this by giving different learners identical tasks, under identical conditions, and recording how rapidly and skillfully they master them. This assumption is called the **principle of indirect measurement.**

● **Repeated observations of the effects of a psychological trait will overcome any imprecision in the observations themselves.**

Consistency, or redundancy, of measurement is of critical importance in indirect measurement. We can infer little about reading ability, for example, by observing a learner reading a single word. But we can draw conclusions about reading ability from having a student read an essay made up of many words, sentences, and paragraphs. This assumption is called the **redundancy principle.**

● **Ability is best measured as a quantity rather than as a cognitive process.**

The pioneers of the psychometric approach developed tests to measure the diverse abilities of large groups of individuals. The tests had to be short (requiring about an

Psychometric approach. A set of beliefs about ability testing that assumes that the effects of traits can be systematically observed and recorded, that repeated observations of the effects of a trait will overcome observational imprecision, that ability is best measured as a quantity rather than as a cognitive process, and that the amount of ability can be established through relative rather than absolute measurement.

Principle of indirect measurement. The assumption that ability can be measured by giving different learners identical tasks under identical conditions and recording how rapidly and skillfully each masters them.

Redundancy principle. The assumption that conclusions about a learner's abilities can be accurately measured by observing the learner using these abilities in a variety of circumstances and contexts.

hour to administer) and easily scored. These practical limitations did not allow for analysis of the thought processes behind the responses. Thus the idea of ability as a single, monolithic quantity was established.

● **We can establish the amount of the ability a learner possesses through relative rather than absolute measurement.**

The scores derived from ability tests that follow the psychometric tradition are relative, not absolute. In other words, the score tells us how much ability a person possesses relative to others who have taken the test, not specifically what the individual knows or doesn't know.

Now let's examine the procedures involved in translating this set of beliefs into a test whose purpose is to measure learning ability.

Developing Ability Tests: Initial Considerations

Figure 11.1 outlines the steps involved in the psychometric approach to test construction. Psychologists who use this approach follow a particular theory of learning ability and choose a certain method of test administration. These two considerations guide the initial selection of test questions; let's examine both more closely.

Theories of Learning Ability. Some of the earliest theories of learning ability focused on the relationship between sensory processes and learning. Sir Francis Galton, an Englishman, and James Cattell, an American, developed some of the first ability tests that measured, for example, the highest pitch someone could audibly detect, color discrimination, estimation of lengths and weights, grip strength, and speed of hand movement.

Modern tests of ability focus on cognitive abilities rather than sensorimotor processes. The designers of these tests assume that cognitive abilities involving attention, memory, comprehension, and reasoning underlie differences among learners in reading, writing, science, math, and so on. For example, Alfred Binet, a Frenchman who developed the first practical IQ test, wanted his test to include questions that assessed a child's ability to gain information from regular classroom instruction—for example, to solve simple math problems, understand spoken language, and see similarities and differences between objects and ideas. He created (and sometimes borrowed from other tests) questions and tasks that reflected his ideas about what underlies learning ability. He did not, however, precisely define the abilities his items were intended to re-

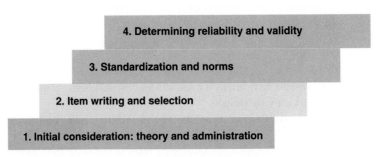

Figure 11.1
The steps involved in the psychometric approach to test construction.

flect, nor did he comprehensively sample all the skills involved in comprehension, arithmetic, reasoning, or memory. Binet's method was to build a test that (1) was consistent with his views about what underlies learning ability, (2) was practical to use in a one-to-one assessment format, and (3) accurately separated those learners who needed special instruction from those who did not.

Figure 11.2 illustrates some of the types of questions and tasks used by present-day ability tests. Notice the emphasis on cognitive as opposed to sensory abilities. Thus, modern test developers build ability tests that assess cognitive skills rather than sensory, physical, or social skills. In addition, they measure ability as either a single, unidimensional trait or a multidimensional trait. The former preference results in general ability tests, while the latter results in multiple ability tests.

General ability tests assume that a single, general trait or aptitude underlies the differences in school achievement among learners. Success or failure on different questions and tasks on the test is assumed to reflect the effects of this one underlying trait. These tests assign a single score (usually an IQ score), which is intended to represent the test-taker's learning ability.

Multiple ability tests do not assume that any single, general trait underlies learning. Rather, the tasks and questions on these tests are designed to measure the effects of several specific and distinct abilities. Such tests assign several separate scores to learners, each of which represents a distinct aspect of the overall ability to learn.

Method of Administration.
Some ability tests include questions and tasks that the learner answers in a one-to-one format. The examiner orally delivers the questions, presents any stimulus material (for example, pictures, blocks, figures) to the learner, and records the correctness of the responses. These are called **individual ability tests.**

Other ability tests are designed to be given in groups. These tests typically assemble large numbers of examinees in a room or auditorium. Each examinee responds to a written set of questions on a standardized, often computer scorable, answer sheet. These tests are called **group ability tests.**

Thus, current ability tests fall into one of four categories depending on whether test developers view learning ability as a single or multidimensional trait and whether they

General ability tests. Tests that assume that a single, general trait or aptitude underlies differences in school achievement among learners.

Multiple ability tests. Tests that do not assume that a single trait underlies differences in school achievement between learners and instead measure a number of specific and distinct abilities. These tests assign several separate scores representing different aspects of learning ability.

Individual ability tests. Ability tests administered by one examiner to one learner at each testing session.

Group ability tests. Ability tests designed for administration to large groups of learners on one occasion.

Ability tests can be given in either group or individual assessment formats. While group testing allows many learners to be assessed in a short period of time, individual assessment allows the examiner to judge the extent to which the examinee did his or her best on the test.

1. Verbal tests	Type of item
A. Information—Amount of general information about life	How many nickels are there in a dime?
B. Similarities—Ability to analyze information	In what way are a dog and a bird alike?
C. Arithmetic—Ability to do simple arithmetic computations in a story problem within a time limit	Seven children picked 42 apples and divided them equally. How many apples did each child receive?
D. Vocabulary—Knowledge of word meanings	What does "ridiculous" mean?
E. Comprehension—Knowledge of and judgment about real-life situations	Why do we need firefighters?

Figure 11.2
Skill descriptions and sample items from the *Wechsler Intelligence Scale for Children.* Simulated items similar to those in the *Wechsler Intelligence Scale for Children–Revised.* Copyright © 1974 by The Psychological Corporation. Reproduced by permission. All rights reserved.

choose individual or group administration. Table 11.1 lists some of the ability tests currently used in each of these four categories.

Item Writing and Selection

The kinds of questions that appear on a given ability test reflect both the test developers' preference for mode of administration and their theory of learning ability (for example, whether it is presumed to be a unidimensional or a multidimensional trait). These two factors guide the initial development and selection of ability test questions and tasks. Screening and editing, test tryouts, and statistical analyses determine the final selection of test items (questions). These latter processes involve two distinct types of item selection procedures: qualitative item analysis and quantitative item analysis. Let's see how each is put to work to select items for a learning ability test.

Qualitative Item Analysis. **Qualitative item analysis** involves screening and editing test items for clarity, style, cultural content and conciseness. Since these tests are given to all examinees using the same instructions and procedures, the person giving the test follows a single, well-rehearsed format. Thus, test developers make a great effort to know the nature of their audience and write instructions and questions that examinees will understand. At this stage of test development, questions are also screened for cultural content. This means that test developers discard or rewrite test questions or tasks containing knowledge or pictures that are more familiar to one segment of the population (for example, one cultural group) than another. Questions also are carefully screened for ethnic, racial, and gender stereotypes.

Quantitative Item Analysis. **Quantitative item analysis** involves trying out the edited test questions on a sample of individuals for whom the test is designed. After this

Qualitative item analysis. The process by which test developers check questions, tasks, and directions for clarity, style, bias, and conciseness.

Quantitative item analysis. The process by which test developers examine each test question to determine whether it is of appropriate difficulty and whether each item reflects the overall trait or ability that the test is presumed to measure.

2. Performance tests   **Type of item**

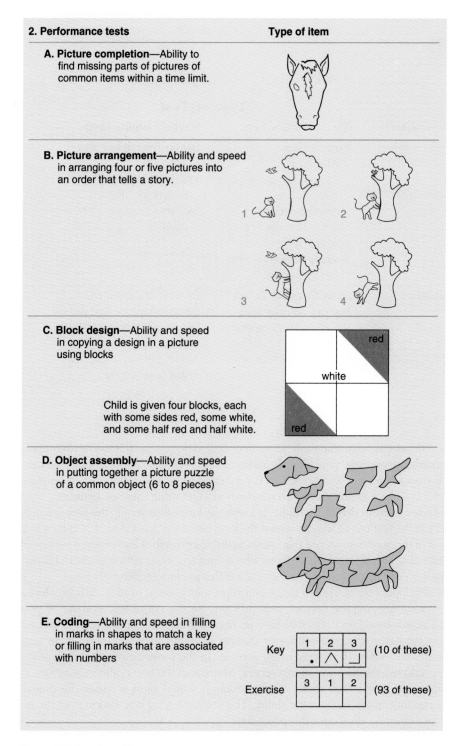

A. Picture completion—Ability to find missing parts of pictures of common items within a time limit.

B. Picture arrangement—Ability and speed in arranging four or five pictures into an order that tells a story.

C. Block design—Ability and speed in copying a design in a picture using blocks

Child is given four blocks, each with some sides red, some white, and some half red and half white.

red
white
red

D. Object assembly—Ability and speed in putting together a picture puzzle of a common object (6 to 8 pieces)

E. Coding—Ability and speed in filling in marks in shapes to match a key or filling in marks that are associated with numbers

Key

1	2	3
•	∧	⌐

(10 of these)

Exercise

3	1	2

(93 of these)

Figure 11.2 (continued)

Table 11.1

Commonly Used Ability Tests

	Type of Test	
Mode of Administration	**General Ability Tests**	**Multiple Ability Tests**

Individually administered	Wechsler Scales:
	  WIPPSI
	  WISC-III
	  WAIS-R
	Stanford-Binet
	Columbia Mental Maturity
	  Scale
	Peabody Picture Vocabulary
	  Test
		Detroit Tests of Learning
		  Aptitude
		KABC-Kaufman Assessment
		  Battery for Children
		McCarthy Scales of Children's
		  Abilities

Group administered	Lorge Thorndike IQ Test
	Test of Cognitive Skills
	School and College Ability
	  Tests
	Otis-Lennon School Ability
	  Test
		Differential Aptitude Test
		General Aptitude Test Battery
		SRA Primary Mental Abilities
		  Test
		Armed Services Vocational
		  Aptitude Battery

tryout, test developers examine each question or task to determine if it meets two important standards: appropriate difficulty (the index of item difficulty) and whether each item reflects the overall trait or ability the test is presumed to measure (the item discrimination index). Let's look at how these two standards are met using these procedures.

Index of item difficulty. The appropriateness of an ability test question for its intended audience. It is represented by the proportion of individuals in a test tryout who answered the item correctly.

The **index of item difficulty** (indicated with the letter p) is simply the proportion of individuals in the test tryout who answered the item correctly. A p-value of 90 means that 90 percent of those who answered that question did so correctly. Conversely, a p-value of 25 indicates that only 25 percent of those who attempted the question answered it correctly. An item with a p-value of 90 is easy; one with a p-value of 25 is difficult.

Test developers try to choose items that represent a range of item difficulty levels with the goal of keeping the average item difficulty for the entire test at about 50 percent. Test scores based on items that have an overall average difficulty level of 50 percent allow for better discrimination—or ranking of individuals by ability—than tests that average, say, either 10 percent or 90 percent. In the former case, almost all of the learners would receive low overall test scores, whereas in the latter, almost everyone in the group would have a high score. Neither example would allow accurate discrimination between individuals by learning ability. The accompanying box, *Calculating the Index of Item Difficulty,* illustrates this procedure.

Index of item discrimination. An ability test question's or task's actual reflection of the overall trait or ability that the test is presumed to measure.

Another important standard for test item development is the **index of item discrimination.** The reasoning behind this index is that every question or task on an ability test should reflect the ability that the test is measuring. If the test measures reasoning ability, then every question should require this ability. However, while on the surface a particular question may look as though it measures reasoning ability, the thought

Applying Your Knowledge:

Calculating the Index of Item Difficulty

To determine the difficulty index (indicated with the letter p) for a particular test item, the test developer divides the number of students selecting the correct answer for a test item by the total number of students attempting the item. For example, suppose students chose the options to a four-alternative multiple-choice item the following numbers of times, with option C the correct answer (indicated with *)

A	B	C*	D
3	0	18	9

$$p = \frac{\text{number of students selecting correct answer}}{\text{total number of students attempting answer}}$$

$$p = \frac{18}{30} = .60$$

We learn from this index that the item was moderately difficult (60 percent of the class got it right) and that option B should be modified. When p levels are less than about .25, the item is considered relatively difficult. When p levels are about .75, the item is considered relatively easy. Test developers try to build tests that have most items between p levels of .20 and .80, with an average p level of about .50.

process used by learners to arrive at the correct answer may actually require only memorization. The index of item discrimination compares the answers to individual items of students who did well on the entire test with the answers of students who did poorly on the entire test. It thus allows test developers to distinguish items that measure the ability underlying the test from those that do not. The accompanying box, *Calculating the Index of Item Discrimination*, illustrates this procedure.

These two statistics are the principal criteria used by the developer of a standardized test to decide whether to include particular items in the final version of the test. Our list of suggested readings at the end of this chapter provides more details on each of these procedures.

Standardization and Norms

As stated earlier, IQ tests allow us to rank or compare learners on the basis of how much learning ability each possesses. Standardization and norms are required to accomplish this.

Standardization involves administering the test to all persons in a defined group in the same way under the same conditions. The group of individuals upon whom the test is standardized is called the **norm group.** Standardization thus results in **norms:** statistical standards that allow the comparison of a learner's score with those of the original norm group.

Let's apply the concepts of standardization and norms to Jarad, a learner in your first-grade class who is 7 years and 2 months old. Jarad earned failing grades in all subject areas for the first marking period. You ask a school psychologist to give him a test

Standardization. The administration of a test to all persons in a defined group in the same way under the same conditions.

Norm group. The group of individuals upon whom a test is standardized.

Norms. Statistical standards that allow the comparison of a learner's score with those of a defined reference, or norm, group.

Applying Your Knowledge:

Calculating the Index of Item Discrimination

To determine the discrimination index (indicated by the letter D for a particular test item), the test developer follows these steps:

1. Arranges the scores on the total test from highest to lowest.
2. Divides the total test scores into the top half and bottom half (or similar division, such as top third and bottom third).
3. Counts the number in the upper group and the number in the lower group that chose each response alternative for that item.
4. Records the information in the following format:

Example for Item X

Options	A	B	C*	D
Upper	1	0	11	3
Lower	2	0	7	6

5. Computes the discrimination index with the following formula:

$$D = \frac{\text{(number who got item correct in upper group)} - \text{(number who got item correct in lower group)}}{\text{number of students in upper (or lower) group}}$$

Using the numbers above for test item X,

$$D = \frac{11-7}{15} = .267$$

The discrimination index is .267, which is positive. This means that more students who did well on the overall test answered the item correctly than students who did poorly on the overall test. A test item with a D = .267 would be considered a moderately difficult item that has positive (desirable) discrimination. Generally, test items that have positive D values are considered adequate. Other factors being equal, a test's discrimination will be greatest when the average *p* level (difficulty) is about .50.

that will determine whether he has the ability to succeed in your class. After Jarad takes the test, you have the following conversation with the psychologist:

You: Well, how did Jarad do?

Psychologist: He got a raw score of 59.

You: What's that mean?

Psychologist: He answered 59 questions correctly.

You: Is that good or bad?

Psychologist: Good.

You: But he only got 59 right?

Psychologist: On a standardized test the number right doesn't tell you specific information. It's not like a spelling test. It only makes sense when you compare it with how others did. And his score of 59 in comparison with others is good.

You: How good?

Psychologist: Seventy-seven percent of the learners who took this test scored lower than Jarad.

You: Who else took the test? I thought you only gave it to Jarad.

Psychologist: I compared his score with a group that was made up of learners like Jarad.

You: How intelligent is Jarad?

Psychologist: I don't know. But his score on this test, which measures ability to learn in school, indicates that he did better than most learners of similar age and grade.

You: Is there cause for concern?

Psychologist: Not about what this test measures. You'll have to look elsewhere for an answer to his poor grades.

Types of Norms. From the dialogue we see that norms, established during the standardization process, allow you to compare a student's score with the scores of others like him. To determine how well Jarad did in comparison to others, the psychologist computed his number of correct answers and converted the resulting *raw score* into a **percentile rank.** In this case, Jarad's raw score of 59 is at the seventy-seventh percentile for a child who is in the middle of the first grade. This means that 77 percent of learners in the middle of the first grade in the norming sample received scores lower than Jarad on this ability test. Thus the psychologist concluded that Jarad's ability is not the cause of his learning failure.

An ability test like that given to Jarad typically provides two other types of scores that allow you to interpret a learner's test result: age-equivalent scores and standard scores. Since these terms will frequently appear in your learners' school records, you should be familiar with them.

Age-equivalent scores describe a learner's raw score on an ability test in terms of the age of those in the norm group who earned similar scores. For example, in Table 11.2 we see that a raw score of 59 for a learner whose age is 7 years and 0 months (usually written as 7.0) is equivalent to a score typical of the average learner who is 8 years and 3 months old (8.3). In other words, Jarad has scored about a year above what would be expected, given his chronological age.

Percentile rank. Scores that indicate where an individual's score ranks in comparison with others of the same age or grade.

> **How do I explain the results of standardized tests to learners and parents?**

Age-equivalent scores. The obtained scores of those in a norming sample who are of various ages.

Teachers must be able to use norms tables and other technical information to interpret the standardized test scores of their learners. Typically, these scores tell teachers how their learners compare to a representative state or national sample of learners regarding a particular ability.

Table 11.2

Example of Age-Equivalent Scores for an Ability Test

Chronological Age

Raw Score	6-0	6-6	7-0	7-6	8-0	8-6	9-0	9-6	Raw Score
40	6-7	6-4	6-2	6-0	5-7	5-6	5-3	5-2	40
41	6-8	6-5	6-3	6-1	5-8	5-6	5-3	5-2	41
42	6-9	6-6	6-3	6-2	5-9	5-7	5-4	5-2	42
43	6-10	6-6	6-4	6-2	6-0	5-7	5-4	5-3	43
44	7-0	6-7	6-5	6-3	6-0	5-7	5-5	5-3	44
45	7-2	6-8	6-6	6-4	6-1	5-8	5-5	5-3	45
46	7-3	6-9	6-8	6-5	6-2	5-9	5-6	5-4	46
47	7-4	7-1	6-9	6-6	6-3	6-0	5-7	5-4	47
48	7-5	7-2	7-0	6-7	6-4	6-1	5-8	5-5	48
49	7-6	7-3	7-1	6-8	6-5	6-1	5-8	5-5	49
50	7-8	7-5	7-2	6-8	6-5	6-2	5-8	5-6	50
51	7-10	7-6	7-3	6-9	6-6	6-2	5-9	5-6	51
52	8-0	7-8	7-4	7-0	6-7	6-3	5-9	5-7	52
53	8-2	7-9	7-5	7-1	6-8	6-4	6-0	5-7	53
54	8-4	8-0	7-6	7-2	6-9	6-5	6-1	5-8	54
55	8-5	8-1	7-7	7-3	7-0	6-6	6-2	5-9	55
56	8-7	8-3	7-8	7-4	7-1	6-7	6-3	6-0	56
57	8-10	8-5	8-0	7-6	7-2	6-9	6-5	6-1	57
58	9-1	8-7	8-2	7-7	7-3	6-9	6-5	6-1	58
59	9-3	8-10	**8-3**	7-8	7-4	7-0	6-6	6-2	59
60	9-6	9-1	8-5	7-9	7-5	7-1	6-7	6-3	60
61	9-9	9-3	8-7	8-1	7-6	7-2	6-7	6-4	61
62	10-3	9-6	8-9	8-3	7-8	7-3	6-8	6-5	62
63	10-6	10-0	9-4	8-9	8-3	7-8	7-3	6-8	63
64	11-0	10-6	10-0	9-5	8-8	8-1	7-5	7-0	64

If, on the other hand, Jarad's chronological age were 9.0, his score of 59 would be 2 years and 4 months below ($9.0 - 6.6 = 2.4$) what we would expect someone of his age to earn. An age-equivalent score tells us whether an individual's ability as measured on a given test is higher, lower, or similar to that of other learners of the same age. It does not indicate specifically how well the learner performs on specific tasks, such as reading or computing.

Standard scores like percentile ranks allow you to determine where a particular learner's raw score ranks among the scores of other learners in the norming group. You are already familiar with standard scores, although you may not know it. SAT scores and IQ scores are examples of standard scores.

You may recall that SAT scores of 300, 500, and 700 represent low, average, and high scores, respectively. Likewise, you have a fairly good idea what the IQ scores of 75,

How do I use a norms table to determine how well my learners are performing?

Standard scores. Scores that indicate where a particular learner's raw score ranks among the scores of other learners in the norming group.

100, and 125 represent. These scores tell not only how well someone scored in relation to the national average, but precisely how far below or above the average that individual's score fell. From an appropriate norms table, we would learn that an IQ score of 116 is at about the eighty-fourth percentile, indicating that 84 percent of those taking the IQ test scored below 116. Similarly, an SAT score of 600 is at the eighty-fourth percentile, indicating that 84 percent of those taking the SAT scored below 600.

The Normal Distribution. As we have seen, deviations from the norm are useful in interpreting test scores. They are especially useful in interpreting test score results that follow a normal curve, or **normal distribution,** such as Jarad's ability test and the IQ and SAT tests described above. The distributions of scores from these tests, and many other tests that measure naturally occurring physical and social phenomena, take the form of a normal distribution: many learners score in the middle of the distribution, representing its mean or midpoint, while decreasing numbers of learners score toward each of its tails, giving it the bell-shaped appearance shown in Figure 11.3.

In a normally distributed set of scores, we know that scores are symmetrically distributed around the mean, which also represents the median, or fiftieth percentile. The degree to which scores are spread out around the mean is referred to as the *variability* of scores. A useful measure of variability is the **standard deviation.** The smaller the standard deviation, the more scores tend to cluster closely around the mean. The larger the standard deviation, the more scores tend to spread out toward the tails of the distribution. Figure 11.4 shows two distributions of scores with the same mean but with different standard deviations. Note that the scores in distribution B display more variability than those in distribution A.

Normal distribution. A classic distribution of scores in which most scores fall symmetrically around the mean with fewer scores on the upper and lower ends, which makes a frequency distribution of scores look bell-shaped.

Standard deviation. A measurement of variability and clustering around a mean.

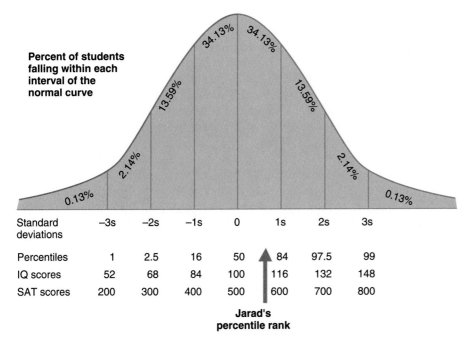

Figure 11.3
Jarad's performance in reference to the normal curve and other normally distributed scores.

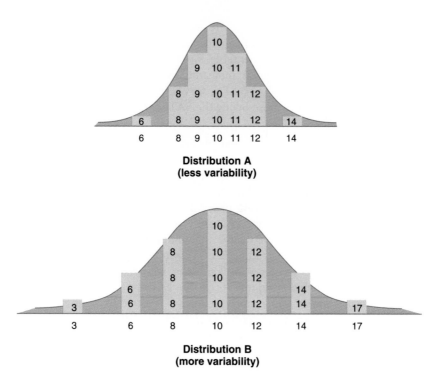

Figure 11.4
Two distributions of scores with the same mean but different standard deviations.

Now refer back to Figure 11.3. As this figure shows, in a sufficiently large set of normally distributed scores, about 68 percent of the scores will be clustered within one standard deviation above or below the mean. Similarly, about 95 percent of the scores will be clustered within two standard deviations of the mean.

Since scores in a normal distribution are symmetrically distributed about the mean, we know that a score that falls one standard deviation above the mean is at the eighty-fourth percentile. That is, one half of 68 percent of the scores plus the mean (which represents the fiftieth percentile) equals the eighty-fourth percentile. Thus, if the mean of the norming sample for the SAT is 500 and the standard deviation is 100, we know that those who score 600 on the SAT are one standard deviation above the mean, at about the eighty-fourth percentile. Similarly, if the standard deviation of an IQ test was 16, we would know that someone who scored 116 is at about the eighty-fourth percentile—in other words, 84 percent of those in the norming sample scored lower than this individual. The relationship of these scores to the normal curve is illustrated in Figure 11.3. The accompanying box, *Calculating the Standard Deviation,* illustrates this procedure for the two distributions in Figure 11.4.

Reliability and Validity. Test developers establish norms during the standardization process. Out of this same process come the data used to determine test reliability and validity.

The concepts of reliability and validity are particularly important for tests that purport to measure psychological constructs such as intelligence, learning ability, or cre-

Applying Your Knowledge:

Calculating the Standard Deviation

Distribution A ($\overline{X}=10$)			Distribution B ($\overline{X}=10$)		
X	$(X-\overline{X})$	$(X-\overline{X})^2$	X	$(X-\overline{X})$	$(X-\overline{X})^2$
14	4	16	17	7	49
12	2	4	14	4	16
12	2	4	14	4	16
11	1	1	12	2	4
11	1	1	12	2	4
11	1	1	12	2	4
10	0	0	10	0	0
10	0	0	10	0	0
10	0	0	10	0	0
10	0	0	10	0	0
9	−1	1	8	−2	4
9	−1	1	8	−2	4
9	−1	1	8	−2	4
8	−2	4	6	−4	16
8	−2	4	6	−4	16
6	−4	16	3	−7	49
		54			186

To calculate the standard deviation:

1. Find the mean of the scores, written $\overline{X}$.
2. Substract the mean from each of the scores, written $X-\overline{X}$.
3. Square each difference, written $(X-\overline{X})^2$.
4. Add all the squared differences, written $\Sigma(X-\overline{X})^2$

$$\text{A} \qquad\qquad \text{B}$$
$$\Sigma(X-\overline{X})^2=54 \qquad \Sigma(X-\overline{X})^2=186$$

5. Divide this total by the number of scores, written $\dfrac{\Sigma(X-\overline{X})^2}{N}$

$$\text{A} \qquad\qquad\qquad \text{B}$$
$$\frac{\Sigma(X-\overline{X})^2}{N}=\frac{54}{16}=3.37 \qquad \frac{\Sigma(X-\overline{X})^2}{N}=\frac{186}{16}=11.62$$

6. Find the square root, written $\sqrt{\dfrac{\Sigma(X-\overline{X})^2}{N}}$, which is the formula for the standard deviation (s).

$$\sqrt{\frac{\Sigma(X-\overline{X})^2}{N}}=\sqrt{3.37}=1.84 \qquad \sqrt{\frac{\Sigma(X-\overline{X})^2}{N}}=\sqrt{11.62}=3.41$$

$$s_A=1.84 \qquad\qquad s_B=3.41$$

ativity. **Reliability** is the degree to which a test produces consistent scores on repeated testings. **Validity** tells us whether a test measures what the test developer says it measures. Let's see how these two standards are met.

The Correlation Coefficient. Reliability and validity are expressed as correlation coefficients. A **correlation coefficient** is a statistic that indicates the degree to which two sets of scores are related to one another. While the mathematical concept of a correlation coefficient may not be familiar to you, the concept of a relationship is. In fact, you ask questions involving correlations all the time without consciously thinking about it.

For example, we often ask the following questions about learners: Does the amount of time a learner spends doing homework relate to her grades? What is the relationship between hours spent watching television and school achievement? How are parents' levels of education and their children's achievement related? Do the IQ scores achieved by learners in June change from the same learners' scores of the previous September?

Notice how all these questions involve (1) a relationship and (2) a set of scores (homework and grades, hours spent watching TV and grades, parents' education and grades, scores from two points in time). A correlation coefficient allows you to express these relationships quantitatively—that is, as a numerical index. The correlation coefficient (expressed as *r*) is a statistic that ranges from -1.0 to +1.0 and tells you two things: (1) its size indicates the strength of a relationship and (2) its sign (+ or -) indicates the direction of the relationship.

Reliability. The degree to which a test produces consistent scores on repeated testings.

Validity. The degree to which a test measures what the test is intended to measure.

How will I know if a standardized test is a reliable and valid measure of a learner's ability?

Correlation coefficient. A numerical index on a -1.0 to +1.0 scale that indicates the degree to which two sets of scores are related.

The Strength of r. A zero correlation indicates the absence of a relationship between the two characteristics being studied. As *r* increases from zero, whether positive or negative, the degree of the relationship gets stronger. An index of +1.0 is the highest positive *r* obtainable and indicates that the two sets of scores are perfectly related. An index of 0 means that no relationship exists.

Direction. As we have seen, sets of scores can be positively or negatively related. With positive relationships, the higher the scores on one behavior (for example, hours spent studying), the higher the score on the other behavior, with which it is correlated (for example, grades). Family income and years of education are positively related. So too are scores on an ability test and school achievement. Amount of time spent watching television is probably related to grades, but in a negative direction: the greater the number of hours a student spends in front of the TV, the lower his or her grades will be.

Correlation and Reliability. The best indicator of the reliability of an ability test score is how stable the score is over a period of time. If an important educational decision about a child is made in September on the basis of an ability test score, we would like to have confidence that this score will be the same in October or November.

We evaluate a test's stability by correlating the scores of a group of learners taken on one occasion with the scores of the same learners taken on another occasion. This is called **test-retest reliability.** For an ability test to be reliable, test-retest correlations need to be about .80 or higher, indicating very strong reliability. In other words, with high test reliability you feel confidant that the scores your learners earned on the standardized ability test will remain stable over time. This also means that you can make educational decisions based on these scores with confidence.

Correlation and Validity. Another important question about a test score is its validity. With standardized ability tests, the type of validity we are most concerned about is **predictive validity.** Predictive validity tells us how useful a test is for predicting how much learners will benefit from a future instructional program. The predictive validity of an ability test is determined by correlating a learner's ability before an instructional program with his achievement (for example, course grades, scores on standardized achievement tests, and sometimes teacher ratings of learning) at the end of the pro-

Test-retest reliability. The correlation of the scores of one group of learners taken on one occasion with the scores of the same group of learners taken on another occasion.

Predictive validity. In instruction, the usefulness of a test for predicting how much learners will benefit from some future instructional program; the correlation between a learner's ability before an instructional program and his or her achievement after the program.

All standardized tests must meet rigid standards of reliability and validity in order to be useful in the understanding of strengths and weaknesses of learners. Educators must be knowledgeable about these standards before choosing tests to assess learners.

gram. If the ability and achievement scores are correlated moderately or strongly, the ability test can be said to be valid. Predictive validity coefficients tend to be lower than reliability coefficients, usually ranging from about +.50 to +.80 or higher when a test is valid.

Over the past four decades, educational psychologists have conducted hundreds of research studies in order to establish the predictive validity of IQ tests. These studies have correlated scores on ability tests with academic achievement for nearly all ages of learners across almost all grade levels. Each of these studies has produced a correlation coefficient. The average of all these correlations is about +.50 (Eysenck, 1979; Gage & Berliner, 1988). In other words, students' IQ scores do allow us to predict, with a moderate degree of accuracy, how much each one will achieve in a course of instruction.

The Relevance of Standardized Ability Tests

Now that we have seen how standardized ability tests are constructed and interpreted, let's answer the three questions we raised earlier concerning their relevance to the classroom:

- How much does classroom learning depend on the skills that are measured by an ability test?
- Are these tests fair to learners from diverse cultures and ethnic backgrounds?
- Do such tests provide information useful for making instructional decisions in the classroom?

How Much Does School Learning Depend on Measured Ability?

Think of school learning as a pie and IQ as a slice of it. If we conceptualize school learning in this manner, we can ask the question: How large a piece of the classroom learning pie is taken up by IQ? Another way to ask this same question is this: Of all the factors that make a child successful in school, how important is IQ? Scarr (1981) indicates that many factors besides IQ will contribute to your learners' success: motivation, health, support from parents and friends, quality of teaching, prior knowledge, use of learning strategies, emotional stability, and feelings of acceptance and trust while in school, to name only a handful. Scarr classifies these factors under the term *social competence*. What percentage of school learning can we assign to IQ and what percentage to all the other factors that Scarr calls social competence? The answer, illustrated in Figure 11.5, is that about 25 percent can be attributed to IQ and about 75 percent to social competence.

> **How do I answer the question: "Is there a relationship between IQ and what my students learn in school?"**

So how important is IQ in predicting the degree to which a group of learners will benefit from school? IQ is important but, as we see, not as important as social competence. However, ability tests do allow us to predict with some confidence the degree to which certain learners will profit from instruction. Proponents of ability testing argue that if you had to predict who among a group of learners would learn the most in school, and you could choose only one piece of information about these learners, IQ scores would be the best choice (Eysenck, 1979). Even opponents of IQ testing agree that ability tests predict future achievement better than any other single measure. They acknowledge that ability tests allow educators to predict which children are most likely to learn at below-average, average, or above-average rates.

However, opponents of IQ testing also point out that such identification is of little value if (1) it stigmatizes learners, restricting rather than expanding their opportunities

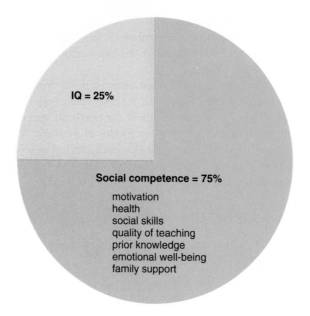

Figure 11.5
Factors contributing to school learning.

for growth and development, and (2) provides information that is of little use for making important instructional decisions in the classroom. The accompanying box, *Twenty Ways to Increase Your Learner's Social IQ*, describes some of the ways you can improve your learners' success in school. These can be posted in your classroom to remind students of some worthy personal goals. With these concerns in mind, let's turn to our next question, concerning the fairness of ability tests.

Are Ability Tests Fair to Learners from Diverse Cultures and Ethnic Backgrounds?

It is sometimes assumed in our culture that standardized tests are biased against certain minority groups, particularly African Americans and Hispanic Americans (Cole, 1981; Haney, 1981). You've probably said at some point in your education that "standardized tests are biased." So pause for a moment, and answer the question "Biased in what way?" Do you mean biased because they contain information or words that favor one racial, ethnic, or gender group over another? Or do you mean they are biased because they contain pictures or refer to specialized topics of greater significance to one group than to others? Test developers today screen test questions scrupulously for racial, ethnic, and gender insensitivity, making this source of bias much less a problem than in the past (Thorndike et al., 1991). Let's look at several other sources of test bias.

> Are ability tests fair to learners from various cultures and ethnic backgrounds?

Bias in Group Differences.   Maybe by bias you mean the fact that certain groups, on average, score higher than other groups on IQ tests. For example, on ability tests Asian Americans score higher than Anglo-Americans, who score higher than African Americans. These differences are cited as evidence of bias because of the assumption that all cultural groups should have the same average scores and distributions of scores on IQ tests (Reschly, 1981).

This assumption would be valid if IQ tests measured intelligence. As we learned earlier, one definition of intelligence is a global trait signifying a person's overall ability to adapt to and succeed in his or her environment. In this respect, no one cultural group

Applying Your Knowledge:

Twenty Ways to Increase
Your Learners' Social IQ

Post the following "IQ builders" in your classroom to remind learners how they can increase their social IQ:

1. Be self-motivating
2. Control your impulses
3. Persevere in the face of difficulties
4. Use your strengths, not your weaknesses
5. Translate your thoughts into actions
6. Acquire a product orientation
7. Complete tasks and follow through with details
8. Initiate actions on your own
9. Become independent of others
10. Delay gratification until the job is done
11. See the big picture you are working toward
12. Strike a balance between critical thinking and creative thinking
13. Become self-confident, but not overly so
14. Don't be afraid of failing
15. Don't postpone or put off tasks
16. Don't blame others for your mistakes
17. Don't engage in self-pity
18. Don't spread yourself too thin
19. Don't wallow in personal difficulties
20. Don't become distracted by events around you

Based on Sternberg, 1989.

can be said to be superior to another in "intelligence." However, IQ and other ability tests do not measure intelligence as a global trait. Instead, they measure certain cognitive processes such as attention, memory, comprehension, and logical reasoning, which are assumed to underlie school learning but which may or may not be strongly related to the ability to adapt to and succeed in one's environment. In other words, ability tests measure a limited set of skills, not the global quality "intelligence." Therefore, there may not be reason to assume that all groups should score the same on IQ tests.

Sample Bias. Some say that ability tests are biased because certain cultural groups are not represented in the norm group to the extent that they are represented in the general population. As with item bias, sample bias was present in some early IQ tests but is seldom a problem today. Test publishers would have difficulty marketing, and therefore do not develop, ability tests whose norms are based on unrepresentative groups (Jensen, 1980). This does not, however, preclude the need to check the characteristics of the norm group (given in the test manual) with the characteristics of the individuals to whom the test is given to insure that the most appropriate test and set of norms has been chosen.

Examiner and Language Bias. Most psychologists are Anglo-American and speak standardized English. Psychologists, educators, and parents concerned about test bias sometimes attribute the lower IQ scores of minority learners to this fact. The implication is that minority learners would obtain higher scores on ability tests if they were tested by members of their own culture. However, there is no research that substantiates this claim. Furthermore, most research indicates that IQ tests do not underestimate the school achievement of minority learners (Reynolds & Kaiser, 1990).

Predictive Validity Bias. A fifth type of bias is predictive validity bias. IQ tests exhibit this type of bias if they predict lower achievement for members of minority groups than members of these groups actually attain following instruction. Thus, IQ tests would be biased against African American or Hispanic American children if they predicted lower reading or math test scores than these learners actually achieved. Despite what some opponents of IQ tests assert, hundreds of studies have failed to find evidence of such predictive validity bias (Jensen, 1980; Kaufman, Harrison, & Ittenbach, 1990; Reynolds & Kaiser, 1990).

Bias in Test Use. Dan Reschly (1981), an educational psychologist at Iowa State University, has a unique perspective on bias in test use. Reschly believes that the tests themselves are not biased. His own research (Reschly, 1978; Reschly & Reschly, 1979; Reschly & Sabers, 1979), as well as that of others (Reynolds & Kaiser, 1990), presents evidence that current ability tests measure the cognitive abilities of learners from minority cultures as accurately as they measure the abilities of learners from the majority culture. According to Reschly, the group differences between majority and minority groups on ability tests reflect real differences in certain aspects of learning ability. African American, Native American, and Hispanic American learners earn lower IQ scores than Anglo-Americans and Asian Americans, and these tests predict the achievement of all groups of learners with about the same accuracy ($r = .50$).

Nevertheless, while the scores themselves may be unbiased, the use to which they have been put may have been to the disadvantage of minority children. Rather than being used to design educational environments that promote learning and development, these scores have been used to place some learners in lower-track classrooms, in low-ability reading groups, and in special education programs of unknown instructional effectiveness. To back up his claims of bias in test use, Reschly cites statistics that demonstrate that African American, Hispanic American, Native American, and economically disadvantaged learners are overrepresented in special education programs for the mentally retarded. At the same time, these groups are underrepresented in programs for the gifted.

Reschly, like Edmund Gordon and Molidawn Terrell (Gordon & Terrell, 1981), points out that our social values should encourage the development of ability tests that enhance opportunities for all individuals. All three argue that the IQ tests used in grade schools, as well as college tests such as the Scholastic Aptitude Test (SAT), Graduate Record Exams (GRE), Law School Admissions Test (LSAT), and Medical College Admission Tests (MCAT), perform a gatekeeping function. They admit members of some groups to the best educational programs while denying access to these programs to other groups.

In order to examine Reschly's position on test bias, it is important to recall the original purpose for which ability tests were created. The need for such tests arose out of concerns for providing appropriate educational services to individuals who could not benefit from regular classroom instruction. The expectation was that such tests would increase the educational opportunities for this special population of learners. Thus the original purpose of the psychological assessment of learning ability was to individualize education in order to promote learning and development. Reschly argues that ability assessment as it is practiced in public schools today may have abandoned this mission. In its place is an emphasis on labeling, identification, and placement in special education programs, which may not always benefit the learner. In Chapter 14 we will examine research on the effectiveness of some of these programs (Ysseldyke & Marston, 1990).

Standardized tests have been criticized for performing a gatekeeping function vis-à-vis minority groups; they admit too many minority learners to programs for learners with mental retardation and learning disabilities and too few to programs for the gifted and talented.

Reschly concludes that our current social and multicultural context requires a return to the original mission of psychological assessment: to expand the learning opportunities for all children. He advocates that ability assessment abandon its current emphasis on testing, classification, and placement, replacing it with testing for instructional planning and intervention.

Now, let's answer our third and final question.

Do Ability Tests Provide Information Useful for Instructional Decision Making?

After reading Reschly's claims about the misuse of IQ scores, you may be asking, "Well, why aren't these tests used for instructional planning and intervention?" Bergan and Dunn (1976) have a straightforward answer to this question: They aren't designed to! Here is their argument. As you study it, recall what was said earlier about the assumptions that underlie the psychometric tradition.

Argument 1: Instructional Validity. Bergan and Dunn and others (for example, Elliott & Shapiro, 1990; Gipps, 1995; Ysseldyke & Marston, 1990) have been advocating for two decades that we hold ability assessment to a higher standard than the traditional one of predictive validity. As you will recall, IQ test proponents base the usefulness of such tests on research showing that they are the single best predictors of school achievement.

Bergan and Dunn contend that it isn't enough for assessment scores to correlate with learner achievement; they must also show the way to attain higher achievement. Instead, as Reschly illustrates, they sometimes have been used to label, classify, place, and even deny educational opportunities to diverse learners. Bergan and Dunn,

> **Can knowing my learners' IQs help me make day-to-day instructional decisions in my classroom?**

A test has instructional validity if its results can be used to improve instruction and learning.

Instructional validity. The belief that tests must be valid for improving instruction and learning.

therefore, advocate that tests should be required to demonstrate **instructional validity.** That is, they must be valid for improving instruction and learning.

Unfortunately, as Bergan and Dunn go on to show, current ability tests can't have instructional validity because they lack two fundamental properties: (1) behavioral definitions of the abilities that are measured and (2) specification of how the skill being measured was chosen or sampled from all the possible skills that could measure that ability.

Argument 2: Behavioral Definition. If you read the test manuals of the widely used ability tests, such as the Wechsler Scales, Stanford-Binet, McCarthy Scales, or Kaufman Assessment Battery for Children, you will see the following abilities highlighted: verbal reasoning, word fluency, verbal ability, numerical ability, rote memory, spatial ability, sequential processing, simultaneous processing, perceptual speed and accuracy, and inductive reasoning.

The manuals typically list these abilities, identify test questions that require them, and present reliability and validity correlation coefficients as evidence that these abilities are being measured. But, as Bergan and Dunn point out, the tests fail to behaviorally define what these abilities are. They do not describe precisely which observable functions the learner must perform to exhibit each ability. They lack an *operational definition.* Bergan and Dunn state that ability tests have instructional value only when they can describe in observable terms the precise cognitive processes or mental operations that make up spatial ability, verbal fluency, sequential processing, and so forth.

As a point of reference, compare this lack of behavioral definition for spatial ability or numerical ability with Gagné's behavioral definition of "conservation ability" described in Chapter 4. Notice that Gagné identifies precise concepts and rules that a learner must acquire in order to exhibit the ability to conserve. Similarly, one can define that ability in terms of the intellectual skills (facts, concepts, principles, and so on) a learner must acquire and demonstrate.

For an ability test to have instructional validity, the intellectual skills that underlie numerical, spatial, reasoning, or verbal ability must be defined with the same level of detail. If such detailed definition is lacking, teachers who know the ability test results of their learners still do not know which specific skills to teach them in order to improve their abilities. They only have a statistic (percentile) that indicates how the learner performed relative to a norm group.

Argument 3: Sampling Specificity. One of the consequences of not having a precise behavioral definition for the abilities being measured is the lack of sampling specificity. *Sampling specificity* refers to the clarity with which a test developer describes the test sampling plan or blueprint for test question development and selection (Kubiszyn & Borich, 1996). For example, suppose that you are preparing a multiplication test for your learners to measure the following skills:

- recall of multiplication facts
- multiplication of two-digit numbers by a one- or two-digit number without carrying
- multiplication of two-digit numbers by a one-digit number with carrying.

Many problems (called the *universe of test content*) could be devised to assess these skills. But due to limitations in testing time, your test can contain only a small sample of test items. Therefore, you need a test sampling plan that describes how you will select the content for a relatively few items from the universe of test content. This test plan requires that you make explicit your decisions about (1) how many test items you will write to measure each skill, (2) what content will be covered, and (3) how many items must be answered correctly for you to conclude that the skill was mastered.

Figure 11.6 shows a test developed from such a plan and a learner's responses. By noting the commonality among wrong answers (circled), we find that this learner needs more practice on multiplication problems that require carrying, a skill that was identified in the test plan.

Ability test developers, however, did not intend for their tests to have Bergan and Dunn's instructional validity, so it is unfair to fault them for failing to accomplish a purpose they never set out to achieve. Nevertheless, their point (and that of Reschly) is that we are at a time in our development as a nation when identification, labeling, selection, and placement of learners (the goals of ability tests) should have lower priority than equality of access to effective instructional programs.

Summary Comments About Present-Day Ability Tests

IQ tests are used in many settings other than education—for example, in business, law, and psychiatry, and for psychological diagnosis in clinical practice, in which they function effectively for the purposes for which they are used. The use of ability tests in the classroom for matching instruction to the abilities of diverse learners has become controversial, however. For most of the twentieth century and continuing to the present day, educational psychologists, public school administrators, and teachers have turned to ability tests to help them understand why some learners fail in school. They expect

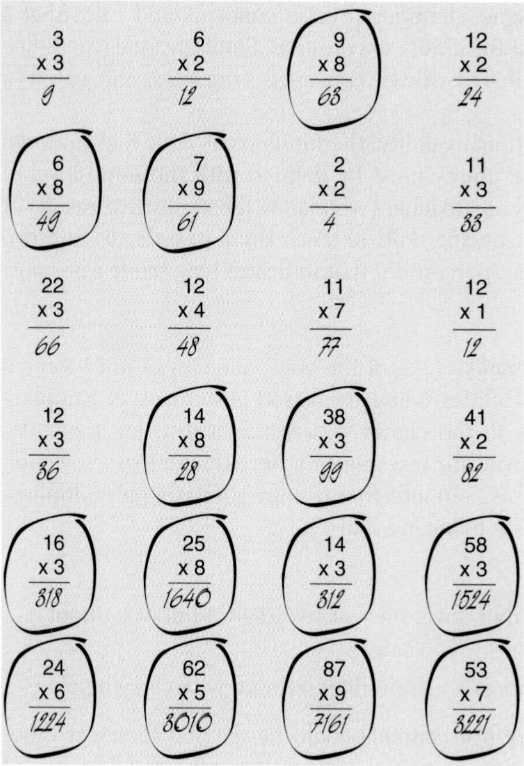

3 × 3 = 9	6 × 2 = 12	9 × 8 = 68	12 × 2 = 24
6 × 8 = 49	7 × 9 = 61	2 × 2 = 4	11 × 3 = 33
22 × 3 = 66	12 × 4 = 48	11 × 7 = 77	12 × 1 = 12
12 × 3 = 36	14 × 8 = 28	38 × 3 = 99	41 × 2 = 82
16 × 3 = 318	25 × 8 = 1640	14 × 3 = 312	58 × 3 = 1524
24 × 6 = 1224	62 × 5 = 3010	87 × 9 = 7161	53 × 7 = 3221

Figure 11.6
Results of a multiplication test derived from a test plan indicating specific skills to be remediated.

such tests to help identify the basis of learning problems and point the way to resolving them.

As we have seen, IQ tests measure some but not all of the abilities that are required for classroom learning. While the scores on IQ tests predict classroom learning with some accuracy, they explain only about 25 percent of what accounts for school learning. The scores from IQ tests alone, therefore, are not sufficient for diagnosing learning deficits and planning effective instruction.

Although the psychometric approach has not resulted in tests for instructional planning, it has yielded a technology for making assessment tools that are predominantly free from socioeconomic, cultural, ethnic, gender, and other forms of bias. Before the pioneering work of Alfred Binet, characteristics such as physical appearance, sensorimotor ability, economic resources, gender, and race routinely were considered in deciding who was and was not capable of learning (Matarrazo, 1972). As we have seen, out of the psychometric approach has come a set of standards for item development, item selection, norm development, and reliability and validity that all tests should meet.

Alternative Ways of Assessing Learning Ability

If traditional ability tests lack instructional validity, are there assessment procedures that do have that validity? Furthermore, if IQ scores are insufficient for grouping learners to better match their learning needs, what do we use in their place? Or is ability grouping an ineffective educational practice regardless of the assessment procedures used? Let's look at some practical alternatives to ability tests.

Getting Along Without IQ Tests

You may be asking yourself why we don't abandon the search for tests of learning ability and assess only learner achievement. This approach might be taken if there were little difference in the amount of knowledge that individual learners acquire in school. Instead, there are wide variations among learners in reading, arithmetic, science, language, and writing achievement. As long as such variability exists, we need to know why.

Similarly, there will always be a need to identify learners who require special educational services, but in a way that informs us precisely what these services should entail. As we have seen, current ability tests allow us to reliably identify students who have learning problems but often fail to provide instructional guidance for resolving them. What is needed are standardized, nondiscriminatory tests that allow us to identify students with special learning needs and then point the way to diagnosing and remediating learning deficits.

The goal of an effective test of learning ability, therefore, should be to provide reliable and valid information about learner characteristics that can be used to design and improve classroom instruction. One shortcoming of the psychometric approach applied to the classroom was that it resulted in tests that only minimally met this goal. As we learned, out of this tradition came tests that provide only relative information about broadly defined learner characteristics.

Are there learner characteristics that would be useful for teachers, learners, and their parents to know about? Suppose you were designing reading or math instruction for a group of 25 fourth-grade learners. Is there information you would want to know at the start of the school year? If some learners were experiencing difficulty with your instruction, what would you want to know to help you understand and improve their performance? A logical approach to answering these questions would start with the basic question: What cognitive processes are involved in the act of learning? Let's review what learners do as they acquire new knowledge, and learn about some recent developments in how learning ability can be assessed.

Assessing Learning Ability: The Cognitive Approach

The psychometric tradition set out to determine how learners differ from one another in learning ability. The expectation was that by identifying how and in what ways learners differ, we could better match instruction to these individual differences. But as we have seen, the psychometric approach tends to describe these differences in terms of global, broadly defined abilities rather than observable and teachable behaviors.

How can I use the cognitive approach to learning to understand and improve my students' performance?

The cognitive approach to learning ability examines the information-processing activities that learners engage in when acquiring new knowledge. Hunt (1976, 1978) and Sternberg (1977, 1988) are two proponents of this approach. They have identified three broad components of learning behavior that can be measured and that are potentially useful for assessing learning ability: memory stores, memory processes, and executive processes (see Chapter 5 for a review of the information-processing model).

Memory Stores. As we learned in Chapter 5, the information-processing model of learning has identified three types of memory: short-term sensory memory (STSM), short-term memory (STM), and long-term memory (LTM). The cognitive approach to learning ability has focused on the importance of STM in acquiring new knowledge.

Information on the holding capacity and processing speed of your learners' STM can be potentially useful in planning instruction. For example, if you know that a particular learner has a limited STM, you could adopt the techniques in the accompanying box, *How to Increase Your Learners' Memory and Processing Speed*.

How to Increase Your Learners' Memory and Processing Speed

- Reduce the amount of information that must be held in memory in order to solve a problem. For example, rather than requiring the learner to remember several rules simultaneously to solve a problem, provide a written list of the rules.
- Teach techniques for increasing the holding capacity of short-term memory, such as jingles or trigger sentences, narrative chaining, number rhyme or peg word, and chunking, as described in Chapter 5. For example, group bits of information into sets of five to seven logical categories, such as memorizing food types by splitting them into diary products, vegetables, beverages, etc.
- Make sure your learners can perform, automatically and correctly, the prerequisite skills for problem solving. Provide activity sheets, problem sets, and handouts with which to practice and assess prerequisite skills. Eventually, teach your learners how to make paper-and-pencil memory aids for themselves, in the form of outlines, flowcharts, and diagrams.
- Organize your lessons around a limited set of interdisciplinary ideas, called key understandings and principles. These may include *concepts,* such as "freedom," "cooperation," "conflict," "discovery," "change," or "culture"; or *topics,* such as "individual," "society," "community," "relationships," "war," or "partnerships"; or *categories,* such as "time," "laws," "experiences," "living things," or "numbers." By connecting content under common labels, it will be more easily remembered.

Memory Processes. Memory processes involve attention, rehearsal, storage or encoding, and retrieval. The cognitive approach to assessing learning ability holds that learners who differ in reading or math achievement also differ in the ability to focus attention on relevant instructional stimuli, spontaneously rehearse new information, organize information for storage, and quickly retrieve information from LTM. Each of these memory processes can be assessed with methods that involve presenting new information to learners while observing and recording their responses. Many of these assessment techniques use computers to present learning stimuli and record learner performance.

Such techniques allow us to describe a particular student's learning strengths and weaknesses in terms of skills, which can be taught, rather than in terms of abilities, which cannot. Instead of being puzzled about why a particular learner has trouble solving math problems or understanding what she reads, the cognitive approach would have us ask questions such as these: What can we do to improve a learner's skill in focusing attention, rehearsing information, organizing information, or remembering it when needed?

Executive Processes. Cognitive psychologists like Hunt (1976) have devised reliable tests of memory capacity and processes. However, they have not yet done the same for most of the executive processes or cognitive learning strategies, such as comprehension monitoring or IDEAL, which were described in Chapter 5. Nevertheless, some preliminary work is being done in this regard, particularly with learners identified as having specific learning disabilities and mental retardation (Mayer, 1987). We will study about such learners in Chapter 14. Research on the learning abilities of these individuals holds the promise of being able to reliably measure and teach some of the cognitive strategies that are significant for acquiring new knowledge.

Some Final Comments on the Assessment of Learning Ability

The cognitive approach to assessing learning ability is not the only alternative to the psychometric tradition. However, whatever approach may come to supplement our current IQ and ability tests, it will likely address the following characteristics of learning.

Learning Is a Process. The psychometric tradition sought to measure the outcomes of learning (vocabulary, information, sequencing, relationships, and so forth), rather than the processes involved in achieving these outcomes. Any new approach to assessing learning ability is likely to emphasize the process of learning. For example, new assessment instruments might present information to learners while observing and recording both the product (what they learn) and the process (how they learn).

Learning Ability Can Be Improved. The psychometric approach originated at a time when people believed that learning ability was inherited, fixed, and largely immutable. These beliefs exerted a strong influence on the manner in which tests of learning ability were constructed and interpreted. We now know that some types of learning ability can be enhanced and that many skills can be instrumental in doing so. New approaches to ability testing are likely to be based on the modifiability of learning ability and the identification of learning abilities that can be changed through instruction.

Learning Occurs in a Social Context. Tests derived from the psychometric approach viewed learning as a largely private act. The results of such tests placed learners in programs emphasizing self-paced mastery learning, in which the teacher served as manager and the presence of other learners was tangential to the learning process. One goal of the assessment of learning ability in the future, however, may be to better measure children's learning needs within the social context of the classroom. As we saw in Chapter 8, classrooms are social settings, and most classroom learning takes place in a social context. Consequently, since learning is an inherently social act, new approaches to ability testing are likely to take into account the effect that teachers and peers have on the process of learning.

Tracking: Grouping Learners by Ability

For nearly 80 years, IQ scores and other ability tests have been the principal basis by which many public school learners have been organized into groups. Some schools use these scores to sort learners into high-ability, average-ability, and low-ability classes to better provide for learner differences. Are such arrangements equitable and effective?

While an increasing number of educational researchers and policy makers are convinced that such ability grouping, or **tracking,** should be abandoned, this view is not shared by everyone. Here is a sample of some of the diverse opinions on this controversial practice.

Advocates of Heterogeneous Grouping

If tracking would help us accomplish our goals at this school, then we would use it. But we believe in producing active thinkers, critical thinkers, and risk-takers, and tracking our students by ability quite simply doesn't allow us to achieve our goals. (John D'Auria, in Wheelock, 1992, p. 6)

Tracking. Grouping learners into different classes according to scores on standardized tests of learning ability.

Heterogeneous grouping. In education, assigning learners to classes or learning groups in a manner that insures that these groups will include a diverse mixture of learners.

Research is calling into question the practice of grouping learners in classrooms by ability—a process called tracking. While proponents of tracking argue that homogeneous grouping is the best way to help learners achieve their potential, opponents argue that homogeneous grouping stigmatizes slow learners while not necessarily improving the achievement of rapid learners.

I've never worked so hard being creative, but I'm also convinced I'm teaching better. (Rene Comack, in Wheelock, 1992, p. 10)

What I've stopped seeing is very talented, bright children feeling they're not worth a bit of salt because they haven't made it into an elitist program for students labeled "gifted." I'm seeing all kids realize that there are lots of kids who can contribute to learning even when what they contribute is different from them. (Sue Galletti, in Wheelock, 1992, p. 10)

Advocates of Homogeneous Grouping

Homogeneous grouping. The tracking or ability grouping of learners into instructional clusters that are defined by aptitude as measured by ability tests.

People are making decisions on the basis of political considerations. . . . It is not a time for sweeping change. Our schools are already in jeopardy. . . . When grouping is not used, high-ability children will suffer. For the most part, they get no special attention in mixed classrooms. . . . For children who are very precocious to sit in a classroom and be offered nothing but the normative level of instruction is deadly boring and unmotivating. (John Feldhausen, in Mansnerus, 1992, p. 16)

What the administration is saying in terms of cooperative education is that people like my son become an example for the others. Their job is being a model, and I think it's very stressful for young children. (Christine Platt, in Mansnerus, 1992, p. 16)

As I see it, tracking here means identifying different special populations of children and then providing for their specific needs. [Our] students are working a grade level ahead and I don't think it's fair to hold them back just to help others catch up. (Brenda Lanclos, in Suro, 1992, p. 18)

Who's right? Who's winning? Both sides of the "tracking war" can present arguments to support their respective positions. Let's see what the most up-to-date research says about the effects of tracking. First, review Table 11.3 to check your understanding of some important terms heard in the debate.

Table 11.3

Terms Used in the Tracking Debate

Term	Definition
Ability grouping	Any sorting or arrangement of learners for instructional purposes, usually on the basis of standardized test scores. This includes grouping students into different classes or within a single class, as when learners are grouped for math instruction.
Between-class grouping	The practice of assigning learners to separate classes of low-, middle-, and high-achieving groups. These assignments are usually based on standardized IQ or achievement test scores, and sometimes on teacher recommendations.
Within-class flexible grouping	As the expression suggests, assigning learners to homogeneous math or reading skills groups within a class, but only for teaching specific skills and with regrouping as skills are mastered and new ones are introduced.
Cooperative learning	Assigning students with diverse abilities to a single group to work on specific projects; each learner has a specific role to play to help the group achieve its goal.
Detracking (untracking)	The dismantling of between-class (but not within-class) ability groups.
Heterogeneous grouping	Assigning learners to classes or groups more or less randomly. While cooperative learning involves heterogeneous grouping, children are not randomly assigned.
Tracking	Often used synonymously with "ability grouping" and "homogeneous grouping." Historically, tracking refers to the practice of separating learners for nearly all subjects into different career tracks—for example, a vocational track or a college preparatory track. More recently, however, it has come to represent ability or homogeneous grouping for particular subjects.

Tracking: What the Research Says

Approximately 80 percent of secondary schools and 60 percent of elementary schools use some form of tracking (O'Neil, 1992). The argument typically offered in favor of ability grouping is a convincing one: It allows schools to better differentiate instruction by giving high achievers the challenge and low achievers the support each needs to learn.

Opponents of tracking attack it on two grounds: (1) It is undemocratic, and (2) it fails to increase learner productivity. Let's examine some of the questions that researchers have studied to support or refute these claims.

How Representative Are the Tracked Groups? Figures 11.7 and 11.8 present data relating ability grouping to race, ethnicity, and socioeconomic status. These data were gathered from a national study involving 14,000 eighth-grade students in public schools. Figure 11.7 indicates that Asian and Anglo learners were more likely to be grouped into the high-ability category in English and math classes, while the opposite was true for Hispanic, African American, and Native American students.

Figure 11.8 shows how learners in the top and bottom quarters in socioeconomic status fared in terms of ability grouping. Learners in the top socioeconomic quarter were more likely to be categorized in the high-ability group than learners in the bottom socioeconomic quarter (Mansnerus, 1992). Thus the argument of opponents of ability

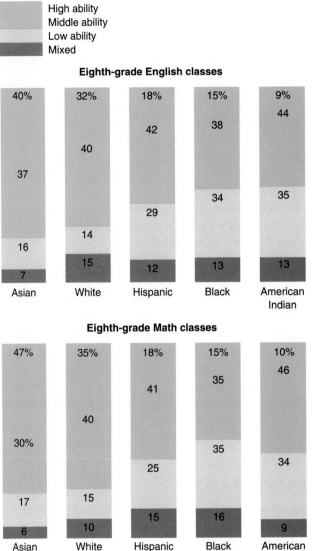

Figure 11.7
Ability grouping by race and ethnicity. *Source:* From the Education Life section of the *New York Times,* November 1, 1992. Copyright © 1992 by The New York Times Company. Reprinted by permission.

grouping that such a practice is biased against certain groups appears to rest on some evidence. Some feel that these data alone are reason enough to avoid grouping by ability. Cloyd Hastings, principal of McCoy Elementary School in Carrollton, Texas, is one of them:

> The answer to the debate on ability grouping is not to be found in new research. There exists a body of philosophic absolutes that should include this statement: The ability grouping of students for educational opportunities in a democratic society is ethically unacceptable. (In Gamoran, 1992, p. 14)

Others agree with Hastings. The National Governors' Association endorsed detracking in its national education goals. The Carnegie Foundation's "Turning Points," a 1988 task force report on middle grades, came out strongly against tracking, as did the National

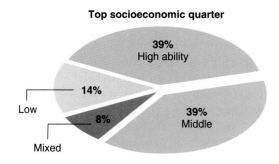

Top socioeconomic quarter

39% High ability

14% Low

8% Mixed

39% Middle

Figure 11.8
Ability grouping by socioeconomics. *Source:* Illustration by Philippe Weisbecker, from the Education Life section of the *New York Times,* November 1, 1992. Copyright © 1992 by The New York Times Company. Reprinted by permission.

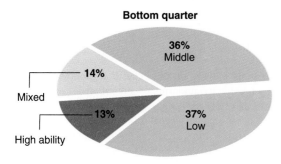

Bottom quarter

36% Middle

14% Mixed

13% High ability

37% Low

Education Association (Mansnerus, 1992). But are there educational benefits to tracking that offset its inequality?

Has Tracking Improved Overall School Achievement? Studies by Slavin (1987, 1991), Fogelman (1983), and Kerchoff (1986) conclude that little evidence supports the claim that tracking increases overall school achievement compared to heterogeneous grouping. These studies have been conducted at the elementary level only. There are few secondary schools that do not use some form of ability grouping. Although Slavin (1987) found that between-class ability grouping fails to raise school achievement, he reports that subject-specific, within-class, flexible grouping for math and reading does have positive effects.

Has Tracking Narrowed or Widened the Achievement Gap Between High- and Low-Ability Learners? Gamoran (1992) conducted a national survey that followed more than 20,000 learners in grades 10 through 12 who were academically tracked into high- and low-ability classes. His data show that in the progression through high school, high-track students gain, while low-track learners fall farther behind. In addition, Gamoran reports an even greater disparity in achievement between those assigned to different tracks than between learners who dropped out of school in the tenth grade and those who remained in school. Gamoran's surprising conclusion is that the program a learner pursued in school had more to do with achievement than whether or not the learner was in school.

Do High Achievers Benefit From Tracking? Although tracking does not increase a school's overall achievement, do certain groups of learners benefit from it? For example, do high achievers who are in high-ability classes learn more than high achievers in heterogeneously grouped classes?

Slavin (1987, 1990a) has gathered extensive research data to answer this question. His research makes a distinction between high achievers and the gifted. High achievers are those learners who score in the top 33 percent on standardized tests of ability and achievement, whereas gifted learners represent the top 3 to 5 percent. Slavin compared high achievers in ability-grouped classes with high achievers in mixed-ability classes in the areas of reading vocabulary, reading comprehension, language mechanics, language expression, math computation, and math concepts and applications. He found no significant advantages for ability-grouped high achievers. He did find, however, that gifted learners placed in accelerated programs (those in which a grade could be skipped or advanced courses taken) gained over similar learners who were not so placed. Slavan found no evidence to justify enrichment programs for gifted learners. Enrichment programs, which make up the overwhelming majority of gifted and talented education programs, do not allow acceleration or advanced course placement, according to Slavin.

Slavin drew the following conclusions about tracking:

> Since arguments for ability grouping depend entirely on the belief that grouping increases achievement, the absence of such evidence undermines any rationale for the practice. The harm done by ability groups, I believe, lies not primarily in effects on achievement but in other impacts on low and average achievers. For example, low track students are more likely to be delinquent or to drop out of school than similar low achievers not in the low track [Wiatrowski, Hansell, Massey, & Wilson, 1982]. Perhaps, most important, tracking works against our national ideology that all are created equal and our desire to be one nation. The fact that African-American, Hispanic, and low socioeconomic students in general wind up so often in the low tracks is repugnant on its face. Why would we want to organize our schools this way if we have no evidence that it helps students learn? (Slavin, 1991, p. 70)

Will Untracking Increase Overall School Achievement? The research reviewed so far fails to make a strong case for continuing the practice of tracking—nor does it make a case for abolishing tracking as a way to improve achievement. Moreover, if untracking were to result simply in untracked classes resembling low-tracked ones (for example, reduced content, overreliance on direct instruction, repetitive practice), an overall reduction in school achievement could result.

Schools seeking to untrack can learn some lessons from those that have already done so. Since 1990, the Massachusetts Advocacy Center has made site visits to over 250 untracked middle schools and interviewed administrators, teachers, parents, and learners. Here is some of what they learned about successful alternatives to tracking (Wheelock, 1992):

> **What can my school do to ensure that both high- and low-ability learners experience the same effective instruction?**

- The motivation for untracking should be to improve the education of all learners. All learners should experience more indirect and self-directed modes of instruction.

- Successful untracking springs from a belief that all students can learn. Schools that have successfully untracked are characterized by high expectations for all learners.

- Breaking down ability groups should proceed hand in hand with building up the curriculum for all learners. This includes making important reforms in curriculum development, instruction, assessment, and counseling. The overall learning environment should be leveled up, not scaled down.

- Parents should be involved in the planning and implementing of heterogeneous grouping. Principals of untracked schools report that parents can make or break the process.

- Schools should phase in implementation and have a multiyear plan: eliminate bottom tracks first, and merge them into middle tracks, or set up heterogeneous groups at the lower grades and move up a grade per year.

- Teachers should be trained in instructional techniques suitable for diverse learners. They should be allowed to learn and experiment with techniques such as cooperative learning, peer tutoring, and within-class flexible grouping.

Untracked classes require teachers who are skilled enough, and flexible enough, to meet the needs of students of varying ability levels simultaneously. Developing those skills will be the topic of Chapter 14, which covers exceptional and at-risk learners. Meanwhile, however, in Chapters 12 and 13 we will consider two additional topics that involve the assessment of learners: assessing learners in the classroom through the use of objective measures of achievement, and constructing performance assessments of learning.

Summing Up

This chapter introduced you to ability and standardized assessment. Its main points were these:

- Intelligence includes not only the ability to learn academic subjects, deal with abstractions, and solve problems but also the ability to withstand stress and distraction, and be motivated, emotionally stable, interested in learning, and socially competent.
- The psychometric approach comprises the following set of assumptions: (1) a psychological attribute or trait can be measured by systematically observing and recording its effects; (2) repeated observations of a psychological trait will overcome any imprecision in the observations themselves; (3) ability is best measured as a quantity rather than as a cognitive process; and (4) the amount of ability possessed can be established through relative rather than absolute measurement.
- The first practical IQ test for the purpose of measuring the ability of learners to benefit from regular classroom instruction, developed by Alfred Binet, (1) was consistent with a unidimensional theory of intelligence, (2) could be used in a one-on-one assessment format, and (3) accurately distinguished learners who needed special instruction from those who did not.
- Qualitative item analysis includes checking test directions for clarity, style, and conciseness and screening items for bias and ethnic, racial, and gender stereotypes. Quantitative item analysis consists of trying out the test on a sample of individuals for whom it is designed and computing the index of item difficulty and index of item discrimination.
- The index of item difficulty is the proportion of individuals in the test tryout who answered the item correctly. The index of item discrimination is the degree to which a test item measures the same ability measured by every other item.

- The process of standardization involves administering the test to a defined group in the same way under the same conditions. The group of individuals upon whom the test is standardized is called the norm group.
- Percentile ranks indicate where a person's score ranks in comparison with others of the same age or grade.
- A correlation is a numerical index that indicates the degree to which two sets of scores are related.
- The best indicator of the reliability of an ability test score is how stable the score is over a period of time (test-retest reliability).
- The best indicator of the validity of an ability test is the extent to which it can predict future achievement (predictive validity).
- Test bias can consist of (1) ethnic, race, and gender bias; (2) group difference bias; (3) sample bias; (4) examiner and language bias; (5) predictive validity bias; or (6) bias in test use.
- Instructional validity is the ability of a test to improve instruction and learning by diagnosing specific learning deficits and providing guidance for planning effective instruction.
- The cognitive approach to learning ability examines the information-processing activities that learners engage in when acquiring new knowledge. Three categories of learning behavior that can be tested and possibly improved with this approach are memory stores, memory processes, and executive processes.
- Research on tracking indicates that the practice may be inherently unfair and does not seem to benefit learners, with the possible exception of the gifted.

For Discussion and Practice

°1. What was Jim Nehring's principal argument against heterogeneously grouped classes? Do you agree with his position? If not, why not?

°2. Create two different definitions of intelligence and explain how you would measure them.

°3. In your own words, explain why the use of intelligence testing in schools is controversial.

°4. Identify and give one example of each of the four assumptions that underlie the psychometric approach.

°5. Describe two characteristics that distinguish individual from group ability tests and two characteristics that distinguish general from multiple ability tests.

°6. What were Alfred Binet's specific goals in developing the first practical IQ test? In your opinion, have they been met?

°7. Using Table 11.2, find and interpret the age-equivalent score for an 8-year-old learner whose raw score is 50. Overall, how would you describe this learner's performance?

°8. How is test-retest reliability determined? What minimal standard of test-retest reliability should a standardized test meet?

Questions marked with an asterisk are answered in the appendix.

*9. Describe how a test developer would go about establishing the predictive validity of an ability test. What minimal standard of predictive validity should a standardized test meet?

*10. Approximately what percent of school learning can be predicted from IQ? What other factors contribute to school learning?

11. Create an example of your own choosing that illustrates each of the following examples of test bias: racial bias, gender bias, bias in group differences, sample bias, examiner bias, predictive validity bias, bias in test use. Which appears to be the most pervasive today?

*12. In your own words, pose three arguments against the usefulness of ability tests for diagnosing learning deficits and planning effective instruction.

*13. Select two tests with which you are familiar, one that you believe has instructional validity, and another that does not. What characteristics distinguish the two tests?

*14. Imagine for a moment that you have been given the responsibility of developing a new kind of ability test. What characteristics would you want your test to have?

*15. Citing evidence from the research literature and your own experience, answer the question "Are there educational benefits to tracking?"

Suggested Readings

Chariot of Software. (1994). *STatView student.* This easy-to-use computer program performs the statistical analyses most used by the classroom teacher, including correlations and the standard deviation. See also Micrograde 2.0 and Microtest III by the same company for item analysis, grading, and test construction programs for your PC. Available from 3659 India St., San Diego, CA 92103 (telephone: 619-298-0202).

Gutkin, T., & Reynolds, C. (1990). *The handbook of school psychology* (2nd ed.). New York: Wiley. Contains detailed discussions of ability testing and how it is used in school settings. Also includes chapters that examine alternatives to IQ testing, particularly for exceptional learners.

Kubiszyn, T., & Borich, G. (1996). *Educational testing and measurement: Classroom application and practice* (5th ed.). New York: HarperCollins. Explains classroom testing and statistics in a readable style. Offers plenty of examples and practice for computing the statistics most used by classroom teachers.

Matarazzo, J. D. (1972). *Wechsler's measurement and appraisal of adult intelligence* (5th ed.). Baltimore: Williams & Wilkins. This is the book to read for those interested in theories of intelligence and some of the attempts to measure it.

Assessing for Learning:
Objective and Essay Tests

This chapter will help you answer the following questions about your learners:

- How can I make sure that my assessments are fair to students?
- How can I make sure my classroom tests measure what I teach?
- How can I write test questions that require learners to use the same thought processes emphasized during my instruction?
- How do I choose among test item formats for an objective test?
- How do I write objective test questions that accurately measure what I have taught?
- How do I write multiple-choice items that measure higher-order thinking skills?
- How do I write essay questions that accurately measure what I have taught?
- Can essay tests be scored reliably?
- Should I base my grades on how a learner's achievement compares with the achievement of other learners, or should I base them on a standard of mastery that I determine?
- How do I combine different indicators of achievement, such as classwork, homework, quizzes, and projects, into a final grade?

Geri Dalton is principal of Fawkes Middle School. Last summer she attended a workshop on the assessment of classroom learning. As a result of three days of rigorous training in assessment techniques, she decided that her major goal this year will be to improve classroom testing and grading at Fawkes Middle School.

It is now the fall term, just six weeks after the first grades have been sent home. Ms. Dalton has planned individual meetings with her teachers to discuss their testing and grading practices, beginning with her first-year teachers. Richard Steele is first on her list.

Ms. Dalton: Come in, Richard. Please sit down. I reviewed the description of your grading system that you sent home to parents at the start of the year, and I'd like to ask a few questions.

Mr. Steele: Fine. But please be kind. I never had a course in testing in college and it's been trial and error for me.

Ms. Dalton: What about during student teaching?

Mr. Steele: Well, my supervising teacher had a pretty complicated system, but she never really explained it. So what I eventually came up with is a mixture of things I remember from when I was in grade school, practices I saw in college, and whatever I picked up last year from observing other teachers.

Ms. Dalton: That's pretty typical. Most teachers develop a testing and grading system based on the very things that you considered.

Mr. Steele: I'd appreciate any suggestions you have.

Ms. Dalton: OK. Let's first look at what you base a grade on. You're using chapter tests 30 percent, daily quizzes 10 percent, homework 20 percent, notebook 20 percent, and class participation 20 percent. Why did you choose those activities and those percentages?

Mr. Steele: Well, those are the things I have them do in my class, and the percentages are small enough to all add up to 100 percent, yet large enough to be meaningful. That way, if the students don't do the notebook, for example, their grade drops 20 percent. That motivates them.

Ms. Dalton: So tests make up 40 percent of the grade, while homework, a notebook, and participation count 60 percent. You're implying that tests are less important for assessing learning than informal measures. Is that what you want? Do you think parents realize when they see a grade of 90 that most of that was not based on tests?

Mr. Steele: I never looked at it that way. I was just trying to balance everything out.

Ms. Dalton: How do you grade the notebook and participation?

Mr. Steele: Well, it's somewhat subjective. I base each grade on 100 points, and I assign a certain number of points at the end of the six weeks depending on the quality of the notebook and the quality of participation.

Ms. Dalton: I didn't see any criteria for assigning these points in your classroom evaluation plan, so I assume you didn't write anything down. Is that right?

Mr. Steele: Yes.

Ms. Dalton: So the most subjective aspects of your grading system count as much as the most objective—your tests. Is that what you intended?

Mr. Steele: I really didn't look at my system that analytically. I was just doing what I saw other teachers do.

Ms. Dalton: You have a really diverse group of learners in your class. Some are better at writing than speaking, and vice versa. Some have good memories but may be weak in problem solving. Others reason well when you're talking to them but can't do it under the time constraints of an essay test. How do you take into consideration all these diverse learning needs in your grading system? It seems to be based primarily on the written word.

Mr. Steele: I have to give the same kind of test to everyone, don't I?

Ms. Dalton: That depends. Are you assessing to promote learning or assessing to assign a grade?

Mr. Steele: You ask tough questions. I guess to assign a grade, although I really want my tests to improve learning.

Ms. Dalton: Sounds as though your grades may not measure what you value. I guess a more basic question is, Do you teach what you value? Let me make one other observation. Your tests are all essay. Why?

Mr. Steele: I hated multiple-choice and true-false tests in college. All they did was measure good guessing. I'm more interested in how my students think.

Ms. Dalton: That's a good value. But look at your essay questions on your first chapter test. They all ask your students to recall information. Not one question measures thinking or reasoning. Since you're only measuring memory, wouldn't a multiple-choice or true-false or fill-in test be easier to grade? This test had ten questions, and each question required about 50 words to answer. When you multiply that times the 150 students in all your classes, that comes out to 75,000 words that you had to read and comment on. How long did it take you to grade all those tests?

Mr. Steele: Two entire weekends.

Ms. Dalton: If you used a machine-scored answer sheet for multiple-choice questions, it would have taken you about 30 minutes.

Mr. Steele: Do you mean we should just use multiple-choice tests?

Ms. Dalton: No. But if all you're measuring is recall, objective-type tests save a lot of time and your learners get feedback sooner. You've got to be fair not only to your students but also to yourself.

Mr. Steele: I guess there's more to grading than I thought.

Classroom Evaluation Activities: An Overview

Most teachers, from elementary school through college, think of making tests and assigning grades as one of the more bothersome aspects of teaching. They view it as a chore, something they have to do to please administrators and parents, rather than an integral part of teaching.

However, skilled evaluation can have a substantial impact on learners in both the short and the long term (Crooks, 1988). At the lesson and unit level, skilled evaluation can:

- reactivate previously learned skills and knowledge
- focus learner attention
- provide opportunities for learners to practice and consolidate new information
- help learners keep track of their own learning and progress
- give learners a sense of accomplishment.

Over time, skilled evaluation can help learners acquire individual habits of learning that:

- increase their motivation to study
- influence their choice of study patterns and learning strategies
- influence their choice of future activities and courses
- establish a realistic picture of their own abilities and competence.

While most teachers would enthusiastically support these outcomes and acknowledge that evaluation is essential to bringing them about, they also are concerned that their efforts at evaluation may be inadequate (Crooks, 1988).

Teachers use a wide range of evaluative activities. Some are informal, such as questions during a class discussion, written notes on assignments and homework, and oral comments during a practice activity. Others are more formal and systematic, such as teacher-written tests. Significant numbers of teachers have had no formal training in assessing classroom learning, while many of those who have had such training find it of little use or relevance in evaluating their learning activities (Gullickson & Ellwein, 1985).

Given a lack of teacher enthusiasm for evaluation, it is not surprising that learners feel the same way. Just as some teachers fail to view evaluation as a meaningful requirement for learning, so do many learners view tests and grades as chores not worth the effort.

The unskilled practice of evaluation has many unfortunate results, as the dialogue between Mr. Steele and Ms. Dalton attests. It can lead to assessment techniques and grades that are unfair not only to learners, but also to both their parents and the teacher. It can mask what learners actually achieve during instruction. Some tests, both those made by teachers and those published, bear little relationship to what learners actually do during instruction. This discrepancy is a major reason why some learners fail to prepare for tests. Furthermore, unskilled evaluation practices clearly put certain learners at a disadvantage. Classroom assessment techniques that rely almost exclusively on paper-and-pencil tests may ignore the strengths of some learners in a diverse classroom and provide them little incentive to study and to improve.

Ineffective evaluation practices are unfair not only to learners but also to parents. Most parents are keenly interested in what their children are learning. In many schools, report cards are the only means parents have of determining that their children *are* learning. Depending on your evaluation skills, your grades may or may not tell them what was learned.

Finally, an unskilled pattern of evaluation practice is unfair to you. You will spend countless hours developing, scoring, and grading homework, class assignments, and tests. Your time is one of the most precious commodities you have. The time you spend on assessment should be on activities that accurately indicate the success of your teaching efforts.

Fairness in Assessment

The major goal of this chapter is to help you develop a pattern of evaluation practice that you, your learners, and their parents will perceive to be fair and that is genuinely fair. A fair pattern of assessment is built on the following values. **Test fairness** means that your expert pattern of evaluation practice should:

1. Provide a valid assessment of what you teach.
2. Motivate learners to higher degrees of effort.
3. Be sensitive to differences in gender, culture, and abilities.
4. Communicate performance and progress accurately to learners and their parents as well as to future teachers, admissions officers, and employers.
5. Be efficient, saving you and your learners time and effort.

We will discuss each of these characteristics in the remainder of this chapter. Before we do, let's turn to one other goal of student assessment: the need to be practical and realistic.

While it is important that you teach what you value and measure what you teach, the technology of measurement does not always allow you to do this with scientific precision. Many things you value and teach may be difficult, even impossible, to measure.

Test fairness. A pattern of evaluation in which the teacher provides an authentic assessment of what has been taught, motivates learners toward higher levels of effort, is sensitive to learner differences, accurately communicates performance and progress to learners and other parties, and efficiently uses teacher and learner time and effort.

How can I make sure that my assessments are fair to students?

Tests that measure what students learn and practice in the classroom can produce high levels of effort and student success.

Furthermore, it is unlikely that you will be able to adjust your tests to individual learners. Inevitably, therefore, some of your tests will be too difficult for some learners and too easy for others, more suited to some of your learners' testing styles than to others, and more motivating for some learners than for others. Be aware that your tests will not be perfect assessments of your learners' performance and progress. Tests, even when well constructed, are only *samples* of your students' behavior that *estimate* their true level of performance and progress. This is why a balanced set of assessment techniques, chosen from those to be described in this and the following chapter, will be important in establishing an effective pattern of evaluation practice.

Validity in Assessment

The single most discouraging time during my first year of teaching was after I scored my first test. I put a lot of time and effort into my lessons and I was hoping everyone would do well. I wanted everyone to get an A. No one did, and more than half the class failed. Hadn't they studied? Had I done a poor job of teaching? Was my test bad? They seemed to understand what I was teaching. They did the lab assignments correctly, used the equipment properly, filled out the activity sheets, took notes on what they saw. They answered all my questions during the lessons. I had no idea what went wrong. So I curved all the grades to make everyone happy. That left a bad taste in my mouth, which lingers to this day. (Author, personal experience)

In the fields of psychology and education, most tests that have been developed to appraise a particular mental state or trait, such as intelligence, creativity, attitude, or achievement, do so indirectly. In other words, the behaviors that learners demonstrate on these tests (for example, choosing the correct option on a multiple-choice question, agreeing or disagreeing with attitude statements, identifying whether a statement is true or false) are not of themselves of interest. Rather, they provide an indication—or behavioral sign—of an underlying trait or ability.

Classroom assessment of learning, particularly beyond the early elementary grades, is almost exclusively based on paper-and-pencil tests, which also indicate, rather than directly measure, what children have learned (Gullickson & Ellwein, 1985). For example, we may measure an understanding of the scientific method not by having learners plan, conduct, and evaluate an experiment (a direct measure), but by asking them to list the steps in conducting an experiment, to write about the difference between a hypothesis and a theory, or to choose the correct definition of a control group from a list of choices (all indirect measures). Or we may measure children's understanding of money not by observing them select food, pay for it, and get the correct change (direct assessment) but by asking them to recall how many pennies there are in a dollar, or to write down how much change they would get back from a $10 bill if they paid $6.75 for a T-shirt (indirect assessment).

There are obvious advantages to indirect assessment of achievement and learning, not the least of which is efficiency. It would be very time-consuming to measure directly all learning that goes on in a classroom. But indirect assessment raises a thorny problem: How do you know that the test is measuring what you say it is? In other words, how do you know it has **test validity**? Recall that *validity* is the degree to which a test measures what it says it measures—and what you want it to measure.

Test validity. The capacity of a test to measure what it says it is measuring.

No test is completely valid or invalid. A test is valid or invalid only for a particular purpose—the purpose for which it was built, such as measuring knowledge, self-concept, or problem-solving ability. Without reference to purpose, the concept of test validity would make no sense. A test may be valid or invalid for assigning children to special classes for the gifted (for a test that measures aptitude). Or a test may be valid or invalid for determining which learners are in need of remedial work in a particular subject (for a test that measures prior achievement).

In the previous chapter we learned about the importance of predictive validity in standardized tests. Recall that the *predictive validity* of a test indicates the extent to which a test score anticipates or predicts how an individual will perform at some future time related to what the test is measuring. For example, it indicates how someone might perform in college on the basis of a standardized ability test score received in high school, or how well someone performs on the job after taking a job selection test.

In this chapter we will learn about content validity. **Content validity** is a measure of the degree to which a test covers all the content that was taught in the manner in which it was taught—how well, in other words, the content of your test matches the content of your classroom instruction. In this chapter we will take a close look at content validity.

Ensuring Content Validity

Most teachers respond with "Of course!" when asked if their classroom tests measure what they taught. However, one of the most common complaints of learners, whether in grade school or in college, is that their tests often do not measure what they've been taught (Tuckman, 1988). Very likely, the reason behind the poor test performance of the learners described in the vignette that opened Part IV of this book is that their test lacked content validity. Although the learners may have acquired all the goals and objectives the teacher emphasized, the test may not have measured them. How can this happen?

For a test to have content validity, it must have two qualities.

- It must reflect the goals and objectives of your lessons.
- It must give the *same emphasis* to your goals and objectives as did your lessons.

In other words, content-valid tests ask learners to do what they have learned in class. Not all tests do this. As you will see shortly, tests routinely measure skills different from those intended or taught. Moreover, many classroom tests over- or underemphasize certain content areas compared with the emphasis and amount of time devoted to that content during instruction.

To put it another way, content-valid tests measure what teachers teach and learners learn. They ask learners to do what was modeled, coached, and practiced during instruction. If learners saw a teacher demonstrate how to focus a microscope, were coached to do this, and practiced doing it, a content-valid test would ask them to focus a microscope—not to label the parts of the microscope on a diagram.

In discussing how to build tests to ensure content validity, we will focus on two types of assessment techniques: **restricted-response tests,** which include true-false, multiple-choice, matching, fill-in, and restricted essays for measuring knowledge, comprehension, and application behaviors, and **flexible-response tests,** which include extended essays, term papers, research reports, and other performance-based assessments of learning that measure higher thought processes such as analysis, synthesis, and decision-making behaviors. In this chapter we will focus on restricted-response tests, and in the next chapter we will turn our attention to flexible response tests representing performance-based assessments. Table 12.1 summarizes behaviors that are best measured by each type of test (Bloom, Englehart, Hill, Furst, & Krathwohl, 1956).

Content validity. A measure of the degree to which a test covers all the content that was taught in the manner in which it was taught.

Restricted-response tests. Assessment methods that limit the range of possible answers, such as true-false or multiple-choice tests, and are usually intended to test knowledge, comprehension, and application behaviors.

Flexible-response tests. Tests that measure higher thought processes such as analysis, synthesis, and decision-making behaviors usually through performance-based assessments.

Table 12.1

Classification of Behaviors in the Cognitive Domain by Test Type

Type of Test	Level of Behavioral Complexity	Expected Student Behavior	Instructional Process	Key Words
Restricted-response	Knowledge (remembering)	Student is able to remember or recall information and recognize facts, terminology, and rules	Repetition Memorization	define describe identify
	Comprehension (understanding)	Student is able to change the form of a communication by translating and rephrasing what has been read or spoken	Explanation Illustration	summarize paraphrase rephrase
	Application (transferring)	Student is able to apply the information learned to a context different from the one in which it was learned	Practice Transfer	apply use employ
Flexible-response	Analysis (relating)	Student is able to break down a problem into its component parts and draw relationships between the parts	Induction Deduction	relate distinguish differentiate
	Synthesis (creating)	Student is able to combine parts to form a unique or novel solution to a problem	Divergence Generalization	formulate compose produce
	Evaluation (decision making)	Student is able to make decisions about the value or worth of methods, ideas, people, or products according to expressed criteria	Discrimination Inference	appraise decide justify

Building Content-Valid Restricted-Response Tests

Learners spend much of their time completing tests or assessments of various types. Evaluation activities such as written, teacher-made tests; standardized tests; classwork; homework; questions embedded in texts; and questions during class occupy a significant percentage of a learner's school day. Merely taking teacher-made paper-and-pencil tests has been estimated to consume an average of 5 to 15 percent of the school day, with the higher percentage being typical of secondary school learners (Haertel, 1986).

Teachers usually fall into three traps when making pencil-and-paper tests:

● They test content areas they didn't teach. This typically occurs when teachers hold learners accountable for chapter content that was not discussed in class, assigned for homework, or encountered in workbook exercises. Often this occurs when the

Paper-and-pencil tests can be valid and reliable measures of what students know. They need to be designed with instructional goals and objectives in mind.

teacher decides that even though a certain content or skill was not taught, the "good student" should have learned it anyway.

- They place more emphasis on certain content areas on the test than when they were actually teaching these content areas. A common complaint from students is that some or many of the questions on the test covered areas only briefly discussed in class.

- They ask questions in a manner that requires students to use intellectual skills that do not match the way they were taught or the teacher's intended goals and objectives. For example, they use true-false questions to test whether learners can express relationships, or they use essay questions to test recall.

The Test Blueprint

Test blueprint. A table used to identify the type of behavior and content to be tested.

One way to avoid these testing traps is to construct a **test blueprint.** Table 12.2 shows a teacher's blueprint for a test in a physical science class. The topics covered are listed down the first column, and the intellectual skills emphasized in class are identified across the top. The percentages indicate the instructional emphasis for both content and intellectual skill. This test is worth 100 points. The totals for rows and columns reflect the emphasis (in total points) that the test must have to match the instructional emphasis provided in class. The cells identify item types that measure the intent of the lesson and the number and point totals of these items.

How can I make sure my classroom tests measure what I teach?

There is a variety of systems for constructing test blueprints (Kubiszyn & Borich, 1996). Ideally, they should be constructed at the time you plan your lessons and are presenting them to your learners. That way, the content you actually teach and the emphasis placed on it is easily remembered. Using a test blueprint is the best way to assure yourself, your learners, and their parents that your grades reflect what your students have learned from your instruction.

Table 12.2

Test Blueprint for a Physical Science Test

Topics	Memory for Facts and Terms 25%	Understanding of Concepts 40%	Application and Analysis of Data 35%	Totals
Weathering (15%)	5 fill-ins (1 pt each)	5 multiple-choice (2 pts each)		15 pts
Physical weathering (15%)	5 true-false (1 pt each)	5 multiple-choice (2 pts each)		15 pts
Volcanic activity (25%)	5 fill-ins (1 pt each)	5 multiple-choice (2 pts each)	1 essay (10 pts)	25 pts
Folded structures (15%)	5 fill-ins (1 pt each)		1 essay (10 pts)	15 pts
Faults (30%)	5 fill-ins (1 pt each)	5 multiple-choice (2 pts each)	1 essay (15 pts)	30 pts
TOTALS	25 pts	40 pts	35 pts	100 pts

Matching Test Questions and Objectives

The skilled test writer prepares questions that ask the learner to use the same thought processes that were identified in class activities, used in the text, and required by homework. In other words, the test items should ask learners to do exactly what is specified by the objectives that guided your instruction. For example, if you want your learners to recall from memory five major battles of the American Revolution in their correct chronological order, you would ask them, "List five important battles of the American Revolution and arrange them in the order in which they occurred." You would not ask them whether America won the Battle of Bunker Hill (true-false), since this question would not call for the same mental processes required by knowing all five battles in their chronological order. Similarly, if you want your learners to distinguish a noun from an adjective, you would ask them to compare the words "beauty" and "beautiful," not to define these two words. Recalling definitions would tell you little about the learner's ability to distinguish the difference between nouns and adjectives. Furthermore, if you want to assess whether a learner can design and execute a scientific experiment, you might ask the learner to carry out an actual experiment that could be rated for thoroughness, completion, accuracy, objectivity, and so forth, and not simply to list the steps of the scientific method.

When you assemble your test, you will either create test questions or use those provided by your textbook publisher or by other teachers. In each case, the best way to ensure a match between your goals and objectives and your test items is to follow the three

How can I write test questions that require learners to use the same thought processes I emphasized during my instruction?

Matching Test Questions to Instructional Objectives

- Have the goals and objectives of each of your lessons in front of you as you write or select test questions. Do not rely on memory to tell you if you intended your learners to memorize or to apply the processes involved in physical weathering.
- Take the learner's perspective. Reread each test question and ask yourself, "What thought process or intellectual skill is needed to answer this question correctly?" That is, at what level of behavioral complexity is the learner being asked to respond? Have you asked students to list the steps in a process, to compare that process to another, or to analyze its effects?
- Finally, refer back to the objective that corresponds with this question and ask, "Does this question reflect the level of behavioral complexity specified in the objective?" "Does the question reflect what I actually taught in the classroom?"

steps outlined in the accompanying box, *Matching Test Questions to Instructional Objectives*. If the level of behavior required by the test question matches your objective, you have a content-valid test item. If it doesn't, rewrite the item to match the objective.

Summary

The expert practice of developing classroom tests requires first that you develop and follow a test blueprint to ensure that the content coverage and emphasis of the questions match your instruction. Second, it requires that you carefully write test items that demand of the learner the same intellectual skills or behaviors that are specified in your goals and objectives. Your decisions about item formats (true-false, fill-in, multiple-choice, essay) will be based largely on which format best helps you measure the desired behavior, thereby achieving content validity.

Choosing Test Item Formats: General Considerations

How do I choose among test items formats for an objective test?

In the following sections, we cover specific considerations involved in writing content-valid restricted-response test items (we turn to the techniques involved in flexible-response assessment methods in Chapter 13). Two broad categories of restricted-response test item formats can be used to measure instructional goals and objectives:

- *Objective test items,* which include true-false, fill-in-the-blank, multiple-choice, and matching items.
- *Restricted essay items,* which pose a specific problem for which the student recalls information, organizes it in a suitable manner, derives a defensible conclusion, and expresses it within specified guidelines.

The following sections discuss some considerations that can increase the content validity of your restricted response tests.

Objective Test Items

Objective test items have four common formats: true-false, matching, multiple-choice, and completion (fill-in). How you write your objectives may predetermine the format, but in many instances you will have a choice between several item formats. In the following sections, we consider the construction and use of true-false, matching, multiple-choice, and completion items.

How do I write objective test questions that accurately measure what I have taught?

True-False Items

True-false items are popular with teachers because they are quick and easy to write, or at least they seem to be. True-false items do take less time to write than good objective items of any other format, but *good* true-false items are not so easy to prepare.

As you know from your own experience, every true-false item, regardless of how well or poorly written, gives the student a 50 percent chance of guessing the right answer correctly, even without his or her reading the item! In other words, on a 50-item true-false test, we would expect individuals who were totally unfamiliar with the content being tested to answer about 25 items correctly. Fortunately, ways exist to reduce the effects of guessing. Here are some:

● Encourage *all* students to guess when they do not know the correct answer. Because it is virtually impossible to prevent certain students from guessing, encouraging all students to guess equalizes the effects of guessing. The test scores will then reflect a more or less equal "guessing factor" *plus* the actual level of each student's knowledge. This will prevent test-wise students from having an unfair advantage over students who are not test-wise.

● Require revision of statements that are false. In this approach, you provide space at the end of the item for students to alter false items to make them true. Usually the student is asked to first underline or circle the false part of the item and then add the correct wording, as in these examples:

T (F)   High IQ students (always) get good grades.
        often; tend to

T (F)   Panama is (north) of Cuba.
        south

T (F)   (September) has an extra day during leap year.
        February

With this strategy, you would award full credit only if the student's revision is correct. The disadvantage of such an approach is that more test time is required for the same number of items, and scoring time is increased.

The accompanying box, *Writing True-False Questions,* gives specific suggestions for writing these test items.

Matching Items

Like true-false, matching items are a popular and convenient testing format. Like good true-false items, however, good matching items are not easy to write. Imagine you are back in your ninth-grade American history class and the following item shows up on your test:

Directions: Match A and B

A	B
1. Lincoln	a. President during the twentieth century
2. Nixon	b. Invented the telephone
3. Whitney	c. Delivered the Emancipation Proclamation
4. Ford	d. Only president to resign from office
5. Bell	e. Black civil rights leader
6. King	f. Invented the cotton gin
7. Washington	g. Our first president
8. Roosevelt	h. Only president elected for more than two terms

See any problems? Compare the problems you identified with the descriptions of faults that follow.

Homogeneity. The lists are not homogeneous. Column A contains names of presidents, inventors, and a civil rights leader. Unless these are specifically taught as a set of related people or ideas, this is too wide a variety for a matching exercise.

Order of Lists. The lists are reversed: column A should be in place of column B, and column B should be in place of column A. As the exercise is now written, the student reads a name and then has to read through all or many of the more lengthy descriptions to find the answer—a time-consuming process. It also is a good idea to introduce some sort of order—chronological, numerical, or alphabetical—to your list of options. This saves the student time.

Easy Guessing. Notice that there are equal numbers of options and descriptions. This increases the chances of guessing correctly through elimination. If there are at least three more options than descriptions, the chance of guessing correctly is reduced to one in four.

Poor Directions. The instructions are much too brief. Matching directions should specify the basis for matching. For example, "Column A contains brief descriptions of historical events. Column B contains the names of U.S. presidents. Indicate who was president when the historical event took place by placing the appropriate letter to the left of the number in column A."

Multiple Correct Responses. The description "President during the twentieth century" has three correct answers: Nixon, Ford, and Roosevelt. Also, always include first and last names to enhance recall and avoid ambiguities. Here is a corrected version of the matching items we critiqued above:

Writing True-False Questions

- Tell students clearly how to mark *true* or *false* (for example, circle or underline the *T* or *F*) before they begin the test. Write this instruction at the top of the printed test as well.
- Construct statements that are definitely true or definitely false, without qualifications. If the item is true or false on the basis of someone's opinion, make sure the source is part of the item. For example, "According to the head of the AFL-CIO, workers' compensation is below desired standards."
- Write true and false statements that are approximately the same length—avoid the mistake of adding so many qualifying phrases that true statements are almost always longer than false ones. Similarly, include approximately equal numbers of true and false items.
- Avoid using double-negative statements. They take extra time to decipher and are difficult to interpret. For example,

avoid statements such as "It is not true that addition cannot precede subtraction in algebraic operations." Instead write "Addition can precede subtraction in algebraic operations."
- Avoid terms denoting indefinite degree (for example, *large, long time, regularly*), or absolutes (*never, only, always*). These often cue students that a statement must be false. For example, "Congress and the President always cooperate to produce the federal budget."
- Avoid placing items in a systematic pattern that some students might detect (for example, true-true-false-false, true-false-true-false, and so on).
- If you use statements directly from the textbook, make sure that you are not taking them out of context.

Column A

_____ 1. Only president not elected to office.
_____ 2. Delivered the Emancipation Proclamation.
_____ 3. Only president to resign from office.
_____ 4. Only president elected for more than two
      terms.

Column B

a. Gerald Ford
b. Thomas Jefferson
c. Abraham Lincoln
d. Richard Nixon
e. Franklin Roosevelt
f. Theodore Roosevelt
g. George Washington
h. Woodrow Wilson

Notice that we now have complete directions, more options than descriptions, homogeneous lists (all items in Column A are descriptions of U.S. presidents and all items in Column B are names of presidents), and unambiguous alternatives.

The accompanying box, *Writing Matching Items*, contains some additional suggestions for writing these types of questions.

Multiple-Choice Items

Another popular item format is the multiple-choice question. Multiple-choice tests are more common in high school and college than in elementary school. Multiple-choice items are unique among objective test items because if properly written they enable you to measure some limited types of higher-level cognitive objectives. However, multiple-choice items are more difficult to write than are the other types we have discussed so far. In the following sections, we discuss some common problems with multiple-choice items and provide specific suggestions for you to use when writing them. Following

Applying Your Knowledge:

Writing Matching Items

- Keep both the descriptions list and the options list short and homogeneous. They should fit together on the same page. Title the lists to ensure homogeneity (e.g., Column A, Column B) and arrange the options in a logical (e.g., alphabetical) order.
- Make sure that all the options are plausible distractors (wrong answer choices) for each description to ensure homogeneity of lists. In other words, make them logically parallel: don't include one famous general in a list of U.S. presidents, or one U.S. president in a list of foreign heads of state.
- The descriptions list should contain the longer phrases or statements, while the options should consist of short phrases, words, or symbols.
- Number each description (1, 2, 3) and letter each option (a, b, c,).
- To reduce the effects of guessing, include more options than descriptions.
- In the directions, specify the basis for matching (for example, "Match the civil rights leaders' names with the demonstrations they led," or "Match the procedure with the step of the scientific process in which you would use it"). Also, be sure to specify whether students can select each option more than once.

these suggestions will allow you to avoid inadvertently providing students with clues to the correct answer.

Stem. The statement portion of a multiple-choice question.

Response alternatives. The answer-choices portion of a multiple-choice question.

Stem Clue. The statement portion of a multiple-choice item is called the **stem,** and the answer choices are called *options* or **response alternatives.** A *stem clue* occurs when an identical or similar term appears in both the stem and an option, thereby clueing the test-taker to the correct answer. For example:

The free-floating structures within the cell that synthesize protein are called _____.
A. chromosomes
B. lysosomes
C. mitochondria
D. free ribosomes

In this item the word *free* in the option is identical to *free* in the stem. Thus, the wise test-taker has a good chance of answering the item correctly without mastery of the content being measured.

Grammatical Clue. Consider this item:

U. S. Grant was an _____.
A. cavalry commander

    B. navy admiral
    C. army general
    D. senator

Most students would pick up on the easy grammatical clue in the stem. The article *an* eliminates options A, B, and D, because "*an* navy admiral," "*an* cavalry commander," or "*an* senator" are grammatically incorrect. Option C is the only one that forms a grammatically correct sentence. A way to eliminate the grammatical clue is to replace *an* with *a/an.* Similar examples are *is/are, was/were, his/her,* and so on. Alternatively, place the article (or verb, or pronoun) in the options list:

Christopher Columbus came to America in _____.
    A. a car
    B. a boat
    C. an airplane
    D. a balloon

Redundant Words/Unequal Length. Two very common faults in multiple-choice construction are illustrated in this item:

When 53 Americans were held hostage in Iran, _____.
    A. the United States did nothing to free them
    B. the United States declared war on Iran
    C. the United States first attempted to free them by diplomatic means and later attempted a rescue
    D. the United States expelled all Iranian students

The phrase "the United States" is included in each option. To save space and time, add it to the stem: "When 53 Americans were held hostage in Iran, the United States _____." Second, the length of options could be a giveaway: the correct option, C, is much longer than any of the others. Multiple-choice item writers have a tendency to include more information in the correct option than in the incorrect options. Test-wise students know that the longer option is the correct one more often than not. Avoid making correct answers look different from incorrect options.

All of the Above/None of the Above. In general, use "none of the above" sparingly. Some item writers use "none of the above" only when no clearly correct option is presented. However, students catch on to this practice and guess that "none of the above" is the correct answer without knowledge of the content being measured. Also, at times it may be justified to use multiple correct answers, such as "both a and c" or "both b and c." Again, use such options sparingly, because inconsistencies can easily exist among alternatives that logically eliminate some from consideration. Avoid using "all of the above," because test items should encourage discrimination, not discourage it.

Higher-Level Multiple-Choice Questions

A good multiple-choice item is the most time-consuming type of objective test item to write. Unfortunately, most multiple-choice items are written at the knowledge level in the taxonomy of educational objectives. As a new item writer, you will tend to write items at this level, but you should learn to write multiple-choice items that measure cognitive objectives beyond the knowledge level. Following are some suggestions to make your higher-level multiple-choice questions more effective. In the next chapter we will show you how to measure cognitive objectives at the analysis, synthesis, and decision-making levels with performance-based assessments.

Use Justification to Assess Reasons Behind an Answer. Follow up on multiple-choice items with open-ended questions that ask students to specify why they chose their answers. This allows students to demonstrate knowledge at the comprehension level. For example:

Directions: Choose the most appropriate answer and cite evidence for your selection in the space below.

The principal value of a balanced diet is that it _____.
A.   increases your intelligence
B.   cures disease
C.   promotes mental health
D.   promotes physical health
E.   improves self-discipline
What evidence from the text did you use to choose your answer?

_____

_____

Use Pictorial, Graphic, or Tabular Stimuli. Presenting pictures, drawings, graphs, or maps that the student must use to choose the correct answer to a multiple-choice question can require the student to think at least at the application level and may involve even higher cognitive processes (see Table 12.1). Also, such stimuli often can generate several higher-level multiple-choice items, as the questions below and Figure 12.1 illustrate:

Which of the following cities (identified by their grid locations on the accompanying map) would be the best location for a steel mill?
A.   Li   (3A)
B.   Um   (3B)
C.   Cot   (3D)
D.   Dube   (4B)

Approximately how many miles is it from Dube to Rag?
A.   100 miles
B.   150 miles
C.   200 miles
D.   250 miles

In what direction would someone have to travel to get from Wog to Um?
A.   northwest
B.   northeast
C.   southwest
D.   southeast

Use Analogies to Show Relationships Between Terms. To answer analogies correctly, students must not only know what the terms mean (knowledge) but they also must understand how they relate to each other (comprehension or application). For example:

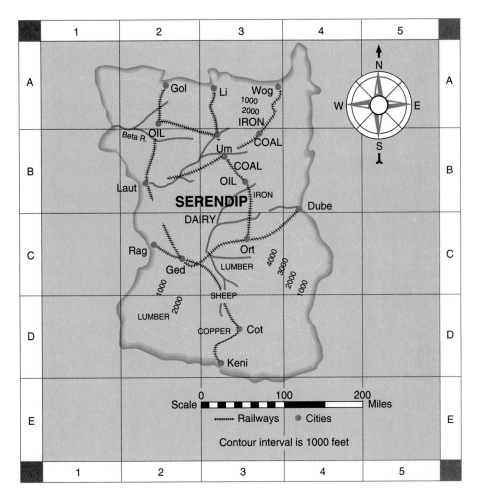

Figure 12.1
Use of a pictorial stimulus to measure a higher-level cognitive process.

Physician is to humans as veterinarian is to:
A. fruits
B. animals
C. minerals
D. vegetables

Require Application of Principles or Procedures. To test whether students comprehend the implications of a procedure, have them use the principle or procedure with new information or in a novel way. This requires them to do more than just follow the steps in solving a problem: They must also demonstrate an ability to apply their knowledge to a new context (application). Consider this example from a math test. The material covered was a division lesson on computation of ratios and proportions:

After filling his car's tank with 18 gallons of gasoline, Mr. Watts said to his son, "We've come 450 miles since the last fill-up. What gas mileage are we getting?" Which is the best answer?

> **Applying Your Knowledge:**
>
> # Writing Multiple-Choice Items
>
> - Be sure that there is one—and only one—correct or clearly best answer.
> - Be sure that all wrong answer choices (*distractors*) are plausible. Eliminate unintentional grammatical clues, and keep the length and form of all the answer choices equal. Rotate the position of the correct answer from item to item randomly.
> - Use negative questions or statements only if the knowledge being tested requires it. In most cases it is more important for the student to know what the correct answer *is* rather than what it is *not*.
> - Include three to five options (two to four distractors plus one correct answer) to optimize testing for knowledge, comprehension, or application rather than encouraging guessing.
> - Use the option "none of the above" sparingly and only when all the answers can be classified unequivocally as wrong.
> - Avoid using "all of the above," especially as the correct answer. It makes it easy for students who have only partial information to guess the correct answer.

    A. 4 miles per gallon
    B. 25 miles per gallon
    C. Between 30 and 35 miles per gallon
    D. It can't be determined from the information given

This item tests not only knowledge of division but also application skills.

The accompanying box, *Writing Multiple-Choice Items,* gives some specific guidelines to follow when you write items of this type.

Completion Items

Like true-false items, completion items are relatively easy to write. The first tests constructed by classroom teachers and taken by students often are completion tests. Like items of all other formats, there are good and bad completion items. Here are some suggestions for writing completion items:

- Require a single-word answer or a brief, definite statement. Avoid items so indefinite that they may be logically answered by several terms:

    Poor item: World War II ended in _____.
    Better item: World War II ended in the year _____.

- Be sure the item poses a specific question. An incomplete statement is often clearer than a question because it provides more structure for an answer.

> *Poor item:* Who was the main character in the story "Lilies of the Field?" _____.
>
> *Better item:* The main character in the story "Lilies of the Field" was called _____.

- Be sure the answer is factually correct. Precisely word the question in relation to the concept or fact being tested. Make sure that the answer is included in the students' text, workbook, or class notes.

- Omit only key words; don't eliminate so many elements that the sense of the content is impaired.

  > *Poor item:* The _____ of test item usually is graded more _____ than the _____ type.
  >
  > *Better item:* The multiple-choice type of test item is usually graded more objectively than the _____ type.

- Word the statement so the blank is near the end. This prevents awkwardly phrased sentences. For example:

  > *Poor item:* In _____ , John F. Kennedy was elected president.
  >
  > *Better item:* John F. Kennedy was elected president in the year _____.

- If the question requires a numerical answer, indicate the units in which it is to be expressed (for example, pounds, ounces, minutes).

Advantages and Disadvantages of Objective-Item Formats

Table 12.3 summarizes the advantages and disadvantages of each of the objective item formats we have discussed: true-false items, matching items, multiple-choice items, and completion items.

Restricted Response Essay Items

In essay items, the student supplies, rather than selects, the correct answer. An essay test requires that the student compose a response to a question for which no *single* response or pattern of responses can be cited as correct to the exclusion of all others. The accuracy and quality of a response to such a question often can be judged only by a person skilled in the subject area.

Like objective test items, essay items can be well constructed or poorly constructed. The well-constructed essay item tests complex cognitive skills by requiring the student to organize, integrate, and synthesize knowledge; to use information to solve novel problems; or to be original and innovative in problem solving. The poorly constructed essay item may require the student to do no more than recall information as it was presented in the textbook or lecture. Worse, the poorly constructed essay item may leave the learner unclear about what is required for a satisfactory response.

An essay item that allows the student to determine the length and complexity of a response is called an **extended-response essay** item. This type of essay is most useful at the analysis, synthesis, and evaluation levels of cognitive complexity. Because of the length of this type of item and the time required to organize and express the response, the extended-response essay is sometimes better assigned as a term paper, literary script, or research report. The extended-response essay often is of value both in assessing communication ability and in assessing achievement. We will have more to say about extended-response essays in the next chapter, on performance-based assessment.

Extended-response essay. An essay question that allows the student to determine the length and complexity of a response; it is a good means of assessing communication ability as well as achievement.

Table 12.3

Advantages and Disadvantages of Various Objective Item Formats

True-False Items

Advantages	**Disadvantages**
Tend to be short, so more material can be covered than with any other format; thus, use T-F items when extensive content has been covered.	Tend to emphasize rote memorization of knowledge (although complex questions sometimes can be asked using T-F items).
Faster to construct (but avoid creating an item by taking statements out of context or slightly modifying them).	They assume an unequivocally true or false answer (it is unfair to make students guess at your criteria for evaluating the truth of a statement).
Scoring is easier (tip: provide a "T" and an "F" for them to circle, because a student's handwritten "T" or "F" can be hard to decipher).	Allow and may even encourage a high degree of guessing (generally, longer examinations compensate for this).

Matching Items

Advantages	**Disadvantages**
Simple to construct and score.	Tend to ask trivial information.
Ideal for measuring associations between facts.	Emphasize memorization.
Can be more efficient than multiple-choice questions because they avoid repetition of options in measuring association.	Most commercial answer sheets can accommodate only five options, thus limiting the size of a matching item.
Reduce the effects of guessing.	

Multiple-Choice Items

Advantages	**Disadvantages**
Versatile in measuring objectives, from the knowledge level to the application level.	Time-consuming to write.

Restricted-response essay. An essay that poses a specific problem for which the student must recall proper information, organize it in a suitable manner, derive a defensible conclusion, and express it according to specific criteria.

An essay that poses a specific problem for which the student must recall information, organize it in a suitable manner, derive a defensible conclusion, and express it according to specific criteria is called a **restricted-response essay** item. The statement of the problem specifies limitations on the response that guide the student in responding and provides evaluation criteria for scoring. Following is an example of a well-written restricted-response essay item. Note how it specifies exactly what information is required, how it should be organized, and how the response will be graded.

> List the major similarities and differences between U.S. participation in the Korean War and World War II, being sure to consider political, military, economic, and social factors. Limit your answer to one page. Your score will depend on accuracy, organization, and conciseness.

Using Restricted Essay Questions

Specific situations that lend themselves to restricted-response essay questions are those that require high-level thought processes, those in which it is necessary to set precise

Multiple-Choice Items (continued)

Advantages

Since writing is minimal, considerable course material can be sampled quickly.

Scoring is highly objective, requiring only a count of correct responses.

Can be written so students must discriminate between options varying in correctness, avoiding the absolute judgments of T-F tests.

Reduce effects of guessing.

Amenable to statistical analysis, so you can determine which items are ambiguous or too difficult (see Kubiszyn & Borich, 1996, Chapter 8).

Disadvantages

If not carefully written, can have more than one defensible correct answer.

Completion Items

Advantages

Question construction is relatively easy.

Guessing is reduced because the question requires a specific response.

Less time is needed to complete than multiple-choice items, so more content can be covered.

Disadvantages

Encourage a low level of response complexity.

Can be difficult to score (the stem must be general enough not to communicate the answer, leading unintentionally to multiple defensible answers).

Very short answers tend to measure recall of specific facts, names, places, and events instead of more complex behaviors.

---

time or length limits for responses, and those in which you wish to tap more than one learning objective. The following criteria will help you write valid restricted-response essay questions.

How do I write essay questions that accurately measure what I have taught?

- The instructional objectives for essay questions should specify higher-level cognitive processes. In other words, your aim in requiring essay answers is for students to supply information, not just recall information. The processes of analysis and synthesis often cannot be measured with objective items.

- Restricted-response essay tests are appropriate in situations where relatively few areas of content are to be tested. If you have 30 students and design a test with six restricted-response essays, you will spend a great deal of time scoring. Use restricted essays when class size is small, or use them in conjunction with objective items. Design your test blueprint to include a number of objective questions and only one or two essays.

- Essay responses help to maintain test security. If you are afraid test items will be passed on to future students, it is best to use an essay test format. In

Well-written essay questions give learners clearly defined tasks and explicitly described standards for answering correctly. Answers to questions written in this manner are easier to rate or score.

general, a good essay test takes less time to construct than a good objective test.

- Restricted-response essays are a good choice when you want to test any of the following learning objectives:

  Analyze relationships
  Compare positions
  State necessary assumptions
  Identify appropriate conclusions
  Explain cause-and-effect relations
  Formulate hypotheses
  Organize data to support a viewpoint
  Point out strengths and weaknesses
  Integrate data from several sources
  Evaluate the quality or worth of an item, product, or action

The accompanying box, *Writing Restricted-Response Essay Questions,* provides specific suggestions that will help you write good essay questions.

Scoring Essays

Essays are difficult to score consistently. That is, the same essay answer may be given an A by one scorer and a B or a C by another scorer. Or the same answer may be graded A on one occasion, but B or C on another occasion by the *same* scorer (Coffman, 1972). What can you do to avoid such scoring problems?

Can essay tests be scored reliably?

Write Good Essay Items. Poorly written questions are one source of scorer inconsistency. Questions that do not specify response length are another. In general, longer essay responses are more difficult to score consistently than shorter responses. This is due to student fatigue and consequent mechanical errors as well as to a tendency for grading criteria to vary from response to response or, for that matter, from page to page, or even paragraph to paragraph within the same response.

Applying Your Knowledge:
Writing Restricted-Response Essay Questions

- Be clear about what mental processes you want the student to use before starting to write the question. Refer to the mental processes required at the various levels in the taxonomy of educational objectives (see Table 12.1). For example, if you want students to apply what they have learned, determine what mental processes would be needed in the application process.

    Poor item: Criticize the following speech by our president.

    Better item: Consider the following presidential speech. Focus on the section dealing with economic policy and discriminate between factual statements and opinions. List these statements separately, label them, and indicate whether each statement is or is not consistent with the President's overall economic policy.

- Make sure that the question clearly and unambiguously defines the task for the student. Tasks should be explained either in the overall instructions at the beginning of the test or in the test items themselves. Clearly state the writing style required (for example, scientific versus descriptive prose), whether spelling and grammar will be counted, and whether organization of the response will be an important scoring element. Also, indicate the level of detail and supporting data required.

    Poor item: Discuss the value of behavioral objectives.

    Better item: Behavioral objectives have enjoyed increased popularity in education over the years. In your text and in class the advantages and disadvantages of behavioral objectives have been discussed. Take a position for or against the use of behavioral objectives in education and support your position by using at least three of the arguments covered in class or in the text.

- Begin restricted-response essay questions with such words or phrases as *compare, contrast, give reasons for, give examples of, predict.* These words tell the student clearly what the answer must contain. Do not begin with such words as *what, who, when,* and *list,* because these words generally lead to tasks that require only recall of information.

    Poor item: List three reasons behind America's withdrawal from Vietnam.

    Better item: After almost 20 years of involvement, the United States withdrew from Vietnam in 1975. Predict what might have happened if America had *not* withdrawn at that time.

- A question about a controversial issue should ask for, and be evaluated in terms of, the presentation of evidence rather than the position taken. You should not demand that students accept your specific conclusion or solution. You can, however, require students to present and use evidence to support their own conclusions, whatever they may be.

    Poor item: What laws should Congress pass to improve the medical care of all citizens in the United States?

    Better item: Some feel that the cost of all medical care should be borne by the federal government. Do you agree or disagree? Support your position with at least three logical arguments.

- Establish reasonable time or length limits for each answer. This helps students complete the entire test and also indicates the level of detail you require. Indicate the time limit either in the statement of the problem or close to the question number.

Use Several Restricted-Response Items. Rather than a single lengthy restricted-response essay, use several smaller essays. This will provide students a greater opportunity to show off their skills and a greater variety of criteria to respond to.

Use a Predetermined Scoring Scheme. All too often, essays are graded without the scorer having specified in advance what he or she is looking for in a "good" answer. If you do not specify the criteria beforehand, your scoring consistency will be greatly reduced. If these criteria are not readily available (in written form) for scoring each question, the criteria themselves may change (you may grade harder or easier after scoring several papers, even if the answers are similar). Or your ability to keep these criteria in mind will be influenced by fatigue, distractions, frame of mind, and so on. Because we all are human, we all are subject to these factors.

We will go into greater detail about the procedures involved in scoring open-ended responses in the next chapter, on performance assessment. Now we turn to potential questions of the content validity and reliability of restricted-response essay questions, and consider some ideas about how to solve these problems.

Some Unresolved Problems

Content Validity. Although multiple-choice questions and restricted-response essay questions can be written in a manner that requires thinking and problem solving, the learner's response may not always indicate that either of these processes took place. Depending on the degree of similarity between what was taught and what was tested, and on how clearly the teacher demonstrated the thinking and problem-solving skills, the learner could have arrived at the answer in a variety of ways—some involving thought and inquiry, some simply involving recall. For example, suppose that you posed the question "What are the reasons trade agreements do or do not work?" just after covering the details of the North American Free Trade Agreement (NAFTA). This might evoke a genuine problem-solving response involving some analysis, or simply a paraphrase of the conditions required by NAFTA given in class. Therefore, even though you follow a test blueprint and write questions to match the performance desired, the actual thought process students use may differ from what you intended.

The most valid way to measure higher thought processes involving inquiry, problem solving, and decision making is to observe the learner's performance related to the skill or behavior in question. In other words, assessment of higher thought processes seldom can be separated from the application of those processes to real-world problems. We will address this issue and provide examples in the following chapter.

Reliability Versus Validity. Teachers must be concerned about a test's reliability as well as its content validity. Recall that *validity* is the degree to which a test measures the traits, abilities, or skills for which it was intended. A test's *reliability*, on the other hand, is the degree to which the test dependably or consistently measures that trait, ability, or skill.

One way to think about reliability is in terms of an assessment instrument with which we are already familiar: the bathroom scale. A bathroom scale is *valid* if it measures how many pounds you weigh rather than how tall you are. It is *reliable* if it registers your 150-pound weight every time you step on it. If you weigh 150 pound but the scale sometimes reads 145, other times 160, and still other times 155, you have an unreliable scale. A reliable test, therefore, is one that dependably and consistently gives approximately the same score regardless of how many times you take it (assuming you don't improve with practice).

Reliability is a quality we want for all our tests, but it is sometimes hard to attain. For example, unclear test questions may be interpreted differently by the learner each time they are read. In such cases, the learner's score will not accurately reflect what she knows or can do. Unclear instructions may produce test scores that are similarly unreli-

Improving the Reliability of Your Tests

- Write test instructions and questions in simple, uncomplicated language. This way, learners won't have to struggle to untangle complicated phrases or clauses. When in doubt, have a student in a lower grade read the item and tell you what the question means.
- Include enough questions on the test to adequately cover all that the learner is expected to know. The more items, the greater the sample of performance obtained and the higher the test reliability.
- Allow students sufficient time to take the test. A rushed student is more likely to make foolish errors, which will lower the reliability of the test.
- Make sure the testing conditions (temperature of the room, noise level, seating arrangements) are conducive to maximum performance. If the testing situa-

tion is uncomfortable, learners are more easily distracted and less likely to demonstrate what they really know.
- Follow a test blueprint so that you adequately sample all that has been taught—and all that the learner knows. The test blueprint will enable you to construct enough test items to adequately measure what you've taught.
- Write objective questions that have easily identifiable right and wrong answers. When using restricted-response essay questions, prepare a model answer or scoring guide before grading. This way the correct answer will be scored "right" every time, or a "good" answer given a high rating, because it reflects your scoring guide, not your mood or temperament at the time of grading.

able. Poorly constructed tests often produce scores that are unreliable because both the instructions and the items are poorly worded. Also, keep in mind that when a scoring guide is not used for essays, the essays may be scored subjectively, further decreasing the test's reliability.

Several steps can be followed to increase test reliability. They are summarized in the accompanying box, *Improving the Reliability of Your Tests*.

Reporting Learner Progress: Your Grading System

Consider the following comments about grading made by these first-year teachers:

> Of all the paperwork, grading is the nitty-gritty of teaching for me. Students take their grade as the bottom line of your class. It is the end-all and be-all of the class. To me, a grade for a class is, or at least should be, a combination of ability, attitude, and effort. Put bluntly: How do you nail a kid who really tried with an F? Or how do you reward a lazy, snotty punk with an A? (Ryan, 1992, p. 4)

> I have been amazed at comments they make about grades. Those with A's ask if they are flunking; others who rarely hand in assignments ask if I think they'll get a B. They make no connection between their own efforts and the grade they receive.... Of course,

there is some truth in their view of the arbitrariness of grading. But I don't like the powerlessness it implies. "I don't give you your grade," I tell them. "You do!" (Ryan, 1992, p. 96)

Grading is still kind of a problem with me. . . . I try not to play favorites [even though I have them]—I don't like S's personality . . . I do like J's, isn't it unfair? You want to be easier on someone you like. Or harder on someone you don't. . . . I wouldn't mind taking a class on grading. I think grading could be hit much harder in college. . . . I just don't know what to do, kind of. (Bullough, 1989, p. 66)

These comments from first-year teachers highlight the confusion, uncertainty, and even fear that surround the responsibility of assigning grades. Most of these negative feelings are related to two facts about grades: (1) They become part of a learner's permanent record viewed by parents, teachers, and future employers; and (2) while there are many procedures for assigning grades, there is little research to support one over another. Consequently, teachers' choices of grading procedures reflect largely their own values, past experiences, and the norms and traditions of the schools in which they work. Their awareness of the significance of grades and the sometimes arbitrary decisions on which they are based understandably gives new teachers cause for concern.

In this section we will identify the most important of the decisions you must make when assigning grades and provide a number of specific recommendations. Although your choice of a grading procedure will reflect your own values, it should also reflect the following beliefs:

- The primary purpose of assigning a grade should be to communicate what the student has learned from your instruction.

- Grades should be based on a variety of indicators of learning, including both written and oral formats, process criteria as well as product criteria, and formal and informal assessments.

- The criteria you use to make up your grading procedure should always be known to learners and parents.

The Purpose of a Grade

> **Should I base my grades on how a learner's achievement compares with the achievement of other learners, or should I base them on a standard of mastery that I determine?**

Most educators agree that the purpose of assigning a grade in reading, social studies, math, science, or any other academic subject should be to communicate how well the learner achieved your instructional goals and objectives (Hills, 1981; Kubiszyn & Borich, 1996; Thorndike, Cunningham, Thorndike, & Hagen, 1991; Tuckman, 1988). This will be accomplished if two criteria are met: (1) Your teaching focuses on your goals and objectives and (2) your assessments measure what you teach. Therefore, the most important consideration in deciding what grades to assign is how well learners have achieved your goals and objectives.

When the basis for a grade is linked to a standard of mastery or achievement you have determined, the grade is said to be criterion-referenced (Thorndike et al., 1991). An example of **criterion-referenced grading** would be to assign a grade of A to learners who averaged 90 percent across all your tests, a grade of B to those who averaged 80 to 89 percent, a grade of C to those who averaged 70 to 79 percent, and so on. In criterion-referenced grading, the grade is compared with a fixed standard of achievement.

> **Criterion-referenced grading.** The linking of grades to a standard of mastery or achievement.

If, however, the basis for assigning a grade is the comparison of a learner's performance with the performance of other learners, a norm-referenced grading system is being used. **Norm-referenced grading** refers to a procedure for assigning grades or scores based on how one learner's achievement compares to the achievement of other learners. In one such system, called "grading on a curve," the teacher decides, for example, that the top 10 percent of learners will get As, the next 20 percent Bs, the next 40 percent Cs, the next 20 percent Ds, and the bottom 10 percent Fs.

"Normal curve grading" refers to a system whereby the percentages of As, Bs, Cs, Ds, and Fs are set in reference to the bell-shaped distribution of scores called the *normal curve*, which we studied in Chapter 11. One version of this system, illustrated in Figure 12.2, uses the standard deviation (also studied in Chapter 11) to indicate the particular percentage cutoff chosen for each letter grade, assuming that the test scores are normally distributed as shown.

Figure 12.3, in contrast, shows the kind of distribution of scores that typically occurs in criterion-referenced grading. In criterion-referenced grading, divisions between As, Bs, Cs, Ds, and Fs are made on the basis of the number or percentage of test items answered correctly as established by the teacher—not by how well others perform on the test, as in the case of a norm-referenced test. For example, in Figure 12.3, this teacher decided that getting 90 percent or more of the items correct on the test deserved the grade of A, getting 80 to 89 percent of the items correct deserved the grade of B, and so on. If the instruction has been effective, more students will score at the high end of the distribution with the criterion-referenced approach than with the norm-

Norm-referenced grading. The assignment of grades or scores based on how one learner's achievement compares with the achievement of other learners.

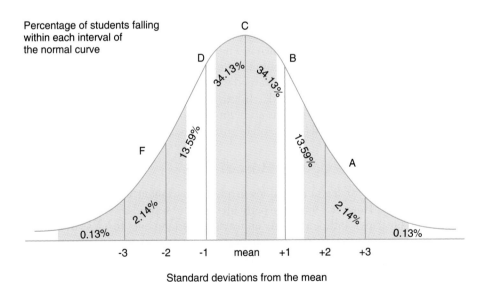

Standard deviations from the mean	Letter grade	Approximate percentage of students
+1.50	A	7
+0.75 to +1.49	B	16
mean ± 0.74	C	54
-0.75 to -1.49	D	16
-1.50	F	7

Figure 12.2
A normal curve, illustrating examples of percentages for distributing grades on a norm-referenced test.

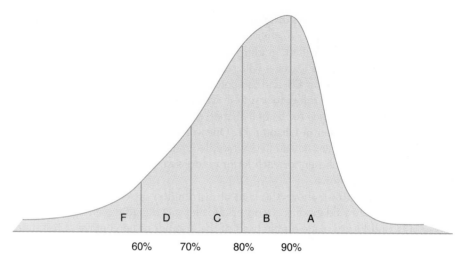

Figure 12.3
A negatively skewed curve, illustrating the distribution of test scores and grades on a criterion-referenced test.

referenced approach. This creates a *negatively skewed* distribution, with the longer tail of the curve extending to the left, as shown in Figure 12.3.

An assigned grade in a criterion-referenced grading system is more directly influenced by the degree to which a student learned what was taught than by how many others received the same or a higher grade. In other words, the standard for assigning grades in criterion-referenced grading is *absolute*—established by the teacher—as opposed to *relative*—as established by how other students performed.

On What Should a Grade Be Based?

There are many ways for learners to demonstrate achievement consistent with your goals and objectives. However, teachers, particularly at the secondary level, tend to rely predominantly on paper-and-pencil tests and written assignments to measure learner achievement. This reliance on the written over the spoken word may place certain learners at a disadvantage, particularly in culturally diverse classrooms (Bennett, 1990). By using a variety of assessment techniques, and balancing your assessments between paper-and-pencil objective tests and performance assessments, you are more likely to be fair to all learners. We discuss the subject of performance assessments in depth in Chapter 13 and that of culture-fair instruction in Chapter 15.

Including a variety of indicators of achievement raises the question of the importance or weight each component carries in the overall final course grade. **Grade weighting** involves assigning degrees of importance to the different performance indicators that are combined to determine a grade. For example, a teacher may decide that homework and classwork count for 20 percent of the grade, quizzes 20 percent, performance assessments 30 percent, formal tests 20 percent, and a journal or notebook 10 percent.

The more weight a grading component plays in your final grade, the more accountable for that component learners will be (Emmer, Evertson, Clements, & Worsham, 1994). Learners are more likely to make a special effort to do classwork and homework

How do I combine different indicators of achievement, such as classwork, homework, quizzes, and projects, into a final grade?

Grade weighting. Assigning different degrees of importance to different performance indicators that are then combined into a grade.

Students are more likely to devote effort to homework assignments if they know that homework will make up a significant portion of their final grade.

well when they represent a significant portion of the final class grade. Additionally, you will want to give more weight to the indicators that you judge to be the most valid and reliable indicators of achievement. Formal tests, for example, usually are better indicators that students have mastered basic facts and rules than either responses to oral questions or class participation.

Finally, be aware that if the different indicators of achievement are graded on different point scales (for example, tests are worth 100 points, quizzes 10 points, projects 50 points, homework 20 points, and so on), simply weighting them and then combining them into a final score may not give the components the importance they deserve. The accompanying box, *Using Grading Formulas,* illustrates three formulas commonly used in schools that attempt to balance these concerns.

Report cards are one of the principal means by which parents learn about their children's achievement. Learners and their parents should know on what the grade was based and how the grade was computed.

Using Grading Formulas

Following are examples of three commonly used grading formulas.

Example 1: The One, Two, Three Times Plan

One Time: All grades recorded for *homework* and *class work* are totaled and averaged. The average grade will count *one time* (one-sixth of the grade). For example, a student's homework and class work grades are:

84, 81, 88, 92, 96, 85, 78, 83, 91, 79, 89, 94 = 1040/12 = 86.6, or 87 average

Two Times: All of the *quizzes* are totaled and averaged. This average grade will count *two times* (one-third of the grade). For example:

82, 88, 80, 91, 78, 86 = 505/6 = 84.2, or 84 average

Three Times: All of the *tests* and *major projects* are totaled and averaged. This average will count *three times* (one-half of the grade). For example:

81, 91, 86 = 258/3 = 86 average

Final Grade: The final grade would be computed as follows:

87 (one time) + 84 + 84 (two times) + 86 + 86 + 86 (three times) = 513/6 = 85.5 = 86

Example 2: The Percentages Plan

A teacher determines a percentage for each area to be included in the grade. For example, homework and class work will count for 20 percent; quizzes, 40 percent; tests and major projects, 40 percent. Using the same scores listed above, a student's grade would be computed as follows:

20 percent of the 86.6 for homework and class work = 17.3

40 percent of the 84.2 for quizzes = 33.7

40 percent of the 86 for tests and major projects = 34.4.

To compute the final grade, add these three weighted averages: 17.3 + 33.7 + 33.4 = 85.4 = 85 as the final grade. (The average is different because the "weight" put on each area varies in the two examples.)

Example 3: The Language Arts Plan

A language arts teacher determines that four grades, those for publishing, goal meeting, keeping a journal, and daily process, each count for one-fourth (25 percent) of the grade.

The grade is computed as follows:

The publishing grade (issued at the end of the marking period) = 88

The goal-meeting grade (issued at the end of the marking period) = 86

The journal grades are 82 + 92 + 94 + 90 + 88 + 86 = 532 ÷ 6 = 88.7 = 89

The daily process grades are 78 + 82 + 86 + 94 + 94 + 91 = 525 ÷ 6 = 87.5 = 88

The six-weeks grade is 88 + 86 + 89 + 88 = 351 ÷ 4 = 87.75 = 88

Making Public Your Decisions About Grading

Learners are often uncertain about their grades at any given point in the school year and confused about how the grade is determined. Likewise, parents are often unaware of what goes into a grade and the relative importance placed on homework, participation, formal tests, and other components.

Once you have developed your grading system, you should present it to your learners, both orally and in a handout that can be sent home. Use numerical examples in both cases. While learners in the early elementary grades may not understand all of the complexities of assigning a grade, their parents will. At both the elementary and the secondary levels, a handout of your grading procedures will communicate a feeling of your accountability to parents and your values regarding achievement and grades.

Summing Up

This chapter introduced you to objective and essay tests. Its main points were these:

- Content validity is the degree to which a test covers all the content that was taught with the degree of emphasis in which it was taught.
- Two general types of test item formats are restricted-response and flexible-response. Restricted-response item formats include true-false, fill-in, multiple-choice, matching, and restricted essays. Flexible-response item formats include extended essays, term papers, research reports, and other performance-based assessments.
- Restricted-response test formats are best suited for measuring behavior at the knowledge, comprehension, and application levels; flexible-response test formats are best suited for measuring behavior at the analysis, synthesis, and decision-making levels.
- A test blueprint is a table that identifies the behaviors and content to be tested. The number and types of test questions are provided for each behavior, by content area, to indicate the instructional emphasis given to each.
- True-false questions are quick and relatively easy to construct but tend to emphasize memorization and guessing.
- Matching questions are suitable for measuring associations between facts but tend to ask trivial information and, depending on the number of alternatives, may not be adaptable to commercial answer sheets.
- Multiple-choice questions are versatile in measuring objectives from the knowledge to application levels but can be time-consuming to write and, if not carefully written, can have more than one defensible answer.
- Completion items reduce guessing but can be difficult to score, leading to multiple defensible answers.
- Restricted-response essay tests can measure behavior at higher levels of behavioral complexity but can be time-consuming to grade and require a scoring key or model answer prepared in advance.
- Criterion-referenced grades are based on standards of mastery or achievement that the teacher has determined. Norm-referenced grades are based on the relative performance of others who have taken the test.

For Discussion and Practice

°1. Identify three problems with Mr. Steele's grading practices that became apparent during his conversation with Ms. Dalton. How could each be remedied?

2. Provide one example each of how a properly constructed test could

reactivate previously learned skills and knowledge.

influence students' choice of study patterns and learning strategies.

establish a realistic picture of students' own abilities and competence.

°3. Provide one example each of how you might increase the fairness of your

Questions marked with an asterisk are answered in the appendix.

tests by making allowances for (a) gender, (b) culture/ethnicity, and (c) ability.

°4. Explain in your own words why a test, even when well constructed, will not be a perfect assessment of your learners' performance and progress.

°5. What would be an indirect assessment—or behavioral sign—for measuring the following objectives:

> How to get the correct change in a convenience store
>
> How to determine the maximum price you could pay for gasoline to travel two thousand miles if you had only $100 and your car gets 32 miles to the gallon
>
> How to determine the angle of a roof with a 3-foot slope for every 10 feet of surface area.

°6. In your own words, describe the concept of test validity. What would be the result on your learners' scores of using a test that is not valid?

°7. What three traps do teachers generally fall into when constructing paper-and-pencil tests? In your opinion, which do you believe occurs most frequently?

8. Prepare a test blueprint for a subject of your own choosing that includes at least five content areas and three levels of behavior. Indicate the number and type of test items you will include in each cell of your blueprint and the totals for each content area and behavior.

°9. Provide a sequence of steps that can be used during the item-writing process to ensure a match between your objectives and your test items.

°10. What does a restricted essay test question require of the learner? Provide an example in your teaching area.

11. Write one multiple-choice test question that asks for justifications and one true-false question that asks for revisions. Provide written instructions to your students for completing each type of question.

°12. If you taught three classes of the same subject, each with 30 students to whom you have given two essay questions requiring approximately 150 words each to answer, how many words would you be required to read? About how long do you think it would take you? Assume you will read the essays at 300 words per minute.

13. Prepare a higher-level multiple-choice question in your teaching area requiring the application of principles or procedures.

°14. Describe in your own words the concepts of validity and reliability. What would be the effects on your learners' scores of an unreliable test?

°15. What six steps can help you increase the reliability of your tests? In your opinion, which is the most difficult to achieve?

°16. Contrast the way in which a grade would be determined using a norm-referenced test with the way it would be determined using a criterion-referenced test.

17. Choose one formula for computing and weighting grades from the box titled *Using Grading Formulas* (p. 418) and show with specific assess-

ments how you would apply it during a six-week grading period in your classroom.

Suggested Readings

Kubiszyn, T., & Borich, G. (1996). *Educational testing and measurement* (5th ed.). New York: HarperCollins. Classroom teachers will find particularly helpful the discussions of essay grading, performance assessments, and the measurement of learner attitudes.

Popham, W. (1990). *Modern educational measurement.* Englewood Cliffs, NJ: Prentice-Hall. This text provides comprehensive treatment of issues surrounding testing and grading. It offers numerous practical examples of grading systems as well as insightful critiques of traditional grading procedures.

Thorndike, R. M., Cunningham, G. K., Thorndike, R. L., & Hagen, E. P. (1991). *Measurement and evaluation in psychology and education* (5th ed.). New York: Macmillan. This text devotes extensive coverage to planning, classroom tests, and rules for writing a variety of test items. It also gives a thorough treatment to standardized tests.

Assessing for Learning: Performance Assessment

This chapter will help you answer the following questions about your learners:

- Can complex cognitive outcomes, such as critical thinking and decision making, be more effectively learned with performance tests than with traditional methods of testing?
- How can I construct performance tests that measure self-direction, ability to work with others, and social awareness?
- Can standardized performance tests be scored reliably?
- How do I decide what a performance test should measure?
- How do I design a performance test based on real-life problems important to people who are working in the field?
- How can I use a simple checklist to score a performance test accurately and reliably?
- What are some ways of using rating scales to score a performance test?
- How do I decide how many total points to assign to a performance test?
- How do I decide what conditions to place on my learners when completing a performance test to make it as authentic as possible?
- What are student portfolios and how can they be graded fairly and objectively?
- How do I weight performance tests and combine them with other student work, such as quizzes, homework, and class participation, to create a final grade?

L ori Freeman, the chair of the seventh-grade science department at Sierra Blanca Junior High School, is holding a planning session with her science teachers. The topic is evaluation of the seventh-grade life science course. Ms. Freeman had previously assigned several faculty to a committee to explore alternatives to multiple-choice tests for assessing what seventh-graders achieved after a year of life science, so she begins this second meeting with a summary of the decisions made by the committee.

Ms. Freeman: Recall that last time we decided to try performance assessment on a limited basis. To begin, we decided to build a performance assessment for our unit on photosynthesis. Does anyone have anything to add before we get started?

Ms. Brown: I think it's important that we look at different ways our students can demonstrate that they can do science rather than just answer multiple-choice and essay questions. But I also want to make sure we're realistic about what we're getting into. I have 150 students in seventh-grade life science. From what I heard last time, a good performance assessment is very time-consuming. I don't see how we can make every test performance based.

Ms. Freeman: Nor should we. Paper-and-pencil tests will always be a principal means of assessment, but I think we can measure reasoning skills, problem solving, and critical thinking better than we're doing now.

Mr. Hollyfield: And recognize that there are a variety of ways students can show they're learning science. Right now there's only one way—a multiple-choice test.

Mr. Moreno: I think Jan's concerns are real. We have to recognize that performance assessment takes a lot of time. But don't forget that a good performance assessment, basically, is a good lesson. A lot of performance testing is recording what learners are doing during the lesson. We just have to do it in a more systematic way.

In this chapter you will also learn the meanings of these terms:

authentic assessment
holistic scoring
multimodal assessment
performance testing
portfolio assessment
primary trait scoring
rubrics
testing constraints

Ms. Ellison: I'm concerned about the subjectivity of these types of assessments. From what I know, a lot of performance assessment is based on our own personal judgment or rating of what students do. I'm not sure I want to defend to a parent a low grade that is based on my personal feelings.

Ms. Freeman: That can be a problem. Remember, though, you make some subjective judgments now when you grade essays or select the multiple-choice questions you use. And as with paper-and-pencil tests, there are ways to score performance assessments objectively and reliably. I think knowing that all our learners will have to demonstrate skills in critical thinking, problem solving, and reasoning will make us do a better job of teaching. I know we shouldn't let tests dictate what we teach. But in the case of performance assessment, maybe that's not such a bad idea.

What exactly is performance assessment? What form does it take? How, when, and why is it used? What role does performance assessment have in conjunction with more traditional forms of assessment? How does a teacher acquire proficiency in designing and scoring performance tests? In this chapter, we will introduce you to performance assessment. First we will describe performance assessment by showing examples of performance tests currently being used in elementary and secondary schools. We will show the progress educators have made at the state and national levels in developing performance tests that are objective, practical, and efficient. Then we will show you how to start developing and using performance tests in your own classroom.

Performance Testing

In Chapters 4, 5, and 6, you learned that children acquire a variety of skills in school. Some of them require learners to take in information by memorizing vocabulary, multiplication tables, dates of historical events, and so on. Other skills involve learning action sequences or procedures to follow when performing mathematical computations, dissecting a frog, focusing a microscope, writing, or typing. In addition, you learned that students must acquire concepts, rules, and generalizations that allow them to understand what they read, analyze and solve problems, carry out experiments, write poems and essays, and design projects to study historical, political, or economic problems.

Some of these skills are best assessed with paper-and-pencil tests. But other skills—particularly those involving independent judgment, critical thinking, and decision making—are best assessed with **performance testing.** Although paper-and-pencil tests currently represent the principal means of assessing these more complex cognitive outcomes, in this chapter we will study other ways of measuring them in more authentic contexts.

Performance testing. Tests that use direct measures of learning rather than indicators that suggest that learning has taken place.

Performance Tests: Direct Measures of Competence

In Chapters 11 and 12 you learned that many psychological and educational tests measure learning indirectly. That is, they ask questions whose responses indicate that something has been learned or mastered. Performance tests, on the other hand, use direct measures of learning rather than indicators that simply suggest cognitive, affective, or psychomotor processes have taken place. In athletics, diving and gymnastics are examples of performances that judges rate directly. Likewise, at band contests judges directly see and hear the competence of a trombone or tuba player and pool their ratings to decide who makes the state or district band and who gets the leading chairs.

Teachers can use performance tests to assess complex cognitive learning as well as attitudes and social skills in academic areas such as science, social studies, or math. When doing so, you establish situations that allow you to directly observe and rate learners as they analyze, problem solve, experiment, make decisions, measure, cooperate with others, present orally, or produce a product. These situations simulate real-world activities that students might be expected to perform in a job, in the community, or in various forms of advanced training.

Performance tests also allow teachers to observe achievements, habits of mind, ways of working, and behaviors of value in the real world. In many cases, these are outcomes that conventional tests may miss. Performance tests can include observing and rating learners as they carry out a dialogue in a foreign language, conduct a science experiment, edit a composition, present an exhibit, work with a group of other learners to design a student attitude survey, or use equipment. In other words, the teacher observes and evaluates student abilities to carry out complex activities that are used and valued outside the immediate confines of the classroom.

> Can complex cognitive outcomes, such as critical thinking and decision making, be more effectively learned with performance tests than with traditional methods of testing?

Performance Tests Can Assess Processes and Products

Performance tests can be assessments of processes, products, or both. For example, at the Darwin School in Winnipeg, Manitoba, teachers assess the reading process of each student by noting the percentage of words read accurately during oral reading, the number of sentences read by the learner that are meaningful within the context of the story, and the percentage of story elements that the learner can talk about in his or her own words after reading.

At the West Orient school in Gresham, Oregon, fourth-grade learners assemble portfolios of their writing products. These portfolios include both rough and polished drafts of poetry, essays, biographies, and self-reflections. Several math teachers at Twin Peaks Middle School in Poway, California, require their students to assemble math portfolios, which include the following products of their problem-solving efforts: long-

A performance test can evaluate process as well as product and thus can measure more of what actually goes on in the classroom and in everyday life than can a pencil-and-paper test.

term projects, daily notes, journal entries about troublesome test problems, written explanations of how they solved problems, and the problem solutions themselves.

Social studies learning processes and products are assessed in the Aurora, Colorado, public schools by engaging learners in a variety of projects built around this question: "Based on your study of Colorado history, what current issues in Colorado do you believe are the most important to address, what are your ideas about the resolutions of those issues, and what contributions will you make toward the resolutions?" (Pollock, 1992). Learners answer these questions in a variety of ways involving individual and group writing assignments, oral presentations, and exhibits.

Performance Tests Can Be Embedded in Lessons

The examples of performance tests just given involve performances that occur outside the context of a lesson and are completed at the end of a term or during an examination period. Many teachers use performance tests as part of their lessons. In fact, some proponents of performance tests hold that the ideal performance test is a good teaching activity (Shavelson & Baxter, 1992). Viewed from this perspective, a well-constructed performance test can serve as a teaching activity as well as an assessment.

For example, Figure 13.1 illustrates a performance activity and assessment that was embedded in a unit on electricity in a general science class (Shavelson & Baxter, 1992). During the activity the teacher observes and rates each learner on the method he or she uses to solve the problem, the care with which he or she measures, the manner of recording results, and the correctness of the final solution. This type of assessment provides immediate feedback on how learners are performing, reinforces hands-on teaching and learning, and underscores for learners the important link between teaching and testing. In this manner, it moves the instruction toward higher-order thinking.

Other examples of lesson-embedded performance tests might include observing and rating the following as they are actually happening: typing, preparing a microscope slide, reading, programming a calculator, giving an oral presentation, determining how plants react to certain substances, designing a questionnaire or survey, solving a math problem, developing an original math problem and a solution for it, critiquing the logic of an editorial, or graphing information.

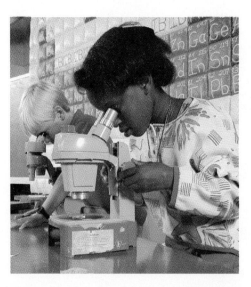

A good performance test is very much like a good lesson. During the test, learners have the opportunity to "show off" what they have been working hard to master.

HANDS-ON ELECTRIC MYSTERIES INVESTIGATION

Find out what is in the six mystery boxes A, B, C, D, E, and F. They have five different things inside, shown below. Two of the boxes will have the same thing. All of the others will have something different inside.

Two batteries:

A wire:

A bulb:

A battery and a bulb:

Nothing at all:

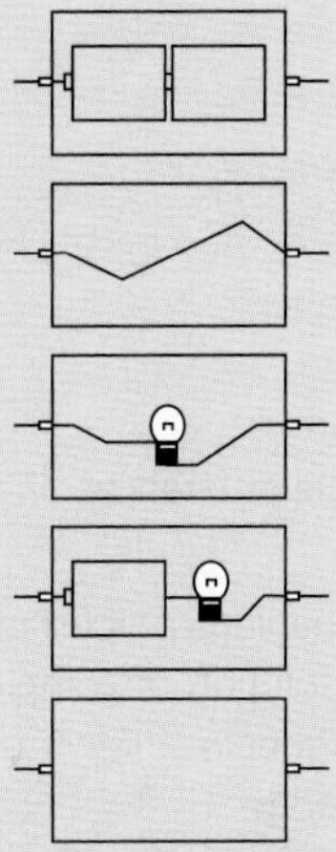

You can use your bulbs, batteries, and wires any way you like. Connect them in a circuit to help you figure out what is inside.

When you find out what is in a box, fill in the spaces on the following pages.

Box A: Has _____ inside.

Draw a picture of the circuit that told you what was inside Box A.

How could you tell from your circuit what was inside Box A?

_____

_____

_____

Do the same for Boxes B, C, D, E, and F.

_____

_____

Figure 13.1
Example of a performance activity and assessment.

Performance Tests Can Assess Affective and Social Skills

Educators across the country are using performance tests to assess not only higher-level cognitive skills but also noncognitive outcomes such as self-direction, ability to work with others, and social awareness (Redding, 1992). This concern for the affective domain of learning reflects an awareness that the skilled performance of complex tasks involves more than the ability to recall information, form concepts, generalize, and problem solve. It also involves habits of mind, attitudes, and social skills.

The Aurora public schools in Colorado have developed a list of learning outcomes and their indicators for learners in grades K through 12. These are shown in Table 13.1. For each of these 19 indicators, a four-category rating scale has been developed to serve as a guide for teachers who are unsure how to define "assumes responsibility" or "demonstrates consideration." While observing learners during performance tests in social studies, science, art, or economics, teachers recognize and rate those behaviors that suggest learners have acquired the outcomes.

Teachers in Aurora are encouraged to use this list of outcomes when planning their courses. They first ask themselves what content—key facts, concepts, and principles—all learners should remember. In addition, they try to fuse this subject area content with the five district outcomes by designing special performance tests. For example, a third-grade language arts teacher who is planning a writing unit might choose to focus on

> How can I construct performance tests that measure self-direction, ability to work with others, and social awareness?

Table 13.1

Learning Outcomes of the Aurora Public Schools

A Self-Directed Learner
1. Sets priorities and achievable goals
2. Monitors and evaluates progress
3. Creates options for self
4. Assumes responsibility for actions
5. Creates a positive vision for self and future

A Collaborative Worker
6. Monitors own behavior as a group member
7. Assesses and manages group functioning
8. Demonstrates interactive communication
9. Demonstrates consideration for individual differences

A Complex Thinker
10. Uses a wide variety of strategies for managing complex issues
11. Selects strategies appropriate to the resolution of complex issues and applies the strategies with accuracy and thoroughness
12. Accesses and uses topic-relevant knowledge

A Quality Producer
13. Creates products that achieve their purpose
14. Creates products appropriate to the intended audience
15. Creates products that reflect craftsmanship
16. Uses appropriate resources/technology

A Community Contributor
17. Demonstrates knowledge about his or her diverse communities
18. Takes action
19. Reflects on his or her role as a community contributor

indicators 8 and 9 to address district outcomes related to "collaborative worker," indicator 1 for the outcome "self-directed learner," and indicator 13 for the outcome "quality producer." She would then design a performance assessment that allows learners to demonstrate learning in these areas. She might select other indicators and outcomes for subsequent units and performance tests.

Likewise, a ninth-grade history teacher, having identified the important content for a unit on civil rights, might develop a performance test to assess district outcomes related to "complex thinker," "collaborative worker," and "community contributor." A performance test (adapted from Redding, 1992, p. 51) might take this form: "A member of a minority in your community has been denied housing, presumably on the basis of race, ethnicity, or religion. What steps do you believe are legally and ethically defensible, and in what order do you believe they should be followed?" This performance test could require extensive research, group collaboration, role-playing, and recommendations for current ways to improve minority rights.

Performance tests represent an addition to the testing practices reviewed in the previous chapter. They are not intended to replace these practices. Paper-and-pencil tests are the most efficient, reliable, and valid instruments available for assessing knowledge, comprehension, and some types of application. But when it comes to assessing complex thinking skills, attitudes, and social skills, properly constructed performance tests can do a better job. On the other hand, if they are not properly constructed, performance assessments can have some of the same problems with scoring efficiency, reliability, and validity as traditional approaches to testing. In this chapter, we will guide you through a process that will allow you to properly construct performance tests in your classroom. Before doing so, let's look at what educators and psychologists are doing at the national and state levels to develop standardized performance tests. As you read about these efforts, pay particular attention to how these forms of standardized assessment respond to the needs for scoring efficiency, reliability, and validity.

Standardized Performance Tests

In the past decade several important developments have highlighted concerns about our academic expectations for learners and how we measure them. Several presidential commissions completed comprehensive studies of the state of education in American elementary and secondary schools (Goodlad, 1984; Holmes Group, 1990; Sizer, 1984). They concluded that instruction at all levels is predominantly focused on memorization, drills, and workbook exercises. They called for the development of a curriculum that focuses on teaching learners how to think critically, reason, and problem solve in real-world contexts.

Four teachers' organizations—the National Council of Teachers of Mathematics, the National Council for Social Studies, the National Council for Improving Science Education, and the National Council of Teachers of English—took up the challenge of these commissions by publishing new curriculum frameworks. These frameworks advocate that American schools adopt a "thinking curriculum" (Mitchell, 1992; Parker, 1991; Willoughby, 1990). Finally, the National Governors' Association (NGA) in 1990 announced six national goals for American education, two of which target academic achievement:

> Goal 3: American students will achieve competency in English, mathematics, science, history, and geography at grades 4, 8, and 12 and will be prepared for responsible citizenship, further learning, and productive employment in a modern economy.

> Goal 4: U.S. students will be the first in the world in science and mathematics achievement.

The NGA commissioned the National Educational Goals Panel to prepare an annual report on the progress made by American schools toward achieving these goals. Its first report, in September 1991, concluded that since no national examination system existed, valid information could not be gathered on the extent to which American schools were accomplishing Goals 3 and 4. The goals panel then set up two advisory groups to look into the development of a national examination system: the National Council on Education Standards and Testing and the New Standards Project. Both groups concluded that Goals 3 and 4 would not be achieved without the development of a national examination system to aid schools in focusing their curricula on critical thinking, reasoning, and problem solving. Moreover, these groups agreed that only a performance-based examination system would adequately accomplish the task of focusing schools on complex cognitive skills.

The challenge for these groups was to overcome the formidable difficulties involved in developing a standardized performance test. At a minimum, such tests must have scoring standards that allow different raters to compute similar scores regardless of when or where the scoring is done. How then does the New Standards Project propose to develop direct measures of learning in science, mathematics, and the social studies with national or statewide standards that all schools can measure reliably?

To help in this process, several states, including California, Arizona, Maryland, Vermont, and New York, have developed standardized performance tests in the areas of writing, mathematics, and science. They have also worked out procedures to achieve scoring reliability of their tests. For example, New York's Elementary Science Performance Evaluation Test (ESPET) was developed over a number of years with the explicit purpose of changing how teachers taught and students learned science (Mitchell, 1992). It was first administered on a large scale in 1989. Nearly 200,000 fourth-grade students in 4,000 of New York's public and nonpublic schools took the ESPET. They included students with learning disabilities and physical handicaps as well as other learners traditionally excluded from such assessment. The fact that all fourth-grade learners took this test was intended to make a statement that science education and complex learning are expected of all students.

ESPET contains seven sections. Some contain more traditional multiple-choice and short-essay questions, and others are more performance based. Following is a description of the manipulative skills section of the test:

Five balances are seemingly randomly distributed across the five rows and five columns of desks. The balances are obviously homemade: the shaft is a dowel; the beam is fixed to it with a large nail across a notch; and the baskets, two ordinary plastic salad bowls, are suspended by paper clips bent over the ends of the beams. Lumps of modeling clay insure the balance. On the desk next to the balance beam are a green plastic cup containing water, a clear plastic glass with a line around it halfway up, a plastic measuring jug, a thermometer, and ten shiny new pennies.

Other desks hold electric batteries connected to tiny light bulbs, with wires running from the bulbs ending in alligator clips. Next to them are plastic bags containing spoons and paper clips. A single box sits on other desks. Another desk holds pieces of paper marked A, B, and C, and a paper container of water. The last setup is a simple paper plate divided into three parts for a TV dinner, with labeled instructions and a plastic bag containing a collection of beans, peas, and corn. . . .

Children silently sit at the desks absorbed in problem solving. One boy begins the electrical test, makes the bulb light, and lets out a muffled cry of satisfaction. The instructions tell him to test the objects in the plastic bag to see if they can make the bulb light. He takes the wire from one of the plastic bags and fastens an alligator clip to it. Nothing happens and he records a check in the "bulb does not light" column on his answer sheet. He gets the same result from the toothpick. He repeats the pattern for all five objects. . . .

Meanwhile, in the same row of desks, a girl has dumped out the beans and peas into the large division of the TV dinner plate as instructed and is classifying them by placing them into the two smaller divisions. She puts the Lima beans and the kidney beans into one group and the pintos, peas, and corn into the other group. The first group, she writes, is "big and dull"; the second is "small and colorful."

At the end of seven minutes, the teacher instructs them to change desks. Every child must rotate through each of the five science stations. In one day, the school tests four classes each with about twenty-five children. One teacher is assigned to set up and run the tests. The classroom teachers bring in their classes at intervals of about one hour. (Mitchell, 1992)

A Test Worth Studying For

The ESPET is a syllabus-driven performance examination. In other words, its development began with the creation of a syllabus: a detailed specification of the content and skills on which learners will be examined and the behaviors that are accepted as indicators that the content and skills have been mastered. A syllabus does not specify how the content and skills will be taught. These details, which include specific objectives, lesson plans, and activities, are left to the judgment of the teacher. The syllabus lets the teacher (and learner) know what is on the exam by identifying the real-world behaviors, called *performance objectives,* learners must be able to perform in advanced courses, other programs of study, or in a job.

Teachers of different grades can prepare learners for these objectives in numerous ways, a preparation that is expected to take several years. The examination and the syllabus and performance objectives that drive it are a constant reminder to learners, parents, and teachers of the achievements that are to be the end products of their efforts. Tests like the ESPET, by virtue of specifically defining the performances to be achieved, represent an **authentic assessment** of what is taught.

Authentic assessment. Testing that covers the content that was taught in the manner in which it was taught and that targets specific behaviors that have applicability to advanced courses, other programs of study, or careers.

A Test Worth Teaching To

But if teachers know what's on the ESPET, won't they narrow their teaching to include only those skills and activities that prepare students for the exam? Performance test advocates, such as Resnick (1990) and Mitchell (1992), argue that teaching to a test has not been a concern when the test involves gymnastics, diving, piano playing, cooking, or repairing a radio. This is because these performances are not solely test-taking tasks but also job and life tasks necessary for adult living. Performance tests, if developed cor-

Performance tests are worth studying for and teaching to. Well-designed performance tests can produce high levels of motivation and learning.

rectly, should also include such tasks. Here is Ruth Mitchell's description of a worst-case scenario involving teaching to the ESPET:

> Suppose as the worst case (and it is unlikely to happen) that a Grade 4 teacher in New York State decides that the students' scores on the manipulative skills test next year will be perfect. The teacher constructs the whole apparatus as it appeared in the test classroom . . . and copies bootlegged answer sheets. And, suppose the students are drilled on the test items, time after time. By the time they take the test, these students will be able to read and understand the instructions. They will know what "property" means in the question, "What is another property of an object in the box?" (This word was the least known of the carefully chosen vocabulary in 1989.) The students will be able to write comprehensible answers on the answer sheets. Further, they will have acquired extremely important skills in using measuring instruments, predicting, inferring, observing, and classifying. In teaching as opposed to a testing situation, it will become clear that there is no right answer to a classification, only the development of a defensible criterion. . . . In every case, the students' manipulative skills will be developed along with their conceptual understanding.
>
> A class that did nothing beyond the five stations might have a monotonous experience, but the students would learn important science process skills. (Mitchell, 1992, p. 62)

Mitchell is not advocating teaching to the manipulative section of the ESPET. Her point is that such instruction would not be fragmentary or isolated from a larger purpose, as would be the case if a learner were prepared for a specific multiple-choice or fill-in test. Important skills would be mastered, which could lead to further learning.

Scoring the ESPET

The five stations in the manipulative skills section of the ESPET require a total of 18 responses. For the station requiring measurements of weight, volume, temperature, and height the test developers established a range of acceptable responses. Answers within this range received 1 point. All others are scored 0 with no partial credit allowed.

At the station that tests prediction, learners are expected to drop water on papers of varying absorbency and then predict what would happen on a paper they could not see or experiment with. Their predictions receive differential weighting: three points for describing (within a given range) what happened when the water was dropped, 1 point for predicting correctly, and 1 point for giving an acceptable reason. When scoring these responses, teachers must balance tendencies to generosity and justice, particularly when responses were vague or writing illegible.

Rubrics. Scoring standards composed of model answers that are used to score performance tests.

The scoring standards are called **rubrics.** The classroom teachers are the raters. They are trained to compare a learner's answers with a range of acceptable answers prepared as guides. However, the rubrics acknowledge that these answers are *samples* of acceptable responses, rather than an exhaustive list. Thus, raters are required continually to judge the quality of individual student answers. All ESPET scoring is done from student responses recorded on answer sheets.

Protecting Scoring Reliability

Can standardized performance tests be scored reliably?

Performance tests such as the ESPET, which require large numbers of raters across schools and classrooms, must be continually monitored to protect the reliability of the ratings. That is, the science achievement scores for learners in different fourth grades in different schools or school districts should be scored comparably. There are several ways to accomplish this.

For some performance tests, a representative sample of tests is rescored by the staff of another school. Sometimes teachers from different schools and school districts get together and score all their examinations in common. In other cases, a "recalibration" process is used, whereby individual graders pause in the middle of their grading and grade a few tests together as a group to ensure that their ratings are not drifting away from a common standard. We will describe this process in more detail in the next section.

Community Accountability

Performance tests such as the ESPET do not have statewide or national norms that allow comparison with other learners in order to rank the quality of achievement. How, then, does a parent or school board know that the learning demonstrated on a science or math performance test represents a significant level of achievement? How does the community know that standards haven't simply been lowered or that the learner is not being exposed to new but possibly irrelevant content?

The answer lies with how the content for a performance test is developed. For example, the syllabus on which the ESPET is based was developed under the guidance of experts in the field of science and science teaching. In addition, the recalibration process ensures that science teachers at one school or school district will read and score examinations from other schools or school districts. Teachers and other professionals in the field of science or math can be expected to be critics for one another, ensuring that the syllabus will be challenging and the tests graded rigorously.

Experience with standardized performance testing in science and history in New York State and in mathematics and writing in California and Arizona has shown that cross-grading between schools and school districts provides some assurance that student learning as demonstrated on performance tests represents something of importance beyond the test-taking skills exhibited in the classroom. Nevertheless, as we will see next, research examining the cognitive complexity, validity, reliability, transfer, generalizability, and fairness of teacher-made, statewide, or national performance tests has only just begun (Herman, 1992).

What Research Suggests About Performance Tests

Some educators (for example, Herman, 1992) believe that traditional multiple-choice exams have created an overemphasis on basic skills and a neglect of thinking skills in American classrooms. Now that several states have implemented performance tests, is there any evidence that such tests have increased the complexity of cognitive goals and objectives? Herman (1992) reports that California's eighth-grade writing assessment program, which includes performance tests based on portfolios, has encouraged teachers to require more and varied writing of their learners. In addition, the students' writing skills have improved over time since these new forms of assessment were first implemented. Mitchell (1992) reports that since the ESPET was begun in 1989, schools throughout New York State have revamped their science curricula to include thinking skills for all learners.

Both Herman and Mitchell, however, emphasize that the development of performance tests without parallel improvements in curricula can result in undesirable or inefficient instructional practices, such as teachers drilling students on performance test formats. In such cases, improved test performance will not indicate improved thinking

Performance tests challenge learners with real-world problems that require higher level cognitive skills to solve.

ability, nor will it generalize to other measures of achievement (Koretz, Linn, Dunbar, & Shepard, 1991).

Do Performance Tests Measure Generalizable Thinking Skills?

Although tests such as the ESPET appear to assess complex thinking, research into their validity has just begun. While the recent developments in cognitive learning reviewed in Chapter 5 have influenced the developers of performance tests (Resnick & Klopfer, 1989; Resnick & Resnick, 1991), there is no conclusive evidence at present to suggest that important metacognitive and affective skills are being learned and generalized to tasks and situations that occur outside the performance test format and classroom (Linn, Baker, & Dunbar, 1991).

Shavelson and his colleagues (Shavelson, Gao, & Baxter, 1991) caution that conclusions drawn about a learner's problem-solving ability on one performance test may not hold for performance on another set of tasks. Similarly, Gearheat, Herman, Baker, and Wittaker (1992) have pointed out the difficulties in drawing conclusions about a learner's writing ability based on portfolios that include essays, biographies, persuasive writing, and poetry, which can indicate substantial variation in writing skill depending on the type of writing undertaken. We will return to the assessment of student portfolios later in the chapter.

Can Performance Tests Be Scored Reliably?

Little research into the technical quality of standardized performance tests has been conducted. Nevertheless, current evidence on the ability of teachers and other raters to reliably and efficiently score performance tests is encouraging (Herman, 1992). Studies of portfolio ratings in Vermont, science scoring in New York, and hands-on math assessment in Connecticut and California suggest that large-scale assessments can be administered and reliably scored by trained teachers working individually or in teams.

Summary

Statewide performance tests have been developed, administered, and reliably scored for a number of years. National panels and study groups are developing a set of standardized performance exams that all American students will take in grades 4, 8, and 12 (Resnick & Resnick, 1991). It is not yet clear whether performance tests will become as common an assessment tool in American classrooms as traditional forms of assessment are now.

Nevertheless, many developments in the design of performance tests are occurring at a rapid pace. Curriculum and measurement experts have developed tests at the statewide level that can be reliably scored and efficiently administered by teachers. These tests have encouraged more complex learning and thinking skills and in some cases, as in New York, have led to performance-based revisions of the curriculum. Accounts by Mitchell (1992), Wiggins (1992), and Wolf, LeMahieu, and Eresh (1992) suggest that teachers who have used performance tests report improved thinking and problem solving in their learners. Also, school districts in Colorado, Oregon, California, New York, New Hampshire, Texas, Illinois, and other states have taken it on themselves to experiment with performance tests in their classrooms (*Educational Leadership,* 1992). In the next section we will present a process for developing, scoring, and grading performance tests based on the cumulative experience of these teachers and educators.

Developing Performance Tests for Your Learners

Four years ago, Crow Island Elementary School began a project which has reaped benefits far beyond what any of us could have imagined. The focus of the project was assessment of children's learning, and the tangible product is a new reporting form augmented by student portfolios. . . . The entire process has been a powerful learning experience. . . . We are encouraged to go forward by the positive effects the project has had on the self-esteem and professionalism of the individual teachers and the inevitable strengthening of the professional atmosphere of the entire school. We have improved our ability to assess student learning. Equally important, we have become, together, a more empowered, effective faculty. (Hebert, 1992, p. 61)

Brian doesn't like to write. Brian doesn't write. When Brian does write, it's under duress, and he doesn't share this writing. Last year I began working with a technique called portfolio assessment. . . . Over the year Brian began to write and share his writing with others. His portfolio began to document success rather than failure. His voice, which has always been so forceful on the playground, had begun to come through in his writing as well. (Frazier & Paulson, 1992, p. 65)

As we learned in the previous section, performance assessment has the potential to improve both instruction and learning. As the quotations above illustrate, many educators around the country have decided to give it a try. What these educators have found is that performance assessment has not replaced traditional paper-and-pencil tests. Rather, it has supplemented these measures with tests that allow learners to demon-

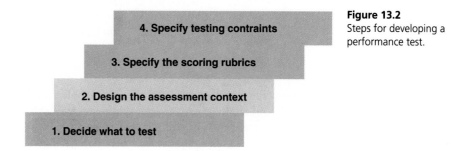

Figure 13.2
Steps for developing a performance test.

strate thinking skills through writing, speaking, projects, demonstrations, and other observable actions.

But as we have also learned, there are both conceptual and technical issues associated with the use of performance tests that teachers must resolve before performance assessments can be effectively and efficiently used. In this section we will discuss some of the important considerations in planning and designing a performance test. We will identify the tasks around which performance tests are based, and describe how to develop a set of scoring rubrics for these tasks. Also included in this section will be suggestions on how to improve the reliability of performance test scoring, including portfolios. Figure 13.2 shows the major steps in building a performance test. We discuss each step in detail below.

Deciding What to Test

Performance tests, like all authentic tests, are syllabus- or performance objectives-driven. Thus, the first step in developing a performance test is to create a list of objectives that specifies the knowledge, skills, attitudes, and indicators of these outcomes, which will then be the focus of your instruction. There are three general questions to ask when deciding what to test:

How do I decide what a performance test should measure?

1. What knowledge or content (i.e., facts, concepts, principles, rules) is essential for learner understanding of the subject matter?

2. What intellectual skills are necessary for the learner to use this knowledge or content?

3. What habits of mind or attitudes are important for the learner to successfully perform with this knowledge or content?

Performance objectives that come from answering question 1 are usually measured by paper-and-pencil tests (discussed in Chapter 12). Objectives derived from answering questions 2 and 3, although often assessed with objective or essay-type questions, can be more authentically assessed with performance tests. Thus, your assessment plan for a unit should include both paper-and-pencil tests, to measure mastery of content, and performance tests, to assess skills and attitudes. Let's see what objectives for these latter outcomes might look like.

Performance Objectives in the Cognitive Domain. Designers of performance tests usually ask these questions to help guide their initial selection of objectives:

● What kinds of essential tasks, achievements, or other valued competencies am I missing with paper-and-pencil tests?

- What accomplishments of those who practice my discipline (historians, writers, scientists, mathematicians) are valued but left unmeasured by conventional tests?

Typically, two categories of intellectual skills are identified from such questions: (a) skills related to acquiring information, and (b) skills related to organizing and using information. The accompanying box, *Designing a Performance Test,* contains a suggested list of skills for acquiring, organizing, and using information. As you study this list, consider which skills you might use as a basis for a performance test in your area of expertise. Then study the list of sample objectives in the bottom half of the box, and consider how these objectives are related to the list of skills.

Performance Objectives in the Affective and Social Domain. Performance assessments require the curriculum not only to teach thinking skills but also to develop positive dispositions and habits of mind. Habits of mind include such behaviors as constructive criticism, tolerance of ambiguity, respect for reason, and appreciation for the significance of the past. Performance tests are ideal vehicles for assessing positive attitudes toward learning, habits of mind, and social skills (for example, cooperation, sharing, and negotiation). Thus, in deciding what objectives to teach and measure with a performance test, you should give consideration to affective and social skill objectives. The following are some key questions to ask for including affective and social skills in your list of performance objectives:

- What dispositions, attitudes, or values characterize successful individuals in the community who work in your academic discipline?

- What are some of the qualities of mind or character traits possessed by good scientists, writers, reporters, historians, mathematicians, musicians, and so on?

- What will I accept as evidence that my learners have developed or are developing these qualities?

- What social skills for getting along with others are necessary for success as a journalist, weather forecaster, park ranger, historian, economist, mechanic, and so on?

- What evidence will convince my learners' parents that their children are developing these skills?

Performance tests can be used to assess habits of mind, such as cooperation and social skills.

Designing a Performance Test

Following are lists of skills appropriate for performance tests in the cognitive domain. Below these lists are a number of sample performance-test objectives derived from the listed skills.

Skills in Acquiring Information

Communicating
explaining
modeling
demonstrating
graphing
displaying
writing
advising
programming
proposing
drawing

Measuring
counting
calibrating
rationing
appraising
weighing
balancing
guessing
estimating
forecasting

Investigating
gathering references
interviewing
using references
experimenting
hypothesizing

Skills in Organizing and Using Information

Organizing
classifying
categorizing
sorting
ordering
ranking
arranging

Problem solving
stating questions
identifying problems
developing hypotheses
interpreting
assessing risks
monitoring

Decision making
weighing alternatives
evaluating
choosing
supporting
defending
electing
adopting

- Write a summary of a current controversy drawn from school life and tell how a courageous and civic-minded American you have studied might decide to act on the issue.
- Draw a physical map of North America from memory and locate 10 cities.
- Prepare an exhibit showing how your community responds to an important social problem of your choosing.
- Construct an electrical circuit using wires, a switch, a bulb, resistors, and a battery.
- Describe two alternative ways to solve a mathematics word problem.
- Identify the important variables that accounted for recent events in our state, and forecast the direction they might take.

- Design a freestanding structure in which the size of one leg of a triangular structure must be determined from the other two sides.
- Program a calculator to solve an equation with one unknown.
- Design an exhibit showing the best ways to clean up an oil spill.
- Prepare a presentation to the city council, using visuals, requesting increased funding to deal with a problem in our community.

The accompanying box, *Identifying Attitudes for Performance Assessment*, displays some examples of attitudes, or habits of mind, that could be the focus of a performance assessment in science, social studies, and mathematics. Use it to select attitudes to include in your design of a performance assessment in these areas.

In this section, we illustrated the first step in designing a performance test by helping you identify the knowledge, skills, and attitudes that will be the focus of your instruction and assessment. The next step is to design the task or context in which these outcomes will be assessed.

Designing the Assessment Context

The purpose of this step is to create an authentic task, simulation, or situation that will allow learners to demonstrate the knowledge, skills, and attitudes they have acquired. Ideas for these tasks may come from newspapers, reading popular books, or interviews with professionals as reported in the media (for example, an oil tanker runs aground and creates an environmental crisis, a drought occurs in an underdeveloped country causing famine, a technological breakthrough presents a moral dilemma). The tasks should center on issues, concepts, or problems that are relevant to your subject matter. In other words, they should be the same issues, concepts, and problems faced every day by important people working in the field.

How do I design a performance test based on real-life problems important to people who are working in the field?

Here are some questions to get you started, suggested by Wiggins (1992):

- What does the doing of mathematics, history, science, art, writing, and so forth look and feel like to professionals who make their living working in these fields in the real world?

- What are the projects and tasks performed by these professionals that can be adapted to school instruction?

- What roles—or habits of mind—do these professionals acquire that learners can re-create in the classroom?

The tasks you create may involve debates, mock trials, presentations to a city commission, reenactments of historical events, science experiments, or job responsibilities (for example, a travel agent, weather forecaster, or park ranger). Regardless of the specific context, they should present the learner with an authentic challenge. For exam-

Applying Your Knowledge:

Identifying Attitudes for Performance Assessment

Science*

- Desiring knowledge. Viewing science as a way of knowing and understanding.
- Being skeptical. Recognizing the appropriate time and place to question authoritarian statements and "self-evident truths."
- Relying on data. Explaining natural occurrences by collecting and ordering information, testing ideas, and respecting the facts that are revealed.
- Accepting ambiguity. Recognizing that data are rarely clear and compelling, and appreciating the new questions and problems that arise.
- Willingness to modify explanations. Seeing new possibilities in the data.
- Cooperating in answering questions and solving problems. Working together to pool ideas, explanations, and solutions.
- Respecting reason. Valuing patterns of thought that lead from data to conclusions and eventually to the construction of theories.
- Being honest. Viewing information objectively, without bias.

Social Studies†

- Understanding the significance of the past to their own lives, both private and public, and to their society.

- Distinguishing between the important and inconsequential to develop the "discriminating memory" needed for a discerning judgment in public and personal life.
- Preparing to live with uncertainties and exasperating, even perilous, unfinished business, realizing that not all problems have solutions.
- Appreciating the often tentative nature of judgments about the past, and thereby avoiding the temptation to seize on particular "lessons" of history as cures for present ills.

Mathematics‡

- Appreciating that mathematics is a discipline that helps solve real-world problems.
- Seeing mathematics as a tool or servant rather than something mysterious or mystical to be afraid of.
- Recognizing that there is more than one way to solve a problem.

*From Loucks-Horsley et al., 1990, p. 41.
†From Parker, 1991, p. 74.
‡From Willoughby, 1990.

ple, consider the following social studies performance test (adapted from Wiggins, 1992):

> You and several travel agent colleagues have been assigned the responsibility of designing a trip to China for 12- to 14-year-olds. Prepare an extensive brochure for a month-long cultural exchange trip. Include itinerary, modes of transportation, costs, suggested budget, clothing, health considerations, areas of cultural sensitivity, language considerations, and other information necessary for parents to decide whether they want their child to participate.

Notice that this example presents learners with the following:

1. A hands-on exercise or problem to solve, which produces
2. an observable outcome or product (typed business letter, a map, graph, piece of clothing, multi-media presentation, poem, and so forth), which enables the teacher to
3. observe and assess not only the product but also the process used to arrive at it.

Designing the content for a performance test involves equal parts inspiration and perspiration. While no formula or recipe guarantees a valid performance test, the criteria given here can help guide you in revising and refining the task (Resnick & Resnick, 1991; Wiggins, 1992).

1. Make the requirements for task mastery clear, but not the solution. While your tasks should be complex, the required final product should be clear. Learners should not have to question whether they have finished or provided what the teacher wants. They should, however, have to think long and hard about how to complete the task. As you refine the task, make sure you can visualize what mastery of the task looks like and identify the skills that can be inferred from it.

2. The task should represent a valid sample from which generalizations about the learner's knowledge, thinking ability, and attitudes can be made. What performance tests lack in breadth of coverage they can make up in depth. In other words, they force you to observe a lot of behavior in a narrow domain of skill. Thus, the tasks you choose should be complex enough and rich enough in detail to allow you to draw conclusions about transfer and generalization to other tasks. Ideally, you should be able to identify 8 to 10 important performance tasks for an entire course of study (one or two per unit) that assess the essential performance outcomes you want your learners to achieve (Shavelson & Baxter, 1992).

3. The tasks should be complex enough to allow for multimodal assessment. Most assessment tends to depend on the written word. Performance tests, however, are designed to allow learners to demonstrate learning through a variety of modalities. This is referred to as **multimodal assessment.** In science, for example, one could make direct observations of students while they investigate a problem using laboratory equipment, give oral explanations of what they did, record procedures and conclusions in notebooks, prepare exhibits of their projects, and solve short-answer paper-and-pencil problems. A multimodal assessment of this kind is more time-consuming than a multiple-choice test, but it will provide unique information about your learners' achievements untapped by other assessment methods. Shavelson and Baxter (1992) have shown that performance tests allow teachers to draw different conclusions about a learner's problem-solving ability than do higher-order multiple-choice tests or restricted-response essay tests, which ask learners to analyze, interpret, and evaluate information.

Multimodal assessment. The evaluation of performance through a variety of forms.

4. The tasks should yield multiple solutions where possible, each with costs and benefits. Performance testing is not a form of practice or drill. It should involve more than simple tasks for which there is one solution. Performance tests should, in the words of Resnick (1987), be nonalgorithmic (the path of action is not fully specified in advance), be complex (the total solution cannot be seen from any one vantage point), and involve judgment and interpretation.

5. The tasks should require self-regulated learning. Performance tests should require considerable mental effort and place high demands on the persistence and determination of the individual learner. The learner should be required to use cognitive strategies to arrive at a solution rather than depend on coaching at various points in the assessment process.

We close this section with three boxes, *Designing a Performance Assessment: Math, Communication,* and *History.* Each contains an example of a performance assessment task that contains most of these design considerations. Note that the first of these, the math assessment, also contains a scoring rubric, which is the subject of our next section.

Applying Your Knowledge:

Designing a Performance Assessment: Math

Joe, Sarah, José, Zabi, and Kim decided to hold their own Olympics after watching the Olympics on TV. They needed to choose the events to have at their Olympics. Joe and José wanted weight lifting and Frisbee toss events. Sarah, Zabi, and Kim thought a running event would be fun. The children decided to have all three events. They also decided to make each event of the same importance.

One day after school they held their Olympics. The children's mothers were the judges. The mothers kept the children's scores on each of the events.

The children's scores for each of the events are listed below:

Child's Name	Frisbee Toss	Weight Lift	50-Yard Dash
Joe	40 yards	205 pounds	9.5 seconds
José	30 yards	170 pounds	8.0 seconds
Kim	45 yards	130 pounds	9.0 seconds
Sarah	28 yards	120 pounds	7.6 seconds
Zabi	48 yards	140 pounds	8.3 seconds

Now answer the question "Who won the Olympics?" and give an explanation of how you arrived at your answer (4 points).

Sample Responses

Student A

Who would be the all-around winner?

ZABI

Explain how you decided who would be the all-around winner. Be sure to show all your work.

I decided by how each person came in and that is who won.   **2 pts**

Student B

Who would be the all-around winner?

ZABI

Explain how you decided who would be the all-around winner. Be sure to show all your work.

I wrote in order all the scores from first place to fifth place. Then I added them up.   **3 pts**
Whoever had the least amount won.

Student C

Who would be the all-around winner?

ZABI

Explain how you decided who would be the all-around winner. Be sure to show all your work.

Zabi got one first place and two third places. I counted 3 points for every first   **4 pts**
place they got and 2 points for second place and 1 point for third place. Zabi got
the most points.

Source: From Blumberg, Epstein, MacDonald, & Mullis, 1986.

Applying Your Knowledge:

Designing a Performance Assessment: Communication

1. You are representing an ad agency. Your job is to find a client in the school who needs photos to promote his or her program. (Examples: the future teachers club, the fine arts program, Student Council.)

2. Your job is to research all the possibilities, select a program, learn about that program, and then record on film the excitement and unique characteristics that make up the program you have selected. Your photos will be used to advertise and stimulate interest in that area.

3. Visualize how you will illustrate your ideas either by writing descriptions or by drawing six of your proposed frames. Present these six ideas to your instructor (the director of the ad agency) before you shoot.

Source: Redding, 1992, p. 49.

Specifying the Scoring Rubrics

One of the principal limitations of performance tests is the time required to score them reliably. Just as these tests require time and effort on the part of the learner, they demand a similar commitment from teachers when scoring them. True-false, multiple-choice, and fill-in items are significantly easier to score than projects, portfolios, or performances. In addition, these latter accomplishments force teachers to make difficult choices about how much qualities like effort, participation, and attitude count in the final score.

Given the challenges confronting teachers who use performance tests, there is a temptation to limit the scoring criteria to the qualities of performance that are easiest to rate (e.g., keeping a journal of problems encountered) rather than the most important required for doing an effective job (e.g., the thoroughness with which the problems encountered were resolved). Wiggins (1992) cautions teachers that scoring the easiest or least controversial qualities can turn a well-thought-out and authentic performance test into a bogus one. Thus, your goal when scoring performance tests is to do justice to the time spent developing them and the effort expended by students taking them. You can accomplish this by developing carefully articulated scoring systems, or rubrics.

By giving careful consideration to rubrics, you can develop a scoring system for performance tests that minimizes the arbitrariness of your judgments while holding learners to high standards of achievement. Following are some of the important considerations in developing rubrics for a performance test.

Applying Your Knowledge:

Designing a Performance Assessment: History

You and your colleagues (groups of three or four) have been asked to submit a proposal to write a U.S. history textbook for middle school students. The publishers demand two things: that the book hit the most important events, and that it be interesting to students. Because of your expertise in eighteenth-century American history, you will provide them with a draft chapter on the eighteenth century, up to but not including the American Revolution, field-tested on some middle school students. They also ask that you fill in an "importance" chart with your responses to these questions:

1. Which event, person, or idea is most important in this time period, and why?
2. Which of three sources of history—ideas, people, events—is most important?

You will be expected to justify your choices of "most important" and to demonstrate that the target population is likely to be interested in your book.

Source: Wiggins, 1992, p. 28.

Developing Rubrics. You should develop scoring rubrics that fit the kinds of accomplishments you want to measure. In general, performance tests require four types of accomplishments from learners:

- **Products:** Poems, essays, charts, graphs, exhibits, drawings, maps, and so forth.
- **Complex cognitive processes:** Skills in acquiring, organizing, and using information.
- **Observable performances:** Physical movements, as in dance, gymnastics, or typing; oral presentations; use of specialized equipment, as in focusing a microscope; following a set of procedures, as when dissecting a frog, bisecting an angle, or following a recipe.
- **Attitudes and social skills:** Habits of mind, group work, and recognition skills.

As this list suggests, the effect of your teaching may be realized in a variety of ways. The difficulty in scoring some of these accomplishments should not deter your attempts to measure them. Shavelson and Baxter (1992), Kubiszyn and Borich (1996), and Sax (1989) have shown that if they are developed carefully and the training of those doing the scoring has been adequate, performance measures can be scored reliably.

Choosing a Scoring System. Choose a scoring system best suited for the type of accomplishment you want to measure. In general, there are three categories of rubrics to use when scoring performance tests: checklists, rating scales, and holistic scoring (see Figure 13.3). Each has certain strengths and limitations, and each is more or less suitable for scoring products, cognitive processes, performances, or attitudes and social skills.

Checklists. Checklists contain lists of behaviors, traits, or characteristics that can be scored as either present or absent. They are best suited for complex behaviors or perfor-

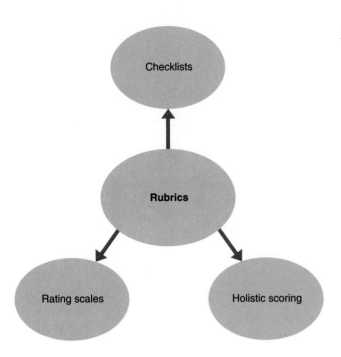

Figure 13.3
Types of scoring rubrics.

mances that can be divided into a series of clearly defined specific actions. Dissecting a frog, bisecting an angle, balancing a scale, making an audiotape recording, or tying a shoe are behaviors requiring sequences of actions that can be clearly identified and listed on a checklist. Checklists are scored on a yes/no, present/absent, 0 or 1 point basis and should also allow the observer to indicate that she had no opportunity to observe the performance. Some checklists also list common mistakes that learners make when performing the task. In such cases, a score of + 1 may be given for each positive behavior, − 1 for each mistake, and 0 for no opportunity to observe. Figures 13.4 and 13.5 show checklists for using a microscope and a calculator.

Rating Scales. Rating scales are typically used for aspects of a complex performance that do not lend themselves to the yes/no or present/absent type of judgment. The most common form of rating scale is one that assigns numbers to categories of performance. Figure 13.6 (p. 449) shows a rating scale for judging elements of writing in a term paper. This scale focuses the rater's observations on certain aspects of the performance (accuracy, logic, organization, style, and so on) and assigns numbers to five degrees of performance.

Most numeric rating scales use an analytical scoring technique called **primary trait scoring** (Sax, 1989). This type of rating requires that the test developer first identify the most salient characteristics, or traits of greatest importance, when observing the product, process, or performance. Then, for each trait, the developer assigns numbers (usually 1–5) that represent degrees of performance.

Figure 13.7 (p. 450) displays a numerical rating scale that uses primary trait scoring to rate problem solving (Szetela & Nicol, 1992). In this system, problem solving is subdivided into the primary traits of understanding the problem, solving the problem, and answering the problem. For each trait, points are assigned to certain aspects or qualities

> How can I use a simple checklist to score a performance test accurately and reliably?

> What are some ways of using rating scales to score a performance test?

Primary trait scoring. An analytical scoring technique that requires a test developer to first identify the most salient characteristics or primary traits when observing a product, process, or performance.

No opportunity to observe	Observed	
☐	☐	Wipes slides with lens paper
☐	☐	Places drop or two of culture on slide
☐	☐	Adds few drops of water
☐	☐	Places slide on stage
☐	☐	Turns to low power
☐	☐	Looks through eyepiece with one eye
☐	☐	Adjusts mirror
☐	☐	Turns to high power
☐	☐	Adjusts for maximum enlargement and resolution

Figure 13.4
Checklist for using a microscope.

No opportunity to observe	Observed	
☐	☐	Turns calculator on
☐	☐	"Keys in" ten numbers consecutively without hitting adjacent keys
☐	☐	Quickly adds three two-digit numbers without error
☐	☐	Knows how to position keyboard and to rest arm and elbow for maximum comfort and accuracy
☐	☐	Knows how to reposition display screen to reduce reflection and glare, when necessary
☐	☐	Pushes keys with positive, firm motions
☐	☐	Can feel when a key touch is insufficiently firm to activate calculator

Figure 13.5
Checklist for using an electronic calculator.

Quality and accuracy of ideas

1	2	3	4	5
Very limited investigation; little or no material related to the facts.		Some investigation and attention to the facts are apparent.		Extensive investigation; good detail and representation of the facts.

Logical development of ideas

1	2	3	4	5
Very little orderly development of ideas; presentation is confusing and hard to follow.		Some logical development of ideas, but logical order needs to be improved.		Good logical development; ideas logically connected and build upon one another.

Organization of ideas

1	2	3	4	5
No apparent organization; lack of paragraphing and transitions.		Organization is mixed; some of the ideas not adequately separated from others with appropriate transitions.		Good organization and paragraphing; clear transitions between ideas.

Style, individuality

1	2	3	4	5
Style bland and inconsistent or "borrowed."		Some style and individuality beginning to show.		Good style and individuality; personality of writer shows through.

Wording and phrasing

1	2	3	4	5
Wording trite; extensive use of clichés.		Some word choices awkward.		Appropriate use of words and phrasing works to sharpen ideas.

Figure 13.6
Rating scale for themes and term papers that emphasizes interpretation and organization.

of the trait. Notice how the designer of this rating scale identified characteristics of both effective and ineffective problem solving.

Two key questions are usually addressed in the design of scoring systems for rating scales using primary trait scoring (Wiggins, 1992):

- What are the most important characteristics that show a high degree of the trait?
- What are the errors most justifiable for achieving a lower score?

Answering these questions can prevent raters from assigning higher or lower scores on the basis of performance that may be trivial or unrelated to the purpose of the perfor-

Understanding the problem

0   No attempt
1   Completely misinterprets the problem
2   Misinterprets major part of the problem
3   Misinterprets minor part of the problem
4   Complete understanding of the problem

Solving the problem

0   No attempt
1   Totally inappropriate plan
2   Partially correct procedure but with major fault
3   Substantially correct procedure with major omission or procedural error
4   A plan that could lead to a correct solution with no arithmetic errors

Answering the problem

0   No answer or wrong answer based upon an inappropriate plan
1   Copying error; computational error; partial answer for problem with multiple
     answers; no answer statement; answer labeled incorrectly
2   Correct solution

Figure 13.7
Analytic scale for problem solving. *Source:* From Szetela & Nicol, 1992, p. 42.

mance test, such as the quantity rather than the quality of a performance. One of the advantages of rating scales is that they focus the scorer on specific and relevant aspects of a performance. Without the breakdown of important traits, successes, and relevant errors provided by these scales, a scorer's attention may be diverted to aspects of performance that are unrelated to the purpose of the performance test.

Holistic Scoring. **Holistic scoring** is used when the rater estimates the overall quality of the performance and assigns a numerical value to that quality, rather than assigning points for specific aspects of the performance. Holistic scoring is typically used in evaluating extended essays, term papers, or artistic performances, such as dance or musical creations. For example, a rater might decide to score an extended essay question or term paper on an A–F rating scale. In such a case, it would be important for the rater to have a model paper that exemplifies each score. After having created or selected these models from the set to be scored, the rater again reads each paper and then assigns each to one of the categories. A model paper for each category (A–F) helps to assure that all the papers assigned to a given category are of comparable quality.

Holistic scoring systems can be more difficult to use for performances than for products. For the former, some experience in rating the performance (for example, dramatic rendition, oral interpretations, or debate) may be required. In these cases, audiotapes or videotapes from past classes can be helpful as models representing different categories of performance.

Combined Scoring Systems. As was suggested, good performance tests require learners to demonstrate their achievements through a variety of primary traits, such as cooperation, research, and delivery. In some cases, therefore, the best way to arrive at a total assessment may be to combine several ratings, from checklists, rating scales, and

Holistic scoring. Estimating the overall quality of a performance by giving a single value that represents a specific category of accomplishment.

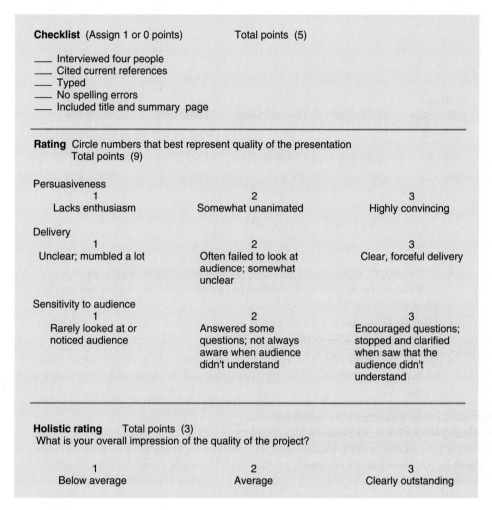

Checklist (Assign 1 or 0 points)   Total points (5)

____ Interviewed four people
____ Cited current references
____ Typed
____ No spelling errors
____ Included title and summary page

Rating   Circle numbers that best represent quality of the presentation
        Total points (9)

Persuasiveness

1	2	3
Lacks enthusiasm	Somewhat unanimated	Highly convincing

Delivery

1	2	3
Unclear; mumbled a lot	Often failed to look at audience; somewhat unclear	Clear, forceful delivery

Sensitivity to audience

1	2	3
Rarely looked at or noticed audience	Answered some questions; not always aware when audience didn't understand	Encouraged questions; stopped and clarified when saw that the audience didn't understand

Holistic rating   Total points (3)
What is your overall impression of the quality of the project?

1	2	3
Below average	Average	Clearly outstanding

Figure 13.8
Combined scoring rubric for a current events project: Total points equal 17.

holistic impressions. Figure 13.8 shows how scores across several traits for a current events project might be combined to provide a single performance score.

Comparing the Three Scoring Systems. Each of the three scoring systems has strengths and weaknesses. Table 13.2 serves as a guide in choosing a particular scoring system for a given type of performance, according to the following criteria:

- **Ease of construction:** the time involved in coming up with a comprehensive list of the important aspects or traits of successful and unsuccessful performance. Checklists, for example, are particularly time-consuming, while holistic scoring is not.

- **Scoring efficiency:** the amount of time required to score various aspects of the performance and calculate these scores as an overall score.

Table 13.2

Comparison of Three Performance-Based Scoring Systems

	Ease of Construction	Scoring Efficiency	Reliability	Defensibility	Feedback	More Suitable For
Checklist	low	moderate	high	high	high	procedures, attitudes
Rating scale	moderate	moderate	moderate	moderate	moderate	products, social skills
Holistic scoring	high	high	low	low	low	products and processes

- **Reliability:** the likelihood that two raters will independently come up with a similar score, or the likelihood that the same rater will come up with a similar score on two separate occasions.
- **Defensibility:** the ease with which you can explain your score to a student or parent who challenges it.
- **Quality of feedback:** the amount of information the scoring system gives to learners or parents about the strengths and weaknesses of the performance.

Assigning Point Values. When assigning point values to various aspects of the performance test, it is a good idea to limit the number of points the assessment or component of the assessment is worth to that which can be reliably discriminated. For example, if you assign 25 points to a particular product or procedure, you should be able to distinguish 25 degrees of quality. When faced with more degrees of quality than can be detected, a typical rater may assign some points arbitrarily, reducing the reliability of the assessment.

How do I decide how many total points to assign to a performance test?

On what basis should points be assigned to a response on a performance test? On the one hand, you want a response to be worth enough points to allow you to differentiate subtle differences in response quality. On the other hand, you want to avoid assigning too many points to a response that does not lend itself to complex discriminations. Thus, assigning one or two points to a math question requiring complex problem solving would not allow you to differentiate between outstanding, above average, average, and poor responses. But assigning 30 points to this same answer would seriously challenge your ability to distinguish a rating of 15 from a rating of 18. Two considerations can help in making decisions about the size and complexity of a rating scale.

First, the scoring model should allow that rater to specify the exact performance—or examples of acceptable performance—that correspond with each scale point. The ability to successfully define distinct criteria, then, can determine the number of scale points that are defensible. Second, although it is customary for homework, paper-and-pencil tests, and report cards to use a 100 point (percent) scale, scale points derived from performance assessments do not need to add up to 100. We will have more to say later about assigning marks to performance tests and how to integrate them with other aspects of an overall grading system (for example, homework, paper-and-pencil tests, classwork), including portfolios.

Specify Testing Constraints

Should performance tests have time limits? Should learners be allowed to correct their mistakes? Can they consult references or ask for help from other learners? Performance tests confront the designer with the following dilemma: If the test is designed to confront learners with real-world challenges, why shouldn't they be allowed to tackle these challenges as real-world people do? In the world outside the classroom, mathematicians make mistakes and correct them, journalists write first drafts and revise them, weather forecasters make predictions and change them. Each of these workers can consult references and talk with colleagues. Why, then, shouldn't learners who are working on performance tests that simulate similar problems be allowed the same working (or testing) conditions?

Even outside the classroom, professionals have constraints on performance, such as deadlines, limited office space, or outmoded equipment. So how does a teacher decide which conditions to impose during a performance test? Before examining this question, let's look at some of the typical conditions, or **testing constraints,** imposed on learners during tests. Wiggins (1992) includes the following among the most common forms of testing constraints:

- **Time.** How much time should a learner have to prepare, rethink, revise, and finish a test?
- **Reference material.** Should learners be able to consult dictionaries, textbooks, or notes as they take a test?
- **Other people.** May learners ask for help from peers, teachers, and experts as they take a test or complete a project?
- **Equipment.** May learners use computers or calculators to help them solve problems?
- **Prior knowledge of the task.** How much information about the test situation should learners receive in advance?
- **Scoring criteria.** Should learners know the standards by which the teacher will score the assessment?

Wiggins recommends that teachers take an "authenticity test" to decide which of these constraints to impose on a performance assessment. His authenticity test involves answering the following questions:

- What kinds of constraints authentically replicate the constraints and opportunities facing the performer in the real world?
- What kinds of constraints tend to bring out the best in apprentice performers and producers?
- What are the appropriate or authentic limits one should impose on the availability of the six resources just listed?

Indirect forms of assessment, by the nature of the questions asked, require numerous constraints during the testing conditions. Allowing learners to consult reference materials or ask peers for help during multiple-choice tests would significantly reduce their

How do I decide what conditions to place on my learners when completing a performance test to make it as authentic as possible?

Testing constraints. The amount of time, reference material, degree of help (if any) from others, specialized equipment, prior knowledge of the task, and scoring criteria that test-takers can have during a performance assessment.

validity. Performance tests, on the other hand, are direct forms of assessment in which real-world conditions and constraints play an important role in demonstrating the competencies desired.

Portfolio Assessment

Portfolio assessment. Assessment of a learner's entire body of work in a defined content area in order to demonstrate the student's growth and achievement.

What are student portfolios and how can they be graded fairly and objectively?

According to Paulson and Paulson (1991), portfolios "tell a story." The story, viewed as a whole, answers the question, "What have I learned during this period of instruction and how have I put it into practice?" Thus **portfolio assessment** is assessment of a learner's entire body of work in a defined area, such as writing, science, or math. The object of portfolio assessment is to demonstrate the student's growth and achievement.

Some portfolios represent the student's own selection of products—scripts, musical scores, sculpture, videotapes, research reports, narratives, models, and photographs—that represent the learner's attempt to construct his or her own meaning out of what has been taught. Other portfolios are preorganized by the teacher to include the results of specific products and projects, the exact nature of which may be determined by the student.

Whether portfolio entries are preorganized by the teacher or left to the discretion of the learner, several questions must be answered prior to the portfolio assignment:

- What are the criteria for selecting the samples that go into the portfolio?
- Will individual pieces of work be evaluated as they go into the portfolio, or will all the entries be evaluated collectively at the end of a period of time—or both?
- Will the amount of student growth, progress, or improvement over time be graded?
- How will different entries, such as videos, essays, artwork, and reports, be compared and weighted?
- What role will peers, parents, other teachers, and the student him- or herself have in the evaluation of the portfolio?

Shavelson, Gao, and Baxter (1991) suggest that at least eight products or tasks over different topic areas may be needed to obtain a reliable estimate of performance from portfolios. Therefore, portfolios are usually built and assessed cumulatively over a period of time. These assessments determine the quality of individual contributions to the larger portfolio at various time intervals and the quality of the entire portfolio at the end of instruction.

Various schemes have been devised for evaluating portfolios (Paulson & Paulson, 1991). Most involve a recording form in which (1) the specific entries are cumulatively rated over a course of instruction, (2) the criteria with which each entry is to be evaluated are identified beforehand, and (3) an overall rating scale is provided for rating each entry against the criteria given.

Frazier and Paulson (1992) and Hebert (1992) report successful ways in which peers, parents, and students themselves have participated in portfolio evaluations. Figure 13.9 represents one example of a portfolio assessment form intended for use as a cumulative record of accomplishment over an extended course of study.

Many teachers use portfolios to increase student reflections about their own work and encourage the continuous refinement of portfolio entries. Portfolios have the ad-

Student: _Julia Coe_ Grade: _8_ Date: _4/16_ Rater: _Mrs. Hartley_	**A1 Understanding of Task:** SOURCES OF EVIDENCE • Explaining of task • Reasonableness of approach • Correctness of response	**A2 How—Quality of Approaches/Procedures** SOURCES OF EVIDENCE • Demonstrations • Descriptions (oral or written) • Drafts, scratch work, etc.	**A3 Why—Decisions Along the Way** SOURCES OF EVIDENCE • Revisions in approach • Explanations (oral or written) • Validation of final solution
Entry 1 Title: _Photosynthesis_ D (I) A O Demonstration Investigation Application Other	4 *Good oral presentation*	2 *Graphing procedures not uniform*	2 *Logical conclusions with supporting data*
Entry 2 Title: _Game of chance_ D I (A) O Demonstration Investigation Application Other	3 *Practical example*	2 *Lacks some sources from text*	4 *Shows careful thinking*
Entry 3 Title: _____ D I A O Demonstration Investigation Application Other			
Entry 4 Title: _____ D I A O Demonstration Investigation Application Other			
Entry 5 Title: _____ D I A O Demonstration Investigation Application Other			
Overall Ratings ➡	**A1 Understanding of Task** **Final Rating** 1 Totally misunderstood 2 Partially understood 3 Understood 4 Generalized, applied, extended	**A2 How—Quality of Approaches/Procedures** **Final Rating** 1 Inappropriate or unworkable approach/procedure 2 Appropriate approach/procedure some of the time 3 Workable approach/procedure 4 Efficient or sophisticated approach/procedure	**A3 Why—Decisions Along the Way** **Final Rating** 1 No evidence of reasoned decision making 2 Reasoned decision making possible 3 Reasoned decisions/adjustments inferred with certainty 4 Reasoned decisions/adjustments shown/explicated

Figure 13.9
Example of portfolio assessment form. *Source:* Adapted from *Looking Beyond "The Answer," the Vermont Mathematics Portfolio, 1992,* report of the Vermont Mathematics Portfolio Assessment Program, publication year 1990–91. Montpelier, VT: Vermont Department of Education.

vantage of containing multiple samples of student work completed over time that can represent finished works as well as works in progress. Entries designated "works in progress" are cumulatively assessed at regular intervals on the basis of student growth or improvement and on the extent to which the entry increasingly matches the criteria given.

Performance Tests and Report Card Grades

How do I weight performance tests and combine them with other student work, such as quizzes, homework, and class participation, to create a final grade?

Performance tests require a substantial commitment of teacher time and learner-engaged time. Consequently, the performance test grade should have substantial weight in the report card grade. Here are two approaches to designing a grading system that includes performance assessments.

One approach to scoring quizzes, tests, homework assignments, performance assessments, and so forth. is to score each on the basis of 100 points. Computing the final grade, then, simply involves averaging the grades for each component, multiplying these averages by the weight assigned, and adding these products to determine the total grade. The box titled *Using Grading Formulas* at the end of Chapter 12 provided examples of three formulas for accomplishing this. But as discussed above, these methods require that you assign the same number of points (usually 100) to everything you grade.

Another approach is to use a "percentage of total points" system. With this system you decide how many points each component of your grading system is worth on a case-by-case basis. For example, you may want some tests to be worth 40 points, some 75, depending on the complexity of the questions and the performance desired. Likewise, some of your homework assignments may be worth only 10 or 15 points. The accompa-

Table 13.3

Example of Grade Components and Weights

Component	Weight
Homework	15%
Objective tests	20%
Performance tests	20%
Portfolio	20%
Classwork	15%
Notebook	10%
TOTAL	100%

Component	Homework							Objective tests			Performance tests			Port-folio	Classwork						Note-book
Dates	8/20	9/7	9/14	9/20	9/28	10/6	TOTAL	9/17	10/7	TOTAL	9/23	10/8	TOTAL	10/7	9/2	9/6	9/14	9/23	10/5	TOTAL	10/8
Cornell	10/10	8/10	14/15	10/10	8/15	0/10	50/70	20/30	25/30	45/60	15/20	18/20	33/40	18/20	9/10	7/15	10/10	9/10	4/5	39/50	5/10
Rosie	10/10	5/10	12/15	8/10	12/15	8/10	55/70	15/30	20/30	35/60	20/20	19/20	39/40	15/20	8/10	14/15	0/10	10/10	5/5	37/50	8/10

Figure 13.10
Sample grade recording sheet, first marking period.

nying box, *Using a Combined Grading System,* describes procedures involved in setting up such a grading scheme for a six-week grading period. Table 13.3 and Figure 13.10 provide some example data for how such a system works.

Final Comments

Performance assessments create challenges that restricted-response tests do not. Performance grading requires greater use of judgment than do true-false or multiple-choice questions. These judgments can become more reliable if (1) the performance to be judged is clearly defined, (2) the ratings or criteria used to make the judgments are determined beforehand, and (3) two or more raters independently grade the performance and an average is taken.

Using videotapes or audiotapes can enhance the validity of performance assessments when direct observation of performance is required. Furthermore, performance assessments need not take place at one time for the whole class. Learners can be assessed at different times, individually or in small groups. For example, learners can rotate through classroom learning centers (Shalaway, 1989) and be assessed when the teacher feels they are acquiring mastery.

Finally, don't lose sight of the fact that performance assessments are meant to serve and enhance instruction rather than being simply an after-the-fact test given to assign a grade. When tests serve instruction, they can be given at a variety of times and in as many settings and contexts as instruction requires. Some performance assessments can sample the behavior of learners as they receive instruction or be placed within ongoing classroom activities rather than consume extra time during the day.

Summing Up

This chapter introduced you to performance-based assessment. Its main points were these:

- Performance tests use direct measures of learning that require learners to analyze, problem solve, experiment, make decisions, measure, cooperate with others, present orally, or produce a product.

Applying Your Knowledge:

Using a Combined Grading System

Step 1: Identify the components of your grading system and assign each component a weight. A weight is the percentage of total points a particular component carries. Table 13.3 displays components and weights for a six-week grading plan.

Step 2: Record the actual points each student earned out of the number of points possible in the grade book. Leave a column for totals. (See Figure 13.10.) As you can see, each component and each separate assignment has varying numbers of possible points that can be earned. Assign points to each component based on the complexity of the required performance, the length of the assignment, and your perception of your ability to assign reliable ratings.

Step 3: Total the actual points earned for each component and divide the total by the possible points. The results represent the percentage of points earned for each particular component. Thus, in our example from Figure 13.10, Cornell and Rosie earned the following points and totals:

	Cornell	Rosie
Homework	50/70 = 71%	55/70 = 79%
Objective tests	45/60 = 75%	35/60 = 58%
Performance tests	33/40 = 83%	39/40 = 98%
Portfolio	18/20 = 90%	15/20 = 75%
Classwork	39/50 = 78%	37/50 = 74%
Notebook	5/10 = 50%	8/10 = 80%

Step 4: Multiply each of these percentages by the weights assigned, as shown in Table 13.3, and total these products.

	Cornell	Rosie
Homework	71 $\times$ .15 = 10.6	79 $\times$ .15 = 11.8
Objective tests	75 $\times$ .20 = 15	58 $\times$ .20 = 11.6
Performance tests	83 $\times$ .20 = 16.6	98 $\times$ .20 = 19.6
Portfolio	90 $\times$ .20 = 18	75 $\times$ .20 = 15
Classwork	78 $\times$ .15 = 11.7	74 $\times$ .15 = 11.1
Notebook	50 $\times$ .10 = 5	80 $\times$ .10 = 8
Totals	76.9	77.1

Step 5: Record the grade either as a letter grade (A = 90–100 percent, etc.) or as the percentage itself, depending on your school's system.

- Performance tests can assess not only higher-level cognitive skills but also noncognitive outcomes, such as self-direction, ability to work with others, and social awareness.
- Rubrics are scoring standards composed of model answers that are used to score performance tests. They are samples of acceptable responses against which the rater compares a student's performance.
- Research on the effects of performance assessment indicates that when teachers include more thinking skills in their lesson plans, higher levels of student performance tend to result. However, there is no evidence yet that the thinking skills measured by performance tests generalize to tasks and situations outside the performance test format and classroom.
- The four steps to constructing a performance assessment are deciding what to test, designing the assessment context, specifying the scoring rubrics, and specifying the testing constraints.
- A performance test can require four types of accomplishments from learners: products, complex cognitive processes, observable performance, and attitudes and social skills. These performances can be scored with checklists, rating scales, or holistic scales.
- Constraints that must be decided on when a performance test is constructed and administered are the amount of time allowed, use of reference material, help from others, use of specialized equipment, prior knowledge of the task, and scoring criteria.
- Two approaches to combining performance grades with other grades are (1) to assign 100 total points to each assignment that is graded and average the results, and (2) to use the percentage-of- total-point systems.

For Discussion and Practice

°1. Compare and contrast some of the reasons for giving conventional tests with those for giving performance assessments.

°2. Using an example from your teaching area, explain the difference between direct and indirect measures of behavior.

3. Describe some habits of mind that might be required by a performance test in your teaching area. How did you learn about the importance of these attitudes, social skills, and ways of working?

°4. Describe how at least two school districts have implemented performance assessments. Indicate the behaviors they assess and by what means they are measured.

5. Would you agree or disagree with this statement: "An ideal performance test is a good teaching activity"? With a specific example in your teaching area, illustrate why you answered as you did.

6. List at least two learning outcomes and describe how you would measure them in your classroom to indicate that a learner is (1) self-directed,

---

Questions marked with an asterisk are answered in the appendix.

(2) a collaborative worker, (3) a complex thinker, (4) a quality producer, and (5) a community contributor.

°7. Describe what is meant by a scoring rubric and how such rubrics were used in New York State's Elementary Science Performance Evaluation Test.

°8. What two methods have been used successfully to protect the scoring reliability of a performance test? Which would be more practical in your own teaching area or at your grade level?

°9. What is meant by the community accountability of a performance test and how can it be determined?

°10. In your own words, how would you answer a critic of performance tests who says they don't measure generalizable thinking skills outside the classroom and can't be scored reliably?

11. Identify for a unit you will be teaching several attitudes, habits of mind, and/or social skills that would be important to using the content taught in the real world.

12. Create a performance test of your own choosing that (1) requires a hands-on problem to solve and (2) results in an observable outcome for which (3) the process used by learners to achieve the outcome can be observed. Use the five criteria by Wiggins (1992) and Resnick and Resnick (1991) to help guide you.

13. For the performance assessment above, describe and give an example of the accomplishments—or rubrics—you would look for in scoring the assessment.

14. For this same assessment, compose a checklist, rating scale, or holistic scoring method by which a learner's performance would be evaluated. Explain why you chose that scoring system, which may include a combination of the above methods.

15. For your performance assessment above, describe the constraints you would place on your learners pertaining to the time to prepare for and complete the activity; references that may be used; people that may be consulted, including other students; equipment allowed; prior knowledge about what is expected; and points or percentages you would assign to various degrees of their performance.

16. Imagine you have to arrive at a final grade composed of homework, objective tests, performance tests, portfolio, classwork, and notebook, which together you want to add up to 100 points. Using Figure 13.10 and Table 13.3 as guides, compose a grading scheme that indicates the weight, number, individual points, and total points assigned to each component. Indicate the percentage of points required for the grades A–F.

Suggested Readings

ASCD (1992). Using performance assessment [special issue]. *Educational Leadership, 49*(8). This special issue contains clear, detailed examples of what teachers around the country are doing to give performance tests a try.

Linn, R. L., Baker, E., & Dunbar, S. B. (1991). Complex performance based assessment: Expectations and validation criteria. *Educational Researcher, 20*(8), 15–21. A clear, concise review of the strengths and limitations of performance tests. Also discusses the research that needs to be done to improve their validity and reliability.

Mitchell, R. (1992). *Testing for learning: How new approaches to evaluation can improve American schools.* New York: Free Press. The first comprehensive treatment of alternative approaches to traditional testing. Includes excellent discussions of the problems of current testing practice and the advantages of performance tests. The examples of performance tests are especially helpful.

What Teachers Need to Know About Learner Diversity

This evening's school board meeting of the Brownwood Consolidated School District has one agenda item: the district budget. Brownwood's tax base has been slowly but steadily eroding over the past decade. To compound the problem, the state has been reimbursing the district less and less for its pupil expenditures. Consequently, the school trustees are caught in a familiar dilemma: maintaining quality of education without raising taxes.

The first two hours of the meeting are taken up with citizen comment on the proposed budget. Speakers address such choices as cutting funds for the gifted and talented education program (GATE), closing the alternative learning center for children with emotional and behavior problems (ALC), eliminating the positions of several counselors and school psychologists, and delaying the renovation of the high school gym.

Now it is time for the school board members to begin discussion on the budget. The chairperson recognizes Mr. O'Neill.

Mr. O Neill: In general I support the idea of mainstreaming, but I just don't see how we can close down the ALC. It would be too disruptive to the education of the regular kids to have these kinds of behavior problems in the regular classroom.

Mr. Stover: Most of the kids in the ALC stay there forever. As long as the place exists, the individual learning needs of these children will continue to be unmet. They belong in the regular classroom, where they can learn in a natural environment.

Ms. Toomey: I was a teacher—and you wouldn't say that if you had to manage a class of 35 kids, even one of whom was disrupting the class. We have a responsibility to the kids who want to learn, especially the gifted ones. With this proposal to cut our GATE program, we'll be doing these kids a disservice.

Ms. Maitland: I agree with Mr. Stover. I'd like to see more rather than less diversity in the classroom. It seems as if we try too hard to homogenize the class. If the kid is gifted, we get him out. If she has learning or behavior problems, we get her out.

Ms. Toomey: But how can we afford to train teachers to deal with this diversity?

Ms. Maitland: The issue may not be to "deal" with diversity like we "deal" with a problem. I think diversity is an opportunity that we should make the most of.

Although the school setting has remained largely unchanged over the past 100 years, the major participants—your students—have not. The typical classroom of today contains a more diverse group of learners than at any point in history. This diversity reflects not only the motivational and cognitive abilities that children bring to school but also the culture that accompanies them.

Added to this medley of cultures in our schools is an assortment of family patterns. In the near future, the majority of children entering school will live with only one parent at some time before their eighteenth birthday, leaving at least 4 million latchkey children of school age at home alone (Hodgkinson, 1988). Even in two-parent families, both parents are likely to be working full time.

The result of this diversity will be an ever-widening increase in the range of individual differences you will find in your classroom. This diversity, however, will be equaled by the diversity of opinion about how teachers should deal with it. There is no consensus in America regarding the goals of education in our culturally diverse, pluralistic society. Some educators view diversity as a problem whose solution lies in administrative arrangements to make classrooms more homogeneous. Others believe that the needs of certain cultural groups are so different from those of the majority that the solution is to create separate schools or curricula specific to particular cultures or genders.

In this section, our view of the goals of schooling will be similar to that of Ms. Maitland: Learner diversity is not an obstacle to be overcome; it is an opportunity to make your classroom a laboratory for living in a democratic society. We see nothing inherently disadvantageous about diversity. The teacher must simply recognize that some of the rules that apply to teaching in a culturally uniform, homogeneous classroom may not always apply to a culturally diverse, heterogeneous class.

Our purpose in the next three chapters is to provide you with a knowledge base for teaching heterogeneous groups of learners. We will conceptualize learner diversity as more than just cultural diversity. Learner diversity encompasses those who differ not only in race, culture, and ethnicity, but also in intellectual abilities, academic achievement, and gender.

Chapter 14 describes several types of learners: those with specific learning or behavioral disabilities, those with specific physical and communication disabilities, and those who are gifted or talented. For each type of learner, we will focus on important issues related to assessment, intervention, and inclusion in regular classrooms.

Chapter 15 addresses cultural diversity, gender differences in achievement, and sex bias in teacher-pupil interactions. You will learn what many concerned educators are doing to inspire cultural diversity, eliminate cultural and gender stereotypes, and promote a nonsexist curriculum.

Finally, Chapter 16 addresses the family-school partnership. In this chapter, we will learn about a systems-ecological perspective on family-school partnerships and the many ways the classroom teacher can promote this partnership. As we will see, meaningful parent participation is an essential ingredient of a successful classroom.

Let's begin our look at these important issues by examining the diversity in learning ability you can expect to find in your classroom.

Teaching Exceptional and At-Risk Learners

This chapter will help you answer the following questions about your learners:

- Will children with severe learning disabilities or mental retardation be in my classroom?
- What instructional arrangements are needed to meet the needs of both exceptional and nonexceptional learners?
- How can schools provide a normal school environment for children with disabilities?
- How can I explain to parents why their learning disabled child isn't achieving up to potential?
- How can I recognize ADHD in a learner?
- What can I do in my classroom to help learners with ADHD?
- How can I identify and assist learners with physical or communication disabilities?
- What specific skills will I need for teaching exceptional learners?
- What activities and experiences will enhance the educational opportunities of a gifted or talented learner?

The faculty members of Fawkes Middle School are milling around the library following a presentation by a state education official, "New Directions in Educating Exceptional Learners." The official, Dr. Bell, has spoken about current practices in the classification and placement of children with physical and learning disabilities, behavior disorders, mental retardation, and the gifted and talented. He has told them that they can expect the inclusion of many of these exceptional learners in their regular classrooms. The teachers, especially those in regular education, have immediately grasped the significance of his message. A glance around the library shows faces with expressions of concern, frustration, and determination. Let's listen to what some of the teachers are saying.

Art: So does this mean that I'll have to teach kids with severe learning disabilities or mental retardation?
Stu: No one expects that. But some of the kids we're now labeling and placing in special classes could benefit from being in our regular classes. That's what Dr. Bell was saying.
Art: Do you think we'll get the support we'll need to teach these kids?

Near the windows several reading teachers are clustered with Jeri, one of the special education teachers.

Terry: How do you feel, Jeri, about losing your job in the resource room?
Jeri: I think Dr. Bell is right. I'd rather work with these kids in their regular classes. It makes them feel too different to leave their regular classes, and I'm not sure what's gained by it.
Mario: But they *are* different. Look at the slow ones. Are we doing them a favor by leaving them in the regular class? How are they going to get the help they need?
Gail: They may not be getting all the help they need now. If the research Dr. Bell cited is correct, some of the labeling and placement we're doing now isn't having the effects we expected. So maybe we need to include them in our regular classes.
Mario: But a lot of teachers don't know much about special ed kids and will need special training.

In this chapter you will also learn the meanings of these terms:

accelerated curriculum
adaptive behavior
attention deficit
attention deficit hyperactivity disorder (ADHD)
communication disability
gifted and talented
hearing disability
hyperactivity
impulsivity
individualized education plan (IEP)
intelligence
IQ–achievement discrepancy
learning disability
least restrictive environment
mainstreaming
mental retardation
normalization
Public Law 94-142
Regular Education Initiative (REI)
task persistence
visual disability

Jeri: I do the same types of things with these kids as any regular teacher. And I'd rather do it in a regular classroom than in a room that doesn't allow for peer interaction.

Gail: Jeri's right. There are ways of organizing a class and directing the work of individual learners that could help us adapt to the change. That was the other half of what Dr. Bell was saying. We have new methods and materials that weren't around when a lot of these learners were in special classes.

Mainstreaming. An approach to educating learners with developmental disabilities that seeks to maximize opportunities for interaction with nondisabled peers.

With the passage of Public Law 94-142 in 1975, learners with disabilities acquired the right to be educated with their nondisabled peers. This law, which requires the public schools to educate learners with disabilities in the least restrictive environment conducive to their development, has come to be known as **mainstreaming.**

We will begin our discussion of the exceptional learner with a brief history of the mainstreaming movement. In particular, we will focus on some of the important legal developments that have contributed to it. Then we will narrow our focus to five categories of exceptional learners: those with mental retardation, those with learning disabilities, those with behavioral disorders, those with sensory and communication disorders, and those who are gifted and talented. For each group we will discuss their assessment, classification, and placement, and we will provide guidelines to help you meet their needs in your classroom. Let's begin with a portrait of Mike, one of the exceptional learners you are likely to meet in your classroom.

Mike, a fifth-grader, is one of the more puzzling individuals to his regular and special education teachers. He looks and speaks just like everyone else outside the classroom, but inside he's withdrawn and easily frustrated.

He starts off his school day by coming to homeroom class. But at the beginning of first period, Mike leaves for the resource room for reading, language, and math. Most of his mornings are spent in a special room with other learners who practice remedial skills, which typically are taught to learners two or three years younger. This is Mike's third year in a resource room, and sometimes he wonders when he's going to be learning the same things his fifth-grade friends are learning. Mike has an average IQ, but he can't seem to make quick enough progress in the regular classroom. One day he seems to learn a new skill; the next day he forgets it.

There are about 17 other learners in the resource room. Some are learning disabled, some have behavior problems, and others are simply labeled slow learners. One teacher and an aide teach them, mostly with individual worksheets and handouts. Theirs is a difficult assignment. There are frequent disruptions in the resource room as kids come and go in the middle of periods. Mike finds it hard to pay attention. Because of the large number of students, he receives only about 10 to 15 minutes of help from his teacher; the rest of the time he spends working through assignments on his own.

He returns to his regular class for physical education followed by lunch. Then he has social studies, science, and fine arts with the regular learners. In his regular classes, Mike's differences stand out. Since he doesn't read and write as well as the others, he's not asked to do what they do during science and social studies. Some of the time he spends completing special worksheets given him by the resource teacher; at other times he just daydreams.

The System of Special Education

Although Mike is considered exceptional, his education is not. His classroom and educational plan are typical of those of many students with learning disabilities. Mike spends nearly half the school day away from his peers. Although individual learners spend different amounts of time in the regular classroom, the system of offering services to learners with disabilities remains largely segregated. It is often referred to as the dual or two-level system: one educational program for regular learners, another for learners with disabilities. In this dual system, special education has its own administration, teachers, budget, psychologists, curriculum, and grading system.

The Regular Education Initiative (Inclusion)

The **Regular Education Initiative (REI),** which Dr. Bell was explaining to the faculty of Fawkes Middle School, represents an attempt to end this dual system (Miller, 1990; Robinson, 1990). It advocates a partnership between regular and special educators in which learners with disabilities would receive individualized services in the regular classroom without the requirement of labeling or special classifications. Figure 14.1 depicts the continuum of special education services, ranging from total exclusion from the regular classroom on one end and total inclusion in the regular classroom on the other. The REI represents the inclusion pole of the continuum, in which the learner is educated with peers in the regular classroom for the entire day.

Advocates of REI (Anderegg & Vergason, 1988; Forest & Pierpoint, 1992; Gersten & Woodward, 1990; Robinson, 1990; Wang, Walberg, & Reynolds, 1992) make these arguments:

- Special education has become a depository for learners who may be difficult to teach but not truly disabled.
- Despite public laws requiring education in the "least restrictive environment," the present system of special education unintentionally imposes barriers to full integration in school and community life.
- The criteria for being placed in a special education category are vague and inconsistently applied. Often the same learner may be declared eligible or ineligible for individualized services depending on who did the assessment.
- African American, Hispanic, Native American, and learners of lower socioeconomic status are often overrepresented in special education programs.

Regular Education Initiative (REI). The mainstreaming of learners with disabilities into regular classrooms where those learners receive individualized services.

Will children with severe learning disabilities or mental retardation be in my classroom?

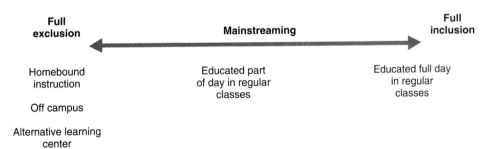

Figure 14.1
The continuum of special education services.

- Typically, the curriculum of pull-out programs is poorly integrated with that of the regular classroom. Thus, students in resource classrooms may not learn the academic or social skills they need when they return to the regular classroom.

The REI is not without its critics, however, even among those who advocate mainstreaming (Kaufman, 1989; Schumaker & Deshler, 1988; Wood, 1992). These critics make the following arguments:

- The rights of learners with disabilities, as presently constituted, are protected by law. But these rights could be jeopardized if labels and categories pertaining to learner disabilities were eliminated. For example, a school district could decide to allot a disproportionate amount of its special services funds to learners other than the disabled.

- Many teachers lack the training and skills to educate diverse groups of learners in their classrooms. Many may also lack the required commitment.

- Behavior problems could increase as learners who need more individualized attention fail to receive it. This would lead to increased numbers of learners being labeled as having behavior problems.

- Regular learners may not be prepared to accept peers with disabilities in their classrooms. This could perpetuate feelings of rejection and lower self-esteem in disabled learners.

As both sides debate the Regular Education Initiative, many public schools across America are beginning to initiate or are being required to develop some form of REI. Since you are likely to become a part of this initiative, you will need to be informed about it and prepared to implement it. Let's begin with a brief history of mainstreaming to better understand the learners who are its focus.

A Brief History of Mainstreaming

The rights of learners with disabilities to an appropriate education has long been an issue for educators and psychologists (Wood, 1992), but not until the 1960s did concerns for protecting these rights receive national attention.

This attention can be attributed in part to the civil rights movement of the 1950s and 1960s, whose objective was equal educational opportunity across racial boundaries. This was achieved in 1954 with the landmark U.S. Supreme Court decision *Brown* v. *Board of Education of Topeka*, which codified the right of African Americans to be educated alongside whites. This case created a precedent for other litigation dealing with the constitutionally protected rights of all learners to equal educational opportunities. Just as "separate but equal" treatment for African American learners was rejected in the public schools, so was "separate but equal" treatment rejected for learners with disabilities. By the close of the 1950s, advocates for these learners began lobbying for national legislation requiring training for special education personnel. This legislation came with the Elementary and Secondary Education Act of 1965 and its various amendments in 1970, which provided federal funds for disabled learners and recognized disabled children as a special needs population.

There are two important results of these and subsequent laws for disabled learners: (1) They clearly established the right to humane treatment and educational opportunities for the disabled; and (2) they required that such learners be identified or classified as disabled in order to qualify for funds to pay for these services. This classification requirement has become a major cause of concern among psychologists, educators, and parents.

From about 1967 through the early 1970s, several major lawsuits brought about by dissatisfied parents of disabled learners further heightened concern for the rights of exceptional children. Thus, from 1950 to 1975, federal legislation and court decisions constructed a legal and educational framework for the treatment of learners with disabilities in public schools. However, there was no single federal mandate that parents could turn to to activate the rights of disabled children. They and their advocacy groups had to sift through many court decisions and federal laws to learn what different learners with different disabilities were entitled to. The need for a major, all-encompassing federal mandate was finally met when President Gerald Ford signed Public Law 94-142, the Education for All Handicapped Children Act, on November 29, 1975.

Public Law 94-142, the Education for All Handicapped Children Act of 1975

Public Law (PL) 94-142 is universally regarded as a landmark piece of education law, as significant for public school education as the 1954 *Brown* v. *Board of Education of Topeka* decision. It accomplished the following:

- It guaranteed that all children who required special education would receive it.
- It assured fairness in how learners with disabilities would be assessed and educated.
- It established standards of accountability for appropriate services at all levels of government.
- It provided federal funds to assist state and local governments to meet provisions of the law.

These goals were accomplished through five major components of the law that affect the identification of learners with disabilities, where they will be educated, and how instruction will be delivered. Let's examine some of the more important aspects of these components to better understand the law and the dual system of education that it began.

Major Components of PL 94-142

The Right to a Free Appropriate Public Education (FAPE). Prior to this law, parents had to pay for private services for their disabled children. As a result, many learners went without needed services. With the passage of PL 94-142, learners with disabilities between the ages of 6 and 21 were guaranteed free and appropriate educational services in public schools.

Nondiscriminatory Evaluation Procedures. As we saw in Chapter 11, the early tests of learning ability reflected various forms of bias. PL 94-142 provided specific guidelines for the reliability and validity of tests used to assess learners with disabilities as well as for the training of personnel who would administer these tests.

Public Law 94-142. The Education for All Handicapped Children Act of 1975, which guaranteed that all children who needed special education would receive a free individualized education plan, assured instructional fairness for learners with disabilities, established procedural due process, and provided federal funding to meet the provisions of the law.

Procedural Due Process. Parents of exceptional children, whose lawsuits in the 1960s and 1970s began the movement toward equal educational opportunity, could not be ignored in the educational assessment and placement process. With PL 94-142, they acquired the right to:

- determine whether their child should be evaluated for special services
- determine whether their child should be placed in a special education program, and also to withdraw this permission at any time
- examine and challenge the confidential records of their child
- request an independent evaluation of their child's performance from professionals outside the public school setting
- disagree with a school district's decision that either qualifies a child for special education or finds the child ineligible for services. In such cases, both the parents and the school can present evidence, call witnesses, and have lawyers present. Both parties also have the right to appeal.

Individualized education plan (IEP). A written educational plan, revised annually, that provides a detailed road map of the kinds of services a child will receive and how those services will be evaluated.

An Individualized Education Plan (IEP) for Each Learner. The **individualized education plan (IEP)** is a written educational plan, revised annually, that provides a detailed road map to the kinds of services a child will receive and how these services will be evaluated. It includes:

- individualized goals and objectives with timelines
- a description of the child's current skill level with respect to the above
- a description of the services to be received in order to achieve the goals and objectives.

Least restrictive environment. According to Public Law 94-142, the environment that maintains "the greatest degree of freedom, self-determination, dignity, and integrity of body, mind, and spirit for the individual while he or she participates in treatment or receives services."

The requirement that the child be educated in his or her least restrictive environment is the most debated aspect of PL 94-142. **Least restrictive environment** refers to the objective of maintaining the greatest degree of freedom; self-determination; dignity; and integrity of body, mind, and spirit for the individual while he or she participates in treatment or receives services. Figure 14.2 portrays the concept of least restricted environment (LRE) as it applies to school learners.

What instructional arrangements are needed to meet the needs of both exceptional and nonexceptional learners?

The school committee that designs an exceptional learner's IEP has wide latitude in constructing the least restrictive environment. Public Law 94-142 requires that the committee first consider quadrant A for all learners. If this committee (which includes regular classroom teachers, special education teachers, a school administrator, a school psychologist, the parent, and sometimes the learners themselves) rules out these LREs, it next considers quadrant B, followed by quadrants C and D. However, state education agencies and local school districts increasingly encourage or require schools to provide most services in quadrants A and B of the LREs.

Legislation Since PL 94-142

Since 1975, three other legislative mandates have influenced the education of individuals with disabilities.

- PL 99-457, Education of the Handicapped Act Amendments of 1986. This law expanded the provisions of PL 94-142 to include learners with disabilities between ages 3 and 5. In addition, it extended services to infants and toddlers with disabilities and their families.

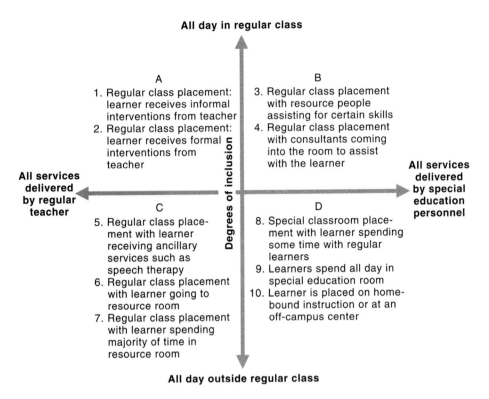

All day in regular class

Degrees of inclusion

All services delivered by regular teacher

All services delivered by special education personnel

A
1. Regular class placement: learner receives informal interventions from teacher
2. Regular class placement: learner receives formal interventions from teacher

B
3. Regular class placement with resource people assisting for certain skills
4. Regular class placement with consultants coming into the room to assist with the learner

C
5. Regular class placement with learner receiving ancillary services such as speech therapy
6. Regular class placement with learner going to resource room
7. Regular class placement with learner spending majority of time in resource room

D
8. Special classroom placement with learner spending some time with regular learners
9. Learners spend all day in special education room
10. Learner is placed on home-bound instruction or at an off-campus center

All day outside regular class

Figure 14.2
Alternative educational environments for learners with disabilities.

- PL 101-336, The Americans with Disabilities Act of 1990. This law protects the rights of all individuals with disabilities by:

    Prohibiting employment discrimination.
    Requiring that individuals with handicaps have access to appropriate transportation.
    Requiring ramps for wheelchairs and removal of barriers to the access of public institutions by persons with handicaps.
    Requiring telephone companies to assist the visually and hearing impaired.
- Education of the Handicapped Act Amendments of 1990. This act added "autism" and "traumatic brain injury" to the list of handicapping conditions that receive services under PL 94-142. In addition, it requires IEPs to provide for "transition services," which spell out the precise process by which learners return to their LREs. Finally, it changed the way we refer to exceptional learners: not as "handicapped children" but as "children with disabilities."

The Principle of Normalization

Underlying this nearly two-decade legal struggle to protect the rights of exceptional learners is a principle called **normalization.** This principle provides the standards by

Normalization. The principle that learners are entitled to programs that allow them to experience the respect and dignity to which any person in their culture or society is entitled.

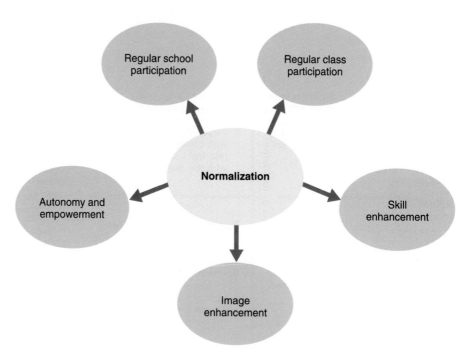

Figure 14.3
Dimensions of normalization.

which current services for learners with disabilities are to be provided. In essence, it states that such learners are entitled to programs that allow them to experience the respect and dignity to which any person in our society is entitled.

Normalization requires that programs for exceptional learners reflect the culture of which these learners are a part. This applies both to what the program achieves for the learners (social skills, academic skills, personal appearance, and so on) and how it does it (physical setting, method of grouping learners, activities provided, staff serving the program, language used to describe the program). Five dimensions encompass the major themes of normalization as they apply to public school learners with disabilities (Gardner & Chapman, 1985, 1990): regular school participation, regular class participation, skill enhancement, image enhancement, and autonomy and empowerment (see Figure 14.3). Let's take a closer look at each of these.

> **How can schools provide a normal school environment for children with disabilities?**

Regular School Participation

According to the principle of normalization, all learners—regardless of disability—should have the opportunity to participate in the routine life of the school. Learners in wheelchairs should be able to attend basketball games. Individuals with mental retardation should be able to attend school dances and other social events. Learners who are excluded from the regular classroom for severely disruptive behavior may still be allowed to have some access to their peers, for example, to eat in the cafeteria and attend assemblies.

Regular Class Participation

As discussed in our analysis of the least restrictive environment, this dimension emphasizes the importance of allowing learners with disabilities to have opportunities to develop normal social relationships with a regular classroom of peers.

Skill Enhancement

The focus of special education programs should be to teach individuals skills that will make their lives as normal as possible. Learners classified as severely emotionally disturbed (SED) who lack social skills should be taught them as part of their IEP. Behavior modification programs should spend as much time teaching learners appropriate behaviors as they spend on reacting to inappropriate ones. Learners who have difficulty spelling, writing, or reading should be taught to master these skills in ways that do not label or stigmatize.

For example, it violates the principle of normalization not to teach handwriting skills to a learner who finds this particularly difficult, assuming the learner has the physical capability to write. Likewise, individuals with mental retardation who lack skills in toileting, dressing, feeding, using public transportation, or crossing streets should be taught these skills and not be left dependent on others to handle these aspects of life.

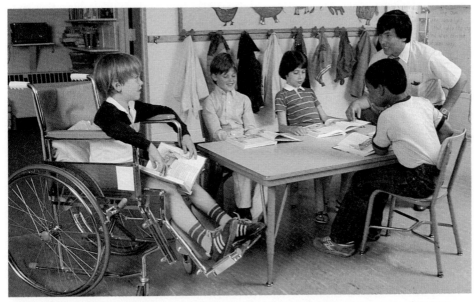

Learners with disabilities should learn in settings that allow them to experience age-appropriate peer relationships and to be treated with dignity and respect.

Image Enhancement

Special education programs violate the principle of normalization when they engage in practices that reinforce stereotypes about individuals with mental retardation, learning disabilities, or emotional disturbance. Common examples are:

- referring to exceptional children using stereotypic labeling, such as "MR," "LD," "ED," or derogatory phrases
- using signs in the school such as "resource room," "alternative learning center," "remedial reading," or "adaptive PE instructor," which can stigmatize or psychologically separate students from their peers
- using educational activities and materials that are inappropriate for the chronological age of the learner; for example, using toys and other materials that are usually used exclusively by toddlers and preschoolers with older children with mental retardation.

Autonomy and Empowerment

As much as possible, individuals with disabilities should be given as many of the same choices as their nondisabled peers with respect to what they do, when and where they do it, with whom, for how long, and in what way. This dimension, when practical, reminds educators to transfer power and control to persons with disabilities and to encourage their participation in the regular classroom and the development of their educational program.

Special Class Versus Regular Class Placement

Concerns about how "special" special education is have never been as prominent as they are today (Hilliard, 1992; Kavale, 1990; Skrtic, 1991). Some educators believe that special education as it is now practiced violates principles of normalization and should turn more toward mainstreaming most learners (Skrtic, 1991). Others have suggested that minority learners are overrepresented in programs for the mentally retarded and learning disabled, and underserved in programs for the academically gifted. Still others have asked whether special education has achieved its intended effects. We might ask whether learners with specific learning disabilities, mental retardation, or emotional disturbance would have been better off had they been left in their regular classes.

Kavale (1990) refers to this as the efficacy question. Research investigating the efficacy question by Carlberg and Kavale (1980) and Kavale (1990) fails to find an advantage for exceptional learners as a result of special class placement. Learners who were two or three years behind their peers in reading or math achievement before being placed in special education classes gained no ground on their peers after two, three, or more years of special education.

Furthermore, special education students classified as having mild mental retardation (IQs of 50 to 70) or as slow learners (IQs of 70 to 90) not only failed to gain ground in math or reading achievement, but actually lost some ground. In other words, for these groups of learners, special class placement resulted in fewer gains than if they had been left in their regular classes. Keogh (1988), Hallahan, Keller, McKinney, Lloyd, and Bryon (1988), Hilliard (1992), Lipsky and Gartner (1989), and Skrtic (1991) all conclude that special class placement does not have a direct instructional benefit on exceptional learners. Advocates of the Regular Education Initiative have examined these data and concluded that there is little justification for special class placement for large numbers of the learners who are now in special classes (Pugack & Lilly, 1984; Skrtic, 1991; Stainback & Stainback, 1984; Wang, Reynolds, & Walberg, 1982; Wang, Walberg, & Reynolds, 1992).

Understanding Exceptional Learners

Over the past decade there has been some debate over the most appropriate expressions to use when describing learners with disabilities (Wood, 1992). Clinical psychologists and physicians traditionally have had the greatest impact on special education terminology. Thus expressions such as "mentally retarded," "learning disabled," "emotionally disturbed," and "physically handicapped" reflect a perspective often referred to as the "medical" or "pathological" model. In other words, the professionals who use such terms tend to view the problem as existing within the person.

How Should We Refer to Learners with Disabilities?

Until recently, legislation governing services for exceptional learners has reflected primarily this medical model. PL 94-142, for example, requires that school psychologists and educational diagnosticians assign labels such as "mentally retarded" or "learning disabled" as a condition for receiving special education services. The primacy of the medical model, however, is diminishing because of concerns that such a perspective runs contrary to the principle of normalization. Recall that one of the themes of this principle is that of image enhancement. Many advocates of learners with disabilities believe that current classifications stigmatize learners and encourage stereotypic thinking about them (Wang, Walberg, & Reynolds, 1992).

Recent legislation reflects a concern for image enhancement. As we saw above, Education of the Handicapped Act Amendments of 1990 changed the way we refer to exceptional learners from "handicapped children" to "children with disabilities." Such expressions, and others like them (for example, learners with mental retardation, children with attention-deficit disorder, learners with visual impairment), are attempts to affirm that exceptional learners are people first, who incidentally have certain physical, cognitive, or emotional characteristics.

Let's look now at some of the learners whose mastery of important educational skills is sufficiently below "normal" or below expectations to identify them as having a specific learning or behavior disability.

Students with Mental Retardation

Less than three decades ago, some psychologists, psychiatrists, educators, and policy makers believed that children with mental retardation could not profit from schooling (Cipiani, 1991). Such children were often confined to large institutions, where they received strictly custodial care. With the passage of PL 94-142, even learners with severe mental retardation have the right to an education in the least restrictive environment.

But there are obstacles in the way of providing education for students with mental retardation. Some of them are due to a lack of knowledge about the best ways to teach these learners, while others are due to misinformation and stereotypes pertaining to individuals with mental retardation (Jacobson, 1991). Since you will probably teach and interact with children who have some form of mental retardation, it is important that you know about them. In this section, we will investigate (1) the more common causes

Mental retardation. A developmental disability characterized by significantly below-average intellectual functioning and significantly below-average adaptive behavior.

of mental retardation, (2) problems encountered in the attempt to classify learners with mental retardation, (3) the learning needs of these children, and (4) challenges that confront teachers because of the unique communication problems experienced by students with mental retardation.

The Definition of Mental Retardation

PL 94-142 defines **mental retardation** in this way:

> Significantly subaverage general intellectual functioning existing concurrently with deficits in adaptive behavior manifested during the developmental period, which adversely affects the child's educational performance.

Mental retardation is generally considered to be a developmental disability that occurs between conception and the eighteenth year. Presently, a normal individual who suffered severe brain damage after the nineteenth birthday would not be considered to have mental retardation—even if he or she displayed many of the same cognitive deficits as individuals with mental retardation before this age.

The most widely accepted method for diagnosing mental retardation today is based on performances on standardized ability, achievement, and adaptive behavior tests. Tests of **adaptive behavior** measure the extent to which a person has learned the skills that most of us learn without need for formal instruction: personal care, feeding, toileting, language, pedestrian skills, social skills, use of leisure time, and so forth.

Adaptive behavior. Skills that most people learn without formal instruction, such as personal care, feeding, and social skills.

To be diagnosed as having mental retardation, a person must score below 70 on an individually administered IQ test and show significant deficits on measures of achievement and adaptive behavior during the developmental period. Most states rely more on the IQ score in diagnosing mental retardation than on measures of adaptive behavior (Morgenstern & Klass, 1991). In other words, mental retardation primarily is defined in terms of a score on a standardized test of ability. Knowing that a child has mental retardation indicates that he or she scored far below average on a standardized ability test. This diagnosis does not reveal what caused the condition, the person's learning needs, what skills the person has and lacks, or how to teach him or her.

The Causes of Mental Retardation

The causes of mental retardation are many and varied, but they can be categorized as (1) genetic disorders, (2) chromosomal disorders, (3) prenatal complications, (4) infections, and (5) social and environmental factors. The first four causes usually adversely affect brain development by causing premature closure of the skull bones, abnormalities in the formation of certain brain structures, or biochemical disorders that affect brain nourishment. Social and environmental factors, which account for approximately 75 percent of all cases of mental retardation, can be traced to psychological and social deprivation in infancy and early childhood (Menke, McClead, & Hansen, 1991). The myth that most school learners with mental retardation are brain injured has been a major obstacle in the way of setting higher expectations and developing instructional programs for them.

Issues in the Educational Classification of Learners with Mental Retardation

Throughout most of this century, school learners with mental retardation have been classified according to certain diagnostic categories. Table 14.1 shows the classification system recommended by the American Psychiatric Association (APA, 1994), and Table

Table 14.1

Classification of Mental Retardation Used by the American Psychiatric Association

IQ Range	Severity	Expectations
50 or 55–70	Mild	Educable—can learn basic academic skills
30–49	Moderate	Can be trained to learn basic daily living skills
20–29	Severe	Can learn some basic living skills but never be fully independent
Under 20	Profound	Will always require full-time care and constant supervision

14.2 shows the system used in most school settings. These classification systems have several features in common.

- The lower the IQ, the more likely the individual will have other disabilities, such as hearing and vision problems, as well as a general lack of muscular coordination.
- Learners are classified on the basis of IQ tests and not specific learning deficits or weaknesses.
- Information is not provided about how individuals should or can be taught.

Currently, many professionals prefer a system of classification that categorizes learners with mental retardation on the basis of skills they need to learn rather than their deficits. These are called noncategorical approaches (Cipiani, 1991). For example, compare the following definition of mental retardation with that on page 476:

> Mental retardation refers to the need for specific training of the skills that most people acquire incidentally and that enable individuals to live in the community without supervision. (Dever, 1990, p. 149)

Table 14.2

Classification of Mental Retardation Used in Most School Settings

IQ Range	Severity	Expectations
50–70	Educable	Can learn some basic academic skills
30–49	Trainable	Can learn self-help skills and routine work skills
Below 30	Severe	Will always require full-time supervision and care

This definition avoids labeling, setting limits on learning, or focusing exclusively on what the person cannot do. Rather, it specifies that persons with mental retardation are those who must be taught to do things that most of us learn naturally as we grow and develop. It provides general direction to what must be taught (for example, skills that allow one to live without supervision) and implies not only that individuals with mental retardation *can* learn, but also that the limits of their skill attainment may be unknown. Finally, it places some of the responsibility for seeing that learners with mental retardation acquire necessary life skills with public education.

Focus on

Anne M. Donnellan, University of Wisconsin-Madison

After receiving a psychology degree from Queens College in 1969, I moved to San Diego, no job prospect in sight, but armed with optimism born of ignorance and a knowledge of operant conditioning. I opened a preschool for children labeled "autistic" in 1970 when almost nothing was known about their learning. I began a relentless search for information and understanding that still continues. Two major convictions drove me forward in this research: Then and now people with communication and behavior challenges rarely receive the respect and care that are every citizen's right, and little is truly "known" about these individuals compared to what is presumed or assumed to be true. That my work on analyzing the communicative functions of behavior is heralded as groundbreaking leaves me feeling both honored and sad. People with disabilities ought not to have had to prove they had a need and desire to communicate.

Communication and relationships are essential to being human. In the late sixties behavioral control techniques were being researched in laboratories as political freedom was being sought on the streets and campuses. The interplay of these concepts affected the direction of my research. These experiences left me ever more committed to the belief that both power and responsibility lie within the individual rather than in the institution or a technology.

Growing up in an immigrant family I learned vivid firsthand accounts of the evils of colonialism which shaped my philosophy regarding hierarchies in both personal and cultural ways, and led me to a sharper perception of the perspectives of people whose lives are controlled by others. It remains a regret that my first contribution to the field—demonstrating and arguing that the use of coercion to control behaviors of vulnerable people who cannot give clear consent is unnecessary, inherently dangerous, wrong and inevitably doomed to fail—continues to be a subject of controversy. Aversive control in as well as outside the classroom ought to be relegated to an historical footnote.

Presently my research focuses on the impact of movement disturbances on learners' ability to communicate. It is becoming clear to me that our construct of retardation has been based on some assumptions that cannot be supported by fact, and that we have only begun to recognize the fundamental importance of communication to the demonstration of competence. A century of mental mismeasurement misled us into believing that there are people whose minds fail to develop. Instead, Vygotsky's notion that a child with an impediment does not fail to develop but develops differently seems more apt.

As evidence mounts of unsuspected competencies masked by communication problems, teachers will find themselves on the front lines in another battle for civil rights—the right not to remain silent, and the right not to be excluded from full citizenship because of policies and regulations that deny access to experience and expression to those learners who must communicate in augmented ways. Research in communication is undergoing a veritable explosion today. Teachers need to be aware of current research and methods for teaching a population of special learners whose disabilities require them to communicate in nontraditional ways. But, also, a lesson in history for those of us who support an empirical approach to knowledge is that we should examine our assumptions as carefully as we review our data.

Table 14.3

IQ and Reading Data from the University of Washington Experimental Education Unit Project: Data from the Du Vergeas' Follow-Up Study

Child	Age	Stanford-Binet IQ	Grade Level in Reading
1	14.10	43	2.2
2	14.3	59	4.1
3	15.0	45	3.8
4	13.6	52	6.9
5	14.8	46	2.5
6	14.3	53	2.7

Source: Rynders & Horrobin, 1990.

Learning Needs of Students with Mental Retardation

Only 15 years ago, many learners with low IQs were considered uneducable (Restak, 1975; Sinclair & Forness, 1983). In other words, it was not worth teaching them fundamental academic skills. Table 14.3 displays the chronological age, IQ, and grade-equivalent reading scores of six learners who were enrolled in an early education program from the time they were 18 months old. As can be seen, all learners earned grade-equivalent reading scores on the Wide Range Achievement Test (WRAT) that indicate substantial learning of basic reading skills (Rynders & Horrobin, 1990). Project

Learners with mental retardation can learn a variety of skills that eventually allow them to achieve independence from caregiver supervision. Carefully designed instruction and training are the primary needs of persons with mental retardation.

EDGE at the University of Minnesota (Rynders & Horrobin, 1980) and the Portsmouth Project (Buckley, 1987) present similar data showing that learners with Down's syndrome and even those with IQs below 50 can learn to read with comprehension.

These data and the work of educators like Dever, Donnellan, and LaVigna (1990), and Donnellan, LaVigna, Negri-Shoultz, and Fassbender (1988) are convincing evidence that the possible level of skill attainment for any person with retardation is unknown. It is clear that such persons can learn, but we do not yet know how much. Given this fact, Dever specifies five principles as guides for instructional programs for children with retardation (Dever, 1990). These are explained in the accompanying box, *Meeting the Learning Needs of Students with Mental Retardation.*

Students with Learning Disabilities

We began this chapter by describing Mike, a fifth-grader with learning disabilities. Why can't students like Mike, who has normal cognitive ability, learn basic math or reading skills as quickly as other learners his age? Since about 1970, the answer to this question has been that he has a specific **learning disability.** But what exactly does it mean to have a specific learning disability? Here's how PL 94-142 defines it:

Learning disability. Any learning disorder presumed to be the cause of a learner achieving significantly below what his or her IQ predicts.

> A disorder in one or more of the basic psychological processes involved in understanding or using language, spoken or written, that manifests itself in the imperfect ability to listen, speak, read, write, spell, or do mathematical calculations; the term includes such conditions as perceptual handicaps, brain injury, minimal brain dysfunction, dyslexia, and developmental aphasia; the term does not include children who have learning problems that are primarily the result of visual, hearing, or motor handicaps, of mental retardation, or of environmental, cultural, or economic disadvantage.

Notice that this definition is derived from a medical or pathological perspective. In other words, the underlying cause of the child's inability to master reading, writing, or language is to be found with the child—a "disorder of the basic psychological processes." Second, it suggests that the learning failure is not influenced by economic or social conditions, educational disadvantage, or insufficient instruction, nor to such factors as mental retardation, emotional disturbance, or physical disabilities. Thus, this definition directs the school psychologist or educational diagnostician to search primarily within the individual for the source of the learning problem and only secondarily to develop an academic program or instructional procedures to remediate the problem (Weisberg, 1990). Let's examine more closely how psychologists assess a child for learning disabilities.

Assessing Learning Disabilities

Public Law 94-142 guarantees that each student believed to have a learning disability will receive fair, objective assessment by trained examiners before being diagnosed as learning disabled. The diagnostic process involves the use of standardized IQ and achievement tests to confirm the presence of a learning disability. We studied standardized ability tests in Chapter 11. Let's now examine some of the more important characteristics of standardized achievement tests for assessing learning disabilities.

Standardized Achievement Tests. Standardized achievement tests have nearly all the characteristics of standardized ability or IQ tests: professional item development,

Meeting the Learning Needs of Students with Mental Retardation

Principle 1. Instruction Is the Central Need of Individuals with Mental Retardation. Individual educational programs for individuals with mental retardation, regardless of the degree of retardation, should primarily focus on instructional goals and objectives—not on medical, psychological, or social goals and service objectives.

The failure of learners with mental retardation to acquire skills should lead to improved instructional programs. Weisberg (1990) makes the point that learners with mental retardation primarily require efficient and effective educational programs and instructional procedures. He stresses that the expert practice of instruction for learners with mental retardation is no different from that for learners with normal abilities, except that it must be practiced with far greater precision. Instructional programs for students with mental retardation should focus on:

- maintaining learner attention
- introducing concepts in a logical sequence
- using a variety of examples
- providing immediate feedback.

Principle 2. The Goal of All Instruction Should Be Independence. Dever proposes the following definition of independence:

> Independence is exhibiting behavior patterns appropriate to the behavior settings normally frequented by others of the individual's age and social status in such a manner that the individual is not seen as requiring assistance because of his/her behavior. (Dever, 1990, p. 151)

Thus the goals of instructional programs for those with mental retardation should focus on development of the skills that enable these persons to meet this definition of independence. Such programs should allow students to:

- go where their peers go
- participate in ordinary school activities
- fit in with other learners in terms of dress and behavior.

Principle 3. The Amount and Intensity of Instruction Required to Make Learners Independent Should Be the Basis by Which Severity of Mental Retardation Is Defined. The determinant of the level of retardation should be the amount of instructional effort required to eliminate the term "retarded"

from the words we use to describe a person. Therefore, instructional programs should:

- refer to learners by functional abilities rather than IQ level
- keep records of time spent and materials used for each learner.

Principle 4. Independence Should Be the Aim of Instruction for All Learners with Mental Retardation, Despite the Fact That Some Will Never Achieve It. Decisions not to teach skills to certain individuals with mental retardation are often based on notions of "inability to learn." We now know that such individuals can learn. Nevertheless, we also know that some individuals with mental retardation are disabled to such a degree that they will always require some level of supervision. When schools decide not to teach some things to some learners, such decisions should be based on:

- available resources
- possible benefit to the learners
- the wishes of parents and learners.

Principle 5. Instructional Priority Should Be Assigned to Communication Training. Children with mental retardation have significant communication deficits. They must learn to communicate if they are to gain access to desired activities and objects, get a teacher's attention, or make their needs and desires known (Donnellan, LaVigna, Negri-Shoultz, & Fassbender, 1988; Donnellan, Mirenda, Mesaros, & Fassbender, 1984).

Durand (1988, 1990) demonstrated that behaviors such as aggression, tantrums, throwing objects, and self-injury become more frequent and more intense as the tasks given to learners with mental retardation get more difficult. When simpler tasks are substituted, behavior problems decrease significantly. In other words, problem behaviors can serve a communicative function. Simply punishing or ignoring these behaviors is thus ineffective. The following specific strategies (based on Donnellan et al., 1988, and the techniques discussed in Chapter 9) will help learners expand their communication skills:

- teach students appropriate ways to make their needs known
- reinforce only appropriate behavior
- seek medical or psychological help for learners who need relief of pain or other symptoms.

standardization, norms, reliability, and validity. They differ from IQ tests primarily in terms of the test content.

There are standardized achievement tests for nearly every academic area taught in grades K through 12: reading, math, handwriting, biology, algebra, geography, and so forth. Since the overwhelming majority of students with learning disabilities experience problems in math, reading, or both areas, standardized reading and math tests are the principal instruments for assessing learning disabilities.

One of the goals of constructing these tests is to develop questions that cover the most important math and reading skills across a given grade level. Thus a fourth-grade reading or math test must be comprehensive enough to allow adequate assessment of what a fourth-grader knows, yet short enough to be administered in about an hour. It also must contain questions that any school across the country is likely to include in its fourth-grade math or reading curriculum.

As we learned in Chapter 11, scores on standardized tests are interpreted with the use of norms: percentile ranks, standard scores, and grade- or age-equivalent scores. For example, if Mike was making normal progress and was given a standardized math test in November of his fifth grade, his grade placement would be represented by 5.3: fifth grade/third month of the school year. A grade-equivalent score of 5.3 means that Mike got as many items correct as did the average child in the fifth grade, third month of school in the standardization sample. Had Mike earned that score, we would have no concerns about his ability to learn math. But if Mike had earned a grade-equivalent score of 2.3, his performance would have been typical of a learner in November of the second grade. His math skills would be three years below what we would expect, given his current grade level.

The Assessment Process. Why is Mike doing so poorly in reading and math? His teacher observes that he attends school regularly and seems to be trying to learn. He appears to have normal cognitive ability. To determine whether Mike has a specific disability that qualifies him for special services, his teacher refers him to a school psychologist.

Before an educational program is developed for learners with disabilities, learners first receive a comprehensive individualized assessment in all relevant intellectual, physical, and personal-social domains.

To rule out environment or other psychological conditions as factors in the learning problem, the psychologist conducts interviews with present and former teachers, reviews records, and may even observe Mike in class. She then gives Mike a battery of tests, which include an individually administered IQ test; standardized reading, language, and math achievement tests; tests of vision, hearing, and perceptual abilities; and perhaps a personality test to determine whether Mike has a psychological problem. This assessment process takes about three weeks.

Following these tests, a psychological evaluation is written and presented to a committee, which must decide whether Mike qualifies for special education services under PL 94-142.

Mike's evaluation is typical of that used to determine the presence of a learning disability. Two points are worth noting. First, evidence of a learning disability may not be observed during the assessment process. Mike's teacher referred him for evaluation because he noticed that he was not doing well in class and scored low on a group achievement test. But during the evaluation process, the psychologist may not test Mike to determine the cognitive processes or strategies he uses to learn. Second, the effects of prior schooling on Mike's learning problem also may not be known. Mike's present problems could be attributed to inadequate or insufficient instruction in an earlier grade. Since the assessment process does not involve actually teaching Mike a math or reading skill he has not learned, we do not know whether Mike's learning problem is a result of earlier circumstances.

The IQ–Achievement Discrepancy

Since a specific learning disability cannot be directly seen or measured, its presence must be inferred. The logic behind this inference is as follows:

> **How can I explain to parents why their learning disabled child isn t achieving up to potential?**

1. Children should achieve in school at a level consistent with their abilities. If they have an IQ within normal range, their academic achievement should be there as well. Figure 14.4 shows this condition.

2. If a child's IQ is within normal range and his or her achievement is not, then the discrepancy is due either to a specific learning disability or to some other factor, such as inadequate instruction or lack of prior instruction, cultural differences, vision or hearing problems, or emotional disturbance. Figure 14.5 shows this condition.

3. By confirming that a child has a normal IQ and that achievement is below normal, and by ruling out factors such as environmental deprivation or emotional disturbance, the presence of a specific learning disability is confirmed.

Thus the presence of a specific learning disability is confirmed by a significant **IQ–achievement discrepancy.** Since IQ and standardized achievement tests report performance in terms of similar norms (usually percentile ranks and standard scores), performance on one test can be compared with performance on the other to determine the size of the discrepancy between aptitude and achievement.

> **IQ–achievement discrepancy.** An achievement level different from what would be predicted given a learner's score on an ability test.

Summary

Earlier we asked what it means to have a specific learning disability. As we found out, it means that a learner's score on a standardized achievement test is significantly below what you would predict, given his or her IQ score, and that this discrepancy cannot be attributed to environmental factors or physical and emotional problems. Diagnosis of a child as learning disabled indicates a need for special education services. Given that the

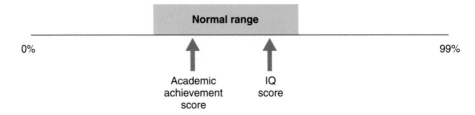

Figure 14.4
Percentile ranks indicating that the child is performing consistently with his or her abilities. No learning disability is present.

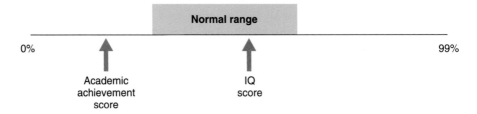

Figure 14.5
Percentile ranks showing an IQ–achievement discrepancy. A specific learning disability may be present.

child has normal cognitive abilities but a specific learning deficit, the goal of these services is to remediate the deficit and help the learner make up ground that he or she has lost in math or reading achievement. Before this can be done, some other questions must be answered:

- What specific information, intellectual skills, or cognitive strategies does the learner lack that may explain why he or she is failing to master math or reading skills?
- What are the critical knowledge, intellectual skills, and learning strategies that the learner must be taught to help him or her to read, calculate, or solve math problems at or above grade level?
- What is the most appropriate way to sequence instructional objectives and design instructional strategies to help the learner return to grade level?

We will return to these questions when we present guidelines for teaching the exceptional learner. Before we do, let's look at another group of learners whom you may also find in your classroom.

Students with Behavioral Disorders

As a teacher, you will have to deal with a wide range of learning, behavioral, and psychological problems. Some of these were discussed in Part III when we studied classroom management. At that time, we distinguished behavior problems arising out of group dynamics from those arising out of a failure to meet an individual learner's needs for recognition, power, and achievement. The problems we were referring to in those chapters were not serious. They were the normal psychological challenges that many learners experience in the course of growing up: doubts about friendships and self-esteem, sadness over the loss of a friend, poor grades, arguments with classmates over who gets what privilege, worries about tests. These are not pathologies or persistent behavioral problems.

But there is another category of behavior problems, called *behavioral disorders,* that are more intense and persistent, usually lasting six months or longer. They include depression, attention deficit disorders, the effects of child abuse, and conduct disorders. These disorders genuinely place learners at risk for serious psychological harm, school failure, and life-long disturbances. Their symptoms, when looked at in isolation, often appear no different from the more transitory behavior problems we discussed in Chapter 9. The fact that many behavioral disorders and mild behavior problems look the same in the classroom can be confusing to the teacher who must decide whether professional help may be needed.

There are different theoretical perspectives and approaches to treating behavioral disorders. School psychologists trained in the behavioral science tradition (Chapter 4) have a different perspective from those trained in the cognitive tradition (Chapters 5 and 6). Developmental psychologists assert that many behavior and psychological problems cannot be explained in terms of any single perspective. Rather, the root of these problems is often as complex as the learners themselves. These developmental psychologists point out that chronic problems have both historical and developmental roots.

The majority of learners you teach will not have these disorders, but you will encounter learners who do. Bee (1995) estimates that 3 to 5 percent of learners ages 0 to 18 experience attention deficit disorder, 5 to 7 percent experience conduct disorder (such as serious aggression), and 2 to 10 percent experience severe depression. In other words, 14 to 20 percent of learners experience some form of behavioral disorder during their school-age years (Brandenberg, Freedman, & Silver, 1990). The majority of these learners can benefit from special help in school or from a community or social service agency. In this section, we will promote an understanding of these problems by discussing the nature and causes of attention deficit hyperactivity disorder (ADHD).

Attention Deficit Hyperactivity Disorder

Todd is a 10-year-old who never seems to settle down. When he's asked to sit quietly and read, he wriggles and squirms in his seat. Although he reads at an appropriate grade level, he can't seem to focus on assigned tasks. During seatwork, he appears distracted. During formal lessons, he calls out without raising his hand, makes inappropriate comments, or seems unaware of what is going on around him. Since kindergarten, his teachers have made similar comments on his evaluation forms: "can't seem to focus"; "disruptive"; "bright but uncooperative."

Once learners like Todd were described as "hyperactive," or "fidgety," or "distractible." They were at risk of being labeled troublemakers because their behavior so often disrupted classroom routine. Today the descriptors used for Todd have been superseded by the term **attention deficit hyperactivity disorder,** or ADHD. Learners with ADHD have short attention spans, are easily distracted, and have heightened levels of physical activity. However, many learners display all these symptoms, yet do not have ADHD (Deutsch & Kinsbourne, 1990). Thus, immediately describing a learner's overactive, restless, inattentive behavior as "hyperactive" or as a sign of ADHD is fraught with problems.

We can better appreciate the problems in diagnosing hyperactivity or ADHD by studying Table 14.4, which lists the hallmarks of ADHD used by psychologists as an aid to diagnosis. However, a problem with this approach to diagnosis is that it is based on

Attention deficit hyperactivity disorder (ADHD). A disorder that has its onset before age 7, lasts at least six months, and is characterized by an inability to sustain attention, impulsivity, hyperactivity, and deficits in rule-governed behavior.

Table 14.4

Diagnostic Criteria for Attention-Deficit/Hyperactivity Disorder

I. Either (A) or (B):

A. six (or more) of the following symptoms of *inattention* have persisted for at least 6 months to a degree that is maladaptive and inconsistent with developmental level:

Inattention

1. often fails to give close attention to details or makes careless mistakes in schoolwork, work, or other activities
2. often has difficulty sustaining attention in tasks or play activities
3. often does not seem to listen when spoken to directly
4. often does not follow through on instructions and fails to finish schoolwork, chores, or duties in the workplace (not due to oppositional behavior or failure to understand instructions)
5. often has difficulty organizing tasks and activities
6. often avoids, dislikes, or is reluctant to engage in tasks that require sustained mental effort (such as schoolwork or homework)
7. often loses things necessary for tasks or activities (e.g., toys, school assignments, pencils, books, or tools)
8. is often easily distracted by extraneous stimuli
9. is often forgetful in daily activities

B. six (or more) of the following symptoms of *hyperactivity-impulsivity* have persisted for at least 6 months to a degree that is maladaptive and inconsistent with developmental level:

Hyperactivity

1. often fidgets with hands or feet or squirms in seat
2. often leaves seat in classroom or in other situations in which remaining seated is expected

3. often runs about or climbs excessively in situations in which it is inappropriate (in adolescents or adults, may be limited to subjective feelings of restlessness)
4. often has difficulty playing or engaging in leisure activities quietly
5. is often "on the go" or often acts as if "driven by a motor"
6. often talks excessively

Impulsivity

7. often blurts out answers before questions have been completed
8. often has difficulty awaiting turn
9. often interrupts or intrudes on others (e.g., butts into conversations or games)

II. Some hyperactive-impulsive or inattentive symptoms that caused impairment were present before age 7 years.

III. Some impairment from the symptoms is present in two or more settings (e.g., at school [or work] and at home).

IV. There must be clear evidence of clinically significant impairment in social, academic, or occupational functioning.

V. The symptoms do not occur exclusively during the course of a Pervasive Developmental Disorder, Schizophrenia, or other Psychotic Disorder and are not better accounted for by another mental disorder (e.g., Mood Disorder, Anxiety Disorder, Dissociative Disorder, or a Personality Disorder).

Source: From American Psychiatric Association (1994).

quantitative deviations from an unspecified norm. "Often," for example, is a relative term. Shifting from one activity to another six times in one hour might be considered "often" in one class but not in another. Therefore, your judgment may be influenced by the behavioral norms of your class.

Similarly, your judgment about how often is "often" is influenced by age. "Often loses things" means one thing in a class of 5-year-olds and another in a class of 9-year-olds. We also know that as normal children get older, parents and teachers report declines in attention, declines in impulse control, and increased restlessness.

Moreover, we know that the symptoms of ADHD increase following certain traumatic experiences. These increases often last beyond six months but then subside with proper intervention (Davidson & Baum, 1990; Deutsch & Kinsbourne, 1990). Thus many transitory problems may be mistakenly diagnosed as ADHD.

Further complicating the diagnosis of ADHD is the fact that quantitative criteria fail to convey the qualitative aspects of the behavior of hyperactive children. Whalen and Henker (1985) and Whalen and colleagues (1979) have completed numerous studies of hyperactive children that show that their overall activity levels do not differ significantly from those of their peers. Rather, the qualitative aspects of their behavior—intensity, severity, inappropriateness—are what generally catch the teacher's eye. Lists like those in Table 14.4 fail to consider these features of hyperactive behavior.

Yet it is precisely these factors that appear to best distinguish learners with ADHD from their peers. Were you to view a videotape of a classroom that included an ADHD learner who had not been brought to your attention, you probably would recognize him or her because of inattention, impulsiveness, and frequency of social behavior inappropriate to the time and setting. Let's examine some of these signs of ADHD and the research that supports them.

Recognizing ADHD

Developmental psychologists identify four hallmarks or primary symptoms of ADHD: (1) inability to sustain attention, (2) impulsivity, (3) hyperactivity, and (4) deficits in rule-governed behavior.

How can I recognize ADHD in a learner?

Inability to Sustain Attention. In comparison to their classmates, learners with ADHD have difficulty staying with or completing an activity over a period of time. This difficulty isn't as evident during activities such as watching TV or playing video games as it is during dull, boring, effortful, and repetitive tasks such as copying from a blackboard, doing practice worksheets, listening to a speaker, or silent reading. In other words, it occurs during many common classroom activities.

Studies of hyperactive learners show that this problem, an **attention deficit,** isn't necessarily one of distractibility, although that is commonly assumed. In other words, the problem of sustained attention is not so much being drawn off task by irrelevant sounds, sights, or movements that may occur during an activity (called *overselective attention*). Rather, learners with ADHD become more easily bored and disinterested in activities in comparison with their classmates (Douglas, 1983; Ross & Ross, 1982).

Attention deficit. Difficulty staying with or completing an activity over a period of time; becoming easily bored and uninterested in activities relative to others.

Impulsivity. Psychologists define **impulsivity** as the failure to stop and think before responding to a task (Braswell & Bloomquist, 1991). Rather than ask themselves "What am I supposed to do?" or "What is the best plan?" before starting on a new task or answering a question, learners with ADHD more typically jump in and start writing or answering with no plan in mind.

There is some debate among developmental psychologists as to whether impulsivity is a genuine component or primary symptom of ADHD separate from either activity level or attention (Achenbach & Edelbrock, 1983; Milich & Kramer, 1985). Some psychologists (Barkley, 1989) suggest that impulsivity is just one more facet of the problem of sustaining attention. Nevertheless, the consensus is that impulsivity is a useful concept for describing some of the qualitative aspects of the behavior of hyperactive learners.

Impulsivity. A failure to stop and think before responding to a task.

Research suggests that learners with ADHD have difficulty sustaining attention to tasks and learn better in environments that provide immediate consequences for behavior.

Hyperactivity. A greatly increased rate of activity and/or restlessness.

Hyperactivity. Current research calls into question the notion that overactivity or **hyperactivity** is the most significant feature of ADHD (Barkley, 1990). Although numerous studies have demonstrated that ADHD learners are more active or restless than other children (Barkley & Cunningham, 1979; Porino et al., 1983), many studies fail to show this (Firestone & Martin, 1979; Sandberg, Rutter, & Taylor, 1978; Shaffer, McNamara, & Pincus, 1974; Whalen et al., 1979). Despite the lack of consensus on the importance of activity level in diagnosing ADHD, hyperactivity continues to remain one of the primary symptoms of the disorder.

Deficits in Rule-Governed Behavior. In Chapter 9 we discussed the importance of rules in classroom management. Rule-governed behavior in the classroom has three aspects: immediate compliance with requests; persistence in continuing assigned tasks; and use of problem-solving strategies to cope with unfamiliar situations. Barkley (1990) believes that learners with ADHD have particular problems with the second aspect of rule-governed behavior, persistence. His research indicates that many ADHD learners are initially compliant but have difficulty maintaining this compliance.

Barkley makes the point that the problems hyperactive learners have with sustaining attention may be better viewed as problems with rule-governed behavior. In other words, hyperactive learners have particular difficulty sustaining attention to rules and less difficulty sustaining attention during situations in which there are few rules. That is, hyperactive learners do not behave differently from nonhyperactive learners at lunchtime, recess, on the playground, or in other low-demand settings. Rather, their attention deficits become pronounced in settings of high demand with many rules, such as the classroom.

Barkley believes that ADHD learners are more contingency-shaped than rule-governed. In other words, the expectation of reward or fear of punishment has a greater effect on their behavior than the stimulus control typically exerted by rules or requests.

Prevalence and Risk Potential for ADHD

Exact figures on the percentage of learners who have ADHD are difficult to obtain. Information from parents and teachers is a prime source determining the frequency of this disorder. However, the data from these sources are not as objective as researchers would like. Nevertheless, most studies conclude that 3 to 5 percent of the school-age population has ADHD (Barkley, 1990, Ross & Ross, 1982). Boys are nearly twice as

Applying Your Knowledge:
Teaching Learners with ADHD

Minimize Extraneous Demands. The more rules, demands, and requests in a classroom, the more likely the symptoms of ADHD will appear (Barkley, 1990). Children with ADHD learn best in classrooms where there are only necessary rules, where children are allowed frequent choices, and where the teacher does not continually make unnecessary demands.

Provide Continuous Monitoring. Once instructions are given to ADHD children, attention deficits are less likely to occur if the teacher monitors what they are doing and repeats instructions when called for (Douglas, 1980, 1983). A key symptom of ADHD is sustained noncompliance with instruc-

tions. This problem can be minimized if, after giving instructions, the teacher continuously monitors the children's activities.

Maintain a High Rate of Instructional Feedback and Reinforcement. Barkley (1990) maintains that ADHD learners have deficits in rule-governed behavior and are better controlled by consequences of behavior than by antecedents. His research and that of others (Douglas & Parry, 1983; O'Leary, 1980; Wielkiewicz, 1992) reports sizable reductions in ADHD symptoms in classrooms where there are high rates of both feedback on performance and positive reinforcement.

likely as girls to have ADHD: 5 to 7 percent of boys versus 2 to 4 percent of girls have been diagnosed.

What can teachers do to improve the behavior of the ADHD school-age learner? Research by Barkley (1990) offers some hints. The accompanying box, *Teaching Learners with ADHD*, provides some specific guidelines, based on the research we described above about the difficulty ADHD learners have in maintaining compliance over time.

What can I do in my classroom to help learners with ADHD?

Students with Communication Disabilities

Another category of learners with special needs that you may encounter in your classroom is composed of those with disabilities involving communication. As with other learners we have considered in this chapter, such students should be part of regular classes whenever possible, and teachers should focus on students' specific learning needs, not on their disabilities.

How can I identify and assist learners with physical or communication disabilities?

Because spoken language is so central to all facets of human experience, and to education in particular, learners with communication disabilities require your patience and care. A **communication disability** is an impairment that involves speech, language, vision, or hearing. It is important to remember that speech and language are not the same thing, although the terms are commonly used interchangeably. Educational psychologists use the term *speech* to refer to the production of sounds. Disabilities that involve speech include problems with producing particular sounds or with vocal pitch patterns. *Language* disabilities, which involve impairment of the ability to understand or communicate, are typically much more severe than speech disabilities. You are therefore more likely to teach learners with speech disabilities in your regular classroom.

Communication disability. An impairment that involves speech, language, vision, or hearing.

Speech Disabilities

Speech disabilities can take many forms. Young children commonly distort, omit, or substitute one sound for another (for example, "sreight train" rather than "freight train"). Some speech sounds, such as *r, l,* and *s,* are difficult for many children. Such *articulation* difficulties are common in the early years but commonly disappear after grade 2 or 3. Therefore, speech therapists often delay working with a child until after that time. However, you should make sure that such articulation problems are neither keeping children from being understood nor making them the butt of teasing. Children who experience social isolation as a result of articulation disorders should be referred for speech therapy.

Stuttering is a less common but more distressing disability that involves the repetition of the first sound of a word ("Ccccccome here") or sometimes the inability to make any sound at all. Learners who stutter may have difficulty with particular sounds, or they may have difficulty only when they feel anxiety.

A third type of speech disability involves problems with the voice. Learners who have such *voice disabilities* may speak in an unusually high-pitched tone or in a monotone (a monotonous, single-pitched speech) or may speak too softly to be heard.

Classroom teachers should remember that speech disabilities are common in young children, but that they generally rectify themselves over time. You can best assist learners with speech disabilities in the following ways:

- Provide a role model to other children for acceptance of the disability; avoid display impatience or irritation toward the learner.
- Avoid finishing a learner's sentences, and do not allow other learners to do so.
- Avoid correcting a learner's articulation in the presence of peers.
- Avoid putting learners with speech disabilities into high-pressure situations that may exacerbate the difficulty.

Language Disabilities

Language disabilities are problems with the ability either to understand language (*receptive language disability*) or to express one's ideas in language (*expressive language disability*). A learner whose native language is not English but who has difficulty communicating his or her ideas in English does *not* have a language disability (see Chapter 2). Such a learner simply needs additional assistance in learning English.

You should suspect a language disability in a child who seldom speaks, who uses very few words or only very short sentences, or who relies almost solely on gestures to communicate. Language disabilities may arise from physical problems, such as hearing disorders, from mental retardation, or from a learning disability. Children who are neglected, or whose home environments do not include rich verbal experiences, may come to school with seeming language disabilities. Such children's language skills usually can catch up with those of their peers if they are given sufficient verbal experiences. All children who are suspected of having language disabilities should be referred to a psychologist or language specialist.

Visual and Hearing Disabilities

The great majority of visual disabilities can be corrected with prescription lenses. In fact, only 1 out of every 1,000 children has a **visual disability** so severe that his or her educational needs cannot be met in a regular class. Most of the learners who need special services for their visual impairments can read with the aid of large-print books or

Visual disability. An inability to see well that cannot be corrected with eyeglasses.

magnifying glasses. A smaller group of students, those classified as educationally blind, must use hearing and touch rather than vision as primary learning tools (Kirk, Gallagher, & Anastasiow, 1993).

A **hearing disability** may range from a mild impairment to profound deafness. Learners with mild hearing impairments may need no more assistance than a seat at the front of the room; those with profound deafness, on the other hand, may communicate entirely in sign language. Approximately 3 or 4 learners in 1,000 have partial hearing impairments. Such students, whose disabilities may range from mild to moderate, are likely to be part of your regular classroom. Those with profound disabilities are unlikely to be mainstreamed unless they have received special training in communication skills.

Hearing disability. An inability to hear well; may range from mild disability to total deafness.

Guidelines for Better Special Education

While the Regular Education Initiative (REI) continues to gain prominence, many educators and policy makers conclude that some form of special education classification and placement will always be necessary (Case, 1992; Villa & Thousand, 1992). The real issue, therefore, may be how to adapt the current special education system to make it more responsive to the need for academic achievement and normalization. Here are some of the steps school districts across the country have taken to adapt their schools and classrooms to the needs of mainstreamed learners.

1. Classify exceptional learners in terms of instructional needs—not cognitive deficits. The Winooski School District in Vermont no longer assigns special education labels to students, staff, materials, rooms, instructional procedures, or behavior management practices. When classifications are used for learners, they are based strictly on current educational needs (Dever, 1990). Thus, such classifications may only be relevant for a brief time. Learners are not blind, deaf, mentally retarded, learning disabled, or emotionally disturbed. Instead, they are learners who require intensive instruction in mobility, pedestrian skills, signing, reading recognition, money management, housekeeping, word recognition, or social skills. In the Winooski School District, programs—rather than children—have labels (Villa & Thousand, 1992).

2. Assess learning environments—not psychological processes. In the Minneapolis Public Schools, school psychologists are spending more time assessing the adequacy of instructional environments and less time testing for the hypothesized inadequacies of exceptional learners (Ysseldyke & Marston, 1990). They spend more time in classrooms evaluating how well teachers teach and model appropriate behavior rather than taking children out of classrooms to measure IQ.

Weisberg (1990) asserts that the key to discovering why certain students do not learn specific skills, and understanding what must be done to teach them, lies in a logical analysis of program design and teacher presentation procedure. In the former case, he advocates that exceptional learners be taught learning strategies (see Chapters 5 and 6) continuously, that skills be sequenced in such a way that learners acquire preskills before being asked to apply them, that easier skills be taught before harder ones, and that easily confused strategies and skills be separated. For the latter, Weisberg emphasizes the importance of assessing how well teachers secure and maintain attention; monitor, correct, and diagnose errors; provide practice and review; and program for generalization and transfer.

3. The key need for exceptional learners is the need for faultless instruction. Dever (1990) reminds us that lack of skills and low achievement are the symptoms that lead teachers to refer their learners for special education services. Assuming that all students can learn, then the focus of special education should be on designing instructional programs to help exceptional learners acquire skills. Although many of these learners will have needs for social, psychological, nutritional, and health services, the justification for special education services should be in terms of instructional needs. Moreover, skill learning should be the principal criterion by which the effectiveness of special education is judged.

4. Set up teaching teams to help all learners. The Edmunds School District in Lynnwood, Washington, believed that the various categorical program regulations were a major hurdle to improving the achievements of low-achieving learners and those traditionally served by special education programs (Fink, 1992). Job titles like special education teacher, chapter 1 reading teacher, or adaptive PE teacher no longer exist. In their place are learning support teams, which collaborate in regular classrooms. They provide instruction to those students making the slowest progress by offering small-group or one-to-one instruction without regard for labels or classifications. They also help to adapt the regular classroom for learners who are making rapid progress.

5. Prepare regular education students for mainstreaming. School districts like Winooski and Edmunds make special efforts to help regular learners work cooperatively with special students. Following suggestions by Wood and Reeves (1989), they help regular students to understand the nature of disabling conditions through special instructional units and simulation activities. One elementary school teacher prepared her class to accept a learner with physical handicaps by having them construct puppets portraying themselves. She constructed a puppet personifying the new classmate. Students' puppets asked the teacher's puppet questions like "Can I help you?" and "Can you play with the rest of the class?"

We turn now to an examination of our final group of exceptional learners, the gifted and talented. We will examine issues related to their assessment, classification, and placement and provide guidelines for teaching the gifted and talented in your classroom.

Gifted and Talented Learners

A student who reads rapidly, comprehends quickly, has an exceptional memory, is imaginative and creative, has a long attention span, and is comfortable with abstract ideas is described with words like "bright," "exceptional," "gifted," or "talented." Not all schools have programs or classes for the learning needs of the gifted and talented. However, awareness is growing that **gifted and talented** students are an important natural resource that must be encouraged, activated, directed, and fully developed.

The size and scope of most specialized school programs, such as those for other groups of exceptional learners, make programs for the gifted look pale by comparison. But teaching the gifted remains an important objective of virtually every school. Because of their importance to your school's objectives and because of the distribution of gifted and talented learners across every social class, community, and type of school, you should be aware of the needs of these exceptional learners. In this section we will identify the characteristics that make students gifted and talented and some of the ways you can plan your teaching to meet their learning needs.

Defining Giftedness

Because of the different ways in which gifted students are identified, the words *gifted* and *talented* often represent considerable diversity in ability and learning style. No single standard or definition of giftedness has been agreed on. However, the Gifted and Talented Act of 1978 provides a broad definition:

Gifted and talented. Children and youth who are identified as possessing abilities that offer evidence of high performance in areas such as intelligence, achievement, creativity, and task persistence.

A variety of abilities should be included under the definition of gifted in addition to intellectual abilities. Among them are creative abilities, leadership abilities, social aptitudes, and specific skills in the cultural arts.

Gifted and talented children means children, and whenever applicable youth, who are identified at the preschool, elementary, or secondary level as possessing demonstrated or potential abilities that give evidence of high performance capability in areas such as intellectual, creative, specific academics, or leadership abilities, or in the performing and visual arts, and who by reason thereof require services or activities not ordinarily provided by the school. (Public Law 95-561, Section 902)

While a consensus exists as to which general abilities and behaviors compose giftedness, there is considerable variation in how to measure both the degree of ability and the proper combination of abilities that represent giftedness. The following are some of the most important behavioral elements from which an individual school district's definition of giftedness is likely to be composed.

Intelligence. Among the characteristics of giftedness is general **intelligence.** We noted in Chapter 5 that ability in a specific area is more predictive of future productivity and accomplishments (in that area) than is general intelligence (Gardner & Hatch, 1989; Sternberg, 1989). Nevertheless, many formulae for defining giftedness include general as well as specific measures of intelligence. This is particularly true in the elementary grades, where it is believed that learners are still developing their specialized intellectual capacities. The emphasis on general intelligence for aiding identification of giftedness at the elementary level is also a function of the difficulty of measuring specific abilities at that age.

At the junior high and secondary levels, measures of specific intelligence are more likely to be substituted for general intelligence. The most common are verbal and mathematical abilities, scores for which can be derived from most general IQ tests. For example, a sufficiently high score on verbal intelligence could qualify a learner for gifted English but not for gifted math, and vice versa. Also, increasingly specific signs of intel-

Intelligence. A global trait signifying an individual's overall ability to adapt to and succeed in his or her environment.

ligence, such as "linguistic intelligence," or "logical-mathematical intelligence" are being substituted for general IQ, when suitable forms of assessment, such as work samples, are available.

How high must a student score on tests of general or specific intelligence to be considered gifted? This depends on the school district's criteria. Recall from Chapter 11 that intelligence is distributed in a normal or bell-shaped distribution. Most individuals score in or near the middle of the distribution, which represents an IQ score of 100. From the shape of this curve, we also know that less than 1 percent of the population will attain an IQ score of 145 or higher, 2 to 3 percent an IQ score of 130 or higher, and approximately 16 percent an IQ score of 115 or higher.

Although these percentages vary slightly depending on the test, they are often used as a general guideline in selecting gifted learners. An IQ score of about 130 or higher generally makes one eligible for gifted instruction (Colangelo & Davis, 1991). However, because giftedness almost always is defined in conjunction with at least several other behaviors, in practice, admission to gifted programs and classes usually is far less restrictive. It is not uncommon to accept learners with scores below 130 as eligible for gifted instruction, especially when work samples, such as student portfolios indicating high degrees of specific intelligence, are available. In some cases, tested IQ may not be considered at all, in which case the learner must exhibit unusual ability in one or more other areas.

Because IQ tests rely on standard language usage that predominates in the middle class, a school district with a high concentration of lower-socioeconomic students may not require a high level of tested intelligence (at least not as measured by standardized tests). In most cases, however, specific and general intelligence are among several behaviors that constitute giftedness.

Achievement. Another behavior frequently used to determine giftedness is the learner's achievement, usually in the area for which gifted instruction is being considered. Achievement is measured by yearly standardized tests that cover areas such as math, social studies, reading comprehension, vocabulary, and science. Cutoff scores in the form of percentile ranks are determined in each subject area, with a percentile score of 90 to 95 representing a typical cutoff. Although cutoff percentiles differ among school districts, a cutoff percentile of 90 means that a learner is eligible for gifted instruction if his or her score on the appropriate subscale of a standardized achievement test is higher than the scores of 90 percent of all those who took the test.

Creativity. In addition to intelligence and achievement, indices of creativity often are considered in selecting gifted learners. Inclusion of this behavioral dimension has broadened the definition of this type of learner. However, not all gifted learners are talented, nor are all talented learners gifted. The phrase "gifted and talented," which is widely used, can mean talented but not gifted, gifted but not talented, mostly talented with some giftedness, mostly gifted with some talent, or both gifted and talented.

These alternative categorizations are made possible by inclusion of creativity indices in the eligibility standards. Because creative behaviors generally are considered in selecting gifted students, this type of learner more appropriately might be called gifted and/or talented. Some observable signs of creativity used to classify a learner as gifted include:

- applying abstract principles to the solution of problems
- being curious and inquisitive
- giving uncommon or unusual responses

- showing imagination
- posing original solutions to problems
- discriminating between major and minor events
- seeing relationships among dissimilar objects.

In identifying the gifted and talented learner, the creative component usually is composed of recommendations from teachers based on these and other observable signs of creativity—for example, from a learner's portfolio and performance assessments, (see Chapter 13), or from a rating scale used to identify creative students, such as that shown in Table 14.5. Studies with children of normal intelligence have shown a modest relationship between intelligence and creativity (Torrance, 1981).

Task Persistence. A fourth behavior sometimes used in selecting gifted and talented learners involves recommendations from teachers and other knowledgeable sources concerning a learner's **task persistence.** This behavior is difficult to evaluate, but it often is considered indispensable for satisfactory achievement in a gifted and tal-

Task persistence. An attribute usually determined by such characteristics as a learner's ability to concentrate on detail, impose high standards on herself or himself, persist in achieving personal goals, evaluate personal performance, and devote a high level of energy to academic tasks.

Table 14.5

Rating Scale for Identifying Creative Students

Trait	Rating (Circle One Number)*	Trait	Rating (Circle One Number)*
1. Ability to concentrate	1 2 3 4 5	21. Lack of tolerance for boredom	1 2 3 4 5
2. Ability to defer judgment	1 2 3 4 5	22. Need for supportive climate	1 2 3 4 5
3. Above-average IQ	1 2 3 4 5	23. Nonconformism	1 2 3 4 5
4. Adaptability	1 2 3 4 5	24. Openness to experience	1 2 3 4 5
5. Aesthetic appreciation	1 2 3 4 5	25. Playfulness	1 2 3 4 5
6. Attraction to the complex and mysterious	1 2 3 4 5	26. Willingness to take risks	1 2 3 4 5
7. Curiosity	1 2 3 4 5	27. Self-confidence	1 2 3 4 5
8. Delight in beauty of theory	1 2 3 4 5	28. Sense of identity as originator	1 2 3 4 5
9. Delight in invention for its own sake	1 2 3 4 5	29. Sense of mission	1 2 3 4 5
10. Desire to share products and ideas	1 2 3 4 5	30. Sensitivity	1 2 3 4 5
11. Eagerness to resolve disorder	1 2 3 4 5	31. Ability to see that solutions generate new problems	1 2 3 4 5
12. Extensive knowledge background	1 2 3 4 5	32. Spontaneity	1 2 3 4 5
13. Flexibility	1 2 3 4 5	33. Commitment to task	1 2 3 4 5
14. Good memory, attention to detail	1 2 3 4 5	34. Tolerance for ambiguity and conflict	1 2 3 4 5
15. High energy level, enthusiasm	1 2 3 4 5	35. Willingness to face social ostracism	1 2 3 4 5
16. Humor (perhaps bizarre)	1 2 3 4 5	36. Willingness to daydream and fantasize	1 2 3 4 5
17. Imagination, insight	1 2 3 4 5		
18. Independence	1 2 3 4 5		
19. Internal locus of control and evaluation	1 2 3 4 5		
20. Inventiveness	1 2 3 4 5		

*Rating Scale: 1 Not present; 2 Minimally present; 3 Somewhat present; 4 Moderately present; 5 Strongly present.
Source: From Sattler, 1988.

ented program, because both the quantity and the quality of the work expected are likely to be considerably above that in the regular classroom. Obviously this trait alone would not be sufficient for qualifying a learner for gifted instruction, but if such instruction is indeed geared to the extremely able student, students will need unusual levels of task persistence to succeed. Behaviors teachers look for in determining task persistence include:

- ability to devise organized approaches to learning
- ability to concentrate on detail
- self-imposed high standards
- persistence in achieving personal goals
- willingness to evaluate own performance, and ability to do so
- sense of responsibility
- high level of energy, particularly in academic tasks.

In evaluating these behaviors, parents and teachers play the greatest role in influencing a child's eligibility for gifted instruction. By providing testimony about the ability of a child to work hard, accept additional responsibility, and live with increased performance and grading expectations, teachers and parents can provide data that the learner can profit from gifted instruction.

Present Trends in Gifted Education

In Chapter 11 we learned that there is little evidence to support the claim that homogeneously grouped—or tracked—classes increase overall school achievement relative to heterogeneously grouped classes (Kerchoff, 1986; Slavin, 1991). However, this research excluded gifted learners, who represent the top 3 to 5 percent of the school population. Research tends to support programs and classes specifically targeted to the gifted and talented when they are allowed to pursue an **accelerated curriculum.** In an accelerated curriculum, gifted students can skip a grade or take advanced courses, such as advanced placement (AP) courses for college credit (Slavin, 1990a). Other gifted and talented programs that simply enrich—or add to—existing curricula by allowing students to pursue games and simulations to promote creativity and problem solving, conduct individual investigations, or simply use computers or other technology tend to be less successful in increasing the achievement of these learners (Kulik & Kulik, 1984). Gifted and talented programs that are exclusively enrichment programs have been criticized for providing few activities that would not benefit all learners. Their primary advantage tends to be that they provide beneficial opportunities for learners who can master the regular curriculum rapidly enough to take advantage of them.

This has led to the increasing popularity of *magnet schools,* whose primary purpose is to provide curricula in specialized areas—such as science, language arts, and the creative arts—to a broad range of students whose interests and abilities qualify them. Some magnet schools are within a school, thereby promoting heterogeneous interactions among learners while providing advanced and accelerated coursework leading to college credit and/or early high school graduation to those who can master the curriculum more quickly. The magnet school concept, as well as other alternatives, such as advanced placement credits and early graduation, that move the gifted learner more rapidly through the school curriculum, are increasingly coming to define programs for the gifted and talented.

Accelerated curriculum. Programs for the gifted and talented that offer advanced courses and/or grade skipping.

Teaching the Gifted and Talented Learner

Pose Challenging Problems. Gifted learners benefit from the freedom to independently explore issues and ideas of concern to them. You can give them this opportunity by posing challenging questions and problems. Focus the problem so the learner must make key decisions about what is important for a solution (e.g., what references, materials, documents, and equipment will be needed). This feeling of responsibility and control over the inquiry is essential if the learner is to see it as truly his or her own. Throughout the inquiry, let learners feel your support, encouragement, and availability to provide additional references and materials relevant to the directions they wish to explore.

Plan Instruction Involving Group Activities. Gifted students are among the most capable of picking up ideas from others and creating from them new and unusual variations. Brainstorming sessions, group discussions, panels, peer interviews, teams, and debates are among the ways you can involve gifted learners with the whole class. When carefully organized, these activities can create a "snowballing" of ideas that can turn initially rough ideas about a problem into polished and elegant solutions in which the whole class participates.

Include Real-Life Problems that Require Problem Solving. Let your gifted students become actual investigators in solving real-world dilemmas in a content area. This will force them to place newly acquired knowledge and understandings in a practical perspective and to increase the problem-solving challenge. Ask them pointed questions that do not have readily available answers: "How would you reduce world tensions among the superpowers?" "How would you eliminate acid rain?" "How could we harvest the seas?" "How could life be sustained on the moon?" Make clear that their inquiry into the nature of a problem should incorporate the same methods used by the professionals—scientists, engineers, political scientists—who must answer these questions in daily life. Require actual library or laboratory research that produces not just opinions, but objective evidence and a product or answer leading to a possible solution.

Draw Out Knowledge and Understanding. Since gifted learners tend to be verbally fluent, it can be difficult to determine whether an articulate response substitutes superficiality and glibness for an in-depth understanding. Such responses may even be purposefully composed to intimidate the listener, whether teacher or classmate. Testing and questioning the gifted, therefore, should draw out the knowledge and understanding that lie within, to separate superficiality from in-depth understanding. Use authentic or performance assessments (Chapter 13) to make your gifted learners go beyond knowing and remembering facts, to explain the reasons behind their answers, to put together the known facts into something new, to judge the outcome of their own inquiry, and to create a product that results from these activities.

Instructional Strategies for Gifted and Talented Learners

You may consider one of your students gifted as a result of her previous assignment to gifted classes, or you may arrive at this conclusion from an independent assessment of the student's intelligence, achievement, creativity, and task persistence. In either case, there are several methods for managing and teaching the gifted learner in the regular classroom. The accompanying box, *Teaching the Gifted and Talented Learner,* suggests some of the ways you can plan your teaching to meet such students' needs.

What activities and experiences will enhance the educational opportunities of a gifted or talented learner?

Summing Up

This chapter introduced you to teaching exceptional learners. Its main points were these:

- The Regular Education Initiative (REI) represents a partnership between regular and special educators in which learners with disabilities receive individualized services in the regular classroom without the requirement of labeling or special classifications.

- The need for a major, all-encompassing federal mandate for the public schools to educate the disabled learner in the least restricted environment was met by Public Law 94-142, Education for All Handicapped Children Act of 1975.
- The medical or pathological model of handicapping conditions assigned labels, such as "mentally retarded" or "learning disabled," as a condition for receiving special education services. The model currently embraced by many professionals is a system of classification that categorizes learners on the skills they need rather than on their deficits.
- The principle of normalization states that exceptional learners are entitled to programs that allow them to experience respect and dignity. This includes regular school participation, regular class participation, skill enhancement, image enhancement, autonomy, and empowerment.
- In order for a child to be diagnosed as having mental retardation, he or she must score below 70 on an individually administered IQ test and show significant deficits on measures of achievement and adaptive behavior, between the time of conception and his or her eighteenth year.
- An alternative to the present-day system of determining retardation is to categorize learners with mental retardation based on the skills they need to learn rather than on their deficits. In this manner, mental retardation would refer to the need for specific training that would allow individuals to live in the community without supervision.
- Assessing students with learning disabilities is a complicated process that includes intelligence and achievement tests. The presence of a learning disability is confirmed by an IQ–achievement discrepancy.
- Attention deficit hyperactivity disorder (ADHD) is a behavior disorder characterized by a short attention span, impulsivity, heightened physical activity, and deficits in rule-governed behavior (such as compliance, tracking, and problem solving). Most studies conclude that 3 to 5 percent of the school-age population has ADHD, with boys nearly twice as likely as girls to have ADHD.
- The effects of ADHD can be minimized in the classroom by avoiding unnecessary demands, continuously monitoring the behavior of the ADHD learner, and maintaining a high rate of instructional feedback and reinforcement.
- Your goal for students with communications disorders is to identify them and make sure they receive appropriate instructional resources.
- Some of the criteria most often used for selecting students for gifted and talented programs are intelligence, achievement, creativity, and task persistence.

For Discussion and Practice

1. Describe some of the apparent contradictions in Mike's behavior that make him a puzzle to his regular and special education teachers. What would be your initial reaction if Mike were in your class?

°2. In your own words describe the Regular Education Initiative and how it is likely to change your classroom in the future.

°3. Describe the concept of mainstreaming and cite some of the legislation that has brought it to prominence.

Questions marked with an asterisk are answered in the appendix.

°4. Describe the purpose of an individualized educational plan (IEP). What kinds of information must it contain?

°5. Describe four possible educational environments for learners with disabilities and give some examples of the types of services that would be provided within each. Which of these environments do you feel is most relevant to your classroom?

°6. In your own words, describe the principle of normalization. What are some of the themes it represents?

°7. Explain how standardized ability and achievement tests are used in the classification of learners with certain disabilities.

°8. How would a school psychologist most likely answer a teacher's questioning "Why is Mike (as described in this chapter) doing so poorly, when he attends school regularly and seems to be trying to learn?" What might be some additional questions that might get at the reason for Mike's problem?

°9. What is the most widely accepted method for diagnosing mental retardation? How low must someone's score on an IQ test be to indicate some degree of mental retardation?

°10. What early signs, if taken together, might signal the onset of ADHD in an early elementary school learner?

°11. What would you do in your classroom to improve the behavior of an ADHD learner?

°12. What is a communication disability? What are some specific things you would look for in your learners in diagnosing a communication disability?

13. From your own experience, what are some qualities you would associate with a gifted person? How well do they match the four characteristics described in this chapter?

°14. Describe one trend in gifted education that is supported by research.

Suggested Readings

Colangelo, N., & Davis, G. (eds.) (1991). *Handbook for gifted education.* Needham, MA: Allyn & Bacon. This book explores in depth the various definitions of gifted learners and describes a variety of programs to meet their educational and psychological needs.

Donnellan, A. M., LaVigna, G. W., Negri-Shoultz, N., & Fassbender, L. L. (1988). *Progress without punishment: Effective approaches for learners with severe behavior problems.* New York: Teachers College Press. Presents an effective argument for why learners with disabilities should not experience aversive behavior modification programs and offers numerous practical alternatives to punishment.

Matson, J. L., & Mulick, J. A. (1991). *Handbook of mental retardation* (2nd ed.). New York: Pergamon Press. The most comprehensive resource available for those interested in the assessment, treatment, and prevention of mental retardation and social policy regarding it.

Skrtic, T. M. (1991). The special education paradox: Equity as the way to excellence. *Harvard Educational Review, 61*(2), pp. 148–206. Must reading for anyone interested in understanding the Regular Education Initiative. This article gives a thorough airing and analysis to the views of all players in this important debate.

Wood, J. W. (1992). *Adapting instruction for mainstreamed and at-risk students* (2nd ed.). New York: Macmillan. This book points out how schools can make mainstreaming a shared responsibility on the part of administrators, teachers, parents, and learners. It gives extensive advice to teachers on how to meet the learning and emotional needs of mainstreamed students.

Multicultural and Gender-Fair Instruction

This chapter will help you answer the following questions about your learners:

- In what ways do learners from different ethnic and cultural groups learn and think differently?
- How do I recognize cultural bias in textbooks and in classroom conversation?
- What difficulties does the social organization of the typical classroom present for minority learners?
- How can I adapt my conversational style to encourage minority learners to participate more?
- How can I meet the needs of minority students' unique learning styles?
- What is the difference between a learner's learning style and his or her cognitive style?
- What instructional strategies are most appropriate for specific cognitive styles?
- What is "culturally responsive teaching" and how is it achieved?
- What prevalent sex-role stereotypes pertaining to curriculum, grouping, and classroom management should I avoid?
- How can I teach my class in ways that are free of gender bias?

The United States differs from nearly all other industrialized nations in the diversity of its classroom learners. It is not uncommon, in a single classroom, for teachers to find themselves facing male and female learners not only of different intellectual abilities but also of diverse cultural, linguistic, ethnic, and racial backgrounds. In this chapter we will study what teachers need to know about these aspects of learner diversity. Let's begin by looking in on Professor Thomas's educational psychology class as his students discuss the topic of cultural differences and learning.

Professor Thomas: This week you read about "culturally responsive teaching." What are your opinions on what some of these authors had to say?

Howard: I guess my views are a lot like my father's. He's a junior high teacher. He thinks that trying to adjust your teaching to ethnic or cultural learning styles may be more trouble than it's worth. It's hard enough to adjust to differences in abilities, personalities, and motivation. Now we're expected to adapt to ethnicity, race, and gender. At what point do we say "Forget that stuff and just do the best job you can with each individual learner"?

Professor Thomas: So your point is that if you just treat everybody as individuals, you don't need to worry about differences in culture and learning styles. Does everyone agree?

Julie: I think Howard misses the point. Every teacher would agree that we have to treat each learner as an individual. It's a cliché. Every teacher who has ever set foot in a classroom has had "individualization" drummed into her head. Yet many minority students don't do well in our schools. Something's not getting across!

Leon: And what's not getting across is that different groups learn differently, think differently about what they're learning, and think differently about their classrooms and teachers. But some teachers treat learners as though everyone were alike.

Scott: But *everybody* thinks differently. There are probably as many differences within a group as there are between groups. I think ethnic and racial differences in learning style are just stereotypes.

Professor Thomas: Janet, as an African American woman, did the information you read on the learning styles of minority learners strike a familiar chord?

Janet: Well, the discussions of cooperation and competition, and language differences, rang a little true. The stuff on learning styles I don't relate to. But maybe that's because I grew up in a middle-class home.

Scott: That's just my point. A lot of this literature makes it sound as though all members of a group think the same.

Roselia: The point is that schools may not be educating minority learners as well as the majority. And it may be because schools don't respect or appreciate the differences we bring to school. They just see the differences as problems.

Betty: I don't know about anyone else, but I found the readings helpful. I don't know if I'd teach a whole lot differently in a culturally diverse classroom, but I'd think differently about the learning problems of minority students. I wouldn't just assume it was their problem to learn, but that it was my responsibility to organize my classroom in a way that would help them.

Introduction

Prospective teachers, school administrators, and educational policy makers often want information about how to make their schools and classrooms responsive to the culturally diverse learner. Some educators assume that we already know enough to achieve success in teaching these learners. But as you will discover in this chapter, there are many divergent opinions about culture- and gender-specific learning. Let's look in on what some prominent educators and psychologists have to say about culture and teaching.

> We know that African American children who are neurologically intact and otherwise in good health show no deficits in intellectual functioning during the first years of postnatal life. Yet, many of these same children will be at risk for school failure after a year or two of formal schooling. What accounts for deflection of skill acquisition and intellectual performance in these children? The more meaningful questions for informing educational practice and policy as it pertains to poor minority students must address students' functional abilities, adaptive skills, cognitive strategies, and social competencies, and how they "fit" with the context of the classroom. (Nelson-LeGall & Jones, 1991, p. 27)

> Responsive instructional conversations and successful group and individual problem solving activities will be different for different cultures: students' experience, values, knowledge, and taste will vary by culture and will necessarily be reflected in responsive instruction. In the absence of school/cultural compatibilities, the relationship between teacher and child becomes the ground for struggle, and the relationship issues themselves absorb all of the energy of teacher and child that should be directed toward learning academic skills. (Tharp, 1989, p. 356)

> A word of caution is necessary here. . . . Research in this area [cultural learning styles] indicates that there are as many within-group as there are between-group differences. Lumping all Hispanic students together, for instance, has its dangers. . . . Although it is important to be able to adapt the learning environment to children with different cognitive and learning styles, it is also true that new learning styles can be suggested and encouraged. What is important is that what children bring with them to school be understood and valued, not ignored, deplored, or despised. (Cushner, McClelland, & Safford, 1992, p. 114)

Minority group. A social group that occupies a subordinate position with respect to the society as a whole and that shares a sense of collective identity.

In discussing the educational experiences of different cultural groups in this chapter, we will refer to various minority groups. **Minority group** is the sociological term for a social group that tends to occupy a subordinate position in our society and whose members share a sense of collective identity and common perception of the world around them (Cushner et al., 1992). Educators and psychologists concerned about cultural differences and their effects on school learning typically have studied three minority groups: African Americans, Hispanic Americans, and Native Americans. In this chapter, we will primarily address the school-related problems and research pertaining to these three groups.

Many teachers in American schools teach learners from a variety of cultural backgrounds. While some of these learners have succeeded in our schools, others have not. Many African American, Hispanic, and Native American learners, for example, are believed to be not achieving at their potential. One explanation for the discrepancy between what Anglo-Americans and African, Hispanic, and Native Americans achieve focuses on the concept of cultural compatibility.

Cultural compatibility refers to the belief that different cultural groups have different ways of learning and thinking, as well as needs for different motivational, instructional, and classroom management strategies. Those who study topics related to cultural compatibility believe that American schools historically have not sufficiently adapted to the learning styles, preferences, and needs of various cultural groups. They argue that insufficient adaptation of classroom instruction to the learning styles and preferences of learners is a major reason for the comparatively low achievement of minority learners (Tharp, 1989).

Cultural compatibility. The goal of designing instruction to incorporate relevant features of the learners' culture.

In what ways do learners from different ethnic and cultural groups learn and think differently?

The importance of cultural compatibility in the classroom is receiving increased attention among educators. Some have recommended that teachers adapt their instructional, classroom management, and motivational strategies to the needs of different cultural groups. The topic of "culturally responsive teaching" has appeared frequently in popular teacher magazines (*Educational Leadership*, vol. 49, January 1992); scholarly journals (*Education and Urban Society*, vol. 24, November 1991; *Exceptional Children*, vol. 59, 1992) and textbooks used for teacher training (Bennett, 1990; Cushner et al., 1992; Garcia, 1991). Nevertheless, as the discussion in Dr. Thomas's class illustrates, there is no consensus that culturally responsive teaching is possible or even desirable. And there is little agreement that the lack of cultural compatibility is an adequate explanation for lower school achievement by some minorities.

In this chapter, we will address the issue of how best to deal with two groups of diverse learners: those whose diversity is based on cultural differences—for example, African Americans, Hispanic Americans, and Native Americans—and those whose difference is based on gender.

To help you teach these two groups of learners, we will first trace the positions that minority groups and girls and boys have historically held in our schools. We will examine what some schools have done to perpetuate cultural and gender bias and what effect this has had on the academic achievement of minority groups and of girls. Then we will analyze the concepts of cognitive and learning styles, the research supporting their existence, and the results of educational programs that have tried to incorporate these concepts into culturally responsive teaching. Finally, we will address what teachers need to know about how to teach diverse learners by presenting a conceptual model that suggests the important questions to ask when planning, delivering, evaluating, and revising instruction.

Cultural Differences and Schooling

To understand the cultural backgrounds of students of color and to teach them successfully, it is important to understand how their cultures have been and are accepted in

A classroom made up of a diverse group of learners requires that the teacher accommodate her instruction to a variety of learning and cognitive styles.

school and society (Grant, 1991). Although most of us have heard and read that lack of understanding of cultural differences and underachievement characterize the minority experience in American schools, you may be less aware why some have expressed this viewpoint. Consequently, in this section we will review two important aspects of the school experience of minority groups: (1) how schools have valued minority culture, and (2) how well schools have taught minority students (Grant, 1991; Grant & Secada, 1990).

Minority Learners and Teachers

One symbol of how well schools respect different cultures is the number of minorities in the teaching force. As Grant asserts, "Teachers of color indicate to students of color that their cultural group is respected and academically capable" (1991, p. 243). Grant and Sleeter (1986) conducted interviews with minority learners who expressed a preference for teachers of their own minority background. From the work of Albert Bandura, which we studied in Chapter 3, we would expect teachers to be more effective as role models when they have characteristics in common with their learners.

Despite the recognition that minority teachers are important role models for students, and especially for minority learners, the likelihood that a minority learner will encounter a teacher of a similar background is minimal. Harris and Harris (1988) report that at the beginning of the 1980s, 91.5 percent of public school teachers were Anglo, 7.8 percent were African American, and 0.7 percent belonged to other groups. By 1986, the numbers were 89.6 percent Anglo, 7 percent African American, and 3.4 percent other. Anglo women represented nearly 67 percent of the teaching force. All indications are that this situation will continue well into the next century (Cushner et al., 1992).

Minority Learners and Textbooks

The textbook is the most frequently used instructional tool in middle schools and high schools and is, in many cases, the only tool (Eisner, 1987). Thus, textbooks provide an excellent opportunity to communicate examples of cultural respect and equality. Although progress has been made in eliminating racial and ethnic stereotyping in texts,

Ornstein (1992) reports that this was not the case through the early 1980s. Studies of textbooks completed in the 1970s reported underrepresentation of African American and Hispanic American men and women, who rarely were depicted in higher-status or decision-making roles. In comparison with the Anglo culture, the culture of minority groups has not been portrayed in an esteemed or respected manner (Butterfield, Demas, Grant, May, & Perez, 1979; Dumfee, 1974).

Sleeter and Grant (1991) recently analyzed K through 9 textbooks with publication dates between 1980 and 1987. They report that these texts depict the Anglo culture as superior to the cultures of people of color. Anglos received the most attention, were represented in a greater variety of professional and nonprofessional roles, and typically dominated the story line and lists of accomplishments. In addition, Sleeter and Grant report that minority group cultures were rarely discussed in relationship to each other. Rather, they were shown in relationship to the Anglo culture. For example, African American cowboys of the West were discussed in a context of Anglo culture rather than in the context of their interactions with Native or Hispanic Americans who also lived in that region at that time. Thus, although textbooks offer the opportunity for teachers to present minority cultures in a favorable light, this has not always been the case (Grant, 1991).

> **How do I recognize cultural bias in textbooks and in classroom conversation?**

Minority Learners and the Language of the Classroom

Bowers and Flinders (1990) cite numerous examples of how the verbal and nonverbal language of the classroom frequently communicate disrespect for the cultural heritage of certain minority groups. For example, Native American culture views forests as the natural state of the world. Yet textbooks and teachers sometimes speak of forests as wild places needing to be tamed or harnessed. Also, stories of other cultures sometimes use the expressions "primitive," "undeveloped," or "backward" to describe minority cultures.

Bowers and Flinders also remind us that the nonverbal aspects of communication signify different things to different cultures:

> Depending on the cultural background of the student, a smile can signify rapport, embarrassment, or potential hostility; eye contact can signify respect or disrespect; close physical proximity can signify friendship or aggressiveness; and slow speech (relative to what the student perceives as normal) can signify interest and consideration or rudeness and indifference. (1990, p. 51)

Their point is that one way for schools to show respect for the culture of different groups is to make teachers aware of how their own verbal and nonverbal language patterns may differ from those of their culturally diverse learners. However, Bowers and Flinders report that these issues are seldom addressed in either teacher training programs or in-service programs for classroom teachers.

Minority Learners and Tracking

Grant (1991) believes that another way schools fail to acknowledge the culture of minority learners is through the practice of tracking and the use of tests to decide who is placed in which track. Despite some evidence that tracking lowers the achievement and self-esteem of minority learners and that standardized ability testing may disproportionately place minority learners in low-ability tracks, these practices continue in many schools throughout the United States.

Minority Learners and School Achievement

Although African, Hispanic, or Native American learners can and do achieve as well as and better than many Anglo-Americans in school, as groups, these learners tend to score lower than Anglo or Asian American students, indicating that many of these learners may not be achieving their potential in school. The school achievement of many Native American learners is substantially lower than that of Anglos (Tharp, 1989), and their dropout rate is the highest of all minority groups—nearly 42 percent (Bennett, 1990).

As a group, Hispanic Americans are the most undereducated of Americans (Bennett, 1990). Only 40 percent have completed high school, and the dropout rate of 39.9 percent is second only to that of Native Americans. Their reading, writing, and math skills also lag behind the national average (see Table 15.1).

African Americans consistently score below the national average on scholastic achievement measures (see Table 15.1). Their dropout rate approaches 25 percent (compared with 14.3 percent for Anglos). On measures of scholastic ability, such as the Scholastic Assessment Test (SAT) or group and individual IQ tests, African Americans typically score from 10 to 15 IQ score points below Anglos (Jensen, 1980).

A recent analysis of how African American learners are faring in the Milwaukee Public Schools exemplifies their achievements in many urban centers (Holt, 1992).

- Between 1978 and 1985, 94.4 percent of all students expelled from the Milwaukee Public Schools were African Americans.

Table 15.1

National Assessment of Educational Progress, by Subject and by Ethnic Group*

Reading, 1987–1988	9-year-olds	13-year-olds	17-year-olds
National average	211.8	257.5	290.1
White	217.7	261.3	294.7
Black	188.5	242.9	274.4
Hispanic	193.7	240.1	270.8
Writing, 1988	**fourth-graders**	**eighth-graders**	**eleventh-graders**
National average	173.3	208.2	220.7
White	180.0	213.1	225.3
Black	150.7	190.1	206.9
Hispanic	162.2	197.2	202.0
Mathematics, 1985–1986	**9-year-olds**	**13-year-olds**	**17-year-olds**
National average	222.0	269.0	302.0
White	227.0	274.0	309.0
Black	202.0	249.0	279.0
Hispanic	205.0	254.0	283.0

*Range: From 0 to 500.

Source: "National Assessment of Educational Progress Scales in Reading, Writing, and Mathematics," 1990, *Digest of Education Statistics* (pp. 113, 116, 118, 120, 121), 1991, Washington, DC: National Center for Education Statistics, U.S. Department of Education.

Carl A. Grant, University of Wisconsin-Madison

I began my career working as a teacher and administrator and realized that students of color were continually being marginalized and oppressed and were not the recipients of social justice because of school policy and practices. The culture of peoples of color was treated as subordinate to the culture of Anglos, and instructional materials were often racist and sexist and ignored students with disabilities.

My research into multicultural issues grew out of the civil rights struggles of the 1960s. Social change was being demanded in colleges and K–12 schools. The policies and practices of many educational institutions at that time often worked against people of color and women. Multicultural education research began to investigate the interactions of race, ethnicity, class, gender, and disability as they were being played out in schools and the classroom.

Most recently, research has studied the practice of tracking and the use of tests to decide who gets tracked. Its results suggest that tracking serves to lower the achievement and self-esteem of minority learners, and standardized tests may disproportionately place minority learners in low-ability tracks. Another finding from the research is that what teachers know about their students' cultural backgrounds can influence student learning. Their training needs to include a history of schooling from the perspective of people of color, a discussion of the need for teachers to understand their own biographies and enculturation, and an examination of what the literature says (or does not say) about the influence of culture on the teaching and learning of students of color.

For teachers to use effectively any information they do receive about the culture of their students, they must understand their own biographies and enculturation and how these give direction to their thoughts and actions. Finally, research indicates that the educational problems experienced by students of color are not the main cause for students' lack of educational success. The overall structures of school and society play a major role in the lack of academic success of students of color.

I hope that teachers use the results from this research to better understand how to make their teaching more appropriate and engaging for their students, especially when they have males and females of color, low-income students, students with disabilities, and white students who have limited knowledge about race, class, and gender issues. To understand the cultural background of students of color and to teach them successfully it is necessary to understand how their culture has been and is accepted in school and society. Also, the results of this research should help teachers understand the importance of providing students with curriculum and instruction that empower them and that teaches them to understand the importance of making wise life choices.

One of the most important perspectives I believe teachers should take away from multicultural education is that it is a way of thinking, a way of seeing the world that is consistent with the words and statements in many of our national documents dealing with equity, equality, liberty, and justice. It is an education that starts when each of us examines our own attitudes, beliefs, privileges, and behavior. Multicultural education is not static. It requires that each of us continually examine ourselves, our homes, and our communities for a lifelong, deep concern for humankind.

- During the 1986–1987 school year, Milwaukee's African American high school students had an average grade point average of D (1.46 GPA).

- During the 1989–1990 school year, 50 percent of the male students suspended from school were African Americans, although they represented only 27.6 percent of the students in the school district.

Although many explanations have been advanced for the underachievement of minority groups, the one that has increasingly gained support is the *cultural compatibility*

Historically, schools have not succeeded with minority learners as well as they have with majority learners. Some research suggests that this may result in part from the failure of schools to understand and appreciate minority group culture fully.

hypothesis (Tharp, 1989). This hypothesis states that the social structure of many American classrooms (for example, whole-group instruction, competitive orientation, and learning from text) and cognitive abilities required to learn (verbal/analytic) may not be compatible with the social structure and cognitive learning styles of some minority learners. It is this incongruence that some believe undermines minority group achievement.

The cultural compatibility hypothesis has influenced research on instructional methods that has the potential to raise the achievement of minority learners. It has also given rise to a strategy of teaching called *culturally responsive teaching*. Increasingly, methods textbooks, scholarly journals, and popular teacher magazines recommend that teachers of minority learners adopt various versions of this type of teaching.

Cultural Compatibility and Minority Learner Achievement

The nontraditional school day begins with a period of learning readiness whose purpose is to build self-esteem and motivation, and to teach children how to resolve conflicts. Children then are engaged in two two-hour blocks of academic time: reading and language arts in the morning; and math, science, and social studies in the afternoon.

All teachers require students to do a great deal of reciting and memorization, tying in with the oral tradition of griot (African story telling). Every morning Willene Wallace's second graders recite "The Pledge of Allegiance," sing "The Black National Anthem," and repeat aloud poems by black American authors. In class, teachers tell stories, and then often ask children to improvise a variation of the story, possibly with an African or African American motif if the story didn't originally have one.

To provide a showcase for students and to create a nurturing environment, all children belong to a "school family" composed of three to four multi-grade classes. Family meetings occur every two weeks, and the programs planned by a team of teachers often feature students in performances and peer teaching. (Scherer, 1992, p. 17)

The school described here is attempting to create a classroom environment that is compatible with the home culture of African American learners. Similar culturally compatible or culturally responsive experiments in education are being carried out in other schools. For example, the Kamehameha Early Education Program (KEEP) for more than 20 years has been studying the effects of a culturally compatible language arts program on the reading and language achievement of K–3 learners of Hawaiian ancestry (Tharp et al., 1984). In Shiprock, New Mexico, a similar project is under way among elementary school-age Navaho learners (Vogt, Jordan, & Tharp, 1987). The Milwaukee public schools are experimenting with African American Immersion Schools (Holt, 1992). These and other projects are attempts to investigate whether culturally diverse learners can achieve on a par with Anglo-American learners when placed in classrooms whose group and classroom management strategies, methods of communication, instructional practices, and motivational techniques are attuned to native cultural patterns.

In this section we will examine the cultural compatibility hypothesis. We will begin with a description of the culture of the typical American classroom and point out incompatibilities between this process of schooling and the home culture of certain minority groups. Then we will review the research supporting the cultural compatibility hypothesis. We will analyze the recommendations for how teachers should teach minority groups and propose a framework for integrating cultural knowledge about learners with instructional practice in a manner that acknowledges cultural group differences.

Education and Schooling

Educators often make a distinction between education and schooling, or informal and formal learning. They use the term **education** to refer to the varied and informal ways children learn the customs, attitudes, beliefs, values, social skills, and other behaviors they require to be successful members of a family, cultural group, or society (Cushner et al., 1992). Most education is informal and occurs outside the school. It occurs in contexts that are immediately meaningful, face-to-face, and influenced by group dynamics. Cooperation, not competition, predominates. A common language is the medium of learning, and the motivation to learn is often influenced by familial, peer, and similar emotionally laden relationships.

Schooling, on the other hand, often takes place apart from a real-world context. As we learned in Chapters 8 through 10, schools and classrooms have their own sets of normative beliefs, methods of social organization, rules, routines, and instructional strategies. Whereas learning outside school is largely observational and occurs through the social learning processes, learning inside school is characterized by a reliance on words, explanations, and questions. Both teaching and evaluation occur in an academic context (although, as we saw in Chapter 12, performance assessments are beginning to change this).

Roland G. Tharp, who has researched the effects of culture on schooling, uses the term *psychocultural variables* to refer to features of learning outside the school that differ from those inside it and that potentially cause frustration and lack of achievement for culturally different learners (Tharp, 1989). Tharp and his colleagues have focused on four classes of psychocultural variables that are most relevant for understanding the differences between learning and schooling: social organization, sociolinguistics, learning style, and cognitive style. Tharp believes that American schools may be working better for Anglo-Americans than for African Americans, Native Americans, or Hispanic Americans because the typical social organization, sociolinguistics, and instructional strategies

Education. The varied and informal ways in which children learn the customs, attitudes, beliefs, values, social skills, and other behaviors that they require to be successful members of a family, cultural group, and society. Most such education takes place outside the school.

Schooling. Learning that takes place within the special academic context and culture of formal educational structures, primarily through words, processes, and questions.

used in schooling are more compatible with the former culture. Let's examine the basis for that assertion.

Social Organization

Social organization. The relationships—roles, functions, and common goals—between adults and children during learning.

What difficulties does the social organization of the typical classroom present for minority learners?

In the school context, **social organization** refers to the relationships between adults and children during learning: their roles, functions, and common goals. We discussed these terms in Chapter 8 when we looked at group processes in the classroom. In American schools, the standard social organization is characterized by whole-group direct instruction. Learners typically are seated at individual desks arranged in rows or in small groups around a table. Children listen to a teacher explain and demonstrate, engage in some type of independent practice, and take tests. Although cooperative learning may be used from time to time, typically children work independently and competitively.

Tharp and others (Bennett, 1990; Cushner et al., 1992; Franklin, 1992; Garcia, 1991) believe that this type of social organization is more compatible with the culture of the Anglo culture than with that of the three principal minority groups. The result may be that Anglo children make an easier transition to school, which encourages academic success.

These educators believe that certain minority groups experience a difficult home–school transition because the social organization of their informal learning is incompatible with that of the typical American classroom. For example, Tharp (1989) states that Hawaiian and Navaho children, two groups whose reading achievement and language development are well below that of Anglo children, grow up with a social organization characterized by small-group cooperation, collaboration, and assisted performance.

Franklin (1992), Tharp (1989), and Williams (1981) report that African American children are raised in a social organization where relationships between siblings and peers are more cooperative than competitive, and the relationships between adults and children are characterized by a focus on feelings and emotions rather than on skill learning (called *affective-oriented* versus *task-oriented*). Clark (1991) concludes that African American learners experience a noncompetitive, mutually supportive learning environment at home, where egalitarianism, informality, and humor are valued. These researchers believe that schools create dissonance and stress for minority learners by exposing them to classrooms that encourage individuality, competition, task orientation, and formality, and that lessen the importance of relationships.

Sociolinguistics

Sociolinguistics. The study of how cultural groups differ in the courtesies and conventions of language rather than in the grammatical structure of what is said; the social conversation of speech.

Sociolinguistics is the study of how cultural groups differ in the courtesies and conventions of language. Sociolinguistics examines the rules governing social conversation: with whom to speak, how to speak, when to pause, when to ask and answer questions, how to interrupt a speaker. Sociolinguists study, for example, aspects of communication as revealed by the average length of utterances, time between utterances, speech rhythms, and rules for when, how, and about what people converse with each other. Among these aspects of communication, the most frequently studied are wait-time, rhythm, and participation structure.

Wait-time 1. The amount of time a teacher gives a learner to respond to a question.

Wait-Time. Sociolinguists report that cultures differ significantly in the manner in which they pause during conversation, called "wait-time." There are two types: wait-time 1 and wait-time 2. With reference to classroom conversation, **wait-time 1** refers to

Teachers need to be aware that members of different groups have different conversational styles.

the amount of time a teacher gives a learner to respond to a question. Teachers who use short wait-time 1s do not give learners much time to think before answering a question. Such a teacher repeats the question or calls on another learner to answer the same question after a pause of only 2 or 3 seconds.

Wait-time 2 refers to the interval of time after a learner's response before the teacher speaks. Teachers who use long wait-time 2s wait several seconds before asking a follow-up question, correcting the answer, or otherwise commenting on what the learner has said. Teachers who use short wait-time 2s frequently interrupt learners before they finish answering.

Wait-time 2. The interval of time after a learner's response before the teacher speaks.

Rowe (1986) has found that increasing either wait-time has the following effects on learners' responses.

- Learners give longer answers to questions.
- They volunteer more responses.
- There are fewer unanswered questions.
- Learners are more certain of their answers.
- Learners are more willing to give speculative answers.
- The frequency of learner questions increases.

Tharp (1989) reports that different cultures often have different wait-times. Navaho children, for example, are raised in a culture with longer wait-time 2s than are Anglo children. As a result, Anglo teachers more frequently interrupt Navaho children than do Navaho teachers. Some studies show that Navaho children speak in longer sentences and volunteer more answers when taught by teachers who use longer wait-time 2s. Hawaiian children, on the other hand, prefer shorter wait-time 2s. Tharp reports that in Hawaiian culture, interruptions are a sign of interest in what the speaker is saying. Conversely, long wait-time 2s suggest to Hawaiian learners that the speaker is uninterested or bored with the conversation.

Rhythm. *Rhythm* refers to the tempo, inflections, and speed of a conversation. Young (1970) and Piestrup (1973) have observed that African American children and their mothers converse with one another using rapid rhythms and a "contest" style of interaction. Mothers encourage their children to be assertive. Directions for household chores and the children's responses to these directions take on an almost debate-like tone, with the mother directing or calling and the children responding. Franklin (1992) suggests that this style of interaction creates a high-energy, fast-paced home environment, which contrasts with the low-energy, slow-paced environment of the typical classroom, and speculates that this contrast between the pace of conversation at home and in school may be one reason why some African American children are referred for behavior problems in the classroom.

Similarly, Anderson (1992) states that many Anglo teachers overreact to the conversational style of African American adolescents, which may explain the disproportionate referral of these children to programs for learners with behavior disorders. Anderson recommends that teachers allow African American learners to use in the classroom the conversational style they bring from home. This would include speaking more rhythmically, using greater variation of tone, and engaging in more fast-paced verbal interplay.

Participation Structure. The typical classroom conversation occurs in a one-to-one, question-and-answer format. A teacher looks directly at a child, asks him a question, and waits for an answer before making a follow-up response.

Tharp (1989) observes that such a **participation structure** results in very little participation by Hawaiian or Navaho children. At home and in their communities, the typical participation structure when adults are present involves a relatively small group of children together with an encouraging, participating, but nondirective adult in an informal setting. When the classroom participation structures are based on those in the culture, both Hawaiian and Navaho children, who otherwise rarely participate in classroom discussions or question-and-answer formats, become surprisingly verbal (Au & Mason, 1981; Watson-Gegeo & Boggs, 1977).

Sociolinguists point out that children are more comfortable in classrooms where the sociolinguistic patterns (including wait-times, rhythms, participation structures) are compatible with those of their home and community. Baratz and Baratz (1970) and Lein (1975) point out that schools often view African American or Hispanic migrant children as nonverbal. Yet when observed in familiar home or neighborhood environments, these same children use vibrant, expressive, and creative language. Because the sociolinguistic patterns of the typical American classroom make certain minority group learners uncomfortable, these learners participate less in class, speak in ways that Anglo-American teachers view as deficient or inappropriate, and consequently achieve less.

Learning Styles

Take a minute and reflect on the circumstances under which you learn best and how you tend to think about and solve problems:

1. Do you prefer studying in a group or by yourself?
2. When learning about a short story, poem, song, picture, or dance, do you first try to grasp the overall theme, message, or point of view, or do you tend to first analyze the characters, plots, relationships, or movements?

How can I adapt my conversational style to encourage minority learners to participate more?

Participation structure. The social structure that governs classroom conversation. The most common form of participation structure is a one-to-one question-and-answer format.

3. Do you learn better when teachers provide visual aids, or do you prefer verbal explanations and examples?

4. Do you tend to relate on a personal level to what you read and listen to, or do you approach information and tasks in an impersonal, disinterested manner?

5. Do you prefer large blocks of time in which to master something, or would you rather distribute your efforts over smaller time periods?

6. When you look at pictures such as those shown in Figure 15.1, can you easily see the simple geometric figures embedded in the complex pattern, or do you have difficulty separating the simple figure from the background?

7. Do you learn better in noisy or quiet environments?

8. Are you quick to jump to conclusions, or do you reflect for long periods of time before making a decision?

9. Do you prefer teachers who use an overhead projector or the blackboard?

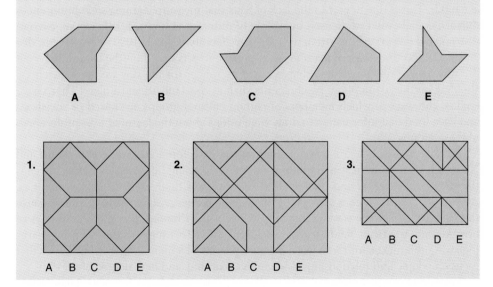

This is a test of your ability to tell which of five simple figures (A–E) can be found in a more complex pattern. Beneath the row of figures is a row of patterns. Each pattern has a row of letters beneath it. Indicate your answer by putting an X through the letter of the figure that you find in the pattern.

Note: There is only one of these figures in each pattern, and this figure will always be right side up and exactly the same size as one of the five lettered figures.

Figure 15.1
Hidden figures test. *Source:* Adapted from "Hidden Figures Test" (Cf-1), *Kit of Factor Referenced Cognitive Tests.* Copyright © 1962 by Educational Testing Service. Reprinted by permission of Educational Testing Service, the copyright owner.

10.   Do you have to see the purpose or larger reason for learning something
      in order to grasp and understand it, or can you learn things even if they
      have little relevance for you at the moment?

In the above list, the odd-numbered questions pertain to learning style preferences, while the even-numbered questions pertain to how you process or think about what you learn. The former measure your *learning style* and the latter your *cognitive style*. In this section, we will address learning styles; in the next, cognitive styles.

Learning style. The classroom or environmental conditions under which an individual prefers to learn.

Technically speaking, **learning style** refers to the classroom or environmental conditions under which an individual prefers to learn. Learning style preferences fall into the following categories:

Physical environment: seating arrangements, lighting, temperature, noise level, and so on.

Social environment: working alone versus in pairs or small groups; cooperative versus competitive instructional formats; working with or without the presence of adults.

Emotional environment: friendly, helpful versus aloof, solitary; preference for a nurturing, people-oriented versus a self-reliant, materials- or text-oriented learning environment.

Instructional environment: lecture versus discussion; preference for certain types of tests; direct, indirect, self-directed instructional formats; preference for activities involving visual, tactile, or kinesthetic sense modalities.

Managerial environment: many versus few rules; written-down versus unstated rules; clear versus implied consequences; number of classroom routines; preferences for particular leadership styles (referent, expert, and so on as discussed in Chapter 8).

Do different cultures have learning style preferences? There is surprisingly little research comparing the learning style preferences of different cultural groups (Cushner et al., 1992). This is due in part to the lack of tests that measure learning style preferences that are equally valid when used by people of different cultures. Furthermore, current instruments do not exhibit strong validity or reliability (Snider, 1990). Most of the discussion supporting cultural learning style preferences is based on the assumption that the way we are raised at home shapes our preferences for the way we learn at school. Building on this assumption, psychologists such as Asa Hilliard and Roland Tharp have studied the ways in which members of certain cultural groups are raised or socialized and have used that information to draw conclusions about the learning style preferences of these groups.

We have already learned about some of these preferences. Native Americans and Native Hawaiians prefer small-group cooperative learning because this better matches the social organization and participation structures of their homes and communities. African American learners prefer a fast-paced, high-energy style of instruction because this better matches the conversational patterns of their homes. Based on his studies of how African American children are raised, Hilliard (1976) suggests the following learning style preferences for these learners: energetic involvement in activities, lessons that focus on people and relationships, cooperative learning, and high degree of novelty.

In one of the few cross-cultural studies of learning style preferences, Jalali (1989) used the Learning Style Inventory (Renzulli & Smith, 1978) with 300 culturally different fourth-, fifth-, and sixth-graders and found the following learning style preferences: *African Americans* preferred quiet, warmth, bright light, mobility, routine and patterns, frequent feedback from authority figures, action-oriented instructional experiences, and afternoon or evening learning sessions rather than morning. *Hispanic Americans* preferred low light, structure, mobility, learning alone (some researchers, like Kagan [1983] and Ramirez & Castaneda [1974], suggest the importance of group learning), tactile and visual instruction, and feedback from an authority figure.

Cognitive Styles

In Chapter 5 we studied a model of cognitive learning (Figure 5.1). From it you learned that the *learning process* is what goes on inside the learner's head as a result of receiving instructional stimuli. The learning process refers to how learners attend to, assimilate, accommodate, and use learning strategies to acquire knowledge.

Cognitive style refers to individuals' preferred ways of engaging in the learning process. Some learners are quick to respond when presented with a problem to solve or question to answer. Others are more reflective, even though they may be as informed and expert. The even-numbered questions in the list on pages 512–514 reflect examples of cognitive style. Although there are a number of cognitive styles (convergent versus divergent thinking, reflectivity versus impulsivity), the one most studied in cross-cultural research has been that of field-dependence versus field-independence.

Field-Dependence Versus Field-Independence.   Much has been written about how African American, Native American, and Hispanic American children are more "global" than "analytic" in the way they approach learning (Franklin, 1992). Some use the terms "holistic/visual" to describe "global" learners and "verbal/analytic" to describe the opposite style or orientation (Tharp, 1989). Still others (Hilliard, 1976) prefer the term "field sensitive" to describe the holistic/visual cognitive style and "field insensitive" to refer to the verbal/analytic cognitive style.

All of these researchers are referring to a traditional distinction between cognitive styles usually referred to as **field-dependence** and **field-independence.** These terms refer to two different ways of viewing the world. People who are field-dependent see the world in terms of large, connected patterns. Looking at a volcano, for example, a field-dependent person would notice its overall shape and the larger colors and topographical features that make it up. A field-independent person, on the other hand, would tend to notice the discrete, individual parts of a scene. Thus, she might notice the individual trees, the different rocks, the size of the caldera, where the caldera sits in relation to the rest of the structure, topographical features showing the extent of lava flow, and so forth.

To better understand what field-dependence and field-independence mean and what these terms suggest about how culturally different children learn, let's look at how researchers have studied these concepts. Witkin and Goodenough (1977) were among the first psychologists to explore how individuals perceive situations and respond to problems. They used two types of tests to determine whether a person tended to be field-dependent or field-independent: the rod-and-frame test and the embedded figures test. Figure 15.2 depicts the rod-and-frame test. In a darkened room, subjects were shown a tilted rod inside a tilted frame with no other visual information (Position A, Figure 15.2). Subjects were then asked to adjust the rod so that it was perpendicular to the ground. Some subjects, even though they had no visual cues such as floor or walls, adjusted the rod correctly (Position B) despite the tilt of the frame. These subjects were called field-independent because they used internal information from their senses to gauge space and movement and ignored contradictory information from the visually tilted frame.

How can I meet the needs of minority students' unique learning styles?

What is the difference between a learner's learning style and his or her cognitive style?

Cognitive style. The means by which individuals process and think about what they learn.

Field-dependence. A cognitive style that influences learners to perceive complex stimuli in terms of larger patterns and relationships.

Field-independence. A cognitive style that influences learners to perceive complex stimuli in terms of the discrete, individual elements that constitute it.

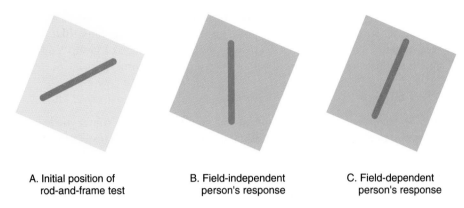

A. Initial position of
rod-and-frame test

B. Field-independent
person's response

C. Field-dependent
person's response

Figure 15.2
Field-dependence in perception and personality.

Other subjects, however, adjusted the rod so that it was perpendicular to the frame (Position C). Witkin called these individuals field-dependent. They depended more on the external information provided by the frame than on the internal information coming from their senses. They were more dependent on external sources of information to solve the problem than were members of the field-independent group.

Refer back to Figure 15.1, a hidden figures test. Field-dependent people find it difficult to focus their gaze and attention away from the global pattern to locate the simple figures embedded within the pattern. In other words, they focus on the whole figure rather than its parts. Field-independent people, on the other hand, have no difficulty separating the simple figures from the background. As in the rod-and-frame test, they are able to use internal sources of information to solve the problem. They engage in an internal dialogue with themselves and analytically break the whole into its constituent parts. Thus, the term *verbal/analytic* is used to describe the field-independent problem-solving style. On the other hand, *visual/holistic* and *global* are terms used to describe the cognitive style used by field-dependent people.

Educational Implications. Witkin and his colleagues believe that field-dependence and field-independence are stable traits of individuals that affect different aspects of their lives—especially their approaches to classroom learning. Table 15.2 summarizes the characteristics associated with both types of learners.

Witkin, Moore, Goodenough, and Cox (1977) and Garger and Guild (1984) believe that the different personality characteristics or traits of field-dependent and field-independent learners suggest that at least some learners employ different cognitive processes during classroom learning activities. These researchers also suggest that each group would profit from different instructional strategies. The accompanying box, *Matching Teaching Strategies with Learners' Cognitive Styles*, suggests some instructional strategies for each of these two groups of learners.

As you study the table and box, keep in mind two points:

1. The two contrasting cognitive styles have not been directly observed. These descriptions are assumptions or inferences about how the groups approach and think about instructional situations and stimuli, based on their performances on the various tests used by Witkin and his col-

> **What instructional strategies are most appropriate for specific cognitive styles?**

Table 15.2

Characteristics of Field-Dependent and Field-Independent Learners

Field-Dependent (Field-Sensitive) Learner	Field-Independent Learner
Perceives global aspects of concepts and materials.	Focuses on details of curriculum materials.
Personalizes curriculum—relates concepts to personal experience.	Focuses on facts and principles.
Seeks guidance and demonstrations from teacher.	Rarely seeks physical contact with teacher.
Seeks rewards that strengthen relationship with teacher.	Formal interactions with teacher are restricted to tasks at hand—seeks nonsocial rewards.
Prefers to work with others and is sensitive to their feelings and opinions.	Prefers to work alone.
Likes to cooperate.	Likes to compete.
Prefers organization provided by teacher.	Can organize information by himself or herself.

leagues. In other words, these descriptions come from a logical rather than an empirical analysis.

2. Little research supports the notion that one group requires a different instructional strategy than another to achieve in school (Cronbach & Snow, 1977; Kampwerth & Bates, 1980; Mayer, 1987). Rather, the teaching style preferences identified in the box only suggest the most efficient way to teach learners who tend to approach learning in a field-dependent or field-independent manner.

Cognitive Style and Culture. Educators and psychologists have been interested in the relationship between cognitive style and culture. The work of several researchers has suggested that Native Americans, Hispanic Americans, and African Americans tend to be more field-dependent than either Anglo-Americans or Asian Americans (Bennett, 1990; Cushner et al., 1992; Garcia, 1991; Hilliard, 1992; Tharp, 1989). They therefore advocate that teachers who work with these groups of learners use more field-dependent teaching styles.

What evidence have these studies found to suggest that minority groups have different patterns of cognitive functioning than Anglo-Americans? While the evidence is scattered and sometimes inconsistent, in general there is some support that minority learners are more holistic/global/visual or field-sensitive in their approaches to learning than are Anglo-Americans. For example, Native Americans consistently score higher on tests that require spatial ability and manipulation skills (arranging puzzles, solving

Matching Teaching Strategies with Learners' Cognitive Styles

Strategies for Field-Dependent Learners

- Display physical and verbal experiences of approval or warmth; show referent power.
- Motivate by use of social and tangible rewards.
- Use cooperative learning strategies.
- Minimize corrective feedback.
- Allow interaction during learning.
- Structure lessons, projects, homework, and so forth.
- Assume role of lecturer, demonstrator, checker, reinforcer, grader, materials designer.

Strategies for Field-Independent Learners

- Be formal in interactions with learners; show expert power.
- Motivate by use of nonsocial rewards, such as grades.
- Use mastery learning and errorless teaching strategies.
- Use corrective feedback.
- Emphasize independent projects.
- Allow learners to develop their own structure.
- Assume role of consultant, listener, negotiator, facilitator.

mazes, drawing figures) than on tests that require primarily verbal abilities (detecting similarities and differences in concepts, analyzing proverbs for their underlying meaning) (Cohen, 1985; Gallimore, Tharp, Sloat, Klein, & Troy, 1982; Tharp, 1987).

Lesser, Fifer, and Clark (1965) found that Hispanic American and African American first-grade learners had different patterns of mental abilities than did Chinese American or Jewish American first-graders. The former groups performed better in those abilities that suggest a field-sensitive cognitive style, while the latter showed strengths in tasks requiring verbal/analytic abilities.

Shade (1982), Cohen (1969), and Hilliard (1976) present evidence suggesting that African American learners have a cognitive style emphasizing field-sensitive abilities as well as a preference for person-oriented classroom activities: cooperative learning and activities that focus on people and what they do rather than on things or objects.

Some researchers (Knight & Kagan, 1977; Ramirez & Castaneda, 1974) conclude that Mexican Americans are more field-sensitive as a group than Anglo-Americans. They explain the superior relative performance of this group on measures of field-sensitivity by pointing out that their child-rearing practices stress strong family ties and a respect and obedience to elders—experiences that may lead to a more field-sensitive cognitive style.

Summary and Conclusions

We have presented the evidence that minority groups differ from Anglo-Americans in certain aspects of learning and cognitive style. Some educators and psychologists suggest that these differences are a significant factor in the failure of minority groups to achieve their potential (Tharp, 1989). These educators and psychologists believe that many American classrooms use teaching styles that are incompatible with the more field-sensitive, person-oriented, cooperative learning preference of the majority of Native Americans, Hispanic Americans, or African Americans.

Is there sufficient justification to advocate field-sensitive teaching styles in classrooms with significant numbers of minority learners? Should teachers make greater use of instructional practices that emphasize cooperative learning, action-oriented activities, and visual/holistic learning when they teach significant numbers of African, Hispanic, or Native American learners? Before embracing culturally responsive teaching, consider the following cautions.

Beware of Perpetuating Stereotypes. Grant cautions that cultural information such as that described here may be used to "perpetuate ideas from the cultural deficit hypothesis and encourage teachers to believe that these students have deficits and negative differences and, therefore, are not as capable of learning as white students" (1991, p. 245). Others (Weisner, Gallimore, & Jordan, 1988) claim that cultural explanations of differential achievements of minority groups often result in global and stereotypical descriptions of how minority cultures behave that go beyond available evidence. Kendall (1983) argues that it is one thing to be aware of the potential effect of culture-specific learning and cognitive styles on classroom achievement, but another to expect a child of a particular group to behave and learn in a particular way.

Focus on Within-Group Differences. Almost all studies of the learning style preferences and cognitive styles of different minority groups have shown that differences within the cultural groups studied were as great as those between cultural groups (Cushner et al., 1992; Henderson, 1980; Tharp, 1989). In other words, Native Americans, Hispanic Americans, African Americans, and Anglo-Americans vary considerably on tests of field-dependence and field-independence. Some Anglo-Americans are field-dependent in their patterns of scores and some Native Americans are similarly field-independent. On average, the groups may differ. But around these averages are ranges of considerable magnitude. Thus, using a field-dependent teaching style—even in a monocultural classroom—may fail to match the preferred learning and cognitive styles of at least some learners.

Focus on "Expert Practice." Some educators, such as Englemann (1982) and Lindsley (1992a), argue that before assuming that differences in achievement result from characteristics within the learner (for example, learning and cognitive styles), the teacher should rule out factors external to the learner, such as ineffective teaching practices. Also, minority learners, like all other learners, require high-quality instruction. All learners should be given equal resources; motivation; high expectations; and expert instruction before their teachers embrace techniques specifically adapted to minorities. Although there is some evidence that African American and Native American children improve in reading and math with culturally responsive teaching techniques (Franklin, 1992; Tharp, 1989), studies fail to indicate that expert instruction using traditional instructional methods could not have achieved the same or similar results.

Culturally Responsive Teaching

If the research supporting the practice of **culturally responsive teaching** has yet to provide explicit prescriptions for teaching culturally different learners, what does it tell us about better understanding students in multicultural classrooms? For the answer to

Culturally responsive teaching. Instructional methods designed to be compatible with the learning and cognitive styles of a particular ethnic or cultural group.

this question, let's examine the research of Professor Deborah Dillon of Purdue University. We will integrate what she has learned with a perspective on multicultural schooling that places subject matter at the center of what teachers need to know about teaching culturally diverse learners.

Professor Dillon spent a year observing one teacher, Mr. Appleby, teach a class of low-track African American learners in a high school serving primarily children of low socioeconomic status (Dillon, 1989). She wanted to determine what makes a teacher of culturally different learners effective. Let's listen to what Mr. Appleby says in one of the interviews:

> Kids need to know where you are and how you stand on things and you have to be predictable and dependable. . . . I'm not as strict with them (students), you know . . . I let them run their mouths more; I challenge them more, maybe I talk to them more, ask them for feedback, get personal and use nicknames. . . . I let them work together more than most of their other teachers would do, I imagine. A lot of their teachers would look at this as cheating . . . I pretty much give them responsibility for their own behavior . . . with some of these kids they're not going to remember who wrote "The Pearl" or "Of Mice and Men"—but . . . they got involved in a book, and they got involved in something—they used their imagination—they had a good experience . . . they opened up and shared some of their thoughts and feelings . . . we can create an atmosphere in the classroom where kids can feel free to express themselves. (Dillon, 1989, p. 244)

Dillon concluded that Appleby's effectiveness as a classroom teacher was based on his ability to assume the role of "translator and intercultural broker" between the middle-class culture of the school and the lower-class African American culture of his students. As a cultural broker and translator, Appleby was thoroughly knowledgeable about the backgrounds of his learners, and as a result he was able to bridge the differences between school and community/home cultures.

With this cultural knowledge, Appleby created a classroom with three significant attributes:

Some teachers are successful with minority group learners because they act as cultural brokers, helping their students adapt to the classroom and vice versa.

- He created a social organization where teacher and learners knew one another, trusted one another, and felt free to express their opinions and feelings. In other words, Appleby created a climate characterized by the type of cohesiveness discussed in Chapter 8.

- He taught lessons that were built around the prior knowledge and experiences of his learners. His knowledge of his learners' backgrounds allowed him to represent the subject matter in ways that encouraged his students to link it with what they already knew and felt.

- He used instructional methods that allowed learners to actively participate in lessons and to use the language and social interaction patterns with which both he and his learners were familiar.

Here is how Appleby's students describe this style of teaching:

I act differently in his class—I guess because of the type of teacher he is. He cuts up and stuff . . . he is hisself—he acts natural—not tryin' to be what somebody wants him to be . . . he makes sure that nobody makes fun of anybody if they mess up when they read out loud. (Melinda, in Dillon, 1989, p. 241)

Appleby's fun, he helps you when you feel bad, he'll talk to you. Appleby's got his own style, he makes his own self . . . he's not a brag . . . Appleby always has this funny grin. Everybody call him Magnum—like Tom Selleck—he don't know that yet . . . he's funny, he tells jokes, laughs with the class. He makes me want to work, he makes me want to give and do something . . . he show me that I can do it. (LaVonne, in Dillon, 1989, p. 242)

Dillon concludes that in order to teach successfully in multicultural classrooms, teachers need to know more about the values, socialization practices, interests, and concerns of their learners than about presumed learning style preferences and cognitive styles and the dos and don'ts of teaching learners with these traits. Rather, Dillon believes that the cultural knowledge that teachers like Appleby have about their learners allows them to represent subject matter content in ways that are meaningful to them, to develop lessons that gain their active participation, and to create social organizations in the classroom within which learners feel free to be themselves.

Culture and Teaching:
What Teachers Need to Know and Understand

Dillon's in-depth study suggests that, in order to be successful, teachers of culturally different learners must understand the importance of three relationships: (1) learner-subject matter relationships, (2) teacher-subject matter relationships, and (3) teacher-learner relationships (McDiarmid, 1991). Successful teachers of culturally different learners must understand all three relationships, including how these relationships have been formed and how they can be improved.

In Figure 15.3, we conceptualize the teaching act as a triadic relationship between teacher, learner, and subject matter (McDiarmid, 1991). What distinguishes the teacher-learner relationship from other adult-child relationships is that in the former case both parties have a mutual involvement in and concern for subject matter.

McDiarmid asserts that successful teachers of culturally different learners should recognize that their primary obligation is to teach their subject matter. However, teachers must also recognize that their way of thinking and portraying the knowledge they

> **What is "culturally responsive teaching" and how is it achieved?**

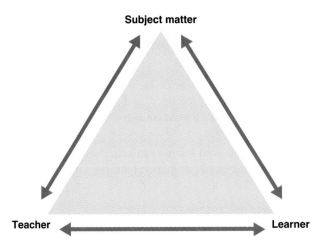

Figure 15.3
Triadic relationship among teacher, learner, and subject matter.

teach may not match the way their learners think about it (teacher-subject matter relationship); that their learners have prior knowledge, attitudes, and experiences with the subject matter that may facilitate or frustrate learning (learner-subject matter relationship); and finally, that teacher-student (as well as student-student) relationships, as expressed in the social organization of the classroom, can facilitate or frustrate subject matter learning.

McDiarmid suggests that successful teachers like Mr. Appleby must be knowledgeable about the cultures from which their learners come, sensitive to the differences between the school culture and that of the community, and appreciative of the importance of good teacher-student and student-student relationships. In addition to these characteristics, they must also have a thorough understanding of the subjects they teach in order to make them meaningful to diverse learners. Cultural knowledge alone will not make one an effective teacher of content. Likewise, subject matter expertise, in and of itself, will not make a teacher effective if he or she does not understand the importance of how learners relate to the subject and to all classroom participants. In other words, knowledge of subject matter, of learners, and of the relationships between the two are essential for teaching in multicultural classrooms. The accompanying box, *Integrating Cultural Knowledge with Subject Matter Expertise*, presents some important guidelines for forging these relationships.

Gender Differences and Schooling

So far we have discussed cultural diversity and how it is experienced in schools. Gender differences are yet another aspect of learner diversity that concerns educators. In this section we will discuss what teachers need to know about gender differences and gender-fair teaching. But, before doing so, consider two factors that limit our understanding of the gender differences in schools.

● Much of what we know about how girls and boys learn and about sex roles at home and in school comes from research on middle-class Anglo children (Cushner et al., 1992). We know relatively little about how children of other cultures are affected by the sex-role socialization practices at home and at school.

● Most research has focused on the effects of sex-role stereotypes on girls rather than on boys. For example, there is much discussion in both the popular media and

Integrating Cultural Knowledge with Subject Matter Expertise

Guidelines for Learner-Subject Matter Relationships

1. Know how your learners perceive the knowledge you teach. Their friends, family, and community have influenced these perceptions. For example, among poor, working-class, and minority students, the exclusive use of formal texts and a competitive classroom environment may be looked on with some degree of skepticism.
2. Know what kinds of knowledge, skills, attitudes, and values are respected in your students' cultures. This knowledge will allow you to present subject matter in ways that bridge the cultural gap between school and community.
3. Be aware of your learners' prior knowledge and experience with the subject matter of your lessons. Their misconceptions and the degree to which you anticipate them will have a lot to do with how well your students learn.
4. Learn what your students think, understand, and value about the subject matter. This will help you create a positive classroom climate and establish a context for learning in which learners feel free to talk about themselves and how they feel about school and school subjects.

Guidelines for Teacher-Subject Matter Relationships

1. Your knowledge and understanding of your subject will affect the activities you use, the type of practice you provide, and the sense modalities you use to represent your subject.
2. Represent ideas, concepts, and procedures in a variety of ways in order to adapt to the experiences and understandings of culturally different learners. Given knowledge of your learners' cultures, you should be able to judge the appropri-

ateness of the examples you use to teach concepts, the language you use to describe these concepts, and the media selected to express them.

3. Be aware of how your subject matter relates to the world around your learners and how to help your learners understand these connections. All learners, and in particular culturally diverse ones, should be taught the connection between what they learn in school and what they experience outside it.

Guidelines for Teacher-Learner Relationships

1. You are a role model for your learners. How you think about a subject will affect your learners' attitudes toward it. If you represent science as difficult, mathematics as boring, or history as a collection of facts, that is how your learners will view them.
2. You can limit your learners' access to important subject matter by the social organization you create in the classroom. Ability grouping, tracking, and competitive learning arrangements can limit learners' access to important knowledge and generalizations.
3. The style of leadership you assume in the classroom (authoritarian, laissez-faire, democratic) or the type of power you exercise (expert, referent, legitimate, coercive, reward) can affect the willingness of culturally different learners to engage in subject matter learning tasks. If you want your learners to explore problems and ideas with others, consider how your own behavior and the relationships you establish with learners inhibit or promote such cooperation.

scholarly journals of how socialization practices limit the social, educational, and occupational choices of girls. Very little is known or has been studied about how such practices inhibit the choices made by boys (Cushner et al., 1992).

Despite these limitations, research on the different ways boys and girls experience gender at home and in school has sensitized educators and psychologists to some inequities. We will address these inequities in this section. First, let's explore some sex-role stereotypes and the ways in which schools may unintentionally perpetuate them. We will then return to McDiarmid's triadic perspective on cultural diversity to illustrate how it applies to helping teachers deal with issues of gender.

What prevalent sex-role stereotypes pertaining to curriculum, grouping, and classroom management should I avoid?

Think back to some of your experiences as a student or reflect on a classroom with which you are familiar as a visitor or observer. Which of the following practices did you observe?

- Textbooks (or other curriculum materials) that portray females as housewives and males as outside-the-home wage earners.
- Teachers who use the female gender with the roles of teacher, nurse, or social worker but the male gender when referring to engineers, doctors, and lawyers.
- Girls and boys grouped for certain types of activities during recess that reflect sex-role biases.
- Teachers calling on boys more for answers during math or science but girls more during language arts.
- Different career advice given to girls and boys.
- Teachers who address boys from across the classroom but girls from an arm's length distance or less.
- Teachers who reprimand boys more sharply and in front of students more often than girls for the same behavior.
- Teachers who praise girls when they choose activities associated with traditional gender roles.
- Female teachers who express misgivings about math more often than do male teachers.
- Boys are more often corrected for academic mistakes and more often told to get it right than girls who make similar mistakes.
- Teachers who call on boys more often than on girls.

Sex-role stereotypes. The overextension of sex roles as well as the rigid application of sex roles to individuals without taking personal qualities into account.

This list describes some of the ways schools can perpetuate **sex-role stereotypes.** We use sex-role stereotypes when we overextend sex roles or apply them too rigidly to people without taking their individual qualities into account. When we say that men are unemotional or can't nurture children as well as women, we are applying a stereotype. If we say that women are intuitive and less analytic than men, we are applying another stereotype. Boys are often described (and expected to be) more aggressive, dominant, competitive, and risk-taking, while girls are cast as dependent, nurturing, helping, generous, sociable, compliant, and emotional.

In addition to these personality stereotypes about males and females, there are occupational stereotypes. Girls are expected to be housewives, nurses, social workers, elementary school teachers, law paraprofessionals, dental assistants, secretaries, clerks, and bank tellers, while boys are expected to be auto mechanics, electricians, construction workers, high school math teachers, lawyers, doctors, or executives.

Boys and girls are also stereotyped according to mental abilities, creating intellectual stereotypes. For most of the twentieth century girls were assumed to be born with less mathematical ability than boys. Thanks to the work of Eccles and her colleagues (Eccles, Adler, & Kaczala, 1982; Eccles et al., 1983; Eccles & Jacobs, 1986), we know that the parents' stereotypes about female math ability, the mothers' beliefs about the difficulty of math, and the perceived value of math to the student—not inherited abilities—account for much of the difference in male-female scores on math ability tests. Girls also are mistakenly believed to have less spatial ability than boys. However, re-

Research shows that boys receive more attention from teachers than do girls. Teachers tend to correct the misbehavior of boys in ways that give them a more prominent role in the classroom.

search has shown that science, spatial, mathematical, and even verbal abilities have very little to do with gender (Jacklin, 1989).

How Schools Perpetuate Sex-Role Stereotypes

Despite our awareness of such stereotypes, they continue to persist, because of both the power of norms and social sanctions or punishments. Norms, as we learned in Chapter 8, are expectations shared by members of a group regarding how they should think, feel, and behave. We learned that norms are powerful regulators of group behavior. Sex-role stereotypes—attitudes, beliefs, values, and behavior associated with gender—are coded by one's social group into norms. Because these norms are part of our everyday thinking, we view them as natural, normal, and appropriate. In other words, we take them for granted and rarely challenge their validity.

We also learned from Chapter 8 that when group norms are present, so too are group sanctions against violating those norms. Thus, both males and females are reluctant to challenge and deviate from their respective group norms because of the punishments (both real and imagined) that can occur when one behaves in an "unmanly" or "unwomanly" manner.

But adherence to male or female group norms or stereotypes may incur costs. Stereotypes have significantly constrained women's occupational, educational, and social opportunities. Expectations for how women should look have led females to be more at risk for developing serious eating disorders such as bulimia or anorexia (Attie, Brooks-Gunn, & Petersen, 1990). For boys, different expectations for behavior, and different reactions by adults to inappropriate behavior, have been considered factors in their being at higher risk than girls for developing conduct disorders, elimination disorders such as night-time bed wetting (enuresis), and ADHD (Barkley, 1990; Liebert & Fischel, 1990; Martin & Hoffman, 1990).

Despite the fact that stereotypes and their harmful effects are recognized and appreciated by educators and psychologists, schools may persist in a number of practices that perpetuate them. In the following sections, we consider curriculum bias, academic differentiation, classroom management practices, and school staffing patterns (Sadker & Sadker, 1988; Sadker, Sadker, & Steindam, 1989).

Curriculum Bias. Just as curriculum bias historically has affected the achievement of certain minority groups, it also has contributed to the stereotyping of females. Although progress has been made in recent years in eliminating sex-role stereotyping from textbooks and other educational materials and in exposing learners to examples of boys and girls who engage in a wider variety of activities (girls playing marbles, boys babysitting), some stereotypes still prevail (Cushner et al., 1992). Sadker and Sadker (1990) have identified six types of curriculum bias that can be used as a guide for judging the presence of sex-role stereotypes in teaching materials. Some examples of these six types of bias appear in the accompanying box, *Detecting Gender-Specific Curriculum Bias.*

Academic Differentiation. Despite the fact that boys and girls are born with similar spatial, mathematical, and verbal abilities, and despite the fact that girls typically earn better grades than boys, boys are awarded 64 percent of all National Merit Scholarships and outperform girls on all sections of the American College Testing Program Examination (ACT), the Scholastic Aptitude Test (SAT), the Graduate Record Exams (GRE), the Medical College Admission Test (MCAT), and the Graduate Management Admissions Test (GMAT) (Cushner et al., 1992). While parental attitudes and peer group norms play a certain role, we also know that teachers inadvertently contribute to the differential treatment of male and female learners.

For example, Sadker and Sadker report that

> . . . girls are more likely to be invisible members of classrooms. They receive fewer contacts, less praise, fewer complex and abstract questions, and less instruction on how to do things for themselves. (1990, p. 115)

Boys are also more likely to be corrected for academic mistakes and urged to practice skills until they achieve mastery. Girls, on the other hand, particularly high-achieving girls, are ignored persons in the classroom. They are asked fewer questions and receive

Schools can make significant contributions in breaking down the sex-role stereotypes that sometimes appear in textbooks. Teachers must be prepared to present their subject matter in ways that confront the stereotypic perceptions of their learners.

Detecting Gender-Specific Curriculum Bias

Linguistic Bias. Examples of linguistic bias are history texts that use masculine terms such as "cavemen," "forefathers," "mankind," or "servicemen" to refer to groups composed of both men and women. Likewise, occupational titles like fireman, policeman, mailman, businessman, or deliveryman ignore the fact that women also assume these roles. Similarly, be careful about associating human service professions (teacher, social worker, nurse) with the female pronoun and business or science professions with the masculine.

Referring to boats, countries, or hurricanes as "she" is another form of linguistic bias. Also, watch out for expressions like "John Williams and his wife," which imply that the wife is John's possession. "John Williams and Susan Williams" is a more appropriate expression.

Stereotyping. Stereotyping occurs when textbooks or other curriculum materials identify males or females with particular personality traits or particular occupational roles. Thus, females are typically depicted as nurses, housewives, and teachers, while males are doctors, soldiers, and farmers. Girls are depicted in situations where they are dependent, passive, cooperative, docile, or fearful, while boys are brave, active, courageous, risk-taking, and adventuresome.

Invisibility. Invisibility occurs when history books ignore the important roles women have played throughout world history. It is also evident when the achievements of women in the arts, sciences, and mathematics are omitted from textbooks.

Imbalance. Women played a prominent role in the suffrage movement in America in the 1920s. Yet, in the past, history books devoted more space to discussing their style of dress during that period than to their political movement. An imbalance results when the role women played in the history of a country, the development of a particular scientific process, or the creation of an important invention is given less importance than that of men.

Unreality. Unreality refers to portraits of historical periods of contemporary life or culture that gloss over controversial topics or issues like prejudice, discrimination, divorce, or alternative family living arrangements. Books that ignore the fact that more than one-third of American children live in single-parent, female-headed households present an unrealistic picture of the American family to school learners.

Fragmentation. Textbooks in history or science often feature boxes with the particular achievements of a woman but do not integrate this material into the text. The impression left with the reader is that the accomplishment is out of the ordinary and that women haven't made contributions to the mainstream of development of the country or a scientific discipline.

less feedback than boys (Sadker & Sadker, 1985, 1986). Sadker, Sadker, and Klein (1991) estimate that from preschool through college graduation, girls receive nearly 1800 fewer hours of instruction and attention than boys.

The result of this differential is that by the time they graduate from high school, some girls show declines in career commitment (Eccles, 1986). This decline has been attributed to feelings of social helplessness and a notion that boys don't want to associate with "smart" girls (Cushner et al., 1992). Moreover, Farmer and Sidney (1985) report that guidance counselors and classroom teachers tend to give more praise and encouragement to girls when they choose careers more in line with traditional sex-role stereotypes than when they choose nontraditional ones such as engineering.

Classroom Management Practices. In both elementary and secondary school classrooms, teachers manage boys and girls differently (Grossman, 1990). Boys receive more criticism than girls (Dunkin & Biddle, 1974). Teachers react more to the misbehavior of boys than to that of girls (Serbin, O'Leary, Kent, & Tonick, 1973). When teachers correct learners for misbehaving, they typically talk to girls in private but call out to boys from across the room and in a harsher fashion (Katz, 1986; Meyer & Thompson, 1956; Serbin et al., 1973). The effect of these practices is to give boys a more prominent role in the classroom and to reinforce the notion that boys and girls are different.

School Staffing Patterns. There are two principal concerns regarding how schools are staffed. The first has to do with the so-called feminization of schooling. As we have mentioned, the overwhelming majority of teachers are Anglo females. The percentage of female teachers is greatest at the elementary school level. Some educators and psychologists attribute the fact that boys experience more disciplinary and conduct problems in schools than girls to the predominance of women teachers (Cushner et al., 1992).

Holt (1992) believes that African American males, in particular, are put at a disadvantage by being taught by female teachers. He advocates the establishment of African American immersion schools in which African American males will be taught a multicultural curriculum exclusively by African American male teachers. Although these ideas are controversial (Ravitch, 1992), there is some acceptance for this point of view.

A second feature of school staffing patterns is the predominance of men as leaders, supervisors, and bosses but of women as workers (i.e., teachers, secretaries, paraprofessionals). Many educators believe that the underrepresentation of women as administrators (although this is rapidly changing) reinforces sex-role stereotypes that relegate women to lesser roles not only in schools but in the larger society as well (Cushner et al., 1992).

Promoting Gender-Fair Schooling

We conclude this section by revisiting McDiarmid's triadic perspective on cultural diversity to see how it applies to gender diversity. Just as the academic achievement of minority learners should be the overriding goal of teachers who teach in multicultural settings, likewise it should be the primary goal of **gender-fair instruction.** Just as the successful teaching of culturally different learners demands teachers' expert knowledge of subject matter, of learners, and of the relationships between these two factors, so also is this true of gender-fair schooling.

The accompanying box, *Promoting Gender-Fair Instruction,* lists some guidelines based on the triad shown in Figure 15.3.

Gender-fair instruction. The use of educational strategies, curriculum materials, and instructor-learner interactions that counteract sex-role stereotypes.

How can I teach my class in ways that are free of gender bias?

Summing Up

This chapter introduced you to what teachers need to know about culture and gender diversity. Its main points were these:

- A minority group is a social group that tends to occupy a subordinate position in our society and whose members share a sense of collective identity and a common perception of the world around them.
- Cultural compatibility refers to the belief that minority learners have ways of learning and thinking and needs for motivational, instructional, and classroom management strategies that differ from those of majority learners.
- The results of tests of scholastic achievement indicate that Native Americans, Hispanic Americans, and African Americans consistently perform below Anglo-Americans, and frequently have higher dropout rates, indicating that many minority learners may not be achieving their potential.

Promoting Gender-Fair Instruction

Guidelines for Learner-Subject Matter Relationships

- Recognize that some females have certain attitudes, beliefs, and values about school subjects such as math and science that have been acquired from their parents, peer group, and society at large. Many parents have gender-stereotyped beliefs about some subjects, like math, that are acquired by their daughters.
- Be aware of these beliefs and be prepared to represent subjects such as math and science in ways that bridge or confront the perceptions of your learners.
- Remember that learners' prior experiences with math or science may have convinced them that they lack an ability in these subjects. Teach the subjects in ways that overcome these attributions.

Guidelines for Teacher-Subject Matter Relationships

- Recognize your own gender-stereotyped beliefs about certain subjects—whether math, science, or home economics.

- Teach your subject in ways that overcome the negative attributions regarding ability that female learners often make when the subject is math or science.
- Use various examples and ways of representing your subject that do not reinforce gender stereotypes. For example, curriculum materials and teaching activities in math and science should depict competent female models.

Guidelines for Teacher-Learner Relationships

- Remember that you are a role model for your learners. Do not communicate gender stereotypes about occupations and subjects during informal conversations with learners.
- Group learners in ways that promote gender-free attitudes and beliefs about subject matter, occupations, and recreational activities.

- Psychocultural variables, which potentially cause frustration and lack of achievement for minority learners, include the social organization of the classroom, sociolinguistics, learning style, and cognitive style.
- Sociolinguists point out that children are more comfortable in classrooms where sociolinguistic patterns (for example, wait-times, rhythms, and participation structures) are compatible with those of their home and community.
- Learning style refers to the physical, social, emotional, instructional, and managerial environment in which an individual prefers to learn. Different cultures are purported to have different learning styles, although little research evidence is available.
- Cognitive style refers to individual preferences for assimilating, accommodating, and using learning strategies to acquire knowledge. The cognitive style of field-dependence refers to "holistic/visual," or "global" learners who tend to see the world in terms of large, connected patterns. The cognitive style of field-independence refers to "verbal/analytic" learners who tend to see the world in terms of discrete parts.
- There is some evidence that minority learners are more holistic/global/visual or field-dependent than verbal/analytic or field-independent.
- In order to teach in multicultural classrooms, teachers need to know more about the values, socialization practices, interests, and concerns of their learners.

Specifically, they need to be knowledgeable about learner-subject matter, teacher-subject matter, and teacher-learner relationships.

- Sex-role stereotyping occurs when we overextend sex roles or apply them too rigidly to people without taking into account individual qualities. At least three male-female stereotypes persist: personality stereotypes, occupational stereotypes, and intellectual stereotypes.

- Six types of curriculum bias that can foster sex-role stereotypes are linguistic bias (for example, use of masculine terms) stereotyping (limiting male/female occupations), invisibility (ignoring female/male roles or influences), imbalance (not giving the proper weight to women's/men's contributions), unreality (ignoring or glossing over some facts), and fragmentation (omitting or poorly integrating some accomplishments of one gender).

For Discussion and Practice

°1. What individual characteristics come to mind when you hear the phrase "minority group member"? What three characteristics do sociologists agree minority groups tend to possess?

°2. In your own words, explain the cultural compatibility hypothesis.

°3. Provide some indications that schools may have undervalued minority culture and may not have taught minority learners as well as Anglo-American learners. Which of these do you believe has been most detrimental to the performance of minority learners?

°4. How do Native Americans, Hispanic Americans, and African Americans fare with respect to school achievement in comparison to Anglo-American learners? What is the approximate dropout rate for each group, respectively, compared with Anglo-American learners?

°5. What is the difference between education and schooling? Why is this difference important to the understanding of minority learners?

°6. Identify and give an example of each of the psychocultural variables relevant to educating the minority learner.

°7. How would you explain the difference between a field-dependent and a field-independent learner? Identify which you believe you are closest to, and give an example of how your preferred cognitive style came to your attention.

°8. What cognitive style does research suggest some minority groups tend to have? What are some cautions in implementing these findings in the classroom?

°9. What three types of relationships are important for successfully teaching culturally different learners? From your own experience, give an example of the importance of each.

°10. What two factors limit our understanding of gender differences in schools? How would either or both of these factors affect your thinking about male-female stereotypes?

Questions marked with an asterisk are answered in the appendix.

11. From your own experience, provide an example of a personality sex-role stereotype, an occupational sex-role stereotype, and an intellectual sex-role stereotype. Which is likely to be found with the school-age learner you are most likely to teach?

°12. What are some examples of linguistic sex-role stereotypes? What are some of the steps you would take to avoid this type of bias in your classroom?

°13. In your own words, describe the research you would cite in convincing a colleague that boys aren't born smarter than girls in mathematical and spatial ability. What are some of the reasons this stereotype has prevailed?

°14. In your subject matter and grade level, what are some examples of classroom practices that might treat boys and girls differently?

15. Using McDiarmid's triadic perspective on cultural diversity, suggest one thing you might do in your classroom to promote each of his three types of relationships.

Suggested Readings

Bennett, C. I. *Comprehensive multicultural education: Theory and practice.* (1990). Needham, MA: Allyn & Bacon. Presents numerous real-world vignettes designed to pique the reader's interest in the topic of how best to teach learners of different cultures. Integrates knowledge from the social sciences, the humanities, and instructional theory.

Cushner, K., McClelland, A., & Safford, P. (1992). *Human diversity in education: An integrative approach.* New York: McGraw-Hill. A comprehensive treatment of the various forms of human diversity found in schools: cultural, gender, class, language, and handicapping conditions.

Kennedy, M. M. (Ed.). (1991). *Teaching academic subjects to diverse learners.* New York: Teachers College Press. Presents the view that expert teaching is the antidote to the problems of minority group underachievement. This book has two chapters on the issue of what teachers should know about teaching culturally different learners.

Family Systems and Home-School Partnerships

This chapter will help you answer the following questions about your learners:

- What are some ways to bring the parents of my learners closer to my school and classroom?

- What are some of the reasons parents of my learners might not be involved in school as much as I would like?

- How can I help uninvolved parents become more interested and concerned?

- How can I plan, organize, and execute a parent conference that is cordial and upbeat?

- What are some ways I can let parents know more about my classroom and their child's progress?

- How can I help parents become more involved with their child's homework?

- What can I do to encourage greater involvement among parents who are linguistically and culturally different from the majority?

Tamara, a first-year teacher at Cedar Creek Elementary, and Christie, Tamara's mentor, are carpooling this week. Tamara looks forward to the drives to and from school as a time to share with Christie her thoughts, flashes of insight, and frustrations because they rarely have time to talk at school.

Tamara: I went to this great workshop last Saturday on teaching students how to write. They talked about how to get children to write poetry, short stories, fables, biographies, and all sorts of things from their personal experiences.

Christie: Teaching writing takes a lot of time when you consider all the editing and correcting you have to do. Giving students feedback on their writing and getting them to rewrite is the problem. Long delays in getting things back really slow things down.

Tamara: Having only about 10 students would be nice.

Christie: Dream on. But have you thought about getting some volunteers who can answer student questions and correct things like spelling and grammar?

Tamara: Sure, but from where?

Christie: Well, a few years ago when I got involved in the "Write to Read" program for my first-graders I had the same problem. Here was this company ready to donate some computers, software, workbooks, the whole nine yards. But I had 27 in my class, none of whom knew the first thing about keyboards and computers. So I put the word out in my class newsletter that I needed some parents every day from 9 to 10:30 to help with the program.

Tamara: What was the response?

Christie: I was amazed. From October through June I had one or two parents almost every day.

Tamara: How good were they?

Christie: Well, at first they were as unfamiliar with computers as the kids, so I held a Saturday workshop for all the volunteers. After that things went fine. I was surprised at how much writing got done and how fast the kids improved in punctuation, spelling, and grammar, as well as computer literacy. I couldn't have run the program without the help of those parents.

Tamara: Did the kids like having parents there?

Christie: More than that. They improved their classroom behavior because of it. Even more important, it gave parents a chance to meet each other and to learn what a teacher's life is like. I can't tell you how many parents commented on the respect they had for me after seeing what I do each day in my classroom.

Tamara: Was it just the parents of some of the kids who came?

Christie: No. And that's what was so great. It really helped bridge the different cultures I had to work with in that class.

Tamara: I never thought about involving parents; they never seemed to care—or maybe that was just my perception. In my university classes the only time we discussed parents was how to get them to help you make their kids behave and do their homework. It never occurred to me that they could be a part of my classroom.

Christie: That's the whole point. If the only time we involve parents is when there are problems, we're wasting a valuable resource.

Introduction

In 1990, the National Governors' Conference for educational reform set forth a formidable agenda for psychologists and educators. At this conference, the following goals were to be achieved by the first decade of the twenty-first century:

1. All children in America will start school ready to learn.

2. The high school graduation rate will increase to at least 90 percent.

3. American students will leave grades 4, 8, and 12 having demonstrated competency over challenging subject matter in the sciences and humanities.

4. American students will be the best in the world in mathematics and science achievement.

5. Every adult American will be literate and will possess the knowledge and skills to compete in a global economy and exercise the rights and responsibilities of citizenship.

6. Every school in America will be free of drugs and violence and will offer a disciplined environment conducive to learning.

A theme throughout the commentaries on the governors' agenda was the realization that schools will have to develop genuine partnerships with parents to achieve these goals. Only the active participation of parents, community groups, and educators in partnership with one another will bring about the desired objectives (Lambert, 1991).

In the dialogue above, Christie created such a partnership. Her partnership—or network of parents—not only improved learner behavior and achievement but also helped bridge the different cultures with which she had to communicate in her classroom. In addition, it gave Christie a nearly inexhaustible supply of motivated adults to help in the daily work of teaching a culturally diverse classroom of learners.

When parents and teachers become partners, student achievement can increase and parents can learn about you and your school. Research studies confirm that coordination and collaboration between home and school improve learner achievement, attitude toward school, classroom conduct, and parent and teacher morale (Christenson, Rounds, & Franklin, 1992; Cochran & Dean, 1991). Establishing genuine partnerships with the parents and guardians of your learners is as essential to expert teacher practice as building a cohesive classroom climate, establishing a well-managed work environment, developing goals and objectives, conducting effective instruction, and using authentic assessments of student performance.

The expert practice of parent involvement requires that you develop and strengthen, throughout the school year, linking mechanisms for parent participation and collaboration. **Linking mechanisms** are opportunities for school and family involvement that may involve parent-teacher conferences, home visits, participation of teachers in community events, newsletters, phone calls, personal notes, volunteering as classroom aides, and the use of home-based curriculum materials. These efforts require more than just a handout sent home to parents at the beginning of the school year, an obligatory presentation during back-to-school night, or an occasional note home. In this chapter we will examine how you can establish more enduring linking mechanisms in your classroom.

> **Linking mechanisms.** Opportunities for interaction between the various systems and subsystems within the family-school environment.

The opportunities to develop and nurture linking mechanisms will be the culmination of your efforts to build a successful classroom workplace. The challenge of the twenty-first century will be to establish such linking mechanisms in your classroom as a routine pattern of effective teaching practice. The goal of this chapter is to prepare you to meet this challenge by:

- presenting a practical rationale for the use of linking mechanisms
- reviewing research on the effects of such mechanisms on learner achievement, attitudes, and classroom behavior
- describing attitudes, beliefs, and skills essential for building and nurturing teacher-parent partnerships
- providing examples of linking mechanisms that successful schools and teachers have developed.

As the cartoon in Figure 16.1 illustrates, tension, fear, indifference, hostility, and even condescension and disrespect can sometimes characterize the relationships between teachers and parents. These frustrations can occur for beginning as well as experienced teachers in both multicultural and culturally homogeneous classrooms (Delgado-Gaitan, 1991).

Such conflict may be surprising. Teachers and parents share similar goals and expectations for learners. Both groups genuinely value the other and respect the roles each plays in the development of the child (Cochran & Dean, 1991). Teachers and parents also share the same responsibilities—the child is simultaneously a responsibility of both and a link between them. Why, then, do some teachers view parent-teacher involvement as a burden rather than an advantage, a duty instead of a choice? Why do some parents, as Delgado-Gaitan (1991) indicates, feel estranged and intimidated by the school and its staff? To help you better understand the roots of parent-teacher conflict and see more clearly how you can develop an effective family-school partnership, we will study the school, community, and classroom from a systems—or *ecological*—perspective.

A Systems-Ecological Perspective

You were probably first acquainted with a **systems-ecological perspective** when you were taught how plants and animal species depend on each other in natural environments. This perspective suggests that we view nature as an **ecosystem** made up of numerous systems and subsystems. These systems and subsystems coexist in dynamic,

> **Systems-ecological perspective.** A view of child development that considers the family, school, and peer group as a type of social ecosystem in which each part is dependent on and affected by the other parts.

> **Ecosystem.** Systems and subsystems coexisting in dynamic, mutually dependent relationships.

Figure 16.1
Family-School Conflict: The Frustrations of Parent Involvement. *Source: Austin-American Statesman,* May 5, 1992. DOONESBURY copyright © 1992 G. B. Trudeau. Reprinted with permission of UNIVERSAL PRESS SYNDICATE. All rights reserved.

mutually dependent relationships. Events affecting one subsystem (the extermination of a predator) affect other subsystems (an explosion in the population of the predator's prey), which in turn affect different systems and their subsystems (a decrease in certain types of vegetation, which affects the growth of other plant and animal species dependent on this vegetation).

Bronfenbrenner (1979, 1989) urges us to view child development from a systems-ecological perspective. Bronfenbrenner looks at the child's world as a naturalist looks at nature—as an ecosystem. Like ecosystems, children develop in the context of a process

The young child's ecosystem primarily consists of the home environment. There is much that parents can do at home to help children achieve success in school.

of mutual accommodation. In the child's ecosystem the major systems include the family, school, and peer group.

The child's ecosystem may be visualized as a series of layers or concentric circles, as shown in Figure 16.2. Each of these layers or circles and their connections has a special term. The most central layer is called the **microsystem.** It includes all those settings where the child lives or spends significant portions of his or her time: home, the school, classroom, day care setting, playground, even a job setting if the child is old enough. Bronfenbrenner refers to these settings as *subsystems.*

Each subsystem can be viewed within itself as a system. The school system is made up of subsystems that include teachers, administrators, support personnel, school board members, and learners. The family system includes a marital, parental, sibling, and often a grandparent subsystem. The peer system includes social friendships, academic friendships, and sports or hobby friendships.

The next layer of the system includes subsystems that the child does not directly experience but that affect the child because of the influence they exert on the microsystem. This layer is called the **exosystem.** It may include the parents' workplace, their friends, the PTA, the school board, and other groups.

Finally, both microsystems and exosystems exist in a larger setting, the macrosystem. By **macrosystem,** Bronfenbrenner refers to the larger culture or society in which the microsystem and exosystems function. Figure 16.3 shows some of the functional relationships between the three levels of systems.

Microsystem. The most central layer of a child's ecosystem, including all of the settings and subsystems where the child lives or spends significant amounts of time.

Exosystem. A subsystem beyond the immediate environment of the child that can indirectly influence the behavior of the child.

Macrosystem. The outermost layer of a child's ecosystem, consisting of the larger culture or society in which the exosystem and microsystem exist.

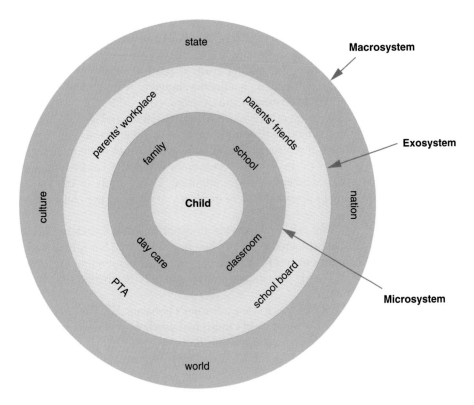

Figure 16.2
The child from a systems-ecological perspective.

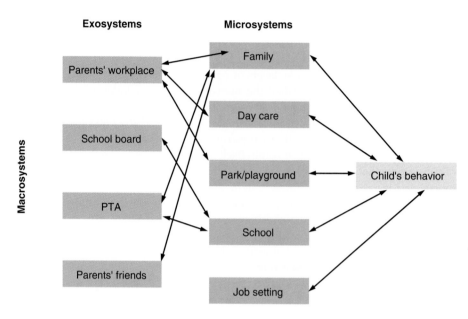

Figure 16.3

The child's ecosystem. Lines indicate linkages or mesosystems. *Source:* Adapted from *The Developing Child,* 6th ed. (p. 495), by H. Bee, 1992. New York: HarperCollins. Copyright © 1992 HarperCollins College Publishers. Reprinted by permission.

Bronfenbrenner urges us to look at child development in the context of the relationships between and among these systems. When the relationships or linkages between systems are characterized by mutual trust, a positive orientation, and goal consensus, as we discussed in Chapter 8, healthy development results. Conflict among these systems adversely affects child growth and development.

In this perspective, the actions of individual parents, teachers, and learners (i.e., the subsystems) are viewed as products of the interrelationships among them. For example, the parent who never signs and returns graded assignments may not be an uninterested and uninvolved parent, as might be assumed. Dynamics within the family system (for example, other siblings who demand extensive attention, loss of a job, or marital conflict) may explain the parent's apparent lack of involvement in his or her child's education.

Similarly, the teacher who refuses to provide an opportunity for a student who is at risk of dropping out to earn extra credit may not be uncaring. His or her refusal may be motivated by a recent memo to teachers from the principal (responding, in turn, to pressure from the school board) demanding that all students be treated equally and given the same opportunities.

Finally, Bronfenbrenner urges us to view a learner's behavior, whether in school or at home, as a product not only of that child's individual psychological development but also of the demands and forces operating within the systems of which the child is a member. Family experiences, and the culture of the family system, influence school behavior and performance, which in turn affect the family system. For example, school adjustment problems, which may be influenced by problems within the family, may in turn exacerbate conditions within the family system itself.

Thus, when you are trying to understand the behavior of parents, teachers, and learners, the systems-ecological perspective recommends that you first ask yourself, "What forces within the system (subsystem relationships) or outside the system (exosystems) impel the person to act this way?" When your goal is to promote the development of members of the ecosystem (for example, your learners), the systems-ecological perspective focuses concern on the relationships or linkages between the systems.

Bronfenbrenner refers to relationships between systems as **mesosystems** (represented by the arrows in Figure 16.3) and considers them to be as influential in the child's development as events occurring within the specific systems themselves. Thus for Bronfenbrenner the quality of the linkage between family and school is as significant for the healthy development of learners as the quality of instruction within the classroom or nurturing within the family.

Mesosystems. Relationships between systems or linking mechanisms in a child's ecosystem, which are often as important as the events that occur within systems.

Extent of Family-School Linkages

Although professional opinion over the past two decades supports Bronfenbrenner's views about the importance of effective family-school linkages (Fine & Carlson, 1992), parent involvement in American schools remains low (Christenson et al., 1992). Chaukin and Williams (1985) conducted a survey of over 3,000 parents in schools in the southern United States. They found that parents were interested in assuming a variety of roles, such as paid school staff member, school program supporter, decision maker, co-learner, or home tutor. Despite their professed interest, however, actual participation was minimal. For example, 75 percent of parents indicated an interest in decision making, but only 21 percent actually participated in such an activity. A similar discrepancy was evident between parents' interest in being an advocate (meeting with school officials to recommend changes in instructional and other educational practices) and their actual participation in this role.

Surveys indicate that teachers and administrators feel little interest in having parents assume the roles of decision makers and advocates (W. Snider, 1990). This is not the case, however, for the roles of home tutor and supporter of school programs. Teachers encourage these roles, and parents actually participate in them more than in roles involving in-school activities. In general, surveys indicate that only about 4 percent of parents are active at school—approximately one or two parents per classroom (Dauber & Epstein, 1989; Epstein, 1985, 1986). The parents who are involved at school tend to be parents of elementary school children. Their involvement, however, takes a dramatic decline once children enter the fourth grade. Not surprisingly, involvement by parents in school activities is lowest in secondary school.

Effects of Family-School Linkages

When answering the question "How effective is parent involvement in schools?" it is important to carefully define the types of involvement we mean and what types of effects we are looking for. "Family-school linkages" and "parent involvement" are terms that encompass a host of activities and roles on the part of parents. Table 16.1 displays these roles or linking mechanisms on a continuum extending from most passive to most active involvement. Research on the effects of parent involvement has examined primarily effects resulting from Roles II and III. There is relatively little research on the beneficial effects for learners of Roles I and IV.

The beneficial effects of parent involvement principally involve academic achievement. Relatively few studies have examined attitudes and behavior. Finally, some stud-

What are some ways to bring the parents of my learners closer to my school and classroom?

Table 16.1

Family-School Linking Mechanisms

I Parent as Information Receiver	II Parent as Learner	III Parent as Teacher	IV Parent as Decision Maker
More Passive ←			→ **More Active**
Parent-teacher conference	Parenting skills classes	Volunteers doing housekeeping clerical tasks	PTA
Group conference	Teaching skills classes	materials gathering and	School advisory council
Notes home	English-as-second	development	Parent advisory council
Newsletters	language classes	tutoring	Site-based management teams
Phone calls		evaluation activities	
Prerecorded messages			
Home visits by teacher			
Parent visits to class			

ies have looked at the beneficial effects of parent involvement on parents and teachers. Here are some of the findings of this research.

Academic Effects on Learners. Leler (1983) reviewed 18 studies designed to examine the effects of parenting skills classes and home tutoring programs on the academic achievement of learners. Thirteen of these programs showed positive gains in reading vocabulary and reading comprehension as a result of parents' establishing homework routines, reading to their children, reading in the presence of their children, asking questions about their children's work, and setting up a quiet place to study. Five programs showed no differences between experimental and control groups as a result of these activities.

Grave, Weinstein, and Walberg (1983) analyzed 29 experimental programs designed to improve the achievement of elementary school learners by making the home a more educationally stimulating environment. They concluded that home instruction programs have positive effects on children's academic learning.

Other Positive Effects. Epstein (1982) found that the fifth-grade classrooms of teachers who emphasized parent involvement (Types I, II, and III in Table 16.1) had learners with better attitudes toward school and homework including higher homework completion rates. S. L. Kagan (1984) reports improved attendance, a reduction in suspension rates, and improved attitudes toward homework on the part of learners whose parents involved themselves in activities of Types I, II, and III. Similar positive results arising out of parent involvement have been found for school attendance (Haynes, Comer, & Hamilton-Lee, 1989), student sense of well-being (Cochran, 1987), positive attitudes toward school and behavior (Becher, 1984; Henderson, 1989), student readiness to do homework (Rich, 1988), increased student time spent with parents (Rich, 1988), and higher educational aspirations among students and parents (McHill, Rigsby, & Meyers, 1969).

Effects on Parents and Teachers. Kagan and Schraft (1982) found that the more active a parent's role, the higher the parent's own personal aspirations and perceptions of power. This was true for low-income but not middle-income parents. Kagan (1984) and Becher (1984) report more favorable attitudes toward school as a result of parent involvement activities as well as a greater understanding and support for various school goals and activities.

The few studies that have examined the effect of parent involvement on teachers report that teachers who more frequently use activities such as those described in Table 16.1 allocate more time to instructional activities and to improving group cohesiveness and relationships than teachers who rarely use family-school linking mechanisms (Becher, 1983; Epstein, 1986).

Barriers to Family-School Linkages

When we first went into the New Haven schools we observed the difficult interactions between home and school. Parents had no faith in the school. They had this hope in September that the school would make a difference for their kids. But, by October, they knew that it wouldn't. All of the potential animosity between home and school came out as the kids didn't do well in school. Parents were angry that the school only wanted to see them when their kids were in trouble. Racial issues, class issues, low expectations—all became manifest in a variety of ways because of the disappointment that developed on the part of parents and staff.

Eventually, we viewed the problem this way: On the one side you have parents whose attitudes, values, and experiences are consistent with their social network. On the other, you have a school with expectations the kids can't necessarily meet, given their experiences. Now you get a clash as a result of that, a clash that staff is not prepared to deal with. (Comer, 1991, p. 3)

Educators and psychologists have little doubt about the beneficial effects of parent involvement for learners, parents, and teachers themselves. The question, then, is not whether family-school linking mechanisms help learners, but rather how to promote

Parental involvement in the school can lead to positive outcomes not only for students but also for their parents.

What are some of the reasons parents of my learners might not be involved in school as much as I would like?

them. But as we saw above, relatively few parents make use of these linkages. Before discussing how to actively encourage and develop family-school partnerships, let's look at some of the barriers that inhibit effective collaboration between these two components of the child's ecosystem. Four barriers to family-school partnerships have been identified: (1) different priorities, (2) a tradition of separation, (3) a tradition of blame, and (4) changing demographics.

Different Priorities. At first glance, one would expect that friendly partnerships between families and schools could be easily and naturally achieved. Both systems share overlapping goals: educating children and teaching them appropriate social behavior. Many teachers are themselves parents and can identify with the concerns of parents and the day-to-day frustrations and pressures that are played out within the family system. Likewise, parents experience the complexities of managing several children and can appreciate the enormous skill and energy a teacher requires to manage 25 to 35 children.

But clashes between families and schools almost inevitably arise. When you probe deeper into the structure of the systems themselves, you can readily discern the sources of these clashes. While the systems have overlapping goals—the socialization and education of children—the priority they assign to these goals is different. The family as a primary socialization group has the interests of the individual child at heart. Parents want the school to do what's best for their child. The school, however, has primary responsibility for groups of children. Sometimes it may not be possible to reconcile the needs of the school to provide group instruction with the demands of a family that something different be done for a particular child (Comer, 1988).

Lightfoot (1978) views family-school relations as inherently conflict-ridden because of the family system's paramount concern for the individual child and the school system's overall responsibility for large numbers of children. For example, from the family's perspective, the best thing for a child who has severe test anxiety during final exam week would be for tests to be given orally without time limits. The school, however, has developed certain rules and routines for giving final exams that it perceives to be in the best interests of all children. The school would find it impossible to accommodate the individual needs of each child for fair testing.

Another example would be parents' demands for more homework for their child. Some parents would like their children to have an hour or more of homework each school night. From the family's perspective, more homework may be just what a child needs to raise his level of achievement. But from the teacher's perspective (particularly for the junior or senior high teacher who may have as many as 150 papers to grade), extra homework may place impractical demands on his or her time.

A Tradition of Separation. Surveys of parent-school communication conducted over the past 20 years show a persistent finding that parents desire more communication with the school but in fact experience very little communication (Gallup, 1978; Gallup & Elam, 1988; Swap, 1987). In these surveys, parents frequently complain that teachers show poor attitudes in communicating with parents and report a sense of meaningless dialogue and covert ostracism when approaching their children's schools. When they do hear from teachers, parents charge that the content of the communcation is largely negative and centers on complaints about student achievement or behavior.

Williams and Stallworth (1984) report that teachers and school administrators historically have been more comfortable with passive than with active involvement roles

Many parents seek an active collaboration with their child's teacher. Parental involvement increases learner achievement and empowers parents.

for parents—although parents seek the latter type of involvement. Clark's research (1983) reveals that educators are most comfortable with parent involvement activities that focus on school-to-home transmission of information from professionals to parents rather than on approaches that involve genuine collaboration and partnerships.

A Tradition of Blame. Heath and McLaughlin (1987) assert that since the 1980s surveys of teachers' attitudes toward parents have indicated an increasing tendency to blame parents for the lack of achievement and the inappropriate behavior of their children. Research by Davies (1991) reports a similar orientation on the part of teachers. They tend to view the homes of low-achieving learners—particularly minority group learners—as deficient in values, stimulation, and socialization practices. Not surprisingly, many parents blame the school for the academic and behavior problems of their children. This readiness of teachers and parents to blame one another for the failures of learners is a significant barrier to the development of home-school linkages (Huang & Gibbs, 1992).

Changing Demographics. As we have emphasized throughout this book, American society is becoming increasingly diverse and is experiencing rapid social and economic change. Periodic economic, racial, and social crises produce many conflicting ideas about the role of the school. As a result, parents often place conflicting demands on the school, and the school has expectations for the family that it may not be able to meet. As more and more families have two working parents or are headed by a single working parent, the demands of the school for certain types of parental involvement may become increasingly unrealistic.

Delgado-Gaitan (1992) explains how poorly equipped and prepared some schools are for dealing with the family systems of culturally diverse learners. She reports that parents of ethnically and linguistically diverse learners fail to participate in school to the same extent as their Anglo counterparts, a finding shared by others (Clark, 1983; Comer, 1984). The reason for this lack of participation, according to Delgado-Gaitan, has less to do with lack of interest or skill on the part of the parents (which she refers

Concha Delgado-Gaitan, University of California-Davis

Compelled by academic theory and an ardent belief that literacy is a powerful tool for liberation, my research has focused on ethnographic studies in three California communities (Carpinteria, Redwood City, and West Sacramento) and Commerce City, Colorado. Carpinteria has been the community where I have conducted the major part of my work. There, as a researcher, I participated in the growth and development of Latino families, and they in turn have influenced my understanding of literacy, parent involvement, and cultural change and research in the Latino community, which I described in the *Harvard Educational Review* (December 1993).

My ethnographic inquiry into family-school relationships in Carpinteria, California, began in the homes of Latino children with the question "What literacy practices exist in the family?" I followed children from the classroom who were placed in different levels of reading ability. Teachers suspected that the children who were in more advanced reading groups in the classroom had parents who read to them, and those students who were in less advanced groups had parents who did not read to them or did not pay much attention to their academic work.

The essence of my research emphasizes the notion that educators must communicate effectively with parents and incorporate the culture of the home just as much as they should involve parents and teach them about their children's learning. My research has shown that Latino parents care a great deal about their children's education and that the more educators involve parents in the student's learning, the higher the academic results.

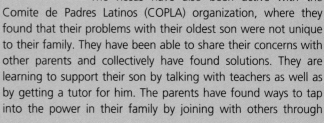

A classic example is the Rosa family. This family is representative of many families with whom I have worked who have found their strength with each other in a variety of ways. I got to know the Rosas extremely well over the years of observations while studying family-school communication and family literacy activities.

The Rosas live in a small apartment with their four children, an adult cousin with two children, and Mrs. Rosa's parents. Although work consumes the parents' full day when they are employed, it could be considered fortunate, since there have been times when those same endless hours were spent looking for a job when they have been unemployed. On certain weeknights, Mr. Rosa attends Alcoholics Anonymous (AA) meetings to deal with an ongoing challenge he has had. The family is quite proud of all of their children's achievement in school, even of their oldest son, who has continuously faced traumatic problems in learning. The Rosas talk with him and try to encourage him to stay in school and deal with the difficulties he has in several classes.

The Rosas have also been active with the Comite de Padres Latinos (COPLA) organization, where they found that their problems with their oldest son were not unique to their family. They have been able to share their concerns with other parents and collectively have found solutions. They are learning to support their son by talking with teachers as well as by getting a tutor for him. The parents have found ways to tap into the power in their family by joining with others through

to as a "deficit model" of parent participation) than with the barriers that inevitably arise between a school system founded on one culture and a family system from another.

Delgado-Gaitan explains that ethnically diverse families living in poor socioeconomic conditions often face sustained isolation from the school culture, not only as a result of language and value differences but also because they have not learned how the school system works. Some schools may unintentionally facilitate this exclusion by establishing activities that require knowledge and behaviors specific to the cultural major-groups like AA, which Mr. Rosa attends, and COPLA, in which both parents participate. There they find support, resources, and directions that strengthen their goals for education. They have also found their loving center through family stories about their experiences, which inspire their goals for success. Nurturing gestures like baking cookies for everyone when they need to talk about conflicts or difficult matters also show how the family has tapped into a ritual that enables them to create a safe environment to communicate. Whether it's baking cookies, telling stories, or other joint activities like listening, the bonding that occurs salutes their ability to transcend the strain of adversity and to focus on their power of human potential.

For many children in these families, their ability to learn comfortably in school is often impeded by emotional stress compounded by unresponsive schools until this cycle is interrupted. How can families like this one who face oppressive difficulties find their source of strength and power? I believe that all families, regardless of color, religion, socioeconomic standing, place of residence, ethnicity, or educational attainment, have strengths and power. How to access those strengths has been illustrated by the Rosa family in their ability to confront stressful situations related to their children's schooling. Their courage comes from their connectedness with others in a supportive situation that redirects their pain outward rather than inward.

Specifically, teachers can be advocates for families like the Rosas by recognizing that.

- When parents participate in children's schooling, academic performance increases.
- Parents have a great deal of knowledge to share about their children that can assist teachers in the classroom.

- Parents must be involved as an integral part of the curriculum.
- Frequent communication between teachers and parents must be established through written messages, personal meetings, or phone calls to share information that can enhance the students' learning opportunities.
- Teachers must also utilize the home culture as part of the classroom curriculum by making the students' language, culture, and history part of the daily program. Literacy activities (reading and writing) can reflect much of the children's native knowledge.
- Children are different (linguistically, culturally, socially, academically), and these differences do not make them deficient in comparison with others.
- In order to maximize the students' long-term opportunity for learning, the family must be involved every step of the way. Teachers must make parents co-teachers so that when the child goes home, parents stand a better chance of reinforcing what is learned at school. Learning is a collaborative effort between home, school, and community.

We can't always find power on our own when our lives feel out of control. But it is important to recognize that our experience of isolation is not unique, and that by sharing with others there is a potential for us to change our lives—be it in relation to the larger community or on a much closer level, our heart, which is the real source of our power. Social networks are opportunities for us to become connected with others around common issues and to learn that we are not alone in dealing with our problems—as overwhelming as they may seem. By joining families and teachers, schools can discover alternatives to the many issues involving them.

ity that are assumed but not made explicit. The absence of knowledge about how the school system works can limit participation in formal school activities, resulting in isolation for some parents, especially those who may not have been schooled in the United States and/or are limited in English proficiency.

Thus, the increasing numbers of culturally diverse family systems that schools must serve, together with the conflicting priorities of schools and families, as well as traditions of separation and blame, can limit the participation of parents in schools, and can eventually create frustration, apathy, and discord. According to Seligman and Darling (1989)

The American family is undergoing significant changes. For instance, more mothers are working than ever before, and schools should be responsive to this reality when planning parent involvement.

the factors contributing to the complexity of parent-teacher, or school-family, encounters are these:

- the varied social, economic, educational, ethnic, racial, and religious backgrounds of families and school personnel
- past experiences of parents in interacting with schools and professionals
- past experiences of school personnel in interacting with parents
- differences in the level of interpersonal communication skill possessed by parents and school personnel
- their respective beliefs about schooling and parenting
- their expectations and stereotypes
- their personal value systems.

These differences can be bridged, discord can be minimized, and proactive partnerships between families and schools can be developed by the establishment of mechanisms for family-school coordination and communication. We have referred to these mechanisms as *linking mechanisms,* or, as Bronfenbrenner calls them, mesosystems. Delgado-Gaitan refers to these linkages as *mechanisms for parent empowerment* (1990, 1991, 1992). In the remainder of this chapter, we offer specific suggestions you can use for maximizing them.

Building Home-School Linkages

Developing partnerships with the parents of your learners should be as much a focus of your planning for the new school year as your classroom rules, routines, instructional goals, and objectives. As educators like Delgado-Gaitan and Bronfenbrenner advocate, and as the research suggests, your learners' achievement of academic goals, their adherence to rules and routines, and their attitudes and expectations about school can be enhanced by having parents as partners. But working toward these common goals demands mutual effort and interpersonal and communication skills on your part.

Principles of Family-School Partnership

Following are principles for creating genuine family-school partnerships, based on the writings and research of Delgado-Gaitan, Bronfenbrenner, Comer, and other experts.

View the Family from a Systems-Ecological Perspective. As Bronfenbrenner suggests, avoid viewing the behavior of your learners or their parents as simply products of individual psychological forces. Instead, recognize that the family system is made up of several subsystems including the marital subsystem, the parental subsystem, the sibling subsystem, and extrafamily or exosystems such as grandparents and employers. Changes in one subsystem inevitably bring about changes in another.

Problems in school can affect a child's other systems. For example, phone calls to parents during working hours about their child's school behavior can result in an employer reprimanding the employee, an argument at home between husband and wife, punishment of the child, teasing by siblings, and concern and criticism by in-laws. Likewise, demands by school staff that parents make the child complete homework inevitably reverberate throughout the entire family system. These effects may be so great as to preclude any change in parental behavior.

Thus, when you ask a parent to take greater responsibility for getting her child to bed earlier at night, or to supervise her child's homework more closely, or to take away privileges for school misbehavior, these demands may affect more than that one parent. Indeed, it very likely will affect a variety of family subsystems.

Taking a systems perspective with respect to family intervention will help you anticipate and avoid the sources of conflict and resistance within the family system. For example, if you recognize that the father is part of both a marital subsystem and a parental subsystem, you will make special efforts to involve him in any communication or conferences about the child. Similarly, if you know that a child's older brother (sibling subsystem) has primary responsibility for supervision while the single parent is at work, you will be more likely to communicate with both him and the parent when you have concerns and recommendations.

> How can I help uninvolved parents become more interested and concerned?

Considering the family situation from a systems prespective will help you remember that parents experience periodic emotional, familial, and economic problems that you may be unaware of. Make a special effort to give the benefit of the doubt, particularly when parents fail to respond in a timely manner to your requests. Carlson (1992) documents the overwhelming economic, divorce, custody, and career problems of single parents. A parent's failure to monitor her child's homework, attendance, or tardiness to class may result less from lack of interest than from her need to cope with day-to-day personal, social, and economic problems. When parents do not live up to your expectations, try to avoid assigning personal blame.

Acknowledge the Changes in the American Family. Most families include two working parents. Research shows that teachers believe that working parents are less involved with their children's education (Linney & Vernberg, 1983). However, a study conducted by Medrich, Roizen, Rubin, and Burkley (1982) concludes that working and nonworking mothers spend the same amount of time in child-related activities. Furthermore, their data show that children of working mothers are just as involved in extracurricular activities as are the children of nonworking mothers.

Single-parent families make up about 25 percent of the families of children in school. Yet many teachers view this family pattern as an abnormality (Carlson, 1992). Teachers often have lower expectations for the achievement of children from single-parent families, despite the fact that no data support this opinion (Epstein, 1987).

Some researchers suggest that the requirements single-parent families have for organization, schedules, routines, and division of responsibilities better prepare children to accept such structures in schools (Linney & Vernberg, 1983). Carlson (1992) concludes that it is family income, not single or dual parenting alone, that affects children's achievement in school.

View Parent Participation from an "Empowerment Model." Delgado-Gaitan (1991) proposes that we view parent participation from an **empowerment model** that involves giving parents both the power and the knowledge to deal with the school system. Typically, the **deficit model** has been used to explain why minority parents have not become involved with schools. These perspectives sometimes have portrayed parents as passive, lazy, incompetent, or unskilled at helping their children. They propose that parents are unable to become involved in their children's education because they work long hours away from the home or are simply not interested. But as Delgado-Gaitan points out, when conditions are examined closely, research has shown that Hispanic families who speak a different language and have a different culture from that of the school do indeed care about their children and possess the capacity to advocate for them. This holds true for African Americans, Hispanic Americans, Native Americans, and other cultural and linguistic groups. The question is not whether they can become genuine partners with the school, but how to empower them to do so.

Recognize the Unique Needs of Mothers and Fathers. Turnbull and Turnbull (1986) urge teachers to promote nonsexist views of parenting and parent involvement. They recommend that teachers recognize the importance of both mothers and fathers when designing home-school linkages. Encourage visiting opportunities for both parents, develop flexible schedules to accommodate both parents, send information about children and schooling to both parents, and seek to promote teaching skills in fathers as well as mothers. Finally, give consideration to the father's interests and needs when suggesting ways for parents to work with their children at home.

Understand the Variety of Possible School-Family Linkages. As you plan for parent involvement early in the school year, consider and evaluate the full range of ways in which parents can participate. These activities can be placed on a continuum anchored on one end by activities involving parents as receivers of information and on the other end by involving parents as active educational decision makers, as shown in Table 16.1. The accompanying box, *Planning Family-School Linkages*, offers some suggestions. In the remainder of this chapter, we'll take a closer look at some of the ways teachers can involve parents in classroom learning: parent conferences, group conferences, written communications with parents, telephone calls, skills classes, homework, and language classes.

The Parent Conference

Parent conferences will be one of your most important linking mechanisms in Category I linkages. There are many reasons for holding conferences with parents or guardians.

Empowerment model. A view of parent participation that involves giving parents both the power and the knowledge to deal successfully with the school system.

Deficit model. A view of parent participation that assigns the blame for the lack of participation on parents attitudes, temperament, and conditions.

Planning Family-School Linkages

Plan Ahead. At the beginning of the year, try to anticipate your needs for parent involvement. Will you need help implementing a new computer system or writing program? Would you like to have a series of career seminars for students? Do you need "Reading Parents" to read to kindergartners several times a week?

Communicate Your Needs. Once you know what your needs are, let parents know about them. Send home a checklist during the first few weeks of school, indicating what your needs for parent involvement are, exactly what tasks will be involved, and what time commitment will be required.

Delegate Responsibility. Enlist the help of class parents to organize activities, or organize committees for ongoing events. Assign one father to be in charge of scheduling for the "Reading Parent" program; one mother will get in touch with each child's family to gather information to be used in planning career seminars.

Accommodate Parents' Scheduling Needs. Perhaps a single mother has a busy schedule but could manage to come in for reading one morning a month. Make your schedule flexible enough to accommodate her desire to be involved.

Teachers typically have a parent conference when they want to discuss their concerns about a learner's academic progress or classroom behavior (Shalaway, 1989). Sometimes conferences can be threatening to both parents and teachers. While their purpose is *reactive*—to correct a specific problem that has arisen at school—they can become emotionally charged confrontations between parent and teacher.

> How can I plan, organize, and execute a parent conference that is cordial and upbeat?

Proactive parent conferences have a different agenda. You request such a conference because you want to understand a learner better, establish a relationship with the parents, elicit a commitment from parents to serve as partners in their child's education, or inform parents about your goals and aspirations for their child. While such conferences are the exception rather than the norm, many schools, such as those participating in the Accelerated Schools Program developed at Stanford University (Hopfenberg, Levin, Meister, & Rogers, 1990), have successfully used such a proactive approach to increase parent participation.

Several general guidelines, based on professional practice and research, can promote family-school partnerships through a proactive perspective and effective communication skills. Let's see how they work to help you plan, conduct, and evaluate a parent conference.

Planning

Planning the conference involves determining goals, an agenda, materials, and the setting.

Parent conferences require careful planning on the part of teachers. They also require that teachers demonstrate good communication skills, such as active listening.

Goals. Give careful consideration to your purpose or goal for meeting with parents and the outcome you expect to achieve. Typical purposes for holding a proactive conference can be to help you:

- get to know parents and child better
- discuss the child's learning and behavior problems
- inform the parents about the child's success
- persuade the parents to seek professional help for the child
- persuade the parents to supervise the child's homework and study time more closely
- teach the parents a particular skill that can be used at home to help the child
- find out the parents' expectations for their child and for you
- explain the results and implications of the child's grades or scores
- determine the parents' preferences for family-school involvement.

Once you have decided on the goals of the conference, identify a concrete outcome you expect as proof you have met your goal. This could be a written home-school intervention plan to improve the learner's behavior, a commitment to attend parenting classes held at school, an agreed-upon time for a home visit, or a contract spelling out mutual obligations and commitments. The Stanford Accelerated School Program requires both parents and school personnel to sign an agreement delineating the responsibilities of parents, learners, and school staff (Hopfenberg et al., 1990).

Agenda. Prepare and send home an agenda that states the purpose of the conference, describes the topic you would like to discuss, and invites the parents to meet with you. Provide a sufficient number and variety of times to accommodate the schedules of working parents and guardians. When you have received a commitment from the parent to meet, record your perceptions of the student's strengths and needs on Part 1 of the form shown in the accompanying box, *Planning a Parent Conference*. This will set the stage for Part 2, in which you can record at the start of the conference the parents' perceptions of their child's strengths and needs. These perceptions may reveal contradic-

Planning a Parent Conference

Name of Child _____

Parent(s) _____

Date_____ Grade _____

Part 1: (To Be Completed Prior to Conference)
Student strengths observed by teacher:

Student needs observed by teacher:

Part 2: (To Be Completed at Start of Conference)
Student strengths observed at home by parent:

Student needs observed at home by parent:

Part 3: (To Be Completed at End of Conference)
Suggestions for action
Home setting:

School setting:

tions that, if left unaddressed during the conference, can present a stumbling block to effective parent-teacher communication. This information can provide an agenda for action, which can be recorded on Part 3 of the form at the close of the conference.

Materials. Before the conference, write down questions you wish to ask, points you want to make, and suggestions you will offer. Collect the learner's work samples, grades, test scores, and other information you plan to share ahead of time, to avoid fumbling through stacks of papers during the conference.

Setting. Many parents are understandably nervous when they first meet with teachers. Take pains to put them at ease by providing a quiet place to talk, comfortable chairs, and, if possible, some refreshment, such as a soft drink, coffee, or a snack.

Conducting the Parent Conference

In addition to these general guidelines, during the parent conference you will be expected to use several communication skills (Swap, 1987).

Plain Talk. Practice speaking plainly. Here are just some of the terms that educators use naturally but that mean little to most parents:

norms	fine-motor skills
behavioral objectives	learning set
negative reinforcement	developmental needs
homogeneous grouping	cognitive skills
discovery learning	percentiles
linguistic approach	knowledge acquisition
prosocial behavior	standardized test
higher-order thinking	basic skills
portfolios	prerequisite skills

New teachers—particularly when they first meet parents or address them at group meetings—rely on professional jargon that may be incomprehensible to parents. Remember that jargon, however familiar to you, will diminish rather than increase your credibility with most parents.

Listening. Listening is your most important communication skill. Parents, particularly when they are upset, want to be heard. One of the most frequent complaints leveled by parents against teachers is that they don't listen (Gordon, 1974). The Appalachian Educational Laboratory (Shalaway, 1989) offers the following list of hints for you to become a good listener:

- maintain eye contact
- face the speaker and lean slightly forward
- nod or give other noninterrupting acknowledgments
- when the speaker pauses, allow him or her to continue without interrupting
- ignore distractions
- wait to add your comments until the speaker is finished
- ask for clarification when necessary
- check your understanding by summarizing the essential aspects of what the speaker tried to say or the feeling he or she tried to convey.

Active listening. A technique whereby the listener summarizes essential aspects of what the speaker has tried to say or the feeling the speaker tried to convey.

Gordon (1974) refers to this last skill as **active listening.** It is particularly valuable during reactive parent conferences or conferences requested by parents who are upset over something they perceive you said or did, as such conferences can be emotionally charged. Teachers typically take a defensive or aggressive posture when confronted by an angry parent. Rather than listen to what the parent has to say, the teacher follows the parents' statement with a denial, a defensive statement, or a refusal to talk further.

Gordon believes that active listening, in which the listener provides feedback to the speaker on the message that was heard and the emotion that was conveyed, opens doors to further communication by letting the speaker know that he or she was understood and respected. Active listening is an essential communication skill to be used with the parents of learners and the learners themselves—but it is difficult to learn. It requires an ability to concentrate on what someone is saying even when you strongly object to what is being said. As with any skill, you must practice it before you can use it naturally and automatically.

Use "I" Messages. We discussed Ginott's model of congruent communication (Ginott, 1972) in Chapter 9 in reference to conduct management of learners. The use of congruent messages is just as important when you speak with parents. Particularly when you are upset about the actions of a learner or the words or actions of a parent, it is important that you clearly communicate your feelings. However, the way to do this is not by criticizing or blaming (with a "you" message) but rather by (1) describing what was offensive ("When you . . ." or "When your . . ."); (2) describing the feeling or emotion you experience when the offensive condition occurs ("I feel . . ."); and (3) offering a statement of the reason for the feeling (because . . .").

For example, you might say, "When Amanda talks back to me, her behavior disrupts the entire class, and that makes me angry because I have to take time away from all the other students in the class to deal with her." This message focuses on your reaction to the problem rather than on what the child said or did. It opens up avenues to further communication rather than setting up barriers, which might be the case if you used the following "you" message: "What gives Amanda the right to talk back to me in my own classroom?"

Evaluating the Parent Conference

At the end of the conference, summarize what was said and agreed on, and make a list of any actions to be taken by you or the parent, using Part 3 of the form shown in the box *Planning a Parent Conference*. Make follow-up calls, send notes, and follow through on the tasks you committed yourself to. Finally, take a moment to reflect on how well you communicated with the parents and achieved your goals, and what you might do differently the next time you have a parent conference. This moment of reflection will be one of the most important aids to sharpening your parent conferencing skills.

Other Parent Involvement Techniques

The Group Conference

Bringing parents together in one group can save you the time of having to repeat information about your goals, objectives, teaching methods, and evaluation activities to all interested parents. Group conferences also give parents the opportunity to meet one another and develop a rapport.

Some elementary school teachers conduct group conferences by allowing parents to follow their children throughout a regular school day. When the learners are at art, music, or physical education, the teacher talks to all the parents. Teachers who have tried this technique report that it makes the individual conference more meaningful and interesting to the parent (Shalaway, 1989).

Other forms of group conferences that have been found to contribute to learner achievement and improvement in classroom behavior are monthly parents' nights, neighborhood meetings with school staff, early morning breakfasts, and monthly Dads' or Moms' nights in which parents get together at the school to play basketball, volleyball, or softball (Lucas, Henze, & Donato, 1990). Some schools have instituted popular "authors' nights," when each child in the class reads his or her best work aloud. When it is feasible, have translators if non–English-speaking parents are present.

Certificate of Achievement

Strike up the band for

_____

who is doing excellent work in

_____

_____
signature   date

Figure 16.4
Example of a Happy Gram.

Written Communications

What are some ways I can let parents know more about my classroom and their child's progress?

Teachers can also inform parents about their children through Happy Grams (see Figure 16.4), activity calendars (see Figure 16.5), and informal notes (see Figure 16.6, p. 556). Shalaway (1989) urges teachers to contact parents when their children are behaving well—not just when problems occur. Glasser (1990), whose ideas we studied in Chapter nine, makes the same recommendation.

Surveys of parents indicate that they read school newsletters and find them helpful if they contain specific content about the classroom and school (Shalaway, 1989). Items to include in newsletters are the following:

- lists of household items that could be saved for class projects
- calendars of upcoming events
- successful home learning activities
- calls for volunteers
- highlights of available community resources
- successful parenting hints
- lists of learning resources to have in the home.

Telephone Calls

Telephone calls allow an exchange of ideas and information that cannot be achieved with written messages. Traditionally, a phone call from the teacher has been a harbinger of bad news. Phone messages should be used more to praise, reward, and inform than to

Calendar Activities

Run off copies of these activities
and paste them on the calendars.

Primary

For June

1 List 10 things you want to do this summer.

2 Start a list to keep track of every book you read this summer.

4 Start a stamp collection. Cut the stamp off any envelope that will be thrown away. Look for different ones every day.

5 World Environment Day.

6 Write a letter to your teacher. Thank him or her for helping you this year.

8 Be an architect today and build yourself a secret hideaway.

10 Draw a picture of the main character of the book you're reading.

12 Take a walk and look for animal tracks. Compare them to the size of your feet. Try to identify them.

13 Make an original flag and fly it tomorrow on Flag Day.

14 Flag Day. Count the flags you see today.

15 Make a Father's Day gift by drawing a picture of your dad.

19 Father's Day.

21 Summer solstice—the longest day of the year. What time does the sun set tonight?

22 Find out on what day of the week you were born. That's your lucky day!

23 Draw a picture of your favorite animal. Give it a name.

24 Poet John Ciardi was born on this day in 1916. Read some poems from his book I Met a Man.

25 Stand in the sunlight and see how small you can make your shadow.

27 Start a leaf collection. Press leaves between the pages of an old book.

28 Write a letter to your favorite author. Send it to the book's publisher.

For July

1 What if ET invited you to a party on his planet? Draw a picture of what the party would look like.

3 Decorate your bicycle for the Fourth of July.

4 Independence Day

5 Read a book by Beatrix Potter to celebrate her birthday.

7 Read from the tale of Pinocchio, first published this day in 1891.

8 The Liberty Bell cracked on this day in 1835. Draw a picture of the bell.

9 Ask your parents to help you make a family tree.

10 Today begins National Ice Cream Week.

11 Celebrate author E. B. White's birthday by reading from Stuart Little.

12 Look at yourself in the mirror. Draw what you see.

13 Write a letter to your teacher telling what you've been doing this summer.

14 Bastille Day. France's independence day. Draw the French flag.

15 Read your favorite poem to your parents.

18 Pull 15 weeds in your lawn.

20 First landing on the moon in 1969. Look at Erich Fuch's book Journey to the Moon.

21 Write a letter to a friend you haven't seen since the end of school.

22 Tell a story to a friend and make up a new ending.

23 Interview your parents about what you were like as a baby.

25 Draw a map of your house.

26 Make a sandwich and cut it into fourths.

27 What flower grows between the nose and the chin? Tulips! Make up your own riddle.

29 Give a name to an imaginary planet and draw a picture of the planet's surface.

30 Stand in the sunlight and make your shadow's arms disappear.

For August

1 Sing "The Star-Spangled Banner" in honor of Francis Scott Key's birthday.

3 Crickets, ladybugs, and spiders can bring good luck. Can you find any of these bugs?

4 Write a letter to a relative you haven't seen this summer.

6 Make a funny hat from a newspaper or a paper bag.

7 National Family Day.

8 Collect a pile of stones, twigs, and leaves. Arrange them on newspaper to make an animal portrait.

9 Write out the alphabet. After each letter write an item of food that begins with that letter.

10 Draw a picture of your home from the outside.

11 Measure your brother, your sister, or a friend.

13 Hold a rope-skipping contest today. Run a skipping relay race and skipping marathon.

15 Balance on one foot. Try it with your eyes closed. Have a one-footed race with your friends.

16 Guess how many windows are in your home. Count them. How close were you?

17 Read some of Ogden Nash's funny poems in honor of his birthday.

19 Design your own bumper sticker.

21 Play a game of basketball in honor of Wilt Chamberlain's birthday.

22 Read your favorite comic strip to someone.

23 Write out your first name. Under each letter write all the names you can think of that begin with that letter.

25 Have a picnic with friends.

26 Hold some beach ball races. Try running with the ball between your knees and ankles.

29 Make a collage of pictures cut from old magazines.

30 Stand in the sunlight with three friends and make the biggest shadow you can.

31 Make a list of things you hope to do in school this year.

Intermediate

For June

1 Start a list to keep track of every book you read this summer.

2 Start a summer diary. Write or draw a message in it every day.

4 Write 10 things you want to do this summer.

5 World Environment Day.

6 Write a letter to your teacher. Thank him or her for helping you this year.

8 Celebrate Gwendolyn Brooks's birthday by reading from Bronzeville Boys and Girls.

9 Make up two word problems and ask someone to solve them.

10 Design your own bumper sticker.

11 Start a stamp collection. Look for a different stamp on a used envelope everyday.

13 Make an original flag and fly it tomorrow on Flag Day.

14 Flag Day.

15 Today in 1752, Ben Franklin proved that lightning is a form of electricity. Read a biography of Franklin.

Make a Father's Day gift by drawing a picture of your dad.

21 Summer solstice—the longest day of the year. What time does the sun set tonight?

22 Read a newspaper article. Write five facts that you learned.

23 Draw a picture of your favorite animal.

24 Poet John Ciardi was born on this day in 1916. Read from his book John J. Plenty and Fiddler Dan.

25 Meet with two friends. How much do you weigh together?

27 Helen Keller was born in 1880. Read about her life in The Helen Keller Story by Catherine Owens Peare.

28 Find out on what day of the week you were born. That's your lucky day!

30 Draw a picture of the main character of the book you are reading.

For July

1 Start a leaf collection. Press leaves between the pages of an old book.

3 Decorate your bicycle for the Fourth of July.

4 Independence Day.

6 Draw a picture of yourself doing your favorite summer activity.

7 Compare the amounts of vitamins and minerals listed on two different breakfast cereal boxes.

8 The Liberty Bell cracked on this day in 1835. What does the inscription on the bell say?

9 Draw a picture of your home from the outside.

10 Today begins National Ice Cream Week.

Figure 16.5
A classroom activity calendar for a parent newsletter.

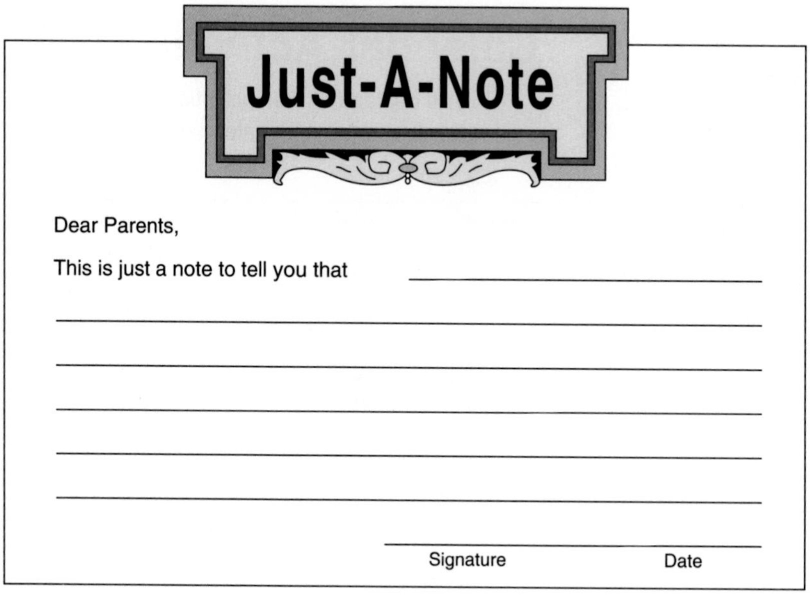

Just-A-Note

Dear Parents,

This is just a note to tell you that ______________________

____

____

____

____

____

Signature Date

Figure 16.6
Example of informal notes for encouraging parent involvement.

scold. Many teachers keep track of phone contacts using a log similar to that shown in the accompanying box, *Recording Telephone Contacts.*

Teaching Skills Classes

Parent participation activities that have involved educating parents to teach their children have been the most successful in improving learner achievement (Berger, 1991). Such classes can teach parents skills to help them develop their children's language, reading, and math abilities. Parenting classes are also popular activities for involving parents as learners. For example, Dorothy Rich, president of the Home and School Institute, has developed the MegaSkills Program, which empowers parents to teach children the 10 MegaSkills of confidence, motivation, effort, responsibility, initiative, perseverance, caring, teamwork, common sense, and problem solving. Research on the effects of the MegaSkills Program has found that children of parents enrolled in the program spend more time on homework, less time watching TV, and more time with their parents (Rich, 1988).

Homework

Homework is an important linking mechanism between home and school. It is one of the few visible signs parents have of their child's learning and your teaching. It is also a vehicle for parents to participate in educating their child. However, depending on the community in which you teach, homework can be an emotionally charged issue. Some parent organizations are demanding more homework. Some school boards, responding to parental pressure, have been regulating the types and amounts of homework teachers

Applying Your Knowledge:

Recording Telephone Contacts

School-Family Telephone Record

Teacher _____

Student _____

Parent _____

Telephone number called:

You may wish to use this same record for calls from the family to you. Simply record "H" in the Response column.

Day/Date _____ Time _____ Response* _____ Comments _____

1. _____
2. _____
3. _____
4. _____
5. _____
6. _____
7. _____
8. _____

Additional comments/record: _____

_____

*Response List A. Spoke with parent

B. Busy signal

C. No answer

D. Disconnected telephone

E. Scheduled call back

F. No adult home

G. Declined to speak

H. Family initiated call

I. Other: _____

should and must assign. Teachers are justifiably concerned. The process of developing, assigning, collecting, correcting, grading, recording, and returning homework occupies substantial amounts of teacher time. Are the results and benefits to learners worth the costs?

How can I help parents become more involved with their child's homework?

A number of recent studies have found a complex relationship among homework, school achievement, and parent involvement in school. Epstein (1989) found that the children who failed to complete their schoolwork and homework were the same students who disliked talking to parents about school and felt tense when working with a parent. Also, the parents of these children tended to have low levels of education, and their homes lacked items necessary for completing assignments, such as reference books.

On the other hand, Chandler and her colleagues (1986) found that low-income parents benefited from the knowledge of their children's schoolwork they obtained by re-

Involving Parents in Homework

- Make homework assignments, especially nightly assignments, short enough that they can be completed in a reasonable period of time.
- Make sure that parents review their children's homework. Either require that parents sign each assignment, or send home all the child's assignments at the end of each week or each academic unit with a form requesting a parent's signature.
- Provide an opportunity for parents to comment on their child's work. For example, staple a brief form letter to the weekly set of homework papers. The form should provide a blank line for a parent's signature, as well as space for a parent to write a brief, positive comment about the child's work.

viewing homework assignments: homework made the parents aware of what was going on in school and led them to seek out their children's teachers. This same study found that teachers expected more of students whose parents sought them out, so homework might have indirectly helped improve the children's school achievement.

The accompanying box, *Involving Parents in Homework,* provides some specific suggestions for enlisting parental interest in homework assignments.

Language Classes

Delgado-Gaitan (1991, 1992) advocates that schools set up English as a second language (ESL) classes for non–English-speaking parents. She reports that the Carpinteria Project in California has been particularly successful in empowering parents through such classes. In examining the results of a research project aimed at promoting the success of Spanish-speaking students in six high schools, Lucas et al. (1990) report that on-campus ESL classes for parents were among the most important factors contributing to academic achievement of their children.

> **What can I do to encourage greater involvement among parents who are linguistically and culturally different from the majority?**

Teachers play an important role in Category II activities by motivating parents to attend these classes, communicating their availability through newsletters and other written materials, diagnosing transportation problems, and informing the school district and principal about them (Greenwood and Hickman, 1991).

Summary

Parents are an underutilized resource for improving learner achievement. Full exploitation of this resource may require a shift in the way the school system views the educational role of the family system. Conventional types of parent participation activities, such as parent conferences, will probably encompass the majority of your efforts to create family-school linkages. They are important and necessary. However, they are only part of an overall parent participation plan.

Serious efforts at family-school linkage should also involve creating opportunities to involve parents as learners, teachers, and decision makers. These types of activities represent our best attempts to have parents participate in the schools and learn how to help their children succeed. Activities such as language classes, having parents serve as tutors, and on site-based management teams and school advisory councils enhance parent involvement as an ongoing process that is crucial to classroom instruction—and to learner achievement. These efforts place parents in an active role in their children's education.

Summing Up

This chapter introduced you to the family-school partnership. Its main points were these:

- Linking mechanisms are opportunities for school and family involvement that include parent-teacher conferences, home visits, participation by teachers in community events, newsletters, phone calls, personal notes, parent volunteers as classroom aides, and the use of home-based curriculum materials.
- Bronfenbrenner's systems-ecological perspective urges teachers to view a learner's behavior at school and at home not simply as a product of the child's individual psychological development but as a product of the demands and forces operating within all the systems of which the child is a member.
- Research indicates that positive effects on learner achievement were produced by projects that taught parents to teach their children at home and involved parents as teachers in their children's classrooms. In addition to improved achievement, parent involvement results in better attitudes toward school, higher homework completion rates, better attitudes toward homework, and improved attendance.
- Guidelines for successful parent-teacher conferences include having specific proactive goals, making an agenda that parents know about beforehand, designing a conference plan with preselected questions and documents, and providing a comfortable and relaxed setting.
- Activities that involve parents as information receivers include written communications (notes and newsletters), phone calls, prerecorded messages, home visits, and parent visits.
- Activities that involve parents as learners and home tutors include parenting skill classes, teaching skill classes, and English as a second language classes.
- Activities that involve parents as volunteers and teacher aids include housekeeping and clerical tasks, materials gathering and development, tutoring, grading, and recording.
- Activities that involve parents as decision makers in running the school include PTAs, school advisory councils, parent advisory councils, and site-based management teams.

For Discussion and Practice

°1. If you were Christie, what advice would you give Tamara for (1) how to go about finding parents to volunteer in the classroom and (2) making them effective at their assigned tasks?

°2. What four outcomes has research found from the collaboration between home and school?

°3. Explain what is meant by a "linking mechanism" and give four examples between a school and community.

°4. Identify what you believe is the most significant reason frustrations develop between parents and teachers and what you, personally, would do in your classroom to reduce parent-school conflicts.

°5. With a specific example, explain the meaning of an ecosystem.

°6. Provide an example of an exosystem that influences the behavior of the school-age learners you are likely to teach.

°7. After a parent-teacher conference, the father says that all past homework due will be turned in and personally checked by him for accuracy. The homework never gets turned in. Explain some possible reasons for the parent's behavior from a systems-ecological perspective.

°8. Using your response to question 7, define and identify the meso-systems that might play a role in accounting for the father's unresponsiveness.

°9. How would Delgado-Gaitan explain the lack of involvement by minority parents in school?

°10. What might you do on open-school night to encourage the participation of Hispanic parents? What might you do to encourage the participation of African American parents?

°11. Identify six principles for creating family-school partnerships based on the writings of Delgado-Gaitan, Bronfenbrenner, and Comer. Which do you believe should receive the highest priority?

°12. Identify four categories of parent involvement and give an example of an activity in each. Identify one unique activity in each category that has not been mentioned and that you would try in your own school and/or classroom.

°13. What is the difference between proactive and reactive parent conferences?

Questions marked with an asterisk are answered in the appendix.

°14. Express concerns about a student regarding each of the following areas with an "I" message:

   talking back

   missing homework

   tardiness

   acting out

15. Create an outline of content you would put in a class newsletter to send home to parents. Identify any features that would attract the attention of the parents (for example, pictures, personal stories, classroom achievements) that might make them want to become involved in your classroom.

Suggested Readings

Elementary School Journal 91(3) (1991). Chicago: University of Chicago Press. This entire issue is devoted to establishing educational partnerships among home, family, and school. It contains a variety of articles by experienced educators that offer specific suggestions for improving family-school relations.

Fine, M. J., & Carlson C. (1992). *The handbook of family-school intervention: A systems perspective.* Needham, MA: Allyn & Bacon. This text presents a thorough study of the systems perspective on family-school partnerships. It demonstrates the application of systems interventions to a wide range of family-school problems.

McAfee, O. (1984). *A resource notebook for improving school-home communications.* Charleston, WV: Appalachia Educational Laboratory. This resource notebook is a compendium of specific techniques used by teachers around the country for building school-family partnerships.

Appendix:

Discussion and Practice Answers

Chapter 1

1. Survival stage—behavior management concerns; task stage—delivery of instruction; impact stage—fulfillment of learner potential.
2. Concerns theory grew out of the analysis of recorded interviews with teachers. Implications are that a teacher's concerns change over time. For most teachers, concerns about survival or self diminish rapidly after several months of teaching. What follows is a new set of concerns about how best to help students learn.

Chapter 2

1. It could temper a tendency to explain a learner's behavior as exclusively the result of either nature *or* nurture and prompt an explanation that might include both.
3. The concept of permanence and the realization that changing shape doesn't change mass.
4. Schemata are information and understandings that the child acquires from the environment and that allow coordinated actions and action sequences to occur. For example, sensorimotor: grasps a cup; preoperational: recognizes the American flag as a symbol; concrete operational: understands law of conservation of liquids; formal operational: draws logical conclusions from propositional statements.
5. Organization and adaptation are two basic cognitive processes that occur throughout a learner's life. They allow a learner to simplify and make sense of new information gained as a result of experience. They also allow a learner to restore any cognitive disequilibrium that new information may create.
6. During a science lesson a child learns that the earth revolves around the sun. This child previously thought that the sun moved around the earth. As a result of the lesson the learner organizes new information about the movement of the solar system and creates a new cognitive schema to put this information into. In the process of doing this the learner adapts prior schemata or notions about planetary movement to accept these new ideas.
7. It (a) was the first theory to sketch the general principles of cognitive development and (b) showed that children think qualitatively differently at different stages of development. It (a) tends not to explain variations in the onset of specific

stages, (b) does not explain how learners move from one stage to another, and (c) tends to downplay social influences on learning.
8. His metaphor is the zone of proximal development: a zone that, when stimulated by the teacher, affords the learner the greatest opportunity to respond and encompasses the range of skills or abilities bounded on one side by what the learner can do independently and on the other side by the skills a learner needs adult assistance to perform.
9. His theory helps us recognize (a) that learning is a social process and (b) the importance of assessing not just a child's present level of functioning but also his or her potential level of learning (zone of proximal development).
10. Changes taking place in a learner are due to social experiences (Vygotsky), not altered schemata (Piaget) or the accumulation of learned intellectual skills or capabilities (Gagné).
11. The interactionist perspective holds that while children are born with certain innate abilities (LAD) that predispose them to varying degrees of language competence, this competence can be altered and enhanced by both the environment and the social experiences of the learner. This perspective can help explain how a learner uses certain language expressions (slang, for example) that cannot be explained by reference to an innate LAD.
12. a. Teach question-asking skills.
    b. Teach the use of subvocal speech.
13. In bilingual instruction the native language is taught for the first and second years of school in the same classroom where exposure to the second language takes place. Both languages are then maintained for several years, after which the learner is expected to perform entirely in the second language. Total immersion teaches only the second language. English as a second language provides instruction in both languages but in separate classrooms.

Chapter 3

1. The biological approach holds that how we develop affectively is due to temperaments we inherit from our parents. The social learning approach holds that our affective development is determined largely through the learning process, in particular the process of modeling. The psychoanalytic approach holds that affective development is the result of

the interplay between maturational forces, cognitive development, and experience.

2. Identical twins reared apart were more similar to one another in terms of their emotionality, adaptability, and activity level than were fraternal twins.
   a. Activity level.
   b. Adaptability.
   c. Emotionality.
3. He has a high activity level, has a hard time getting along with others, and becomes easily upset, which are traits inherited from his parents.
4. Children have demonstrated more or less aggressive behavior depending on which models they have observed.
   a. Maturation.
   b. Exposure to increasingly complex verbal and physical behavior models.
   c. Increasing ability to attend, recall, imitate, and be motivated.
5. He probably has observed aggressive models and has never been taught the skills necessary to get along with peers and adults.
6. The drive for identity.
7. Stage 4: Industry versus inferiority. The child must successfully respond to demands to master academic tasks, get along with others, and follow the rules.
   Stage 5: Identity versus role confusion. The child must establish a sense of who he is and who he hopes to be.
8. Children of divorced parents showed more signs of depression, substance abuse, and emotional and behavioral disturbance than children of intact families. Joe failed to successfully resolve the identity crisis of trust versus mistrust during the infancy stage of his life.
9. Personal-social development begins with inborn temperament. It is then influenced by child-rearing practices and modeling processes and later by the family environment, which in turn influences the child's self-image.
10. Self-esteem contributes to a positive attitude, social ability, and adaptability, which may influence school achievement over time.
11. Vertical relationships represent the child's attachment to parents and teachers for purposes of safety, security, and protection. Horizontal relationships represent the child's attachment to other children for purposes of belonging, cooperation, competition, and intimacy.
12. They are intentional, voluntary behaviors intended to help another. For example, Joe might be expected to explain to another student the importance of handing in assignments or to follow the rules to be admitted to a sporting event.
13. How one thinks and becomes concerned about other people's actions and feelings. Rebecca becomes concerned that Robert is embarrassed by being scolded in front of the class.
14. Level 0: "A friend is someone you like."
    Level 1: "A friend is someone who thinks like you."

Level 2: "A friend is someone who helps me when I need it."

15. Level I: A child doesn't take an extra piece of candy when told not to because he may be seen and punished.
    Level II: A child doesn't take an extra piece of candy because he knows his father would disapprove.
    Level III: A child doesn't take an extra piece of candy because lunchtime is near and he doesn't want to spoil his appetite for a healthier meal.

Chapter 4

1. a. Environment that stimulates correct and rapid performance.
   b. Focus on observable performance.
   c. Abundant opportunities for feedback and reinforcement following performance.
   In the ABC model, antecedents (A) in the environment elicit the desired behavior (B), which becomes strengthened when followed by appropriate consequences (C).
2. It is reinforcing a correct response after it has occurred to increase the likelihood that it will recur. Example: praising a student after a correct answer to increase the likelihood that the student will raise his or her hand again later.
3. Whether the learner possesses the prerequisites for it.
4. Task analysis. To identify and sequence prerequisite skills.
5. The instruction should be designed to allow as few errors as possible and to increase correct responses as much as possible.
6. It is when stimuli in the environment automatically bring about the correct answer. Some examples are (a) a list of posted rules that precludes misbehavior, (b) a bell that when rung signals the class to silence, or (c) an overhead projector that when turned on elicits the attention of learners.
8. Active: writing sentences, calculating an answer, focusing a microscope.
   Passive: listening to a lecture, looking at an overhead projection, waiting for assistance.
   Students should be actively responding about 75 percent of the time.
9. a. Giving directions that focus only on the response you want.
   b. Allowing learners to respond actively.
   c. Allowing learners to produce correct answers 70 to 90 percent of the time.
10. (a) Your example should tell learners not only what was correct, but also why. (b) Your example should give the right answer, point out how to get the right answer, have learners correct the answer, or provide some extra problems.
11. Positive consequences encourage learners to continue their good efforts and motivate them to do better. Only when

they actually increase the frequency of the target behavior are they positive reinforcers.

12. Your conditions should include: (a) Baseline measurement; (b) assessment of reinforcer preferences; (c) immediate, continuous reinforcement; and (d) gradual fading of extrinsic reinforcers to natural reinforcers.

13. They are reinforcers that are naturally present in the setting where the behavior occurs (for example, grades in a classroom) or represent a change in stimulation due to the behavior itself (for example, seeing the right answer on the display of a calculator).

14. (a) Verbal reprimands, (b) overcorrection, (c) response cost, and (d) exclusion. They would have to reduce the frequency of the targeted behavior.

Chapter 5

1. To describe the unobservable workings of the mind. The mind as a computer or information-processing system.

2. Relevant learner characteristics, instructional manipulations, cognitive processes, cognitive outcomes, outcome performance.

3. Behavioral approach: Only observable outcomes and right/wrong answers are studied on simple learning tasks. Cognitive approach: Cognitive processes and outcomes and information processing are studied on complex human thinking tasks. The behavioral psychologist attempts to build a model that accounts for all learning; the cognitive psychologist limits the study of learning to complex thought processes.

4. General methods of thinking that improve learning and problem solving across a variety of subject areas that go beyond the processes naturally required for carrying out a task.

5. Rehearse: Repeat to themselves what was read or heard.
   Elaborate: Relate what was learned to an image or to past learning.
   Organize: Place information learned in related groups.

6. Setting goals, focusing their attention, reinforcing themselves, and coping with difficult problems.

8. You will need to teach them to:
   a. attend to the effective strategies
   b. attribute differences to the relative effectiveness of a particular strategy
   c. use the more effective strategy in future decision making.

9. Domain-specific knowledge is useful for learning facts, concepts, and principles in a specific area or topic, for example, how to solve an equation with two unknowns. General knowledge is useful for learning across a variety of school tasks, for example, how to spell.

10. Declarative knowledge, for example, how to add and subtract. Procedural knowledge, for example, how to tie a shoe lace.

11. (1) Relate new information to existing information.
    (2) Allow learners to think about information in working memory with strategies such as notetaking, discussion, practice, and comprehension monitoring.

12. They help store and retain information longer using verbal representations and images.

14. The former, revisionist view, holds that intelligence can be altered; the latter, classical view, holds it is immutable or difficult to change. Gardner believes there are seven specific areas of intelligence. Sternberg believes there is a common set of strategies that apply to all areas of learning. Both believe intelligence should only be studied in the context of important cultural problems and products.

Chapter 6

1. Mr. Robbins's lesson was heavily influenced by the behavioral science approach advocated by Lindsley and Englemann. His activities elicited practice of correct responses followed by immediate feedback in a teacher-directed lesson. Mrs. Greer's lesson, on the other hand, followed the cognitive science approach advocated by Pressley, Ball, and Bruner. Her lesson focused on thought processes involving reflection, problem solving, analysis, and inquiry.

2. Constructivism is a term used by cognitive psychologists to represent an approach to teaching and learning that emphasizes the active role of the teacher and helps the learner build internal connections or relationships among the ideas and facts they are learning. It encourages learners to use their experiences to actively construct understanding that makes sense to them, rather than acquiring understanding by having it "told" to them in a preorganized format.

4. For example, discovery, relationships, conflict, responsibility. It will make learners more likely to acquire meaning and understanding by being able to connect the new subject matter with what they already know.

6. Conceptual conflict results when our existing beliefs or ways of explaining things do not produce the outcomes we predict, challenging our long-established beliefs about certain events. Conceptual conflict is represented by the Piagetian process of disequilibrium discussed in Chapter 2.

8. Hint: Have your learners view the writing assignment as a problem-solving activity requiring problem exploration, planning, revising, and editing.

9. Bruner says that good teaching is helping learners discover for themselves the generalizations under which lie related concepts and facts, rather than "telling" them to the learner. Rather than teach the rules for manipulating fractions, Mrs. Greer helped her learners construct the rules for themselves.

Chapter 7

1. Intrinsic motivation is what influences learners to choose, get energized about, and persist until they accomplish a task successfully, regardless of whether it brings an immediate reward.
2. Jared began to understand that he had to do what the teacher was asking to achieve some of his own goals.
3. Such theories view the person as not making conscious choices. They see people as operating without volition—their behavior is fixed and routine.
4. a. Primary drives are forces within the individual that are triggered by biological needs, such as hunger and thirst.
   b. Acquired drives are learned through the process of association with some primary drive, such as desires for money, for love, or to play sports.
5. Physiological, safety, belongingness and love, self-esteem (deficiency needs); and self-actualization (growth needs).
6. a. Locus of causality (internal versus external).
   b. Stability (changeable and unstable versus unchangeable and stable).
   c. Controllability (uncontrollable versus controllable).
7. a. Luck.
   b. Effort.
8. a. Situational cues, for example, time-on-task.
   b. Prior beliefs or causal schemata, for example, "hard work pays off."
   c. Self-perceptions, for example, "I can do it."
9. a. Monitor your attributional messages.
   b. Focus on learning strategies.
   c. Refrain from ability grouping.
   d. Promote cooperation.
   e. Teach realistic goal setting.
10. a. Past experiences (for example, a good grade on an earlier assignment).
    b. Persuasion from teacher (for example, teacher says, "You can do it!").
    c. Physiological cues (for example, rapid breathing during a test).
    d. Modeling (for example, seeing a classmate perform well).
11. a. Help them set goals.
    b. Teach them learning strategies.
    c. Find adults and peers to model confidence and persistence.
12. That attribution and self-efficacy theories make motivation appear too cognitive, abstract, and devoid of energy and passion. They fail to account for the needs of learners to feel competent and independent.
13. The needs, for competence, relationships, and autonomy.
15. For example, the project should emphasize the learning process, not just the product (attribution theory); the project should let learners set their own goals (self-efficacy the-

ory); the project should help each learner become competent (self-determination theory).
17. a. Present a challenge.
    b. Allow for learner's choice and control.
    c. Be doable within time and resource limitations.
    d. Require collaboration.
    e. Result in a product or artifact.

Chapter 8

1. Developmental psychologists, such as Piaget, would account for perceptions, feelings, thoughts, and actions by the forming of schemata—or cognitive structures—mostly through the child's interactions with the environment. Social psychologists, such as the Schmucks, would account for perceptions, feelings, thoughts, and actions by the relationships, goals, and social structure of the group(s) to which the individual belongs.
4. Sharan and Sharan (1976); Cohen (1984, 1986); Cohen and Intele (1981); Webb (1982); Slavin (1984, 1990b). You might use cooperative learning to achieve some of your lesson objectives.
6. a. Through the unfolding of genetic and instinctual tendencies or dispositions.
   b. Through associations with people—parents, siblings, peers, and teachers.
7. a. Forming—acceptance and responsibilities: "What's expected of me?"
   b. Storming—shared influence: "How can my voice be heard?"
   c. Norming—how work gets done: "Who do I go to for help?"
   d. Performing—freedom, control, self-regulation: "What things can I do independently of the teacher?"
8. Distancing: "Why do I gotta do this stuff?"
   Centering: "What's in it for me if I do it?"
9. Your examples should have in common that
   a. they were probably unspoken and unwritten, and
   b. not to follow them would bring social disapproval.
10. Expert power: by being in command of your subject matter.
    Referent power: by being trustworthy, fair, and concerned about your students.
    Legitimate power: by being invested with authority by the school district.
    Reward power: by dispensing reinforcements.
    Coercive power: by dispensing punishment.
    New teachers should work toward expert and referent power.
11. (a) On the basis of what you read, hear, or see, you expect certain behavior; (b) you look for this behavior more; (c) your students become aware that you expect this behavior to occur and behave accordingly; and (d) you find what you are looking for.
12. Every teacher showed some bias by favoring one student classification over another.

13. a. Orient group members to appropriate social interactions.
    b. Create group identification and cohesiveness.
    c. Promote academic achievement and positive relationships.
15. a. Create a list of norms.
    b. Conduct a discussion about class norms.
    c. Appoint a class committee to recommend ways of improving group behavior.
    d. Model normative behavior.
16. Achievement: Slavin (1987, 1990b, 1991); Cohen (1985). Productivity: Kafer (1976); Reynolds (1977).
17. a. Construct a bulletin board around friendships.
    b. Have students write brief autobiographies.
    c. Form a friendship circle.
    d. Select pals.
    e. Publish a directory.
    f. Form heterogeneous groups.
18. a. Problems learners bring with them.
    b. Problems from learners who choose not to abide by classroom rules and norms.
    c. Problems that mutually occur during the group development process, such as distancing and centering.

Chapter 9

1. a. Rosalyn standing in doorway talking.
   b. Carlos refusing to sit down.
   c. Adam making a face.
   d. Jeanne talking back to the teacher.
   e. Two late students slamming the door.
   f. Carlos and Rosalyn tapping their pencils.
   g. Tina and Joan making bobbing movements.
2. a. Everyone must be in their seats at the time of the bell.
   b. No talking until you are acknowledged by the teacher.
   c. Late students must report to the principal before coming to class.
   d. Disparaging, demeaning, or humiliating comments may not be made about another student.
3. You could, for example, combine a mutually agreed upon set of rules with a consistently applied system of reward and reinforcement.
5. a. Humanistic: Ginott (1972), Glasser (1990). Strong on teaching self-control, weak on prevention.
   b. Applied behavior analysis: Cooper, Heron, and Heward (1987). Strong on stopping major disruptive behavior, weak on prevention.
   c. Classroom management: Kounin (1970); Emmer, Evertson, and Anderson (1980); Hunter (1982). Strong on prevention, weak on stopping major disruptive behavior.
6. Communicate that the behavior is unacceptable; accept students' feelings; avoid use of labels; use praise only when deserved; elicit students' cooperation; communicate displeasure with inappropriate behavior.
7. Develop rules with students; set aside an area for disruptive students; confer privately with disruptive students; remove disruptive students, but provide an opportunity for them to return.
8. a. Giving praise after a correct answer.
   b. Sending a student (who was bored with your lesson) to the library, which results in his avoiding classwork that he did not want to do.
   c. Specifically praising a student for good work after every third or fourth assignment.
   d. Sounds, sights, people, or materials that can trigger a reaction; for example, a math worksheet, the principal, the sound of the final bell.
10. The more effective managers tended to emphasize group cohesiveness and communicated well-worked-out rules and routines during the first weeks of school. The less effective classroom managers did not have well-worked-out rules and routines, were ineffective monitors of student behavior, failed to deliver rewards and reprimands consistently, and used vague or unclear disciplinary messages.
12. a. Figure 9.3: High task orientation, mostly teacher-initiated interchanges, unsolicited student responses discouraged.
    b. Figure 9.4: Students have a say in establishing limits of their behavior, student spontaneity and risk-taking behavior allowed, teacher acts as moderator or participant.
13. Engaged learning time is the actual time students are actively involved in learning the lesson content. Allocated time is the time you plan for, or allocate to, the lesson.
14. Beginning class routine, ending class routine, getting-help-from-the-teacher routine, use of room routine.
15. Strategies that stop misbehavior without disrupting the flow of a lesson. Anticipation: student squirms in seat; deflection: teacher moves closer to student; reaction: if student doesn't stop, teachers removes privilege of going to the learning center for a day.

Chapter 10

1. To identify precise learning outcomes and bind classroom activities together into a coherent sequence that makes sense to learners.
3. Verbal information, intellectual skills, cognitive strategies, attitudes, motor skills.
5. Memorization, concepts, principles, problem solving. Mental operations lower in the hierarchy are required for the successful completion of operations at higher levels in the hierarchy.
7. Knowledge: recalling, memorizing.
   Comprehension: translating, restating, summarizing.

Application: using information in a new and different context.

Analysis: comparing and contrasting, differentiating, inferring.

Synthesis: combining parts in new or unique ways.

Evaluation: making value judgments and decisions, supporting, justifying.

9. Direct (or didactic), indirect (or inquiry), and self-directed (or self-regulated). Your patterns should involve the teaching skills of structuring, modeling, coaching, and fading.

10. She had a lesson that included rules, routines, expectations for student behavior, and a classroom management plan. Ms. Freeman used the indirect instructional method, which included some elements of structuring, modeling, coaching, and fading.

11. a. Gaining attention.
    b. Informing the learner of the objective.
    c. Stimulating recall of prerequisite learning.
    d. Presenting stimulus material.
    e. Guiding learning.
    f. Eliciting the desired behavior.
    g. Providing feedback.
    h. Enhancing retention.
    i. Promoting transfer.

12. a. Structuring: review, anticipatory set, and objectives and purpose.
    b. Modeling: input, modeling, and checking for understanding.
    c. Coaching: guided practice and closure.
    d. Fading: independent practice.

13. a. Psychophysical, for example, vary intensity of your voice.
    b. Emotional, for example, use a word in the student's native language.
    c. Discrepancy, for example, introduce a contradiction or mistake.
    d. Commanding stimuli, for example, point out what should be attended to.

14. a. Attention.
    b. Retention.
    c. Production.
    d. Motivation.

15. a. Focus learner attention.
    b. Stress value of demonstration.
    c. Talk conversationally.
    d. Make steps simple and obvious.
    e. Help learners remember.

16. a. Prompt fading gradually reduces the length and frequency of physical or verbal cues given to learners to help them attain a correct response. For example, using fewer words and shorter explanations.

    b. Reinforcer fading gradually reduces or transfers the motivation for performing a skill from extrinsic reinforcers to intrinsic reinforcers. For example, reduce use of stickers or tokens so learner can develop natural satisfaction for performing correctly.

17. It should (a) emphasize the mastery of prerequisite tasks, (b) be similar to performance in the real world, (c) contain a variety of examples, (d) vary the context in which the performance is expected, and (e) promote self-direction by allowing the use of personal examples.

18. The use in new and different contexts of facts, rules, and action sequences; concepts, patterns, and abstractions; and strategies for learning.

19. a. Emphasize mastery.
    b. Have real-world similarity.
    c. Provide variety.
    d. Offer flexibility.
    e. Promote self-direction.

Chapter 11

1. How do you teach, for example, one child to understand Marx's theory of class struggle while teaching another, in the same class, the correct spelling for "wuz"?

2. a. The ability to learn academic subjects, deal with abstractions, and solve problems; for example, measure performance with a paper-and-pencil test using context-free problems.

    b. The ability to withstand stress and distraction; to be motivated, emotionally stable, interested in learning, and socially competent; and to display grace and balance. For example, measure performance in a social setting using real-world problems.

3. Some educators feel it deprives certain individuals access to learning opportunities from which they can benefit.

4. a. Psychological attributes or traits can be measured indirectly.
    b. Repeated observations will overcome imprecision in observation.
    c. Ability is best measured as a quantity as opposed to a process.
    d. Measurement of ability can be relative rather than absolute.

5. Individual versus group ability tests: the former are given in a one-to-one format and are orally delivered, the latter are given in group settings and are paper-and-pencil tests. General versus multiple ability tests: the former measure a single underlying trait and assign a single score that measures that trait, the latter measure multiple traits and assign individual scores that measure those traits.

6. To develop a test that (a) was consistent with a general (unidimensional) theory of intelligence, (b) was practical to use

in a one-to-one assessment format, and (c) accurately separated learners who needed special instruction from those who did not.

7. The learner's raw score indicates an age-equivalent score of 6.5, or 6 years, 5 months. Overall, this learner is performing below students of his or her age.

8. By correlating the scores of the same learners taken on one occasion with their scores on another occasion. About +.80 or higher.

9. Scores on the test from a group of learners would be correlated with the scores from the same learners on an achievement test after a program of instruction. It should be at about +.50 to +.80 or higher.

10. About 25 percent. Motivation, health, social skills, quality of teaching, prior knowledge, emotional well-being, family support.

12. Their lack of (a) instructional validity, (b) behavioral definition, and (c) sampling specificity.

13. The former is more useful for improving instruction and learning, the latter is more useful for labeling and classifying learners.

14. You might require the test to (a) measure learning as both process and product, (b) focus on learning abilities that can be improved, (c) measure learning in a group as well as in an individual context, and (d) exhibit instructional validity.

15. Studies by Slavin (1987, 1990a, 1991), Fogelman (1983), Kerchoff (1986), and Gamoran (1992) indicate the lack of educational benefits of tracking. The personal testimonies of some teachers, parents, and students, however, argue for the benefits of tracking.

Chapter 12

1. a. The manner in which he weighted grades did not reflect the emphasis desired.
   b. His tests were primarily based on a single format using the written word.
   c. His essay format was not appropriate for the level he was testing.

3. For example, (1) using a variety of testing techniques, including performance assessments; (2) using test items that provide the opportunity for justifications and revisions to gain insight into each learner's line of reasoning, and awarding partial credit where appropriate.

4. It is only a *sample* of students' behavior that *estimates* their true levels of performance and progress.

5. (1) A test of subtraction; (2) a test of multiplication and division; (3) a test involving principles of trigonometry.

6. Validity is the degree to which a test measures what it says it measures—and what you want it to measure. It would not represent what you wanted it to measure.

7. They (a) test over content areas they didn't teach, (b) place more emphasis on certain content areas in the test than was actually taught, and (c) ask questions in a manner that requires students to use intellectual skills that were not taught in class.

9. a. Place your goals and objectives in front of you as you write test items.
   b. Ask yourself what thought process or intellectual skill is needed to answer each test item.
   c. Determine whether your objectives include the needed thought process or skill.

10. It must pose a specific problem for which the student recalls information, organizes it in a suitable manner, derives a defensible conclusion, and expresses it within specified guidelines.

12. $3 \times 30 = 90$ students; $90 \times 150 = 13,500$ words per question; $13,500 \times 2 = 27,000$ words total. At a reading rate of about 300 words per minute, it would take 90 minutes, or about an hour and a half, not counting time for writing comments and corrections and recording grades.

14. Validity is the degree to which a test measures the traits, abilities, or skills for which it was intended. Reliability is the degree to which the test dependably or consistently measures that trait, ability, or skill. The use of an unreliable test would mean your students' scores would not be consistent, if they were retested.

15. a. Write test instructions and questions in simple language.
    b. Write enough questions to cover all the content.
    c. Allow the students sufficient time to take the test.
    d. Make the test conditions comfortable.
    e. Follow a test blueprint.
    f. Prepare restricted response questions that have clearly identifiable right and wrong answers.

16. A norm-referenced grade is determined by use of a relative standard established by the naturally occurring distribution of scores in a class (for example, percentage of students receiving a particular grade or higher). A criterion-referenced grade is determined by use of an absolute standard established by the teacher indicating the minimum levels of achievement required at various grade intervals (for example, number of items correct).

Chapter 13

1. Conventional tests are given to provide data on which to base grades, to indicate how much has been learned, to facilitate decisions about instructional placement, to discuss with parents, and to help others make employment decisions. Performance assessments are given to stimulate higher-order thinking in the classroom and to simulate real-world activities.

2. An indirect measure, such as knowledge shown in a multiple-choice test, will suggest only that something has been learned. A direct measure, such as a problem-solving activity, requires that what has been learned can be applied and exhibited in the context of a real-world problem.

4. The Darwin School records percentage of words read accurately during oral reading, number of sentences read with understanding, and number of story elements that learners can talk about on their own. The West Orient School requires portfolios of poetry, essays, biographies, and self-reflections.

7. Scoring rubrics are model answers with which a learner's performance is compared. They can be a detailed list of what an acceptable answer must contain or a sample of typical responses that would be acceptable.

8. (a) Rescoring of a sample of your learner responses by other teachers and (b) the coming together of a group of teachers during the scoring process to score a sample of learner responses together.

9. It decides whether the learner demonstrated a significant level of achievement. It is determined by matching the performance assessment to the curriculum guide and having teachers from other schools or school districts read the test and critique its contents.

10. There is a lack of evidence at this time concerning the generalizability of the skills measured by performance assessments; but examples in a number of states (Vermont, New York, Connecticut, and California, among others) and research (Herman, 1992) have shown that performance assessments can be scored reliably.

Chapter 14

2. REI is a partnership between regular and special educators in which learners with disabilities receive individualized services in the regular classroom without labeling or special classifications.

3. Mainstreaming places learners with disabilities in the least restrictive environment conducive to their development. PL 94-142 and PL 99-457.

4. An IEP is a road map to the kinds of services the child will receive and how they are to be delivered. It includes goals and objectives, current skill levels, and services to be provided.

5. The four environments are (a) all day in a regular class with a regular education teacher, (b) all day in a regular class with special education personnel assisting, (c) some or all of the day outside the regular class with the regular education teacher assisting, (d) some or all of the day outside the regular class with special education personnel.

6. Normalization is the principle that learners are entitled to programs that allow them to experience the respect and dignity to which any person is entitled. It represents regular school and class participation, skill and image enhancement, autonomy, and empowerment.

7. They are used to determine the size of the discrepancy, if any, between a learner's aptitude and achievement at a particular grade level.

8. Mike has a learning disability in one or more areas of content, such as math or reading. Other questions might be "Did Mike receive adequate prior instruction in the problem areas?" and "Was Mike's early childhood conducive to learning the prerequisite skills?"

9. The most widely used method is based on the learner's performance on standardized ability, achievement, and adaptive behavior tests. A score below 70 on an IQ test usually indicates mental retardation.

10. Oppositional, noncompliant, aggressive behavior; restlessness; inattention; and impulsivity.

11. You might minimize extraneous demands, closely monitor the child's behavior, and provide high levels of feedback and reinforcement.

12. A communication disability is an impairment that involves speech or language. You would look for difficulty in producing particular sounds or vocal pitch patterns (for example, distorting or substituting one sound for another) and for a child who seldom speaks and relies almost solely on gestures to communicate.

14. Research tends to support programs and classes specifically targeted to the gifted when they are allowed to pursue accelerated programs and when a grade can be skipped and/or advanced courses taken.

Chapter 15

1. a. A subordinate position in society.
   b. A sense of collective identity.
   c. A common perception of the world around them.

2. Culturally diverse children have ways of learning and thinking and needs for motivational, instructional, and classroom management strategies that differ from those of Anglos and that, if provided, would raise their achievement levels to be comparable to those of Anglos.

3. a. Only a small percentage of teachers are members of minorities, thus limiting minority role models.
   b. Textbooks have sometimes failed to communicate cultural respect and equality.
   c. Teachers and textbooks have sometimes failed to consider the verbal and nonverbal language patterns of minorities.

d. Disproportionate numbers of minority learners have sometimes been tracked into lower-level classes.

4. All groups score below Anglo learners on measures of scholastic ability. Their dropout rates are 42, 40, and 25 percent, respectively, compared with 14 percent for Anglos.

5. Education refers to the varied and informal ways in which children learn the customs, attitudes, beliefs, values, social skills, and other behaviors required at home and in society. Schooling refers to the formal classroom in which students learn subject matter characterized by a reliance on words, explanations, and questions. Research has shown that school performance improves when the method of education used at home matches the process of schooling used in the classroom, which can negatively affect minority learners.

6. a. Social organization (for example, whole-group instruction).
   b. Sociolinguistics (for example, wait-time).
   c. Learning style (for example, preference for a certain type of emotional environment).
   d. Cognitive style (for example, field-independence/dependence).

7. Field-dependent: holistic/visual, global. They focus on the whole picture and rely more on external sources of information.
   Field-independent: verbal/analytical. They focus on the parts and rely more on internal sources of information.

8. According to some research, Native Americans, Hispanic Americans, and African Americans tend to be more field-dependent than Anglo-Americans and Asian Americans. The cautions are these:
   a. Perpetuating stereotypes.
   b. Large within-group differences.
   c. Difficulty in matching instruction to many different learning styles.
   d. Directing the focus away from expert instruction.

9. a. Learner-subject relationships.
   b. Teacher-subject matter relationships.
   c. Teacher-learner relationships.

10. Much of the research has studied only middle-class Anglo children and girls rather than boys. You should be cautious in generalizing gender research to other groups.

12. For example, using only masculine terms, using stereotyped personalities or occupations, ignoring the accomplishments of one gender or incompletely representing them, and failing to integrate the accomplishments of one sex into the larger picture.

13. This stereotype has prevailed because of parents' stereotypes about female math ability, mothers' belief about the difficulty of math, and perceived value of math to the student. Research by Eccles and colleagues (1982, 1983, 1986) has found that these factors—not inherited abilities—

account for much of the difference in male/female scores on math ability tests.

14. For example, correcting boys from across the room but speaking privately to girls, giving different career advice to girls than to boys, correcting boys more often than girls for making mathematics mistakes, calling on girls more than boys during a poetry lesson.

Chapter 16

1. (1) Create a classroom newsletter in which you issue a call for help; (2) train them to accomplish the tasks you would like them to perform.

2. Improved (a) learner achievement, (b) attitudes toward school, (c) classroom conduct, and (d) parent and teacher morale.

3. Opportunities for school and family involvement such as parent-teacher conferences, home visits, participation by teachers in community events, and newsletters.

4. Parents want schools to do what is best for their child, but the school's primary responsibility is to groups of children.

5. An ecosystem is a system made of subsystems that must co-exist and are mutually dependent on each other. For example, the learner must coexist with and is dependent on the school, family, and peer group systems.

6. (a) The state and national political system that influences school standards, (b) the legislative system that influences funding for schools, (c) the economic system that employs family members, and (d) the social service system that cares for families in need.

7. The parent and family may be undergoing stress at home due to divorce or separation, financial crisis, a change in job, or problems outside the family that may be momentarily capturing the parent's attention.

8. These are the relationships between forces outside the school-family relationship that can cause the parent to act in a certain way. For example, a job offer in another city may create sibling concerns about giving up the stability of their existing peer relationships, which in turn may capture the exclusive attention of the father in this example.

9. She would point to the fact that some minority parents may not be proficient in the English language, may espouse different values than the cultural majority, or may not understand how the school system works.

10. Provide bilingual student guides for parents who need them and/or provide classroom visitation instructions in Spanish. Exhibit student work that shows the relationship between the African American culture and the community.

11. These authors suggest that teachers
    a. view the family from a systems-ecological perspective.

b.   acknowledge changes in the American family.

c.   use a parent empowerment model instead of a deficit model.

d.   recognize equally the needs of mother and father or the unique needs of single parents when involving parents.

e.   take into account the possible presence of familial and economic crises.

f.   offer a variety of possible school-family linkages that provide for different degrees of school participation.

12. Activities can involve parents as (a) information receivers (e.g., notes home), (b) learners and home tutors (e.g., parenting skills classes), (c) volunteers and teacher aids (e.g., tutoring), and (d) active decision makers in running the school (e.g., parent advisory council).

13. A proactive conference would inform the parent about the child's success and the possible reasons improvement might be necessary. A reactive conference would blame the parent or child for the inappropriate behavior.

14. For example, "When Mark acts out I really get upset because I have to stop what I'm doing and spend precious time getting the class back on track."

Glossary

ABC model of learning. A model that considers antecedents in the environment that elicit desired behavior, which is then strengthened when followed by appropriate consequences.

Accelerated curriculum. Programs for the gifted and talented that offer advanced courses and/or grade skipping.

Accommodation. Altering or adjusting cognitive structures affected by new information.

Active listening. A technique whereby the listener summarizes essential aspects of what the speaker has tried to say or the feeling the speaker tried to convey.

Active responding. Learner behavior that emphasizes asserting, volunteering, or actively seeking out information.

Adaptation. As identified by Piaget, a central drive of humans to adapt to the world as they experience it.

Adaptive behavior. Skills that most people learn without formal instruction, such as personal care, feeding, and social skills.

Advance organizer. A summary of the concepts, generalizations, and themes to be learned, presented at a general and inclusive level.

Affectional bonds. Long-lasting bonds between a child and a parent.

Age-equivalent scores. The obtained scores of those in a norming sample who are of various ages.

Antecedents. Stimuli present in an environment that make a behavior more likely to occur.

Anticipatory set. An organized framework usually presented to learners at the beginning of a lesson that helps them relate past with present learning and that places the lesson into a context that the learners can relate to and focus on.

Applied behavior analysis. An approach to classroom management that applies behavioristic principles to modify behavior in socially important areas.

Assimilation. Expanding or enriching cognitive structures with new information or perceptions.

Attention deficit hyperactivity disorder (ADHD). A disorder that has its onset before age 7, lasts at least six months, and is characterized by an inability to sustain attention, impulsivity, hyperactivity, and deficits in rule-governed behavior.

Attention deficit. Difficulty staying with or completing an activity over a period of time; becoming easily bored and uninterested in activities relative to others.

Attribution theory. A perspective on motivation that assumes that people seek to understand why they succeed or fail.

Authentic assessment. Testing that covers the content that was taught in the manner in which it was taught and that targets specific behaviors that have applicability to advanced courses, other programs of study, or careers.

Authentic problems. Problems encountered in the real world for which the expected solution is uncertain and the task then yields multiple solutions, each with advantages and disadvantages.

Automaticity. Learning a procedure so thoroughly that it can be carried out quickly with little thinking or effort.

Behavioral schemata. Patterns of action or sequences of behavior that the child uses to explore and respond to objects in her environment.

Behavioral setting. The immediate environment in which a behavior occurs.

Behaviorism. A school of thought in psychology whose cardinal tenet is that any conclusion made about human development must be based on scientific observations of overt behavior and the observable events that strengthen and elicit it.

Case study. An intensive study of persons or situations singly or in small numbers.

Categorization. The process by which the mind simplifies information that enters short-term memory.

Causal schemata. Beliefs about the sequential nature of observed data in which effects are attributed to causes.

Centering. The questioning by a member of a group about how that individual will personally benefit from the group; a preoccupation with fairness.

Classical conditioning. The process by which an unconditioned, neutral stimulus and an unconditioned response are paired repeatedly to become a conditioned stimulus that elicits a conditioned response.

Classroom management tradition. An approach emphasizing the organization and management of instructional activities in order to prevent misbehavior.

Clinical method. Research that studies a small group of subjects in everyday, natural settings.

Coaching. An aspect of instruction by which the teacher helps learners master particular skills through the skillful use of practice and prompts.

Coercive power. Leadership based on punishment or coercion.

Cognitive apprenticeship. The notion that learners can best become more skilled at gathering and using knowledge for themselves by observing experts.

Cognitive strategies. General methods of thinking that improve learning across a variety of subject areas.

Cognitive style. The means by which individuals process and think about what they learn.

Commanding stimuli appeal. The use of assertive commands or statements by an instructor to focus learner attention.

Communication disability. An impairment that involves speech, language, vision, or hearing.

Comprehension monitoring. Cognitive strategies that help learners derive meaning from what they read.

Conceptual conflict. The result when our existing beliefs or ways of explaining things don't produce the outcomes we predicted.

Concerns theory. A view that conceptualizes the teacher's growth and development as a process of passing through concerns for self (teacher) to task (teaching) to impact (pupil).

Concrete operational stage. The third of Piaget's cognitive developmental stages, characterized by an understanding of the laws of conservation and a readiness to engage in other mental operations using concrete stimuli.

Conditioned response. In classical conditioning, a response that is elicited by some previously neutral stimulus; occurs by pairing the neutral stimulus with an unconditioned stimulus.

Conditioned stimulus. A stimulus that through the conditioning process has acquired the power to generate a conditioned response.

Congruent communication. Communication that uses statements that are directed at a learner's actions, that reflect an accurate or honest evaluation of learner performance, that help learners believe in themselves and their own abilities, and that attribute learner achievement to internal rather than external factors.

Consequences. Stimuli or events that follow behavior; consequences can be negative or positive.

Constructivism. An approach to learning in which learners are provided the opportunity to construct their own sense of what is being learned by building internal connections or relationships among the ideas and facts being taught.

Content validity. A measure of the degree to which a test covers all the content that was taught in the manner in which it was taught.

Continuous reinforcement schedule. Reinforcement of every occurrence of a behavior.

Control group. The baseline group against whom changes in the experimental group are compared. The experimental group's stimulus is withheld from the control group.

Cooperative learning. A teaching method that uses heterogeneous groups of learners who are responsible for one another's learning with respect to a common goal.

Cooperative learning. The assignment of students of varying abilities and ethnicities and of both genders to small groups with a common goal in which each member has a role.

Correlational study. Research that tries to determine whether a relationship exists between two variables.

Correlation coefficient. A numerical index on a -1.0 to $+1.0$ scale that indicates the degree to which two sets of scores are related.

Criterion-referenced grading. The linking of grades to a standard of mastery or achievement.

Cultural compatibility. The goal of designing instruction to incorporate relevant features of the learners' culture.

Culturally responsive teaching. Instructional methods designed to be compatible with the learning and cognitive styles of a particular ethnic or cultural group.

Decay theory. A theory that holds that information dissolves or dissipates from our working memory unless it is rehearsed.

Declarative knowledge. Verbal information: the facts, concepts, principles, and theories we learn from lectures, studying textbooks, or watching television.

Deficiency/growth needs theory. A theory of motivation that posits that humans have an innate hierarchy of needs that drives all activity.

Deficit model. A view of parent participation that assigns the blame for the lack of participation on parents attitudes, temperament, and conditions.

Dependent variable. The variable that is the presumed effect of an independent variable.

Descriptive research. A means of measuring variables through questionnaires, interviews, or systematic observation, or a combination of these practices.

Developmental stage. A period of development during which a person's physical, mental, or psychological functioning is different from the periods preceding and following it.

Developmental theories. Theoretical approaches for explaining the process of human development. The four major theories are biological, learning, cognitive-developmental, and psychoanalytic.

Direct explanation teaching. A variety of teaching methods that make explicit to learners at the outset of a lesson the academic competencies, strategies, generalizations, or procedures to be taught.

Direct instruction. Instructional methods that present information explicitly through lecturing, questioning, and demonstration. Direct instruction is particularly suited to the acquisition of facts, rules, and action sequences.

Discovery learning. The organization of knowledge around fundamental themes and principles rather than discrete facts.

Discrepancy appeal. The use of novel, unique, or surprising stimuli to focus the attention of learners.

Discrimination training. Reinforcement that occurs only in the presence of a particular stimulus in order for the subject to discriminate the occasions when a reward will occur and when it will not.

Displacement theory. A theory that holds that, once new information enters working memory, existing information is pushed out and replaced by incoming data.

Distancing. Behaviors that challenge authority and leadership to test the limits of group commitments.

Domain-specific knowledge. Knowledge of facts, concepts, and principles pertaining to a specific area or topic.

Drive theory. A theory of motivation that is based on the assumption that all activity is directed toward reducing the tension triggered by needs and drives.

Dual-coding theory. A theory that holds that complex networks of verbal representations and images reside within long-term memory to promote long-term retention.

Ecosystem. Systems and subsystems coexisting in dynamic, mutually dependent relationships.

Education. The varied and informal ways in which children learn the customs, attitudes, beliefs, values, social skills, and other behaviors that they require to be successful members of a family, cultural group, and society. Most such education takes place outside the school.

Educational psychology. A discipline that focuses on theoretical and empirical instructional knowledge.

Elaboration. Associating what you are learning with a particular image or relating old learning to new.

Emotional appeal. A characteristic of an instructional stimulus that draws on the emotional response of learners to focus learner attention.

Empathy. The ability to read someone else's feelings and match them to the observer's own feelings.

Empowerment model. A view of parent participation that involves giving parents both the power and the knowledge to deal successfully with the school system.

Engaged learning time. The amount of time learners spend thinking about, acting on, or working with a learning task.

Equilibrium. The result of accommodation; the restoration of cognitive balance by altering cognitive structures to take into account new data.

Ethnography. A research technique in which the researcher acts as an observer, recorder, and interpreter and makes his or her point of view explicit.

Exosystem. A subsystem beyond the immediate environment of the child that can indirectly influence the behavior of the child.

Expectancy (Pygmalion) effect. Often referred to as a "self-fulfilling prophecy," the correlation between high teacher expectations and high learner achievement and low teacher expectations and low learner achievement.

Experimental group. A group that is given a stimulus (such as a program of instruction) that presumably causes a change in the group members' behavior.

Experimental study. Research in which the independent variable is changed so that its effects on the dependent variable can be seen.

Expert power. The legitimation of an individual's leadership because others perceive that individual as an expert.

Extended-response essay. An essay question that allows the student to determine the length and complexity of a response; it is a good means of assessing communication ability as well as achievement.

Extinction. A procedure that involves identifying and eliminating the specific reinforcer for a particular inappropriate behavior.

Fading. The removal of external learning supports and the simultaneous provision of independent practice to promote transfer.

Field-dependence. A cognitive style that influences learners to perceive complex stimuli in terms of larger patterns and relationships.

Field-independence. A cognitive style that influences learners to perceive complex stimuli in terms of the discrete, individual elements that constitute it.

Flexible-response tests. Tests that measure higher thought processes such as analysis, synthesis, and decision-making behaviors usually through performance-based assessments.

Formal operational stage. The fourth and final of Piaget's developmental stages, characterized by abstract thinking, logical reasoning, and other forms of higher-order conceptualization.

Gender-fair instruction. The use of educational strategies, curriculum materials, and instructor-learner interactions that counteract sex-role stereotypes.

General ability tests. Tests that assume that a single, general trait or aptitude underlies differences in school achievement among learners.

Generalizability. The reproducibility of research results across contexts, settings, and learners.

General knowledge. Knowledge useful for learning across a variety of school tasks.

Gifted and talented. Children and youth who are identified as possessing abilities that offer evidence of high performance in areas such as intelligence, achievement, creativity, and task persistence.

Goal conflicts. Conflicts that arise as a result of learner-teacher or learner-learner disagreement about what should be accomplished in the classroom.

Goals. Educational priorities that focus on the subject matter, societal concerns, and/or learner interests and are used to guide the formation of objectives.

Grade weighting. Assigning different degrees of importance to different performance indicators that are then combined into a grade.

Group. Two or more persons engaged in interactions around a common goal so that each member of the group influences the others.

Group ability tests. Ability tests designed for administration to large groups of learners on one occasion.

Group cohesiveness. The degree to which members of a group have relationships, common goals, and a social structure within that group.

Group conflict. Disruptions that destabilize group relationships, structures, and goals.

Guided practice. Teacher-provided activities used to encourage learners to organize a response to what has been modeled or demonstrated, often with prompts and questions.

Hearing disability. An inability to hear well; may range from mild disability to total deafness.

Heterogeneous grouping. In education, assigning learners to classes or learning groups in a manner that insures that these groups will include a diverse mixture of learners.

Holistic scoring. Estimating the overall quality of a performance by giving a single value that represents a specific category of accomplishment.

Homogeneous grouping. The tracking or ability grouping of learners into instructional clusters that are defined by aptitude as measured by ability tests.

Horizontal relationships. Students' relationships with peers.

Humanistic tradition. An approach to classroom management that emphasizes the critical role of communication and problem solving between teacher and students.

Hyperactivity. A greatly increased rate of activity and/or restlessness.

Hypothesis. A prediction about how the variables in a question are related to one another.

Hypothetico-deductive reasoning. The ability to pose hypotheses and draw conclusions from observations.

Immediate memory. Our information-storage capacity that holds sensory data for less than a second before it is lost or transferred to our working memory.

Impact stage. The stage of teaching when instructors begin to view their learners as individuals with individual needs.

Impulsivity. A failure to stop and think before responding to a task.

Independent practice. The solitary attempt of a learner to master skills.

Independent variable. A variable that is thought to produce a desired effect or outcome.

Index of item difficulty. The appropriateness of an ability test question for its intended audience. It is represented by the proportion of individuals in a test tryout who answered the item correctly.

Index of item discrimination. An ability test question's or task's actual reflection of the overall trait or ability that the test is presumed to measure.

Indirect instruction. Instructional methods best suited for the learning of concepts, patterns, and abstractions. Indirect instruction involves the expression of learner ideas, teacher-mediated discussion, and group problem solving.

Individual ability tests. Ability tests administered by one examiner to one learner at each testing session.

Individualized education plan (IEP). A written educational plan, revised annually, that provides a detailed road map of the kinds of services a child will receive and how those services will be evaluated.

Information-processing model. A model of learning that examines how we learn using the "mind as computer" metaphor.

Instinct theory. An early school of thought about motivation that assumed that individual and collective actions and thoughts were a result of inherited and innate instincts.

Instructional events. Elements of the teaching process that allow learners to acquire and transfer new information and skills.

Instructional management. Two broad components of teaching skill: (1) expertise in planning for instruction and (2) expertise in delivering instruction.

Instructional validity. The belief that tests must be valid for improving instruction and learning.

Intelligence. A global trait signifying an individual's overall ability to adapt to and succeed in his or her environment.

Intentional learners. Students who find their own approaches or systems for achieving educational goals.

Interference theory. A theory that holds that subsequent learning competes with prior learning and interferes with what is contained in working memory.

Intermittent reinforcement schedule. A procedure by which only certain responses are followed by the delivery of a reinforcer.

Interpersonal conflicts. Conflicts between members of a class group over individual needs for affiliation, power, and achievement.

Interval schedule. Delivery of reinforcers after the first response made following a predetermined period of elapsed time.

Intrinsic motivation. Motivation to engage in an activity for its own sake.

Intrinsic reinforcement. A strengthening of behavior that occurs in the absence of any external uses of reinforcers.

IQ–achievement discrepancy. An achievement level different from what would be predicted given a learner's score on an ability test.

Joint cognitive venture. An activity focused on a clear cognitive goal whose various components are carried out by different classroom participants: learner, peers, and teachers.

Keyword method. An elaboration strategy whereby the learner transforms one of two related pieces of information into a keyword familiar to him- or herself to help remember the other piece.

Language acquisition device. A built-in neurological device programmed to pick up the regular features of any language or communication.

Laws of conservation. The understanding that changes in certain properties of an object (e.g., shape) do not change other properties of the object (e.g., mass).

Lead management. Use of expert and referent power to develop self-control and to persuade students to enjoy the satisfaction of doing good work.

Learning disability. Any learning disorder presumed to be the cause of a learner achieving significantly below what his or her IQ predicts.

Learning style. The classroom or environmental conditions under which an individual prefers to learn.

Least restrictive environment. According to Public Law 94-142, the environment that maintains "the greatest degree of freedom, self-determination, dignity, and integrity of body, mind, and spirit for the individual while he or she participates in treatment or receives services."

Least-to-most prompting. Prompting learners with the least intrusive methods before progressing to relatively more intrusive forms of prompting.

Legitimate power. Leadership based on a specific role rather than on the nature of an individual.

Limit testing. Challenges to teacher authority and leadership; the questioning by an individual of how he or she will personally benefit from a group. Often occurs during the storming stage of group development.

Linking mechanisms. Opportunities for interaction between the various systems and subsystems within the family-school environment.

Locus of causality. In attribution theory, a generalized belief about the causes of success and failure of our actions.

Long-term memory. The information storage capacity in which new information is integrated through rehearsal, elaboration, and organization with information that is already known or residing within long-term memory.

Low-profile classroom control. A set of coping strategies and techniques used to stop misbehavior, especially surface behaviors, without disrupting the flow of a lesson.

Macrosystem. The outermost layer of a child's ecosystem, consisting of the larger culture or society in which the exosystem and microsystem exist.

Mainstreaming. An approach to educating learners with developmental disabilities that seeks to maximize opportunities for interaction with nondisabled peers.

Mediation. Thinking that uses symbols to represent objects or events in one's environment.

Mental retardation. A developmental disability characterized by significantly below-average intellectual functioning and significantly below-average adaptive behavior.

Mesosystems. Relationships between systems or linking mechanisms in a child's ecosystem, which are often as important as the events that occur within systems.

Metacognition. Thinking about thinking; the use of cognitive strategies for finding and organizing information and remembering when and where to use them.

Microsystem. The most central layer of a child's ecosystem, including all of the settings and subsystems where the child lives or spends significant amounts of time.

Minority group. A social group that occupies a subordinate position with respect to the society as a whole and that shares a sense of collective identity.

Modeling. Demonstrating what learners are about to learn; the process of being attentive to, remembering, imitating, and being rewarded for imitating specific behaviors.

Multimodal assessment. The evaluation of performance through a variety of forms.

Multiple ability tests. Tests that do not assume that a single trait underlies differences in school achievement between learners and instead measure a number of specific and distinct abilities. These tests assign several separate scores representing different aspects of learning ability.

Natural reinforcers. Reinforcers that occur naturally in the setting where a behavior occurs; also, changes in stimulation due to the behavior itself, such as hitting the correct keys on a piano when trying to play a particular song.

Nature/nurture question. A longstanding debate about the relative importance to development of genetic influences and environmental factors.

Negative reinforcement. A procedure that increases the likelihood of a response being repeated by removing an aversive stimulus immediately following that response.

Normal distribution. A classic distribution of scores in which most scores fall symmetrically around the mean with fewer scores on the upper and lower ends, which makes a frequency distribution of scores look bell-shaped.

Normalization. The principle that learners are entitled to programs that allow them to experience the respect and dignity to which any person in their culture or society is entitled.

Norm crystallization. The convergence of expectations into a shared perspective by the group.

Norm diffusion. The formation of expectations among a group of learners as a result of past individual experiences and expectations.

Norm group. The group of individuals upon whom a test is standardized.

Norm-referenced grading. The assignment of grades or scores based on how one learner's achievement compares with the achievement of other learners.

Norms. Shared expectations among group members regarding how they should think, feel, and behave; the principal regulators of group behavior.

Objectives. Statements that specify the skills learners acquire in order to achieve important goals.

Object permanence. The knowledge that objects that are not currently visible (such as a car that has passed) still exist. This knowledge typically develops when a child has reached 6 months.

Operant conditioning. A type of learning in which the probability or likelihood of a behavior occurring is changed as a result of procedures that follow that behavior.

Operational definition. The description of a variable in the precise manner in which it will be measured or demonstrated.

Operational schemata. Mental operations performed on objects or events, the results of which lead to some logical outcome.

Organization. As a form of information processing, ordering and systematizing new information so that one can remember and use it efficiently.

Parallel distributed processing model. A model of learning that suggests that learners may not always learn in orderly, sequential ways, but instead use sources of information simultaneously to construct their own meanings.

Participation structure. The social structure that governs classroom conversation. The most common form of participation structure is a one-to-one question-and-answer format.

Passive responding. Learner behavior in which the learner receives or waits for information.

Perceived self-efficacy. An appraisal or evaluation that a person makes about his or her personal competence at a particular task; an individual's personal expectations, internal standards, and self-concept.

Percentile rank. Scores that indicate where an individual's score ranks in comparison with others of the same age or grade.

Performance testing. Tests that use direct measures of learning rather than indicators that suggest that learning has taken place.

Portfolio assessment. Assessment of a learner's entire body of work in a defined content area in order to demonstrate the student's growth and achievement.

Positive reinforcement. The condition of administering a stimulus, following a response, that increases the likelihood of that response occurring again.

Pragmatics. The cultural rules of language usage.

Predictive validity. In instruction, the usefulness of a test for predicting how much learners will benefit from some future instructional program; the correlation between a learner's ability before an instructional program and his or her achievement after the program.

Preoperational stage. The second of Piaget's stages of cognitive development; characterized by egocentrism and the increasing ability to mediate, but with a continued dependence on immediate experience.

Primary trait scoring. An analytical scoring technique that requires a test developer to first identify the most salient characteristics or primary traits when observing a product, process, or performance.

Principle of indirect measurement. The assumption that ability can be measured by giving different learners identical tasks under identical conditions and recording how rapidly and skillfully each masters them.

Procedural conflicts. Disagreements between members of a group over classroom rules and routines.

Procedural knowledge. Know-how knowledge: action sequences we use to complete tasks, such as booting a floppy disk or writing an outline.

Project-based learning. An approach to learning that argues that intrinsic motivation is marshaled, generated, and sustained in a learning environment that recognizes the importance of the interrelationships among learning tasks, learner disposition, and teachers.

Prompts. Supplementary or additional aids that teachers use to increase the likelihood that learners will engage in successful practice.

Propositional networks. Extensive networks of interconnected ideas stored in long-term memory that provide representations and images that help us retain information for a long time.

Prosocial behaviors. Intentional, voluntary behaviors intended to help others.

Psychometric approach. A set of beliefs about ability testing that assumes that the effects of traits can be systematically observed and recorded, that repeated observations of the effects of a trait will overcome observational imprecision, that ability is best measured as a quantity rather than as a cognitive process, and that the amount of ability can be established through relative rather than absolute measurement.

Psychophysical appeal. Any variation in the color, size, intensity, or pitch of stimuli in the visual field of learners that results in the learners' making an attending response.

Public Law 94-142. The Education for All Handicapped Children Act of 1975, which guaranteed that all children who needed special education would receive a free individualized education plan, assured instructional fairness for learners with disabilities, established procedural due process, and provided federal funding to meet the provisions of the law.

Punisher. A stimulus received following a response that decreases the likelihood that the response will happen again.

Punishment. In operant conditioning, an action taken following a response that decreases the likelihood that the response will happen again.

Qualitative item analysis. The process by which test developers check questions, tasks, and directions for clarity, style, bias, and conciseness.

Qualitative research. Research conducted to describe or create hypotheses about the relationship between independent and dependent variables.

Quantitative item analysis. The process by which test developers examine each test question to determine whether they are of appropriate difficulty and whether each item reflects the overall trait or ability that the test is presumed to measure.

Quantitative research. Research conducted to test previously stated relationships between independent and dependent variables.

Randomization. A process to help ensure experimental generalizability by giving large numbers of individuals an equal opportunity to be included in a study in either the experimental or the control group.

Ratio schedule. Application of reinforcers after a set number of responses, such as every third response.

Reciprocal teaching. Teaching that provides alternative representations or elaborations of the content to be learned through the vehicle of group discussion.

Redundancy principle. The assumption that conclusions about a learner's abilities can be accurately measured by observing the learner using these abilities in a variety of circumstances and contexts.

Referent power. Leadership earned because of a perception of an individual's trustworthiness, fairness, and concern for members of the group.

Regular Education Initiative (REI). The mainstreaming of learners with disabilities into regular classrooms where those learners receive individualized services.

Rehearsal. Repeating to yourself what you are reading or hearing.

Reinforcement. In operant conditioning, actions taken following a response that increase the likelihood that the response will occur again. Reinforcement can be both positive and negative.

Reliability. The degree to which a test produces consistent scores on repeated testings.

Response alternatives. The answer choices portion of a multiple-choice question.

Restricted-response essay. An essay that poses a specific problem for which the student must recall proper information, organize it in a suitable manner, derive a defensible conclusion, and express it according to specific criteria.

Restricted-response tests. Assessment methods that limit the range of possible answers, such as true-false or multiple-choice tests, and are usually intended to test knowledge, comprehension, and application behaviors.

Reward power. Leadership based on rewards or benefits that an individual can give to members of a group.

Routine. A procedure organized around a particular time, concept, or place that helps guide learners through the day.

Rubrics. Scoring standards composed of model answers that are used to score performance tests.

Rules. General statements defining acceptable and unacceptable behaviors.

Schedule of reinforcement. A rule for when reinforcers will be given following performance of a desired behavior.

Schema of attachment. Positive cognitive structure influencing vertical relationships.

Schemata. Elaborate cognitive structures or networks made up of ideas and concepts that are used to interpret one's environment and guide behavior.

Schema theory. Cognitive structures of integrated units that organize large amounts of information.

Schooling. Learning that takes place within the special academic context and culture of formal educational structures, primarily through words, processes, and questions.

Self-concept. A schema that an individual holds toward him- or herself.

Self-determination theory. An approach that holds that an attitude of determination is the foundation for motivated behavior.

Self-directed instruction. An instructional method that places much of the responsibility for learning on the learner by using metacognition, subvocal rehearsal, guided practice, and self-evaluation.

Self-efficacy theory. An approach to motivation that emphasizes an individual's personal expectations, internal standards, and self-concept.

Self-esteem. A global evaluation or judgment of one's worth.

Self-fulfilling prophecy. The correlation that has been observed between expectations and performance.

Sensorimotor stage. The first of Piaget's stages of cognitive development, characterized initially by only reflex actions but later by the learning of object permanence and the beginnings of internal cognitive mediation.

Sex-role stereotypes. The overextension of sex roles as well as the rigid application of sex roles to individuals without taking personal qualities into account.

Situated learning. The teaching of cognitive and metacognitive skills specific to an academic discipline.

Situational cues. Stimuli in the learner's behavioral environment that predispose the learner to behave in a certain manner.

Social cognition. How one thinks and becomes concerned about other people's actions and feelings.

Social needs. Needs for affiliation, power, and achievement that are either not present or not as strong outside a group context.

Social organization. The relationships—roles, functions, and common goals—between adults and children during learning.

Social structure. Roles and functions that members of a group assume.

Sociolinguistics. The study of how cultural groups differ in the courtesies and conventions of language rather than in the grammatical structure of what is said; the social conversation of speech.

Stage of group formation. In social psychology, a period of group development in which the concerns of the group and functioning of the group are different from the periods preceding and following.

Stages of identity. Discrete periods of personality development during which the individual confronts an identity crisis he or she must overcome to pass successfully to the next stage.

Standard deviation. A measurement of variability and clustering around a mean.

Standardization. The administration of a test to all persons in a defined group in the same way under the same conditions.

Standard scores. Scores that indicate where a particular learner's raw score ranks among the scores of other learners in the norming group.

Stem. The statement portion of a multiple-choice question.

Stimulus control. In operant conditioning, the control of the occurrence of a response by a dependable signal or cue, which indicates that a reinforcer will occur if the correct response is emitted.

Structuring. Getting learners ready to learn by selecting, organizing, and previewing the content to be presented.

Surface behaviors. Normal developmental behaviors children find themselves doing when confined to a small space with large numbers of other children.

Survival stage. The first stage of teaching during which beginning teachers focus primarily on their own well-being rather than on their learners or the process of teaching.

Symbolic schemata. The mental representations of objects, events, and experiences without the need to perform some type of action on them.

Systems-ecological perspective. A view of child development that considers the family, school, and peer group as a type of social ecosystem in which each part is dependent on and affected by the other parts.

Task analysis. A process for identifying the behavioral components of more complex skills and arranging them in a hierarchical sequence.

Task persistence. An attribute usually determined by such characteristics as a learner's ability to concentrate on detail, impose high standards on herself or himself, persist in achieving personal goals, evaluate personal performance, and devote a high level of energy to academic tasks.

Task stage. The second stage of teaching in which a teacher's concerns focus on improving his or her teaching skills and mastering the content being taught.

Test blueprint. A table used to identify the type of behavior and content to be tested.

Test fairness. A pattern of evaluation in which the teacher provides an authentic assessment of what has been taught, motivates learners toward higher levels of effort, is sensitive to learner differences, accurately communicates performance and progress to learners and other parties, and efficiently uses teacher and learner time and effort.

Testing constraints. The amount of time, reference material, degree of help (if any) from others, specialized equipment, prior knowledge of the task, and scoring criteria that test-takers can have during a performance assessment.

Test-retest reliability. The correlation of the scores of one group of learners taken on one occasion with the scores of the same group of learners taken on another occasion.

Test validity. The capacity of a test to measure what it says it is measuring.

Tracking. Grouping learners into different classes according to scores on standardized tests of learning ability.

Transfer of learning. The process whereby skills learned in one situation or under one set of conditions are demonstrated in a different situation or under a different set of conditions.

Unconditioned response. A reaction that automatically follows an unconditioned stimulus.

Unconditioned stimulus. A stimulus that naturally or automatically elicits an unconditioned response.

Validity. The degree to which a test measures what the test is intended to measure.

Variables. Variations in conditions in a given situation.

Vertical relationships. Students' relationships with adults, such as parents and teachers.

Visual disability. An inability to see well that cannot be corrected with eyeglasses.

Wait-time 1. The amount of time a teacher gives a learner to respond to a question.

Wait-time 2. The interval of time after a learner's response before the teacher speaks.

Working memory. The information storage capacity that receives data from immediate memory and holds them for about 10 to 20 seconds.

Zone of proximal development. Vygotsky's metaphor describing the range of skills and abilities bounded by what a learner can do independently and what a learner needs adult assistance in performing.

References

Aber, J. L., & Allen, J. (1987). The effects of maltreatment on young children's socioemotional development: An attachment theory perspective. *Developmental Psychology, 23,* 406–414.

Abramson, L. Y., Seligman, M.E.P., & Teasdale, J. (1978). Learned helplessness in humans: Critique and reformulation. *Journal of Abnormal Psychology, 87,* 49–74.

Achenbach, T. M. (1982). *Developmental psychology.* New York: Wiley.

Achenbach, T. M. (1990). Conceptualization of developmental psychopathology. In M. Lewis & S. M. Miller (Eds.), *Handbook of developmental psychopathology* (pp. 3–14). New York: Plenum.

Achenbach, T. M., & Edelbrock, C. (1983). *Manual for the child behavior checklist and revised child behavior profile.* Burlington, VT: University of Vermont Department of Psychiatry.

Ainsworth, M.D.S. (1972). Attachment and dependency: A comparison. In J. L. Gewirtz (Ed.), *Attachment and dependency* (pp. 97–138). Washington, DC: Winston.

Ainsworth, M.D.S. (1982). Attachment: Retrospect and prospect. In C. M. Parks & J. Stevenson-Hinde (Eds.), *The place of attachment in human behavior* (pp. 3–30). New York: Basic Books.

Ainsworth, M.D.S. (1989). Attachments beyond infancy. *American Psychologist, 44,* 709–716.

Alberto, P., & Troutman, A. (1986). *Applied behavior analysis for teachers: Influencing student performance* (2nd ed.). Columbus, OH: Merrill.

Allison, P. D., & Furstenberg, F. F., Jr. (1989). How marital dissolution affects children: Variations by age and sex. *Developmental Psychology, 25,* 540–549.

Allport, G. (1924). *Social psychology.* Boston: Houghton Mifflin.

Allport G. (1955). *Becoming: Basic considerations for a psychology of personality.* New Haven: Yale University Press.

American Psychiatric Association. (1994). *Diagnostic and statistical manual for mental disorders* (4th ed.). Washington, DC: Author.

Ames, C. (1992). Classrooms: Goals, structures and student motivation. *Journal of Educational Psychology, 84,* 261–271.

Ames, C., & Ames, R. (1984). Goal structures and motivation. *The Elementary School Journal, 85,* 39–52.

Anderegg, M. L., & Vergason, G. A. (1988). An analysis of one of the cornerstones of the regular education initiative. *Focus on Exceptional Children, 20*(8), 1–8.

Anderson, C. W. (1991). Policy implications of research on science teaching and teachers' knowledge. In M. M. Kennedy (Ed.), *Teaching academic subjects to diverse learners.* New York: Teachers College Press.

Anderson, C. W., & Roth, J. R. (1989). Teaching for meaningful and self-regulated learning of science. In J. Brophy (Ed.), *Teaching for meaningful understanding and self-regulated learning* (pp. 265–309). Greenwich, CT: JAI.

Anderson, J. R. (1983). *The architecture of cognition.* Cambridge, MA: Harvard University Press.

Anderson, M. G. (1992). The use of selected theater rehearsal technique activities with African-American adolescents labeled "behaviorally disordered." *Exceptional Children, 59,* 132–140.

Anderson, R. C., & Pearson, P. D. (1984). A schema-theoretic view of basic processes in reading. In P. D. Pearson (Ed.), *Handbook of reading research.* New York: Longman.

Applebee, A. N. (1984). *Contexts for learning to write.* Norwood, NJ: Ablex.

Argyus, C. (1972). *Intervention, theory and method: A behavioral science view.* Reading, MA: Addison-Wesley.

Arlin, P. K. (1975). Cognitive development in adulthood: A fifth stage? *Developmental Psychology, 11,* 602–606.

Arlin, P. K. (1977). Piagetian operations in problem solving. *Developmental Psychology, 13,* 297–298.

ASCD Update. (1991, September). John O'Neil (Ed.), *The complex art of motivating students.* Alexandria, VA: Association for Supervision and Curriculum Development.

ASCD Update. (1992, February). John O'Neil (Ed.), Alexandria, VA: Association for Supervision and Curriculum Development.

Atkinson, J. W. (1957). Motivational determinants of risk-taking behavior. *Psychological Review, 64,* 359–372.

Atkinson, J. W. (1964). *An introduction to motivation.* Princeton, NJ: Van Nostrand Reinhold.

Atkinson, M. L. (1984). Computer-assisted instruction: Current state of the art. *Computers in the Schools, 1,* 91–99.

Atkinson, R. C. (1968). Computerized instruction and the learning process. *American Psychologist, 23,* 225–239.

Attie, I., Brooks-Gunn, J., & Petersen, A.C. (1990). A developmental perspective on eating disorders and eating problems. In M. Lewis & S. M. Miller (Eds.), *Handbook of developmental psychopathology* (pp. 409–420). New York: Plenum.

Atwell, N. (1987). *In the middle: Reading, writing, and learning from adolescents.* Portsmouth, NH: Heinemann.

Au, K. H., & Mason, J. M. (1981). Social organizational factors in learning to read: The balance of rights hypothesis. *Reading Research Quarterly, 17*(1), 115–152.

Ausubel, D. P. (1960). The use of advanced organizers in the learning and retention of meaningful verbal material. *Journal of Educational Psychology, 51,* 267–272.

Ausubel, D. P. (1968). *Educational psychology: A cognitive view.* New York: Holt, Rinehart & Winston.

Ausubel, D. P. (1977). The facilitation of meaningful verbal learning in the classroom. *Educational Psychologist, 12,* 162–178.

Ausubel, D. P., & Robinson, F. G. (1969). *School learning: An introduction to educational psychology.* New York: Holt, Rinehart & Winston.

Bachrach, S. (1966). *Ethiopian folk tales.* Oxford: Oxford University Press.

Backman, E. W., & Secord, P. F. (1968). *A social psychology of education.* New York: Harcourt, Brace & World.

Baer, D. M., & Wolf, M. M. (1970). The entry in natural communities of reinforcement. In R. Ulrich, T. Stachnik, & J. Mabry (Eds.), *Control of human behavior: Vol. 2* (pp. 319–324). Glenview, IL: Scott, Foresman.

Baer, D. M., Wolf, M. M., & Risley, T. R. (1968). Some current dimensions of applied behavior analysis. *Journal of Applied Behavior Analysis, 1,* 91–97.

Bailey, S. M. (1993). The current status of gender-equity research in American schools. *Educational Psychologist, 28*(4), 321–339.

Baillargeon, R. (1987). Object permanence in 3½ and 4½-month-old infants in a nonsearch AB task. *Developmental Psychology, 23,* 655–664.

Ball, D. L. (1991). Teaching mathematics for understanding: What do teachers need to know about subject matter? In M. M. Kennedy (Ed.), *Teaching academic subjects to diverse learners* (pp. 63–83). New York: Teachers College Press.

Bandura, A. (1969). *Principles of behavior modification.* New York: Henry Holt.

Bandura, A. (1973). *Aggression: A social learning analysis.* Englewood Cliffs, NJ: Prentice-Hall.

Bandura, A. (1977a). Self-efficacy: Toward a unified theory of behavioral change. *Psychological Review, 84,* 191–215.

Bandura, A. (1977b). *Social learning theory.* Englewood Cliffs, NJ: Prentice-Hall.

Bandura, A. (1982a). The self and mechanisms of agency. In J. Suls (Ed.), *Psychological perspectives on the self: Vol. 1* (pp. 3–40). Hillsdale, NJ: Lawrence Erlbaum.

Bandura, A. (1982b). Self-efficacy mechanism in human agency. *American Psychologist, 37,* 122–147.

Bandura, A. (1986). *Social foundations of thought and action: A social cognitive theory.* Englewood Cliffs, NJ: Prentice-Hall.

Bandura, A. (1988). Self-regulation of motivation and action through goal systems. In V. Hamilton, C. H. Bower, & N. D. Frijda (Eds.), *Cognitive perspectives on emotion and motivation* (pp. 37–61). Dordrecht, The Netherlands: Kluwer.

Bangert, R., Kulik, J., & Kulik, C. (1983). Individualized systems of instruction in secondary schools. *Review of Educational Research, 53,* 143–158.

Barahal, R., Waterman, J., & Martin, H. (1982). The social-cognitive development of abused children. *Journal of Consulting and Clinical Psychology, 49,* 508–516.

Baratz, S. S., & Baratz, J. C. (1970). Early childhood intervention: The social science base of institutional racism. *Harvard Educational Review, 40,* 29–50.

Barkley, R. A. (1989). The problem of stimulus control and rule governed behavior in children with attention deficit disorder with hyperactivity. In J. Swanson & L. Bloomingdale (Eds.), *Research on attention deficit disorders.* New York: Pergamon.

Barkley, R. A. (1990). Attention deficit disorders: History, definition and diagnosis. In M. Lewis & S. M. Miller (Eds.), *Handbook of developmental psychopathology* (pp. 65–76). New York: Plenum.

Barkley, R. A., & Cunningham, C. (1979). Stimulant drugs and activity level in hyperactive children. *American Journal of Orthopsychiatry, 49,* 491–499.

Barkley, R. A., Fisher, M., Newby, R., & Breen, M. (1988). Development of a multi-method protocol for assessing stimulant drug responding in ADHD children. *Journal of Clinical Child Psychology, 3,* 231–244.

Barrel, J. (1991). *Teaching for thoughtfulness.* New York: Longman.

Bar-Tal, D. (1979). Interactions of teachers and pupils. In I. H. Frieze, D. Bar-Tal, & J. S. Carroll (Eds.), *New approaches to social problems: Applications of attribution theory* (pp. 344–355). San Francisco: Jossey-Bass.

Bartlett, F. C. (1932). *Remembering: A study in experimental and social psychology.* Cambridge, UK: Cambridge University Press.

Bartz, K., & Levine, E. (1978). Child rearing by black parents: A description and comparison to Anglo and Chicano parents. *Journal of Marriage and the Family, 40,* 709–719.

Baxter, G., Shavelson, S. S., Goldman, S., & Pine, J. (1992). Procedure based scoring for hands-on science assessment. *Journal of Educational Measurement, 29*(1), 1–17.

Bean, T. W., & Steenwyck, F. L. (1984). The effect of three forms of summarization instruction on sixth graders' summary writing and comprehension. *Journal of Reading Behavior, 16,* 297–306.

Beane, J. A. (1991). Sorting out the self-esteem controversy. *Educational Leadership, 49,* 25–30.

Bear, T., Schenk, S., & Buller, L. (1992/1993, December/January). Supporting victims of child abuse. *Educational Leadership, 50,* 42–47.

Becher, R. M. (1983). *Problems and practices of parent-teacher school relationships and parent involvement.* Unpublished manuscript, University of Illinois–Urbana.

Becher, R. M. (1984). *Parent involvement: A review of research and principles of successful practice.* Washington, DC: National Institute of Education.

Bechtel, W. & Abrahamsen, A. (1991). *Connectionism in the mind.* Cambridge, MA: Basil Blackwell.

Bee, H. (1995). *The developing child* (7th ed.). New York: HarperCollins.

Benard, B. (1993). Fostering resiliency in kids. *Educational Leadership, 51*(3), 44–48.

Benedict, R. (1959). *Patterns of culture.* Boston: Houghton Mifflin.

Bennett, C. I. (1990). *Comprehensive multicultural education: Theory and practice* (2nd ed.). Needham, MA: Allyn & Bacon.

Bereiter, C. (1990). Aspects of an educational learning theory. *Review of Educational Research, 60,* 603–624.

Bereiter, C., & Engelmann, S. (1966). *Teaching disadvantaged children in the preschool.* Englewood Cliffs, NJ: Prentice-Hall.

Bereiter, C., & Scardamalia, M. (1989). Intentional learning as a goal of instruction. In L. B. Resnick (Ed.), *Knowing, learning, and instruction: Essays in honor of Robert Glaser* (pp. 361–392). Hillsdale, NJ: Lawrence Erlbaum.

Berg, C. A., & Claugh, M. (1991). Hunter lesson design: The wrong one for science teaching. *Educational Leadership, 48*(4), 73–76.

Bergan, J. R., & Dunn, J. A. (1976). *Psychology and education: A science for instruction.* New York: Wiley.

Berger, E. H. (1991). Parent involvement: Yesterday and today. *The Elementary School Journal, 91*(3), 209–220.

Berk, L. E. (1993). *Infants, children and adolescents.* Boston: Allyn & Bacon.

Berliner, D. (1986). The pursuit of the expert pedagogue. *Educational Researcher, 15* (7), 5–13.

Berliner, D. (1988). *The development of expertise in pedagogy.* Washington, DC: American Association of College for Teacher Education.

Bernard, L. L. (1924). *Instinct.* New York: Holt, Rinehart & Winston.

Bialystok, E. (1986). Factors in the growth of linguistic awareness. *Child Development, 57,* 498–510.

Bijstra, J., van Geert, P., & Jackson, S. (1989). Conservation and the appearance-reality distinction: What do children really know and what do they answer? *British Journal of Developmental Psychology, 7,* 43–53.

Billings, A. G., & Moos, R. H. (1983). Comparisons of children of depressed and nondepressed parents: A social environmental perspective. *Journal of Abnormal Child Psychology, 14,* 463–486.

Billings, A. G., & Moos, R. H. (1985). Children of parents with unipolar depression: A controlled 1-year follow-up. *Journal of Abnormal Child Psychology, 14,* 149–166.

Binet, A., & Simon, T. (1916). *The development of intelligence in children* (E. S. Kite, Trans.). Baltimore: Williams & Wilkins.

Bjorklund, D. F. (1989). *Cognitive development.* Monterey, CA: Brooks/Cole.

Blank, S. S., & Covington, M. (1965). Inducing children to ask questions in problem solving. *Journal of Educational Research, 59*(1), 21–27.

Bloom, B. (1981). *All our children learning.* New York: Pergamon.

Bloom, B. S. (1985). *Developing talent in young people.* New York: Ballantine Books.

Bloom, B., Englehart, M., Hill, W., Furst, E., & Krathwohl, D. (1956). *Taxonomy of educational objectives. The classification of educational goals. Handbook I: Cognitive domain.* New York: Longman Green.

Bloom, L. (1973). *One word at a time.* The Hague: Mouton.

Blumberg, E., Epstein, M., MacDonald, W., & Mullis, L. (1986). *A pilot study of higher order thinking skills assessment techniques in science and mathematics.* Final Report. Princeton, NJ: National Assessment of Educational Process.

Blumenfeld, P. C. (1992). Classroom learning and motivation: Clarifying and expanding goal theory. *Journal of Educational Psychology, 84*(3), 272–281.

Blumenfeld, P. C., Soloway, E., Marx, R. W., Krajcik, J. S., Guzdial, M., & Palincsar, A. (1991). Motivation project-based learning: Sustaining the doing, supporting the learning. *Educational Psychologist, 26,* 369–398.

Bohannon, J. N., III, & Warren-Leubecker, A. (1989). Theoretical approaches to language acquisition. In J. Berko Gleason (Ed.), *The development of language* (2nd ed., pp. 167–223). Columbus, OH: Merrill.

Bombeck, E. (1978). *At wit's end.* New York: McGraw-Hill.

Borich, G. (1993). *Clearly outstanding: Making each day count in your classroom.* Needham, MA: Allyn & Bacon.

Borich, G. (1994). *Observation skills for effective teaching* (2nd ed.). Columbus, OH: Merrill.

Borich, G. (1995). *Becoming a teacher: An inquiring dialogue for the beginning teacher.* Washington, DC/London: Falmer Press Ltd.

Borich, G. (1996). *Effective teaching methods* (3rd ed.). New York: Merrill.

Bower, T.G.R., & Wishart, J. G. (1972). The effects of motor skill on object permanence. *Cognition, 1,* 165–172.

Bowers, C. A., & Flinders, D. J. (1990). *Responsive teaching: An ecological approach to classroom patterns of language, culture and thought.* New York: Teachers College Press.

Bowlby, J. (1969). *Attachment and loss: Vol. 1. Attachment.* New York: Basic Books.

Bowlby, J. (1973). *Attachment and loss: Vol. 2. Separation, anxiety and anger.* New York: Basic Books.

Bowlby, J. (1980). *Attachment and loss: Vol. 3. Loss.* New York: Basic Books.

Bowlby, J. (1988). Developmental psychiatry comes of age. *The American Journal of Psychiatry, 145,* 1–10.

Boyer, E. L. (1993, March 27). *Making connections.* Invited address to Association for Supervision and Curriculum Development, Washington, DC.

Brandenberg, N. A., Freedman, R. M., & Silver, S. E. (1990). The epidemiology of childhood psychiatric disorders: Prevalence findings from recent studies. *Journal of the American Academy of Child and Adolescent Psychiatry, 29,* 76–83.

Brandt, R. (1992). Reconsidering our commitments. *Educational Leadership, 50,* 2–5.

Bransford, J. D., & Steen B. (1984). *The IDEAL problem solver.* New York: Freeman.

Brantner, J. B., & Doherty, M. A. (1983). A review of timeout: A conceptual and methodological analyses. In S. Axelrod & J. Apsche (Eds.), *The effects of punishment on human behavior* (pp. 87–132). New York: Academic Press.

Braswell, L., & Bloomquist, M. L. (1991). *Cognitive-behavioral therapy with ADHD children: Child, family and school intervention.* New York: Guilford Press.

Bronfenbrenner, U. (1979). *The ecology of human development.* Cambridge, MA: Harvard University Press.

Bronfenbrenner, U. (1989). Ecological systems theory. In R. Vasta (Ed.), *Annals of child development: Vol. 6* (pp. 187–251). Greenwich, CT: JAI.

Brooks, J. G., & Brooks, M. G. (1993). *The case for constructivist classrooms.* Alexandria, VA: Association for Supervision and Curriculum Development.

Brophy, J. (1986). Classroom organization and management. In D. Smith (Ed.), *Essential knowledge for beginning education.*

Washington, DC: American Association of Colleges for Teacher Education.

Brophy, J. E. (1988). Research linking teacher behavior to student achievement: Potential implications for instruction of Chapter 1 students. *Educational Psychologist, 23*(3), 275–276.

Brophy, J. (1992). Probing the subtleties of subject-matter teaching. *Educational Leadership, 49*(7), 4–8.

Brophy, J., & Good, T. (1986). Teacher behavior and student achievement. In M. C. Wittrock (Ed.), *Handbook of research on teaching* (3rd ed., pp. 328–375). New York: Macmillan.

Brown, A. L. (1980). Metacognitive development and reading. In R. J. Spiro, B. C. Bruce, & W. F. Brewer (Eds.), *Theoretical issues in reading comprehension: Perspectives from cognitive psychology, linguistics, artificial intelligence, and education* (pp. 453–481). Hillsdale, NJ: Lawrence Erlbaum.

Brown, A. L., Bransford, J. D., Ferrara, R. A., & Campione, J. C. (1983). Learning, remembering, and understanding. In J. H. Flavell & E. M. Markman (Eds.), *Handbook of child psychology: Vol. III, Cognitive development* (pp. 77–166). New York: Wiley.

Brown, A. L., & Campione, J. C. (1986). Psychological theory and the study of learning disabilities. *American Psychologist, 41* (10), 1059–1068.

Brown, A. L., & Palincsar, A. S. (1989). Guided cooperative learning and individual knowledge acquisition. In L. B. Resnick (Ed.), *Knowing, learning, and instruction: Essays in honor of Robert Glaser* (pp. 393–452). Hillsdale, NJ: Lawrence Erlbaum.

Browne, D. A. (1984). WISC-R scoring patterns among Native Americans of the northern plains. *White Cloud Journal, 3,* 3–16.

Bruner, J. S. (1960). *The process of education.* Cambridge, MA: Harvard University Press.

Bruner, J. S. (1961). The art of discovery. *Harvard Educational Review, 31,* 21–32.

Bruner, J. S. (1966). *Toward a theory of instruction.* New York: Norton.

Buckley, S. (1987). Attaining basic educational skills: Reading, writing and numbers. In D. Lane & B. Stratford (Eds.), *Current approaches to Down's syndrome* (pp. 315–343). East Sussex, England: Holt, Rinehart & Winston.

Bullough, R. V. (1989). *First-year teacher: A case study.* New York: Teachers College Press.

Burden, P. (1986). Teacher development: Implications for teacher education. In J. Raths and L. Katz (Eds.), *Advances in teacher education: vol. 2.* Norwood, NJ: Ablex.

Burke, P., & Puig-Antich, J. (1990). Psychobiology of childhood depression. In M. Lewis & S. M. Miller (Eds.), *Handbook of developmental psychopathology* (pp. 327–340). New York: Plenum.

Burkell, J., Schneider, B., & Pressley, M. (1990). Mathematics. In M. Pressley & Associates, *Cognitive strategy instruction that really improves children's academic performance* (pp. 147–177). Cambridge, MA: Brookline Books.

Buss, A. (1989). Temperaments as personality traits. In G. A. Kohnstamm, J. E. Bates, & M. K. Rothbart (Eds.), *Temperament in childhood* (pp. 49–58), Chichester, England: Wiley.

Buss, A. H., & Plomin, R. (1986). The EAS approach to temperament. In R. Plomin & J. Dunn (Eds.), *The study of temperament: Changes, continuities, and challenges* (pp. 67–80). Hillsdale, NJ: Lawrence Erlbaum.

Butterfield, R. A., Demas, E. S., Grant, G. W., May, P. S., & Perez, A. L. (1979). A multicultural analysis of the popular basal reading series in the International Year of the Child. *Journal of Negro Education, 57,* 382–389.

Calderhead, J., & Robson, M. (1991). Images of teaching: Student teachers' early conceptions of classroom practice. *Teaching & Teacher Education, 7,* 1–8.

Calonico, J., & Calonico, B. (1972). Classroom interaction: A sociological approach. *Journal of Educational Research, 66,* 165–169.

Canter, L. (1989). *Assertive discipline for secondary teachers.* Santa Monica, CA: Canter and Associates.

Cantwell, D. P. (1990). Depression across the early life span. In M. Lewis & S. M. Miller (Eds.), *Handbook of developmental psychopathology* (pp. 293–310). New York: Plenum.

Carbo, M. (1983). Research in reading and learning style: Implications for exceptional children. *Exceptional Children, 49*(6), 486–494.

Carey, W. B. (1981). The importance of temperament-environment interaction for child health and development. In M. Lewis & L. A. Rosenblum (Eds.), *The uncommon child* (pp. 31–56). New York: Plenum.

Carlberg, C., & Kavale, K. (1980). The efficacy of special versus regular class placement for exceptional children: A meta-analysis. *Journal of Special Education, 14,* 295–309.

Carlson, C. (1992). Single parenting and stepparenting: Problems, issues and interventions. In M. J. Fine & C. Carlson (Eds.), *The Handbook of family-school intervention: A systems perspective* (pp. 188–214). Needham, MA: Allyn & Bacon.

Carnine, D. W. (1976). Effects of two teachers' presentation rates on off-task behavior, answering correctly, and participation. *Journal of Applied Behavior Analysis, 9,* 199–206.

Carnine, D. W. (1983). Government discrimination against effective educational practices. *Proceedings of the Subcommittee on Human Resources Hearing on Follow Through Amendments of 1983.* Washington, DC: U.S. Government Printing Office.

Carnine, D. W., & Fink, W. T. (1978). Increasing the rate of presentation and use of signals in elementary classroom teachers. *Journal of Applied Behavior Analysis, 11,* 35–46.

Carr, E. G., & Durand, V. M. (1985). Reducing behavior problems through functional communication training. *Journal of Applied Behavior Analysis, 18,* 111–126.

Carroll, J. B., & Horn, J. L (1981). On the scientific bases of ability testing. *American Psychologist, 36*(10), 1012–1020.

Carter, K., Cushing, K., Sabers, D., Stein, P., & Berliner, D. (1988). Expert-novice differences in perceiving and processing visual classroom information. *Journal of Teacher Education, 39,* 25–31.

Carter, K., Sabers, D., Cushing, K., Pinnegar, S., & Berliner, D. (1987). Processing and using information about students: A study of expert, novice, and postulant teachers. *Teaching & Teacher Education, 3,* 147–157.

Case, A. D. (1992). The special education rescue: A case for systems thinking. *Educational Leadership, 50*(2), 32–34.

Case, R. (1985). *Intellectual development: birth to adulthood.* Orlando: Academic Press.

Case, R. (1992). Neo-Piagetian theories of intellectual development. In H. Beilin & P. B. Pufall (Eds.), *Piaget's theory: Prospects and possibilities.* Hillsdale, NJ: Lawrence Erlbaum.

Cassidy, J., & Asher, S. R. (1992). Loneliness and peer relations in young children. *Child Development, 63,* 350–365.

Ceci, S. J., & Liker, J. K. (1986). A day at the races: A study of IQ, expertise, and cognitive complexity. *Journal of Experimental Psychology: General, 115,* 255–266.

Chadsey-Rusch, J. (1991). Communication training. In J. L. Matson & J. A. Mulick (Eds.), *Handbook of mental retardation* (2nd ed., pp. 424–435). New York: Pergamon.

Chandler, J., Argyris, D., Barnes, W., Goodman, I., & Snow, C. (1986). Parents as teachers: Observations of low-income parents and children in homework-like tasks. In B. Schieflin & P. Gilmore (Eds.), *Ethnographic studies of learning.* Norwood, NJ: Ablex.

Chandler, M., Fritz, A. S., & Hala, S. (1989). Small-scale deceit: Deception as a marker of two-, three-, and four-year-olds' early theories of mind. *Child Development, 60,* 1263–1277.

Chaukin, N. F., & Williams, D. L., Jr. (1985). *Parent involvement in education project. Executive summary of the final report.* Austin, TX: Southwest Educational Development Lab. (ERIC Document Reproduction Service No. ED 266874)

Chi, M. T. H. (1978). Knowledge structure and memory development. In R. S. Siegler (Ed.), *Children's thinking: What develops?* (pp. 73–96). Hillsdale, NJ: Lawrence Erlbaum.

Chi, M. T. H., Glaser, R., & Farr, M. J. (1988). *The nature of expertise.* Hillsdale, NJ: Lawrence Erlbaum.

Chomsky, N. (1965). *Aspects of a theory of syntax.* Cambridge, MA: MIT Press.

Chomsky, N. (1975). *Reflections on language.* New York: Pantheon.

Chomsky, N. (1986). *Knowledge of language: Its nature, origin and use.* New York: Praeger.

Chomsky, N. (1988). *Language and problems of knowledge.* Cambridge, MA: MIT Press.

Christenson, S. L., & Conoley, J. C. (1993). *Home-school collaboration: Enhancing children's academic and social competence.* Silver Spring, MD: National Association of School Psychologists.

Christenson, S. L., Rounds, T., & Franklin, M. J. (1992). Home-school collaboration: Effects, issues and opportunities. In S. L. Christenson & J. C. Conoley (Eds.), *Home-school collaboration: Enhancing children's academic and social competence.* Silver Spring, MD: National Association of School Psychologists.

Cicchetti, D., Carlson, V., Braunwald, K., & Aber, J. L. (1987). The Harvard child maltreatment project: A context for research on the sequel of child maltreatment. In R. Gelles & J. Lancaster (Eds.), *Research in child abuse: Biosocial perspectives* (pp. 277–298). New York: Aldine.

Cicchetti, D., & Olsen, K. (1990). The developmental psychopathology of child maltreatment. In M. Lewis & S. M. Miller (Eds.), *Handbook of developmental psychopathology* (pp. 261–280). New York: Plenum.

Cipiani, E. (1990). The communicative function hypothesis: An operant behavior perspective. *Journal of Behavior Therapy and Experimental Psychiatry, 21*(4), 239–247.

Cipiani, E. (1991). Educational classification and placement. In J. L. Matson & J. A. Mulick (Eds.), *Handbook of mental retardation* (2nd ed., pp. 181–194). New York: Pergamon.

Clark, C., & Peterson, P. (1986). Teachers' thought processes. In M. R. Wittrock (Ed.), *Handbook of research on teaching* (3rd ed., pp. 255–296). New York: Macmillan.

Clark, M. L. (1991). Social identity, peer relations and academic competence of African-American adolescents. *Education and Urban Society, 24,* 41–52.

Clark, R. M. (1983). *Family life and school achievement: Why poor black children succeed or fail.* Chicago: University of Chicago Press.

Cochran, M. (1987). The parental empowerment process: Building on family strengths. *Equity and Choice, 4*(1), 9–23.

Cochran, M., & Dean, C. (1991). Home-school relations and the empowerment process. *Elementary School Journal, 91,* 261–270.

Coffman, W. E. (1972). On the reliability of ratings of essay examinations. *NCME Reports on Measurement in Education, 3*(3), 1–4.

Cohen, E. G. (1984). Talking and working together: Status, interaction and learning. In P. Peterson, L. C. Wilkinson, & M. Halleman (Eds.), *The social context of instruction: Group organization and group processes.* New York: Academic Press.

Cohen, E. G. (1986). *Designing groupwork: Strategies for the heterogeneous classroom.* New York: Teachers College Press.

Cohen, E. G., & Intele, J. K. (1981). *Interdependence and management in bilingual classrooms.* Final Report II (NIE Contract #NIE-G-80-0217). Stanford, CA: Stanford Center for Educational Research.

Cohen, H. G. (1985). A comparison of the development of spatial conceptual abilities of students from two cultures. *Journal of Research in Science Teaching, 22,* 491–501.

Cohen, R. A. (1969). Conceptual styles, cultural conflict and nonverbal tests of intelligence. *American Anthropologist, 71,* 828–856.

Colangelo, N., & Davis, G. (Eds.) (1991). *Handbook for gifted education.* Needham, MA: Allyn & Bacon.

Cole, N. S. (1981). Bias in testing. *American Psychologist, 36*(10), 1067–1077.

Coleman, A. D., & Bexton, W. H. (1975). *Group relations reader.* Sausalito, CA: Grex.

Collins, A., Brown, J. S., & Newman, S. E. (1989). Cognitive apprenticeship: Teaching the crafts of reading, writing, and mathematics. In L. B. Resnick (Ed.), *Knowing, learning, and instruction: Essays in honor of Robert Glaser* (pp. 453–494). Hillsdale, NJ: Lawrence Erlbaum.

Comer, J. P. (1984). Home-school relationships as they affect the academic success of children. *Education and Urban Society, 16,* 323–337.

Comer, J. P. (1988). Educating poor minority children. *Scientific American, 259*(5), 42–48.

Comer, J. P. (1991). School parents relationships that work: An interview with James Comer. *The best of the Harvard Education Letter.* Cambridge, MA: Harvard Graduate School of Education.

Cooley, C. H. (1956). *Human nature and the social order.* New York: The Free Press.

Cooper, H. (1989). *Homework.* White Plains, NY: Longman.

Cooper, H. M. (1979). Pygmalion grows up: A mode for teacher expectation, communication and performance influence. *Review of Educational Research, 49,* 389–410.

Cooper, H. M., & Good, T. L. (1983). *Pygmalion grows up: Studies in the expectation communication process.* White Plains, NY: Longman.

Cooper, J. O., Heron, T. E., & Heward, W. L. (1987). *Applied behavior analysis.* Columbus, OH: Merrill.

Costa, A., & Lowery, L. (1989). *Techniques for teaching thinking.* Pacific Grove, CA: Midwest Publications.

Coster, W., Gersten, M., Beighly, M., & Cicchetti, D. (1989). Communicative behavior in maltreated toddlers. *Developmental Psychology, 25,* 1020–1029.

Crittenden, P. (1988). Relationships at risk. In J. Belsky & T. Nezworski (Eds.), *Clinical applications of attachment* (pp. 136–174). New York: Plenum.

Cronbach, L. J., & Snow, R. E. (1977). *Aptitudes and instructional methods: A handbook for research on interactions.* New York: Irvington.

Crooks, J. J. (1988). The impact of classroom evaluation practices on students. *Review of Educational Research, 58,* 438–481.

Cushner, K., McClelland, A., & Safford, P. (1992). *Human diversity in education: An integrative approach.* New York: McGraw-Hill.

Dansereau, D. F. (1988). Cooperative learning strategies. In C. E. Weinstein, E. T. Goetz, & P. A. Alexander (Eds.), *Learning and study strategies: Issues in assessment, instruction, and evaluation* (pp. 103–120). San Diego: Academic Press.

Dashiell, F. F. (1935). Experimental studies on the influence of social situations on the behavior of individual human adults. In C. Murchison (Ed.), *A handbook of social psychology* (pp. 1097–1158). Worcester, MA: Clark University Press.

Dauber, S. L., & Epstein, J. L. (1989, April). *Parent attitudes and practices of involvement in inner-city elementary and middle schools.* Paper presented at the annual meeting of the American Educational Research Association, San Francisco.

Davidson, L. M., & Baum, A. (1990). Posttraumatic stress in children following natural and human-made trauma. In M. Lewis & S. M. Miller (Eds.), *Handbook of developmental psychopathology* (pp. 251–260). New York: Plenum.

Davies, D. (1987). Looking for an ecological solution. *Equity and Choice, 4,* 3–7.

Davies, D. (1991). Schools reaching out: Family, school and community partnerships for student success. *Phi Delta Kappan, 72*(5), 376–382.

de Charms, R. (1968). *Personal causation: The internal affective determinants of behavior.* New York: Academic Press.

de Charms, R. (1976). *Enhancing motivation: Change in the classroom.* New York: Irvington.

Deci, E. L., Vallerand, R. J., Pelletier, L. G., & Ryan, R. M. (1991). Motivation and education: The self-determination perspective. *Educational Psychologist, 26,* 325–346.

Delgado-Gaitan, C. (1990, January). *Involving parents in the schools: A process of empowerment.* Paper presented at the symposium on Race, Ethnicity and Schooling, University of California, Davis.

Delgado-Gaitan, C. (1991). Involving parents in the schools: A process of empowerment. *American Journal of Education, 100* (1), 20–46.

Delgado-Gaitan, C. (1992). School matters in the Mexican-American home: Socializing children to education. *American Educational Research Journal, 29*(3), 495–516.

Delguardi, J., Greenwood, C. R., & Hall, R. V. (1979). *Opportunity to respond: An update.* Paper presented at the fifth annual meeting of the Association of Behavior Analysis, Dearborn, MI.

DeLisi, R., & Staudt, J. (1980). Individual differences in college students' performance of formal operational tasks. *Journal of Applied Developmental Psychology, 1,* 201–208.

Dembo, M. (1981). *Teaching for learning: Applying educational psychology in the classroom* (2nd ed.). Glenview, IL: Scott, Foresman.

Deutsch, C. K., & Kinsbourne, M. (1990). Genetics and biochemistry in attention deficit disorder. In M. Lewis & S. M. Miller (Eds.), *Handbook of developmental psychopathology* (pp. 93–108). New York: Plenum.

Dever, R. B. (1990). Defining mental retardation from an educational perspective. *Mental Retardation, 28*(3), 147–154.

Devin-Sheehan, L., Feldman, R. S., & Allen, V. L. (1976). Research on children tutoring children: A critical review. *Review of Educational Research, 46,* 355–385.

Dewey, J. (1938). *Experience and education.* New York: Collier.

Dillard, J. L. (1972). *Black English: Its history and usage in the United States.* New York: Random House.

Dillon, D. (1989). Showing them that I want them to learn and that I care about who they are: A microthnography of the social organization of a secondary low-track English-reading classroom. *American Educational Research Journal, 26*(2), 227–259.

DiSessa, A. (1982). Understanding Aristotelian physics: A study of knowledge based learning. *Cognitive Science, 6,* 37–75.

Dishon, T. J., Patterson, G. R., Stoolmiller, M., & Skinner, M. L. (1991). Family, school and behavioral antecedents to early adolescent involvement with antisocial peers. *Developmental Psychology, 27,* 172–180.

Doherty, W. J., & Needle, R. N. (1991). Psychological adjustment and substance use among adolescents before and after a parental divorce. *Child Development, 62,* 328–337.

Donaldson, M. (1978). *Children's minds.* New York: Norton.

Donnellan, A. M., & LaVigna, G. W. (1990). Myths about punishment. In A. C. Repp & N. N. Singh (Eds.), *Perspectives on the use of non-aversive and aversive interventions for persons with developmental disabilities* (pp. 33–58). Sycamore, IL: Sycamore Publishing.

Donnellan, A. M., LaVigna, G. W., Negri-Shoultz, N., & Fassbender, L. L. (1988). *Progress without punishment: Effective approaches for learners with severe behavior problems.* New York: Teachers College Press.

Donnellan, A. M., Mirenda, P. L., Mesaros, R. A., & Fassbender, L. L. (1984). Analyzing the communication functions of aberrant behavior. *Journal of the Association for Persons with Severe Handicaps, 9,* 201–212.

Douglas, V. I. (1980). Higher mental processes in hyperactive children: Implications for training. In R. Knights & D. Baker (Eds.), *Treatment of hyperactive and learning disordered children* (pp. 65–92). Baltimore, MD: University Park Press.

Douglas, V. I. (1983). Attention and cognitive problems. In M. Rutter (Ed.), *Developmental neuropsychiatry* (pp. 280–329). New York: Guilford.

Douglas, V. I., & Parry, P. A. (1983). Effects of reward on delayed reaction time task performance of hyperactive children. *Journal of Abnormal Child Psychology, 11,* 313–326.

Doyle, R. (1989). The resistance of conventional wisdom to research evidence: The case of retention in grade. *Phi Delta Kappan, 71,* 215–220.

Doyle, W. (1983). Academic work. *Review of Educational Research, 53,* 159–200.

Doyle, W. (1986). Classroom organization and management. In M.C. Wittrock (Ed.), *Handbook of research on teaching* (3rd ed.). New York: Macmillan.

Dreikurs, R., Grunwald, B., & Pepper, F. (1982). *Maintaining sanity in the classroom* (2nd ed.). New York: Harper & Row.

Duit, R. (1995). The constructivist view: A fashionable and fruitful paradigm for science education research and practice. In L. P. Steffe, & J. Gale (Eds.), *Constructivism in education* (pp. 271–286). Hillsdale, NJ: Lawrence Erlbaum.

Dumfee, M. (1974). *Eliminating ethnic bias.* Alexandria, VA: Association for Supervision and Curriculum Development.

Dunkin, M., & Biddle, B. (1974). *The study of teaching.* New York: Holt, Rinehart & Winston.

Dunn, R. S. (1979). Learning—a matter of style. *Educational Leadership, 36,* 430–432.

Dunn, R. S., & Dunn, K. J. (1978). *Teaching students through their individual learning style.* Reston, VA: Reston.

Durand, V. M. (1988). Motivation assessment scale. In M. Hersen & A. Bellack (Eds.). *Dictionary of behavior assessment techniques* (pp. 309–310). Elmsford, NY: Pergamon.

Durand, V. M. (1990). *Severe behavior problems: A functional communication training approach.* New York: Guilford.

Durand, V. M., & Carr, E. G. (1993). An analysis of maintainance following functional communication training. *Journal of Applied Behavior Analysis, 25,* 777–794.

Eccles, J. S. (1986). Gender roles and women's achievement. *Educational Researcher, 15,* 15–19.

Eccles, J. S. (1990). Academic achievement. In R. M. Lerner, A. C. Peterson, & J. Brooks-Gunn (Eds.), *The encyclopedia of adolescence* (pp. 1–5). New York: Garland.

Eccles, J. S., Adler, T. F., Futterman, R., Goff, S. B., Kaczala, C. M., Meece, J. L., & Midgley, C. (1983). Expectations, values and academic behaviors. In J. T. Spence (Ed.), *Achievement and achievement motivation* (pp. 75–146). San Francisco: Freeman.

Eccles, J. S., Adler, T. F., & Kaczala, C. M. (1982). Socialization of achievement attitudes and beliefs: Parental influences. *Child Development, 53,* 310–321.

Eccles, J. S., & Jacobs, J. E. (1986). Social forces shape math attitudes and performance. *Signs, 11,* 367–389.

Eccles, J. S., Lord, S., & Midgley, C. (1991). What are we doing to early adolescents? The impact of educational contexts on early adolescents. *American Journal of Education, 99,* 521–539.

Eccles, J. S., & Midgley, C. (1990). Changes in academic motivation and self-perception during early adolescence. In R. Monte-mayor, G. R. Adams, & T. P. Gullotta (Eds.), *From childhood to adolescence: A transitional period?* (pp. 134–155). Newbury Park, CA: Sage.

Eckenrode, J., Laird, M., & Doris, J. (1993). School performance and disciplinary problems among abused and neglected children. *Developmental Psychology, 29*(1), 53–62.

Eisenberg, N. (1988). The development of prosocial and aggressive behavior. In M. H. Borinstein & M. E. Lamb (Eds.). *Developmental psychology: An advanced textbook* (2nd ed., pp. 461–496). Hillsdale, NJ: Lawrence Erlbaum.

Eisenberg, N. (1990). Prosocial development in early and mid-adolescence. In R. Monte-mayor, G. R. Adams, & T. P. Gullotta (Eds.), *From childhood to adolescence: A transitional period?* (pp. 240–268). Newbury Park, CA: Sage.

Eisner, E. W. (1987, January/February). Why the textbook influences curriculum. *Curriculum Review,* 11–13.

Elbaz, F. (1983). *Teacher thinking: A study of practical knowledge.* New York: Nichols Publishing.

Elliot, E. S., & Dweck, C. S. (1988). Goals: An approach to motivation and achievement. *Journal of Personality and Social Psychology, 54,* 5–12.

Elliot, S. N., & Shapiro, E. S. (1990). Intervention techniques and programs for academic performance problems. In T. B. Gutkin & C. R. Reynolds (Eds.). *The handbook of school psychology* (2nd ed., pp. 637–662). New York: Wiley.

Ellson, D. G. (1976). Tutoring. In N. L. Gage (Ed.), *The psychology of teaching methods* (pp. 130–165). Chicago: University of Chicago Press.

Emmer, E. T., Evertson, C. M., & Anderson, L. M. (1980). Effective classroom management at the beginning of the school year. *Elementary School Journal, 80,* 219–231.

Emmer, E. T., Evertson, C. M., Clements, B. S., & Worsham, M. E. (1994). *Classroom management for secondary teachers* (3rd ed.). Englewood Cliffs, NJ: Prentice-Hall.

Englemann, S. (1991). Teachers, schemata, and instruction. In M. M. Kennedy (Ed.), *Teaching academic subjects to diverse learners* (pp. 218–234). New York: Teachers College Press.

Englemann, S., & Carnine, D. (1982). *Theory of instruction: Principles and applications.* New York: Irvington.

Epstein, J. L. (1982, March). *Student reactions to teacher practices of parent involvement.* Paper presented at the annual meeting of the American Educational Research Association, New York.

Epstein, J. L. (1985, April). *When school and family partnerships work: Implications for changing the role of teachers.* Paper presented at the annual meeting of the American Educational Research Association, San Francisco.

Epstein, J. L. (1986). Parents' reaction to teacher practices of parent involvement. *The Elementary School Journal, 86,* 277–294.

Epstein, J.L. (1987). Toward a theory of family-school connections: Teacher practices and parent involvement. In K. Hurrelmann, F. Kauffman, & F. Losel (Eds.), *Social interventions: Potential and constraints* (pp. 121–136). New York: De Gruyter.

Epstein, J. (1989). *Research report 26.* Baltimore: Center for Research in Elementary and Middle Schools, Johns Hopkins University.

Erickson, M., Egeland, B., & Pianta, R. (1989). The effects of maltreatment on the development of young children. In D. Cicchetti & V. Carlson (Eds.), *Child maltreatment: Theory and research on the causes and consequences of child abuse and neglect* (pp. 647–684). New York: Cambridge University Press.

Erickson, M. F., & Mohatt, G. (1982). Cultural organization of participation structures in two classrooms of Indian students. In G. Spindler (Ed.), *Doing the ethnography of schooling.* Prospect Heights, IL: Waveland.

Erickson, M. F., Sroufe, L. A., & Egeland, B. (1985). The relationship between quality of attachment and behavior problems in preschool in a high-risk sample. In I. Bretherton & E. Waters (Eds.), Growing points of attachment theory and research. *Monographs of the Society for Research in Child Development, 50,* 147–166.

Erikson, E. H. (1950/1963). *Childhood and society.* New York: Norton.

Erikson, E. H. (1964). *Insight and responsibility.* New York: Norton.

Erikson, E. H. (1974). *Dimensions of a new identity: The 1973 Jefferson lectures on the humanities.* New York: Norton.

Eron, L. D., & Huesmann, L. R. (1990). The stability of aggressive behavior—even unto the third generation. In M. Lewis & S. M. Miller (Eds.), *Handbook of developmental psychopathology* (pp. 147–156). New York: Plenum.

Evertson, C. M., & Emmer, E. T. (1982). Effective management at the beginning of the school year in junior high classes. *Journal of Educational Psychology, 74,* 485–498.

Evertson, C. M., Emmer, E. T., Clements, B. S., & Worsham, M. E. (1994). *Classroom management for elementary school teachers* (3rd ed.) Englewood Cliffs, NJ: Prentice-Hall.

Eysenck, H. J. (1979). *The structure and measurement of intelligence.* New York: Springer-Verlag.

Fantuzzo, J., King, J., & Heller, L. R. (1992). Effects of reciprocal peer tutoring on mathematics and school adjustment: A component analysis. *Journal of Educational Psychology, 84,* 331–339.

Farmer, H., & Sidney, J. (1985). Sex equity in career and vocational education. In S. Klein (Ed.), *Handbook for achieving sex equity through education.* Baltimore, MD: Johns Hopkins University Press.

Fine, M. J., & Carlson, C. (1992). *The handbook of family-school intervention: A systems perspective.* Needham, MA: Allyn & Bacon.

Fink, S. (1992). How we reconstructed our categorical programs. *Educational Leadership, 50*(2), 42–43.

Firestone, P., & Martin, J. E. (1979). An analysis of the hyperactive syndrome: A comparison of hyperactive, behavior problem, asthmatic, and normal children. *Journal of Abnormal Child Psychology, 7,* 261–273.

Fischer, K. W. (1980). A theory of cognitive development: the control and construction of hierarchies of skills. *Psychological Review, 87,* 477–531.

Flanders, N. A. (1963). Teacher influence in the classroom. In A. Bellack (Ed.), *Theory and research in teaching* (pp. 37–53). New York: Bureau of Publications, Teachers College.

Flanders, N. A. (1964). Some relationships among teacher influence, pupil attitudes and achievement. In B. Biddle & W. Elena (Eds.), *Contemporary research on teacher effectiveness.* New York: Holt, Rinehart & Winston.

Flavell, J. H. (1979). Metacognition and cognitive monitoring: A new area of cognitive developmental inquiry. *American Psychologist, 34,* 906–911.

Flavell, J. H. (1981). Cognitive monitoring. In W. P. Dickson (Ed.), *Children's oral communication skills* (pp. 35–60). New York: Academic Press.

Flavell, J. H. (1985). *Cognitive development* (2nd ed.). Englewood Cliffs, NJ: Prentice-Hall.

Flavell, J. H. (1987). Speculations about the nature and development of metacognition. In F. E. Weinert & R. H. Klawe (Eds.), *Metacognition, motivation and understanding* (pp. 21–30). Hillsdale, NJ: Lawrence Erlbaum.

Floden, R. F. (1991). What teachers need to know about learning. In M. M. Kennedy (Ed.), *Teaching academic subjects to diverse learners* (pp. 181–202). New York: Teachers College Press.

Fogelman, K. (1983). Ability grouping in the secondary school. In K. Fogelman (Ed.), *Growing up in Britain: Papers from the National Child Development Study.* London: Macmillan.

Forest, M., & Pierpoint, J. R. (1992). Putting all kids in the MAP. *Educational Leadership, 50*(2), 26–31.

Franklin, M. E. (1992). Culturally sensitive instructional practices for African-American learners with disabilities. *Exceptional Children, 59,* 115–122.

Frazier, D. M., & Paulson, F. L. (1992). How portfolios motivate reluctant learners. *Educational Leadership, 49*(8), 62–65.

French, J., Jr., & Raven, B. (1959). The bases of social power. In D. Cartwright (Ed.), *Studies in social power* (pp. 150–168). Ann Arbor: University of Michigan Press.

Freud, S. (1915). Instincts and their vicissitudes. In S. Freud, *The collected papers.* New York: Collier.

Freud, S. (1965). *A general introduction to psychoanalysis* (J. Riviere, Trans.). New York: Washington Square Press. (Original work published 1920)

Froyen, L. A. (1993). *Classroom management: The reflective teacher-leader* (2nd ed.). New York: Macmillan.

Fuller, F. (1969). Concerns of teachers: A developmental conceptualization. *American Educational Research Journal, 6,* 207–226.

Fyano, L. T. (1980). *Achievement motivation.* New York: Plenum.

Gage, N. L., & Berliner, D. C. (1988). *Educational psychology* (4th ed.). Boston: Houghton Mifflin.

Gagné, E. D., Yekovich, C. W., & Yekovich, F. R. (1993). *The cognitive psychology of school learning* (2nd ed.) New York: HarperCollins.

Gagné, R. M. (1968). Contributions of learning to human development. *Psychological Review, 75,* 177–191.

Gagné, R. M. (1970). *Conditions of learning* (2nd ed.). New York: Holt.

Gagné, R. M. (1985). *Conditions of learning* (4th ed.). New York: Holt.

Gagné, R., Briggs, L. & Wagner, W. (1992). *Principles of instructional design.* (4th ed.) Orlando, FL: Harcourt, Brace.

Galambos, S. J., & Goldin-Meadow, S. (1990). The effects of learning two languages on levels of metalinguistic awareness. *Cognition, 34,* 1–56.

Gall, M. (1984). Synthesis of research on questioning in recitation. *Educational Leadership, 42*(3), 40–49.

Gallimore, R., Tharp, R. G., Sloat, K., Klein, T., & Troy, M. E. (1982). *Analysis of reading achievement test results for the Kamahameha Early Education Project: 1972–1979.* (Tech. Rep. No. 102). Honolulu: Kamehameha Schools/Bishop Estate.

Gallup, A., & Clark, D. (1987). The 19th annual Gallup poll on the public's attitudes toward the public schools. *Phi Delta Kappan, 69,* 17–30.

Gallup, A., & Elam, S. (1988). The twentieth annual Gallup poll on the public's attitudes toward the public schools. *Phi Delta Kappan, 70,* 33–46.

Gallup, G. H. (1978). The tenth annual Gallup poll of the public's attitudes toward the public schools. *Phi Delta Kappan, 60,* 33–45.

Gamoran, A. (1992). Synthesis of research: Is ability grouping equitable? *Educational Leadership, 50*(2), 11–13.

Gamoran, A. (1993). Alternative uses of ability grouping in secondary schools: Can we bring high quality instruction to low-ability classes? *American Journal of Education, 102,* 1–22.

Garcia, J. (1981). The logic and limits of mental aptitude testing. *American Psychologist, 36*(10), 1172–1180.

Garcia, R. L. (1991). *Teaching in a pluralistic society: Concepts, models, strategies* (2nd ed.). New York: HarperCollins.

Gardner, H. (1983). *Frames of mind: The theory of multiple intelligences.* New York: Basic Books.

Gardner, H. (1991). *The unschooled mind: How children think and how schools should teach.* New York: Basic Books.

Gardner, H. (1993). *Multiple intelligencies: The theory in practice.* New York: Basic Books.

Gardner, H., & Hatch, T. (1989). Multiple intelligences go to school: Education implication of the theory of multiple intelligences. *Educational Researcher 18*(8), 4–10.

Gardner, J. F., & Chapman, M. S. (1985). *Staff development in mental retardation services: A practical handbook.* Baltimore: Paul H. Brookes.

Gardner, J. F., & Chapman, M. S. (1990). *Program issues in developmental disabilities* (2nd ed.) (pp. 39–57). Baltimore: Paul H. Brookes.

Garger, S., & Guild, P. (1984). Learning styles: The crucial differences. *Curriculum Review, 23,* 9–12.

Gelman R. (1972). Logical capacity of very young children: Number invariance rules. *Child Development, 43,* 75–90.

Gelman, S. A., & Ebeling, K. S. (1989). Children's use of nonegocentric standards in judgments of functional size. *Child Development, 60,* 920–932.

Gearheat, M. J., Herman, J., Baker, E. L., & Wittaker, K. (1992). *Writing portfolios at the elementary level: A study of methods for writing assessment.* CSE Technical Report No. 337. Los Angeles: UCLA Center for the Study of Evaluation.

Gersten, M., Coster, W., Schneider-Rosen, K., Carlson, V., & Cicchetti, D. (1986). The socio-emotional basis of communicative functioning: Quality of attachment, language development and early maltreatment. In M. E. Lamb, A. L. Brown, & B. Rogoff (Eds.), *Advances in Developmental Psychology: Vol. 4* (pp. 105–151). Hillsdale, NJ: Lawrence Erlbaum.

Gersten, R., & Woodward, J. (1990). Rethinking the regular education initiative: Focus on the classroom teacher. *Remedial and Special Education, 11*(3), 7–16.

Gesell, A.L. (1925). *The mental growth of the preschool child.* New York: Macmillan.

Gesell, A. L. (1928). *Infancy and human growth.* New York: Macmillan.

Gesell, A. L. (1954). The ontogenesis of infant behavior. In L. Carmichael (Ed.), *Manual of child psychology* (2nd ed.). New York: Wiley.

Getzels, J. W. (1969). A social psychology of education. In G. Lindzey & E. Aronsen (Eds.), *The handbook of social psychology* (pp. 459–537). Reading, MA: Addison-Wesley.

Ghatala, E. S. (1986). Strategy-monitoring training enables young learners to select effective strategies. *Educational Psychologist, 21,* 43–54.

Ghatala, E. S., Levin, J. R., Pressley, M., & Goodwin, D. (1986). A componential analysis of the effects of derived and supplied strategy-utility information on children's strategy selections. *Journal of Experimental Child Psychology, 41,* 76–92.

Gilligan, C. (1982). *In a different voice: Psychological theory and women's development.* Cambridge, MA: Harvard University Press.

Gilligan, C. (1988). Adolescent development reconsidered. In C. Gilligan, J. U. Ward, J. M. Taylor, & B. Bardige (Eds.), *Mapping the moral domain.* Cambridge, MA: Harvard University Press.

Gilligan, C. (1990). Preface: Teaching Shakespeare's sister. In C. Gilligan, N. Lyons, & T. Hanmer (Eds.), *Making connections: The relational worlds of adolescent girls at Emma Willard School.* Cambridge, MA: Harvard University Press.

Gilligan, C., & Attanucci, J. (1988). Two moral orientations: Gender differences and similarities. *Merrill-Palmer Quarterly, 34,* 223–237.

Ginott, H. G. (1972). *Teacher and child.* New York: Macmillan.

Gipps, C. V. (1995). *Beyond testing: Towards a theory of educational assessment.* Washington, DC: Falmer Press.

Glasersfeld, E. (1995). A constructivist approach to teaching. In L. P. Steffe & J. Gale (Eds.), *Constructivism in education* (pp. 3–16). Hillsdale, NJ: Lawrence Erlbaum.

Glasser, W. (1986). *Control theory in the classroom.* New York: Harper & Row.

Glasser, W. (1990). *The quality school: Managing students without coercion.* New York: Harper & Row.

Glynn, F. L., & Thomas J. D. (1974). Effect of cueing on self-control of classroom behavior. *Journal of Applied Behavior Analysis, 7,* 299–306.

Glynn, F. L., Thomas J. D., & Shee, S. K. (1973). Behavioral self-control of on-task behavior in an elementary classroom. *Journal of Applied Behavior Analysis, 6,* 105–118.

Goetz, E. T., Alexander, P. A., & Ash, M. J. (1992). *Educational psychology: A classroom perspective.* New York: Merrill.

Good, T. L., & Brophy, J. E. (1991). *Looking in classrooms* (5th ed.). New York: Harper & Row.

Good, T., Grouws, D., & Egmeier, H. (1983). *Active mathematics teaching.* New York: Longman.

Good, T. L., & Stipek, D. J. (1983). Individual differences in the classroom: A psychological perspective. In G. Fenstermacher & J. Goodlad (Eds.), *1983 National Society for the Study of Education Yearbook.* Chicago: University of Chicago Press.

Goodlad, J. (1984). *A place called school: Prospects for the future.* New York: McGraw-Hill.

Gordon, E. W., & Terrell, M. D. (1981). The changed social context of testing. *American Psychologist, 36*(10), 1167–1171.

Gordon, T. (1974). *Teacher effectiveness training.* New York: Peter H. Wyden.

Grant, C. A. (1991). Culture and teaching: What do teachers need to know. In M. M. Kennedy (Ed.), *Teaching academic subjects to diverse learners* (pp. 237–256). New York: Teachers College Press.

Grant, C. A., & Secada, W. (1990). Preparing teachers for diversity. In W. R. Houston (Ed.), *Handbook of research in teacher education* (pp. 403–422). New York: Macmillan.

Grant, C. A., & Sleeter, C. (1986). *After the school bell rings.* Philadelphia: Farmer.

Grave, M. E., Weinstein, T., & Walberg, H. J. (1983). School-based home instruction and learning: A quantitative analysis. *Journal of Educational Research, 76*(6), 351–360.

Greenbowe, T., Herron, J. D., Lucas, C., Nurrenbern, S., Staver, J. R., & Ward, C. R. (1981). Teaching preadolescents to act as scientists: Replication and extension of an earlier study. *Journal of Educational Psychology, 73,* 705–711.

Greenwood, C. R., Delguardi, J. C., & Hall, R. V. (1984). Opportunity to respond and student academic achievement. In W. L. Heward, T. E. Heron, D. S. Hill, & J. Trap-Porter (Eds.), *Focus on behavior analysis in education* (pp. 58–88). Columbus, OH: Merrill.

Greenwood, G., Good, T. L., & Siegel, B. (1971). *Problem situations in teaching.* New York: Harper & Row.

Greenwood, G., & Parkay, F.W. (1989). *Case studies for teacher decision making* (pp. 15–20). New York: Random House.

Greenwood, G. E., & Hickman, C. W. (1991). Research and practice in parent involvement: Implications for teacher education. *The Elementary School Journal, 91*(3), 279–288.

Grolnick, W. S., & Ryan, R. M. (1989). Parent styles associated with children's self-regulation and competence in school. *Journal of Educational Psychology, 81,* 143–154.

Grossman, H. (1990). *Trouble-free teaching: Solutions to behavior problems in the classroom.* Mountain View, CA: Mayfield.

Guilford, J. P. (1985). The structure-of-intellect model. In B. B. Wolman (Ed.), *Handbook of intelligence* (pp. 225–266). New York: Wiley.

Gullickson, A. R., & Ellwein, M. C. (1985). Post-hoc analysis of teacher-made tests: The goodness of fit between prescription and practice. *Educational Measurement: Issues and Practice, 4*(1), 15–18.

Gunstone, R. F., & White, R. T. (1981). Understanding of gravity. *Science Education, 65,* 291–299.

Guzzetti, B. J., Snyder, T. E., Glass, G. V., & Gamas, W. S. (1993). Promoting conceptual change in science: A comparative meta-analysis of instructional interventions from reading education and science education. *Reading Research Quarterly, 28,* 117–159.

Haertel, E. H. (1986, April). *Choosing and using classroom tests: Teachers' perspectives on assessment.* Paper presented at the annual meeting of the American Educational Research Association, San Francisco.

Haertel, E. H. (1990). Performance tests, simulations and other methods. In J. Millman & L. Darling-Hammond (Eds.), *The new handbook of teacher evaluation: Assessing elementary and secondary school teachers* (pp. 278–294). Newbury Park, CA: Sage.

Hakuta, K., Freidmann, B. M., & Diaz, R. M. (1987). Bilingualism and cognitive development: Three perspectives. In S. Rosenberg (Ed.), *Advances in applied psycholinguistics: Vol. 2. Reading, writing, and language learning* (pp. 284–319). New York: Cambridge University Press.

Hall, R. V., Delguardi, J., Greenwood, C. R., & Thurston, L. (1982). The importance of opportunity to respond in children's academic success. In E. B. Edgar, N. G. Haring, J. R. Jenkins, & C. G. Pious (Eds.), *Mentally handicapped children: Education and training* (pp. 107–140). Austin, TX: Pro-Ed.

Hallahan, D. P., Keller, C. E., McKinney, J. D., Lloyd, J. W., & Bryon, T. (1988). Examining the research base of the regular education initiative: Efficacy studies and the adaptive learning environments model. *Journal of Learning Disabilities, 21*(1), 29–35.

Haney, W. (1981). Validity, vaudeville and values: A short history of social concerns over standardized testing. *American Psychologist, 36*(10), 1021–1034.

Hansford, B. C., & Hattie, J. A. (1982). The relationship between self and achievement performance measures. *Review of Educational Research, 52,* 123–142.

Harris, K. R., & Graham, S. (1992). Self-regulated strategy development: A part of the writing process. In M. Pressley, K. R. Harris, & J. T. Guthrie (Eds.), *Promoting academic compe-*

tence and literacy in school (pp. 277–309). San Diego: Academic Press.

Harris, S., & Harris, L. (1988). *The teacher's almanac.* New York: Hudson Group.

Harrison, G. V. (1972). *Beginning reading. I: A professional guide for the lay tutor.* Provo, UT: Brigham Young University Press.

Harrow, A. (1969). *A taxonomy of the psychomotor domain: A guide for developing behavioral objectives.* New York: David McKay.

Harter, S. (1988). The determinations and mediational role of global self-worth in children. In N. Eisenberg (Ed.), *Contemporary topics in developmental psychology* (pp. 219–242). New York: Wiley.

Harter, S. (1990). Processes underlying adolescent self-concept formation. In R. Monte-mayor, G. R. Adams, & T. P. Gullota (Eds.), *From childhood to adolescence: A transitional period?* (pp. 205–239). Newbury Park, CA: Sage.

Hartup, W. W. (1989). Social relationships and their developmental significance. *American Psychologist, 44,* 120–126.

Harvard Education Letter. (1992). Adria Sternberg (Ed.). January/February, VIII, 1, Cambridge, MA: Harvard Graduate School of Education. 1–8.

Hasazi, J. E., & Hasazi, S. E. (1972). Effects of teacher attention on digit-reversal behavior in an elementary school child. *Journal of Applied Behavior Analysis, 5,* 157–162.

Hawkins, J., Pea, R. D., Glick, J., & Scribner, S. (1984). "Minds that laugh don't like mushrooms": Evidence for deductive reasoning by preschoolers. *Developmental Psychology, 20,* 584–594.

Haynes, N. M., Comer, J. P., & Hamilton-Lee, M. (1989). School climate enhancement through parental involvement. *Journal of School Psychology, 27,* 87–90.

Heath, S. B., & McLaughlin, M. W. (1987). A child resource policy: Moving beyond dependence on school and family. *Phi Delta Kappan, 68*(8), 576–580.

Hebert, E. A. (1992). Portfolios invite reflection from students and staff. *Educational Leadership, 49*(8), 58–61.

Heguik, R. L., McDevitt, S. C., & Carey, W. B. (1982, August). *Longitudinal stability of temperament characteristics in the elementary school period.* Paper presented at the meeting of the International Society for the Study of Behavioral Development, Toronto.

Heider, F. (1960). The gestalt theory of motivation. In M. R. Jones (Ed.), *Nebraska symposium on motivation: Vol. 8* (pp. 145–171). Lincoln: University of Nebraska Press.

Henderson, A. T. (1989). *The evidence continues to grow: Parent involvement improves student achievement.* Columbia, MD: National Committee for Citizens in Education.

Henderson, R. W. (1980). Social and emotional needs of culturally diverse children. *Exceptional Children, 46,* 598–605.

Henderson, R. W., & Swanson, R. A. (July 1977). *The effects of televised skill instruction, instructional system support, and parental intervention on the development of cognitive skills.* Final report on Grant No. OCD-C3-479 from the Office of Child Development, Department of Health, Education and Welfare. Tucson: Arizona Center for Educational Research and Development, the University of Arizona.

Henderson, R. W., Swanson, R. A., & Zimmerman, B. J. (1974). Inquiry response induction in preschool children through televised modeling. *Developmental Psychology, 11*(4), 523–524.

Henker, B., & Whalen, C. K. (1989). Hyperactivity and attention deficits. *American Psychologist, 44,* 216–223.

Herman, J. L. (1992). What research tells us about good assessment. *Educational Leadership, 49*(8), 74–78.

Herman, J. L., Aschbacher, P. R., & Winters, L. (1992). *A practical guide to alternative assessment.* Alexandria, VA: Association for Supervision and Curriculum Development.

Hess, R. D., & Shipman, V. C. (1965). Early experience and the socialization of cognitive modes in children. *Child Development, 36,* 869–886.

Hilgard, E. R., & Bower, G. H. (1981). *Theories of learning* (5th ed.). Englewood Cliffs, NJ: Prentice-Hall.

Hilliard, A. G. (1976). *Alternatives to IQ testing: An approach to the identification of gifted minority children.* Final report, Sacramento Division of Special Education, California State Department of Education. (ERIC Document Reproduction Service No. ED 147009)

Hilliard, A. G. (1992). The pitfalls and promises of special education practice. *Exceptional Children, 59*(2), 168–172.

Hills, J. R. (1981). *Measurement and evaluation in the classroom* (2nd ed.). Columbus, OH: Merrill.

Hodgkinson, H. (1988). *All one system: demographics of education, kindergarten through graduate school.* Washington, DC: The Institute for Educational Leadership.

Hoffman, M. L. (1982). Development of prosocial motivation: Empathy and guilt. In N. Eisenberg (Ed.), *The development of prosocial behavior* (pp. 281–314). New York: Academic Press.

Hoffman, M. L. (1984). Empathy, its limitations, and its role in a comprehensive moral theory. In W. M. Kurtines & J. L. Gewirtz (Eds.), *Morality, moral behavior, and moral development* (pp. 283–302). New York: Wiley.

Hoffman, M. L. (1988). Moral development. In M. H. Bornstein & M. E. Lamb (Eds.), *Developmental psychology: An advanced textbook* (2nd ed., pp. 497–548). Hillsdale, NJ: Lawrence Erlbaum.

Hoffman-Plotkin, D., & Twentyman, C. T. (1984). A multimodal assessment of behavioral and cognitive deficits in abused and neglected preschoolers. *Child Development, 55,* 794–802.

Holmes Group. (1990). *Tomorrow's schools: Principles for the design of professional development schools.* East Lansing, MI: Author.

Holt, K. C. (1992). A rationale for creating African-American immersion schools. *Educational Leadership, 49,* 18.

Hopfenberg, W. S., Levin, H. M., Meister, G., & Rogers, J. (1990). *Accelerated schools.* Stanford, CA: School of Education, Stanford University.

Horcones. (1985). *Twelve years of applying behavior analysis to cultural design.* Paper presented at the meeting of the American Psychological Association, Los Angeles.

Horcones. (1987). The concept of consequences in the analysis of behavior. *The Behavior Analyst, 10,* 291–294.

Horcones. (1991). Walden Two in real life: Behavior analysis in the design of the culture. In W. Ishag (Ed.), *Human behavior in today's world.* New York: Praeger.

Horcones. (1992). Natural reinforcement: A way to improve education. *Journal of Applied Behavior Analysis, 25*(1), 71–76.

Horn, J. M. (1983). The Texas adoption project: Adopted children and their intellectual resemblance to biological and adoptive parents. *Child Development, 54,* 268–275.

Huang, L. N., & Gibbs, J. T. (1992). Partners or adversaries? Home-school collaboration across culture, race and ethnicity. In S. L. Christenson & J. C. Conoley (Eds.), *Home-school collaboration: Enhancing children's academic and social competency* (pp. 81–110). Washington, DC: National Association of School Psychologists.

Hull, C. L. (1943). *Principles of behavior: An introduction to behavior theory.* New York: Appleton-Century-Crofts.

Hunt, E. (1976). Varieties of cognitive power. In L. B. Resnick (Ed.), *The nature of intelligence.* Hillsdale, NJ: Lawrence Erlbaum.

Hunt, E. (1978). Mechanisms of verbal ability. *Psychological Review, 85,* 109–130.

Hunter, M. (1982). *Mastery teaching.* El Segundo, CA: Instructional Dynamics.

Idol, L., & Croll, V. J. (1987). Story mapping training as a means of improving reading comprehension. *Learning Disability Quarterly, 10,* 214–229.

Iwata, B. A. (1987). Negative reinforcement in applied behavior analysis: An emerging technology. *Journal of Applied Behavior Analysis, 20,* 361–387.

Jacklin, C. N. (1989). Female and male: Issues of gender. *American Psychologist, 44,* 127–133.

Jacobson, J. W. (1991). Administrative and policy dimensions of developmental disabilities services. In J. L. Matson & J. A. Mulick (Eds.), *Handbook of mental retardation* (2nd ed., pp. 3–22). New York: Pergamon.

Jalali, F. A. (1989). *A cross-cultural comparative analysis of the learning styles and field dependence/independence characteristics of selected fourth- and sixth-grade students of Afro, Chinese, Greek, and Mexican-American heritage.* Unpublished doctoral dissertation, St. John's University, New York.

Jensen, A. (1980). *Bias in mental testing.* New York: Free Press.

Johnson, D., & Johnson, R. (1984). *Learning together and learning alone: Cooperation, competition and individualization.* Englewood Cliffs, NJ: Prentice-Hall.

Johnston, D. K. (1988). Adolescents' solutions to dilemmas in fables: Two moral orientations—two problem solving strategies. In C. Gilligan, J. U. Ward, J. M. Taylor, & B. Bardige (Eds.), *Mapping the moral domain.* Cambridge, MA: Harvard University Press.

Jones, F. H. (1987). *Positive classroom discipline.* New York: McGraw-Hill.

Jones, V. F., & Jones, L. S. (1990). *Comprehensive classroom management* (3rd ed.). Needham, MA: Allyn & Bacon.

Kafer, N. (1976). Friendship, choice and performance in classroom groups. *The Australian Journal of Education, 20,* 278–284.

Kagan, S. (1983). Social orientation among Mexican-American children: A challenge to traditional classroom structures. In E. Garcia (Ed.), *The Mexican-American child: Language, cognition and social development.* Tempe, AZ: Center for Bilingual Education.

Kagan, S. (1984). Interpreting Chicano cooperativeness: Methodological and theoretical considerations. In J. L. Martinez, Jr., & R. H. Mendoza (Eds.), *Chicano psychology* (2nd ed.). New York: Academic Press.

Kagan, S. L. (1984). *Parent involvement research: A field in search of itself* (Report No. 8). Boston, MA: Institute for Responsive Education.

Kagan, S. L., & Schraft, C. M. (1982). *When parents and schools come together: Differential outcomes of parent involvement in urban schools.* Boston, MA: Institute for Responsive Education. (ERIC Document Reproduction Service No. ED 281–951)

Kahle, J. B., Parker, L. H., Rennie, L. J., & Riley, D. (1993). Gender differences in science education: Building a model. *Educational Psychologist, 28*(4), 379–404.

Kamps, D. M., Leonard, B. R., Vernon, S., Dugan, E. P., Delguardi, J. C., Gershon, L. W., & Folk, L. (1992). Teaching social skills to students with autism to increase peer interactions in an integrated first-grade classroom. *Journal of Applied Behavior Analysis, 25*(2), 281–288.

Kampwerth, T. J., & Bates, M. (1980). Modality preference and teaching methods: A review of the research. *Academic Therapy, 15,* 597–605.

Kash, M. M., & Borich, G. (1978). *Teacher behavior and pupil self-concept.* Reading, MA: Addison-Wesley.

Katz, P. A. (1986). Modification of children's gender-stereotyped behavior: General issues and research considerations. *Sex Roles, 14,* 591–601.

Kaufman, A. S., Harrison, P. L., & Ittenbach, R. F. (1990). Intelligence testing in the schools. In T. B. Gutkin & C. R. Reynolds (Eds.), *The handbook of school psychology* (2nd ed., pp. 289–327). New York: Wiley.

Kaufman, J. M. (1989). *The regular education initiative as Reagan-Bush education policy: A trickle-down theory of education for the hard-to-teach.* Charlottesville, VA: University of Virginia, Curry School of Education.

Kavale, K. A. (1990). Effectiveness of special education. In T. B. Gutkin & C. R. Reynolds (Eds.), *The handbook of school psychology* (2nd ed., pp. 870–900). New York: Wiley.

Kavale, K. A., & Mattson, P. D. (1983). One jumped off the balance beam: Meta-analysis of perceptual training. *Journal of Learning Disabilities, 16,* 165–173.

Keating, D. (1979). Adolescent thinking. In J. Adelson (Ed.), *Handbook of adolescent psychology* (pp. 211–246). New York: Wiley.

Kelly, H. H. (1967). Attribution theory in social psychology. In D. Levine (Ed.), *Nebraska symposium on motivation, 15,* 192–238. Lincoln: University of Nebraska Press.

Kendall, F. E. (1983). *Diversity in the classroom: A multicultural approach to the education of young children.* New York: Teachers College Press.

Keogh, B. K. (1988). Improving services for problem learners: Rethinking and restructuring. *Journal of Learning Disabilities, 21*(1), 19–22.

Kerchoff, A. C. (1986). Effects of ability grouping in British secondary schools. *American Sociological Review, 51,* 842–858.

King, A. (1989, April). *Improving lecture comprehension: Effects of a metacognitive strategy.* Paper presented at the annual meeting of the American Educational Research Association, San Francisco.

Kirk, S., Gallagher, J. J., & Anastasiow, N. J. (1993). *Educating exceptional children* (7th ed.). Boston: Houghton Mifflin.

Kirk, S. A., McCarthy, J. J., & Kirk, W. D. (1968). *The Illinois Test of Psycholinguistic Abilities* (Rev. ed.). Urbana: University of Illinois Press.

Knight, G. P., & Kagan, S. (1977). Acculturation of prosocial and competitive behaviors among second- and third-generation Mexican-American children. *Journal of Cross-Cultural Psychology, 8,* 273–284.

Knight, P. (1992). How I use portfolios in mathematics. *Educational Leadership, 49*(8), 71–72.

Koestner, R., Ryan, R. M., Bernieri, F., & Holt, K. (1984). Setting limits in children's behavior: The differential effects of controlling versus informational styles on intrinsic motivation and creativity. *Journal of Personality, 52,* 233–248.

Kohlberg, L. (1978). Revisions in the theory and practice of moral development. *New Directions for Child Development, 2,* 83–88.

Kohlberg, L., & Elfenbein, D. (1975). The development of moral judgments concerning capital punishment. *American Journal of Orthopsychiatry, 54,* 614–640.

Koretz, D., Linn, R., Dunbar, S., & Shepard, L. (1991). *The effects of high stakes testing on achievement.* Paper presented at the annual meeting of the American Educational Research Association, Chicago.

Kounin, J. S. (1970). *Discipline and group management in classrooms.* New York: Holt, Rinehart & Winston.

Krathwohl, D., Bloom, B., & Masia, B. (1964). *Taxonomy of educational objectives. The classification of educational goals. Handbook II: Affective domain.* New York: David McKay.

Krumboltz, J. D., & Krumboltz, H. B. (1972). *Changing children's behavior.* Englewood Ciffs, NJ: Prentice-Hall.

Kubiszyn, T., & Borich, G. (1996). *Educational testing and measurement: Classroom application and practice* (5th ed.). New York: HarperCollins.

Kuhn, D. (1989). Children and adults as intuitive scientists. *Psychological Review, 96,* 674–689.

Kulik, J. A., & Kulik, C. C. (1984). Effects of accelerated instruction on students. *Review of Educational Research, 54,* 409–425.

Kulik, J. A., & Kulik, C. C. (1988). Timing of feedback and verbal learning. *Review of Educational Research, 58,* 79–97.

Kuriloff, A., & Atkins, S. (1966). T-Group for a work team. *Journal of Applied Behavioral Science, 2,* 63–94.

Lambert, N. M. (1991). Partnerships of psychologists, educators, community-based agency personnel, and parents in school redesign. *Educational Psychologist, 26,* 185–198.

Langer, J. A., & Applebee, A. N. (1987). *How writing shapes thinking: A study of teaching and learning,* Champaign, IL: National Council of Teachers of English.

Langlois, J. H., & Stephan, C. W. (1981). Beauty and the beast: The role of physical attractiveness in peer relationships and social behavior. In S. S. Brehm, S. M. Kassin, & S. X. Gibbons (Eds.), *Developmental social psychology: Theory and research* (pp. 152–168). New York: Oxford University Press.

Lautrey, J., DeRibaupierre, A., & Rieben, L. (1987). Operational and individual differences. In E. DeCorte, H. Lodewigks, R. Parmentier, & P. Span (Eds.), *Learning and instruction.* Oxford: Lewen UP and Pergamon Press.

Lein, L. (1975). "You were talkin' though, oh yes, you was." Black American migrant children: Their speech at home and school. *Council on Anthropology and Education Quarterly, 6*(4), 1–11.

Leinhardt, G. (1992). What research on learning tells us about teaching. *Educational Leadership, 49*(7), 20–25.

Leinhardt, G., & Greeno, J. G. (1986). The cognitive skill of teaching. *Journal of Educational Psychology, 78,* 75–95.

Leler, H. (1983). Parent education and involvement in relation to the schools and to parents of school-aged children. In R. Hoskins & D. Adamson (Eds.), *Parent education and public policy* (pp. 141–180). Norwood, NJ: Ablex.

Lesser, G. S., Fifer, G., & Clark, D. H. (1965). Mental abilities of children from different social-class and cultural groups. *Monographs of the Society for Research in Child Development, 30*(4, Serial No. 102).

Levin, J. R. (1985). Educational applications of mnemonic pictures: Possibilities beyond your wildest imagination. In A. A. Sheikh (Ed.), *Imagery in Education: Imagery in the educational process* (pp. 63–87). Farmingdale, NY: Baywood.

Levin J., & Nolan, J. F. (1991). *Principles of classroom management: A hierarchical approach.* Englewood Cliffs, NJ: Prentice-Hall.

Lewis, M., & Miller, S. M. (Eds.). (1990). *Handbook of developmental psychopathology.* New York: Plenum.

Lewis R., & St. John, N. (1974). Contribution of cross-racial friendship to minority group achievement in desegregated classrooms. *Sociometry, 37* (1), 79–91.

Liebert, R. M., & Fischel, J. E. (1990). The elimination disorders: Enuresis and encopresis. In M. Lewis & S. M. Miller (Eds.), *Handbook of developmental psychopathology* (pp. 421–430). New York: Plenum.

Lightfoot, S. L. (1978). *Worlds apart: Relationships between families and schools.* New York: Basic Books.

Lindsley, O. R. (1971). From Skinner to precision teaching: The child knows best. In J. B. Jordan & L. S. Robbins (Eds.), *Let's try doing something else kind of thing* (pp. 1–11). Arlington, VA: Council for Exceptional Children.

Lindsley, O. R. (1990). Our aims, discoveries, failures, and problem. *Journal of Precision Teaching, 7,* 7–17.

Lindsley, O. R. (1991). Precision teaching's unique legacy from B. F. Skinner. *Journal of Behavioral Education, 1,* 253–266.

Lindsley, O. R. (1992a). Why aren't effective teaching tools widely adopted? *Journal of Applied Behavior Analysis, 25*(1), 21–26.

Lindsley, O. R. (1992b). Precision teaching: Discoveries and effects. *Journal of Applied Behavior Analysis, 25*(1), 51–57.

Linn, R., Baker, E., & Dunbar, S. (1991). Complex, performance-based assessment: Expectations and validation criteria. *Educational Researcher, 20*(8), 15–21.

Linney, J. A., & Vernberg, E. (1983). Changing patterns of parental employment and the family-school relationship. In C. D. Hayes & S. Kamerman (Eds.), *Children of working parents: Experiences and outcomes* (pp. 73–99). Washington, DC: National Academy Press.

Lippitt, R., & Gold, M. (1959). Classroom social structure as a mental health problem. *Journal of Social Issues, 15,* 40–58.

Lipsky, D. K., & Gartner, A. (1989). School administration and financial arrangements. In S. Stainback, W. Stainback, & M. Forest (Eds.). *Educating all students in the mainstream of regular education* (pp. 105–120). Baltimore: Paul H. Brookes.

Little, W. (1977). *Reading for concepts.* New York: McGraw-Hill.

Livson, N., & Peskin, H. (1980). Perspectives on adolescence from longitudinal research. In J. Adelson (Ed.), *Handbook of adolescent psychology* (pp. 47–98). New York: Wiley.

Loney, J., & Milich, R. (1982). Hyperactivity, inattention and aggression in clinical practice. In M. Woolrach & D. Routh (Eds.), *Advances in behavioral pediatrics: Vol. 2* (pp. 113–147). Greenwich, CT: JAI.

Loucks-Horsley, S., Kapiton, R., Carlson, M. D., Kuerbis, P. J., Clark, P. C., Melle, G. M., Sachse, T. P., & Wolten, E. (1990). *Elementary school science of the '90s.* Alexandria, VA: Association for Supervision and Curriculum Development.

Lovitt, T. C. (1994). Applied behavior analysis; An insider's appraisal. In R. Gardner, D. M. Sainato, J. O. Cooper, T. E. Heron, W. L. Heward, J. W. Eshleman, & T. A. Grossi (Eds.), *Behavior analysis in education* (pp. 312–331). Pacific Grove, CA: Brooks-Cole.

Lucas, T., Henze, R., & Donato, R. (1990). Promoting the success of Latino language minority students: An exploratory study of six high schools. *Harvard Educational Review, 60,* 315–340.

Lytton, H. (1977). Do parents create, or respond to, differences in twins? *Developmental Psychology, 12,* 456–459.

Macfarlane, J. W. (1971). From infancy to adulthood. In M. C. Jones, N. Bayley, J. W. Macfarlane, & M. P. Honzik (Eds.), *The course of human development* (pp. 406–410). Waltham, MA: Xerox College Publishing.

Maehr, M. L., & Midgley, C. (1991). Enhancing student motivation: A schoolwide approach. *Educational Psychologist, 26,* 399–428.

Main, M., & George, C. (1985). Response of abused and disadvantaged toddlers to distress in agemates: A study in the daycare setting. *Developmental Psychology, 21,* 407–412.

Mann, L., & Goodman, L. (1976). Perceptual training: A critical retrospect. In E. Schopler & R. J. Reichler (Eds.), *Psychopathology and child development: Research and treatment.* New York: Plenum.

Mannheim, B. F. (1957). An investigation of the interrelations of reference groups, membership groups and the self-image: A test of the Cooley-Mead theory of the self. *Dissertation Abstracts, 17,* 1616–1617.

Mansnerus, L. (1992, November 1). Should tracking be derailed? *New York Times Magazine, Education Life,* pp. 14–16.

Maratsos, M. (1983). Some current issues in the study of the acquisition of grammar. In J. H. Flavell & E. M. Markman (Eds.), *Handbook of child psychology: Cognitive development: Vol. 3* (pp. 707–786). New York: Wiley.

Marean, J. H. (1987). *Earth science: A laboratory approach investigating the earth.* Reading, MA: Addison-Wesley.

Maribeth, G. (1993). Effects of invented spelling and direct instruction on spelling performance of second-grade boys. *Journal of Applied Behavior Analysis, 26,* 281–292.

Marshall, S. P. (1990). *What students learn (and remember) from word problem instruction.* Paper presented at the annual meeting of the American Educational Research Association, Boston.

Martin, M. & Hoffman, J. A. (1990). Conduct disorders. In M. Lewis & S. M. Miller (Eds.), *Handbook of developmental psychopathology* (pp. 109–118). New York: Plenum.

Maslow, A. H. (1943). A theory of human motivation. *Psychological Review, 50,* 370–396.

Maslow, A. H. (1970). *Motivation and personality* (Rev. ed). New York: Harper & Row.

Masten, A. S. (1989). Resilience in development: Implications of the study of successful adaptation for developmental psychopathology. In D. Cicchetti (Ed.), *The emergence of a discipline: Vol. 1. Rochester Symposium on Developmental Psychopathology* (pp. 261–924). Hillsdale, NJ: Lawrence Erlbaum.

Matarazzo, J. D. (1972). *Wechsler's measurement and appraisal of adult intelligence* (5th ed.). Baltimore: Williams & Wilkins.

Mauer, R. E. (1985). *Elementary discipline handbook: Solutions for the K–8 teacher.* West Nyack, NY: The Center for Applied Research in Education.

Mayer, R. E. (1987). *Educational psychology: A cognitive approach.* Boston: Little, Brown.

McCarthy, J. D., & Hoge, D. R. (1982). Analysis of age effects in longitudinal studies of adolescent self-esteem. *Developmental Psychology, 18,* 372–379.

McClelland, C. (1975). *Power: The inner experience.* New York: Irvington.

McClelland, J. L., & Rumelhart, D. E. (1981). An interactive activation model of context effects in letter perception: Part 1. An account of basic findings. *Psychological Review, 88,* 375–407.

McClelland, J. L., & Rumelhart, D. E. (1986). *Parallel distributed processing: Vol. 2.* Cambridge, MA: MIT Press.

McCormick, L., & Schiefelbusch, R. L. (1984). *Early language intervention.* Columbus, OH: Merrill.

McDiarmid, G. W. (1991). What teachers need to know about cultural diversity: Restoring subject matter to the picture. In M. M. Kennedy (Ed.), *Teaching academic subjects to diverse learners* (pp. 257–269). New York: Teachers College Press.

McDougall, W. (1908). *An introduction to social psychology.* London: Methuen.

McHill, E. L., Rigsby, L., & Meyers, E. (1969). *Educational climates of high schools: Their effects and sources.* Baltimore, MD: Johns Hopkins University, Center for the Study of Social Organization of Schools. (ERIC Document Reproduction Service No. ED 030-205)

McKeachie, W. J. (1990). Learning, thinking, and Thorndike. *Educational Psychologist, 25,* 127–142.

McLean, P. D. (1974, August). *Parental depression: Incompatible with effective parenting.* Paper presented at the Sixth Annual Conference on Behavior Modification, Banff, Alberta, Canada.

McMillan, J. (1980). *The social psychology of school learning.* New York: Academic Press.

McQueen, T. (1992). *Essentials of classroom management and discipline.* New York: HarperCollins.

Mead, G. H. (1934). *Mind, self and society.* Chicago: University of Chicago Press.

Mead, M. (1939). *From the South Seas: Studies of adolescence and sex in primitive societies.* New York: Morrow.

Medrich, E. A., Roizen, J. A., Rubin, V., & Burkley, S. (1982). *The serious business of growing up: A study of children's lives outside school.* Berkeley: University of California Press.

Meichenbaum, D. (1977). *Cognitive behavior modification: An integrative approach.* New York: Plenum.

Meltzoff, A. N. (1988). Infant imitation and memory: Nine-month-olds in immediate and deferred tests. *Child Development, 59,* 217–255.

Menke, J. A., McClead, R. E., & Hansen, N. B. (1991). Perspectives on perinatal complications associated with mental retardation. In J. L. Matson & J. A. Mulick (Eds.), *Handbook of mental retardation* (2nd ed., pp. 139–150). New York: Pergamon.

Merrett, F., & Wheldall, K. (1992). Teachers' use of praise and reprimands to boys and girls. *Educational Researcher, 44,* 73–79.

Metcalfe, B. (1981). Self-concept and attitude toward school. *British Journal of Educational Psychology, 51,* 55–76.

Meyer, W. J., & Thompson, G. G. (1956). Sex differences in the distribution of teacher approval and disapproval among sixth graders. *Journal of Educational Psychology, 47,* 385–396.

Milich, R., & Kramer, J. (1985). Reflections on impulsivity: An empirical investigation of impulsivity as a construct. In K. Gadow & I. Bealer (Eds.), *Advances in learning and behavior disorders: Vol. 3.* Greenwich, CT: JAI.

Miller, G. A. (1956). The magical number seven, plus or minus two: Some limits on our capacity for processing information. *Psychological Review, 65,* 81–97.

Miller, L. (1990). The regular education initiative and school reform: Lessons from the mainstream. *Remedial and Special Education, 11*(3), 17–22.

Miller, S. M., Birnbaum, A., & Durbin, D. (1990). Etiologic perspectives on depression in childhood. In M. Lewis & S. M. Miller (Eds.), *Handbook of developmental psychopathology* (pp. 311–326). New York: Plenum.

Mitchell, R. (1992). *Testing for learning: How new approaches to evaluation can improve American schools.* New York: Free Press.

Moles, O. (1987). *Trends in student misconduct: The 70's and 80's.* Paper presented at the annual meeting of the American Educational Research Association, Washington, DC.

Morgenstern, M., & Klass, E. (1991). Standard intelligence tests and related assessment techniques. In J. L. Matson & J. A. Mulick (Eds.), *Handbook of mental retardation* (2nd ed., pp. 195–210). New York: Pergamon.

Mounoud, P. (1986). Similarities between developmental sequences at different age periods. In I. Levin (Ed.), *Stage and structure: reopening the debate.* Norwood, NJ: Ablex.

Muss, R. E. (1988). Carol Gilligan's theory of sex differences in the development of moral reasoning during adolescence. *Adolescence, 23,* 229–243.

Nehring, J. (1989). *"Why do we gotta do this stuff, Mr. Nehring?" Notes from a teacher's day in school.* New York: Fawcett.

Neisser, U. (1976). *Cognition and reality: Principles and implications of cognitive psychology.* San Francisco: Freeman.

Nelson-LeGall, S., & Jones, E. (1991). Classroom help-seeking behavior of African-American children. *Education and Urban Society, 24,* 27–40.

Nelson-LeGall, S., Kratzer, L., Jones, E., & DeCooke, P. (1990). Children's self-assessment of performance and task-related help seeking. *Journal of Experimental Child Psychology, 49,* 245–263.

Nitko, A. J. (1989). Designing tests that are integrated with instruction. In R. L. Linn (ed.), *Educational assessment* (3rd ed., pp. 13–103). New York: Macmillan.

Nucci, L. P., & Turiel, E. (1978). Social interactions and the development of social concepts in preschool children. *Child Development, 49,* 400–407.

Nussbaum, J., & Novick, S. (1982). Alternative frameworks, conceptual conflict and accomodation: Toward a principled teaching strategy. *Instructional Science, 11,* 183–200.

O'Leary, K. D. (1980). Pills or skills for hyperactive children. *Journal of Applied Behavior Analysis, 13,* 191–204.

O'Leary, K. D., & O'Leary, S. (1977). *Classroom management: The successful use of behavior modification* (2nd ed.). New York: Pergamon.

O'Malley, P. M., & Bachman, J. G. (1983). Self-esteem: Change and stability between ages 13 and 23. *Developmental Psychology, 19,* 257–268.

O'Neil, J. (1992). On tracking and individual differences: A conversation with Jeannie Oakes. *Educational Leadership, 50*(2), 18–21.

O'Neill, R. E., Horner, R. H., Alben, R. W., Storey, K., & Sprague, J. R. (1991). *Functional analysis: A practical assessment guide.* Sycamore, IL: Sycamore Publishing.

Ornstein, A. C. (1992). *Secondary and middle school teaching methods.* New York: HarperCollins.

O'Sullivan, J. T., & Pressley, M. (1984). Completeness of instruction and strategy transfer. *Journal of Experimental Child Psychology, 35,* 275–288.

Padilla, A. M., Lindholm, K. J., Chen, A., Duran, R., Hakuta, K., Lambert, W., & Tucker, G. R. (1991). The English-only movement: Myths, reality, and implications for psychology. *American Psychologist, 46,* 120–130.

Paivio, A. (1971). *Imagery and verbal processes.* New York: Holt, Rinehart & Winston.

Paivio, A. (1986). *Mental representations: A dual coding approach.* New York: Oxford University Press.

Palincsar, A. S. (1987). Reciprocal teaching: Can student discussion boost comprehension? *Instructor, 5*(96), 56–60.

Palincsar, A. S., & Brown, A. L. (1984). Reciprocal teaching of comprehension-fostering and monitoring activities. *Cognition and Instruction, 1,* 117–175.

Palincsar, A. S. & Brown, A. L. (1989). Classroom dialogues to promote self-regulated comprehension. In J. Brophy (Ed.), *Advances in research on teaching* (pp. 35–71). Greenwich, CT: JAI.

Parker, W. C. (1991). *Renewing the social studies curriculum.* Alexandria, VA: Association for Supervision and Curriculum Development.

Pasch, M., Sparks-Langer, G., Gardner, T. G., Starko, A. J., & Moody, C. D. (1991). *Teaching as decision making: Instructional practices for the successful teacher.* New York: Longman.

Patterson, G. R. (1975). *Families. Applications of social learning to family life.* Champaign, IL: Research Press.

Patterson, G. R. (1980). Mothers: The unacknowledged victims: *Monographs of the Society for Research in Child Development, 45* (Serial No. 186).

Patterson, G. R., & Bank, L. (1986). Bootstrapping your way in the nomological thicket. *Behavioral Assessment, 8,* 49–73.

Patterson, G. R., Capaldi, D., & Bank, L. (1991). An early starter model for predicting delinquency. In D. J. Peplery & K. H. Rubin (Eds.), *The development and treatment of childhood aggression* (pp. 139–168). Hillsdale, NJ: Lawrence Erlbaum.

Patterson, G. R., DeBarsyshe, B. D., & Ramsey, E. (1989). A developmental perspective on anti-social behavior. *American Psychologist, 44,* 329–335.

Paulson, P. R., & Paulson, F. L. (1991). Portfolio: Stories of knowing. In P. H. Dryer (ed.), *Claremont Reading Conference 55th Yearbook 1991: Knowing: The power of stories* (pp. 294–303). Claremont, CA: Center for Developmental Studies of the Claremont Graduate School.

Pavlov, I. P. (1927). *Conditioned reflexes.* London: Oxford University Press.

Pavlov, I. P. (1928). *Lectures on conditioned reflexes: Twenty years of objective study of higher nervous activity behavior of animals (Vol. 1)* (W. H. Gantt, Trans.). New York: International Publishers.

Peterson, P. L., & Comeaux, M. A. (1987). Teachers' schemata for classroom events: The mental scaffolding of teachers' thinking during classroom instruction. *Teaching and Teacher Education, 3,* 319–331.

Phillips, S. (1983). *The invisible culture: Communication in classroom and community on the Warm Springs Indian Reservation.* New York: Longman.

Piaget, J. (1959). *The language and thought of the child.* London: Routledge & Kegan Paul.

Piaget, J. (1963). *The origins of intelligence in children.* New York: Norton.

Piestrup, A. (1973). *Black dialect interference and accommodation of reading instruction in first grade* (Monograph No. 4). Berkeley, CA: University of California, Language Behavior Research Laboratory.

Pinker, S., & Prince, A. (1988). On language and connectionism: Analysis of a parallel distributed processing model of language acquisition. *Cognition, 28,* 73–193.

Pintrich, P. R. (1991). Editors' comment. *Educational Psychologist, 26,* 199–205.

Plomin, R. (1989). Environment and genes: Determinants of behavior. *American Psychologist, 44,* 105–111.

Plomin, R., & DeFries, J. C. (1983). The Colorado adoption project. *Child Development, 54,* 276–289.

Plomin, R. & DeFries, J. C. (1985) A parent-offspring adoption study of cognitive abilities in early childhood. *Intelligence, 9,* 341–356.

Plomin, R., & Rende, R. (1991). Human behavior genetics. *Annual Review of Psychology, 42,* 161–190.

Pollock, J. E. (1992). Blueprints for social studies. *Educational Leadership, 49*(8), 52–53.

Porino, L. J., Rappoport, J. L., Behar, D., Sceery, W., Ismond, D. R., & Bunney, W. E. (1983). A naturalistic assessment of the motor activity of hyperactive boys. *Archives of General Psychiatry, 40,* 681–687.

Posner, G. J., Strike, K. A., Hewson, P. W., & Gertzog, W. A. (1982). Accomodation of a science conception: Toward a theory of conceptual change. *Science Education, 66,* 211–227.

Pressley, M. (1995). *Advanced educational psychology for educators, researchers, and policymakers.* New York: Harper-Collins.

Pressley, M., Borkowski, J. G., & O'Sullivan, J. T. (1984). Memory strategy instruction is made of this: Metamemory and durable strategy use. *Educational Psychologist, 19,* 94–107.

Pressley, M., Borkowski, J. G., & O'Sullivan, J. T. (1985). Children's metamemory and the teaching of memory strategies. In D. L. Forrest-Pressley, G. E. MacKinnon, & T. G. Waller (Eds.), *Metacognition, cognition, and human performance* (pp. 111–153). New York: Academic Press.

Pressley, M., & Ghatala, E. S. (1990). Self-regulated learning: Monitoring learning from text. *Educational Psychologist, 25,* 19–34.

Pressley, M. Harris, K. R., & Marks, M. B. (1992). But good strategy instructors are constructivists! *Educational Psychology Review, 4,* 3–31.

Pugack, M., & Lilly, M. S. (1984). Reconceptualizing support services for classroom teachers: Implications for teacher education. *Journal of Teacher Education, 35*(5), 48–55.

Purkey, W. W. (1970). *Self-concept and school achievement.* Englewood Cliffs, NJ: Prentice-Hall.

Putnam, J., & Burke, J. B. (1992). *Organizing and managing classroom learning communities.* New York: McGraw-Hill.

Rabinowitz, M., & McCauley, R. (1990). Conceptual knowledge processing: An oxymoron? In W. Schneider & F. E. Weinert (Eds.), *Interactions among aptitudes, strategies, and knowledge in cognitive performance* (pp. 117–133). New York: Springer-Verlag.

Radke-Yarrow, M., Cummings, E. M., Kuczynski, L., & Chapman, M. (1985). Patterns of attachment in two- and three-year olds in normal families and families with parental depression. *Child Development, 56,* 884–893.

Ramirez, M., & Castaneda, A. (1974). *Cultural democracy: Biocognitive development and education.* New York: Academic Press.

Raven, B. H. (1974). The comparative analysis of power and power preference. In J. T. Tedeschi (Ed.), *Perspectives on social power* (pp. 172–198). Chicago: Aldine.

Ravitch, D. (1992). A culture in common. *Educational Leadership, 49,* 8–11.

Redding, N. (1992). Assessing the big outcomes. *Educational Leadership, 49*(8), 49–53.

Rehm, L. P., & Carter, A. S. (1990). Cognitive components of depression. In M. Lewis & S. M. Miller (Eds.), *Handbook of developmental psychopathology* (pp. 341–352). New York: Plenum.

Reich, P. A. (1986). *Language development.* Englewood Cliffs, NJ: Prentice-Hall.

Reimer, J., Paolitto, D. P., & Hersh, R. M. (1983). *Promoting moral development: From Piaget to Kohlberg* (2nd ed.). New York: Longman.

Renzulli, J. S., & Smith, L. H. (1978). *The learning styles inventory: A measure of student preferences for instructional techniques.* Mansfield Center, CT: Creative Learning Press.

Reschly, D. J. (1978). WISC-R factor structures among Anglos, blacks, Chicanos, and Native American Papagos. *Journal of Consulting and Clinical Psychology, 46,* 417–422.

Reschly, D. J. (1981). Psychological testing in educational classification and placement. *American Psychologist, 36*(10), 1094–1102.

Reschly, D. J., & Reschly, J. E. (1979). Validity of WISC-R factor scores in predicting achievement and attention for four sociocultural groups. *Journal of School Psychology, 17,* 355–361.

Reschly, D. J., & Sabers, D. (1979). Analysis of test bias in four groups with the regression definition. *Journal of Educational Measurement, 16,* 1–9.

Resnick, L. B. (1987). *Education and learning to think.* Washington, DC: National Academy Press.

Resnick, L. B. (1989). *Knowing, learning, and instructions: Essays in honor of Robert Glaser.* Hillsdale, NJ: Lawrence Erlbaum.

Resnick, L. B. (1990). *An examination system for the nation.* Pittsburgh, PA: Learning, Research and Development Center, University of Pittsburgh.

Resnick, L. B., & Klopfer, L. E. (1989). Toward the thinking curriculum: An overview. In L. B. Resnick & L. E. Klopfer, (Eds.), *Toward the thinking curriculum: Current cognitive research.* Alexandria, VA: Association for Supervision and Curriculum Development.

Resnick, L. B., & Resnick, D. P. (1991). Assessing the thinking curriculum: New tools for educational reform. In B. R. Gifford and M. C. O'Connor (Eds.), *Future assessments: Changing views of aptitude, achievement and instruction.* Norwood, MA: Kluwer.

Restak, R. (1975). Genetic counseling for defective parents: The danger of knowing too much. *Psychology Today, 9,* 21–23, 92–93.

Reynolds, C. (1977). Buddy system improves attendance. *Elementary School Guidance and Counseling, 11,* 305–336.

Reynolds, C. R., & Kaiser, S. M. (1990). Test bias in psychological assessment. In T. B. Gutkin & C. R. Reynolds (Eds.), *The handbook of school psychology* (2nd ed., pp. 487–525). New York: Wiley.

Reynolds, W. M. (1980). Self-esteem and classroom behavior in elementary school children. *Psychology in the Schools, 17,* 273–277.

Rich, D. (1988). *Megaskills: How families can help children succeed in school and beyond.* Boston: Houghton Mifflin.

Rinne, C. (1984). *Attention: The fundamentals of classroom control.* Columbus, OH: Merrill.

Rist, R. (1970). Student social class and teacher expectations: The self-fulfilling prophecy in ghetto education. *Harvard Educational Review, 40,* 411–451.

Robinson, F. P. (1946). *Effective study.* New York: Harper & Row.

Robinson, V. (1990, Fall). Regular education initiative: Debate on the current state and future promise of a new approach to educating children with disabilities. *Counterpoint, 5.*

Rodgers, T. A., & Iwata, B. A. (1991). An analysis of error-correction procedures during discrimination training. *Journal of Applied Behavior Analysis, 24,* 775–782.

Roehler, L. R., & Duffy, G. G. (1984). Direct explanation of comprehension processes. In G. G. Duffy, L. R. Roehler, & J. Mason (Eds.), *Comprehension instruction: Perspectives and suggestions* (pp. 265–280). New York: Longman.

Rogan, J., Borich, G., & Taylor, H. P. (1992). Validation of the stages of concern questionnaire. *Action in Teacher Education, 14*(2), 43–49.

Rogoff, B. (1990). *Apprenticeship in thinking: Cognitive development in social context.* New York: Oxford University Press.

Rosenshine, B., & Chapman, S. (1992). *Instructional elements in studies which taught students to generate questions.* Paper presented at the annual meeting of the American Educational Research Association, San Francisco.

Rosenshine, B., & Meister, C. (1992). The use of scaffolds for teaching higher-level cognitive strategies. *Educational Leadership, 49*(7), 26–33.

Rosenshine, B., & Meister, C. (1994). Reciprocal teaching: A review of the research. *Review of Educational Research, 64*(4), 479–530.

Rosenshine, B., & Stevens, R. (1986). Teaching functions. In M. C. Wittrock (Ed.), *Handbook of research on teaching* (3rd ed., pp. 376–391). Englewood Cliffs, NJ: Merrill/Prentice Hall.

Rosenthal, T. L, & Zimmerman, B. J. (1978). *Social learning and cognition.* New York: Academic Press.

Ross, D. M., & Ross, S. A. (1982). *Hyperactivity: Current issues, research and theory* (2nd ed.). New York: Wiley.

Rosser, R. A., & Nicholson, G. I. (1984). *Educational psychology.* Boston: Little, Brown.

Roth, K. J. (1990). Developing meaningful conceptual understanding in science. In B. F. Jones & L. Idol (Eds.), *Dimensions of thinking and cognitive instruction* (pp. 139–175). Hillsdale, NJ: Lawrence Erlbaum.

Roth, K. J. (1991). Reading science texts for conceptual change. In C. M. Santa & D. E. Alvermann (Eds.), *Science learning: Processes and applications* (pp. 48–63). Newark, DE: International Reading Association.

Rowe, M. B. (1974). Wait-time and rewards as instructional variables, their influence on language, logic and fate control: Part 1. Wait-time. *Journal of Research in Science Teaching, 11*, 81–94.

Rowe, M. B. (1986, January/February). Wait-time: Slowing down may be a way of speeding up. *Journal of Teacher Education, 23*, 43.

Rowe, M. B. (1987). Wait-time: Slowing down may be a way of speeding up. *American Educator, 11*(1), 38–43, 47.

Rumelhart, D. E. (1992). Towards a microstructural account of human reasoning. In S. Davis (Ed.), *Connectionism: Theory and practice*. New York: Oxford University Press.

Rutter, M., & Garmezy, N. (1983). Developmental psychopathology. In E. M. Hetterington (ed.), *Handbook of child psychology: Socialization, personality and social development: Vol. 4* (pp. 779–912). New York: Wiley.

Ryan, K. (1992) (ed.). *The roller coaster year: Essays by and for beginning teachers*. New York: HarperCollins.

Rynders, J. E., & Horrobin, J. (1980). Educational provisions for young children with Down's syndrome. In J. Gottleib (Ed.), *Educating mentally retarded persons in the mainstream* (pp. 109–147). Baltimore: University Park Press.

Rynders, J. E., & Horrobin, J. (1990). Always trainable? Never educable? Updating educational expectations concerning children with Down's syndrome. *American Journal of Mental Retardation, 95*(1), 77–83.

Sacks, S. R., & Harrington, C. N. (1982, March). *Student to teacher: The process of role transition*. Paper presented at the meeting of the American Educational Research Association, New York.

Sadker, M., & Sadker, D. (1985, March). Sexism in the schoolroom of the 80's. *Psychology Today*, 54–57.

Sadker, M., & Sadker, D. (1986). Sexism in the classroom: From grade school to graduate school. *Phi Delta Kappan, 68*, 512.

Sadker, M., & Sadker, D. (1988). *Teacher, school & society*. New York: Random House.

Sadker, M., & Sadker, D. (1990). *Sex equity handbook for schools* (2nd ed.). New York: Longman.

Sadker, M., Sadker, D., & Klein, S. (1991). The issue of gender in elementary and secondary education. *Review of Research in Education, 17*, 269–334.

Sadker, M., Sadker, D., & Steindam, S. (1989). Gender, equity and educational reform. *Educational Leadership, 46*, 44–47.

Sadoski, M. (1983). An exploratory study of the relationship between reported imagery and the comprehension and recall of a story. *Reading Research Quarterly, 19*, 110–123.

Sadoski, M. (1985). The natural use of imagery in story comprehension and recall: Replication and extension. *Reading Research Quarterly, 20*, 658–667.

Sandberg, R., Rutter, M., & Taylor, E. (1978). Hyperkinetic disorder in psychiatric clinic attenders. *Developmental Medicine and Child Neurology, 20*, 279–299.

Sattler, J. (1988). *Assessment of children*. San Diego: Author.

Savage, T. (1991). *Discipline for self-control*. Englewood Cliffs, NJ: Prentice-Hall.

Sax, G. (1989). *Principles of educational and psychological measurement and evaluation* (3rd ed.). Belmont, CA: Wadsworth.

Saxe, G. B. (1995). From the field to the classroom: Studies in mathematical understanding. In L. P. Steffe & J. Gale (Eds.), *Constructivism in education* (pp. 287–312). Hillsdale, NJ: Lawrence Erlbaum.

Scardamalia, M., & Bereiter, C. (1985). Fostering the development of self-regulation in children's knowledge processing. In S. F. Chipman, J. W. Segal, & R. Glaser (Eds.), *Thinking and learning skills: Research and open questions* (pp. 563–577). Hillsdale, NJ: Lawrence Erlbaum.

Scardamalia, M., & Bereiter, C. (1986). Research on written composition. In M. C. Wittrock (Ed.), *Handbook of research on teaching* (3rd ed., pp. 778–803). New York: Macmillan.

Scarr, S. (1981). Testing for children: Assessment and the many determinants of intellectual competence. *American Psychologist, 36*(10), 1159–1166.

Scarr, S., & Weinberg, R. A. (1983). The Minnesota adoption studies: Genetic differences and malleability. *Child Development, 54*, 260–267.

Schaefle, A., Rest, J. R., & Thoma, S. J. (1985). Does moral education improve moral judgment? A meta-analysis of intervention studies using the defining issues test. *Review of Educational Research, 55*, 319–352.

Scherer, M. (1992). School snapshot: Focus on African-American culture. *Educational Leadership, 49*, 17–19.

Schmuck, R., (1971). Influence of the peer group. In G. Lesser (Ed.), *Psychology and educational practice* (pp. 502–529). Glenview, IL: Scott, Foresman.

Schmuck, R., & Schmuck, P. (1988). *Group processes in the classroom* (5th ed.). Dubuque, IA: William C. Brown.

Schmuck, R., & Schmuck P. (1992). *Group processes in the classroom* (6th ed.). Dubuque, IA: William C. Brown.

Schneider, W., & Korkel, J. (1989). The knowledge base and text recall: Evidence from a short-term longitudinal study. *Contemporary Educational Psychology, 14*, 382–393.

Schneider, W., Korkel, J., & Weinert, F. E. (1989). Domain-specific knowledge and memory performance: A comparison of high- and low-aptitude children. *Journal of Educational Psychology, 81*, 306–312.

Schneider-Rosen, K., Braunwald, K., Carlson, V., & Cicchetti, D. (1985). Current perspectives in attachment theory: Illustrations from the study of maltreated infants. In I. Bretherton & E. Waters (Eds.), Growing points in attachment theory. *Monographs of the Society For Research in Child Development, 50* (1–2, Serial No. 209).

Schoenfeld, A. H. (1983). Problem solving in the mathematics curriculum: A report, recommendations and an annotated bibliography. *The Mathematical Association of America*, MAA Notes, No. 1.

Schoenfeld, A. H. (1985). *Mathematical problem solving*. New York: Academic Press.

Schoenfeld, A. H. (1989) Exploration of students' mathematical beliefs and behavior. *Journal for Research in Mathematics Education, 20*, 338–355.

Schumaker, J. B., & Deshler, D. D. (1988). Implementing the regular education initiative. *Journal of Learning Disabilities, 21*(1), 36–42.

Schunk, D. H. (1983). Developing children's self-efficacy and skills: The roles of social comparative information and goal setting. *Contemporary Educational Psychology, 8,* 76–86.

Schunk, D. H. (1989a). Self-efficacy and achievement behaviors. *Educational Psychology Review, 1,* 173–208.

Schunk, D. H. (1989b). Self-efficacy and cognitive skill learning. In C. Ames & R. Ames (Eds.), *Research on motivation in education: Vol. 3. Goals and cognitions* (pp. 13–44). San Diego: Academic Press.

Schunk, D. H. (1991). Self-efficacy and academic motivation. *Educational Psychologist, 26,* 207–232.

Schunk, D. H., & Hanson, A. R. (1985). Peer models: Influence on children's self-efficacy and achievement. *Journal of Educational Psychology, 77,* 313–322.

Schunk, D. H., Hanson, A. R., & Cox, P. D. (1987). Peer model attributes and children's achievement behaviors. *Journal of Educational Psychology, 79,* 54–61.

Schutz, W. (1958). *FIRO: A three-dimensional theory of interpersonal behavior.* New York: Holt, Rinehart & Winston.

Seifert, K. L., & Hoffnung, R. J. (1987). *Child and adolescent development.* Boston: Houghton Mifflin.

Seligman, M., & Darling, R. B. (1989). *Ordinary families, special children.* New York: Guilford.

Selman, R. L. (1980). *The growth of interpersonal understanding and clinical analysis.* Orlando: Academic Press.

Selman, R. L. (1989). Fostering intimacy and autonomy. In W. Damon (Ed.). *Child development today and tomorrow* (pp. 175–213). San Francisco: Jossey-Bass.

Serbin, L. A., O'Leary, D. K., Kent, R. N., & Tonick, J. J. (1973). A comparison of the preacademic and problem behaviors of boys and girls. *Child Development, 44,* 796–804.

Shade, B. J. (1982). Afro-American cognitive style: A variable in school success. *Review of Educational Research, 52,* 219–244.

Shaffer, D., McNamara, N., & Pincus, J. H. (1974). Controlled observations on patterns of activity, attention and impulsivity in brain damaged and psychiatrically disturbed boys. *Psychological Medicine, 4,* 4–18.

Shaffer, D. R. (1993). *Developmental psychology: Childhood and adolescence.* Pacific Grove, CA: Brooks/Cole.

Shalaway, L. (1989). *Learning to teach.* Cleveland, OH: Edgell Communications.

Sharan, S., & Sharan, Y. (1976). *Small group teaching.* Englewood Cliffs, NJ: Educational Technology Publications.

Shavelson, R. J., & Baxter, G. P. (1992). What we've learned about assessing hands-on science. *Educational Leadership, 49*(8), 20–25.

Shavelson, R. J., Gao, X., and Baxter, G. (1991). *Design theory and psychometrics for complex performance assessment.* Los Angeles: UCLA Center for Research on Evaluation, Standards and Student Testing.

Sherif, M. (1935). A study of some social factors in perception. *Archives of Psychology, 27,* 187–193.

Short, E. J., & Ryan, E. B. (1984). Metacognitive differences between skilled and less skilled readers: Remediating deficits through story grammar and attribution training. *Journal of Educational Psychology, 76,* 225–235.

Shulman, J. H. (1991). Classroom casebooks. *Educational Leadership, 49*(3), 28–31.

Shulman, L. (1987). Knowledge and teaching: Foundations of the new reform. *Harvard Education Review, 19*(2), 4–14.

Shulman, L. S. (1992). Toward a pedagogy of cases. In J. H. Shulman (Ed.), *Case methods in teacher education.* New York: Teachers College Press.

Simmons, R. G., Burgeson, R., Carlton-Ford, S., & Blyth, D. A. (1987). The impact of cumulative change in early adolescence. *Child Development, 58,* 1220–1234.

Sinclair, E., & Forness, S. (1983). Classification: Educational issues. In J. L. Matson & J. A. Mulick (Eds.), *Handbook of mental retardation.* New York: Pergamon.

Sizer, T. (1984). *Horace's compromise: The dilemma of the American high school.* Boston: Houghton Mifflin.

Skinner, B. F. (1953). *Science and human behavior.* New York: Macmillan.

Skinner, B. F. (1954). The science and the art of teaching. *Harvard Educational Review, 24,* 86–97.

Skinner, B. F. (1971). *Beyond freedom and dignity.* New York: Knopf.

Skinner, B. F. (1974). *About behaviorism.* New York: Knopf.

Skrtic, T. M. (1991). The special education paradox: Equity as the way to excellence. *Harvard Educational Review, 61*(2), 148–206.

Slavin, R. (1984). Students motivating students to excel: Cooperative incentives, cooperative tasks and student achievement. *Elementary School Journal, 85,* 53–64.

Slavin, R. (1985). Team-assisted individualization: A cooperative learning solution for adaptive instruction in mathematics. In M. Wang & H. Walberg (Eds.), *Adapting instruction to individual differences.* Berkeley, CA: McCutchean.

Slavin, R. (1987). Ability grouping and student achievement in elementary schools: A best evidence synthesis. *Review of Educational Research, 57,* 273–336.

Slavin, R. (1990a). Achievement effects of ability grouping in secondary schools: A best evidence synthesis. *Review of Educational Research, 60,* 471–499.

Slavin, R. (1990b). *Cooperative learning.* Englewood Cliffs, NJ: Prentice-Hall.

Slavin, R. (1991). Are cooperative learning and untracking harmful to the gifted? *Educational Leadership, 48,* 68–71.

Slavin, R. E. (1991). Synthesis of research on cooperative learning. *Educational Leadership, 48* (5), 71–82.

Slavin, R. (1993). *Student team learning: An overview and practical guide.* Washington, DC: National Educational Association.

Slavin, R. E., & Karwait, N. (1984). Mastery learning and student teams: A factorial experiment in urban general mathematics classes. *American Educational Research Journal, 21,* 725–736.

Slavin, R. E., Leavey, M. B., & Madden, M. A. (1984). Combining cooperative learning and individualized instruction: Effects on student mathematics achievement, attitudes and behaviors. *Elementary School Journal, 84,* 409–422.

Sleeter, C., & Grant, C. (1991). *Race, class, gender, and disability in current textbooks.* New York: Routledge & Chapman.

Smetana, J. G., Kelly, M., & Twentyman, C. T. (1984). Abused, neglected and nonmaltreated children's conceptions of moral and conventional transgressions. *Child Development, 55,* 277–287.

Snakeshaft, C. (1986). A gender at risk. *Phi Delta Kappan, 67,* 499–502.

Snider, V. E. (1990). What we know about learning styles from research in special education. *Educational Leadership, 48*(2), 53.

Snider, W. (1990, November). Parents as partners: Adding their voices to decisions on how schools are run. *Education Week, 9*(44), 11–15.

Soar, R., & Soar, R. (1983). Context effects in the learning process. In D. C. Smith (Ed.), *Essential knowledge for beginning educators* (pp. 156–192). Washington, DC: American Association of Colleges of Teacher Education.

Solso, R. L. (1988). *Cognitive Psychology* (2nd ed.). Needham, MA: Allyn & Bacon.

Sparks-Langer, G. M., & Cotton, A. B. (1991). Synthesis of research on teachers' reflective thinking. *Educational Leadership, 48*(6), 37–44.

Spaulding, C. L. (1992). *Motivation in the classroom.* New York: McGraw-Hill.

Sperling, G. (1960). The information available in brief visual presentations. *Psychological Monographs, 74*(11).

Spivey, N. N. (1995). Written discourse: A constructivist perspective. In L. P. Steffe & J. Gale (Eds.), *Constructivism in education* (pp. 313–330). Hillsdale, NJ: Lawrence Erlbaum.

Sroufe, L. A. (1983). Infant-caregiver attachment and patterns of adaptation in preschool: The roots of maladaptation and competence. In M. Perlmutter (Ed.), *Minnesota Symposium on Child Psychology* (Vol. 16, pp. 41–84). Hillsdale, NJ: Lawrence Erlbaum.

Sroufe, L. A. (1988). The role of infant caregiver attachment in development. In J. Belsky & T. Nezworski (Eds.), *Clinical implications of attachments* (pp. 18–40). Hillsdale, NJ: Lawrence Erlbaum.

Sroufe, L. A. (1989). Pathways to adaptation and maladaptation: Psychopathology as developmental deviation. In D. Cicchetti (Ed.), *The emergence of a discipline: Vol. 1. Rochester symposium on developmental psychopathology* (pp. 13–40). Hillsdale, NJ: Lawrence Erlbaum.

Stainback, S., & Stainback, W. (1984). A rationale for the merger of regular and special education. *Exceptional Children, 51*(2), 102–111.

Stanford, G. (1977). *Developing effective classroom groups.* New York: Hart.

Stark, K. D., & Brookman, C. S. (1992). Childhood depression: Theory and family-school intervention. In M. J. Fine & V. Carlson (Eds.), *The handbook of family-school intervention: A systems perspective* (pp. 247–271). Needham, MA: Allyn & Bacon.

Stephens, T. M. (1976). *Directive teaching of children with learning and behavior handicaps.* Columbus, OH: Merrill.

Sternberg, R. (1989). *The triarchic mind: A new theory of human intelligence.* New York: Penguin Books.

Sternberg, R. (1994). *Thinking and problem solving.* San Diego: Academic Press.

Sternberg, R. (1995). *The nature of insight.* Cambridge, MA.: MIT Press.

Sternberg, R. J. (1986). A triarchic theory of intellectual giftedness. In R. J. Sternberg & J. E. Davidson (Eds.), *Conceptions of giftedness* (pp. 223–243). Cambridge, UK: Cambridge University Press.

Sternberg, R. J. (1977). *Intelligence, information processing and analogical reasoning: The componential analysis of human abilities.* Hillsdale, NJ: Lawrence Erlbaum.

Sternberg, R. J. (1989). *The triarchic mind.* New York: Viking.

Straker, G., & Jacobson, R. S. (1981). Aggression, emotional maladjustment and empathy in the abused child. *Developmental Psychology, 17,* 762–765.

Stromer, R. (1975). Modifying letter and number reversals in elementary school children. *Journal of Applied Behavior Analysis, 8,* 211.

Sulzer-Azaroff, B., Drabman, R. M., Greer, R. D., Hall, R. V., Iwata, B. A., & O'Leary, S. G. (1988). *Behavior analysis in education 1968–1987.* Lawrence, KS: Society for the Experimental Analysis of Behavior.

Sulzer-Azaroff, B., & Mayer, G. (1986). *Achieving educational excellence using behavioral strategies.* New York: Holt, Rinehart & Winston.

Suro, M. D. (1992, November 1). Selecting the smart set. *The New York Times Magazine, Education Life,* 18–19.

Swanson, R. A., & Henderson, R. W. (1977). Effects of televised modeling and active participation on rule-governed question production among native American children. *Contemporary Educational Psychology, 2,* 345–352.

Swap, S. M. (1987). *Enhancing parent involvement in schools.* New York: Teachers College Press.

Swap, S. M. (1990). Comparing three philosophies of home-school collaboration. *Equity and Choice, 6*(3), 9–19.

Szetela, W., & Nicol, C. (1992). Evaluating problem solving in mathematics. *Educational Leadership, 49*(8), 42–45.

Tarver, S. G., & Dawson, M. M. (1978). Modality preference and the teaching of reading: A review. *Journal of Learning Disabilities, 11,* 5–17.

Tharinger, D. J., & Lambert, N. M. (1990). The contributions of developmental psychology to school psychology. In T. B. Gutkin & C. R. Reynolds (Eds.), *The handbook of school psychology* (pp. 74–103). New York: Wiley.

Tharp, R. G. (1987, August). *Culture, cognition and education: A culturogenetic analysis of the wholistic complex.* Paper presented at the Conference of the Institute on Literacy and Learning, University of California, Santa Barbara.

Tharp, R. G. (1989). Psychocultural variables and constants: Effects on teaching and learning in schools. *American Psychologist, 44,* 349–359.

Tharp, R. G., Jordan, C., Speidel, G., Au, K. H., Klein, T. W., Sloot, K. C. M., Calkins, R. P., & Gallimore, R. (1984). Product and process in applied developmental research: Education and the children of a minority. In M. E. Lamb, A. L. Brown, & B. Rogoff (Eds.). *Advances in developmental psychology: Vol. 3* (pp. 91–144). Hillsdale, NJ: Lawrence Erlbaum.

Thelen, E. (1984). Learning to walk: Ecological demands and phylogenetic constraints. In L. P. Lipsitt & C. Rovee-Collier (Eds.), *Advances in infancy research: Vol. 3* (pp. 213–260). Norwood, NJ: Ablex.

Thomas, A., & Chess, S. (1977). *Temperament and development.* New York: Brunner/Mazel.

Thomas, E. L., & Robinson, H. A. (1972). *Improving reading in every class: A sourcebook for teachers.* Needham, MA: Allyn & Bacon.

Thorndike, R. L. (1913). *The psychology of learning (educational Psychology II).* New York: Teachers College Press.

Thorndike, R. M., Cunningham, G. K., Thorndike, R. L., & Hagen, E. P. (1991). *Measurement and evaluation in psychology and education* (5th ed.). New York: Macmillan.

Tichener, E. B. (1898). The postulates of structural psychology. *Philosophical Review, 7,* 449–453.

Tisak, M. S., & Turiel, E. (1988). Variation in seriousness of transgressions and children's moral and conventional concepts. *Developmental Psychology, 74,* 352–357.

Tombari, M., Fitzpatrick, S. J., & Childress, W. (1985). Using computers as contingency managers in self-monitoring interventions: A case study. *Computers in Human Behavior, 1,* 75–82.

Tomlinson-Keasey, C., Eisert, D. C., Kalle, L. R., Hardy-Brown, K., & Keasey, B. (1978). The structure of concrete operational thought. *Child Development, 50,* 1153–1163.

Torrance, E. P. (1981). Ten ways of helping young children gifted in creative writing and speech. In J. P. Cowan, J. Khalena, & E. P. Torrance (Eds.), *Creativity: Its educational implications.* Dubuque, IA: Kendall/Hunt.

Trecker, J. L. (1977). Women in U. S. history high school textbooks. In J. Potker & A. Fishel (Eds.), *Sex bias in the schools: The research evidence* (pp. 146–161). Cranbury, NJ: Associated University Presses.

Trovato, J., & Bucher, B. (1990). Peer tutoring with or without home-based reinforcement for reading remediation. *Journal of Applied Behavior Analyses, 13*(1), 128–141.

Tuckman, B. W. (1988). *Testing for teachers.* San Diego: Harcourt Brace Jovanovich.

Tulving, E. (1989). Remembering and knowing the past. *American Scientist, 77,* 361–367.

Turiel, E. (1983). *The development of social knowledge: Morality and convention.* Cambridge, UK: Cambridge University Press.

Turnbull, A. P., & Turnbull, H. R. (1986). *Families, professionals and exceptionality.* Columbus, OH: Merrill.

Tyler, R. W. (1974). Considerations in selecting objectives. In D. A. Payne (Ed.), *Curriculum evaluation: Commentaries on purpose, process, product.* Lexington, MA: D. C. Heath.

van Houten, R. (1994). Teaching children with learning problems. In R. Gardner, D. M. Sainato, J. O. Cooper, T. E. Heron, W. L. Heward, J. W. Eshleman, & T. A. Grossi (Eds.), *Behavior Analysis in Education.* Pacific Grove, CA: Brooks-Cole.

Vasta, R. (1976). Feedback and fidelity: Effects of contingent consequences on accuracy of imitation. *Journal of Experimental Child Psychology, 21,* 98–108.

Villa, R. A., & Thousand, J. S. (1992). How one district integrated special and general education. *Educational Leadership, 50*(2), 39–41.

Vogt, L. A., Jordan, C., & Tharp, R. G. (1987). Explaining school failure, producing school success: Two cases. *Anthropology & Education Quarterly, 18,* 276–286.

Vygotsky, L. S. (1962). *Thought and language.* New York: Wiley.

Vygotsky, L. S. (1987). *Thinking and speech* (N. Minick, Ed., Trans.). New York: Plenum.

Wadsworth, B. J. (1984). *Piaget's theory of cognitive development.* New York: Longman.

Walker, C. H. (1987). Relative importance of domain knowledge and overall aptitude on acquisition of domain-related information. *Cognition and Instruction, 4,* 25–42.

Walker, H., & Sylvester, R. (1991). Where is school along the path to prison? *Educational Leadership, 14*–16.

Wallerstein, J. S. (1984). Children of divorce: Preliminary report of a ten-year follow-up of young children. *American Journal of Orthopsychiatry, 54,* 444–458.

Wallerstein, J. S. (1989, January 22). Children after divorce. Wounds that don't heal. *The New York Times Magazine,* 19–21, 41–44.

Wang, M. C., Reynolds, M. C., & Walberg, H. J. (1982). *Handbook of special education: Research and practice: Volume 1. Learner characteristics and adaptive education.* Oxford, England: Pergamon.

Wang, M. C., Walberg, H., & Reynolds, M. C. (1992). A scenario for better—not separate—special education. *Educational Leadership, 50*(2), 35–38.

Watson, J. B. (1926). *Behaviorism.* New York: Norton.

Watson-Gegeo, K. A., & Boggs, S. T. (1977). From verbal play to talk story: The role of routines in speech events among Hawaiian children. In S. Ervin-Tripp & C. Mitchell-Kernan (Eds.), *Child discourse* (pp. 67–90). New York: Academic Press.

Waxman, S., & Gelman, R. (1986). Preschoolers' use of superordinate relations in classification and language. *Cognitive Development, 1,* 139–156.

Webb, N. M. (1982). Interaction and learning in small groups. *Review of Educational Research, 52,* 421–450.

Wechsler, D. (1975). Intelligence defined and undefined: A relativistic appraisal. *American Psychologist, 30,* 135–139.

Weed, K., Ryan, E. B., & Day, J. (1990). Metamemory and attributions as mediators of strategy use and recall. *Journal of Educational Psychology, 82,* 849–855.

Weiner, B. (1977). An attributional approach for educational psychology. In L. S. Shulman (Ed.), *Review of research in education: Vol. 4,* (pp. 345–366). Itasca, IL: E. E. Peacock.

Weiner, B. (1979). A theory of motivation for some classroom experiences. *Journal of Educational Psychology, 11,* 3–25.

Weiner, B. (1980). *Human motivation.* New York: Holt, Rinehart & Winston.

Weiner, B. (1986). *An attribution theory of motivation and emotion.* New York: Springer-Verlag.

Weiner, B. (1991). Metaphors in motivation and attribution. *American Psychologist, 46,* 921–930.

Weinstein, C. E., & Mayer, R. E. (1986). The teaching of learning strategies. In M. C. Wittrock (Ed.), *Handbook of research on teaching* (3rd ed., pp. 315–327). New York: Macmillan.

Weisberg, P. (1990). Academic training. In J. L. Matson (Ed.), *Handbook of behavior modification with the mentally retarded.* New York: Plenum.

Weisner, T., Gallimore, R., & Jordan C. (1988). Unpackaging cultural effects on classroom learning: Native Hawaiian peer assistance and child-generated activity. *Anthropology and Education Quarterly, 19,* 327–353.

Weissman, M. M., Paykel, E. S., & Klerman, G. L. (1972). The depressed woman as a mother. *Social Psychiatry, 7,* 98–108.

Wellington, B. (1991). The promise of reflective practice. *Educational Leadership.* 48(6), 4–5.

Whalen, C. K., & Henker, B. (1985). The social worlds of hyperactive (ADHD) children. *Clinical Psychology Review, 5,* 447–478.

Whalen, C. K., Henker, B., Collins, B. E., Finck, D., & Dotemoto, S. (1979). A social ecology of hyperactive boys: Medication effects in structured classroom environments. *Journal of Applied Behavior Analysis, 12,* 65–81.

Wheelock, A. (1992). The case for untracking. *Educational Leadership, 50*(2), 6–10.

Wiatrowski, M., Hansell, S., Massey, C. R., & Wilson, D. L. (1982). Curriculum tracking and delinquency. *American Sociological Review 47,* 151–160.

Wielkiewicz, R. M. (1992). Behavioral intervention: A home and school approach. In S. L. Christenson & J. C. Conoley (Eds.), *Home-school collaboration: Enhancing children's academic and social competence* (pp. 333–356). Silver Spring, MD: National Association of School Psychologists.

Wiggins, G. (1992). Creating tests worth taking. *Educational Leadership, 49*(8), 26–34.

Wiggins, G. (1993). Assessment: Authenticity, context, and validity. *Phi Delta Kappan, 75* (3), 200–214.

Williams, D. L., & Stallworth, J. T. (1984). *Parent involvement in education: What a survey reveals.* Austin, TX: Southwest Regional Educational Development Lab: Parent Involvement in Education Project. (ERIC Document Reproduction Service No. ED 253–327)

Williams, M. D. (1981). Observations in Pittsburgh ghetto schools. *Anthropology & Education Quarterly, 12,* 211–220.

Williams, M. D., & Hollan, J. D. (1981). The process of retrieval from very long-term memory. *Cognitive Science, 5,* 87–119.

Willig, A. (1985). A meta-analysis of selected studies on the effectiveness of bilingual education. *Review of Educational Research, 55,* 269–317.

Willoughby, S. S. (1990). *Mathematics education for a changing world.* Alexandria, VA: Association for Supervision and Curriculum Development.

Witkin, H. A., & Goodenough, D. R. (1977). Field dependence and interpersonal behavior. *Psychological Bulletin, 84,* 661–689.

Witkin, H. A., Moore, C. A., Goodenough, D. R., & Cox, P. W. (1977). Field-dependent and field independent cognitive styles and their educational implications. *Review of Educational Research, 47,* 1–64.

Wolf, D. P., LeMahieu, P. G., & Eresh, J. (1992). Good measure: Assessment as a tool for educational reform. *Educational Leadership, 49*(8), 8–13.

Wood, J. W. (1992). *Adapting instruction for mainstreamed and at-risk students* (2nd ed.). New York: Macmillan.

Wood, J. W., & Reeves, C. K. (1989). Mainstreaming: An overview. In J. W. Wood (Ed.), *Mainstreaming: A practical approach for teachers.* Columbus, OH: Merrill.

Worrell, J., & Stilwell, W. E. (1981). *Psychology for teachers and students.* New York: McGraw-Hill.

Young, V. H. (1970). Family and childhood in a Southern Georgia community. *American Anthropologist, 72,* 269–288.

Ysseldyke, J. E., & Marston, D. (1990). The use of assessment information to plan instructional interventions: A review of the research. In T. B. Gutkin & C. R. Reynolds (Eds.), *The handbook of school psychology* (2nd ed., pp. 663–684). New York: Wiley.

Zimbardo, P. G. (1996). *Psychology and life* (14th ed.). New York: HarperCollins.

Zimmerman, B. J. (1989). A social cognitive view of self-regulated academic learning. *Journal of Educational Psychology, 81,* 329–339.

Zimmerman, B. J. (1990). Self-regulated learning and academic achievement: An overview. *Educational Psychologist, 25,* 3–18.

Zimmerman, B. J., Banderro, A., & Martinez-Pons, M. (1992). Self-motivation for academic achievement: The role of self-efficacy beliefs and personal goal setting. *American Educational Research Journal, 29*(3), 663–676.

Zimmerman, B. J., & Kleefeld, C. F. (1977). Toward a theory of teaching: A social learning view. *Contemporary Educational Psychology, 2,* 158–171.

Zimmerman, B. J., & Ringle, J. (1981). Effects of model persistence and statements of confidence on children's self-efficacy and problem solving. *Journal of Educational Psychology, 73*(4), 485–493.

Zimmerman, B. J., & Rosenthal, T. L. (1974). Observational learning of rule-governed behavior by children. *Psychological Bulletin, 81*(1), 29–43.

Credits

Photo Credits

Unless otherwise acknowledged, all photos are the property of Scott, Foresman. Abbreviations are as follows: (b) bottom; (c) center; (l) left; (r) right; (t) top.

2 Bill Aron/PhotoEdit; 4 Jim Whitmer; 6 Lawrence Migdale; 7 Jeffry W. Myers/Stock Boston; 13 Andy Sacks/Tony Stone Image; 22(l) Bob Daemmrich/The Image Works, (r) David Young-Wolff/PhotoEdit; 24 Bob Daemmrich/The Image Works; 29 Paul Conklin/PhotoEdit; 34 Peter Brandt; 37 Bob Daemmrich/Stock Boston; 39 Matthew Neal McVay/Tony Stone Images; 51 Billy E. Barnes/Tony Stone Images; 54 Lawrence Migdale/Tony Stone Images; 66 David Young-Wolff/PhotoEdit; 71 Norma Morrison; 73 David Young-Wolff/PhotoEdit; 75 Bill Aron/PhotoEdit; 80 Lawrence Migdale; 89 Steve and Mary Skjold; 100(tl, tr, bl) Bob Daemmrich, (br) Frank Siteman/The Picture Cube; 102 Bob Daemmrich; 108 Charles Gupton/Tony Stone Images; 117 Myrleen Ferguson/PhotoEdit; 121 Bob Daemmrich/Stock Boston; 126 Elizabeth Crews; 129 Bob Daemmrich/The Image Works; 134 Bob Daemmrich; 137 Tony Freeman/PhotoEdit; 141 Charles Gupton/Stock Boston; 142 Jim Whitmer; 148 Tony Freeman/PhotoEdit; 172 Bob Daemmrich; 179 Myrleen Ferguson/PhotoEdit; 186 M. Siluk/The Image Works; 195 Norma Morrison; 208 Frank Siteman/The Picture Cube; 211 Chip Henderson/Tony Stone Images; 213 Jim Whitmer; 217 Jim Whitmer; 223 Elizabeth Crews; 226 Michael Man/PhotoEdit; 240(l) Jim Pickerell/Stock Boston, (c) Jim Pickerell/The Image Works, (r) Mary Kate Denny/PhotoEdit; 242 Jim Pickerell/Stock Boston; 246 Bob Daemmrich/Stock Boston; 250 Elizabeth Crews; 253 David Young-Wolff/PhotoEdit; 258 Mary Kate Denny/PhotoEdit; 267 Bachmann/Stock Boston; 276 Jim Pickerell/The Image Works; 286 Jim Whitmer; 290 Bob Daemmrich/Stock Boston; 294 Tony Freeman/PhotoEdit; 296 Chip Henderson/Tony Stone Images; 309 Bob Daemmrich/Stock Boston; 314 Mary Kate Denny/PhotoEdit; 320 Jim Whitmer; 334 Tony Freeman/PhotoEdit; 338 Bob Daemmrich/Stock Boston; 342 Norma Morrison; 352(l) Bob Daemmrich/Stock Boston, (c) Robert W. Ginn/Unicorn Stock Photos, (r) Myrleen Ferguson/PhotoEdit; 354 Bob Daemmrich/Stock Boston; 359 Mary Kate Denny/PhotoEdit; 365 Henley & Savage/Tony Stone Images; 370 Bob Daemmrich/The Image Works; 375 Bob Daemmrich/The Image Works; 376 Erika Stone; 382 Jim Pickerell/Stock Boston; 390 Robert W. Ginn/Unicorn Stock Photos; 394 Mark Lewis/Tony Stone Images; 398 Richard Hutchings/PhotoEdit; 412 Bob Daemmrich/Tony Stone Images; 419(t) Chip Henderson/Tony Stone Images, (b) Frank Siteman/Stock Boston; 424 Myrleen Ferguson/PhotoEdit; 427 Cameramann/The Image Works; 428 Lawrence Migdale; 433 Elizabeth Crews; 436 Jim Whitmer; 439 Norma Morrison; 462(l) Bob Daemmrich, (c) Frank Siteman/The Picture Cube, (r) Comstock; 464 Bob Daemmrich; 479 Richard Hutchings/PhotoEdit; 482 Bob Daemmrich/Stock Boston; 488 Bob Daemmrich/The Image Works; 493 Peter Brandt; 500 Frank Siteman/The Picture Cube; 504 Cameramann/The Image Works; 508 Lawrence Migdale; 511 Bachmann/The Image Works; 520 Bob Daemmrich/The Image Works; 525 Richard Hutchings/PhotoEdit; 526 Erika Stone; 532 Comstock; 536 Erika Stone; 541 B. Bachmann/Stock Boston; 543 Willie L. Hill Jr./Stock Boston; 546 David Young-Wolff/PhotoEdit; 550 Frank Siteman/Stock Boston.

Figure, Table, Box, and Literary Credits

10 "Teacher Concern Checklist" by Francis F. Fuller and Gary D. Borich from *Effective Teaching Methods*, 2nd ed., by Gary D. Borich. Copyright © 1992 Macmillan College Publishing Company, Inc. Reprinted by permission of Simon & Schuster. 67–68 From *Case Studies for Teacher Deci-*

sion Making by G. Greenwood and F. Parkay. Copyright © 1989 Gordon E. Greenwood and Forrest W. Parkay. Reprinted by permission of the authors. 74 Table 3.1, "Erikson's Eight Stages of Development," from *The Developing Child*, 7th ed., by Helen Bee. Copyright © 1995 by Harper-Collins College Publishers. 77 Fig. 3.1, "An Integrative Model Describing the Formation of Individual Personality," from *The Developing Child*, 7th ed., by Helen Bee. Copyright © 1995 by HarperCollins College Publishers. 79, 93, 241, 262–263, 415–416 From *The Roller Coaster Years: Essays by and for Beginning Teachers* edited by Kevin Ryan. Copyright © 1992 by HarperCollins College Publishers. 84–85 From *Child and Adolescent Development*, 2nd ed., by Kelvin L. Seifert and Robert J. Hoffnung. Copyright © 1987 by Houghton Mifflin Company. Reprinted with permission. 88 Table 3.2, "Securely Attached Infants, at Later Ages, Show a Number of Characteristics," from *The Developing Child*, 6th ed., by Helen Bee. Copyright © 1992 by HarperCollins College Publishers. 92 Table 3.3, "Stages in the Development of Empathy," from *The Developing Child*, 7th ed., by Helen Bee. Copyright © 1995 by HarperCollins College Publishers. 96–97 Table 3.4 From *Piaget's Theory of Cognitive and Affective Development* by Barry J. Wadsworth. Copyright © 1996 by Longman Publishers USA. Reprinted with permission. 103 From "Precision Teaching: Discoveries and Effects" by Ogden R. Lindsley in *Journal of Applied Behavior*, Vol. 25, No. 1, 1992. Reprinted by permission of Society for the Experimental Analysis of Behavior, Inc. and Ogden R. Lindsley. 106, 113 Figs. 4.2, 4.5 From *Developmental Psychology: Childhood and Adolescence* by D. Schaffer, pp. 277–279. Copyright © 1993, 1989, 1982 by Brooks/Cole Publishing Company, a division of International Thomson Publishing Inc., Pacific Grove, CA 93950. Reprinted by permission. 116 Fig. 4.7 Adaptation of "A Learning Hierarchy for Conservation Skills" from "Contributions of Learning to Human Development" by R. M. Gagné, *Psychological Review*, Vol. 75, p. 184. Copyright © by the American Psychological Association. Adapted by permission of the American Psychological Association and Dr. Robert M. Gagné. 139 Fig. 5.1 Adapted from *Educational Psychology: A Cognitive Approach* by R. E. Mayer, p. 55. Copyright © 1987 by HarperCollins College Publishers. 143 "Examples of Several Types of Mnemonics" from *Effective Teaching Methods*, 2nd ed., by Gary D. Borich. Copyright © 1992 Macmillan College Publishing Company, Inc. Reprinted by permission of Simon & Schuster. 152 Fig. 5.2, "Basic Elements of the Human Information-Processing System," from *The Cognitive Psychology of School Learning* by Gagné, Yekovich, and Yekovich, p. 40. Copyright © 1993 by HarperCollins College Publishers. 158 Fig. 5.4 Adapted from *Educational Psychology: A Cognitive Approach* by R. E. Mayer, p. 13. Copyright © 1987 by HarperCollins College Publishers. 164 Table 5.2, "The Seven Intelligences," adapted from "Multiple Intelligences Go to School: Education Implication of the Theory of Multiple Intelligences" by H. Gardner and T. Hatch, *Educational Researcher*, Vol. 18, No. 8, 1989, pp. 4–10. Copyright © 1989 by the American Educational Research Association. Adapted by permission of the publisher. 165 Table 5.3 Adapted from *Mulitple Intelligences* by Howard Gardner. Copyright © 1993 by Howard Gardner. Reprinted by permission of Basic-Books, a division of HarperCollins Publishers, Inc. 176 Figs. 6.2, 6.3 From *Teaching Academic Subjects to Diverse Learners* by M. M. Kennedy, pp. 67–69, 71, 182, 219. Copyright © 1990 by Teachers College, Columbia University. All rights reserved. Reprinted by permission of Teachers College Press, New York. 190 Fig. 6.5 From *Teaching as Decision Making: Istructional Practices for the Successful Teacher* by M. Pasch, et al., 33. Copyright © 1991 Longman Publishers USA. Reprinted by permission. 197, 200 Figs. 6.6, 6.7 From *Effective Teaching Methods*, 3rd ed., by Gary Borich. Copyright © 1996 by Gary Borich. Reprinted by permission of Prentice-Hall Publishers. 216 Fig. 7.2 From "A Theory of Motivation for Some Classroom Experiences" by B. Weiner, *Journal of Educational Psychology*, Vol. 71, p. 7. Copyright © 1979 by the American Psychological Association. Reprinted by permission of the American Psychological Association and Dr. Bernard Weiner. 241, 356 From *Why Do We Gotta Do This Stuff, Mr. Nehring* by James Nehring. Copyright © 1989 by James Nehring. Reprinted by permission of the publisher M. Evans and Company, Inc. 247 Fig. 8.2 From *Group Processes in the Classroom*, 5th ed., by Richard A. Schmuck and Patricia A. Schmuck. Copyright © 1988 Times Mirror Higher Education Group, Inc., Dubuque, Iowa. All rights reserved. Reprinted by permission. 278–279 From *Problem Situations in Teaching* by Gordon Greenwood, Thomas Good, and Betty Siegel. Copyright © 1971 Gordon Greenwood. Reprinted by permission of the author. 360 Fig. 11.2 From *Wechsler Intelligence Scale for Children–Revised*. Copyright © 1974 by The Psychological Corporation. All rights reserved. Reprinted with permission. 384 Fig. 11.7 "Eighth-Grade English and Math Classes" from "Should Teaching Be Derailed?" by Laura Mansnerus, in the Education Life section, *The New York Times*, Sunday, November 1, 1992. Copyright © 1992 by The New York

Name Index

Subject Index

Note: Page numbers followed by *b*, *f*, and *t* indicate terms found in boxes, figures, and tables, respectively.